QUALITY OF LIFE
FOR OLDER PEOPLE
An International Perspective

WILLIAM R. LASSEY

Professor Emeritus
Washington State University

MARIE L. LASSEY

Professor Emerita
University of Idaho

Main ideas / Important points
Definitions
Examples

Prentice
Hall

Upper Saddle River, New Jersey 07458

Library of Congress Cataloging-in-Publication Data

Lassey, William R.
    Quality of life for older people : an international perspective / William R. Lassey, Marie
L. Lassey.
      p. cm.
    Includes bibliographical references and index.
    ISBN 0-13-628777-8 (pbk.)
    1. Aged.   2. Quality of life.   I. Lassey, Marie L.   II. Title.

HQ1061 .l3567 2001
305.26—dc21

                                                                       00-056533

VP, Editorial Director: Laura Pearson
AVP, Publisher: Nancy Roberts
Managing Editor: Sharon Chambliss
Editorial/production supervision
   and interior design: Mary Araneo
Director of Marketing: Beth Gillett Mejia
Cover Art Director: Jayne Conte
Cover Designer: Bruce Kenselaar
Prepress and Manufacturing Buyer: Mary Ann Gloriande

This book was set in 10/12 New Baskerville by A & A Publishing Services, Inc.,
and was printed and bound by RR Donnelley & Sons Company. The cover was
printed by Phoenix Color Corp.

 © 2001 by Prentice-Hall, Inc.
    A Division of Pearson Education
    Upper Saddle River, New Jersey 07458

Printed in the United States of America

10 9 8 7 6 5 4 3 2 1

ISBN 0-13-628777-8

Prentice-Hall International (UK) Limited, *London*
Prentice-Hall of Australia Pty. Limited, *Sydney*
Prentice-Hall Canada Inc., *Toronto*
Prentice-Hall Hispanoamericana, S.A., *Mexico*
Prentice-Hall of India Private Limited, *New Delhi*
Prentice-Hall of Japan, Inc., *Tokyo*
Pearson Education Asia Pte. Ltd., *Singapore*
Editora Prentice-Hall do Brasil, Ltda., *Rio de Janeiro*

This book is dedicated to William Lassey of Cartwright, North Dakota, age 86 and father of one author, and Audie Hallman, of Stockbridge, Georgia, age 86 and aunt of the other. They have both aged optimally and have enjoyed a rich quality of life—deeply inspiring us as we watched them function as caring family members and dedicated citizens in their communities.

CONTENTS

Chapter 11

Japan: Challenges of Aging and Cultural Change   286

Chapter 12

The United Kingdom: Pioneering Geriatric and Hospice Care   317

Chapter 13

The Netherlands: Integrated and Comprehensive Services   345

Chapter 14

Germany: Confronting Aging and Social Integration   367

CONTENTS

PREFACE

Rapid aging of populations throughout the world is causing major reconsideration of public policies and support programs. The proportion of the population age 65 and older in the economically advanced countries will grow from about 15 percent in the year 2000 to more than 25 percent by 2030, with considerable variation by country. Retirees may grow even faster, from 19 percent in 2000 to approximately 37 percent by 2030. The segment of national resources needed and the social organization required for service provision are thus likely to require major upward revisions.[1, 3]

The implications are profound:

- Financing of Social Security, physical health care, mental health care, long-term care, housing, and expenditures for related services will almost certainly need to be substantially increased.
- Older citizen dependence on public and private support services is likely to rise significantly as the number of very old individuals increases.
- The proportion of population under age 65, who will be expected to pay a high proportion of the required taxes, will decline. Financing the needed additional expenditures is likely to mean higher payroll deductions per capita.
- Professionals in many fields devoted to work with the older population are likely to be under considerable stress and in short supply.

The issues have become so significant worldwide that 1999 was declared the United Nations International Year of Older Persons, as a means of focusing on needed changes in policy to accommodate the expanding older population. Social Security, Medicare, Medicaid, and other expenditures to support the elderly were more than

one-third of the United States budget in 1998. That proportion could rise significantly if policy changes are not made.[2]

◆◆◆ GOALS OF THIS VOLUME

Our primary goal is to integrate and expand upon knowledge about optimal aging and
quality of life in economically advanced nations, while examining the issues, policies, and programs supportive of older people. This volume should serve as a basic
resource for students and others who have an interest in knowing more about how to
improve quality of life for older people in the United States and other economically
advanced countries. We draw upon the extensive experience in a range of countries,
although with special emphasis on the United States. More specific objectives include:

- Development of an analytical framework that identifies important contributing factors to optimal aging and quality of life—related to individuals, social
  groups, physical health, mental health, long-term care, residential settings, economic issues, and lifestyle choices (Chapter 1).
- Examination of individual, family, neighborhood, community, and societal participation in optimal aging (Chapters 2 and 3).
- Review and evaluation of other contributing factors to quality of life such as
  physical health, mental health, long-term care, residential environments, economic and financial conditions, and lifestyle (Chapters 4 through 9).
- A summary of the history, experience, and effectiveness of policies and programs to meet the needs of older people in Canada, Japan, the United Kingdom,
  the Netherlands, Germany, Sweden, and France (Chapters 10 through 16).
- A comparison of the international experiences with the United States to develop
  a framework outlining universal factors associated with optimal aging and quality of life (Chapters 17 and 18).

We should acknowledge at the outset that we have prepared this book partially
out of personal concern for older relatives and peers, as well as our own future well-
being as members of the older population. The quality of life, or lack thereof, among
our older friends has had a fundamental impact on us as individuals. We hope this
effort to expand knowledge of issues about aging will provide guidance toward
improved public and private support services while directly enhancing the personal
ability of individual readers to help achieve optimal aging for their family members
and eventually themselves.

◆◆◆ RATIONALE FOR AN INTERNATIONAL EMPHASIS

Several Western European nations and Japan have older populations than the United
States and are thus already experiencing major impacts and the need for adjusting policies and programs accordingly. Public awareness and response to aging varies widely
among countries. Selected new policies in some countries appear to be very effec-

tive in meeting quality-of-life goals at reasonable cost. However, the successes have not always been carefully studied, evaluated, and widely disseminated. Knowledge of effective efforts deserves to be highlighted and disseminated. Each country can presumably benefit from the tested experience of other nations.

Although we intend to take full account of effective policies and programs in each country, it would be presumptuous to assume that we could develop a fully explanatory theory of what works and what doesn't. Our knowledge is not that complete. Rather, we are in search of practical and workable options based on evidence from direct observations, research results, and recorded experience in the United States and other countries.

◆◆◆ THE INTENDED AUDIENCE

We hope the book is useful to:

- Undergraduate and graduate students in gerontology, health services administration, medicine, nursing, public health, social work, sociology, human development, human ecology, and other fields of endeavor focusing on, or serving, older populations.
- Faculty, researchers, and other scholars who are interested in an international perspective on factors that contribute to improved policies, programs, and quality of life for older individuals.
- Administrators and professional staff in various service programs such as health care, mental health care, long-term care, housing, income support, or retirement communities.
- Geriatricians and other physicians, nurses, health care administrators, pharmacists, social workers, and other health professionals involved in care of the elderly.
- Legislative and other government officials responsible for public policies and programs.
- Voluntary organization leaders who represent or serve the elderly.
- Individual citizens who are interested in increasing their ability to enhance quality of life for themselves, relatives, and/or friends.

◆◆◆ ACKNOWLEDGMENTS

Lennie Latham served as research assistant during the early preparation of this volume and became an expert in computer searches via the Internet. Jerry Hands was of great assistance later in the process. Latham, Hazuki Akimoto, Doreen Evans, Gail Hicks, Jan Kaschmutter, Michael McDole, and Ron Peoples were students in a Washington State University class on Aging and Long-Term Care Administration during 1997 and 1998 and were enormously helpful in reviewing some of the draft material. Molly Meier-Thiessen, research and teaching assistant in courses in Social Psychology and Personal and Social Issues on Aging, University of Idaho (1995–96), also provided valuable assistance. Kathy Swanz, Head Librarian at the Washington State University Library in Spokane, and Lydia McNulty, librarian, were immensely helpful in identifying library resources and references. We found our Prentice Hall editor Angie Stone, field representative Larry Armstrong, and project manager Mary Araneo enormously helpful as colleagues in bringing this volume to fruition. We extend our sincere thanks. Finally, the manuscript benefited greatly from several reviewers who were asked by Prentice Hall editors to react to earlier drafts: Patricia S. Baker, University of Alabama at Birmingham; Leonard D. Cain, Portland State University; Suzanne L. Cross, Central Michigan University; Ruth Dunkle, University of Michigan; Dale A. Lund, University of Utah; Sarah Matthews, Cleveland State University; Young Song, California State University, Hayward. We appreciate their suggestions.

◆◆◆ REFERENCES

1. Organization for Economic Cooperation and Development (1996). *Ageing in OECD Countries: A Critical Policy Challenge*, Paris: Organization for Economic Cooperation and Development.
2. Samuelson, Robert J. (1999). The Seduction of Surpluses, *Newsweek*, CXXXIV 134 (2), 74.
3. United States Census Bureau (2000). *International Data Base*. Online at www.census.gov/cgi-bin/ipc/idbpyry.pl.

Part I

INTRODUCTION
Basic Issues

Part I introduces the basic issues associated with an increasingly older population, identifies the individual role in optimal aging, examines family influences, explores neighborhood forces, and clarifies the larger community context. Chapter One identifies the basic factors that make understanding of aging crucially important—such as the rapidly expanding older population, increasing income-support costs, the rising resources needed for health care, and the significance of growth in long-term care requirements.

These challenges affect every older person to some degree, impact every economically advanced country, and demand attention from the younger population responsible for providing a major part of the social and financial support. The allocation of national and international resources is profoundly affected by the need to strengthen social institutions for sustenance of the older population.

In Chapter Two we emphasize that individual characteristics and responsibilities are central to creation of conditions for optimal aging. Good decisions and actions require effective preparation—through adequate socialization and education in the family, neighborhood, community, and larger society. An individual can make good choices that are likely to contribute to success in later life if the tools are available.

Chapter Three emphasizes that personal initiative will be most effective in the context of strong social support from family, friends, the immediate neighborhood, community, and larger society, especially in the event of disability. Opportunities must be provided for older individuals to pursue preferred personal goals while receiving the support they need in times of dependency.

Chapter 1

INTRODUCTION
Optimal Aging and Quality of Life

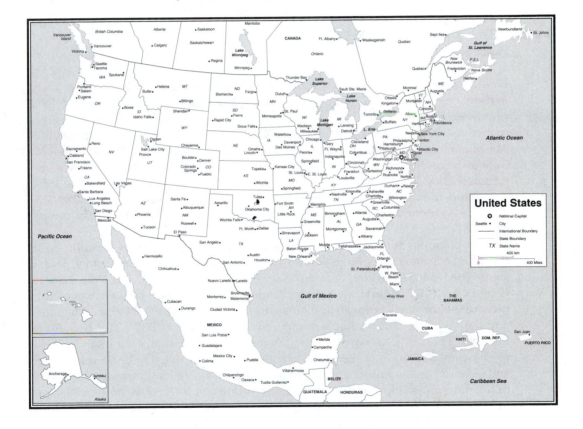

◆◆◆ INTRODUCTION

This chapter summarizes demographic changes in the older populations of economically advanced countries, defines important terminology, and outlines the scope and methods of gerontology. Specific topics include:

- A global and demographic perspective.
- The meaning of older age.
- A philosophy of aging.
- Myths, realities, and other clarifications.
- Key definitions and relationships.
- Primary factors in optimal aging.
- The study of aging.
- Careers in gerontology and geriatrics.

◆◆◆ A GLOBAL DEMOGRAPHIC PERSPECTIVE

By 2030 the population of older people is expected to increase to 20 percent or more in the more economically advanced countries. The proportion may grow to 28 percent in less prosperous countries in Asia, Africa, and Latin America. Major tragedies such as the uncontrolled incidence of AIDS could of course change the projections. The very rapid increase in the elderly population is a direct result of improvements in health conditions, together with lower birthrates, lower infant mortality, and greater average life expectancy. The "baby boom" cohort, born in years 1946 to 1964, contributes to rapid population increases in most of the more economically advanced countries—and will fuel the huge growth of older population early in the twenty-first century.[28, 34, 44, 82]

Populations and proportions of elderly for the eight countries examined in this volume are summarized in Table 1–1. The highest proportions of older people are in The United Kingdom, Germany, Sweden, France and Japan. The United States, Canada, and the Netherlands have had somewhat less growth, but are expected to increase to near the European and Japan averages over the next 30 years. The older population in the United States numbered 34.1 million in 2000—12.7 percent of the total. These numbers are expected to double to more than 69 million by 2030, when nearly 20 percent of the projected population is expected to be 65 years of age and older; 2 percent will be age 85 and older. Figure 1–1 below illustrates the growth in the older population since 1900 with projections for 2010, 2020, and 2030. Note that the growth rate is particularly high after 2010 when the baby boom generations reach age 65 in large numbers.[1, 75]

The proportion of older minority members of the population (especially Hispanics and Asians) will increase considerably more than European Americans—to 25 percent of the older population by 2030. The growth rate is projected to be 226 percent for minorities and only 79 percent for European Americans.[1]

Table 1–1   Populations, Proportions of Elderly, and Life Expectancy in Eight Countries, January 1, 2000

Country	Population (millions)	Proportion Age 65+ (%)	Life Expectancy
United States	273,131	12.7	76.2
Canada	31,006	12.5	79.4
Japan	126,680	16.7	80.1
United Kingdom	59,247	15.6	77.4
Netherlands	15,878	13.5	78.2
Germany	82,081	16.1	77.2
Sweden	8,911	17.3	79.3
France	58,978	16.0	78.6

*Source:*United States Census Bureau, 2000.

Table 1–2 summarizes the changes by age category for 1980, 1990, 1997, with projections to 2025 for the United States. As the table indicates there has been a steady increase in the older population within each category although there was a decline in the age 65–74 group between 1990 and 1997. The most significant increases in the early twenty-first century are a direct result of the baby boom cohort. It is worth noting that the age 85 plus segment is growing with greatest rapidity in the United

FIGURE 1–1   Number of Persons 65+, 1900–2030 (in millions)
Note: Increments in years are uneven.
Source: Based on data from the United States Census Bureau (2000).

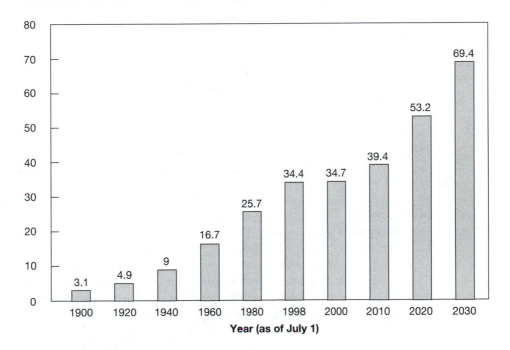

Table 1–2 **Changes and Projected Increases in Proportions of Older People by Age Groups, 1980 to 2025, United States**

Year	Total	Age 65–74	75–84	85 Plus
1980	11.3%	6.9%	3.4%	1.0%
1990	12.5	7.3	4.0	1.2
1997	12.7	6.9	4.4	1.4
2025	18.5	10.6	5.8	2.1

Source: United States Census Bureau, 1998.

States and most other economically advanced countries. When the baby boomers reach 65 they alone are expected to number roughly 19 million or 5 percent of the population. Centenarians (mostly female) have increased to one of every 10,000 people in the United States.[3, 61, 75]

The population pyramid in Figure 1–2 helps illustrate the predominance of women in the older-age categories (especially above age 80), the substantial numbers in younger retirement categories (ages 65–79), and the projected increases in future years as the larger numbers in the middle-age categories (ages 35–64) reach retirement age. The sex ratio is 143 women for every 100 men. Note also that the pyramid is somewhat narrower at the bottom than in the middle, reflecting lower birthrates in recent decades as compared to earlier periods.[40, 75]

Variability of Older Populations

The older population in every country tends to be quite heterogeneous. The historical context and specific experience in various geographic subdivisions of each country contribute to diversity. Variability is also a result of unique cultural factors such as values, attitudes, and behavior patterns progressively shaped over time. Generalizations about the characteristics of the elderly must thus be interpreted as averages that do not precisely fit most members of the population.[32, 64, 68]

Racial and Ethnic Variations. About 15.7 percent of the older population was of minority origin in 1998. Eight percent was African American, 5 percent was Hispanic, 2 percent was Asian or Pacific American, and less than 1 percent was Native American. Only 7.2 percent of these minority groups were age 65 or older, compared to 14.8 percent of European Americans. Minority families tend to be larger and their life expectancy is lower.[1, 3]

It is noteworthy that differences between racial and ethnic groups will continue to be quite substantial in the United States. Although great progress has been made in the improvement of economic and social conditions for minority elderly, life expectancy at birth and at age 65 in 2030 will continue to be lower for African Americans, Native Americans, and Hispanic Americans as compared to European Americans. Asian Americans have higher life expectancies than European, or African, or

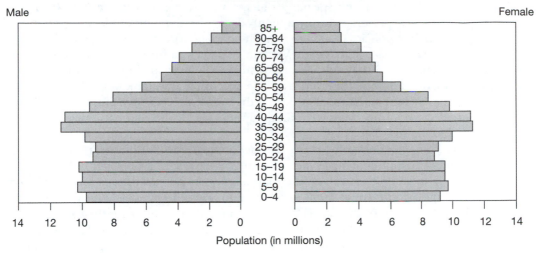

FIGURE 1-2   Population Pyramid for the United States
Source: U.S. Census Bureau, *International Data Base* (2000).

Hispanic Americans, attributable in part to cultural factors such as diet, family support, and higher education. However, minority populations will increase more rapidly overall than the majority, from 16 percent in 1998 to a projected 25 percent by 2030—largely because of higher birthrates, larger families, and in-migration from other countries.[1, 4]

In most European countries, much of the population growth is also among immigrant minority groups from Asia, Africa, the Middle East, and southern Europe—cultures that have quite different family traditions than western and northern Europeans. They have traditionally been much more likely to care for older family members at home, in part because the economic level has allowed fewer resources to support other alternatives. Consequently, as the older population becomes increasingly diverse in economically advanced countries, cultural variations in patterns of aging may require adjustments in government policies. For example, more culturally sensitive health care, long-term care, and housing programs may be needed.[3, 4]

Cohort Effects. The attitudes, values, and other characteristics of any age group thus arise from their specific experience and result in a so-called "cohort effect" on culture and public policy. Individuals in each cohort experience unique historical events, different from predecessor or successor cohorts. Their experience is likely to influence future public policies.[33, 64]

For example, participants were profoundly affected by the worldwide recession of the 1930s and World War II during the early 1940s, contributing to major changes in attitudes, values, expectations for the future, and public policies. The remaining veterans of World War II in Europe, Asia, and the United States are a unique group of elderly individuals with special problems, needs, and attitudes arising from the depth of their experience during a highly disruptive segment of history. A complex of special public policies related to health and long-term care services (administered in the United States by the federal Veteran's Affairs Administration) were developed to serve their specific needs. After World War II the baby boom generation had another kind of unique experience and perspective that will undoubtedly affect public retirement and income policy during the twenty-first century. Similarly, individuals growing up in the 1960s were uniquely affected by the traumatic circumstances related to the Viet Nam war.[38]

Current younger cohorts of older people (ages 65–74) have experienced better education, higher average incomes, and better health than older cohorts. Consequently, their experience and their large numbers are having the effect of raising the averages for the entire older population to higher levels of social and economic well-being. Studies of the oldest cohort—centenarians—indicate they were generally productive, often well educated, and lived a healthy life—much like the current younger cohorts. They apparently learned the secrets of right living long before modern knowledge about aging.[8, 57]

Dependency Ratio Changes

The old-age dependency ratio (the ratio of the number of people age 65 and over to the number from ages 15 to 64) in the United States is expected to increase from about .25 in the year 2000 to about .32 in 2030. The dependency ratio changes will be about the same in Canada, moderately greater in France, the United Kingdom, Sweden, and the Netherlands, and much greater in Japan and Germany. During the same period, the proportion of national income devoted to social security could rise from 8.2 percent to 14.6 percent or more in the United States and even more in the countries with higher proportions of older people.[15, 81]

However, dependency ratio changes should not be given undue weight since many older people remain productive in the workplace and in the community. Older men and women are often very important contributors to community infrastructure and political affairs and are critical informal caretakers for family members and other dependent individuals. Their psychological and emotional support are often crucial to family and community well-being but such contributions do not get fully measured in the public economy.[43]

Life Expectancy and Sex Ratio Implications

A child born in the United States during 2000 could expect to live for an average of 76.2 years—a life expectancy 29 years greater than in 1900. This translates to an average of 73 years for men and 79 for women. There were 143 older women for every 100 older men in 1998 or 20.2 million older women and 14.2 million older men. The ratio of women to men increases with age, from 118 women for each 100 men at age 65–69, to 241 women for each 100 men at age 85 and older.[1, 55, 58]

The life expectancy of women is greater than for men throughout the world. Males have higher mortality rates at every age beginning about age 15—with only 44 males out of every 100 males left by age 85. Consequently, a high proportion of the oldest population is female. Many are alone and without adequate family support or income support. Their needs in older age deserve special consideration as discussed in later chapters.[61]

Differences Between Older Age Categories. Under current conditions roughly 75 percent of the *young old* (ages 65 to 74) in modern societies have relatively good health, vigor, and financial security. Healthiness and vigor at this age were much less common in earlier decades, as noted earlier, and remain less common today in Eastern Europe, in much of Asia and Africa, and in other developing societies, where economic, social, and environmental conditions have so far meant shorter and less healthy lives.[76]

The characteristics of the older population have thus changed significantly over time and will continue to change in the decades ahead which, coupled with the general growth of the older population, suggests profound implications for public policy and the meaning of older age.[62]

◆◆◆ THE MEANING OF OLDER AGE

Age is first of all an indicator of progress through the stages of life and serves as one of the scheduling mechanisms for numerous forms of social and cultural activity such as schooling, dating, marrying, working, and retiring. Every culture is in considerable measure socially and economically organized on the basis of age-related categories of activity, although the specific content of activities and age of qualification vary considerably from one culture to another.[57, 62]

Reaching a specific culturally defined age is the primary criterion of qualification to receive major resource allocations. For example, in the United States age 62 (or 65) has for some time opened the door to Social Security and other pension income, special forms of health care insurance such as Medicare (at age 65), a Golden Age Passport providing free access to the glories of national parks and monuments, substantial discounts at private lodging accommodations or restaurants, and many other very useful benefits.

On the negative side, age 65 is approximately the time when one begins to notice that bodily functions do not work as well as they formerly did. Arthritis has often set in. More medical interventions may become necessary. One's younger co-workers may become impatient with the slowing work pace and may urge retirement. Social roles can begin to change from productive contributor and full participant in community life to, perhaps, a less well-defined retiree status.

These transitions are all part of the aging experience. The challenge for most older people is finding out how to enjoy the opportunities of older age while accepting the declines. Our experience and observations are that aging can be a very meaningful and productive process for most people—if we understand how it works and how to improve it. Understanding of aging requires a broad perspective that takes into account highly diverse conditions and populations. The variability of domestic and international experience with aging is enormous, as later chapters will indicate.[62]

◆◆◆ A PHILOSOPHY OF AGING

We *do not* subscribe to the negative perspective emphasizing the declines of older age as an unhappy and progressive struggle with deterioration and disease, which is not a realistic or appropriate reflection of what aging is like in the present age. We take a more positive view and are deeply interested in how our older peers think and behave individually, within the family, in community groups, in organizations, and as part of the larger society. Similarly, we attempt to understand how families, other small groups, organizations, and the larger society affect the individual older person. As recent entrants ourselves to the retiree population, we have a deep interest in personal understanding of how to improve options and opportunities.[29, 65]

Pessimistic attitudes about aging can have the effect of denying older individuals opportunity, resources, and respect—simply because of their chronological age. Moreover, many well-meaning younger people (including sons and daughters) hold great affection for their parents, grandparents, and other older people, but may nonetheless patronize them, try to make decisions for them, and sometimes attempt to manage their affairs—whether or not help is needed. Similarly, many working professionals who serve the older population hold negative attitudes that are sometimes reinforced during their education. These attitudes arise in part because older people generally suffer from one or more chronic conditions and are hard to fully "cure"—thus frustrating medical professionals and social caregivers.[21, 26, 34]

We do not deny, on the other hand, that there is progressive decline of some organ systems with age, accompanied by other personal losses. Many older persons have severe disabilities and need substantial family and/or public assistance to achieve reasonable quality of life. However, many age-related changes are not necessarily disabling and do not have to interfere with quality of life. Most older individuals remain quite capable of promoting their own health, maintaining their well-being, and continuing to actively contribute to society.[26, 34]

We believe that certain basic public policies, already well established in many countries, can significantly improve quality of life for a high proportion of older individuals:

- Education about the process of health maintenance and optimal aging.
- Social support services tailored to specific individual needs of older people.
- Guaranteed acute, mental, chronic and long-term health care.
- Good quality housing and appealing community environments.
- A basic level of financial security.
- Support for opportunities to achieve a satisfying lifestyle in a community of personal choice.

These public policy initiatives will enable most older citizens to satisfy their basic needs while achieving optimal aging. Before we discuss the issues and options in detail, it is crucial to be clear about some of the myths, realities, language, meanings, and the relationships among important factors associated with aging.

◆◆◆ MYTHS, REALITIES, AND OTHER CLARIFICATIONS

As suggested above, a number of myths and misconceptions have been generated reflecting negative attitudes toward older people.

Ageism

Negative attitudes and beliefs toward older people as a group are referred to as "ageism"—forms of prejudice that denigrate and stereotype the whole group. Such attitudes lead to fear of aging and inaccurate images of older people. The consequences can include various forms of discrimination and even abuse.[29, 42, 57]

We know, however, that decline, dependence, and eventual death are largely a consequence of disease or malfunction rather than a simple result of aging—as later chapters will emphasize. If acute and chronic disease can be avoided, treated effectively, or postponed to very late in life, the human body and mind can continue functioning quite well to very advanced ages, as illustrated by the on-going creative and productive capacities of many older artists, politicians, and other distinguished citizens.[29, 30, 31]

No characterization of ageism is entirely accurate for all societies. Among Native Americans, for example, older individuals have traditionally been viewed as holders of great wisdom, have high social status, and are usually revered by children, grandchildren and the larger community. This positive attitude toward aging may be less prevalent now than in earlier history, but nonetheless remains predominant within some subgroups in the United States and in many other countries.[12, 18, 76]

Ageism unfortunately contributes to the loss of productivity and creativity of many older individuals who could otherwise continue their contributions to society in the work place and in communities. We believe that the wisdom and cultural accumulation available through the older population are greatly needed by society and should not be lost because of ignorance about the consequences of aging.[57]

Privileged and Deprived Retirees

Public programs directed toward older people are often criticized because of the belief that a high proportion of older people are privileged retirees living in affluent conditions with publicly provided social security, other pensions, Medicare, Medicaid, and other expensive services. It is certainly correct that a substantial segment of older people have good incomes and live relatively well. However, a higher proportion have modest incomes and live somewhat frugally. Many supplement a meager income with full- or part-time work and use a high proportion of their personal resources to pay for medical care not covered by Medicare or other health insurance. Rates of poverty remained relatively high in the United States at 10.5 percent in 1998. Moderate- and lower-income older people appear to need every bit of the public support that comes to them if they are to achieve a reasonable quality of life.[1]

The Typical Pattern

An older person in economically advanced countries is likely to be fully alert, active, and living independently in the community with relatively little special assistance. Life satisfaction has not necessarily declined and may in fact be higher than at any previous age. The early years after age 65 are largely positive and satisfying for a high proportion of older citizens. Only a small proportion has difficulty making a reasonably good adjustment to retirement.

The oldest years (age 85 and older) are clearly more difficult, but can also be quite fulfilling if a satisfactory social support system, adequate resources, and comfortable physical environment are available. The age of frailty is constantly being shifted upward in all of the economically advanced countries. The somewhat negative perception of aging held by many people thus conflicts with scientifically generated knowledge about the widely varied but generally positive experience in older age.[25, 69, 76, 77]

◆◆◆ KEY DEFINITIONS AND RELATIONSHIPS

Several basic terms used throughout the book deserve definition to facilitate understanding.

Older People

All individuals age 65 and older are encompassed by the term "older people" which for our purposes is equivalent to "older age" or "elderly." The reality of course is that many people beyond age 65 function as well as younger individuals and dislike being considered "old." The chronological age definition is clearly somewhat arbitrary and is used primarily for classification purposes rather than as a hard and fast indication of functional capacity. The older population is divided into three general categories by the United States Census Bureau: the young old (65–74); the aged (75–84); and the oldest old (85 and older).[3, 28, 74]

Optimal Aging

Optimal aging is defined for our purposes as an extended process of maximizing individual potential to remain physically healthy, mentally strong, and socially satisfied until the end of life. Optimal aging is most likely to occur in societies or circumstances where the context of aging includes adequate social support, health care, mental health care, long-term care, housing, financial security, and a satisfying lifestyle. Individual initiative, understanding of the aging process, and an ability to take advantage of available public and private resources are major contributors to optimal aging and lead directly to quality of life in the later years.

Quality of Life

Quality of life has a relatively recent origin as a term to describe the circumstances of older people; it was hardly used prior to 1975. Since then the concept has become an established part of the lexicon for discussing the features and conditions of older individuals who are healthy and doing well, as well as for those with chronic conditions. Quality of life is used to describe responses to the "intrinsic" characteristics of an individual and the "extrinsic" social, economic, and environmental factors that affect well-being. It is a product of individual experience—which means that what is perceived as "good" quality by one person may not be satisfying to someone else.[13]

Quality of life for an individual is thus both subjective and objective—referring to the degree to which life's possibilities are realized. The subjective dimension has been scientifically studied by directly asking older individuals questions about how they evaluate their lives in terms of satisfaction with their social life, state of their health, adequacy of their housing, sense of mastery or control over their environment, and satisfaction with their financial situation. Objective evaluations include environmental conditions or circumstances, such as level of air pollution, level of income, characteristics of housing, or degrees of health services availability. Quality of life measures can be used to take into account the effects of specific diseases such as Alzheimer's or the consequences of medical interventions.[17, 48, 60, 73]

Quality of life does not have the same meaning in every culture. In some countries financial security may be considered the most important factor, whereas in others it might be psychological well-being, cognitive function, or perceived health status. The important factors may change with age. At the early ages between 65 and 75, financial security and social well-being may predominate; at later ages, stability of health condition might be considered more important. Careful comparative studies of the various countries would be necessary to clarify the degree to which there is a common definition of contributing factors to quality of life. The World Health Organization and the United States National Institute on Aging have initiated such studies and have generated some results which show common attributes for quality of life in several countries.[16, 54]

Contributing Factors to Quality of Life. The degree of quality in later life is thus defined as an outcome of both personal perceptions and the measured conditions associated with aging. The micro or informal local influences, macro or societal factors, and the intermediate or linking mechanisms that tie the individual and society together are each important. The micro level relates to individual behavior and primary social interaction with family and community, whereas the macro level includes factors in the larger society that influence aging.[36, 50]

Several of the key subjective and objective elements are summarized in Table 1–3. The major factors contributing to quality of life are listed in the first column of Table 1–3. Individual, family, and neighborhood factors are most immediate and direct in their influence, whereas the macro or community and societal factors may be less directly influential but are of primary importance in the overall potential for high quality of life.

Table 1-3   Summary of Contributing Factors to Quality of Life

Factors	Quality of Life Measures
Micro Level: Individual, Family, and Neighborhood	
Biological/genetic inheritance	Physical/mental makeup, intellectual ability and skills
Health status	Physical and mental well-being
Personality	Personal adjustment, autonomy, individual uniqueness, self-concept
Social integration and satisfaction with family and neighborhood	Sense of belonging, being loved, personal identity, self-esteem and self-respect, feeling that life is worthwhile
Social class experience	Status and respect in the neighborhood and community
Personal lifestyle	Sum of behaviors, attitudes, activities
Macro Level: Community and Society	
Social support systems	Social participation, religion, meaning in life
Health care system	Access to needed preventive, physical, mental, and long-term care
Housing and community physical environment	Comfort, security, beauty, healthiness
Financial security	Assurance of needed income and mobility to access resources
Lifestyle opportunities	Aesthetic and sensual satisfaction

Source: Data from various sources including: Bond, 1999: 567; Brod et al, 1999: 29; Brayne, 1995: 354; Bytheway, 1997: 8; Clair, Karp, and Yoels, 1993: 18; Raphael et al, 1997: 234; Stewart and King, 1994: 36-37.

Quality of Life Defined by Outcomes. Outcomes are listed in the second column of Table 1–3. Physical and mental capacity, physical and mental well-being, a sense of belonging, love, self-esteem, personal adjustment within a social group, a sense of autonomy, opportunity for intimacy and sexuality, freedom from prejudice, and the pleasures of a satisfying lifestyle all contribute directly to quality of life. Similarly, within the larger community and society, individuals will be better off when they know that health care is available as needed, when they have a satisfying home and community, when they experience a sense of financial security, and when they have access to pleasing lifestyle opportunities.[48]

If any of the attributes are negative or unrealized, quality is less than optimum. Some of the key relationships are summarized in the following paragraphs.

Relationships and Assumptions

Individual, Family, and Neighborhood

• **Biological/genetic structure** at birth establishes physical characteristics, basic intelligence, and skill potential. Greater physical prowess, intelligence, and skill mean that quality of life is likely to be higher.

- **Socialization experiences** in the family and neighborhood, and later, in the community and larger society, have a profound effect on sense of belonging, feeling loved, self-esteem, self-respect, and overall preparation for life. A continuing rich family and neighborhood experience is likely to enhance later life.
- **Personality characteristics** developed through initial social experience will structure personal adjustment and sense of autonomy. A unique and stable personality with a positive self-concept, attitudes, values, and beliefs will serve most people well throughout life.
- **Race and ethnicity** affect quality of aging because of the historical and current tendencies for social and economic discrimination. This leads to fewer opportunities, greater poverty, shorter lives, and lower expectations in later life. Fortunately, family bonds tend to be strong among African Americans, Hispanics, and other minorities in the United States and other countries helping to moderate the effects of discrimination.
- **Socioeconomic status**—education, income, occupation—is an indicator of the manner in which personal standing is evaluated by others in the community. Ordinarily, individuals with higher socioeconomic status have greater resources and more opportunities for choice in later life. However, satisfaction and happiness in older age is not entirely dependent on status—if family and community bonds are strong and resources are sufficient for basic needs.
- **Lifestyle** is the product of work, retirement, leisure and other individual experiences and behaviors in the family, neighborhood, community and society. Lifestyle opportunities such as travel, art, and music bring pleasure to the senses, and provide the aesthetic experiences that can greatly enhance satisfaction and enjoyment. Since each individual is unique, each lifestyle is a result of cumulative personal opportunities and preferences. There is thus enormous variety. A personally satisfying lifestyle in later years is the ultimate good outcome, regardless of its characteristics.

Community and Societal Influences

- **Norms, rules, and laws** are informally and formally created in families, neighborhoods, communities, states, and in the larger society to help regulate social relationships and structure individual expectations. If these regulators are just and enforced, older individuals know what to expect. When the rules are unjust or inadequate, quality of life can be diminished.
- **Public policies** define and guide public social activity and services such as qualification for social security, pension payments, and access to health insurance. Understanding, conforming with, and feeling that policies are adequate and fair lowers stress and contributes to the sense of satisfaction in later life.
- **Education** contributes to the development of knowledge, skills, and competencies that can enhance optimal aging. Gaining and sustaining intellectual stimulation, needed personal skills, and functional values are among the most important contributors to optimal aging.
- **Social support systems** in the community and larger society add important dimensions to family and neighborhood support. These include both informal

social groups and formal government agencies. Organized activities such as churches, civic clubs, senior citizen centers, and a vast array of other possibilities provide opportunity for social interaction, stimulation, spiritual experience, and relationships that are crucial to a sense of belonging and well-being. Public agencies such as Social Security offices, area agencies on aging, and numerous other entities to serve older people can be a source of information and great assistance in providing resources and solving problems.

- **A health care system** that functions effectively, is accessible, and responds to specific physical, mental, and chronic health needs is crucial to the well-being of older individuals. Inadequate insurance or limited access to preventive or curative health care is among the most distressing circumstances faced by those with health problems. Thus, attention to improvement of health care provisions is clearly among the most significant public policy and personal issues affecting quality in later life.

- **Satisfying housing, home, and community environment** are fundamental to comfort, security, healthy living conditions and access to beauty inside and outside in the yard and neighborhood. Older individuals or couples with sufficient resources can design and create the home they prefer in a satisfying setting. However, adequate housing and a pleasing home environment are very often problematic for those with disabilities and lower incomes, especially older women. Communities, states, the federal government, and private enterprise each attempt to provide alternatives that will meet the need for quality elderly environments.

- **Financial security** is fundamental to well-being and a sense of control. Without adequate basic resources, all other quality of life options are difficult. Social Security and work-related pensions provide the needed income for a high proportion of the older population, but many (especially women) depend on state and local welfare and/or Medicaid for basic survival. For example, ability to pay for adequate transportation is essential to secure the basic necessities of life and enjoy the larger environment.

The quality of life for any older individual is impacted somewhat differently by these factors since each has varying experiences, values, and expectations. No common package of outcomes will fit everyone. Achieving optimal aging requires that each individual has the opportunity to fashion his or her unique package of personal attributes, social opportunities, and environmental circumstances to create a rich and fulfilling experience. Community, regional, and national initiatives can improve the quality of opportunities by creating economic and social conditions that facilitate individual choice.

Although the contributors to quality of life outlined above are couched in terms that apply particularly to Americans, they also fit experience in other countries. Most economically advanced countries have policies, institutions, programs, and a variety of opportunities that contribute to quality of life for older people. Our thesis is that Americans have much to learn from these varied experiences.

◆◆◆ PRIMARY FACTORS IN OPTIMAL AGING

The conceptual framework outlined above identifies the primary factors that guide our analysis of aging issues, processes, and outcomes. These major categories, relationships, and assumptions form the basis for the organization of the chapters in this volume.

The Individual Role

Aging is to some degree a biological process established for each individual at conception. Individuals age at a pace and pattern affected by genetic makeup interacting with nutritional, social, economic, and other environmental factors. Complexes of genes exercise substantial control over life expectancy, but are not entirely in control. Physical and chemical agents in the environment may damage an individual and shorten life.[69,70]

Everyone has some degree of choice. The social environment regularly forces us to choose among alternative and sometimes competing options. Opportunity for choice is clearly a high priority for achievement of satisfaction and a sense of personal well-being among older people. The quality of the choices will inevitably shape the life course. Good choices will increase our perception of control and belonging in society. Poor choices will cause us frustrations. The consequent experiences throughout individual development will provide, or may fail to provide, the competencies and functional skills needed for optimal aging.[51, 56, 80]

No single theory or causal factor entirely explains the process of individual aging. A multidisciplinary perspective is required including at least biological, social, economic, and psychological factors.[69]

Family, Neighborhood, Community, and Societal Roles

Socialization in the family, neighborhood, community, and larger society, coupled with genetic makeup, are the primary contributors to formation of personality, personal competencies, and social roles. The family is clearly the most crucial socialization influence in the earliest years of life. In the later years when dependency may occur, the family is the primary caretaker. However, the social context of aging also includes the broader regional, national, and international social system, especially in the age of television and the Internet.

Social interaction and communication within families and other groups, such as recreational organizations, schools, and a range of other possibilities, contribute to the knowledge, skills, attitudes, values, and beliefs held by each older individual— forming who they are, what they are like, what they think, how they feel, and how they behave. The basic structure of personal identity formed in early life usually remains relatively stable into older age. However, personality will gradually change over time as a consequence of personal growth, new experiences such as marriage, parenthood, grandparenthood, retirement, and as the body and mind are affected by acute health problems and chronic diseases.[5, 18]

The larger society contributes cultural values, norms, and rules imposed on the family, community, and the individual older person. Authoritarian and controlling societies have greater direct influence on the family and individual, compared to open and democratic societies. However, cultural conditions and historical circumstances will affect the individual to some degree in any society.[14]

Workplace ageism is a major problem in many countries. Older individuals are often discriminated against because they are considered less productive than younger people or because they are perceived to block advancement of their younger colleagues. In many European countries this sometimes leads to forced retirement programs at earlier ages than preferred by older workers. In some parts of the entertainment industry older professionals have difficulty securing good roles despite their talent.[29]

Cultural traditions play a major role in structuring expectations of how the family, community, and society should respond to the needs of older members, and are the basis for substantial differences among countries, differences among regions within a single country, and differences among ethnic or racial groups within a society. As we shall see in later chapters, some nations place a very high value on national policies and programs for elderly citizens (Canada, The United Kingdom, the Netherlands, and Sweden, for example), while other countries rely somewhat more on family and community support (Japan, Germany, France and the United States). The pattern for allocation of power, influence, and resources between younger and older generations is among the most distinctive cultural differences among countries.[38]

Physical and Mental Health

Health status may be the most important of the broader influences on the quality of later life. Individual initiative is obviously primary in securing exercise, maintaining a nutritious diet, avoiding toxins from smoking or excessive consumption of alcohol or drugs, and undertaking other health producing measures. Maintenance of health is likely to be more effective if preventive services and medical advice are readily available. Preventive health services tailored to personal preferences and individual needs will usually be more effective in maintaining health than forceful medical intervention. Continuing health status is heavily affected by quality of community health services, as well as regional and national public health programs.[11]

Mental function continues with little decline for most people through age 84. After that decline becomes much more common, especially the incidence of Alzheimer's disease and other forms of dementia. About 40 percent of individuals over age 85 (in the United States) have some form of dementia or debilitating mental function that limits their mobility and capacity to live independently. The positive side is that 60 percent continue to function reasonably well into more advanced age. However, societal factors such as socioeconomic status do make a clear difference in mental function. In every country, older individuals at higher socioeconomic levels tend to do better than those with lower incomes, less education, and generally poorer health.[9, 13]

Long-term health care for chronic conditions becomes a permanent requirement for the relatively few older individuals with serious disability who cannot perform

the usual activities of daily living. A much larger number may require residence in nursing homes for short periods while recovering from episodes of serious acute illness
or surgery. However, since long-term care is very expensive, it is of major concern to
individuals who depend upon it and is an issue of great relevance in overall health
policy.

Housing and Community Environment

The quality of the immediate environment is crucial to the well-being and satisfaction
of older individuals. The environment includes the biophysical (air quality, water
quality, natural beauty, etc.) and constructed (housing and other physical structures)
attributes of a community that provide space for living, transportation, sustenance services, and recreation.

Some countries place great emphasis on access to quality housing for the elderly
in an attractive and environmentally healthy community setting and with access to the
full range of needed local services. As a consequence, most older people in these
countries (notably the Netherlands and Sweden) express generally high satisfaction
with available services and their state of well-being. In contrast, many lower-income
elderly in the United States (especially those in poverty) live in housing and community settings that are often rundown and of environmentally poor quality, and
express considerable dissatisfaction with their well-being and quality of life.[10]

Economic and Financial Influences

Individuals in the United States are expected to take the initiative in assuring their own
financial security in older age. This is part of the American ideology although it is
less true in other countries with comprehensive public pensions. A certain proportion
of Americans do not save for retirement, either because they fail to consider their
future or because they do not earn enough for significant savings. They must depend
on government social security and Medicare or Medicaid for their sustenance as they
age.

Policies and programs of state and national governments directly affect the
income and well-being of older people. Most regional units (city, country, state, or
provincial governments) have service programs which assist the elderly (through
state departments of social and health services and area agencies on aging, for example). However, the seamlessness and quality of such programs vary enormously among
state jurisdictions and among nations.

The more affluent nations tend to have more complete and adequate public provisions for financial security and more abundant and well-funded social support programs than less affluent nations. For example, Sweden has one of the
highest per capita incomes in the world and has a range of publicly sponsored programs for provision of high-quality services to facilitate elderly well-being. On the
other hand, Japan is equally affluent but, because of different values and beliefs, families have been expected to care for the majority of older members, and public
programs have been incomplete and inadequate (although new policies have been
initiated, as discussed in detail later).

Economic Challenges. Guaranteeing economic independence for the older population is creating great social and political stress in most modern countries. Because length of life is increasing, pensions and social security needs are growing rapidly—thus raising the required payroll deductions for workers. If no major change is made in the retirement age in the United States, as noted earlier, as of 2050 only two people are likely to be at work for each retired person.[4, 46]

From a national perspective, higher payroll taxes have the effect of increasing labor costs for employers, while potentially reducing overall economic growth. Yet, employment of older individuals in paid employment is declining in most countries despite improved health status and productivity potential.[35, 82]

Laws have been passed in several Western European countries to deliberately ease older workers out of the labor force before the official retirement age. Individuals who are no longer competitive because of antiquated skills or disability are offered disability payments to tide them over until formal retirement. It should be noted that preretirement unemployed status is not welcomed by most older workers, nor is it honored particularly by the larger society. The policies have evolved because of chronic unemployment problems. Predictability of a comfortable retirement has actually diminished in a number of European countries.[35]

A serious danger of competition between generations, as public programs for elderly become more expensive and a threat to adequate educational and other resources for children and younger people, will be a major challenge to public policy in the years ahead. All age groups have a common interest in finding constructive solutions to common problems—since nearly all older people are parents and grandparents in families that collectively want to treat all members well.[37]

Lifestyle

Lifestyle has many dimensions, including elements directly related to financial security. Much of the potential for a high quality lifestyle for most older people depends on public policies with respect to income, health care, long-term care, and housing. Whether or not an older person continues to work or otherwise engages in productive activities is in part dependent on public policies.[42]

A national study funded by the Commonwealth Fund in 1991 found that three out of every four older Americans are actively involved in clearly productive activities. Many continue to work part-time or full-time; others volunteer in service efforts or political activity, locally and nationally. Many care for disabled spouses or other family members. Although such activity may subside with advanced age, most of the elderly remain productive in some capacity.[7]

The functional ability of older workers could be further enhanced if employers deliberately took measures to improve workplace environments, as has been the case in many economically advanced nations. Encouragement of healthy behavior, together with inservice training, can often generate greater returns from older workers than younger replacements.[42, 72]

For those who retire from full- or part-time paid employment, lifestyle depends heavily on social expectations in the community and socioeconomic status. The great majority of individuals remain in their home and community, engaging with family and local social organizations. The more affluent minority may move to a new community, to a warmer climate, or otherwise change their mode of living—as discussed in a later chapter.

◆◆◆ THE STUDY OF AGING

The formal study of aging is a relatively new phenomenon originating largely in the mid-and late twentieth century. Many of the early theories were based on limited perspectives attempting to explain only part of the aging process. For example, *activity or engagement* theory suggested that remaining active and seeking satisfying new roles are the keys to successful aging. *Disengagement* theory focused on the processes of losing roles and altering lifestyles at retirement, suggesting that social roles, especially the work role, are removed in the process of retirement with nothing meaningful as a replacement. Disengagement was thought to benefit both the individual and society.[6, 18, 27, 45, 50]

Continuity theory assumes that what happens to an individual at younger ages structures adaptation to older age; the personality formed at younger ages is continuous throughout the life span—a viewpoint that is somewhat contrary to disengagement theory as noted above. Continuity of personal goals and general patterns of behavior are very common as individuals age, although adaptations are made in response to new information or major life events. *Exchange* theory suggests among other things that continuity can be maintained through the rewards of reciprocity involving engagement and interaction with peers, family, and others in the community. *Symbolic interaction* theory focuses on the interaction between the self and the surrounding society, contributing to development of the self-concept through the the socialization process.[2, 6, 18, 45, 50, 51]

Social scientists have developed these and many other useful theories in attempts to understand aging. This brief summary is intended to indicate that scholars have been at work for decades attempting to explain why individuals are successful or unsuccessful in achieving quality of life in older age.[5, 18, 27, 50]

The study of aging is pursued from several disciplinary perspectives. Each major social science and health care discipline has an aging subfield that may interact with or directly relate to the perspectives of other disciplines. Unifying frameworks and clear guidelines for research remain somewhat inadequate. Nonetheless, the various perspectives come together to form a specific focus referred to as gerontology.[49, 50]

Gerontology. Gerontology is by definition multidisciplinary. The range of applicable disciplines includes biology, sociology, psychology, social psychology, economics, health care policy, law, medicine, nursing, social work, housing, recreation and leisure, and other closely related fields. The research-based knowledge generated by these disciplines is interrelated and becomes mutually reinforcing in the gerontology literature. [12, 53]

Gerontologists engage in scientific research but also attempt to integrate the basic knowledge from the various disciplines. They help develop applications of knowledge that are useful to professional practitioners who directly serve the older population (such as physicians, pharmacists, nurses, social workers, health care administrators, psychologists, and other supportive professionals).[19]

Educators, researchers and working professionals in the field convene regularly in local, state, national, and international forums for exchange of relevant information. For example, the Gerontological Society of America meets on an annual basis and publishes two journals emphasizing scientific and professional practice (*The Gerontologist* and *The Journal of Gerontology*). The American Society on Aging has become an important professional organization as well with its own journal (*Generations*). The National Council on Aging publishes a newsletter that attempts to link together the great variety of organizations working in the field of aging (*Networks*). The National Academy on Aging was created in 1991 in association with the federal Administration on Aging to deepen public understanding of challenges imposed by an aging society. It publishes a journal (*Issues in Aging*) with reports on public policy issues affecting the elderly. The International Association of Gerontology represents gerontological societies around the world and organizes periodic international meetings. Several World Wide Web sites are available with research articles including Ageline (www.aarp.org), GeronLine (www.nig.nl), The National Aging Information Center (www.ageinfo.org), and www.aoa.dhhs.gov.[39, 52]

A European Congress of Gerontology and an International Congress of Gerontology convene periodically with participation from national gerontological and geriatric societies throughout the world. An Observatory on Ageing and Older people was created in 1991 by the European Union, and is designed to gather on-going multidisciplinary data about the impact of social and economic policies on the older populations in all of the European countries. Much of the data is drawn from the Eurobarometer Survey which collects standardized information in each of the countries. *Gerontology, Age and Ageing, Reviews in Clinical Gerontology,* and several other reputable journals are published in Europe.[52, 67, 76, 77]

Geriatrics. Geriatrics deals with the unique health problems and health care alternatives for older individuals. Health professionals trained in the field are prepared to diagnose and treat the unique physical and mental changes that occur with age. Geriatrics is sometimes considered a subfield of gerontology although it is certainly a specialization in its own right. The American Geriatrics Society publishes a newsletter and a journal (*The AGS Newsletter* and the *Journal of the American Geriatric Society*) serving respectively as the most prominent news source and outlet for scientific studies. For example, a 1998 issue of the *AGS Newsletter* reported on the serious shortage of geriatricians to serve the growing elderly population: only 8000 geriatric physicians (including psychiatry) were available, whereas the need was estimated to be approximately 24,000 in 1998.[24, 65]

Geriatrics has only recently been widely accepted in the United States and remains a poorly developed health care specialty in many economically advanced countries. Only about half of the European countries recognize geriatrics as a distinct professional field. The scientific beginnings of the specialty were introduced as early as the eighteenth century through the work of Christoph W. Hufeland in Germany who recommended a scientific approach to health care for older people long before experimental methods were widely adopted. The development of the science of geriatrics is illustrated by growth in publications to 13 international journals and 28 national journals worldwide in 1999.[24, 52, 78]

In addition to these major specializations in aging, many disciplines offer subfields in aging or gerontology, as noted earlier. A wide variety of scientific journals and other periodicals emphasizing aging issues are published. For example, *Modern Maturity*, with a circulation of more than 33,000,000 (published by the American Association for Retired Persons), attempts to apply the results of research and experience to the needs of the older population.

◆◆◆ CAREERS IN GERONTOLOGY AND GERIATRICS

Gerontology and geriatrics are rapidly growing fields of research and practice. New career variations are emerging because of increasing professional response to the growth in the elderly population. Specialization in aging for a physician, pharmacist, lawyer, architect, social worker, psychologist, counselor, sociologist, nurse, health administrator, occupational therapist, physical therapist, speech therapist, recreation therapist, art therapist, case manager, and other professional fields, is likely to provide good job opportunities in the years ahead.[59, 79]

Many universities and colleges have added courses or multidisciplinary training programs. Textbooks for training professionals have become widely available. The Association for Gerontology in Higher Education, with over 300 institutional members, publishes a booklet on *Careers in Aging: Opportunities and Options* and a *National Directory of Educational Programs in Gerontology and Geriatrics.*[39, 66]

In addition to domestic opportunities, international positions are available with the World Health Organization and its subdivisions, the World Bank, The United Nations Centre for Social Development and Humanitarian Affairs, the Agency for International Development and other international organizations, and in technical or research work with professionals in other countries.[47]

◆◆◆ SUMMARY AND CONCLUSIONS

The older population is expanding rapidly in most parts of the world. Pressure on government resources for older people has been increasing rapidly. Major reexamination of policies is underway in most countries—with an emphasis on issues associated with quality of life for the older population.

The elderly are our parents, grandparents, and peers. They have had major influence on our own well-being and deserve our intense attention. The diversity of older populations means that policies and programs must not be rigid, culturally narrow, or ethnocentric. Various income levels, cultural backgrounds, value systems, beliefs, educational levels, and life experiences must be taken into account.

A multidisciplinary approach is essential to adequately appreciate all contributing factors. Although the individual can have a major and creative influence on his or her future well-being, social and biophysical environment outside individual control will also directly affect the quality of life possible in any community.

The change in older population numbers therefore has the potential to profoundly impact families, communities, states, and national governments in every country. Families are the most fundamental social unit providing primary support to elderly members, but they are directly dependent upon local, regional, and national programs to undergird their efforts.

As older populations increase, demand for income security and health services rise rapidly, putting great pressure on allocation of public and private resources. Presumably, a larger proportion of government budgets must be devoted to support of basic income, health care services, long-term care facilities, and specialized housing. Among the important questions to ponder is: How much of our national and local resources should be devoted to providing quality of life for our elderly?

◆◆◆ REFERENCES

1. Administration on Aging (2000). *Profile of Older Americans: 1999*, Online at www.aoa.gov/aoa/stats/profile/default.htm.
2. Aiken, Lewis R. (1995). *Aging: An Introduction to Gerontology*, Thousand Oaks, CA: Sage Publications.
3. American Association of Retired Persons (AARP) (1998). *A Profile of Older Americans*, Washington, DC: AARP.
4. Angel, Ronald J., and Jacqueline L. Angel (1997). *Who Will Care for Us? Aging and Long-Term Care in Multicultural America*, New York: New York University Press.
5. Atchley, Robert C. (1999). *Continuity and Adaptation in Aging: Creating Positive Experiences*, Baltimore: Johns Hopkins University Press.
6. Barrow, Georgia M. (1996). *Aging, the Individual, and Society* (6th ed), Minneapolis/St. Paul: West.
7. Bass, Scott A. (1995). *Older and Active: How Americans over 55 Are Contributing to Society*, New Haven: Yale University Press.
8. Beard, Belle Boon (1991). *Centenarians: The New Generation*, New York: Greenwood Press.
9. Birren, James E., and Marion A. Perlmutter (1990). Measuring Our Psychological Performance, in Robert N. Butler, Mia R. Oberlink, and Mal Schechter, *The Promise of Productive Aging: From Biology to Social Policy*, New York: Springer, 48–69.
10. Blendon, Robert J., Robert Leitman, Ian Morrison, and Karen Donelan (1990). Satisfaction With Health Services in Ten Nations, *Health Affairs*, (Summer), 185–92.
11. Boetzkes, Elisabeth (1993). Autonomy and Advance Directives, *Canadian Journal on Aging*, 12 (4), 441–52.
12. Bond, John (1993). Future Trends in Social Gerontology, *Reviews in Clinical Gerontology*, 3 (4), 407–13.
13. Bond, John (1999). Quality of Life for Older People with Dementia: Approaches to the Challenge of Measurement, *Ageing and Society*, 19 (2), 561–79.
14. Bondevik, Margareth (1994). Historical, Cross-Cultural, Biological and Psychosocial Perspectives of Ageing and the Aged Person, *Scandanavian Journal of Caring*, 8 (2), 67–74.
15. Bosworth, Barry, and Gary Burtless (1998). Population Aging and Economic Performance, in Barry Bosworth and Gary Burtless, *Aging Societies: The Global Dimension*, Washington, DC: Brookings Institution, 1–29.
16. Brayne, Carol (1995). Quality of Life—As Yet Undefined, *World Health Forum*, 16 (4), 352–54.
17. Brod, Meryl, Anita L. Stewart, Laura Sands, and Pam Walton (1999). Conceptualization and Measurement of Quality of Life in Dementia: The Dementia Quality of Life Instrument (DqoL), *The Gerontologist*, 39 (1), 25-35.
18. Brown, Arnold S. (1996). *The Social Processes of Aging and Old Age* (2d ed), Upper Saddle River, NJ: Prentice Hall.
19. Butler, Robert N. (1990). Introduction, in Robert N. Butler, Mia R. Oberlink, and Mal Schechter, *The Promise of Productive Aging: From Biology to Social Policy*, New York: Springer, xxxi-xxxiv.
20. Byers, Bryan (ed.) (1995). *Readings in Social Psychology*. Boston: Allyn and Bacon.

21. Bytheway, Bill (1995). *Ageism*, Buckingham, U.K.: Open University Press.

22. Bytheway, Bill (1997). Talking About Age: The Theoretical Basis of Social Gerontology, in Anne Jamieson, Sarah Harper, and Christina Victor (eds), *Critical Approaches to Ageing and Later Life*, Buckingham, U.K.: Open University Press, 7–15.

23. Clair, Jeffrey Michael, David A. Karp, and William C. Yoels (1993). *Experiencing the Life Cycle: A Social Psychology of Aging*, Springfield, IL: Charles C Thomas, Publisher.

24. Conway, Brian (1998). Special Interest Group on International Activities, *AGS Newsletter*, Second Quarter, 11, 1–12.

25. Cox, Harold G. (1996). *Later Life: The Realities of Aging* (4th ed), Upper Saddle River, NJ: Prentice Hall.

26. Defever, Mia (1991). Long Term Care: The Case of the Elderly, *Health Policy*, 19, 1, 1–18.

27. Encandela, John A. (1997). Social Construction of Pain and Aging, *Symbolic Interaction*, 20 (3), 251–73.

28. Evans, J. Grimley (2000). Ageing and Medicine, *Journal of Internal Medicine*, 247 (1), 159–67.

29. Falk, Ursula, and Gerhard Falk (1997). *Ageism, The Aged, and Aging in America*, Springfield: Charles C Thomas Publishers.

30. Ferraro, Kenneth F. (ed) (1991). *Gerontology: Perspectives and Issues,* New York: Springer Publishing Co.

31. Fetridge, Guild A. (1994). *The Adventure of Retirement*, Amherst, NY: Prometheus Books.

32. Fried, Stephen B., and Chandra M. Mehrotra (1998). *Aging and Diversity: An Active Learning Experience*, London: Taylor and Francis.

33. Fry, Christine L. (1991). Cross-cultural comparisons of aging, in Kenneth F. Ferraro (ed), *Gerontology: Perspectives and Issues,* New York: Springer Publishing Co., 129–46.

34. Green, Bryan S. (1993). *Gerontology and the Construction of Old Age,* New York: Aldine de Gruyter.

35. Guillemard, A. (1996). Equity Between Generations in Aging Societies, in Tamara K. Hareven (ed), *Aging and Generational Relations Over The Life Course: A Historical and Cross-Cultural Perspective*, New York: Walter de Gruyter, 208–24.

36. Hallinan, Maureen T. (1997). A Sociological Perspective on Social Issues, *American Sociologist*, 28 (1), 5–15.

37. Hardy, Melissa A. (1992). Vulnerability in Old Age: The Issue of Dependence in American Society, in Jaber F. Gubrium and Kathy Charmaz (eds), *Aging, Self, and Community*, Greenwich, Connecticut: JAI Press, 255–64.

38. Hareven, Tamara K. (ed). (1996). *Aging and Generational Relations Over the Life Course: A Historical and Cross-Cultural Perspective*, New York: Walter de Gruyter.

39. Heinemann, Gloria D., Elizabeth B. Douglass, and Joy C. Lobenstine (1995). *Careers in Aging: Consider the Possibilities*, Washington, DC: The Association for Gerontology in Higher Education.

40. Hicks, Peter (1997). Impact of Aging on Public Policy, *The OECD Observer*, 203 (January), 19-21. Online at www.oecd.org/publications/observer/203/Article_eng.htm.

41. Hicks, Peter (1998). The Policy Challenge of Ageing Populations, *The OECD Observer*, 212 (July), Online at www.oecd.org/publications/observer/212/Article2_eng.htm.

42. Hoskins, Irene (1995). A Matter of Human Rights, *World Health Forum*, 16 (4), 364–66.

43. Jeffreys, Margot (1995). Further Questions of Equity, *World Health Forum*, 16 (4), 371–72.

44. Kane, Rosalie A., and Mary Olsen Baker (1996). Emerging Trends in Managed Care, presentation to a conference on *Managed Care Issues and Themes: What Next for the Aging Network?* Sponsored by the Administration on Aging, Department of Health and Human Services, Washington, DC

45. Kart, Cary S. (1990). *The Realities of Aging*, Boston: Allyn and Bacon.

46. Kingson, Eric R. (1996). Ways of Thinking About the Long-Term Care and Baby-Boom Cohorts, in Marie E. Coward and Jill Quadagno (eds), *From Nursing Homes to Home Care*, New York: Haworth Press, 3–23.

47. Kosberg, Jordan I. (1999). Opportunities for Social Workers in an Aging World, *Journal of Sociology and Social Welfare*, 26 (1), 7–24.

48. Lawton, M. Powell, Laraine Winter, Morton H. Kleban, and Katy Ruckdeschel (1999). Affect and Quality of Life: Objective and Subjective, *Journal of Aging and Health*, 11 (2), 169–98.

49. Lomranz, Jacob (1998). Introduction: Toward Theories in Mental Health and Aging, in Jacob Lomranz (ed), *Handbook of Aging and Mental Health: An Integrative Approach*, New York: Plenum Press, 1–11.

50. Marshall, Victor W. (1996). The State of Theory in Aging and the Social Sciences, in Robert H. Bin-

stock and Linda K. George (eds), *Handbook of Aging and the Social Sciences* (4th ed), San Diego: Academic Press, 12–30.

51. Michener, H. Andrew, and John D. DeLamater (1994). *Social Psychology*, Fort Worth, TX: Harcourt Brace.

52. Mulley, Graham P. (1999). Journals of Geriatric Medicine and Gerontology, *Age and Ageing*, 28 (1), 1–2.

53. Myer, David. G. (1993). *Social Psychology*, New York: McGraw-Hill.

54. Myers, George C. (1995). Measuring the Needs, *World Health Forum*, 16 (4), 355–57.

55. National Center for Health Statistics, *Health United States 1998*, Washington, DC: U.S. Bureau of the Census.

56. Neal, Arthur G. (1995). Psychological Modernity, in Bryan Byers (ed.), *Readings in Social Psychology*, Boston: Allyn and Bacon, 333–36.

57. Palmore, Erdman B. (1999). *Ageism: Negative and Positive*, New York: Springer.

58. Perls, Thomas T., Kathreen Bochen, Melissa Freeman, Laura Alpert, and Margery H. Silver (1999). Validity of Reported Age and Centenarian Prevalence in New England, *Age and Ageing*, 28 (2), 193–97.

59. Peterson, David A., and Pamela F. Wendt (1990). Employment in the Field of Aging: A Survey of Professionals in Four Fields, *The Gerontologist*, 30 (5), 679–84.

60. Raphael, Dennis, Ivan Brown, Rebecca Renwick, Maureen Cava, Nancy Weir, and Kit Heathcote (1997). Measuring the Quality of Life of Older Persons: A Model With Implications for Community and Public Health Nursing, *International Journal of Nursing Studies*, 34 (3), 231–39.

61. Redburn, David E. (1998). The "Graying" of the World's Population, in David E. Redburn and Robert P. McNamara (eds). *Social Gerontology*, Westport, CT: Auburn House, 5–12.

62. Restrepo, Helena E., and Manuel Rozental (1994). The Social Impact of Aging Populations: Some Major Issues, *Social Science and Medicine*, 39 (9), 1323–38.

63. Rieske, Robert J., and Henry Holstege (1996). *Growing Old in America*, New York: McGraw-Hill, 1996.

64. Riley, Matilda White, and John W. Riley, Jr. (1999). Sociological Research on Age: Legacy and Challenge, *Ageing and Society*, 19 (1), 123–32.

65. Rowe, John W., and Robert L. Kahn (1998). *Successful Aging*, New York: Pantheon Books.

66. Safford, Florence, and George I. Krell (eds) (1992). *Gerontology for Health Professionals: A Practice Guide*, Washington, DC: National Association of Social Workers Press.

67. Schroots, Johannes J. F. (1995). Psychological Models of Aging, *Canadian Journal of Aging*, 14 (1), 44–66.

68. Schulte, Bernd (1996). Social Protection for Dependence in Old Age: The Case of Germany, in Roland Eisen and Frank A. Sloan (eds), *Long-Term Care: Economic Issues and Policy Solutions*, Boston: Kluwer Academic Publishers, 149–70.

69. Slater, Robert (1995). *The Psychology of Growing Old*, Philadelphia: Open University Press.

70. Smith-Sonneborn, Joan (1990). How We Age, chapter 1 in Robert N. Butler, Mia R. Oberlink, and Mal Schechter, *The Promise of Productive Aging: From Biology to Social Policy*, New York: Springer, 7–11.

71. Social Security Administration (1997). *Social Security Programs Throughout the World*, Washington, DC: U.S. Government Printing Office.

72. Sterns, Haravey L., and Anthony A. Sterns (1995). Health and the Employment Capability of Older Americans, in Scott A. Bass (ed), *Older and Active: How Americans Over 55 Are Contributing to Society*, New Haven: Yale University Press, 10–34.

73. Stewart, Anita, and Abby C. King (1994). Conceptualizing and Measuring Quality of Life in Older Populations, in Ronald P. Abeles, Helen C. Gift, and Marcia G. Ory (eds), *Aging and Quality of Life*, New York: Springer, 27–39.

74. United States Census Bureau (1998). *National Data Book*, Washington, DC: U.S. Government Printing Office.

75. United States Census Bureau (2000). *International Data Base*. Online at www.census.gov/cgi-bin/ipc/idbpyry.pl.

76. Walker, Alan, and Tony Maltby (1997). *Ageing Europe*, Philadelphia: Open University Press.

77. Watson, Roger (1996). Conference Report: Third European Congress of Gerontology, *Journal of Advanced Nursing*, 23 (3), 642–43.

78. Wehrmacher, William H. (1992). Conspectus: The Debut of Geriatric Medicine, *Comprehensive Therapy*, 18 (11), 2–3.

79. Weingarten, Tara (1998). For Entrepreneurs, Lawyers, and Doctors, There's Gold in Old, *Newsweek*, October 26, 17.

80. Wielink, Gina, and Robbert Huijsman (1999). Elderly Community Residents' Evaluative Criteria and Preferences for Formal and Informal In-Home Services, *International Journal of Aging and Human Development*, 48 (1), 17–33.

81. Williamson, John B., and Fred C. Pampel (1993). Paying for the Baby Boom Generation's Social Security Pensions: United States, United Kingdom, Germany, and Sweden, *Journal of Aging Studies*, 7 (1), 41–54.

82. World Bank (1994). *Averting the Old Age Crisis: Policies to Protect the Old and Promote Growth*, Washington, DC: The World Bank.

Chapter 2

OPTIMAL AGING
The Individual Role

 **INTRODUCTION**

The goals of this chapter are to identify and explain the primary individual characteristics that impact optimal aging and contribute to a satisfying quality of life. Major topics include:

- Heredity.
- Personality characteristics.
- Social influences.
- Knowledge, skills, and education.
- Physical and mental health.
- Personal financial resources.
- Lifestyle: work, retirement, and leisure.

Successful and contented older people provide ample evidence that a lifestyle can be created that contributes to adjustment during the unavoidable physical and mental changes of later life. Successful adaptation and retention of physical, sensory, and mental capacity arise particularly from a flexible personality and supportive social relationships. Underlying personality characteristics are the basis for individual response to both normal aging and the stresses that inevitably occur. Each individual has some potential to enhance self-conceptions, alter behaviors, and develop capacities to improve his or her future life.[1, 5, 25, 53]

Primary individual factors associated with optimal aging include:

- **Heredity** (physical, intellectual, and skill potential).
- **Personality** (self-concept, personal identity, self-esteem, self-respect, flexibility, independence, interdependence, dependence, autonomy and self-reliance, perception of choices).
- **Social roles** (role flexibility and adaptability to role change).
- **Social class** (upper, middle, lower).
- **Knowledge, skills, and education** (problem-solving skills, coping skills, proclivity for continuing education, interpersonal communication skills, on-going mental curiosity, wisdom).
- **Physical and mental health** (physical health, mental health, sexual function).
- **Economic resources** (income, assets, savings, access to community resources).
- **Lifestyle attributes** (freedom, satisfaction, aesthetic experience).

As the categories and subcategories noted above imply, individual influence on optimal aging encompasses a wide range of variations that lead to individual uniqueness. There is no single formula that will achieve optimal aging for everyone. It is not always clear which attributes are normal and which are atypical or even abnormal. Individuals with highly varied backgrounds and experience have the capacity to thrive in older age.[23, 59]

◆◆◆ HEREDITY

Individuals are born with certain unalterable genetic endowments. Physical capacity, personal skill potential, and intelligence are direct consequences of heredity. However, the basic inherited characteristics can be developed over time with very different outcomes, depending on the socialization and learning process. Overall potential is a consequence of how the basic personal endowment evolves over time.[51]

Physical Potential

Individuals whose parents or grandparents live to a ripe old age seem to have a better chance of surviving disease and living longer. Susceptibility to heart disease, diabetes, some forms of cancer, Alzheimer's disease, and other ailments are higher in some families than in others with similar life experience. Both limitations and potential arise from heredity, but actual outcomes are also a consequence of experience and lifestyle over a lifetime. Living a mentally and physically healthy lifestyle can greatly enhance human potential.[17, 28, 43]

Intellectual Potential

Intelligence is a major contributor to adaptability in older age and is directly associated with greater educational and occupational achievement. Higher levels of education add to intellectual competence and problem-solving skills. Self-direction and self-esteem are enhanced by greater education. These effects tend to be cumulative since the more intelligent person will have greater potential to continue learning through self-education. Knowledge and skills are thus likely to continue to grow.[9, 31]

Moreover, aging does not appear to cause major intellectual decline. Rather, the research evidence indicates that *crystallized* intelligence is associated with acquiring new knowledge and increasing job-relevant skills and may actually increase to some degree with age. Crystallized intelligence is linked to educational level, overall achievement, and acquisition of facts. *Fluid* or creative and inherited intelligence is associated with inductive reasoning and problem-solving skills and may decline somewhat. Decreases in the speed of mental processing usually occur. Memory may decline when other forms of intelligence remain stable. These features of intelligence help illuminate the potential for continuing work and productivity in older age.[18, 21, 23, 37, 62, 64, 69]

Most dimensions of intellectual ability thus continue into advanced old age in the absence of serious disease. Although some decline certainly occurs in reasoning and memory, attention and numerical abilities remain stable until quite advanced age. Overall high intellectual ability appears to slow the process of decline. There is also evidence that a flexible personality helps adjustment as does having a spouse with strong mental abilities. On the other hand, stressful events such as serious illness can cause substantial decline over a short time span. These patterns of change are not uniform and vary by individual abilities and experience. Furthermore, continued use of intellectual skills clearly helps to keep mental function alive and well.[20, 29, 51, 56, 59]

At the most advanced ages (85 and older), decline may be more visible, causing intellectual dysfunction despite higher intelligence. Because of the assorted other declining capacities with older age, functional status is likely to deteriorate—but not necessarily for everyone. Among all older age groupings, functional ability is related to educational level, sensory capacity (vision, hearing), ability to undertake activities of daily living, and any chronic conditions. In sum, the healthiest individuals with the most intellectual capacity and education are more likely to function effectively into more advanced ages. Continuing intellectual function is a primary element in maintaining the ability to remain independent.[1, 33, 63]

A close linkage exists between sensory abilities—especially seeing and hearing—and intellectual function. Sense of smell and taste strongly affect appetite and interest in good nutrition. As the senses decline with advancing age, mental function also declines. If the senses can be improved—through artificial hearing aids, eye glasses, or other measures—intellectual ability and general functional capacity are more likely to continue.[33, 58]

◆◆◆ PERSONALITY

Personality is an enduring, consistent, and unique set of behavioral traits, including a special blend of talents, hopes, loves, hates, and habits that remain relatively stable over time. Personality includes the self-concept, personal identity, self-esteem, values, attitudes, and beliefs that evolve from cumulative socialization and personal experience. While each person has unique traits, the human personality is not static but can change abruptly or gradually over time—especially as a result of major illnesses (e.g., Alzheimer's disease) or trauma, although some unique features are likely to remain recognizable.[1, 22, 26]

Adaptability includes various degrees of tolerance for ambiguity, spontaneity, and future orientation. Older individuals who can tolerate uncertainty are more likely to adapt to changes effectively than are more rigid or inflexible personality types. Spontaneity is associated with feeling pleasure in new experience, as contrasted with a preference for patterned behavior and fear of change. An orientation toward the future and its wide-ranging possibilities leads to flexibility, as contrasted to a preference for tradition and a focus on past experience. A sense of personality integrity, feelings of completeness, and meaningfulness of life become very important at later ages if unhappiness and despair are to be avoided.[1, 13, 18, 21, 44]

Range of Personality Types

The degree of personality integration has varying consequences for the aging process. An integrated or mature personality is likely to make better adjustments than the unintegrated and immature type. For example, immature defensiveness, dependence, anger, and self-disrespect will make adjustment difficult, whereas mature openness, independence, calmness and self-respect will contribute to adjustment. The more integrated personality is likely to fare much better in older age than the less integrated.[27, 55]

The most stable and productive personality type characterizes older individuals who have enjoyed a positive family and community environment and who are effectively realizing their goals for a satisfying life. The integrated personality has high self-esteem and positive self-perceptions. Older individuals with these personalities are more likely to form a stable support system of informal and formal relationships—thus enabling them to maintain considerable independence and personal choice until death, even when illness or severe disability limit their options.[54]

At the other extreme, the older individual with an immature personality may have had difficult family and community experiences, with resulting poor coping abilities and low self-esteem. Such individuals are often not well-adjusted, may be unhappy, and may tend to be dissatisfied with life. They are unlikely to take the initiatives needed to improve themselves and are more likely to feel helpless, suffer depression, feel discouraged, and incur high stress. Most people fall between the two extremes—their personalities function at various levels of success and varying levels of self-esteem.[27, 32]

The Self-Concept

The *self-concept* refers to the perception an individual has of himself or herself as a member of social groups—the family, friends, neighborhood, community, and larger society. An evaluative dimension of self-concept includes beliefs and feelings about personal merit or value, referred to as self-esteem or self-worth. The self-concept also includes *personal identity, self-respect,* and *self-efficacy* (confidence in ability to manage personal affairs).[7, 40]

The various dimensions of the self-concept collectively define the level of confidence an individual has in personal abilities, competencies, and limitations. A positive self-concept contributes to individual *autonomy* and *self-direction* and implies an integrated personality accompanied by confidence in overall ability to function effectively as a member of society.[53, 67]

The self-concept is enhanced for an older person when family members or other close caregivers are reliably available and are responsive and supportive. The older person develops confidence in the availability of assistance and retains feelings of self-worth. This encourages retention of skills to effectively function as an autonomous individual—laying the foundation for on-going emotional stability and a strong personal identity. Self-esteem tends to be sustained when an older individual is treated positively and health is maintained.[19, 24, 60]

On the other hand, if the family or larger social situation does not provide security, is indifferent to needs, or is inconsistent, the older person is likely to be insecure—with accompanying lack of self-confidence and lack of confidence in others. Older people who have a strong sense of self-worth and self-efficacy tend to perform better intellectually and physically, and have greater satisfaction with life.[3, 7]

Older individuals want a distinctive identity, just as younger people do. "Who they are" is very important to them. Loss of roles caused by retirement from a valued job, disability, or loss of a spouse—all key parts of the self-concept—can be very damaging to mental well-being. This may explain in part why the young-old, between 65 and 74, tend not to evaluate themselves as old. They may attribute the common stereotypes of "older people" only to the age groups 80 or older—people who are more likely to be disabled.[1, 30]

Independence, Autonomy, and Choice

Independence appears to be important for older individuals in at least four realms:[4]

1. Social and emotional involvement with others.
2. Maintainance of physical and mental health.
3. Management of house and home.
4. Control of financial resources.

Freedom of choice may be the single most highly valued experience for older individuals. Without choice in the four noted types of customary personal responsibilities, self-esteem can be damaged and a sense of lost power may occur. The ability to exercise some level of control over daily decisions and experiences is clearly important to personal satisfaction and optimal aging.[13]

If personal autonomy is maintained, feelings of self-esteem can actually increase with age, particularly if accompanied by access to fulfilling social networks and satisfying living arrangements. Retirement can create new opportunities and interesting new roles that lead to high levels of personal satisfaction.[11, 24]

Autonomy and independence imply relative freedom from coercion by others. If dependence is to be avoided, the older individual with disabilities must have sufficient power to undertake independent decisions and be able to challenge any attempt by others to impose their choices. The older individual will benefit from having some control mechanism to reward those who support independence—such as an ability to pay for services, signature power to control formal decisions, or enough personal influence to insist on the right to choose. The opportunity to exercise choice has critical effects on quality of life.[14, 35, 50, 70]

Continuing independence, especially in the event of disability, requires a high level of self-confidence. Individual initiative to maintain autonomy is essential if others are to be prevented from assuming inappropriate responsibility for fundamentally personal decisions. However, there is also a limit to exercise of autonomy; at the extreme it can alienate caretakers, who may be unwilling to tolerate undue independence in someone for whom they are trying to care.[32, 62]

Limitations on Choice. Personal choice may be limited by forces other than age, such as illness of caretakers, discrimination based on gender, ethnicity, race, and social class. Many older individuals have no basis for knowing about alternative opportunities for maintaining their well-being and are constrained by external factors beyond their control. Even if alternatives are known, they may not be abe to act on the available choices—because of income limitations, functional disabilities, or other constraints.[54]

The loss of independence and control are among the explanations for the unhappiness of many elderly individuals who are confined to nursing homes or other institutional settings. They lose some of their identity with the diminuation of former roles in the family and community. At the same time, autonomy is lost as they become subject to the rules and limitations of institutional personnel who sometimes do not respect them as human beings.[16]

Self-Reliance and Self-Direction. Self-reliance is an important value in many societies and has particular relevance to older people who grew up in a time of less technology, urbanization, and service density. Capacity to manage personal affairs and take individual responsibility for earning a living were given high priority, especially among men. It is thus very difficult for older generations to become dependent when functional abilities are lost.[46, 54]

When the big decisions of life are constrained because of infirmity, the smaller choices of daily living such as food options and control of personal space become more important. The value of self-reliance continues even though the range of options may necessarily be limited. Some degree of self-direction continues to be necessary for independence and serves as a primary source of identity. Most elderly individuals want to continue controlling certain categories of their lives no matter how old they are. On the other hand, they may choose to delegate some responsibilities considered of lesser consequence.[42, 45, 54]

Similarly, most older people want to manage their personal lives on a daily basis. They want to keep a schedule of activities and engage in recreation they enjoy. They want to relate to friends and family outside the immediate living space, as sources of emotional support. And they want to maintain their preferred habits, personal identity, and individuality.

Interdependence. Appropriate interdependence—with family, friends, and community institutions—is also required for successful adjustment to disability. Dependence and independence may best be considered intertwined rather than opposite ends of a continuum. Maintaining some level of independence involves reciprocity with family, friends, neighbors, and service providers. Interdependence and reciprocity are after all the basis for maintenance of the larger social structure and on-going social order. Older women who exhibit the best adjustment to older age, for example, tend to be well connected to family and other social groups. If interdependence cannot be fully supported by caregivers, relationships may be destroyed with resulting unhappiness.[4, 22, 61, 69]

Dependence. The alternative to healthy independence and interdependence is *dependence*. Some level of dependency is normal at certain stages in the life cycle—during the early socialization process, and later in life when ability to function with complete independence may no longer be possible. Dependence is not necessarily unhealthy, as long as reciprocity with caretakers continues to support a sense of self-worth. Something must be given back to those doing the caretaking—sometimes only expressions of appreciation and a sense of humor—if they are to sustain the effort.

Succumbing to decisions by well-meaning family or health care workers can lead to serious decline in the skills of self-management. It is usually possible for relatives, friends, and service staff to focus on maintaining some level of independence if they are conscious of its importance and have appropriate training.[32]

◆◆◆ SOCIAL INFLUENCES

Family and friends are likely to have highly varied conceptions of appropriate and expected roles for an older person. For example, it is commonplace for adult children to treat their disabled and dependent older parents or grandparents like children, disregarding the fact that the parents continue to feel like adults and want to be treated accordingly. Treating them as children is a put-down and generally inappropriate for preservation of their self-respect.

Role Change

Even for fully competent older adults, adopting radically new roles can be either very stressful or fulfilling. New expectations, performance of new tasks, moving to a new location, and interacting with new people can either create discontinuity or can be positively stimulating, depending in part on whether the changes are voluntary or involuntary. Disengagement from work can be part of a retirement plan with self-chosen and attractive new options, or it can create boredom, frustration and unhappiness. In fact, having free time and continuing high energy is liberating for most people if preceded by adequate preparation.[13, 44, 47]

The potential loss of status associated with giving up a highly valued work role is one of the serious challenges in adjusting to retirement. Alternative roles must be identified, learned and adopted. Many retirees have prepared extensively and find only pleasure in the transition. Others have serious difficulty with the change. They may not have accepted the transition out of the workplace and thus have trouble shifting to other roles with satisfying options. Role transition is more easily achieved by individuals who have deliberately identified desirable new options, especially when the change is gradual. Identification of alternative fulfilling opportunities will help maintain self-esteem.[22, 41]

It is obviously not always possible, however, to control the course of life events, and adjust roles accordingly. Several major changes may unavoidably occur in close proximity. For example, some older individuals suffer a health crisis and become dependent at the same time their potential caregivers experience personal physical health decline or retirement. Normal life processes taken one at a time might be quite manageable, but if bunched together they can lead to personal problems and even depression.[38, 44]

The advent of widowhood is usually a special challenge—since it is clearly a new and unpracticed role for all concerned. The tendency may be for family members to assume some of the deceased spouses responsibilities with the intent of being helpful to the survivor. However, it is important that a widow or widower be encouraged to take charge relatively soon during the bereavement process.[38]

Gender Differences. Possibly the key gender difference is the greater independence and autonomy available to males as compared to females—obviously a cultural rather than biological issue. Many older women have not worked outside the home. If so, they have usually earned much less than their husbands have. Single older women nearly always have less personal retirement income than do older men. The public response to this circumstance varies considerably from one country to another, as we shall see in later chapters. Gender differences are much more pronounced in some countries than others. In all countries, it may be anticipated that gender differences will decrease as the more independent baby boomers enter retirement.[6, 9, 15]

Social Status Influences

Social status is heavily determined by education, income, and occupational prestige. Individuals with higher education tend to participate more in cultural activities, are more likely to be involved in civic and political activities, and are more likely to vote. Higher-income individuals generally have a greater opportunity for access to resources in older age than those with lower incomes, regardless of cultural background. Moreover, high-status individuals are also likely to have better health, greater life expectancy, more stable and happier marriages, a higher level of mental capacity and function, greater sexual activity into later life, and greater satisfaction with the quality of their lives.[9, 31, 54]

Higher education and greater income obviously reduce the dependence of older adults on their children. Similarly, offspring with greater education and resources are better able to assist parents who may not have sufficient resources. Greater material giving and receiving in times of crisis are likely to occur among affluent families as compared to those with fewer resources.[44]

Maintaining social status after the death of a spouse is sometimes a serious problem for older women. As noted, they have less access to personal resources than do men, and they generally have less influence in directing their destiny. Fewer choices can be exercised regarding preferred housing and community environment.[48]

◆◆◆ KNOWLEDGE, SKILLS, AND EDUCATION

Knowledge and skills gained through formal education and experience are major contributors to effective adaptation. Educational level is closely correlated with perceived quality of life and is the single strongest contributor to sustained sense of control. Formal education is of course not the only source of valuable knowledge. The public media are an on-going source of information that can add to knowledge. Computers provide access to the unlimited resources of the Internet, which has become an increasingly important supplemental source of knowledge and skills used by many older Americans.[2, 45, 53]

Problem-Solving and Coping Skills

An ability to solve problems as they occur is a key factor in optimally adjusting to the aging process. The development of *problem-solving skills* is crucial to maintenance of autonomy and self-esteem and to avoid unrealistic responses, frustration, ineffectiveness, and poor adjustment. Problem-solving ability is especially important during the bereavement process after a spouse dies. It may immediately be necessary to deal with a wide range of issues that formerly were the spouse's responsibility. *Coping skills* are closely related to effective problem-solving. Effective coping also requires an ability to deal with stress, anxiety, and ambiguity.[36, 46, 62]

Interpersonal and Communication Skills

Satisfying relationships in marriage and the family, with friends in the community, and with formal institutions such as the health care establishment or the Social Security system are much easier for someone with effective interpersonal skills. Strong communication skills enhance adaptive capacities and can help overcome changes in relationships associated with widowhood or the death of close friends and relatives. The capacity to express one's deepest feelings helps to maintain a sense of balance and control.[41, 52]

Wisdom

Development of wisdom in later life may be the ideal use of intelligence. However, wisdom is obviously a characteristic that has many variations, as all of us know who have encountered wise older people. It is in part a realization of the limitations of knowledge (how little one knows), coupled with an ability to put life in broader perspective. It involves an ability to balance knowledge with emotion, detachment, action and inaction, and doubts. Although wisdom may tend to increase with experience and age, it is clearly not universal among the older population. Wisdom may include some or all of the following attributes:[62]

- Resilience in recovering from the adversities of age.
- Empathy for the experiences of others.
- Caring about other people and sustaining relationships.
- Unselfish concern about intergenerational interactions.
- Capacity for depending on other people as appropriate.
- Concern for the larger society.
- Sense of the complexity of life.
- Humility and the desire for continued learning.
- Humor: recognizing the lighter side of life.
- Acceptance of the life cycle without fear of death.

Many of our distinguished older citizens exhibit this kind of wisdom, as is particularly well illustrated by Mike Mansfield, former United States Senate Majority Leader and Ambassador to Japan, as summarized in Illustration 2–1.

Illustration 2–1
A WISE ELDER STATESMAN: SENATOR MIKE MANSFIELD

Mike Mansfield celebrated his 96th birthday in 1999 at a luncheon in Washington, D.C., with a group of his distinguished colleagues. He was born in New York City but moved to Montana to work in the copper mines after a stint in the United States Marines during World War I. He was elected to the U.S. House of Representatives in 1942 and to the Senate 10 years later. He was elected majority leader and served in that post from 1961 until 1976 without apparently earning any enemies. He then served as Ambassador to Japan from 1977 until 1988.

At age 96, he had not retired but continued to serve as an advisor on Asia to a major investment firm in New York City, maintaining a busy schedule of meetings with officials from around the world. He was considered a wise and monumental figure in Montana where the legislature recently voted to erect a statue in his honor.

Source: Broder, 1999: B7.

◆◆◆ PHYSICAL AND MENTAL HEALTH

Good health is clearly a primary factor in achieving quality of life. It is important to note here that exercise and mental stimulation can facilitate health but cannot guarantee freedom from disease and discomfort beyond a certain level. Arthritis, diabetes, cancer, heart disease, Alzheimer's and other dementias, and other physical ailments can take over despite one's best efforts to avoid them. Disability can prevent fulfillment of normal roles in society and nearly always results in feelings of lost control. Nonetheless, reasonable quality of life can be achieved despite most chronic ailments—assuming good social support and high quality medical and long-term care. Interventions by family, health care professionals or rehabilitation specialists can sometimes off-set the effects of disability while increasing well-being and overall quality of living.[45, 53, 66]

Health Maintenance Activities

Major components of an adequate health maintenance program include exercise, good nutrition, management of stress, careful management of medications, and regular primary health care including physical examinations. Regular physical exercise appears to slow the processes of normal aging—assuming the absence of major disease—while raising the level of mental and physical functioning. Yet, a high proportion of both younger and older people do not take the necessary time and effort.[39, 53]

Aerobic exercise (swimming, jogging, walking, etc.), combined with stretching and use of weights to enhance muscular maintenance, can help to avoid cardiovascular and respiratory problems, while reducing the likelihood of joint problems, osteoporosis, or falls. Vigorous mental exercise appears to have a comparable positive effect. Use of the mind through reading, problem-solving, and skill development leads to greater mental ability in later life. Mental function can be improved at any age.[12, 51, 53 60]

Good nutrition is fundamental to good health and yet it is not achieved by many older people. Inadequate nutrition and obesity contribute to low energy and less initiative. As many as 50 percent of hospital surgeries may be complicated by malnutrition. Malnourished patients stay in the hospital two-thirds longer than those who are adequately nourished. Good nourishment, on the other hand, leads to lower rates of disability, fewer infections, fewer and shorter hospitalizations, and lower death rates.[8]

Regular checkups and immunizations are considered crucial to the prevention or mitigation of acute and chronic problems. On-going guidance from the primary health care system can provide needed health education, as well as a continuing record of health conditions and needs.

Tolerance for stress is greater for healthy individuals, as is overall self-confidence and sense of environmental mastery. Compression of morbidity (limitation of serious health problems) until near the end of life is also enhanced. Diligent work to maintain health thus enhances the overall potential for high-quality aging and greater longevity.[39, 57]

A variety of important health maintenance activities can be initiated to enhance functioning, extend life expectancy, and generally optimize aging while improving quality of life. These issues are discussed in greater detail in later chapters.

◆◆◆ PERSONAL FINANCIAL RESOURCES

Financial security clearly contributes to accessibility of social, medical, material, and other resources needed to fulfill basic needs and generally enhance quality of life. Federal Social Security and private pensions have helped to alleviate financial concerns but usually are not sufficient to fulfill all the needs of retired lower-income workers or women who have no other source of income.[7]

Assets such as a home and savings accounts are important contributors to a sense of well-being and give one an ability to exercise influence with family, friends, and others in the community. On the other hand, having few resources, little education, and poor health, generally means one has little power and influence. Some studies of lower-income older women, however, indicate they tend to see themselves as fortunate in many ways, despite their lower economic status and limited influence.[16]

These issues are further examined in Chapter 8.

◆◆◆ LIFESTYLE: WORK, RETIREMENT, AND LEISURE

Lifestyle includes the combination of activities that characterize an individual pattern of behavior. "Use it or lose it" is an apt phrase to illustrate the importance of consistent and vigorous stimulation of the mind and body during later life. Recreational, intellectual, and aesthetic pursuits are important indicators of an active lifestyle.

Coming to Terms with Life

The degree to which the older individual has come to terms with his or her contribution to the family and society is a key element in structuring a satisfying lifestyle. A sense of peace and integrity can be achieved that makes the retirement lifestyle more fulfilling—somewhat regardless of the living environment. If an individual is unable to come to terms with the contributions of his or her life, a sense of loss, disappointment, and dissatisfaction is a common result.[27]

The older couple described in Illustration 2–2 has created a productive and active retirement lifestyle.

Illustration 2-2
STIMULATION AND PRODUCTIVITY IN RETIREMENT

Frank and Maxine led an active and successful life in Colorado. He was an engineer and contractor, while she helped operate a nursing home and also ran a magazine subscription business from her home. Over the years they had traveled widely throughout the United States and overseas, but they liked Arizona in the winter, where they found the climate and friendships very satisfying.

Upon retirement they continued to travel in their motorhome and also purchased a mobile home in an Arizona RV park as a permanent base where they could contine part-time work and many hobbies. They worked on the magazine subscription business as a way of supplementing their income and staying busy (too busy, they insist!). They traveled around the Southwest to square dance festivals. She had osteoporosis and found square dancing a wonderful form of exercise to help alleviate the pain.

After a few seasons, they had more friends in Arizona than in Colorado! They were realizing their retirement priorities. When we asked them to summarize what was most important to them, they had ready answers.

1. Good health is number one.
2. Enough money to live comfortably.
3. Friendships and opportunity to enjoy them; living is to be with people; going places and sharing experiences, especially while square dancing!
4. The important thing is to get outside of yourself and enjoy your environment. Too many people stay home, watch TV, read, and don't do stimulating things. They tend to die early.
5. Our philosophy is love of family, friendships, money, and time to enjoy each.

The great majority of older individuals have the capacity to create a satisfying and productive retirement lifestyle. Conservation and allocation of energy in pursuit of the most important individual objectives diminishes the likelihood of getting distracted by lesser ends. Careful focus becomes particularly crucial when capacities are lost because of disease or disability.[5, 25, 65]

◆◆◆　SUMMARY AND CONCLUSIONS

Older individuals have, under most circumstances, considerable control over the aging process and outcomes. Personal initiative can improve the chances for an optimal older age, despite the limitations imposed by heredity and any shortcomings in the family and community environment. Knowledge and continuing education can make a clear difference, as can physical health, mental health, and economic resources.

Adjustment to aging is strongly affected by personality characteristics including the strength of one's self-concept and the degree of independence or personal autonomy an individual is able to achieve. Interdependence with family, neighbors, and service systems in the community is important in defining the social support system available on a daily basis and in times of crisis. Although some level of dependence may be necessary because of physical or mental incapacity, the human personality seems to thrive best when reciprocity and interdependence are present. Problem-solving, coping, and communication skills are particularly valuable in making needed role changes at times of crisis.

Opportunity for personal choice is a precious commodity to the elderly. Choice has continuing importance as disability occurs and as decisions are made about housing and support services. The degree of freedom and choice depends in part on cultural tradition; retirement can have very different consequences depending on the chosen lifestyle.

Older individuals can deliberately prepare for and enhance retirement but within certain limitations imposed by heredity and social circumstances. Overall, opportunity for individual initiative and choice may be the most crucial elements in optimal aging and achieving a high quality of life in older age.

◆◆◆ REFERENCES

1. Agronin, Marc E. (1998). Personality and Psychopathology in Late Life, *Geriatrics,* 53 (S1), S35–S40.
2. American Association of Retired Persons (1999). Social Security and Medicare Changes: 1999 Benefits and Changes, *AARP Bulletin,* 40 (2), 8.
3. Andersson, Lars, and Nan Stevens (1993). Associations Between Early Experiences with Parents and Well-Being in Old Age, *Journal of Gerontology,* 48 (3), P109–P116.
4. Arber, Sara, and Maria Evandrou (1993). *Ageing, Independence, and the Life Course,* London: Jessica Kingsley Publishers.
5. Baltes, Margaret, and Frieder R. Lang (1997). Everyday Functioning and Successful Aging: The Impact of Resources, *Psychology and Aging,* 12 (3), 433–43.
6. Barer, Barbara M. (1994). Men and Women Aging Differently, *International Journal of Aging and Human Development,* 38 (1), 29–40.
7. Barusch, Amanda Smith (1997). Self-Concepts of Low-Income Older Women: Not Old or Poor, But Fortunate and Blessed, *International Journal of Aging and Human Development,* 44 (4), 269–82.
8. Becker, Robert J. (1998). The Hidden Costs of Malnutrition, *Business and Health,* 5 (7), 32–33.
9. Bee, Helen L. (1996). *The Journey of Adulthood (3d ed),* Upper Saddle River, NJ: Prentice Hall.
10. Broder, David (1999). Few American Lives Match One Lived by Mike Mansfield, *The Arizona Republic,* March 23.
11. Brown, Arnold S. (1996). *Social Processes of Aging and Old Age,* Upper Saddle River, NJ: Prentice Hall.
12. Butler, Robert N., Myrna Lewis, and Trey Sunderland (1991). *Aging and Mental Health: Positive Psychosocial and Biomedical Approaches* (4th ed.), New York: Macmillan.
13. Charon, Joel M. (1995). *Symbolic Interactionism* (5th ed), Upper Saddle River, NJ: Simon and Schuster.
14. Checkland, David, and Michel Silberfield (1993). Competence and the Three A's: Autonomy, Authenticity, and Aging, *Canadian Journal on Aging,* 12 (4), 453–68.
15. Chrisler, Joan C., and Laurie Ghiz (1993). Body Image Issues of Older Women, *Women and Therapy,* 14 (1-2), 65–75.
16. Clair, Jeffrey Michael, David A. Karp, and William C. Yoels (1993). *Experiencing the Life Cycle: A Social Psychology of Aging,* Springfield, IL: Charles C Thomas, Publisher.
17. Cohen, Gene D. (1988). *The Brain in Human Aging,* New York: Springer.

18. Coon, Dennis (1989). *Introduction to Psychology* (5th ed), New York: West.

19. Duncan, Lauren, and Gail S. Agronick (1995). The Intersection of Life State and Social Events: Personality and Life Outcomes, *Journal of Personality and Social Psychology*, 69 (3), 558–68.

20. Fillit, Howard (1997). Lifestyle Risk Factors for Cognitive Impairment, in H. M. Fillit and R. N. Butler (eds), *Cognitive Decline: Strategies for Prevention*, London: Greenwich Medical Medica, 23–32.

21. Friedman, Rohn S (1993). When the Patient Intrudes on the Treatment: The Aging Personality Types in Medical Management, *Journal of Geriatric Psychiatry*, 26 (2), 149–77.

22. Fry, Christine L. (1991). Cross-cultural comparisons of aging, in Kenneth F. Ferraro (ed), *Gerontology: Perspectives and Issues*, New York: Springer Publishing Co., 129–46.

23. Garfein, Adam J., and A. Regula Herzog (1995). Robust Aging Among the Young-Old, Old-Old, and Oldest-Old, *Journal of Gerontology*, Series B, Psychological Science and Social Science, 506 (2), S77–S87.

24. George, Linda K. (1995). Self-Esteem, in George L. Maddox (ed), *The Encyclopedia of Aging: A Comprehensive Resource in Gerontology and Geriatrics* (2d ed), New York: Springer, 837.

25. George, Linda K. (1990). Social Structure, Social Processes, and Social-Psychological States, in Robert H. Binstock and Linda K. George (eds), *Handbook of Aging and the Social Sciences* (3d ed), San Diego: Academic Press, 186–200.

26. Hareven, Tamara K. (ed) (1996). *Aging and Generational Relations Over the Life Course: A Historical and Cross-Cultural Perspective*, New York: Walter de Gruyter.

27. Hargrave, Terry D., and Suzanne Midori Hanna (1997). Aging: A Primer for Family Therapists, in Terry D. Hargrave and Suzanne Midori Hanna (eds), *The Aging Family: New Visions in Theory, Practice, and Reality*, New York: Brunner/Mazel Publishers, 39-60.

28. Hobfoll, Stevan E., and Jennifer D. Wells (1998). Conservation of Resources, Stress, and Aging: Why Do Some Slide and Some Spring? in Jacob Lomranz (ed), *Handbook of Aging and Mental Health: An Integrative Approach*, New York: Plenum Press, 121–34.

29. Hultsch, David F., Christopher Hertzog, Brent J. Small, and Roger A. Dixon (1999). Use It or Lose It: Engaged Lifestyle as a Buffer of Cognitive Decline in Aging? *Psychology and Aging*, 14 (2), 245–63.

30. Hummert, Mary Lee (1993). Age and Typicality Judgements of Stereotypes of the Elderly, *International Journal of Aging and Human Development*, 37 (3), 217–26.

31. King, Valarie, and Glen H. Elder Jr. (1998). Education and Grandparenting Roles, *Research on Aging*, 20 (4), 450–74.

32. Lemme, Barbara H. (1995). *Development in Adulthood*, Needham Heights, MA: Allyn & Bacon.

33. Lindenberger, Ulman, and Paul B. Baltes (1997). Intellectual Functioning in Old and Very Old Age: Cross-Sectional Results From the Berlin Aging Study, *Psychology and Aging*, 12 (3), 410–32.

34. Lindenberger, Ulman, and Paul B. Baltes (1994). Sensory Functioning and Intelligence in Old Age: A Strong Connection, *Psychology and Aging*, 9 (3), 339–55.

35. Lomranz, Jacob (1998). Memory and Dementia, in Jacob Lomranz (ed). *Handbook of Aging and Mental Health: An Integrative Approach*, New York: Plenum Press, 413.

36. Lund, Dale A. (1989). Conclusions about Bereavement in Later Life and Implications for Interventions and Future Research, in Dale A. Lund (ed), *Older Bereaved Spouses: Research with Practical Applications*, New York: Hemisphere Publishing, 217–31.

37. Lund, Dale A. (1998). Personal Communication.

38. Lund, Dale A. (1993). Widowhood: The Coping Response, in Robert Kastenbaum (ed), *Encylopedia of Adult Development*, Phoenix, AZ: Oryx Press, 537–41.

39. Manton, Kenneth G., Eric Stallard, and H. Dennis Tolley (1991). Limits to Human Life Expectancy: Evidence, Prospects, and Implications, *Population and Development Review*, 17 (4), 603–37.

40. McCrael, Robert M. (1995). Self Concept, in George L. Maddox (ed) (1995). *The Encyclopedia of Aging: A Comprehensive Resource in Gerontology and Geriatrics* (2d ed), New York: Springer, 836.

41. Masterson, James F. (1988). *The Search for the Real Self: Unmasking the Personality Disorders of Our Age*, New York: The Free Press.

42. Mattiasson, Anne-Cathrine, Lars Andersson, Larry C. Mullins, and Linda Moody (1997). A Comparative Empirical Study of Autonomy in Nursing Homes in Sweden and Florida, USA, *Journal of Cross-Cultural Gerontology*, 12 (2), 299–316.

43. McAdams, Dan P. (1990). *The Person: An Introduction to Personality Psychology*, San Diego: Harcourt Brace Jovanovich.

44. Michener, H. Andrew, and John D. DeLamater (1994). *Social Psychology*, Fort Worth, TX: Harcourt Brace.

45. Mirowsky, John (1995). Age and the Sense of Control, *Social Psychology Quarterly*, 58 (1), 31–43.

46. Mirowsky, John (1997). Age, Subjective Life Expectancy, and the Sense of Control: The Horizon Hypothesis, *Journal of Gerontology*, 52B (3), S125–S134.

47. Morrison, Malcolm H. (1986). Work and Retirement in an Older Society, in Alan Pifer and Lydia Bronte (eds), *Our Aging Society*, New York: W.W. Norton, 341–65.

48. Moss, Pamela (1997). Negotiating Spaces in Home Environments: Older Women Living With Arthritis, *Social Science and Medicine*, 45 (1), 23–33.

49. Mutran, Elizabeth, and Donald C. Reitzes (1990). Intergenerational Exchange Relationships in the Aging Family, in Kenneth F. Ferraro (ed), *Gerontology: Perspectives and Issues*, New York: Springer, 149–62).

50. Perlmuter, Lawrence C. and Angela S. Eads (1998). Control: Cognitive and Motivational Implications, in Jacob Lomranz (ed), *Handbook of Aging and Mental Health: An Integrative Approach*, New York: Plenum Press, 45–65.

51. Powell, Douglas H. (1994). *Profiles in Cognitive Aging*, Cambridge, MA: Harvard University Press.

52. Preston, Samuel, and Paul Taubman (1994). Socioeconomic Differences in Adult Mortality and Health Status, in Linda G. Martin and Samuel H. Preston (eds), *Demography of Aging*, Washington, D.C.: National Academy Press, 280–313.

53. Rowe, John W., and Robert L. Kahn (1998). *Successful Aging*, New York: Pantheon Books.

54. Rubinstein, Robert L., Janet C. Kilbride, and Sharon Nagy (1992). *Elders Living Alone: Frailty and the Perception of Choice*, New York: Aldine de Gruyter.

55. Sadler, William (2000). *The Third Age: Six Principles of Growth and Renewal after Forty*, Cambridge, MA: Perseus Books.

56. Schaie, K. Warner (1997). Normal Cognitive Development in Adulthood, in H. M. Fillit and R. N. Butler (eds), *Cognitive Decline: Strategies for Prevention*, London: Greenwich Medical Media, 9–21.

57. Schefft, Bruce K., and Beverly K. Lehr (1990). Psychological Problems of Older Adults, in Kenneth F. Ferraro (ed), *Gerontology: Perspectives and Issues*, New York: Springer, 283–93.

58. Schiffman, Susan S. (1997). Taste and Smell: Losses in Normal Aging and Disease, *Journal of the American Medical Association*, 278 (16), 1357–62.

59. Schroots, Johannes J. F. (1995). Psychological Models of Aging, *Canadian Journal of Aging*, 14 (1), 44–66.

60. Seeman, Teresa E., Judith Rodin, and Marilyn Albert (1993). Self-Efficacy and Cognitive Performance in High-Functioning Older Individuals, *Journal of Aging and Health*, 5 (4), 455–74.

61. Silver, Catherine B. (1998). Cross-Cultural Perspective on Attitudes Toward Family Responsibility and Well-Being in Later Years, in Jacob Lomranz (ed), *Handbook of Aging and Mental Health: An Integrative Approach*, New York: Plenum Press, 383–416.

62. Slater, Robert (1995). *The Psychology of Growing Old*, Philadelphia: Open University Press.

63. Smith, Jacqui, and Paul B. Baltes (1997). Profiles of Psychological Functioning in Old and Oldest Old, *Psychology and Aging*, 12 (3), 458–72.

64. Sterns, Harvey L., and Anthony A. Sterns (1995). Health and the Employment Capability of Older Americans, in Scott A. Bass (ed), *Older and Active: How Americans over 55 Are Contributing to Society*, New Haven: Yale University Press, 10–34.

65. Strawbridge, William J., Richard D. Cohen, Sarah J. Shema, and George A. Kaplan (1996). Successful Aging: Predictors and Associated Activities, *American Journal of Epidemiology*, 144 (2), 135–41.

66. Tennant, A., J. M. L. Geddes, J. Fear, M. Hillman, and M. A. Chamberlain (1997). Outcome Following Stroke, *Disability and Rehabilitation* 19 (7), 278–84.

67. Thomas, Darwin L., Victor Gecas, Andrew Weigert, and Elizebeth Rooney (1974). *Family Socialization and the Adolescent*, Lexington, MA: Lexington Books.

68. Whitbourne, Susan Krauss (1996). *The Aging Individual: Physical and Psychological Perspectives*, New York: Springer.

69. Whitbourne, Susan Krauss, and Charles B. Powers (1994). Older Women's Constructs of Their Lives: A Quantitative and Qualitative Exploration, *International Journal of Aging and Human Development*, 38 (4), 293–306.

70. Wilson, Gail (1993). Money and Independence in Old Age, in Sara Arber and Maria Evandrou (eds.) *Ageing, Independence and the Life Course*, London: Jessica Kingsley Publishers, 46–64.

Chapter 3

SOCIAL SUPPORT SYSTEMS
Family, Friends, Neighborhood, and Community

◆◆◆ **INTRODUCTION**

This chapter examines the relevance and contribution of social-support systems for quality of life among older individuals. The focus is on the roles of family, friends, neighborhood, and community as sources of social support. Specific topics include:

- Social-support relationships.
- The family.
- Friends and other social groups.
- Neighborhood and community.
- Lifestyle impacts.

Social support is among the most basic requirements of older people if they are to achieve a sense of personal well-being and satisfaction with life. The consequence of social isolation is often depression and an increased likelihood of physical illness and mortality. Strong support, on the other hand, appears to decrease the incidence of stress and the probability of declining health. Unfortunately, many older individuals who are mentally or physically disabled, and who can no longer fully manage daily activities by themselves, become socially isolated from family, friends, and community contacts—losing an important part of their traditional support system at this critical time in their lives.[66, 90]

◆◆◆ SOCIAL-SUPPORT RELATIONSHIPS

Social-support systems refer to the structure, characteristics, and organization, of interpersonal relationships through which emotional, material, and other forms of assistance are provided. Such systems are based on cultural expectations about appropriate support in terms of need, security, equity, and the well-being of the person or persons supported. Who is deserving of help depends on varying societal and cultural values. Support systems can be examined from several perspectives.[24, 43]

- Formal and informal.
- Expressive and instrumental.
- Quantity and quality.
- Social networks.
- Reciprocity and beneficence.

Formal and Informal

Most social support is from informal sources—family, friends, or neighbors. Informal support is the primary mechanism for satisfying emotional needs, whereas formal support is primarily for assistance with services from outside the home and neighborhood, such as from local, state, and federal government agencies or private organizations of various kinds. Formal and informal support are often combined when, for example, a home health agency works with the family to provide needed support for a disabled older individual living at home. At times formal support is dependent on the availability of informal support in the home.[10, 43, 80]

Expressive and Instrumental

Social support satisfies two primary requirements for any individual: (1) expressive needs such as love, affection, and admiration that contribute to affirmation as a person, value as a human being, respect, and understanding; and (2) instrumental needs such as financial, material, and informational assistance. For example, family and friends are likely to fulfill the emotional and affirmation needs, while an outside public agency might assist the family in providing financial and other instrumental support. Informal support is likely to have both emotional and instrumental dimensions, whereas formal support is more likely to be largely instrumental. Although both men and women provide both instrumental and emotional support, women are more likely to offer emotional support and men are more likely to provide instrumental support.[58, 90]

Older adults generally want some of their relationships to be expressive, intimate, open, and fulfilling—someone to talk to about whatever is on one's mind as in the case of close friendships. In times of crisis it is clear that a spouse and children are the most important sources of expressive support, but siblings, neighbors, and friends may provide some level of emotional and instrumental support as well. Provision of assistance in times of difficulty is among the most important instrumental values of a supporting relationship. The tendency in older age is to rely on family and to be selective in making and continuing friendships, with emphasis on quality rather than quantity of contacts.[7, 10, 38, 39]

Quantity and Quality

The closeness of a few relationships is more important for an older person than the number of contacts. The quality or intimacy of support from family and friends strongly affects sense of self-worth and fulfillment. However, the quantity of relationships obviously affects the alternative choices and opportunities for interaction. Talking to acquaintances and service providers—some of whom might become close friends—is better than no interaction at all. When deep, intimate, and durable interactions are not continuously available, having some opportunities for conversation is still valuable in avoiding isolation.[39]

The dependency on relatives for social support tends to increase with age, while the number of nonfamily relationships tends to decrease, sometimes as a direct consequence of relative isolation during disabling illness or impending death. Mobility diminishes, thereby limiting access to friends and acquaintances outside of the immediate household. Attention, affection, and direct personal support provided by a daughter or son is more likely to help an older person avoid depression than are occasional contacts with extended family members or acquaintances who cannot provide ongoing personal support.[27, 58]

Social Networks

Social networks refer to contacts with all individuals with whom an individual interacts on a regular basis including either close or impersonal ties. Networks thus define the extensiveness and composition of social relationships. Although someone may have a wide range of contacts with individuals in community organizations and in government agencies, they may receive real support and emotional satisfaction from none of them. Personal values and attitudes serve as the basis for sorting out preferences among members of a social network. Some network members may become close friends if common interests emerge and mutual respect develops.[7, 8, 37, 90]

Social networks of an older person are generated largely as a result of: (1) the cultural, demographic, and community circumstances into which he or she was born; (2) social contacts and lifestyle developed over time, often during educational and career experiences; and (3) through deliberate choices in selecting organizational memberships, such as church or service organizations in the community. For some older individuals who have been highly active in professional endeavors, politics, or in volunteer organizations, the social network continues to be exceedingly important, even though it may not provide the intimate contact and emotional fulfillment of an informal support system. Some combination of informal social support and more formal social networks is essential to meeting the social needs of older individuals.[5]

Reciprocity and Beneficence

The concept of reciprocity implies that relationships, deeds, or goods provided to others will be repaid with something of value that is roughly equivalent to that which is given. Intergenerational reciprocal relationships are important to a sense of well-being. Both giving and receiving signify trust and tend to strengthen bonds between the parties involved. Social exchange is considered of greater value than a one-way flow of communication or material goods. For example, if a daughter or son provides an older parent with ongoing emotional and household support, the parent may provide some form of inheritance or reward. Without the exchange, the likelihood of continued satisfaction with the relationship diminishes. Giving as well as receiving seems to be important to the human psyche.[26]

Reciprocity provides the basis for continued "bonding" between older parents or grandparents and their children and grandchildren. Most older individuals are heavily affected by what is happening in the lives of their children or grandchildren of any age. When a crisis occurs reciprocity demands that a response come from children as a means of preserving the older person's happiness and well-being. Someone who has been helpful to children and grandchildren expects some form of assistance. Reciprocity is more likely to occur when the opportunity for social exchange is relatively local, as contrasted to the situation when geography widely separates generations—as is so often the case in modern society. The quality and frequency of the exchange will directly affect individual satisfaction and well-being.[30, 32, 52]

Older parents in the United States are likely to give money to their children in exchange for services. The incidence of transfers from parent to children are much higher than the reverse, up to about age 80. Such exchanges are evident in other countries as well. In France, for example, about one-third of older parents give money to their adult children. Only about 9 percent of children give financial assistance to parents.[76]

The social norm referred to as *beneficence* applies when reciprocity is not possible because of physical or mental disability. One measure of wisdom, maturity, and adjustment to aging is the ability to receive friendship and affection without necessarily having to reciprocate—such as during the period of illness before death. A history of earlier contributions to family and friends can essentially serve as a substitute for current reciprocity. A mature personality exhibits an ability to receive caring without always needing to reciprocate in the formal sense, as Illustration 3–1 suggests.[84]

Illustration 3–1
LOVE, RECIPROCITY, AND BENEFICENCE

Grace had been a teacher for 28 years and was the mother of four adult children, fifteen grandchildren, and twenty great grandchildren. She and her husband had been very active in the community all their lives. At age 85 she had a disabling stroke and was unable to communicate or respond except for facial expressions. The stroke destroyed her ability to speak.

Fortunately, she was constantly supported by her husband and was surrounded by family and friends who showered her with affection. She did not appear to lose her ability to relate to those around her in loving and affectionate circumstances, despite her obvious pain and great discomfort. She showed her appreciation with smiles as a modest form of reciprocity. She seemed to continue to take great satisfaction in the visits from her extended family, a wide circle of friends, her former students, and others in the community who had experienced her caring personality. She appeared happy and content until her death some weeks later.

Children who have been well treated are very likely to continue providing support for a disabled parent even though the exchange is unequal. Overt gratitude in the form of a smile may be sufficient reciprocity, as Grace's behavior illustrates. Nonetheless, equitable exchanges are generally more satisfying and fulfilling than beneficence over the long term.[7, 92]

◆◆◆ THE FAMILY

Families provide socialization, economic sustenance, marital companionship, co-residence, grandparenting, caretaking, support during widowhood, bereavement help, and proxy decision making, depending on the stage of the life cycle. Families have a major impact on the formation of lifestyles in older age. Furthermore, the family is the most significant support group in times of crisis, regardless of access to public social programs. Families can also be the source of great joy and satisfaction (weddings, births, anniversaries, holidays and celebrations, for example) but can be filled with sorrow and disappointment in the down times (funerals, accidents, illness, economic hardship, etc.). If the family is stable and serves the social-support functions, older members are likely to receive support throughout their lives.

Of those over age 65 who were not institutionalized, roughly 67 percent lived in some form of family setting in 1998 in the United States. (However, this average breaks down to 80 percent of older men and 58 percent of older women.) Most were married couples: 75 percent of men and 43 percent of women, as summarized in Figure 3–1. Many more women than men are widowed without a new spouse, and slightly more women than men are divorced or have never been married.[2, 88]

Roughly 17 percent of women and 7 percent of men lived with other relatives. About 3 percent lived with non-relatives and the remaining 31 percent (41 percent of women and 17 percent of men) lived alone. As suggested by these statistics, older women are particularly vulnerable to isolation at advanced ages, especially when disabled and when siblings and most friends have already died.[4]

About 80 percent of older individuals have living adult children, two-thirds of whom live within 30 minutes travel time and visit at least weekly. Three-quarters have weekly or more frequent phone conversations with children. Thus, interaction of older individuals with family remains a very common pattern, despite the tendency of older people to live alone.[9, 93]

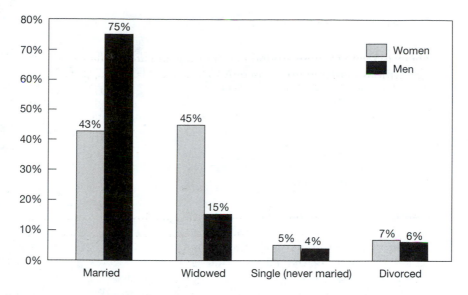

FIGURE 3-1   Marital Status of Persons 65 and Over, 1998
Source: Based on data from the U.S. Census Bureau. See: "Marital Status and Living Arrangements: March 1998 (Update), Current Population Reports, PPL-100.

Unfortunately, some families do not provide a supportive environment and may not fulfill needs of older members when they are in crisis. Conflict between adult children and their older parents usually involves one or both of two issues: (1) disagreements over perceived more favorable treatment of other family members, and/or (2) different viewpoints about lifestyle choices and preferred habits. A parent may be critical of the choices an adult child makes and vice versa. However, even when conflict arises the relationship usually persists and solidarity of the family generally continues.[21]

When the family fails to fulfill the proper role, there is often a problem for older individuals who have poor relationship skills and who lack ability to form and sustain other intimate relationships. Fortunately, a high proportion without good family situations learn to develop other positive friendships and may still achieve a strong self-concept and optimal older age.[23]

Socialization and Older People

Much of the basic cultural knowledge transmitted by the family stays with an older person throughout life. In more traditional societies where extended families are the norm, older members are particularly important as teachers of younger generations. In nations with highly developed educational systems the family role in knowledge transmission has diminished. Nonetheless, intergenerational linkages and the opportunity to transmit knowledge and wisdom have a substantial impact on the sense of purpose, well-being, and life satisfaction of older family members.[22, 62]

Economic Sustenance

The family is the primary unit for sustaining and enhancing the economic well-being of members while accumulating resources for transfer to the next generation. The management of wealth has increasingly become a collective enterprise of the husband and wife, as both work and prepare for their retirement. In relatively affluent families, holding title to accumulated wealth in older years provides the basis for economic power and influence over family affairs, as long as mental and physical alertness continues, enabling them to exercise choice about their personal well-being and about the distribution of their resources. Lower-income older families or widows have much less power.

Marriage

A great majority of older people rate their marriages as happy or very happy. The biggest change in marital patterns during the twentieth century may have been the increased length of marriages, despite high divorce rates. Compared with younger age groups older couples report fewer marital problems. Older families who are most satisfied generally have an enduring and successful marriage.[46] Important marital characteristics are summarized in Table 3–1.

While this summary does not include all the important factors in a successful marriage, presence of these characteristics in the home is likely to mean a satisfying environment supportive of optimal aging. If a husband and wife love and trust one another, depend upon each other, care for one another in times of crisis, and share mutually enjoyable activities on a daily basis, marital satisfaction and success in later life are likely outcomes.

Marital satisfaction consistently improves after children are no longer in the home. Income and assets are stabilized when the daily responsibility for children ends. Retirement means increased time and often more companionship, which

---

TABLE 3–1   Characteristics of an Enduring and Satisfying "Older" Marriage

- Love, intimacy, trust, and mutual satisfaction.
- Agreement on goals and roles in life.
- Strong communication abilities enabling partners to express feelings and disclose themselves.
- High levels of self-esteem.
- An ability to adapt to the faults and foibles of each other.
- Ability to change and adapt as the family situation evolves through initial marriage, young children, mature children, and aging.
- Pleasure and shared humor as best friends, and a desire to spend leisure time together.
- Commitment to the marriage as a permanent institution.

Source: Data from Bengtson, Rosenthal, and Burton, 1990: 269; Smolak, 1993: 278-279; Bee, 1996: 235.

improves communication and intimacy. Older marriages are characterized by greater equality, joint decision making, and decreasing division of traditional male/female tasks. Ill health can of course interrupt the pattern and sometimes requires one partner to provide long-term care to the other. Caregiving is a central feature of the exchange in marriage and is usually accepted with grace in good marriages. It should also be noted that marital satisfaction is among the primary predictors of high quality of life.[10, 45, 70, 73]

The period between age 65 and 75 may be the most pleasant time of life for couples when good health prevails for both members. They can enjoy more freedom and greater leisure than at any earlier time in their marriage. Health may improve because older married people are more likely to eat well, as compared to single individuals, engage in physical activity, and practice other preventive health behaviors.[10, 23, 82]

Overall, members of older married couples have higher morale, greater life satisfaction, better mental and physical health, more adequate economic resources, greater happiness, and lower rates of institutionalization than single individuals. Couples often grow closer and more interdependent as they age, returning to the kind of close and romantic relationship experienced immediately after marriage. Well-functioning older families tend to have a high degree of solidarity, are cohesive, and are interdependent with children and grandchildren of all ages. Relationships with adult children are of particular importance. The usual pattern is that parents and children hold great affection for each other, enjoy living in proximity, interact frequently, and provide mutual assistance in various ways. These nuclear family linkages are generally much stronger than with siblings or more extended family, although such relationships may also remain very important.[11, 68]

Widowhood

Loss of a spouse is one of the most severe forms of stress encountered in older age, especially for individuals who have been married to the same person most of their lives. They may have outlived most of their peers and have relatively few close relatives or confidants. The degree of stress depends somewhat on age and health status, as well as financial well-being and social support. Widows with strong social support and a solid financial base are likely to manage the bereavement process more successfully than individuals without such support and income. Widowed men appear to feel greater loss than widowed women; they experience more depression and difficulty developing new companions after the death of their wives.[27, 57 66, 69]

Many important personal relationships are lost or diminished with widowhood because of the isolation associated with single status as compared to "couple" social relationships. Serious depression may occur and last for a year or more, leading to greater rates of mental disorders, suicide, and mortality than among married peers. Fortunately, most older individuals have close friends who are confidants and do much to fill the marriage vacuum. Adult children often provide regular support and assistance. Single clubs for older individuals have become common in most communities and can provide a very positive outlet.[15, 69]

Remarriage

Remarriage is very common among widowed older people and is much more accept-able than in earlier decades. Most remarriages are between individuals who have previously known each other and who have similar backgrounds. Older women are more likely to remain single after a first marriage (49 percent) than are men (14 percent). Roughly 74 percent of all men over age 65 were married in 1997 compared to 42 percent of women. A significant number of older couples live together but do not marry, sometimes because of concerns about their children's inheritance.[17, 72]

Children sometimes reject the remarriage of a widowed parent and impose a great strain on the new couple. The power relationship in the family is altered by remarriage, sometimes threatening expectations of children. On the other hand, a widowed parent is less likely to be mistreated by children if a strong and indepen-dent new marriage is formed. Fortunately, public values are changing so that remar-riage has become more acceptable to children as a happy alternative to loneliness and isolation of their parent. Second or third marriages are often quite successful as well.[72, 77]

Sexual Fulfillment

Sexual relationships and satisfaction often improve in older age. Sexual arousal and orgasm can continue although response might be slower. Regular sexual activity is among the key factors in maintaining health and vigor, whereas abstinence con-tributes to impotence. Some medications and over-use of alcohol can interfere with sexual response to a greater degree at older ages. When multiple medications are needed to treat chronic diseases, there is a clear possibility of interference with sex-ual activity, including the potential for impotence.[29, 46, 61, 72]

A 1999 survey indicated that men and women find their partners more physi-cally attractive over time. Although the importance of sex to quality of life drops with age, especially for women, more than half of couples continue to thoroughly enjoy sex, although about half of men report some degree of impotence. Most older cou-ples are happy with their sex lives.[47, 86]

Negative social attitudes sometimes interfere with sexual satisfaction of older peo-ple. Younger people often view such activity as inappropriate and not expected. Older people who are conscious of these attitudes may sometimes be constrained in their behavior as a result. Older men are much more likely to have partners for sexual activity than women—because of the much larger numbers of older women than men.

Sexual activity, self-esteem, and self-image are closely interrelated. If one suf-fers losses in any of these categories, the others are affected. Concern about loss of sexual function is sometimes a serious preoccupation (particularly for older men), especially when considering remarriage. However, the evidence is clear that in most cases sexual performance can be regenerated. Appropriate exercise, conditioning, diet, and other physical self-maintenance activities are important if sexual abilities are to be sustained. Sexual counseling and therapy can often fully restore sexual ability.[3, 18, 25]

Frequency of sexual activity in older age is directly associated with the level of sexual involvement during younger years. There is no physiological reason—given good health status—that sexual desire, interest, and activity should not continue until near the end of life. Overall, both older men and women demonstrate a wide range of capacity for sexual enjoyment as they age.[80]

Sexual dysfunction may increase in older age, especially when disease is present. Serious heart disease, emphysema, diabetes (which may cause impotence), and other medical problems can interfere. Some pharmaceuticals diminish sexual function, while others (such as hormone replacement therapy) enhance sexual interest and performance.[81]

Co-Residence of Older Parents with Children

Most married couples, old or young, prefer to maintain households separate from children. Only one-seventh of American households contain more than two generations. A 1994 survey indicated that 84 percent of older Americans preferred to live in their own private home. The universality of this attitude has meant a steady decline in co-residence of older parents and adult children in the United States and many other economically advanced countries. Living alone after the death of a spouse is clearly perceived as having advantages over living with family members or others. It should be noted that co-residence is often for the benefit of the adult child rather than the parent.[36, 71]

As Table 3–2 indicates there are nonetheless substantial variations between countries. High proportions of the elderly live alone, while only a few live with children in the United States, Canada and much of Western Europe. Single parents are much more likely to live with children than are couples, except in Japan where both situations are common. As parents get older or lose their spouse, the incidence of residence with children increases somewhat in the United Kingdom, Germany, Canada, and Japan, but not in the United States.[76]

In Japan and many other Asian, African, and Latin American nations, co-residence continues to be common. But even in these countries the incidence invari-

TABLE 3–2   Co-Residence among Older Adults and Children in Five Countries (1997)

Country	Proportion of Elderly Living Alone (percent)	Proportion of Couples Living with Children (percent)	Proportion of Single Elderly Living with Children (percent)
United States	31	2	13
Canada	38	3	14
United Kingdom	30	5	8
Germany	44	5	10
Japan	8	34	31

Source: Data from American Association for Retired Persons, 1998: 4; Rein and Salzman, 1995: 242.

TABLE 3-3 **Incidence of Older Parents Living with Children in the United States by Sex and Ethnic Group, 1990**

	Incidence	
Ethnic Group	Men (percent)	Women (percent)
European Americans	3.9	5.8
African Americans	5.5	8.6
Hispanic Americans	12.0	20.0
Asian Americans	17.0	32.0

Source: Data from Angel and Angel, 1997: 102; U.S. Census Bureau, 1998.

ably seems to decline as modernization occurs and as an increasing proportion of women enter the workforce. In less economically advanced countries residence with, and dependence on, family continues to be the principle basis of economic well-being and long-term care. since social security and other retirement resources are usually not available.[42, 76]

The incidence of co-residence varies considerably between racial and ethnic groups within the United States, as indicated in Table 3–3. For example, only 5.8 percent of older European-American women and 3.9 percent of men lived with their children in 1990, while the comparable proportions for African Americans were 8.6 percent for women and 5.5 percent for men. Among Hispanic Americans the proportions were much higher, approximately 20 percent for women and 12 percent for men. The highest incidence was with Asian Americans: 32 percent for women and 17 percent for men.[6]

As the data in Table 3–3 imply, Hispanic Americans, African Americans and Asian Americans appear to place greater emphasis on intergenerational responsibility than European Americans—although some of the difference is clearly based on variations in economic capacity of older members to live independently. Family ties appear to be generally stronger in the minority populations.[13]

Co-residence may be as beneficial to the younger relative as the older person. Single children regularly maintain residence with their elderly parents to economize on costs, while also providing various forms of informal care or support. Economic resources are often pooled. Younger members work outside the home providing support for older members who might care for children, help cook, and generally maintain the household to the degree of their ability. A division of labor allows the family to function effectively while providing the needed support.[55]

Grandparenting

The grandparent role has been classified by some authors according to the depth of involvement with grandchildren, as summarized in Table 3–4.

The roles outlined in Table 3–4 are not always sharply differentiated and may vary over the period of the relationship. Normal grandparent behavior is not well defined in many families and depends on the overall family commitment to a close

TABLE 3–4   Types of Grandparent Roles

- *Substituet parent* is commonplace in many single parent families and represents the closest involvement with grandchildren. The grandparent may take full charge while the parent(s) is/are at work or away.
- An *active grandparent* maintains constant interest in and involvement with the grandchild in a mutually pleasurable relationship, but without attempting to be a substitute parent.
- *Teaching grandparent* helps socialize and educate grandchildren on family history and other topics.
- *Social grandparent* plays with grandchildren and enjoys their company on an occasional basis but does not get deeply involved.
- *Absentee grandparent* has only occasional contact at best and does not get at all involved in the lives of grandchildren.

Source: Data from Kart, 1997: 255; Bee, 1996: 203; Cox, 1996: 193; Smolak, 1993: 288–89.

relationship. Cultural traditions in the community also strongly influence the grandparent role. Working grandparents are likely to be less involved with grandchildren than are retired grandparents. The mobility of the grandparent will obviously affect contact with grandchildren.[32, 84]

Diversity.   Contemporary grandparenthood is enormously diverse. Grandchildren may depend on grandparents as role models and companions as they mature and become adults, or they may not identify with them at all. Generally speaking, good relationships and influence from grandparents depend on the closeness of the bond over time. Grandparents can become dependent on their grandchildren for interaction, continuing social involvement, and some personal care during the older years, but this is clearly the exception. Remarried grandparents may behave quite differently than single, divorced, or widowed grandparents.[16, 20, 68, 84]

Grandparents can be a primary source of family cohesiveness by maintaining the history and heritage while supporting the continuity and cultural rootedness of the family. They tend to care what happens and are willing to help resolve problems. Continuity of the family is important to them. Grandparents can be a stabilizing force in providing support to their children (particularly single parents) in times of adversity, by providing childcare, financial assistance, and emotional support.[28, 85] Illustration 3–2 is an example.

Illustration 3-2
THE CLARK FAMILY GRANDPARENTS

John and Mary were married in 1932 during the depths of the Depression. He was a rancher and she was a teacher. They struggled mightily through the 1930s and World War II to raise their four children in very modest circumstances. As conditions improved in the 1950s, and later, they became grandparents and great-grandparents many times over. Their home was the gathering place for Thanksgiving and Christmas holidays, as well as other special events, such as their sixtieth wedding anniversary in 1993, bringing together the entire extended family of some 60 adults and children of all ages.

They paid close attention to each grandchild and great grandchild, celebrating their birthdays, giving gifts at Christmas, and generally treating them as important young people. The affection was happily reciprocated.

They were the repository of family history and wisdom, actually participating in the preparation of a family tree and an informal book outlining the family heritage for generations back. At one time or another they cared for nearly all of the grandchildren in their home, while the parents were away, or simply because the grandchildren loved visiting their grandparents.

When Mary died in 1997 at age 86, every grandchild was at the funeral and at the preceding and post-funeral gatherings at the grandparent home. They were so concerned about their grandfather they organized a phone-call network so that he would receive a call from at least one grandchild every day. Although the bereavement process was difficult after 64 years of marriage, his close relationship with the grandchildren clearly helped greatly to facilitate his adjustment and contentment.

This close grandparenting arrangement applies more consistently in those instances when grandparents live in proximity to grandchildren. When distances are great interaction will obviously be less. However, the Internet and e-mail have become great tools for interaction between grandchildren and their grandparents when they live some distance apart. Grandparents can assume a minimum of responsibility, yet the role provides fulfillment, continuity, and general family satisfaction.[32]

Mutual Benefits of Grandparenting. The relationship between grandparents and grandchildren can satisfy important needs for both, as illustrated in Table 3-5.

As noted earlier, some grandparents feel obligated to take responsibility for grandchildren when parents are unable or unwilling to fulfill the parenting role. This pattern increased by 44 percent between 1980 and 1995 with nearly 4 million children involved. Custodial grandparenting is particularly a challenge for lower-income families when a daughter has children born out of wedlock or when a grandchild

TABLE 3-5 Mutual Benefits from Grandparent/Grandchild Linkages

Grandparent Need	Grandchild Need
To nurture	To be nurtured
To have a life review	To learn about the family past
To share cultural experience	To have a cultural identity
To communicate values	To have positive role models
To leave a legacy	To be connected to previous generations

Source: Data from Newman et al., 1997: 18.

has serious health problems. Grandparents who take full responsibility for grandchildren exhibit a much higher level of stress than those without close responsibility. Inadequate income and health insurance to care for grandchildren can create great difficulties.[19, 31, 36, 64]

Caretaking

As noted earlier, a high proportion of the care needed by older individuals is provided by children or other family members. Older husbands tend to care for their wives and vice versa. Daughters have more frequent contact with their parents than sons and much more frequently become caretakers, especially when widowhood occurs. Adult children clearly feel a major responsibility to offer emotional and other direct help to their parents.

Siblings rarely serve as primary caregivers to disabled brothers or sisters. Nonetheless, bonds between siblings are among the strongest family relationships and tend to extend throughout life. This is more the case in lower-socioeconomic level families with less education and mobility than with higher-income families. Sibling attachments may increase even more in the "baby boom" generation because of relatively smaller families. With few children to depend upon, siblings may seek greater social sustenance from each other.[12,68]

Lifestyle Impacts. The family lifestyle is often drastically altered when an older member becomes dependent—especially when added to other family responsibilities such as raising younger children and professional work requirements. The consequence may be severe stress. Families caught in this circumstance have been referred to as the "sandwich generation" because they feel multiple and somewhat conflicting social and economic responsibilities to children and parents. The stress may eventually limit commitment to ongoing home care for older parents. Women of advanced age are likely to be dependent to some degree on their children or grandchildren for many years.[15, 42] Illustration 3–3 illuminates the point.

Illustration 3–3
A STRESSFUL RETIREMENT FOR BOB AND CAROLYN

Bob and Carolyn retired before age 60 to enjoy a more leisurely and mobile life. Bob was an only son, so his widowed mother lived with them until her severe disability led to a required move to a nursing home. She had enough income to pay the initial costs but most of her social support came from Bob and Carolyn.

Carolyn was the only living child of her widowed mother, who had enough income to pay the costs of an assisted living accommodation but was very dependent on Bob and Carolyn for social support. When one of their children suffered a major health crisis Bob and Carolyn found themselves caught between trying to help their daughter and their mothers at the same time. Fortunately, they were willing to modify their retirement plan at times to serve as the primary family caretakers for both child and parents.

Although neither parent lived with them as they grew older, they were constantly assisting with medical care, shopping, periodic crises, and ongoing social support. Their travel was regularly interrupted by the need to return home for a crisis involving either a child or a parent. They felt constantly responsible for trying to meet the needs of their parents and their children, creating major stresses that seriously affected their own retirement lifestyle.

Many young adult college students are strongly concerned by the financial and personal stress on parent's who are attempting to care for one or more of the grandparents while working full-time and supporting college expenses. The situation is so stressful for some students that they seek counseling, and in some cases, drop out of college to be of assistance to their parents and grandparents.

International Variations. The lifestyle effects are different in those countries where the norm is for grandparents, parents, and children to live in the same household. In many eastern European countries, for example, it is assumed that the oldest adult son and his family become responsible for the social and economic support of parents, with benefits flowing accordingly through inheritance of accumulated resources.[74]

Proxy Decision Making and Legal Arrangements

Disability, especially dementia or other form of mental incompetence, often generates the need for someone within the family to make "proxy" decisions. The ideal situation is for older individuals or family members to anticipate the issue and make plans in advance while mental capacities are intact. Formal steps can be taken to document preferences about future medical, financial, and personal choices using such devices as *durable power of attorney,* a *living trust,* and/or a *living will.* Preparation of such documents can help assure implementation of an older person's preferences, while relieving family members of some of the responsibility for decisions.[53]

Family members are usually chosen for the proxy role because they are in the best position to know the older person well and to understand what actions are preferred. In some instances family members with high integrity are not available. Self-interest may prevail to the disadvantage of the older person when a family member with proxy power has a strong personal interest in the outcome. Formal rules about ethical decision making must sometimes be imposed by the courts to protect the interests of incompetent older individuals.[41]

It is of course very difficult for a frail older person to enforce legal rights in the face of mistreatment or misuse of resources by family members or others. Violation of rights may continue without being addressed unless caring family members, or interested nonfamily parties such as state or local public agencies, are willing to intervene. Even then it may be very difficult to prove malfeasance. If proof is obtained and justice is served, the problem of how to care for the abused elderly person remains.[53]

Implications of Changes in Families

Families are becoming more complex over time as life expectancy increases. Many extended families now include five living generations although each nuclear family is smaller. More adults are present in the older generations and fewer children are born to younger generations. Older people, especially women, have at least a 94 percent probability of being grandparents and a 50 percent chance of becoming great-grandparents.[44, 48, 90]

High rates of divorce, remarriage, and increasing work roles for women are changing the family dramatically. Full- or part-time substitutes for family care are being created on a wider scale in the form of public and private social programs.[34, 37, 55, 71]

Gender Variations. The primary gender challenges arise from the generally poorer economic circumstances of women coupled with greater life expectancy. Widowhood often follows a major reduction in family savings because of health and long-term care costs prior to a husband's death. The probability is thus higher that more women than men will continue to need the help and emotional support of family or will require formal support from public or private agencies. Yet, as a specific consequence of the combination of smaller family size, divorce, and greater life expectancy, large numbers of older women are spending older age without much support from an extended family.[7, 58, 59, 79]

Older and younger women clearly have the major caretaking roles within the family and in formal care settings. As increasing numbers of women assume professional work roles, availability of caretakers has become a serious challenge, especially in the home and within formal care settings. Many older and dependent individuals do not always receive the ongoing attention needed for a reasonable quality of life.

The Baby Boom Generation. The nature of families could change dramatically in the years ahead as the baby boomers reach older age. As noted earlier, this large cohort is characterized by diversity and complexity of family life. The improved economic circumstances of educated and higher-income women means they will be more like older men, with greater choice and freedom whether married or single. Working women often delay child-bearing until age 30 or older and have few children. Divorces have increased to about half of marriages and single-parent families are commonplace. Many divorced and remarried older parents are faced with very uncertain loyalties and support from children and stepchildren. Because of the high divorce rate, male responsibility for more than one family is common, radically altering ability to care for children of two families and/or older parents. Caretaking for parents in older age may become very difficult under these circumstances.[6, 15, 51, 60]

Women who bear children somewhat later in life are more likely than in the past to be caring for children at the same time their elderly parents need care. However, because they tend to have fewer children and higher incomes than their predecessors, they may be better prepared to look after themselves in older age even with fewer available family caregivers.[15]

Consequences of Being Single. Single nonprofessional women may continue to have difficulty achieving adequate economic support for their later years, especially among some minority individuals whose accumulation of assets is very modest. However, single women in their 20s, 30s, and 40s at the end of the 1990s are generally more educated, more likely to have careers, and be better prepared for living alone than their predecessors.[6]

The consequence of older age for the large number of single teenage parents is a very uncertain proposition. Grandmotherhood comes earlier for teenage single mothers because their children are also likely to bear children at a young age. Older women in this situation regularly become responsible for two or more generations of children as well as aging parents, all with very limited education and resources—a very different family structure than the traditional nuclear family. The pattern seriously changes the usual timing of life stages, with serious consequences for self-esteem and ability to manage financially in older age.[15, 64, 68]

Family Mobility. Geographic mobility is increasing, with consequent wide separation of older parents from adult children. Family members may not be close at hand to serve as supporters in times of disability. Dependent older individuals must regularly move away from close friends and a familiar environment to a strange place so as to be near an adult child who can provide care. This situation is especially difficult when financial support, which means even greater dependence, is also needed.[23, 87]

Future Prospects. As longevity increases the relationships between generations will in all likelihood further change. The roles of parents, children, and grandparents may become more complex during the transition periods of life. Greater contact and solidarity among generations is one possibility, as a consequence of many more years of shared lives. Grandparents and grandchildren will have more time to get to know each other if they so choose. The total pool of people to provide caregiving to older family members will often be larger, even though children per nuclear family may be fewer. The collective financial resources to support long-term care will also be greater, if younger family members choose to provide personal or financial support.[14, 75]

Many European countries and Canada have chosen to provide a range of support programs for families to help them to support elderly members. Housing subsidies, financial allowances for children, support for parental leave to care for elderly parents in crisis, and other measures help counterbalance the problems brought on by major social and economic changes. All of these measures have helped to lower poverty and increase the general well-being of the elderly. The United States has so far provided fewer such options.[83]

◆◆◆ FRIENDS AND OTHER SOCIAL GROUPS

Although family relationships may be primary for most older people, friendships in the neighborhood or larger community are often exceedingly important. Family linkages tend to be traditional, somewhat obligatory, and occasionally a source of conflict. Friendships, on the other hand, are optional, self-chosen, and can be more easily broken if not satisfactory. Ability to select and sustain friendships outside the family is an important part of maintaining personal autonomy because friends can also provide affection, affirmation, and assistance in times of need.[7, 84]

The Value of Friendships

Attributes of close friendships include feelings of belonging, integration into a social group, intimate experiences, reassurance of self-worth, assistance when needed, open communication, and information sharing. Feelings of belonging or integration provide opportunity for association with like-minded individuals. Intimate relationships provide a forum in which to confide, share thoughts, and express feelings. Reassurance of self-worth and a sense of respect by someone else increases personal confidence. Reliable sources of assistance are available when needed through informal alliances. Opportunities are also available for providing information, sharing knowledge or skills, offering advice, and giving other forms of assistance to others who need help.[84]

Most older people achieve great satisfaction from good friendships and experience a sense of loneliness when friends are not available for regular interaction. The attachment to friends means that a move from home and neighborhood to a new location, a required move to an institutional setting away from home, or the death of a close friend can be profoundly upsetting.

Close Confidants

The closest friendships are often with peers of similar age and socioeconomic class who have been friends for many years in the work setting, neighborhood, or through organizational activities. Older people of similar age tend to have had comparable life experiences, hold closely related values, and share common interests. The closest confidant outside of marriage is often a long-time friend who is not a family member. A circle of such friendships can be a primary element in a support system after widowhood or decline in health. Fortunately, most older people have a ready-made wide circle of friends (an average of nine according to one national study) and belong to a number of formal and informal social organizations.[7, 10, 13]

Informal self-selected friendships in the neighborhood or wider community are the norm and tend to be more satisfying than the somewhat formal friendships generated at senior-citizen centers or other clubs. The informal friendship-making process is operative in housing complexes with large numbers of older people—in retirement communities, nursing homes, or assisted living facilities. As individuals age confidants become younger; people in the *oldest* age categories are usually widowed and most of their siblings and peers have died. Younger relatives or friends in the neighborhood become the only available close contacts. Proximity becomes a key factor, despite possible incompatibilities. Intimacy and sharing remain very important in older age.[25, 91]

◆◆◆ NEIGHBORHOOD AND COMMUNITY

The importance of family, friendships, neighborhood and community to the elderly is captured in a classic phrase by Scott Peck (in Forschner, 1992: 34):

> We are inevitably social creatures who desperately need each other not merely for sustenance, not merely for company, but for any meaning to our lives whatsoever.

Older individuals in a strong and well-developed neighborhood and community usually receive ongoing support from a variety of sources. Activities and services available in the community provide meaning and stimulation to daily life while fulfilling basic personal and household needs. On the other hand, a poorly developed community can be socially frustrating, short of needed services, dangerous to health and security, and may sharply curtail freedom, autonomy, and overall life quality for its older citizens.[33]

Differentiating the Neighborhood from the Community

The neighborhood is close at hand, often the location of close friendships and important social groups, where most daily activities occur. However, support services may be limited. The larger community is likely to contain several neighborhoods and have all services needed on a daily or weekly basis. The specific delineation of any neighborhood boundary varies depending upon individual perceptions of the geography. Older individuals tend to define a smaller neighborhood than do younger people because their range of mobility may be more limited. Neighborhood and community may largely overlap in many smaller rural locations. Neighborhoods and communities are thus distinguished by the intimacy of social relationships and the scale and scope of accessible support services.

Social Functions

Several important social support functions of well-developed neighborhoods and communities include:

- Social cohesion and integration.
- Social-class differentiation.
- Basic social activities.
- Governmental institutional structure, order and security.
- Provision of services.

Social Cohesion and Integration. Communities can be characterized by their location on a continuum from "socially cohesive, integrated, and mutually supportive" to "lacking cohesion, disintegrative, and nonsupportive." The more supportive communities are obviously at the socially cohesive end of the continuum. Older individuals generally feel a strong sense of belonging to the territory and the people of their neighborhood and community regardless of its cohesiveness, explaining in part why moving to another location is often quite painful and even traumatic for an older person. The feelings of attachment provide the basis for mutuality, interdependency, caring of members for each other, and ongoing social support. When mutuality is missing, delinquency, crime, family breakdown, environmental deterioration, and other forms of disintegration can often be observed—losses that are particularly troubling to the older population.[33]

Social-Class Differentiation. The social class of the neighborhood from which an older person comes can have a profound effect on attitudes, self-concept, and overall likelihood of achieving a successful older age. The social class of the community directly affects perception of choices, retirement opportunities, and alternative lifestyle possibilities.[46, 73]

Older members of middle-class and upper-class families usually have primary political and social control of communities. A socially cohesive and integrated community without sharp distinctions between social classes is more hospitable to the older population than a sharply divided community. Older individuals are quick to perceive the presence of such characteristics or the lack thereof. The appeal of a community to old or new residents is associated in part with the inclination of local governments and voluntary organizations to provide social support and services regardless of social class.[54]

The issue of integrating the elderly at the community level is of great concern in most economically developed countries. Because family support for the elderly with serious disabilities is declining, community-support systems are becoming more important. As noted earlier, social-support networks tend to become less predictable with older age because of deaths of friends and siblings and the uncertainty of family support as disability increases. Support can become strained and problematic to all parties in those instances when the family is not especially functional and the community has no mechanisms to provide assistance.[40, 89]

Social Activities. A variety of local institutions provide opportunities for social interaction and support, including the so-called aging network, churches, informal clubs, and service organizations. Many cities and towns sponsor organized activity groups for the older population. For example, "singles clubs" are very popular in smaller cities and towns around the country. Older individuals gather for card playing, dining, dancing, and a variety of other activities. These gatherings can be the highlight of the week for older men and women who live alone.

The Aging Network. The Aging Network refers generally to all public organizations supported in one way or another at the community and state levels through the federal Older Americans Act. The U.S. Administration on Aging, state units on aging, area agencies on aging, and local units receiving public support, such as information and referral services, nutrition programs, multipurpose senior centers, in-home services, legal assistance, and case management programs, are all part of the network. Most services are offered free of charge to the older person.[35,49]

Multipurpose senior centers serve as important social units for individuals who would otherwise not have good opportunities for human interaction and neighborhood integration. Their goal has been to provide certain basic services that increase the independence and quality of life for older individuals in the community. For those individuals with abundant social alternatives, a senior center is less likely to be viewed as desirable or necessary. Only about 15 percent of older people use such centers, probably because the great majority have long-time affiliations with other preferred alternatives. Studies indicate that low-income elderly are more likely to participate, perhaps because of the meals and other basic services provided. This may be particularly the case for poor African American elderly in some southern states who tend to use the services more than their European American neighbors.[35, 56, 63, 65, 78]

Churches.   Churches provide an important social outlet while also helping to integrate older individuals into the community as they practice their religious beliefs. In Europe older people are four times more likely to be interested in religious life than are young people (1990 survey). Church organizations, such as women's groups, bible-study classes, governance bodies, and choirs perform a very important function for those who need social support. The church is the single most important and fulfilling organization for many older individuals.[89]

Special support services are sometimes provided for older members in the form of food, clothing, study groups, and a variety of other options. Furthermore, church leaders can be of specific assistance to older members through "life review" functions in times of loss and health crises. The focus on religious beliefs enables them to view their life in a larger context, helping older individuals to come to terms with their own impending mortality. By way of reciprocity for the perceived benefits, much of the leadership and maintenance activity for many churches is provided by older members.[32]

Other Organizations.   Every community supports a wide variety of voluntary clubs and service organizations to meet the specialized interest of local citizens. Organizations such as bridge clubs and civic clubs can provide strong social support to older members. Community governments provide a range of public services including police functions, fire protection, road and street construction and maintenance, and a variety of other activities that produce structure, orderliness, and security for citizens. The adequacy and quality of these services will make a very important difference to older citizens. The completeness and quality of services vary widely from one community to another and are an important basis for choice of location by older families or individuals who, for one reason or another, decide to move.

The Contribution of Older People to Communities

Older citizens are major contributors to strong communities and neighborhoods. They volunteer for public activities of many kinds, work in political campaigns, assume leadership roles in community-development projects, and generally carry much of the burden of keeping communities viable and healthy.[32]

Some older individuals volunteer for very taxing service roles such as foster grandparenting—working with young people who need mentors and role models.

This type of activity can be very beneficial for the young people involved and can also be very satisfying for the older person. Many other roles of this type are available for older individuals who seek productive community involvement, as Illustration 3–4 highlights.

Illustration 3—4
CONTRIBUTING TO CHURCH AND THE COMMUNITY

Fred and Mary were married and lived in the same small community all of their lives, constantly offering their talents to important local causes. As they grew older some of these efforts took on increasing importance, particularly the improvement and maintenance of their local church. Fred served as the lay leader and warden for many years while Mary served as church secretary. They contributed substantially to the church budget, and with other church members in the community, helped to upgrade the building with a new church school and social center in the basement.

The church served as a social center and gathering place for the entire community from time to time since there was no other high quality large public building. Fred served as president of the local Farmer's Union and he and Mary hosted many meetings there. It was the principal meeting place for the Women's Homemaker Club in which Mary played a leading role for many of her later years. It was the location of many funerals for the older community members—including Mary's after she passed away in 1997.

As this is written, Fred continues his participation and contributions in his advanced older age.

The role of older citizens in communities may be even stronger in Japan and many European countries where they have traditionally been held in somewhat higher esteem than in the United States. For example, elderly men hold many important positions in private business and public life in Japan. In the Netherlands, many of the maintenance activities which keep communities functional, beautify the countryside, and generally benefit the whole population are performed by the older citizens.

◆◆◆ SUMMARY AND CONCLUSIONS

Satisfying social-support systems provide the primary basis for quality of life in older age, with the family as the key element. Well-functioning families provide the supportive relationships that can lead to strong feelings of belonging and a sense of self-worth. Older individuals often want to move physically and socially closer to their family at crisis points in their lives because they place very high value on such support. However, they generally prefer to maintain independent households rather than live with children or other relatives. Despite the challenges to families in modern society, intergenerational mutual support remains a strong force.

However, social support from one or more close confidants, such as a spouse or a close friend, is of most importance to mental and emotional well-being. Primary relationships are highly valued because they provide a strong measure of satisfying interdependence. Not all relationships in the neighborhood or community provide genuine emotional support because they do not always involve caring or affirmation, even though aid might be provided.

Expectations and obligations among family members are changing. Because of smaller families, increasing employment of women, greater longevity, and other changes that alter family responsibility, the sense of mutual obligation in families appears to be declining. The sense of responsibility for caregiving to disabled older parents may be diminishing. Consequently, other structures to provide support are emerging in the public arena.

Neighborhoods and communities provide a highly important locale for wider social networks, social support, security, and an array of needed services. When community social cohesion, integration, and support systems are adequate, communities help the elderly to survive and thrive. When these social structures are inadequate, as in a poorly developed community, the incidence of drug use, crime, and delinquency, may seriously limit the ability of older people to feel secure. Many rural and urban center communities have physically and socially deteriorated and are no longer able to adequately support the needs of older citizens.

If common values and goals prevail, if economic and social resources are widely shared, and if social and political responsibilities are effectively implemented, a community and its institutions can serve elderly residents very well. If not, a community may be perceived by residents as failing to implement basic social responsibilities.

◆◆◆ REFERENCES

1. Adkins, Vincent K. (1999). Grandparents as a National Asset: A Brief Note, *Activities, Adaptation, and Aging*, 24 (1), 13–18.
2. Administration on Aging (2000). Profile of Older Americans, 1999, online at www.aoa.gov/stats/profile.
3. Aiken, Lewis R. (1995). *Aging: An Introduction to Gerontology*, Thousand Oaks, CA: Sage.
4. American Association of Retired Persons (1998). *Profile of Older Americans*, Washington, DC: American Association of Retired Persons.
5. Andersson, Lars, and Gerdt Sundstrom (1996). The Social Networks of Elderly People in Sweden, in Howard Litwin (ed), *The Social Networks of Older People: A Cross-National Analysis*, Westport, CT: Praeger, 15–29.
6. Angel, Ronald J., and Jacqueline L. Angel (1997). *Who Will Care for Us? Aging and Long-Term Care in Multicultural America*, New York: New York University Press.
7. Antonucci, Toni C. (1990). Social Support and Social Relationships, in Robert H. Binstock and Linda K. George (eds), *Handbook of Aging and the Social Sciences* (3d ed), San Diego: Academic Press, 205–26.
8. Antonucci, Toni C., Rebecca Fuhrer, and Jean-Francois Dartigues (1997). Social Relations and Depressive Symptomatology in a Sample of Community-Dwelling French Older Adults, *Psychology and Aging*, 12, 1, 189–95.

9. Arber, Sara, and Maria Evandrou (eds.) (1993). *Ageing, Independence and the Life Course,* London: Jessica Kingsley Publishers.

10. Atchley, Robert C. (1988). *Social Forces and Aging: An Introduction to Social Gerontology,* Belmont, CA: Wadsworth.

11. Barrow, Georgia M. (1996). *Aging, the Individual, and Society* (6th ed). Minneapolis: West Publishing.

12. Bedford, Victoria Hilkevitch (1995). Sibling Relationships in Middle and Old Age, in Rosemary Blieszner and Victoria Hilkevitch Bedford (eds), *Handbook of Aging and the Family,* Westport, CT: Greenwood Press, 201–19.

13. Bee, Helen L. (1996). *The Journey of Adulthood* (3d ed), Upper Saddle River, NJ: Prentice Hall.

14. Bengtson, Vern L., and W. Andrew Achenbaum (eds) (1993). *The Changing Contract Across Generations,* New York: Aldine de Gruyter.

15. Bengtson, Vern, Carolyn Rosenthal, and Linda Burton (1990). Families and Aging: Diversity and Heterogeneity, in Robert H. Binstock and Linda K. George (eds), *Handbook of Aging and the Social Sciences* (3d ed), San Diego: Academic Press, 263–87.

16. Brussoni, Mariana J., and Susan D. Boon (1998). Grandparental Impact in Young Adults' Relationships with their Closest Grandparents: The Role of Relationship Strength and Emotional Closeness, *International Journal of Aging and Human Development,* 46 (4), 267–86.

17. Burks, Valerie, Dale A. Lund, Charles H. Gregg, and Harry P. Bluhm (1988). Bereavement and Remarriage for Older Adults, *Death Studies,* 12, 51–60.

18. Butler, Robert N., Myrna Lewis, and Trey Sutherland (1991). *Aging and Mental Health: Positive Psychosocial and Biomedical Approaches* (4th ed), New York: Macmillan.

19. Caputo, Richard K. (1999). Grandmothers and Co-resident Grandchildren, *Families in Society: The Journal of Contemporary Human Services,* 80 (2), 120–26.

20. Clair, Jeffrey Michael, David A. Karp, and William C. Yoels (1993). *Experiencing the Life Cycle: A Social Psychology of Aging,* Springfield, IL: Charles C Thomas, Publisher.

21. Clarke, Edward J., Mar Preston, Jo Raksin, and Vern L. Bengtson (1999). Types of Conflicts and Tensions Between Older Parents and Adult Children, *The Gerontologist,* 39 (2), 261–70.

22. Clulow, Christopher (1995). Who Cares? Implications of Caring Responsibilities for Couples and Families, *Sexual and Marital Therapy,* 10 (1), 63–68.

23. Conner, Karen A. (1992). *Aging America: Issues Facing an Aging Society,* Upper Saddle River, NJ: Prentice Hall.

24. Coward, Raymond T., and Stephen J. Cutler (1989). Informal and Formal Health Care Systems for the Rural Elderly, *Health Services Research,* 23 (6), 785–806.

25. Cox, Harold G. (1996). *Later Life: The Realities of Aging,* Upper Saddle River, NJ: Prentice Hall.

26. Craft, Betty J., and Sister Carol Grasser (1998). The Relationship of Reciprocity to Self Health Care in Older Women, *Journal of Women and Aging,* 10 (2), 35–47.

27. Dimond, Margaret, Dale A. Lund, and Michael S. Caserta (1987). The Role of Social Support in the First Two Years of Bereavement in an Elderly Sample, *Gerontologist,* 27 (5), 599–604.

28. Drew, Linda A., and Peter K. Smith (1999). The Impact of Parental Separation/Divorce on Grandparent-Grandchild Relationships, *International Journal of Aging and Human Development,* 48 (4), 191–216.

29. Duffy, Linda M. (1998). Lovers, Loners, and Lifers: Sexuality and the Older Adult, *Geriatrics,* 53 (S1), S66–S69).

30. Dunham, Charlotte Chorn (1995). A Link Between Generations, *Journal of Family Issues,* 16 (4), 450–65.

31. Emick, Michelle A., and Bert Hayslip (1999). Custodial Grandparenting: Stresses, Coping Skills, and Relationships with Grandchildren, *International Journal of Aging and Human Development,* 48 (1), 35–61.

32. Falk, Ursula, and Gerhard Falk (1997). *Ageism, the Aged, and Aging in America,* Springfield, IL: Charles C Thomas Publishers.

33. Forschner, Brian E. (1992). A Sense of Community, *Health Progress,* 73 (5), 34–36, 57.

34. Fry, Christine L. (1991). Cross-cultural Comparisons of Aging, in Kenneth F. Ferraro (ed), *Gerontology: Perspectives and Issues,* New York: Springer, 129–46.

35. Gelfand, Donald E. (1999). *The Aging Network: Programs and Services,* New York: Springer.

36. Genovese, Rosalie G. (1997). *Americans at Midlife: Caught Between Generations,* Westport, CT: Gergin & Garvey.

37. Gierveld, Jenny De Jong, and Theo Van Tilburg (1999). Living Arrangements of Older Adults in the Netherlands and Italy: Coresidence Values and Behavior and Their Consequences for Loneliness, *Journal of Cross-Cultural Gerontology*, 14 (1), 1–24.

38. Groenou, Marjolein Broese van, and Theo van Tilburg (1997). Changes in the Support Networks of Older Adults in the Netherlands, *Journal of Cross-Cultural Gerontology*, 12 (1), 23–44.

39. Groenou, Marjolein Broese van, and Theo van Tilburg (1996). The Personal Network of Dutch Older Adults: A Source of Social Contact and Instrumental Support, in Howard Litwin (ed), *The Social Networks of Older People: A Cross-National Analysis*, Westport, CT: Praeger, 163–82.

40. Hansson, Robert O., and Bruce N. Carpenter (1994). *Relationships in Old Age: Coping with the Challenge of Transition*, New York: Guilford Press.

41. Hardwig, John R. (1994). Justice Within the Family, in Chris Hackler (ed), *Health Care for an Aging Population*, Albany: State University of New York Press, 43–55.

42. Hareven, Tamara K. (1996). Aging and Generational Relations Over the Life Course, in Tamara K. Hareven (ed), *Aging and Generational Relations Over the Life Course: A Historical and Cross-Cultural Perspective*, New York: Walter de Gruyter, 1–12.

43. Hashimoto, Akiko (1998). *The Gift of Generations: Japanese and American Perspectives on Aging and the Social Contract*, Cambridge: University Press.

44. Hogan, Dennis P., David J. Eggebeen, and Sean M. Snaith (1996). The Well-being of Aging Americans with Very Old Parents, in Tamara K. Hareven (ed), *Aging and Generational Relations Over the Life Course: A Historical and Cross-Cultural Perspective*, New York: Walter de Gruyter, pp. 327–37.

45. Hooyman, Nancy R., and H. Asuman Kiyak (1996). *Social Gerontology: A Multidisciplinary Perspective* (4th ed), Boston: Allyn & Bacon.

46. Huyck, Margaret Hellie (1995). Marriage and Close Relationships of the Marital Kind, in Rosemary Blieszner and Victoria Hilkevitch Bedford (eds), *Handbook of Aging and the Family*, Westport, CT: Greenwood Press, 181–97.

47. Jacoby, Susan (1999). Great Sex: What's Age Got To Do With It? *Modern Maturity*, 42W (5), 41–45, 91.

48. Johnson, Katrina W. (1995). *Grandparenting: Some Facts that You May Not Know*, Bethesda, MD: National Institute on Aging.

49. Kane, Rosalie, and Mary Olsen Baker (1996). Emerging Trends in Managed Care, presentation to a conference on *Managed Care Issues and Themes: What Next for the Aging Network?*, Sponsored by the Administration on Aging, Department of Health and Human Services, Washington, DC.

50. Kart, Cary S. (1997). *The Realities of Aging: An Introduction to Gerontology* (5th ed), Boston: Allyn and Bacon.

51. Kingson, Eric R. (1996). Ways of Thinking About the Long-Term Care and Baby-Boom Cohorts, in Marie E. Cowart and Jill Quadagno (eds), *From Nursing Homes to Home Care*, New York: Haworth Press, 3–24.

52. Kirwin, Patricia M. (1991). Intergenerational Continuity and Reciprocity Through the Use of Community-Based Services: Theory and Practice, *Home Health Care Services Quarterly*, 12 (2), 17–33.

53. Knapp, Marshal B. (1991). Legal and Ethical Issues in Family Caregiving and the Role of Public Policy, *Home Health Care Services Quarterly*, 12 (4), 5–28.

54. Koff, Theodore H. (1988). *New Approaches to Health Care for An Aging Population*, San Francisco: Jossey-Bass.

55. Kosberg, Jordan I. (1992). An International Perspective on Family Care of the Elderly, in Jordan I. Kosberg (ed), *Family Care of the Elderly: Social and Cultural Changes*, Newbury Park, CA: Sage, 1–14.

56. Krout, John A. (1989). *Senior Centers in America*, New York: Greenwood Press.

57. Lee, Gary R., Marion C. Willetts, and Karen Seccomber (1998). Widowhood and Depression: Gender Differences, *Research on Aging*, 20 (5), 611–30.

58. Lemme, Barbara Hansen (1995). *Development in Adulthood*, Boston: Allyn and Bacon.

59. Lund, Dale A., Michael S. Caserta, and Margaret F. Dimond (1986). Gender Differences Through Two Years of Bereavement Among the Elderly, *The Gerontologist*, 26 (3), 314–20.

60. Lund, Dale A. (1998). Personal communication.

61. Mayo Clinic (1993). Sexuality and Aging, *Mayo Clinic Health Letter*, February.

62. McCrea, James M., and Thomas B. Smith (1997). Social Issues Addressed by Intergenerational Programs, in Sally Newman, Christopher R. Ward, Thomas B. Smith, Janet O. Wilson, and James M.

McCrea (eds). *Intergenerational Programs: Past, Present, and Future*, London, England: Taylor and Francis.

63. Miner, Sonia, John A. Logan, and Glenna Spitze (1993). Predicting the Frequency of Senior Center Attendance, *The Gerontologist*, 33 (5), 650–57.

64. Minkler, Meredith (1999). Intergenerational Households Headed by Grandparents: Contexts, Realities, and Implications for Policy, *Journal of Aging Studies*, 13 (2), 199–218.

65. Mitchell, Jim (1995). Service Awareness and Use Among Older North Carolinians, *Journal of Applied Gerontology*, 14 (2), 193–209.

66. Murdock, Meliss E., Charles A. Guarnaccia, Bert Hayslip, and Christine L. McKibbin (1998). The Contribution of Small Life Events to the Psychological Distress of Married and Widowed Older Women, *Journal of Women and Aging*, 10 (2), 3–22.

67. Newman, Sally, Christopher R. Ward, Thomas B. Smith, Janet O. Wilson, and James M. McCrea (eds) (1997). *Intergenerational Programs: Past, Present, and Future*, London, England: Taylor and Francis.

68. Norris, Joan E., and Joseph A. Tindale (1994). *Among Generations: The Cycle of Adult Relationships*, New York: W. H. Freeman.

69. O'Bryant, Shirley and Robert O. Hansson (1995). Widowhood, in Rosemary Blieszner and Victoria Hilkevitch Bedford (eds), *Handbook of Aging and the Family*, Westport, CT: Greenwood Press, 440–55.

70. Orbuch, Terri L., James S. House, Richard P. Mero, and Pamela S. Webster (1996). Marital Quality Over the Life Course, *Social Psychology Quarterly*, 59 (2), 162–71.

71. Organization for Economic Cooperation and Development (OECD) (1994). *Caring for Frail Elderly People*, Paris: OECD.

72. Palmore, Erdman B. (1999). *Ageism: Negative and Positive*, New York: Springer.

73. Pearlin, Leonard, and Marilyn M. Skaff (1998). Perspectives on the Family and Stress in Late Life, in Jacob Lomranz (ed), *Handbook of Aging and Mental Health: An Integrative Approach*, New York: Plenum Press, 323–37.

74. Plakans, Andrejs (1996). Retirement, Inheritance, and Generational Relations: Life-Course Analysis in Historic Eastern Europe, in Tamara K. Hareven (ed), *Aging and Generational Relations Over the Life Course: A Historical and Cross-Cultural Perspective*, New York: Walter de Gruyter, 140–57.

75. Qualls, Sara Honn (1993). Family Therapy with Older Adults, *Generations*, 17 (1), 73–74.

76. Rein, Martin, and Harold Salzman (1995). Social Integration, Participation, and Exchange in Five Industrial Countries, in Scott A. Bass (ed), *Older and Active: How Americans Over 55 Are Contributing to Society*, New Haven: Yale University Press, 237–62.

77. Riekse, Robert J., and Henry Holstege (1996). *Growing Old in America*, New York: McGraw-Hill.

78. Roff, Lucinda Lee, and Charles R. Atherton (1989). *Promoting Successful Aging*, Chicago: Nelson-Hall.

79. Rossi, Alice S. (1993). Intergenerational Relations: Gender, Norms, and Behavior, in Bengtson, Vern L., and W. Andrew Achenbaum (eds). *The Changing Contract Across Generations*, New York: Aldine de Gruyter, 191–212.

80. Rowe, John W., and Robert L. Kahn (1998). *Successful Aging*, New York: Pantheon Books.

81. Schiavi, R. C. (1990). Sexuality and Aging in Men, in John Bancroft (ed), *Annual Review of Sex Research*, Lake Mills, IA: Society for the Scientific Study of Sex, 227–50.

82. Schone, Barbara, and Robin Weinick (1998). Health-Related Behaviors and the Benefits of Marriage for Elderly Persons, *The Gerontologist*, 38 (5), 618–27.

83. Skolnick, Arlene, and Jerome Skolnick (1999). Family in Transition, 1997, in Joel M. Charon (ed), *The Meaning of Sociology*, Upper Saddle River, NJ: Prentice Hall, 300–307.

84. Slater, Robert (1995). *The Psychology of Growing Old*, Philadelphia: Open University Press.

85. Smolak, Linda (1993). *Adult Development*, Upper Saddle River, NJ: Prentice Hall.

86. Stepp, Laura Sessions (1999). Not Just Older—Sexier, Too, *Washington Post National Weekly Edition*, 16 (41), 34.

87. Tennstedt, Sharon L., Sybil L. Crawford, and John B. McKinlay (1993). Is Family Care on the Decline? A Longitudinal Investigation of the Substitution of Formal Long-Term Care Services for Informal Care, *The Milbank Quarterly*, 71 (4), 601–24.

88. United States Census Bureau (1998). Marital Status and Living Arrangements: March 1998 (Update), *Current Population Reports*, Washington, DC: United States Census Bureau.

89. Walker, Alan, and Tony Maltby (1997). *Ageing Europe*, Philadelphia: Open University Press.

90. Wenger, G. Clare (1997). Review of Findings on Support Networks of Older Europeans, *Journal of Cross-Cultural Gerontology*, 12 (1), 1–21.

91. Wenger, G. Clare, and Dorothy Jerrome (1999). Change and Stability in Confidant Relationships: Findings From the Bangor Longitudinal Study of Aging, *Journal of Aging Studies*, 13 (3), 269–94.

92. Whitbeck, Les, Danny R. Hoyt, and Shirley M. Huck (1994). Early Family Relationships, Intergenerational Solidarity, and Support Provided to Parents by their Adult Children, *Journal of Gerontology: Social Sciences*, 49 (2), S85–S94.

93. Williams, Mark E. (1995). *Complete Guide to Health and Aging*, New York: Harmony Books and American Geriatrics Society.

Part II

CONTRIBUTING FACTORS TO QUALITY OF LIFE

Part I focused on forces close to the older person that affect his or her long term well-being. Part II identifies and examines the range of factors in the *larger society* that particularly contribute to quality of life. Although the factors exist in every economically advanced country, the chapters in Part II focus primarily on the United States' context. Seven other countries are examined in Part III.

Chapter Four concentrates on the health status of the older population, the potential disease impacts, and the diagnosis and health care system required when illness occurs. The primary illnesses or conditions are identified and evaluated. The older person whose health may be failing is dependent on a very complex health care system that is difficult to understand and use appropriately.

Chapter Five clarifies the meaning of mental health, common mental disorders among older people, and the system of treatment. The incidence of some forms of mental disorder, such as Alzheimer's disease, is higher among older people than among younger people. A high proportion of nursing home residents have disabling mental conditions that have not been adequately treated. The mental health care system is examined and its shortcomings are emphasized.

Chapter Six identifies common chronic conditions and the forms of long-term care used to help individuals with severe and continuing physical and/or mental illness. Home health care is described and evaluated as an alternative to nursing home care. As the number of very old people increases, long-term home care and institutional care become more important, despite the improving health status of the older population. The chapter identifies public policies and actions that need continuing attention.

Chapter Seven focuses on the residential environment as a corollary to Chapter Three, which focused on the social environment. Adequacy of housing is examined in terms of its contribution to health and well-being and particularly as it enables disabled individuals to function independently. Similarly, the neighborhood and community are evaluated as contributors to aesthetic and service needs.

Chapter Eight confronts the issues of financial security, health care insurance, long-term care financing, and the larger economic context in which every older person must function. Income-support programs are evaluated in terms of their adequacy in supporting a high quality of life. Physical health, mental health, and long-term care forms of insurance are reviewed and inadequacies are identified. Policy changes that might help resolve inadequacies are evaluated.

Chapter Nine examines lifestyle options and issues. Lifestyle refers to the total package of experiences, environments, and supports that make up or detract from a good quality of life. A tremendous diversity of opportunity exists, especially for those who have good health and adequate income. In contrast, constraints on quality of life for disabled and/or low-income individuals are emphasized, and the possibilities presented for achieving a satisfying lifestyle through adequate social support and access to needed services.

Chapter 4

HEALTH STATUS
AND HEALTH CARE

 INTRODUCTION

This chapter examines the health status of the older population, the system of care for physical health, and the major challenges associated with improving health maintenance and care. Specific topics include:

- Health status.
- Major health problems.
- Disability and activities of daily living.
- Health maintenance.
- The health care system for older people.
- Geriatric assessment and care.
- Health care challenges.

The older populations in the United States and in most other economically advanced countries are becoming somewhat healthier—particularly the younger cohort, between ages 65 and 74. Attention to nutrition, exercise, stress management, and other positive elements of a healthy lifestyle are improving. A significant proportion of older individuals deliberately engage in health promotion activities. During 1996 about 58 percent (in the United States) maintained appropriate body weight; 68 percent pursued some form of vigorous physical activity; 88 percent ate a full breakfast regularly; and 96 percent did not abuse alcohol. These healthy activities contributed directly to a decline in mortality of about 2 percent per year in the 1980s and 1990s. Overall improvements in health status have enhanced the potential for improved quality of life in older age—an optimistic scenario for the future.[13, 74, 95, 115]

A national survey in 1995 indicated that 63 percent of the older population reported no minor or major activity limitations. Among those age 75 or older, 57 percent reported no activity limitation; 68 percent said their health was very good or excellent. Among those over age 85, about 40 percent considered themselves generally healthy but the other 60 percent have some form of serious chronic condition; about half need assistance with activities of daily living. The increasing numbers of very old individuals means a continuing expansion in the population with long-term disabilities who need chronic health care.[13, 91, 108, 115]

Senior citizens were more active in sports and athletics during the 1990s than in previous decades. For example, participation in the Senior Olympics has been growing rapidly. Approximately 2500 competed in 1987 whereas 12,000 participated in the 1999 games. Nonetheless, a substantial proportion of older people—especially in the lower social classes and among the oldest cohorts—remain relatively sedentary. Involvement in physical activity declines somewhat with age.[31, 112]

A reduction in disabilities of 15 percent was estimated over the decade from 1985 to 1995—a highly significant change in health status contributing directly to improved life expectancy. Disability rates vary substantially by region of the country however; prevalence is much higher in the Southeast and lower in the North and West. Health care for older people with disabilities costs as much as six times more per individual than for relatively healthy older people. Finding better treatment for disabling diseases such as Alzheimer's, osteoporosis, and diabetes has been hugely beneficial, although much more progress is obviously needed.[72, 90, 102, 111]

◆◆◆ HEALTH STATUS

Health status refers to a general health condition such as the existence of acute or chronic disease, illness, impairment or disability, and is based on both objective measurements of physical and mental condition as well as subjective measures of perceived healthiness. As individuals age, acute conditions diminish relative to the more permanent and pervasive chronic conditions.

Genetic inheritance forms the initial basis for health status. However, genes do not constitute destiny. Health status is also strongly affected by the social and cultural background of the family and community; attitudes, beliefs, and values about health maintenance have a major impact. Economic circumstances obviously affect the ability to maintain a good diet, have a good home, and secure health care. Condition of the biophysical environment has major influence on the incidence of disease and illness. Public policies at community, state, and national levels have a major impact on overall health status of the older population because they establish the rules and the programs that provide for public health services, access to insurance, specific health supportive programs, and environmental protection.[63, 95, 108, 129]

Variations in Health Status

African American, Hispanic American, and Native American older people in the United States have poorer health status than their European American counterparts whereas Asian Americans demonstrate better health. Much of the explanation is related to socioeconomic status, educational levels, environmental conditions, access to health insurance, and access to health care—all of which are lower for most "minority" Americans except Asian Americans. As a consequence life expectancy is lower, and rates of hypertension, heart disease, stroke, end-state renal disease, dementia, and prostate cancer are all higher; survival rates from cancer are lower for most minority Americans.[27]

However, a recent study in northern Florida of elderly living alone indicated that African Americans in this region are *not* at higher risk of poor health than elderly European Americans with comparable economic and social conditions, although they tend to perceive themselves as less healthy. In fact, the incidence of mental illness, such as depression, appeared to be somewhat *lower* among the African Americans in this regional study.[27, 50, 88]

African Americans and Hispanic Americans tend generally to rate their health status lower than European Americans. However, when measurements indicate they are comparable on the basis of income, gender, other social factors, they are equally healthy. Likewise, lower-income individuals rate themselves as less healthy than higher-income individuals. Men perceive themselves as healthier than women. Self-perceived health status is closely related to perceived overall quality of life.[34,108]

Normal Health-Status Changes

Several health-status changes correlate with age, are normal, and are relatively universal, such as **vision.** Presbyopia or far-sightedness, increases; peripheral vision diminishes; incidence of cataracts or glaucoma is higher; ability to focus declines; pupil size diminishes; and ability to adapt to darkness decreases. As a consequence, 90 percent of the elderly wear glasses or contact lenses and about 15 percent have seriously impaired vision after age 65, rising to 30 percent after age 85. **Hearing** decreases in one or both ears. Some hearing loss occurs in about 30 percent of the elderly, rising to 50 percent after age 85, and often requiring hearing aids. However, most older people do not suffer enough hearing loss to interfere with normal life activities. **Smell** becomes less sensitive to aromas. **Taste** becomes less perceptive of flavors, and **touch** less responsive to stimuli or pain. **Skin** gets thinner and drier with less elasticity and more wrinkles. Expression lines deepen. Sun damaged skin gets more wrinkled, yellows, gets rough and leathery, and shows spots.[126] **Body Functions** change, with lowered ability to absorb calcium. The decline in ability to absorb calcium can become a very serious problem, especially among women, often requiring dietary supplements to avoid bone loss, osteoporosis, and physical weakness. Wear and tear on joints increase, leading to arthritis. Lung capacity decreases. Kidneys lose mass and decrease speed of filtering the waste from blood. Bladder capacity declines somewhat. Arteries thicken and are less efficient. The level of sex hormones decreases, and sexual inclination declines. Reaction time to stimuli in the environment diminishes somewhat. The immune system is less able to ward off disease, and susceptibility to flu and other transmittable diseases increases. Vulnerability to toxic environmental conditions increases, and side effects of medical treatment rise.[64, 126]

Sleep disorders occur at a higher rate. Sleep problems are reported by about 30 percent of older adults, sometimes leading to shortages of rest that cause sleepiness during the day. More time is needed to fall asleep. Deepness of sleep diminishes. Insomnia is common. Sleep apnea or difficulty breathing is more common. Other difficulties include multiple awakenings, trouble going back to sleep, and early awakening in the morning. Individuals with chronic medical conditions may have even greater difficulty with sleep, especially when pain exists. The usual recommendations of physicians are regular hours for sleeping and rising, avoidance of late dining, avoidance of caffeine, alcohol and tobacco, limiting daytime naps, limiting use of the bed to sleep and sex, daily aerobic exercise, and possibly taking some form of sedative to encourage sleep. In severe cases, sleep therapy might be recommended.[19, 37]

Body composition is altered. Changes in posture, diminished growth of vertebrae, forward bending of the spine, and compression of disks between the vertebrae combine to diminish height by an average of two inches between about age 50 and age 80. Weight usually declines as well, especially in the 70s and 80s, but at a higher rate for men than women. Body fat increases as a proportion of total weight, doubling between age 25 and age 75—but at a slower rate for those who maintain their physical condition.[126]

◆◆◆ MAJOR HEALTH PROBLEMS

Diminished health status may or may not lead to serious acute or chronic problems, disability, or substantially lowered quality of life. The degree of interference with activities of daily living depends on the severity of the problem and how it is treated. Disease in older age is somewhat different than at younger ages. For example: deterioration proceeds more rapidly than at younger ages if not treated; there is a high frequency of multiple conditions; symptoms may not be specific and are often hard to diagnose; secondary complications are common; rehabilitation is often needed; and disease may cause a need for new forms of housing to accommodate disability. The health care system must respond to these differences if treatment is to be effective.[32]

The most common chronic conditions in 1996 for individuals age 65 and over were arthritis (49 percent), hypertension (37 percent), hearing problems (32 percent), and some type of heart disease (30 percent). Arthritis causes more disability than any other ailment, followed by heart disease, lung disease and cerebrovascular disease. Objective measurements indicate that more than 85 percent of the elderly had at least one, and 30 percent had three or more chronic problems in 1996. It is worth emphasizing that only 2 percent of the elderly were confined to bed for any of these or other conditions and 95 percent were able to perform the usual activities of daily living.[108, 115, 126]

Test Material

Doctors find it hard to treat elderly because they usually have more than one ailment.

TABLE 4–1   Eight Major Conditions and Causes of Death, 1996

Condition	Incidence (Annual Cases)	Proportion of Deaths
1. Heart Disease	612,199	39
2. Cancer	342,988	22
3. Cerebrovascular disease	140,488	8
4. Chronic obstructive pulmonary disease	91,470	5
5. Influenza and pneumonia	74,979	4
6. Diabetes	46,376	2
7. Unintentional injury	30,830	2
8. Alzheimer's Disease	21,077	1

Source: Adapted from National Center for Health Statistics, 1998.

From a subjective viewpoint, about half of the older population reported at least one disability in a national survey in 1996; 36 percent reported a minor impairment; about 11 percent indicated a moderate disability; and about 4 percent said they were severely disabled. Between ages 65 and 74 only 13 percent indicated a serious disability. Among those over age 85, more than 71 percent reported some disability and 53 percent reported at least one severe disability. More than 27 percent had difficulty with activities of daily living, and 40 percent had trouble with instrumental activities of daily living such as shopping.[3, 36]

The major chronic health problems and causes of death among older people are summarized in Table 4–1. As the table indicates, heart disease and cancer are the leading causes of death, followed by cerebrovascular disease (in the event of a stroke), chronic obstructive pulmonary disease, influenza and pneumonia, diabetes, injury, and Alzheimer's disease. The most significant and expensive ailments leading to hospitalization are: cancer, circulatory malfunctions, digestive problems, and respiratory illnesses.[31, 43, 69]

Two classes of disease accounted for 69 percent of all deaths among older people in 1996: circulatory ailments were responsible for 47 percent (heart disease and cerebrovascular disease) and 22 percent were caused by all forms of cancer. Deaths from circulatory diseases have been falling in most industrialized countries (especially Japan) while those from cancer have been increasing. Influenza and pneumonia have also been declining, as has pulmonary disease resulting from lowered incidence of smoking.[104, 113]

Heart and Cardiovascular Conditions

Several specific conditions common to older people fall under the heading of heart disease: coronary artery disease, acute myocardial infarction, and congestive heart failure. Coronary artery disease is a progressive narrowing of the arteries which supply blood to the heart and is the most common cause of death in the elderly. Symptoms can include chest, arm, jaw, and abdominal pain.[100]

Acute myocardial infarction arising from coronary artery disease is a major cause of disability as well as the single largest cause of death—greater for women than men. Women who have had an acute attack of myocardial infarction and survived are also at greater risk for early death than men. This disease and other heart diseases are among the most costly in terms of hospitalization and required follow-up care. However, cardiac rehabilitation using carefully monitored aerobic exercise has proven quite successful for increasing muscular strength and endurance, while diminishing disability.[2, 128]

Congestive heart failure is a consequence of the inability of the heart to meet the body's demand for blood—a common problem among older people. It can result from damaged or enlarged heart muscle, high blood pressure, valve narrowing, leaking valves, ineffective heart relaxation, drugs, or other causes. Treatment usually requires some form of medication.[126]

Men suffer higher rates of cardiovascular disease and cancer than women—one of the primary explanations for the longer life expectancy of females. Evidence indicates that heart disease tends to occur in women much later in life than in men, but women are twice as likely to have a second heart attack and to die as a result. Some of these differences are a direct result of the fact that women have such attacks when they are older and more vulnerable.[39, 47, 57, 69]

Cerebrovascular Disease

Restrictions in blood vessels that serve the brain can impair circulation and lead to cerebrovascular disease that can cause blood clots, broken blood vessels, and sometimes a stroke. The amount of brain tissue affected and the area of the brain where the attack occurs determines severity. Consequences can include paralysis, speech disorder or loss, memory impairment, and personality change. These problems are a leading cause of disability and/or admission to mental hospitals, and are particularly pronounced among African Americans—who are twice as likely as European Americans to die of cerebrovascular disease. The disease is less of a problem among Asians in the U.S. or in Japan. Substantial differences thus exist between ethnic groups and among countries in the incidence and severity of heart and circulation problems. Overall, 10 percent or more of deaths in economically advanced countries are a result of strokes. The risk of stroke doubles every 10 years after age 55 and is 25 percent higher for men than women, although women have a higher mortality rate.[59, 99, 113, 126]

Fortunately the overall incidence has been declining in recent decades; heart disease and stroke have decreased in the United States by 44 percent between 1965 and 1995 for the age group 65-70, and by 28 percent for those over age 80—as a direct consequence of improved lifestyles and better preventive health care. Lower-fat diets, exercise, reduction of hypertension through improved medications, use of aspirin, and better rehabilitation have collectively reduced the disabling consequences of strokes. Appropriate drugs and faster treatment have improved survival chances and quality of life, regardless of ethnic background or country of residence. For example, experiments in France indicate that treatment with the drug Nootropil (or piracetam) within the first seven hours can substantially improve the functional condition of stroke victims while lowering the overall costs of care. Depending on the degree of severity, careful self-management can enable most people to live a reasonably active and high-quality life.[69, 89, 113, 126, 129]

Cancer

Cancer is a consequence of an uncontrolled and invasive cell growth that damages or destroys normal cells. The risk of cancer increases with age both as a condition and as a cause of death. Cancers of the stomach, lungs, intestines, bowel, colon, prostate, rectum, breast, cervix and pancreas are the most threatening. Greater incidence with age appears to be a consequence of carcinogens that accumulate in the body over time from smoking, improper diet and other lifestyle factors, although lifestyle is certainly not the only cause. Immune function weakens somewhat with age, and environmental conditions also play a major role. However, it is difficult to pinpoint the precise cause of many types of cancer. Improved treatments such as radiation, chemotherapy, and surgery are increasingly able to intercept the spread of the disease.[15, 126]

Arthritis

Arthritis affects more than 50 percent of the older population. It causes pain and discomfort but does not necessarily lead to significant disability. Three-fourths of those who have it experience no serious limitation on activities of daily living. It is most problematic when it exists in combination with other chronic conditions and appears to be most pronounced among older women with low incomes.[96, 126]

Rheumatoid arthritis (severe inflammation of joints and tendons) is the most severe form. Osteoarthritis is less severe but more common, with gradual deterioration of those joints most associated with stress (knees, hips, and spine). Serious pain, swelling, reduced physical capability, and often some disability are common. Back pain is also quite common as a result of changes in the lower back such as disk compression and instability of the lower vertebrae. Carefully designed and consistent exercise and sufficient rest, as well as use of pain killers, appear to be the best means of counteracting the discomfort of osteoarthritis, rheumatoid arthritis, and related back pain.[15, 49, 126]

Musculoskeletal disorders of these types and back pain are likely to have major impacts on disability and health care costs as the population ages. Hip and knee replacement surgery are widely used to correct problems but are expensive. The rates of surgery are currently highest in those countries with the oldest populations (Sweden, France, and the United Kingdom, among the countries considered here).[7]

Osteoporosis

Osteoporosis is a consequence of gradual loss of bone density, and can lead to brittleness, fractures, and slumped posture. More than half of all women and about one-third of men suffer at some point in their later life from fractures associated with osteoporosis. The disease is a direct consequence of changes in hormonal balance and is associated with menopause in women, who are more likely than men to be disabled. Osteoporosis is among the reasons that women suffer more injuries than men and spend more time bedridden. It leads to limitations on mobility, diminished independence, and sometimes death.[100, 106]

Increasing calcium consumption, estrogen supplements (for women), vitamin D, fluoride, and vigorous exercise can diminish the likelihood of osteoporosis. Vitamin D supplements are recommended for certain groups of older individuals such as nursing home residents who may have dietary deficiencies.[59, 129]

Diabetes

Diabetes is a result of insufficient insulin and an inability to adequately digest carbohydrates, which leads to high blood sugar. It can develop early or late in life. Older individuals are particularly susceptible to Type II diabetes which is not insulin dependent. The disease is more problematic when combined with other chronic conditions. Consequences can include infections, nerve damage, blindness, bowel problems, stroke, poor circulation, limb amputation, comas, and a variety of other outcomes. Although finding a cure has proven difficult, careful management of diet, exercise, and monitoring of insulin level can reduce the likelihood of complications.[126]

Chronic Lung Diseases

Lung diseases such as emphysema, chronic bronchitis, and asthma usually involve some form of obstruction that limits breathing and oxygen intake. Although heredity plays a role, most lung problems are a direct consequence of exposure to smoke, dust, fumes and other carcinogens, and occur much more often in men than women. The symptoms can sometimes be relieved by drug treatment, respiratory therapy, and avoidance of anything that will irritate or infect the lungs.[126]

Gastrointestinal Diseases

Intestinal and gastrointestinal disorders are very common in older people, often resulting from an inadequate diet such as insufficient fiber. Hiatal hernia (failure of the opening between the esophagus and stomach to work properly) and gastroesophageal reflux disease (movement of acid from stomach to the esophagus) are common problems as are diverticulosis and gall bladder disease. Many digestive system problems can be treated with dietary changes (avoidance of caffeine, alcohol, acidic or spicy foods, chocolate, and fat), elevation of the head of the bed, weight reduction, stress reduction, other behavioral modifications and/or medication. Surgery may be necessary in severe cases.[60, 100, 126]

Incontinence and other Elimination Problems

Kidney and urinary maladies are a result of infections, acute illness, stress, prostate infection, and/or gradual decline in the ability of the excretion systems to function properly. Prostate enlargement among men increases after age 50, often making urination difficult. Prostate cancer is the most common cancer among men.[15]

Urinary incontinence (inability to control urine excretion) can lead to serious physical, psychological, and social discomfort. It affects roughly one-third of the elderly in the United States, but is severe for only about 5 percent. An estimated 50 percent of nursing home residents are institutionalized in part for incontinence. The incidence is higher among women than men and comes in a variety of forms, each of which must be treated differently. Accurate assessment is highly important for appropriate treatment. The condition is not considered a normal consequence of aging.[24, 52, 100, 126]

Physicians tend to be somewhat uncomfortable assessing and treating the condition, and hence often do not ask patients about it. Many people are not treated when their condition could be alleviated. Although many older people consider urinary incontinence to be inevitable, irreversible, and a normal part of growing old, it is generally considered by geriatric professionals to be both treatable and reversible in 80 to 90 percent of the cases. Better education of medical professionals and older individuals is needed to help them understand how to deal with this issue.[26, 82, 95, 103, 129]

Chemical or Alcohol Dependency

Roughly 8 percent of the elderly (primarily single men) may be somewhat alcohol dependent. Many have serious health problems associated with alcoholism. Loss of a spouse, poor adjustment to retirement, depression, and anxiety are among the problems that can lead to dependency.[78]

Although drug dependency is not generally a major problem among older people, medically induced iatrogenic chemical dependency occurs on a regular basis. Prescription medication is the treatment of choice for most patient concerns about pain or illness. Individually and collectively these medications have the potential to do great good. However, enormous harm is also possible, if patients are not closely checked for potential negative interactions among medications. Adverse drug reactions lead to 17 percent of all hospital admissions among the elderly. Confusion, memory loss, and a variety of other serious ailments including death are among the consequences.[15, 28]

Accidents

Injurious accidents are the seventh leading cause of death among older people. The rate of automobile fatalities is twice as high for older adults as for younger people. Falls and other accidents are a major cause of mobility loss and consequent lifestyle changes. Hip fractures are very common and often disabling because recovery is much more difficult with increased age. Accidents are often a result of vision and hearing impairments, brittleness of bones, medication side effects, and environmental hazards. The simple fear of accidents (auto related and otherwise) or falls severely restricts mobility for many older individuals.[123, 126]

Parkinson's Disease

Degeneration of the nervous system is the second most common neurological problem after Alzheimer's disease. It becomes more common after age 70 and occurs when there is a loss of pigmented nerve cells in the brain which act as chemical messengers between nerve cells. The initial symptoms are a slowing of movement, usually starting with only one side of the body. Later tremors and shakiness become noticeable. Depression and dementia are common at later stages.[126]

Prospects

The gradual decrease or postponement of many of the diseases leading to premature death is among the primary factors in advancing life expectancy, especially at older ages. Men are gaining years faster than women—with the eventual prospect of more equal length of life between the sexes. Medical science continually expands our knowledge of how to control disease and thus live longer.[53]

◆◆◆ DISABILITY AND ACTIVITIES OF DAILY LIVING

Continuing ability to perform the usual (ADLs) and instrumental (IADLs) activities of daily living is a key factor in quality of life. The primary activities of concern are summarized in Table 4–2.

The great majority of older people (about 83 percent of males and 79 percent of females) in the United States can perform all of the noted self-care activities of daily living and independent activities of daily living until they reach their mid-80s, although married couples are likely to divide the tasks according to traditional female/male responsibilities. About 14 percent reported difficulty in completing usual activities of daily living in 1995 and 21 percent had problems with instrumental activities—usually associated with one or more chronic conditions.[11,13]

Only 9 percent of those age 65 to 69 needed assistance because of disability, whereas among the 75 to 84 year age group 27 percent reported major disability requiring assistance. After age 85, 42 percent of men and 50 percent of women have moderate to severe problems and need assistance. Women tend to have more chronic conditions and more functional limitations than men—and have a steeper rate of functional decline. One study indicated that women have a 36 percent greater likelihood of developing disability between ages 65 and 89 than men. Of course men are more likely to die of a disability at an earlier age than women. African American and Hispanic American women particularly suffer from greater limitations because

TABLE 4–2   Primary Activities of Daily Living

Self-Care Activities (ADLs)	Instrumental Activities (IADLs)
Eating	Preparing meals
Toileting	Taking medications
Dressing	Doing housework
Bathing	Doing laundry
Mobility around the home and from bed to chair	Using the telephone
	Shopping for food and personal needs
	Using public or private transportation
	Handling personal finances

Source: Data from Williams, 1995b: 69.

of their generally poorer health status. When a major illness occurs several of the activities may become very difficult or impossible and alternative housing and/or assistance in the form of home care, home help, assisted living or skilled nursing care become necessary.[4, 7, 108]

◆◆◆ HEALTH MAINTENANCE

The primary goal of health maintenance is to increase the potential for continuing independence and quality of life while lowering the incidence of potentially disabling disease. The 1995 White House Conference on Aging concluded that preventive health care among older people had the potential to save as much as $260 billion annually in health care costs![17, 43, 62]

Preventive health care for older people has not been particularly emphasized in the past because of at least two false assumptions: (1) health problems are part of normal aging, and (2) the condition of an older body will not improve as a result of health maintenance efforts. However, it has become clear that the same general preventive measures that work with young people also improve the health condition of older people. Resistance training and aerobic exercise beyond age 65 have been demonstrated to improve body composition, diminish falls, increase strength, reduce depression, reduce arthritis pain, reduce risk of diabetes and coronary heart disease, and generally increase longevity. Sedentary individuals who improve their physical fitness are less likely to die of all causes than are those who remain sedentary.[23]

Despite the evidence, Medicare had not been willing to pay for most disease prevention and health maintenance activities as of 2000. Annual physical examinations, laboratory tests, health risk assessment, and screening for health problems were not consistently covered except as part of diagnosis for acute or chronic illness. Some immunizations, pap smears, and mammography were covered.[20, 107]

Estimates suggest that up to 80 percent of the chronic diseases that affect older people are a direct consequence of poor health habits. Available evidence also indicates that careful attention to maintaining wellness can help to "compress morbidity" to the latest years of life. Regular physical exercise, for example, can increase bone density, increase oxygen capacity, improve blood sugar balance, diminish unfavorable fats in the blood, add strength, improve the sense of well-being, and improve sleep—all factors that add to the quality of life. More emphasis is also needed on rehabilitation through exercises that can help to restore bodily functions damaged by acute or chronic illnesses.[6, 126]

On-going studies of individuals over age 80 indicate high potential for continuing intellectual and physical health. In one investigation, for example, 86 percent of a sample of men age 80 and over continued to live independently, having effectively postponed disabling health problems to a very late stage in their lives. They maintained a relatively vigorous level of intellectual, interpersonal, cultural and physical activity, suggesting forcefully that good physical and mental health can be maintained much longer than had heretofore been considered normal. Regular vigorous exercise has been demonstrated to greatly reduce the risk of coronary heart disease. The aging process will still occur in cells and organs as they deteriorate over time. Quality of life can significantly improve when serious disease is postponed toward the end of life.[85, 92, 119]

Education and Information

The much lowered incidence of heart disease is heavily attributed to deliberate educational efforts via the mass media, patient counseling, and other efforts to diminish major health risk factors: smoking, overweight condition, saturated fat in diets, stress, and lack of exercise. Obesity does not receive adequate attention, yet it puts older individuals at great risk for arthritis, hypertension, heart disease, diabetes, and early death.[31, 54, 59, 105, 119]

Lack of attention to such issues in some eastern European countries (Russia in particular) has led to *lowered* life expectancy in the 1990s. Better understanding and management of health can clearly help diminish the primary causes of disability and death.[35, 91, 108]

◆◆◆ THE HEALTH CARE SYSTEM FOR OLDER PEOPLE

Health care for older people is based on the so-called "medical model," which emphasizes specialized and compartmentalized services to deal with each kind of disease. On the plus side, older Americans have the benefit of the most technologically advanced and effective disease management in the world. However, the complex and uncoordinated system of care is often difficult for older patients and their families to understand and effectively use. Consequently, many opportunities for preventive care, early intervention, and effective treatment are lost. Specialized knowledge of gerontology and geriatrics is not fully used to help integrate and improve both prevention of disease and ongoing care.[107]

Health Care System Organization

Primary care physicians have responsibility for managing prevention efforts and routine patient health care. When acute or chronic problems occur specialists are called upon to supplement primary care in outpatient and hospital settings. Post-hospital subacute care and skilled nursing care are directed by physicians but are managed primarily by professional administrators, nurses, social-service professionals, and rehabilitation therapists. When complex health problems occur several variously trained specialists may be assisting a patient at the same time with relatively little exchange of information.[94]

Lower-income older people are less likely than are their higher-income counterparts to seek needed care and may not receive appropriate care when it is sought—because of limited knowledge of the system, as well as incomplete insurance coverage.[78] Illustration 4–1 highlights the problem.

Illustration 4–1
PROBLEMS WITH A COMPLEX CARE SYSTEM

Mary is in her early 60s and lives in a small southern town where she worked part-time for years in the local school system—her only source of income. Her medical insurance was covered by the school system. When she became ill she consulted a local general practice physician who was well-known in the community; he concluded that she suffered from a combination of high blood pressure, congestive heart failure, and fibromyalgia (an arthritic condition). She also consulted a second physician in a nearby city who concurred with the diagnoses and placed her on several kinds of heavy medication to treat the diagnosed conditions.

Because she was declared disabled, she had to give up her part-time job and take early retirement on Social Security. This provided a very meager income because of the low wage rates during her working life. She was not yet 65 and did not qualify for Medicare. She was able to continue her medical insurance through the school system for 18 months by paying the premium herself. She had a house, car, furnishings, and a small savings account—too many assets and an income too high to qualify for Medicaid.

After a few months, her health appeared to be seriously deteriorating. High blood pressure threatened a stroke. She was unable to do her own housework, could not manage her personal affairs, and became quite dependent on her friends and family for support with most activities of daily living. One physician advised her that she might have to enter a long-term care facility.

Family and friends urged her to consult a geriatric physician in a nearby larger city. He was also director of a medical residency program in family medicine. After two appointments, this third doctor concluded that she didn't have congestive heart failure or a serious arthritic condition, and the heavy and inappropriate medications were in fact causing most of her problems. He discontinued all but the high blood pressure medication.

After only a week she was again able to take care of her house, manage her personal affairs, drive her car, and function at near normal capacity! Without the intervention of a physician with specialty training related to her needs she might have become permanently disabled. In the meantime, she had accumulated many medical bills that seriously taxed her modest income.

Primary Care Services. Older individuals use primary health services much more often than younger people because of a combination of acute and chronic conditions. The small proportion who have very serious needs have a particularly great impact. Older individuals with higher levels of education and income are more likely than those with lower levels to make appropriate use of primary care services.

Individuals with better educational backgrounds are more likely to understand instructions, to have a personal physician, and are generally more able to understand the complexities of the health care system. Many will have their own home medical guide and a copy of the Physician Desk Reference for prescription drugs.[97]

Hospitalization. Older individuals were responsible for 36 percent of hospital stays and 49 percent of all hospital days of care in 1997. The average length of stay was 6.8 days, contrasted to an average of 5.3 days for individuals under age 65. However, the length of stay for older people has decreased by 5.3 days since 1964.[3]

Although the use of hospitals by older patients has declined, outpatient care, home health care and other post-discharge services offered by hospitals have increased. Lower hospital use arises in part from the Medicare Diagnosis Related Group (DRG) approach, which limits the time and cost of reimbursement for many illnesses. Managed care insurance has forcefully limited hospitalization whenever possible. Post-hospital care in subacute facilities and at home has also improved, making it less necessary for patients to remain hospitalized. Measures to control the high cost of hospitalization have thus been quite effective.

Subacute care is a lower-cost alternative after surgery, stroke, or other hospital procedure—when it is available and when Medicare or other insurance will pay the bill. Many nursing homes provide the needed supportive services and rehabilitation with payments from Medicare.[41]

Many older people continue to remain in the hospital longer than necessary because subacute or nursing care is not immediately available or they have no access to home care. Medicare payment limits are sometimes a serious threat to older people who no longer need hospitalization but remain ill with no good care alternative. In 1997 Medicare and Medicaid paid for half of all hospital services in the United States.[51]

Rehabilitation. Chronic and acute conditions can often be greatly improved through the various forms of physical, speech, occupational and mental rehabilitation available in hospitals or nursing homes. Physical therapy can enhance recovery from surgery, stroke, arthritis, and other disabilities. Occupational therapy can facilitate return of bodily function in many activities of daily living. Speech therapy can facilitate return of ability to speak after stroke or accidents or improve speech capacity. Psychological therapy can improve mental health and self-management.[104]

Pharmaceutical Care. The appropriate use of medications is increasingly important as a medical strategy. High quality pharmacotherapy can make a major difference in the well-being of older patients. A formal interview study revealed that 15 percent of older people were using at least one inappropriate drug.[29, 116]

The consequences of inappropriate medication can take a number of forms including:[84]

- Additional need for primary care.
- Unnecessary hospitalizations.

- False diagnoses of dementia and other diseases.
- Induced illnesses, referred to as iatrogenic disease.
- Unnecessarily high costs for health care.

A drug can affect individuals quite differently especially at older ages. Negative or synergistic side effects are referred to as "adverse drug reactions." Drug dosages with largely positive effects on younger people can generate serious negative effects on the elderly—because of slower metabolism or slower absorption rates. Reduced liver and kidney efficiency can mean that a drug is not absorbed and eliminated efficiently. The widespread use of over-the-counter (OTC) medications complicates pharmaceutical care because physicians and pharmacists are often not aware of what is being used when they write or fill prescriptions. The combination of prescription drugs, over-the-counter preparations, and alcohol may also cause adverse effects.[12, 69]

Approximately 25 percent of all prescribed and 40 percent of over-the-counter drugs consumed in 1995 were for older people. About 25 percent of the older population take three or more prescription drugs per day. One study indicated that older women took an average of 5.7 prescription drugs and 3.2 over-the-counter drugs at the same time. Other studies have revealed that a very high proportion of nursing home residents take multiple prescriptions—an average of seven per patient in one study of twelve nursing homes. One of the medications was clearly inappropriate in 40 percent of the cases and two were inappropriate in 10 percent of patients. Seven percent of all prescriptions were clearly not needed. Such high use is referred to as polypharmacy and increases the potential for adverse drug reactions.[12, 126]

Antipsychotic and hypnotic drugs are often prescribed to modify behavior rather than for a specific physical or mental problem. Several side effects occur such as memory loss, confusion, disorientation, and walking problems. Long-term use of some types of prescription drugs or over-the-counter drugs can also cause nutrient depletion or other nutritional problems, with consequent undernourishment.[12, 114, 126]

Many of these problems can be minimized if pharmacists are involved directly with physicians in drug management. Doctors of Pharmacy are trained to thoroughly understand the chemical and biological effects of drugs in combination and are leading the development of pharmaceutical counseling. They have much greater training in use of medications than most physicians. Pharmacists in retail pharmacies can also play a very helpful role in counseling older patients. Vision and reading problems can be somewhat overcome through personalized explanations.[67, 73]

Drug use evaluation can be very helpful to home-bound individuals. The pharmacist is able to assess what drugs are being taken, inspect the prescription and over-the-counter drugs, and examine use patterns. The information can then be used by the responsible physician in determining an appropriate pharmaceutical plan.[29, 116]

Use of prescription drugs varies enormously between countries. For example, per capita expenditure for drugs is twice as high in Japan, and considerably higher in Germany and France, than in the United States, the Netherlands, Canada, or the United Kingdom.[66]

◆◆◆ GERIATRIC ASSESSMENT AND CARE

Specialization in geriatrics by key health professionals—physicians, nurses, pharmacists, discharge planners, geriatric care managers, and others—has been of great benefit to many older individuals. The goal of geriatric care is to improve health and independence, while promoting high quality, comprehensive, and affordable care. Careful distinctions between disease and the normal changes of aging are a major concern. The field has been promoted and developed with assistance from the American Geriatric Society.[48, 110, 126]

The Geriatric Care Team

Geriatrics requires teamwork among a variety of specialists—usually with a physician as leader. Effective communication among members of the team is crucial if the process is to assure good continuing care.

Physicians. Geriatrics is not particularly popular with physicians, in part because chronic diseases are difficult to treat and are seldom cured. Yet most primary care and specialist physicians must examine and treat older patients on a daily basis. Geriatrics training is probably not needed for most problems, but would be beneficial when complex situations are encountered.[46, 83]

Medical student exposure to geriatrics in most medical schools is quite limited. As of 1996 only 13 of 126 medical schools in the United States offered specialized medical training focusing on geriatrics. Continuing medical education in geriatrics is well developed but is also pursued by relatively few physicians, despite a major effort by the American Geriatric Society to expand interest in the field. Family medicine and internal medicine training programs in many medical schools have begun to implement geriatrics subspecialties.[125]

The shortage of geriatrics specialists in the United States and most other countries is in part a function of the relatively low reimbursements received from health insurance for geriatric assessment, hospital care, and nursing home care. The Medicare fee schedule reimburses at a lower rate for longer visits (often needed by the elderly because of complex problems) than for shorter visits. Fees are particularly modest for home care and nursing home visits.[101]

Nonetheless, some geriatric physicians are inspired by their vocation: ". . . I have realized that part of why I love being a doctor for old people is that it is easy; the rules are simpler and success is clearer than when one is providing primary care for younger adults. With the elderly, there are real problems to confront, real suffering to relieve, and real courage to admire every day."[40]

A few health care institutions—larger hospitals, specialized nursing homes, and a few large health maintenance organizations—employ geriatric physicians on salary. Interest in geriatric care among older patients seems clear. Geriatric physicians in private practice have been able to attract large numbers of patients, although the patients are largely those with good private insurance as a supplement to Medicare.[38, 65]

Other countries have also increased the focus on geriatrics. Canada has considerably expanded training and has increased the use of geriatric assessment in hospitals. The special problems of an aging population have been a major focus of the National Health Service in the United Kingdom, where the field of geriatrics was largely invented. Geriatric care is highly developed in British medical schools and is widely available throughout the health care system.[68]

Nurses. Geriatric nursing has become an increasingly prominent specialty in schools of nursing. Geriatric nurses have assumed very important roles in management and coordination of care for older patients in hospitals and nursing homes, many of them as nurse-practitioners or nurse-administrators. Others are in charge of home health care programs.[126] Their role is discussed further in Chapter 6.

Pharmacists. Pharmacists play a key role in geriatrics, especially when trained at the doctoral level. Improved use of medications is a central part of the geriatric care strategy as noted above.[12, 56]

Discharge and Care Managers. Discharge planners have responsibility for coordinating the delivery of health care services after hospitalization. They gather, validate, and deliver patient information to the responsible health professionals in home health agencies, nursing homes, or to personal physicians who manage home care. Geriatric care management is a relatively new profession with responsibility for advising the frail elderly and families on appropriate uses of the health care system. In the United States they are trained to be experts on Medicare, Medicaid and private insurance. Many of them were educated as social workers or nurses with a specialty in geriatric care.[5, 30]

Geriatric Assessment Units

Organization and management of the multidisciplinary geriatric assessment process is one of the key roles of geriatric physicians and the other noted geriatric specialists. Most geriatric assessment units are associated with medical center hospitals, especially those affiliated with the United States Department of Veteran's Affairs. The primary goal is to increase accuracy of diagnosis and treatment, including identification of personal and social support resources. Assessment procedures and benefits are summarized in Table 4–3.[61, 98, 126]

Assessment intensity can vary considerably depending on indications of client need—from short-term screening to comprehensive assessment and evaluation. Individuals with serious disabilities will benefit from the comprehensive approach, while those with fewer problems may require only screening or intermediate assessment. All levels of assessment can be performed at home, in a physician's office, in a nursing home, or in a hospital. Interdisciplinary teams should be involved in each case with specialties depending on the condition of the patient.[109, 110]

Reimbursement has been a constant challenge. Medicare has not traditionally paid for involvement of nonphysicians members of the assessment team. Comprehensive assessment units are usually located in academic medical centers and

TABLE 4–3   Geriatric Assessment Components and Benefits

Components:

- Measurement of physical status, mobility and ability to function in daily activities.
- Mental status evaluation including cognitive ability and overall mental health.
- Appropriateness of prescribed and over-the-counter medications.
- Subjective well-being, including morale, satisfaction, happiness, and overall adjustment.
- Social support networks and any inadequacies in relationships.
- Economic status.
- Home environment status.
- Unfulfilled basic need for services.

Benefits:

- Improved diagnostic accuracy.
- Targeted improvements in physical and mental status.
- Reduced or improved medications.
- Decreased need for acute care services, home health care and nursing home care.
- More appropriate overall use of health care services.
- Improved living environment.
- Reduced health care costs.
- Improved overall quality of life.
- Prolonged survival.

Sources: Adapted from Kaufman, 1994: 433; Porello et al, 1995: 45–47; Rubenstein et al, 1991: 926; Rubenstein et al, 1995: 216; Larue and Bayly, 1992: 143.

Veterans Administration hospitals because they are subsidized by training and research programs.[61, 65]

The federal Department of Veterans Affairs operated 173 hospitals in 1996 with responsibility for the health care of 26 million war veterans. Geriatric health care has received much of its impetus from the pioneering work conducted in these facilities. The system has been divided into several regions designated as Veterans Integrated Service Networks. Outpatient clinics and home care programs are being created as an alternative to traditional, more expensive, hospital care.[76]

Evidence of Effectiveness

Follow-up studies indicate that geriatric assessment and associated treatment are more cost-effective than conventional medical care for seriously ill older individuals. Positive outcomes have also been documented in experiments with in-home geriatric assessment. The evidence indicated a much higher immunization rate, more attention to treatable disorders, a generally high drug-use compliance rate, improved ability to perform activities of daily living, and a lowered rate of admission to nursing homes.[116]

Other studies at the University of Minnesota have produced similar positive results. Both older patients and their physicians expressed strong satisfaction with contributions to improved physical, psychological, and social well-being. However, as noted earlier, geriatric assessment is not necessarily useful for all older individuals. Age by itself is insufficient as a criterion. If an initial screening examination detects no major problems, comprehensive assessment should not be necessary. Severely demented or terminally ill patients are also not likely to benefit since there is little hope for improvement.[33, 86, 121, 122, 127]

◆◆◆ HEALTH CARE CHALLENGES

Despite the progress noted in the previous pages, a number of major issues are in need of resolution. Attention to these issues would greatly improve quality of care and life for the older population.

Measuring and Improving Quality

Additional quality emphasis appears to be needed in both ambulatory and hospital settings serving larger numbers of older people. Primary options include:[81]

- Wider incorporation of tested quality management techniques.
- Motivation of senior administrators to pursue quality.
- Formation of quality-management teams with representation from administration, staff, and clients.
- More extensive peer reviews to improve performance of health professionals.
- More extensive licensing of providers to assure minimum levels of competence.
- Utilization reviews of health care practices to detect successful methods as well as inadequacies.
- Medication reviews to detect misuse of pharmaceuticals.
- Standardization of data on patients.
- Improvement of management information systems to increase accessibility and better analysis of data.
- Input from older clients about their perception of needs and evaluations of care.
- Measuring medical and behavioral outcomes to detect changes.
- Incorporation of quality-improvement concepts in curricula of geriatric health-professional training programs

Many health care and long-term care organizations pay close attention to the noted procedures and consequently offer outstanding services. However, the practices are not followed in other facilities—to the disadvantage of patients. Medical practice is sometimes based more on tradition than proven results. Use of tested-outcome measures appears to be one of the keys to effective quality assessment—allowing for clear-cut comparisons among various modes of care. For example, comparative studies indicate that rapid treatment of stroke and heart-attack patients with certain drugs has a more favorable effect on long-term survival than invasive procedures (such as bypass surgery or angioplasty) while also reducing costs.[58, 77]

Fraud and Abuse

Older citizens are subjected to a wide range of abuses or outright fraud by health care organizations that take advantage of their limited knowledge of the health care system. Investigations by the Health Care Financing Administration indicate that many large- and small-service providers have inappropriately billed Medicare for services that were not delivered—at great cost to individuals and to the Medicare trust fund.

Physical and psychological abuse, neglect, or misuse of financial resources, can each have very negative effects on health. Manifestations of these abuses are detected in emergency departments of hospitals and sometimes by primary-care physicians or social workers. However, older individuals suffering from these problems often have no good way of seeking the assistance they need, as discussed in more detail in a later chapter.[78]

Fortunately, avenues are available to report fraud and abuse at local and national levels. Medicare has a special hotline for reports of payment or fee abuses. In serious cases, older individuals can report the problem directly to the local police. However, much remains to be done to avoid the expensive effects of illegal or fraudulent practices.

Limitations on Access

Geographic variation in access to health care means that some older individuals are deprived of needed services. For example, availability of physicians and other services tends to be considerably less in rural areas than in urban settings. On the other hand, some suburban areas have abundant services while inner cities are sometimes poorly served. States vary greatly in the overall availability of high-quality medical services for the special problems of older people, thus requiring considerable travel to secure needed specialized treatment.[18, 125]

Many very old individuals have limited resources for extra medical expenses not paid by Medicare. Consequently, they are not able to secure quality care as needed and must often forego medications that would sustain them and improve their quality of life. This problem represents a major gap in access to medical care.[14]

Rationing. Evidence from the national Medical Outcomes Study indicates that rationing procedures used by health maintenance organizations may have detrimental effects for older patients. Physical health outcomes in HMOs appear to be less adequate than outcomes when individuals receive care under a fee-for-service arrangement. In one study, 54 percent of the elderly in the sample suffered health status decline under HMO care as compared to only 28 percent under fee-for-service care.[124]

Outright rationing has been used in some countries and in some health care programs within the United States as a deliberate policy for cutting costs. For example, the United Kingdom has limited the use of kidney dialysis and joint replacements for older people. Although the policy has been modified, many medical procedures remain largely unavailable to the elderly. In Canada, older people must wait for extended periods to secure hip replacements and certain other kinds of medical treatment. The State of Oregon approved a procedure for Medicaid patients that ranks illnesses in priority order. State funds are allocated only for treatment of the higher-priority conditions. Such limitation on allocation of resources, whether through Medicare, Medicaid, or private insurance plans, is clearly detrimental to some older patients.[85]

Although rationing is not a formal national policy in the United States, some of the payment systems have the same effect. For example, the Medicare policy of not paying for prescriptions outside of the formal health care setting means that older individuals with limited resources have their health care rationed. Those with the least resources may qualify for Medicaid, however, and receive medication through that system. Nonetheless, a sizeable number of people in the older population suffer decreased quality of life because they are unable to secure prescribed medications.

Training for Health Professionals

Physicians without appropriate training in geriatrics generally spend less time with older than with younger patients, especially in the nursing home setting. Moreover, older patients are not always encouraged to take preventive measures to the same degree as are younger people. Physicians order fewer breast exams and pap smears for older women, for example, even though the risk of cancer is much higher than it is for younger women.[61]

Multidisciplinary teams seem to offer a clear advantage for older patients. Yet, most health-profession disciplines train in relative isolation from one another. Physicians go to medical schools, nurses to schools of nursing, and pharmacists to pharmacy colleges, with little professional *multidisciplinary* interaction until post-graduate internship or residency work. The tendency is for each discipline to place a very high value on their disciplinary role without adequate understanding of the other critical roles. Some critics argue that the needed common understandings are likely to happen most usefully in the context of joint learning and teamwork during the training process.

The Managed Care Insurance and Delivery System

Managed care is reported to have begun in 1929 when a cooperative health plan was organized in Elk City, Oklahoma. Kaiser Permanente—the largest managed care organization—was formed in 1942 as a social-oriented plan that emphasized prevention, patient education, and cost-effective health care. The concept received a major boost when the Health Maintenance Organization (HMO) Act was passed by Congress in 1973, providing subsidies for the formation of prepaid insurance groups.[10]

The managed care concept promised to offer comprehensive services, greater efficiency, higher quality, and improved convenience for clients. Collaborative care was to be provided by interdisciplinary teams that would engage in disease management, case management and care management as tools to produce better results for patients.[10]

Managed care organizations of various types grew rapidly in the 1990s after a relatively slow start in the 1980s and have now become the predominant form of health care delivery in the United States—although only a relatively small proportion (15 percent) of the older population was enrolled by the end of the 1990s. Lack of adequate information about managed care was highlighted by a national survey in 1998: nearly one-third of older Americans knew nothing about health maintenance organizations (about the same as in the general population), and 89 percent did not know enough to make an informed decision about which Medicare managed care option to choose. This is somewhat troublesome at a time when the available options and choices are increasing.[44]

The HMO approach uses gatekeepers to authorize out-patient and hospital procedures. Formal guidelines help ensure that delivery of care is clinically justifiable, ethical, and used only when clearly needed. In contrast, fee-for-service provision of care keeps the physician and other providers in charge of decisions—with payment coming directly from individual patients or their insurance companies. The orientation of managed care appears in many instances to focus on achieving cost-savings from managing acute care episodes while minimizing treatment of longer-term chronic problems—sometimes to the serious health detriment of older patients.[10, 18, 109]

Clinical studies have indicated that managed care led to 15 percent fewer hospitalizations for patients with chronic diseases (hypertension, diabetes, heart attack, and congestive heart failure) than the norm. Comparable patients under fee-for-service insurance plans had 9 percent more hospitalizations than the norm. Managed care clearly achieved cost-saving, but it was not clear overall whether long-term quality of life was maintained to the same degree as with fee-for-service patients.[93]

Other studies suggest that the quest for cost control diminishes access to services and lowers quality of care for some older patients. When hospitalization is inappropriately denied, or when older patients are discharged from the hospital earlier than their condition warrants, long-term health is threatened. Health services are reduced to save expenditures without necessarily taking full account of the needs of the individual.[18]

Medicare has established formal procedures for appeal when older patients conclude they are not receiving appropriate services from their managed care insurance:[75]

1. The patient must appeal first to the provider organization for "reconsideration." The review must be completed in 60 days or less. A special peer review organization (PRO) has been established to review urgent cases and issue a decision within 48 hours.
2. If redress is not forthcoming, a second appeal can be made to an organization designated by Medicare to handle managed care appeals, often requiring an additional 60 days or more.
3. The third stage involves legal action beginning with a hearing by an administrative law judge.
4. Finally, a fourth stage allows for an appeal to a federal court if the patient is not satisfied after the first three stages.

These complex procedures are obviously difficult for older individuals who may be ill, frail, and have limited income. Despite the noted problems, national policy continues to support use of managed care as the most economical health care delivery mechanism, although it is not clear that savings can continue to be achieved in the long term.

Health Care System Reorganization

Effective use of health services would be much improved if the system were better designed for treatment of older patients. Several practical strategies have been suggested to deal with some of the key issues discussed earlier, such as:[21, 87]

- Further training of professionals in geriatrics to be responsive to characteristics and needs of the elderly.
- Adapting printed information for readability and understandability to older patients.
- Providing formal assistance to older patients for completion of required forms and other paper work, while helping them navigate the various stages of health care.
- Include close relatives or friends (children, siblings, etc.) in medical consultations involving diagnosis and treatment.

Comprehensive Service Centers. An improved service system could respond to several of these strategies. Elements include:[25]

- A network of comprehensive outpatient health centers located within easy distance of residential areas. The Centers would provide diagnosis and follow-up for mental health care, dentistry, podiatry, nutrition, audiology, and physical health care.
- Specialized geriatric assessment units in local hospitals that undertake intensive multidisciplinary evaluation of high-risk patients to assure that diagnosis is accurate and complete, leading to efficient treatment and follow-up.
- Support staff that includes geriatric physicians, nurses, social workers, pharmacists, psychologists, therapists, and possibly other specialists to facilitate application of the full range of health care knowledge.
- Computerized medical information systems that link outpatient, pharmacy, and hospital units to facilitate complete and shared information among health care professionals about health status and medications.
- Case management to assure that care is coordinated and individualized, monitoring is continuous, and the care plan is coupled with personal contact and joint planning with clients and their families.
- More direct communication and organizational linkages between acute-care units and chronic-care services such as physician offices, hospitals, nursing homes, home health agencies, housekeeping providers, transportation units, and medical equipment providers.
- Quality-assurance measurement systems to increase knowledge of treatment consequences and possible needed system adaptations.

- A focus on continuity of care through discharge planning, outreach, and follow-up with primary-care physicians, skilled nursing facilities, home health care and families of patients.

Health care facilities in a number of locations around the United States and in other countries have integrated services roughly as outlined above. For example, the Baptist Health System in Knoxville, Tennessee, has developed a major service thrust for the elderly. Conveniently located senior health centers have been established that cater to elderly citizens. A Senior Select insurance program offers a preferred provider service to supplement Medicare. A Senior Plus Program membership offers complimentary screenings, prescription discounts, free upgrades to a private hospital room if needed, assistance with insurance forms, and wellness educational seminars.[8]

Neighborhood wellness centers for the elderly have been established in many communities, sometimes integrated with home health care. In Toledo, Ohio, for example, such centers provide health screening and assessment, counseling, education, referral when needed, skilled nursing care, and assistance with home modifications to sustain continued residence in private homes.[1]

Improving the Use of Specialized Services

Physicians and hospitals that do a large number of procedures, such as coronary bypass surgery or angioplasty, are much more likely to obtain good results than those that do fewer procedures. The increased skills that come with practice result in fewer failures, as revealed by a series of medical outcome studies. Although such services must be concentrated in a few locations within each state to be cost efficient, the consequence for many older patients is clearly better quality care and longer lives.[55]

Approximately 15 percent of the elderly are subject to some form of surgery each year, and 20 percent of all open heart operations are on people over age 70. The success rate for many kinds of surgery, such as for knee or hip replacement at older and older ages, has improved markedly over the years, greatly improving the quality of life.[126]

Medical specialists tend to focus on narrow problems without necessarily considering the full impact of what they do on the individual. For example, specialists may focus on a specific disease without attending to the larger issues. Great attention to the details of physical condition, mental condition, and social circumstances may be necessary for adequate treatment because of the unique characteristics of health conditions in older age.[32]

The older person is often subjected to interventions to sustain life without adequate consideration of quality of life. It is very difficult for the individual or family to know what treatment is ethical, appropriate, or sufficient to maintain the integrity, individuality and autonomy of the personality. Intervention might sometimes be more appropriately curtailed in the interest of sustaining self-esteem, despite the risk of death. Many older individuals would rather assume some risk than lose their independence and *personhood*.[61]

Compression of Morbidity

Compression of morbidity (delaying chronic diseases until later in life) has become evident as part of the explanation for improved health of the older population. The older an individual is when a potentially disabling disease strikes the sooner they will die from it. Delaying a chronic disease has the potential to reduce its duration and the incidence of disability.[22, 32]

As noted earlier, long-term disability rates dropped 14.5 percent between 1982 and 1994. The incidence of several chronic illnesses, including arthritis, hardening of the arteries, and high blood pressure, has declined. Death from heart attacks has decreased. All of these changes mean that individuals are living longer without serious disability. A higher proportion of deaths now occur at ages beyond 85.[42]

Further improvements are clearly possible. For example, older people are currently less likely than younger people to be given prescriptions that would reduce complications and death from heart attacks. Appropriate use of these drugs could further extend life expectancy. If the positive health maintenance gains continue, per capita medical costs may actually decrease. Prolonging life may be a less expensive proposition if it is possible to diminish the cost of disease and physical deterioration.[42, 71, 79, 131]

Dealing with Developmental Disabilities

A sizeable population of older people have developmental disabilities such as mental retardation, long-term physical problems, or other impairments from childhood. The primary physical problems giving rise to developmental disability are Down syndrome, cerebral palsy, and polio. Individuals with Down syndrome often develop Alzheimer's disease at an earlier age than is the case in the general population. Many developmentally disabled individuals are unnecessarily institutionalized under unhappy conditions simply because knowledge about their needs is limited among institutional administrators and staff.[16, 118]

The population of developmentally disabled elderly was estimated to range from 200,000 to 1,300,000 in 1997. Because many (estimated as high as 40 percent) have not formally entered the service network, the numbers are not precise. The numbers are clearly growing as the population of elderly increases and as medical knowledge has enabled many more to survive into older age.[16]

People in this group need a somewhat different kind of support and assistance than other older individuals. Many qualify for Supplemental Social Security, Medicare, Medicaid, and other special programs available for individuals with serious disabilities. They can benefit particularly from involvement in the arts and other leisure experiences providing meaning, structure, and satisfaction to their daily lives.[120]

When possible, they are likely to be more content and better adjusted if they engage in activities with other older individuals in the community—rather than being segregated as a group. Trained therapists in developmental disabilities can help to optimize the number of developmentally disabled individuals who will be happy and well-adjusted in older age.[9, 45]

◆◆◆ SUMMARY AND CONCLUSIONS

The older population is getting healthier and suffers fewer disabilities than in previous decades. Morbidity and mortality rates have been declining. Further improvement in healthiness of lifestyles among older people is a primary means to slow the growth of public and private health care costs in every country.

The major health problems and causes of death are heart disease, cancer, cerebrovascular disease, and lung disease, although arthritis is the most prevalent chronic condition—partially disabling many older individuals. Influenza, diabetes, and Alzheimer's disease are substantial threats to health as well but affect fewer people.

Disability is usually the result of one or more of the major health problems that sometimes lead to limitations on activities of daily living and requires informal or formal assistance. Limitations can often be avoided if adequate efforts are made to maintain health through preventive behaviors and appropriate use of the primary care system.

Unfortunately, the health care system is not particularly well organized to serve the complex needs of older citizens, especially those who may have minimal education and low incomes. Health professionals often have very little training in geriatrics and fail to understand the special needs of older individuals. Geriatric care remains underdeveloped although it has improved greatly in the last decade. Pharmaceutical care has become much more sophisticated. Appropriate use of medications is a major challenge because of high use by older people and the dangers of adverse drug reactions.

Several major health care issues remain unresolved—especially the quality of care, fraud and abuse in the health care system, limitations on access to care, and the inadequacy of organizations to best serve the older population. Managed care has not yet proven to be an effective alternative for older people. Further integration of health services, more training in geriatrics, and higher quality of care for the elderly are all clearly needed.

The older population of the United States is better served by the health care system than ever before, despite the noted inadequacies. The potential for a high quality of later life has clearly improved. Upcoming generations of older citizens—such as the baby boomers—will generally be much more knowledgeable about the kind of health promotion and care needed to further extend healthiness into older ages.

◆◆◆ REFERENCES

1. Abby, Carol, Judy Didion, Mary Beth Durbin, Kathy Perzynski, and Rebecca Zechman (1994). Neighborhood Wellness Centers: Collaboration Between Home Care and Nursing Education, *Caring Magazine*, 13 (11), 26–31.
2. Ades, Philip A. (1999). Cardiac Rehabilitation in Older Coronary Patients, *Journal of the American Geriatrics Society*, 47 (1), 98–105.
3. Administration on Aging (2000). *Profile of Older Americans*, 1999, Online at www.aoa.gov/stats/profile.
4. American Association of Retired People (1998). *A Profile of Older Americans.* Washington, DC: American Association of Retired Persons.
5. Anderson, Mary Ann, and Lelia B. Helms (1994). Quality Improvement in Discharge Planning: An

Evaluation of Factors in Communication Between Health Care Providers, *Journal of Nursing Care Quality*, 8 (2), 62–72.

6. Austin, Elizabeth (1997). Profile: Mark Meiners, *Advances* (the national newsletter of the Robert Wood Johnson Foundation), Issue 4, 4.

7. Badley, Elizabeth, and Maria Crotty (1995). An International Comparison of the Estimated Effect of the Aging of the Population on the Major Cause of Disablement and Musculoskeletal Disorders, *Journal of Rheumatology*, 22 (10), 1934–40.

8. Baptist Health System (1997). Senior Plus, *Baptist Health News*, Spring, 5.

9. Barret, Diane B., and Claire B. Clements (1997). Expressive Arts Programming for Older Adults both With and Without Disabilities: An Opportunity for Inclusion, in Ted Tedrick (ed), *Older Adults with Developmental Disabilities and Leisure: Issues, Policy, and Practice*, New York: Haworth Press, 53–63.

10. Bateman, William B. (1999). Managed Care: An Evolving Concept, in William B. Bateman, Elizebeth J. Kramer, and Kimberly S. Glassman (eds), *Patient and Family Education in Managed Care and Beyond: Seizing the Treatable Moment*, New York: Springer, 3–17.

11. Bee, Helen L. (1996). *The Journey of Adulthood* (3d ed), Upper Saddle River, NJ: Prentice Hall.

12. Beers, Mark H., Joseph G. Ouslander, Susan F. Fingold, Hal Morgenstern, David B. Reuben, William Rogers, Mira J. Zeffren, and John C. Beck (1992). Inappropriate Medication Prescribing in Skilled-Nursing Facilities, *Annals of Internal Medicine*, 117, 684–89.

13. Besharov, Douglas J., and Keith W. Smith (1999). Neglecting the "Oldest Old," *The Washington Post National Weekly Edition*, 16 (34), 23.

14. Bierman, A., E. S. Magari, and A. M. Jette (1998). Assessing Access as a First Step Towards Improving the Quality of Care for the Very Old, *Journal of Ambulatory Care Management*, 21 (3), 17–26.

15. Blair, Cornelia, Mark A. Siegel, and Jacquelyn Quiram (1998). *Growing Old in America*, Wylie, TX: Information Plus.

16. Boyd, Rosangela (1997). Older Adults with Developmental Disabilities: A Brief Examination of Current Knowledge, in Ted Tedrick (ed), *Older Adults with Developmental Disabilities and Leisure: Issues, Policy, and Practice*, New York: Haworth Press, 7–27.

17. Brody, J. A., and T. P. Miles (1990). Mortality Postponed and the Unmasking of Age-Dependent Nonfatal Conditions, *Aging*, 2 (3), 283–89.

18. Brook, Robert (1995). Medicare Quality and Getting Older: A Personal Essay, *Health Affairs*, 14 (4), 73-81.

19. Bundlie, Scott R. (1998). Sleep in Aging, *Geriatrics*, 53 (Supplement 1), S41–S43.

20. Burton, Lynda C., Donald M. Steinwachs, Pearl S. German, Sam Shapiro, Larry J. Brant, Thomas M. Richards, and Rebecca D. Clark (1995). Preventive Services for the Elderly: Would Coverage Affect Utilization and Costs Under Medicare? *American Journal of Public Health*, 85 (3), 387–91.

21. Butler, Robert N. (1997). Economic and Political Implications of Immunology and Aging on Tomorrow's Society, *Mechanisms of Ageing and Development*, 93 (February), 7–13.

22. Butler, Robert N. (2000). Fighting Frailty, *Geriatrics*, 55 (2), 20.

23. Christmas, Colleen, and Ross A. Andersen (2000). Exercise and Older Patients: Guidelines for the Clinician, *Journal of the American Geriatric Society*, 48 (1), 318–24.

24. Chutka, Darryl S., Kevin C. Fleming, Mary P. Evans, Jonathan M. Evans, and Karen L. Andrews (1996). Urinary Incontinence in the Elderly Population, *Mayo Clinic Proceedings*, 71 (1), 93–101.

25. Coile, Russ (1995). Age Wave: Organizing Integrated Care Networks for an Aging Society, *Health Trends*, 7, 6, 1–8.

26. Coward, Raymond T., Claydell Horne, and Chuck W. Peek (1996). Predicting Nursing Home Admissions Among Incontinent Older Adults: A Comparison of Residential Differences Across Six Years, *The Gerontologist*, 35 (6), 732–43.

27. Coward, Raymond T., Chuck W. Peek, and John C. Henretta (1997). Race Differences in the Health of Elders Who Live Alone, *Journal of Aging and Health*, 9 (2), 147–70.

28. Cummings, Nicholas A. (1993). Chemical Dependency Among Older Americans, in Florence Lieberman and Morris F. Collen (eds), *Aging in Good Health: A Quality Lifestyle in the Later Years*, New York: Plenum Press, 107–14.

29. Der, Elaine Hsia, Laurence Z. Rubenstein, and Gavin S. Choy (1997). The Benefits of In-Home Pharmacy Evaluation for Older Persons, *Journal of the American Geriatrics Society*, 45 (2), 211–14.

30. Dolen, Lenise (1995). The Evolution of For-Profit Geriatric Care Management, *Journal of Long-Term Home Health Care,* 14, 2, 17–24.

31. Elward, Kurt, and Eric B. Larson (1992). Benefits of Exercise for Older Adults, *Clinics in Geriatric Medicine,* 8 (1), 35–50.

32. Evans, J. Grimley (2000). Ageing and Medicine, *Journal of Internal Medicine,* 247 (1), 159–67.

33. Fabacher, Diana, Karen Josephson, Fern Pietruszka, Karen Linderborn, John E. Morely, and Laurence Z. Rubenstein (1994). An In-Home Preventive Assessment Program for Independent Older Adults: A Randomized Controlled Trial, *Journal of the American Geriatrics Society,* 42 (6), 630–38.

34. Ferraro, Kenneth F. (1993). Are Black Older Adults Health-Pessimistic? *Journal of Health and Social Behavior,* 34 (3), 201–14.

35. Foreman, Judy (1997). Americans Living Longer, Better Lives, *The Spokesman-Review* (Spokane, WA), October 19, A8.

36. Freudenheim, Ellen (1997). Chronic Care in America: The Health System That Isn't, *Advances* (the national newsletter of the Robert Wood Johnson Foundation), Issue 4, (1), 9–10.

37. Gentili, A., and J.D. Edinger (1999). Sleep Disorders in Older People, *Aging Clinical Experimental Research,* 11 (3), 137–41.

38. Gerety, Meghan B. (1994). Health Care Reform From the View of a Geriatrician, *The Gerontologist,* 34 (5), 590–97.

39. Glass, Thomas A., Teresa E. Seeman, A. Regula Herzog, Robert Kahn, and Lisa F. Berkman (1995). Change in Productive Activity in Late Adulthood: MacArther Studies in Successful Aging, *Journal of Gerontology,* 50B (2), S65–S76.

40. Goodwin, James S. (1999). Geriatrics and the Limits of Modern Medicine, *New England Journal of Medicine,* 340 (16), 1283–85.

41. Griffiths, Peter (1997). In Search of Therapeutic Nursing: Subacute Care, *Nursing Times,* 93 (26), 54–55.

42. Guralnik, Jack M. (1991). Prospects for the Compression of Morbidity, *Journal of Aging and Health,* 3 (2), 138–54.

43. Guralnik, Jack M., Linda P. Fried, and Maarcel E. Salive (1996). Disability as a Public Health Outcome in the Aging Population, *Annual Review of Public Health,* 17 (1), 25–46.

44. Havemann, Judith (1998). Uninformed Consumers, *Washington Post National Weekly Edition,* June 29, 34.

45. Hawkins, Barbara A. (1997). Health, Fitness, and Quality of Life for Older Adults with Developmental Disabilities, in Ted Tedrick (ed), *Older Adults with Developmental Disabilities and Leisure: Issues, Policy and Practice,* New York: Haworth Press, 29–35.

46. Hellbusch, Joan Swanson, David E. Corbin, James A. Thorson, and Richard D. Stacy (1994). Physicians' Attitudes Towards Aging, *Gerontology and Geriatrics Education,* 15 (2), 55–65.

47. Henderson, Jessica W. (1997). Issues in the Medical Treatment of Elderly Women, *Journal of Women and Aging,* 9 (1, 2)m 107–15.

48. Hodes, Richard J., Vicky Cahan, and Marcia Pruzan (1996). The National Institute on Aging at its Twentieth Anniversary, *Journal of the American Geriatrics Society,* 44 (2), 204–6.

49. Holman, Halsted R., and Kate R. Lorig (1997). Overcoming Barriers to Successful Aging: Self-Management of Osteoarthritis, *Western Journal of Medicine,* 167 (4), 265–68.

50. House, James S., James M. Lepkowski, Ann M. Kinney, Richard P. Mero, Ronald C. Kessler, and A. Regula Herzog (1994). The Social Stratification of Aging and Health, *Journal of Health and Social Behavior,* 35 (3), 213–34.

51. Iglehart, John K. (1999). The American Health Care System: Expenditures, *The New England Journal of Medicine,* 340 (11), 70–76.

52. Iqbal, P., and C. M. Castleden (1997). Management of Urinary Incontinence, *Gerontology,* 43 (3), 151–57.

53. Jacobzone, S., E. Cambois, E. Chaplain, and J. M. Robine (1999). The Health of Older Persons in OECD Countries: Is It Improving Fast Enough to Compensate for Population Ageing? *Occasional Papers No. 37,* Paris: Organization for Economic Cooperation and Development.

54. Johnson, Brett C. (1995). The Case for a New Medical Cohort: Teliatrics, *Journal of Health & Health Policy,* 6, (3), 13–40.

55. Jollis, James G., Eric D. Peterson, and Charlotte L. Nelson (1997). Relationship Between Physician and Hospital Coronary Angioplasty Volume and Outcome in Elderly Patients, *Circulation*, 95 (11), 48.

56. Jones, Judith K. (1992). Assessing Potential Risk of Drugs: The Elusive Target, *Annals of Internal Medicine*, 117 (8), 691–92.

57. Kalache, A. (1998). Preface, in B. Vellas, J. L. Albarede, and P. J. Garry (eds), *Women, Aging and Health*, New York: Springer, 9.

58. Kane, Robert L. (1994). Future of Long-Term Care, in Chris Hackler (ed), *Health Care for an Aging Population*, Albany, NY: State University of New York Press, 199–212.

59. Kane, Robert L., Joseph G. Ouslander, and Itamar B. Abrass (1989). *Essentials of Clinical Geriatrics* (2d ed), New York: McGraw-Hill.

60. Katz, Philip O. (1998). Gastroesophageal Reflux Disease, *Journal of the American Geriatric Society*, 46 (12), 1558–65.

61. Kaufman, Sharon R. (1994). Old Age, Disease, and the Discourse on Risk: Geriatric Assessment in U.S. Health Care, *Medical Anthropology Quarterly*, 8 (4), 430–47.

62. Keller, Ingrid M., and Alexandre Kalache (1997). Promoting Healthy Aging in Cities: The Healthy Cities Project in Europe, *Journal of Cross-Cultural Gerontology*, 12 (1), 287–98.

63. Klinkman, Michael S., Philip Zazove, David R. Mehr, and Mack T. Ruffin IV (1992). A Criterion-Based Review of Preventive Health Care in the Elderly, *Journal of Family Practice*, 34 (2), 205–24.

64. Krauss, Susan (1999). *The Aging Individual: Physical and Psychological Perspectives*, New York: Springer.

65. Larue, Gerald A., and Rich Bayly (1992). *Long-Term Care in An Aging Society: Choices and Challenges for the '90s*, Buffalo, NY: Prometheus Books.

66. Lassey, Marie L., William R. Lassey, and Martin J. Jinks (1997). *Health Care Systems Around the World: Characteristics, Issues, Reforms*, Upper Saddle River, NJ: Prentice Hall.

67. Lau, Hong S., Karin S. Beuning, Ennie Postma-Lim, Liesbeth Klein-Beernink, Anthonius de Boer, and Arjan J. Porsius (1996). Non-compliance in Elderly People: Evaluation of Risk Factors by Longitudinal Data Analysis, *Pharmacy World and Science*, 18, 2, 63–68.

68. Leclere, Helene, Marie-Dominique Beaulieu, Georges Bodage, Andre Sindon, and Martine Couillard (1990). Why Are Clinical Problems Difficult? General Practitioners' Opinions Concerning 24 Clinical Problems, *Canandian Medical Association Journal*, 143, 12, 1305–15.

69. Lemme, Barbara Hansen (1995). *Development in Adulthood*, Boston: Allyn and Bacon.

70. Leveille, Suzanne G., Jack M. Guralnik, Luigi Ferrucci, and Jean A. Langlois (1999). Aging Successfully until Death in Old Age: Opportunities for Increasing Active Life Expectancy, *American Journal of Epidemiology*, 149 (7), 654–64.

71. Leveille, Suzanne G., Brenda W. J. H. Penninx, David Melzer, Grant Izmirlian, and Jack M. Guralnik (2000). Sex Differences in the Prevalence of Mobility Disability in Old Age: The Dynamics of Incidence, Recovery and Mortality, *Journal of Gerontology*, 55B (1), 541–50.

72. Lin, Ge (2000). Regional Assessment of Elderly Disability in the U.S., *Social Science and Medicine*, 50 (2000), 1015–24.

73. Mallet, Louise (1992). Counseling in Special Populations: The Elderly Patient, *American Pharmacy*, NS32 (10), 71–80.

74. Manton, Kenneth G., Eric Stallard, and G. Dennis Tolley (1991). Limits to Human Life Expectancy: Evidence, Prospects, and Implications, *Population and Development Review*, 17 (4), 603–37.

75. Mathany, Meg (1995). Another View of Medicare HMOs: Not Always What the Doctor Ordered, *Health System Leader*, 2 (5), 11–13.

76. McAllister, Bill (1997). A Surgeon for the VA System, *Washington Post National Weekly Edition*, November 10, 32.

77. McClellan, Mark, Barbara J. McNeil, and Joseph P. Newhouse (1994). Does More Intensive Treatment of Acute Myocardial Infarction in the Elderly Reduce Mortality, *Journal of the American Medical Association*, 272 (11), 859–66.

78. McDonald, Alison J., and Susanne T. Abrahams (1990). Social Emergencies in the Elderly, *Emergency Care of the Elderly*, 8 (2), 443–59.

79. McLaughlin, Thomas J., and Donald J. Willison (1996). Adherence to National Guidelines for Drug Treatment of Suspected Acute Myocardial Infarction, *Archives of Internal Medicine*, 156, 799–805 (as summarized in *Research Activities*, Agency for Health Care Policy and Research, 198, 9).

80. Michener, H. Andrew, and John D. DeLamater (1994). *Social Psychology* (3d ed), San Diego: Harcourt Brace.

81. Miller, Douglas K., Rodney M. Coe, James C. Romeis, and John E. Morley (1995). Improving Quality of Geriatric Health Care in Four Delivery Sites: Suggestions from Practitioners and Experts, *Journal of the American Geriatrics Society*, 43 (1), 60–65.

82. Mitteness, Linda S., and Judith C. Barker (1995). Sigmatizing a "Normal" Condition: Urinary Incontinence in Late Life, *Medical Anthropology Quarterly*, 9 (2), 188–210.

83. Mold, James W., David R. Mehr, James N. Kvale, and Richard L. Reed (1995). The Importance of Geriatrics in Family Medicine, *Family Medicine*, 27 (4), 234–41.

84. Monane, Mark, Susan Monane, and Todd Semla (1997). Optimal Medication Use in Elders: Key to Successful Aging, *Western Journal of Medicine*, 167 (4), 233–37.

85. Moody, Harry R. (1994). *Aging: Concepts and Controversies*, Thousand Oaks, CA: Pine Forge Press.

86. Morishita, Lynne, Chad Boult, and Lisa Boult (1998). Satisfaction with Outpatient Geriatric Evaluation and Management, *The Gerontologist*, 38 (3), 303–8.

87. Moschis, G. P., D. N. Bellenger, P.A. Kennett, and L. E. Aab (1996). Targeting the Mature Consumer Market, *Health Services Management Centre*, 9, 2, 90–97.

88. Mouton, Charles P. (1997). Special Health Considerations in African-American Elders, *American Family Physician*, 55 (4), 1243–53.

89. Murphy, N., M. P. Kazek, B. Van Vleymen, M. Melac, and E. Souetre (1997). Economic Evaluation of Nootropil in the Treatment of Acute Stroke in France, *Pharmacological Research*, 36 (5), 373–80.

90. Murray, Christopher J. L., and Alan D. Lopez (1997). Alternative Projections of Mortality and Disability by Cause 1990–2020: Global Burden of Disease Study, *The Lancet,* 349 (May 24), 1498–1504.

91. National Center for Health Statistics (1998). *Health United States 1998,* Washington, DC: U.S. Government Printing Office.

92. Neikrug, Shimshon M., Mati Ronen, David Glanz, Tovia Alon, Shlomo Kanner, Abraham Kaplan, and Clara Kinori (1995). A Special Case of the Very Old: Lifelong Learners, *Educational Gerontology*, 21 (4), 345–55.

93. Nelson, Eugene C., Colleen A. McHorney, and Willard G. Manning (1998). A Longitudinal Study of Hospitalization Rates for Patients with Chronic Disease, *Health Services Research*, 32 (6), 750–58.

94. Newcomer, Robert, Charlene Harrington, and Robert Kane (1997). Managed Care in Acute and Primary Care Settings, in Robert J. Newcomer and Ann M. Wilkinson (eds), Focus on Managed Care and Quality Assurance, *Annual Review of Gerontology and Geriatrics*, Vol. 16, New York: Springer Publishing Company, 1–36.

95. Ory, Marcia G., and Donna M. Cox (1994). Forging Ahead: Linking Health and Behavior to Improve Quality of Life in Older People, *Social Indicators Research*, 33 (1–3), 89–120.

96. Peek, M. Kristen, and Rayond T. Coward (1999). Gender Differences in the Risk of Developing Disability Among Older Adults with Arthritis, *Journal of Aging and Health*, 11 (2), 131-150.

97. Penning, Margaret J. (1995). Health, Social Support, and the Utilization of Health Services Among Older Adults, *Journal of Gerontology: SOCIAL SCIENCES*, 50b (5), s330–s339.

98. Porello, Peter T., Lynn Madsen, Andrew Futterman, and Gary S. Moak (1995). Description of a Geriatric Medical/Psychiatric Unit in a Small Community General Hospital, *Journal of Mental Health Administration*, 22 (1), 38–48.

99. Ramirez-Lassepas, Manuel (1998). Stroke and the Aging of the Brain and Arteries, *Geriatrics,* 53 (S1), S44–S48.

100. Reuben, David B., George T. Grossberg, Lorraine C. Mion, James T. Pacala, Jane F. Potter, Todd P. Semla (1998). *Geriatrics at Your Fingertips*, Belle Mead, NJ: Exerpta Medica.

101. Reuben, David B., Jack Zwanziger, Thomas B. Bradley, Arlene Fink, Susan H. Hirsch, Albert P. Williams, David H. Solomon, and John C. Beck (1993). How Many Physicians Will be Needed to Provide Medical Care for Older Persons? Physician Manpower Needs for the Twenty-First Century, *Journal of the American Geriatrics Society*, 41 (4), 444–53.

102. Rich, Spencer (1997). Curing Disabilities Might Save Medicare, *The Washington Post National Weekly Edition,* 14, 21 (March 24), 35.

103. Robinson, Deirdre, Katherine F. Pearce, and John S. Preisser (1998). Relationship Between Patient Reports of Urinary Incontinence Symptoms and Quality of Life Measures, *Obstetrics & Gynecology*, 91 (2), 224–28.

104. Rogers, Richard G. (1995). Sociodemographic Characteristics of Long-Lived and Healthy Individuals, *Population and Development Review*, 21 (1), 33–58.
105. Roff, Lucinda Lee, and Charles R. Atherton (1989). *Promoting Successful Aging*, Chicago: Nelson-Hall.
106. Ross, P. D. (1998). Osteoporosis: Epidemiology and Risk Assessment, in B. Vellas, J. L. Albarede, and P.J. Garry (eds), *Women, Aging and Health*, New York: Springer, 189–200.
107. Rowe, John W. (1999). Geriatrics, Prevention, and the Remodeling of Medicare, *New England Journal of Medicine*, 340 (9), 720–21.
108. Rowe, John W., and Robert L. Kahn (1998). *Successful Aging*, New York: Pantheon Books.
109. Rubenstein, Laurence Z., William B. Applegate, John R. Burton, Kathryn Hyer, L. Gregory Pawlson, and Carol H. Winograd (1991). Medicare Reimbursement for Geriatric Assessment: Report of the American Geriatrics Society Ad Hoc Committee on Geriatrics Assessment, *Journal of the American Geriatrics Society*, 39 (9), 926–31.
110. Rubenstein, Laurence Z., K. R. Josephson, J. O. Harker, D. K. Miller, and D. Wieland (1995). The Sepulveda GEU Study Revisited: Long-Term Outcomes, Use of Services, and Costs, *Aging Clinical Experimental Research*, 7 (3), 212–17.
111. Seeman, Teresa E., Lisa F. Berkman, Peter A. Charpenlier, Dan G. Blazer, Marilyn S. Albert, and Mary E. Tenetti (1995). Behavioral and Psychosocial Predictors: McArther Studies of Successful Aging, *Journal of Gerontology*, 50A (4), M177–M183.
112. Segal, Doralie Denenberg, Carlos J. Crespo, and Ellen Smit (1998). Active Seniors: Protect Them, Don't Neglect Them, *Public Health Reports*, 113 (2), 137–39.
113. Slater, Robert (1995). *The Psychology of Growing Old*, Philadelphia: Open University Press.
114. Smolak, Linda (1993). *Adult Development*, Upper Saddle River, NJ: Prentice Hall.
115. Steel, Knight (1997). The Elderly: The Single Greatest Achievement of Mankind, *Disability and Rehabilitation*, 19 (4), 130–33.
116. Stuck, Andreas E., Mark H. Beers, Andrea Steiner, Harriet U. Aronow, Laurence Z. Rubenstein, and John C. Beck (1994). Inappropriate Medication Use in Community-Dwelling Older Persons, *Archives of Internal Medicine*, 154 (19), 2195–200.
117. Stuck, Andreas E., Harriet U. Aronow, Andrea Steiner, Cathy A. Alessi, Christophe J. Bula, Maricia N. Gold, Karen E. Yuhas, Rosane Nisenbaum, Laurence Z. Rubenstein, and John C. Beck (1995). A Trial of Annual In-Home Comprehensive Geriatric Assessments for Elderly People Living in the Community, *New England Journal of Medicine*, 333 (18), 1184–89.
118. Sutton, Evelyn (1997). Enriching Later Life Experiences for People with Developmental Disabilities, in Ted Tedrick (ed), *Older Adults with Developmental Disabilities and Leisure: Issues, Policy and Practice*, New York: Haworth Press, 65–69.
119. Taylor, Brian V., Gavin Y. Oudit, and Michael F. Evans (2000). Walking or Vigorous Exercise? Which Best Helps Prevent Coronary Heart Disease in Women?, *Canadian Family Physician*, 46 (February), 316–18.
120. Tedrick, Ted (ed). (1997). *Older Adults with Developmental Disabilities and Leisure: Issues, Policy and Practice*, New York: Haworth Press.
121. Tennant, A., J. M. L. Geddes, J. Fear, M. Hillman, and M. A. Chamberlain (1997). Outcome Following Stroke, *Disability and Rehabilitation*, 19 (7), 278–84.
122. Torres-Gil, Fernando M., and Linda A. Wray (1993). Funding and Policies Affecting Geriatric Rehabilitation, *Clinics in Geriatric Rehabilitation*, 9 (4), 831–40.
123. Wald, Matthew L. (1998). Death Rate on Nation's Roads Dips to Record Low, *Spokesman-Review* (Spokane, WA), October 27, A4.
124. Ware, John E., Martha S. Bayliss, William H. Rogers, Mark Kosinski, and Alvin R. Tarlov (1996). Differences in 4-Year Health Outcomes for Elderly and Poor, Chronically Ill Patients Treated in HMO and Fee-for Service Systems, *Journal of the American Medical Association*, 276 (13), 1039–47.
125. Williams, Mark E. (1995a). Geriatric Medicine on the Information Superhighway: Opportunity or Road Kill? *Journal of the American Geriatric Society*, 43 (2), 184–86.
126. Williams, Mark E. (1995b). *Complete Guide to Aging and Health*, New York: American Geriatrics Society and Harmony Books.
127. Winograd, Carol Hutner (1991). Targeting Strategies: An Overview of Criteria and Outcomes, *Journal of the American Geriatrics Society* (Supplement), 39 (9), S25–S35.
128. Wolinsky, Fredric D., Kathleen W. Wyrwich, and James G. Gurney (1999). Gender Differences in the

Sequelae of Hospitalization for Acute Myocardial Infarction Among Older Adults, *Journal of the American Geriatrics Society*, 47 (2), 151–58.

129. World Health Organization (1998). Preface, in B. Vellas, J. L. Albarede, and P.J. Garry (eds), *Women, Aging and Health*, New York: Springer, 11–73

130. Yelin, Edward H., and Patricia P. Katz (1990). Transitions in Health Status Among Community-Dwelling Elderly People with Arthritis, *Arthritis and Rheumatism*, 33 (8), 1205–15.

131. Zaldivar, R. A. (1997). Elderly Are Healthier Than Ten Years Ago, *Miami Herald*, March 18, 3A.

Chapter 5

MENTAL HEALTH AND MENTAL DISORDERS

 INTRODUCTION

This chapter examines the characteristics of mental health, types of mental disorder, and treatment alternatives for older people. Major topics include:

- Mental health and the origins of mental disorder.
- Types and diagnosis.
- Treatment alternatives.
- Mental health services.
- Legal and ethical issues.

Good mental health is defined as a state of normal mental functioning without disease or disorder, enabling the older individual to think about and manage personal affairs while interacting comfortably with others. Advancing age leads to some deterioration of sensory and cognitive function, but general mental ability continues throughout life in the absence of disorder. Mental health is clearly one of the keys to optimal aging.[44, 77]

About 12 percent of individuals age 65 and over are estimated to have some form of minor or major mental disorder—although estimates vary widely depending on the definition and measurements used. Among the hospitalized older population 40 percent or more appear to have a disorder. The proportion with one or more disorders is estimated to be 50 percent or greater in nursing homes and has grown considerably as a direct result of the decrease in state mental hospital capacity during the 1980s.[97, 103]

Overall mental capacity is structured in part by genetic factors. However, mental health and overall mental ability can be enhanced by effective socialization, education, and other forms of deliberate training. The brain has the capacity to compensate for minor loss of neurons as both volume and weight decline somewhat. Older individuals can generally have a lot to do with maintaining their mental health—through a conscious process of learning about the types of behavior that promote a high level of mental function.[7, 24, 28]

Mental disorder is much less understood and more feared than physical illness. In the absence of knowledge, taboos have evolved that obstruct diagnosis and treatment. Elderly individuals who have mental problems are considerably less likely to be diagnosed and treated than younger people, especially in locations where mental health specialists are not easily available. Unfortunately, intimidating regulations and paper-work requirements also present serious obstacles.[1, 17, 104]

◆◆◆ ORIGINS OF MENTAL DISORDER

A mental problem may have a genetic origin or may be caused by personal or social conditions. Older people are especially at risk because of the numerous losses that occur in later life accompanied by gradual degrading of the psychic immune system. Specific stresses—death of a spouse, physical illness, disability, or a forced move—may trigger a mental disorder for some older people when appropriate support and treatment are not available.[42, 84]

Mental problems may also be a continuation of stress responses or ineffective coping strategies originating at younger ages. Any form of undue psychological stress (external demands or expectations that exceed ability to cope) can aggravate existing mental health problems. Stress can interfere with mental functioning, diminish ability to perform necessary tasks, disrupt concentration, and inhibit good judgment. Stress also has major physiological effects on the body and is associated with a number of mental and physical problems such as hypertension, cardiovascular disease, cancer, insomnia, headaches and emotional disturbances such as anxiety. Older individuals differ greatly in their ability to tolerate stress.[36, 63]

Challenges of Later Life

Many individuals entering older age face the greatest challenges of their life as they begin to lose some of their capacities. They may at the same time lose important social support from peers, siblings, or friends of similar age who become ill or die. They may feel psychologically fragile for the first time in their lives as they suffer loss of personal equilibrium and experience stress or serious depression. The situation is especially troublesome if they do not have the coping skills to manage the multiplicity of changes. Self-esteem, identity, and optimism are difficult to maintain when complicated by grief over the loss of a spouse or close friends. The consequences can lead to problems in concentration, tearfulness, anxiety, sad reflection, and concerns about mortality.[37, 106]

When ability to perform the basic activities of daily living diminishes, and dependence follows, mental disorder is a serious threat. A substantial proportion of older people who have managed quite well throughout their life feel a strong sense of loss, and even depression, when decline of important personal abilities occurs.[45, 63, 97]

Gender and Racial Variations

Older women are more often diagnosed with mental health problems than older men and are more likely to be treated with psychotropic drugs. Several explanations have been offered: greater stress and hardship among women, stereotypes held by medical professionals, and greater willingness to seek help. When older women complain of mental problems they are unfortunately often not taken seriously.[111]

Discrimination clearly contributes to poor mental health. For example, women are not always perceived as independent and autonomous by some mental health professionals. Racism plays a major role in the attitudes of some health care providers towards older Latinos, African Americans, and other minorities—whether female or male. In sum, ageism combined with minority and female status can lead to serious discrimination in both diagnosis and treatment.[83]

◆◆◆ TYPES AND DIAGNOSIS OF MENTAL DISORDERS

Many older individuals are suspicious of mental health practitioners and resist cooperating with them. A common pattern is to request assistance for real or presumed physical problems and only indirectly raise issues of mental condition. Physicians with appropriate training will respond by attempting diagnosis, referring the patient to a mental health specialist, or initiating treatment through counseling and/or medications. Early diagnosis of a mental health problem is clearly advantageous if treatment is to be successful.[26, 78]

Even after seeking help, problems are sometimes not detected, may be misdiagnosed, or may be deliberately overlooked by primary care physicians and nurses. The greatest single risk for nursing home patients suffering from depression or other mental problems may be misdiagnosis from inadequately trained personnel, with consequent misuse of medications. Patients may at times be inappropriately treated with psychotropic medication or other prescriptions, and/or be subject to unskilled counseling with decidedly negative results.[8, 37]

Diagnostic Instruments

Several valid and reliable instruments are available for professional assessment and diagnosis, including the Diagnostic Interview Schedule, the Geriatric Mental State Examination, the Geriatric Depression Scale, and the Mini-Mental State Examination. These and other instruments are used by psychologists, psychiatrists, social

TABLE 5–1   Primary Mental Health Problems of the Elderly

- Depression
    - Major
    - Minor
- Paranoid disorders
    - Simple
    - Schizophrenic
- Delirium
- Dementia
    - Alzheimer's Disease
    - Other dementia
- Drug abuse
    - Alcohol
    - Prescription and over-the-counter medications

Source: Data from Butler, Lewis, and Sunderland, 1991: 155; Reuben et al., 1998: 50–51.

workers, and other mental health professionals as part of the diagnostic process. Assessment by nonprofessionals can be misleading. Individuals showing evidence of dementia, depression, or other disorders should be further examined to refine and verify a diagnosis prior to treatment.[73]

The primary mental health problems particularly affecting older people are summarized in Table 5–1. In addition to the major categories listed in Table 5–1, some older individuals suffer from disorders such as anxiety associated with illness, medication side effects or withdrawal from drugs or medication.[81]

Depression

Depression is the most common problem and is particularly significant among nursing home residents—estimated to be as high as 25 percent. However, older individuals do not generally suffer from depression to any greater degree than younger people. Some studies suggest the rate is lower among older people living at home. Major depression is defined by the *Diagnostic and Statistical Manual of Mental Disorders* (DSM–IV) as a clinical disease requiring professional help and occurs with about 3 percent of the elderly living at home. It may have a biological origin and is usually characterized by serious melancholy mood swings. Symptoms such as those enumerated in Table 5–2 must persist for at least two weeks for classification as major depression.[2, 78, 82, 109]

Minor depression affects about 10 percent of the elderly and is more common, less severe, and of shorter term than major depression. It can be a consequence of psychological or social distress from disturbing major life events, such as loss of a spouse or a move to a nursing home. It does not ordinarily have a biological origin. Older women tend to have higher rates of minor depression than do older men.[56, 84, 92, 102]

Depression is a possible outcome when personal resources have for one reason or another diminished, when important goals have not been reached, when critical social support is lost, or when fear of death becomes prominent. Both major and

TABLE 5–2   Symptoms of Depression

- Depressed mood.
- Loss of interest or pleasure in usual activities.
- Withdrawal from personal contacts.
- Neglect of personal care.
- Muscular aches and pains.
- Difficulty concentrating.
- Pessimism, feeling unhappy, and sadness.
- Feelings of worthlessness; hopelessness, or worrying about the future.
- Fatigue.
- Sleep disturbances.
- Slow thought and action; indecisiveness.
- Decreased appetite and weight loss or gain.
- Agitation.
- Recurrent thoughts of suicide; sometimes a suicide plan.

Source: Adapted from Katz, 1998: 465; Reuben et al, 1998: 48; Schunk, 1999: 227; Slater, 1995: 52; Stafford, 1992: 60.

minor depression can lead to feelings of deep despair, loss of a sense of self-worth, loss of appetite, sleep problems, fatigue, and threats of suicide. About 15 percent of bereaved adults develop such serious grief that formal intervention is necessary. Depression can become a threat especially when bereavement continues for a prolonged period.[9, 56, 84]

Major depression can diminish ability to undertake activities of daily living and may lead to serious disability if not accurately diagnosed and treated. A mental health professional can ascertain whether minor or major depression is evident through application of instruments such as the Geriatric Depression Scale (GDS), or other forms of assessment. Use of the GDS will yield a more accurate diagnosis than informal questions. A history of previous symptoms over a substantial time period is also critical to accuracy of diagnosis.[92, 100, 102]

Depression may be a consequence of physical illness leading to loss of hope, especially if accompanied by hospitalization or a disability that severely limits ability to undertake normal activities of daily living. Although, as noted above, depression is sometimes a consequence of bereavement, it may have previously existed, causing the recovery process to be especially severe. Many older people will attempt to mask depression by blaming it on physical problems such as pain, sleep disturbance, loss of memory ability, or other factors.[38, 66]

Illustration 5-1 describes minor depression after death of a spouse.

Illustration 5-1
DEPRESSION AFTER DEATH OF A SPOUSE

George and Margaret were about to celebrate their 64th wedding anniversary when Margaret suffered a stroke (at age 86) and died after a short period of hospitalization. George was heartbroken and became depressed. He had trouble sleeping, lost his appetite, and wondered if life was worth living without Margaret. His doctor diagnosed minor depression and gave him medication. It took him more than a year to make the adjustment to living alone and recovering his interest in going forward with life.

The turnabout was a consequence in part of the continuing support from his large and affectionate family. A grandson moved into the basement of his house to keep him company and be available in the event of emergency. Two daughters who lived nearby invited him regularly for meals and social occasions. And his grandchildren and great-grandchildren organized a phone call network to be sure that he had one of them to talk to nearly every day. Gradually he regained interest in the future, did some traveling with some of his family, and soon began to enjoy life thoroughly again. After about two years he met a woman about his age from a nearby community and was soon dating weekly, dancing, dining out, and generally appreciating the companionship of someone with whom he could closely identify.

Widowed men, such as George in the illustration, have the highest rates of depression but both widowed women and men suffer more depression than married women or married men. However, as noted earlier, a high proportion of depressed older individuals are not diagnosed and are not treated, despite the strong evidence that antidepressants and other therapies are effective in alleviating depression and generally improving mental function. Since depression often leads to greater physical health care problems and suicide, treatment can also lower use of other health services thus decreasing overall costs.[55, 61, 82, 112]

Suicide. About 70 percent of suicides are a consequence of depression. Approximately 25 percent are among individuals age 60 or older, a much higher rate than in the younger population. Elderly men are the highest risk group, with seven times greater incidence than younger men. However, 75 percent of suicide *attempts*—many unsuccessful—are among women. As many as 75 percent of older individuals, both male and female, who commit suicide have sought help from a physician within a month of their death, and most have also indicated a suicide intent to friends or relatives. Nonetheless, older individuals are somewhat less likely to communicate their intent than are younger people. They are more likely than younger people to use lethal methods (especially firearms) and be successful. An accurate assessment instrument administered by physicians might save many older people from both attempting and succeeding with suicide.[22, 35, 56]

Paranoid Disorders

Simple mistrust, delusions, or hallucinations about persecution by others, as well as severe symptoms such as agitation, aggression against others, and severe distress are indicators of a paranoid disorder—most notably when schizophrenia is the diagnosis. Sometimes the reactions are also a result of sensory impairment. Treatment may require psychological and pharmacological interventions depending on the severity of the case.[81, 94]

Delirium

Delirium is an acute state of confusion or disrupted attention and cognition. It affects at least 14 percent of hospitalized older patients and may be caused by medications, infections, malnutrition, surgery, stress, or other factors. Inadequate hospital care involving inappropriate use or overuse of medications or failure to attend to the needs of patients may also be among the causes. The condition can best be alleviated through accurate diagnosis followed by changes that relieve the causal factors.[48, 49]

Alzheimer's Disease and other Dementias

The most common cause of functional disability in older adults is dementia—defined as a group of disorders characterized by decline in mental function resulting from physiological deterioration or effects of drugs. To qualify as dementia the symptoms must be sufficiently severe to seriously interfere with work, social activities, or relationships. Early indicators include:[16, 22, 31, 36, 54, 67]

- A change in ability to remember.
- Problems with comprehension.
- Impairment of judgment.
- Diminished orientation to time and place.

More than 15 percent of the older population suffers from some form of mild, moderate, or severe dementia—with the prevalence increasing as age rises. Fewer than 3 percent of those 65 to 70 have the problem but the incidence increases dramatically after age 75, rising to 25 percent or greater after age 85. Incidence is higher among women, in part because they live longer. Every economically advanced country reports similar rates.[32, 58, 65, 71, 111]

Some types are reversible while others (such as Alzheimer's Disease) are not. The reversible types are sometimes a consequence of medications such as diuretics, cardiac care drugs, steroids, hypertension medication, and tranquilizers or antidepressants. Many of these problems can be reversed by discovering the cause and removing or changing the offending behavior. However, diagnosis is often delayed for a year or more after the first symptoms appear due to: (1) lack of knowledge about the meaning of symptoms; (2) an unwillingness to admit a problem exists; (3) the time required for physicians to determine whether the symptoms indicate dementia; and (4) communication problems between physicians and caregivers.[10, 36, 94]

Multi-infarct or vascular dementias are irreversible if caused by cell loss, blood vessel damage, or injury to the brain as a result of one or more small strokes. Nutritional deficiencies, brain tumors, strokes, heart problems, severe infections, syphilis, or overuse of alcohol may also cause dementia. Dementia may thus have many causes and progress erratically. Mental ability may decline depending on which area of the brain is damaged. It is sometimes difficult to distinguish multi-infarct dementia from severe depression. Occasionally both problems exist in the same individual.[17, 20, 32, 88]

Alzheimer's is the most prevalent and irreversible form, accounting for approximately 70 percent of all dementia cases and affected more than 4 million people in

1998—90 percent of whom were cared for at home. Approximately 360,000 individuals contracted the disease each year during the 1990s. Alzheimer's is defined as a syndrome with a cluster of symptoms, including memory loss, impaired cognition, language problems, loss of judgment, and behavioral change. The most noticeable effects involve decline of brain function. Deterioration occurs in the nerve cells of the brain, especially in the center of thought, language, and memory. Alzheimer's is progressive and degenerative with an average duration of 8 years from first diagnosis until death. Both physical and mental health are affected. Sleep disorder is often a problem (referred to as "sundowning") and may be accompanied by disorientation and disruptive behavior at night. Women are twice as likely to develop the condition as are men, in part because of their longer life.[5, 15, 53, 81]

Alzheimer's clearly has genetic and family history origins for many victims as revealed in longitudinal studies with large and small samples. However, these factors become less important at older ages when other causes appear to be more important. Dementia is evident in a high proportion of the very old population regardless of family origins and genetic proclivity.[46, 74]

Intensive neurological and psychological evaluations are necessary to clarify the existence and severity of Alzheimer's, particularly after evidence of a stroke, seizure, delirium, or other severe illness. No two individuals react exactly the same or have the same general symptoms. A diagnosis thus requires a careful personal history, administration of a mental status examination, and thorough physical and psychiatric evaluations. The family should be involved in developing the personal history if possible. These procedures will help to distinguish Alzheimer's from depression, delirium, or other forms of dementia, and will help detect whether or not the condition is reversible or irreversible. The diagnosis of Alzheimer's is essentially a process of eliminating other possibilities and can only be clearly determined by an autopsy.[54, 98]

Assessment and diagnosis that distinguish between depression, other mental problems, and types of dementia are among the most serious challenges to physicians and mental health professionals. The American Psychiatric Association has sharpened the definitions in the *Diagnostic and Statistical Manual of Mental Disorders* (DSM–IV), recommending that all other possibilities be ruled out before a diagnosis of Alzheimer's is made.[2, 32, 98, 109]

The symptoms listed in Table 5–3 are summarized in rough sequence of manifestation. The changes noted in the table have been measured using structured instruments such as the Oregon Non-cognitive Inventory for Dementia. Individuals with the disease tend to have great difficulty with communication, comprehension, and relationships with others, depending on the stage of the progression. Falls and injury are also among the serious problems—at twice the rate for those without the disease. Efforts to prevent injury include careful management of medications and organization of the living environment to minimize hazards. Many Alzheimer's patients and other demented older people fortunately retain capacity to enjoy art, music, and other aesthetic experiences until the very late stages. Thus, reasonable quality of life may remain possible.[12, 84, 108]

Effects on Families. Alzheimer's seriously affects caregiver families and is certainly dreaded by those who understand the effects. It is sometimes referred to as a

TABLE 5–3   Common Elements in the Progression of Alzheimer's Disease

Cognitive and Functional Decline
- Forgetting names and dates.
- Gradual loss of recent memory.
- Difficulty in remembering locations.
- Loss of attention span.
- Difficulty learning.
- Loss of orientation of time, place, or personal relationships.
- General confusion.
- Irritability and mood change.
- Problems managing finances.

Functional and Behavioral Problems
- Decline of judgment.
- Difficulty comprehending.
- Difficulty with complex tasks at work or at home.
  Organizing and undertaking everyday activities.
  Selecting clothing and dressing.
  Bathing.
  Proper use of the toilet.
- Anxiety, restlessness, hostility, stubbornness.
- Depression.

Loss of Basic Abilities
- Vocabulary diminishes and ability to speak declines.
- Loss of remote memory.
- Inability to write or follow through on other tasks.
- Incontinence.
- Difficulty walking; unfocused wandering is common.
- Help is needed with many activities of daily living.
- Personality changes occur, such as indifference, paranoia, and jealousy.

The Final Days
- Stupor or coma may begin.
- Complete loss of capacity.
- Death.

Source: Adapted from Butler, Lewis, and Sunderland, 1991: 166; Cobbs and Ralapati, 1998: 137; Filley, 1995: 18; Reuben et al, 1998: 21; Stafford, 1992: 52-56; Williams, 1995: 135.

"family disease." The caregiving process is frustrating and fatiguing. It is impossible to predict how long the progression will take, or the precise symptoms, and is thus very difficult for families to accept. They may try to hide the diagnosis from friends and the community. The on-going decline of a loved family member creates severe emotional turmoil. Moreover, many caregivers work full-time and may also have children living at home as well.[17, 27, 64]

Good information and time are needed to learn how to effectively deal with the challenges. Although many families do their best to take care of an Alzheimer's patient at home, an eventual move to a skilled nursing or assisted living facility is nearly always necessary because the care process in the later stages of the disease is extremely difficult. Confusion or agitation in the evening or at night creates particularly severe stress for family members.[17, 47, 98, 109]

Special Treatment Problems with Alzheimer's. The precise causes of Alzheimer's are not known, making prevention very difficult. The progression can be slowed somewhat with medications such as antioxidents, anti-inflammatories, and estrogen, which prolong independence and have also been found to reduce the risk of contracting the disease.[4, 58, 71]

The best that can sometimes be done is to treat the affected individual as supportively as possible while avoiding negative responses to evolving behaviors. Management through understanding is important, including modification of the living environment to accommodate the losses of ability, giving direction and guidance in daily activities, and medication to control agitation, aggressiveness, and possible hallucinations. Life can be extended and improved somewhat with careful medical attention for infections, pneumonia, and other illnesses, as well as persistent personal caregiving to assure sanitation and good nutrition. Treatment can sometimes be provided to alleviate sleep disturbances and eating problems. Recent advances have increased the availability of pharmaceuticals to alleviate symptoms and to slow progression of the disease.[13, 17, 58, 86]

Treatment often includes support to the caregivers through education, support groups, respite for vacations, and family counseling to minimize depression and fatigue. Professional assistance with the details of caregiving can also delay deterioration somewhat and can help avoid a long period of residence in a nursing home.[67, 72]

Simplification of the environment is a key element in the special care units of nursing homes and can also be a part of the design for assisted living facilities. Some forms of rehabilitation in the form of physical or occupational therapy can be helpful, although the costs may not be covered by Medicare. Programmed activities can help sustain abilities while keeping residents occupied and content.[14, 40, 53, 67, 91]

Opportunity for exercise and outdoor activity appears to be helpful, if the outdoor space is well organized to make it easy for walking and enjoying the setting. Outdoor patios, courtyards, or gardens with sidewalks, trees, flowers, bird feeders, gazebos, and some form of seating are alternatives that may be used for activities such as picnics, exercise groups, and gardening.[23]

Depression accompanying dementia is often a primary cause of inability to manage self-care. Specialists in the treatment of Alzheimer's recommend that soon after diagnosis, while the patient's mind is still relatively intact, plans be made for advanced directives such as a durable power of attorney for health care and a living will with instructions about health interventions to be taken and not taken. The Alzheimer's Association is very active in helping families to cope with these and other issues. Local chapters offer outreach to caregivers through support groups and direct response to requests for assistance.[25, 27, 30, 53]

Special Therapies.   Art therapy has been used as one form of intervention to help counteract depression. The therapy includes a broad range of art forms, including painting, music, dance, theater, sculpture, and writing. Art therapists attempt to increase sensory stimulation, help enrich daily life, and work to make art serve as a satisfying activity. The involvement in art or other creative effort helps enhance self-esteem and provides a basis for socialization with other participants.[29] Illustration 5–2 is an example.

Illustration 5–2
ART THERAPY IN A NURSING HOME

An art therapy program at Covenant House, a nursing home in North Dayton, Ohio, involves four to six residents for two hours per week. The primary focus is to help participants express themselves through various forms of art and be positively stimulated in the process. The art therapist, Dione Greenberg, presents the project for the week and then helps each participant produce a small work of art during each session.

One of her star participants had contracted Alzheimer's. Although the disease had progressed to quite an advanced stage, the art activity clearly helped him to find a renewed interest in life. He was able to produce some beautiful work and demonstrated to other members of the group what might be done with their potential talent.

Art allowed him to demonstrate the use of his remaining and intact abilities. He was able to use his continuing capacity to be creative. With encouragement from the art therapist he helped other participants in the group, providing positive stimulation for them. The experience helped him think of himself as an artist rather than simply a victim of Alzheimer's and gave him a certain dignity and self-respect that somewhat enriched his life and helped to sustain a positive self-concept and sense of well-being. His appreciation of the experience was manifested by his pleasure in noting the arrival of his art therapist for the weekly sessions.

Although involvement in the group was entirely voluntary, the experience was clearly viewed by other participants as a refreshing and stimulating interlude among the routines in the nursing home. Their work was prominently displayed in the social center and on the walls of the home to be admired by other residents, staff, and visitors. Participants were able to demonstrate remaining competencies while taking pride in creation of art for others to admire and enjoy.

Source: Observations by the authors, with reference to Sabat and Collins, 1999: 11–19.

Supportive circumstances and stimulating activities can thus increase the quality of life for an Alzheimer's patient. A satisfying environment increases pleasure, comfort, and ability to function. Exercise, adequate rest, and good nutrition encourage a positive sense of well-being. Pleasant emotional experiences lead to a sense of self-esteem, calm, and contentment. Good relationships with other individuals facilitate emotional satisfaction, a sense of security, and easier daily coping.[11, 18]

Alcohol and Drug Abuse

The National Institute of Alcohol and Alcoholism estimates that as many as 10 to 15 percent of the elderly abuse alcohol to some degree, although abuse is generally lower than among younger people. It may be a lifelong habit or may begin later in life, possibly following the loss of a spouse or some other traumatic life change. The incidence is higher among individuals who suffer from mental health conditions such as depression, anxiety, confusion, and dementia. Interaction of alcohol and medications, with consequent damage to physical health, is a serious problem.[14, 51, 107]

Abuse problems are particularly acute among isolated older individuals with chronic physical illnesses. In many instances polypharmacy (multiple medications) and overuse of alcohol are both present. Isolation and minimal contact with medical care providers or public agencies may result in the problem going undetected unless systematic outreach efforts seek out individuals with a high risk of abuse. An example of a successful outreach program to identify older people with depression, dementia, alcohol abuse, or other mental problems is described in Illustration 5–3.

Illustration 5–3
MENTAL HEALTH OUTREACH: ELDERLY SERVICES OF SPOKANE

Elderly Services has the primary goal of identifying at-risk elderly in the community and maintaining them in their homes if possible. It is a division of the Community Mental Health Center in Spokane, Washington. A gatekeeper network consisting of trained service people who regularly visit homes is used to identify high-risk individuals and report indications of potential need.

Gatekeepers include mail carriers, newspaper delivery people, electrical meter readers, law enforcement officers, bank personnel, pharmacists, telephone service people, and others trained to look for signs of potential stress. Roughly 40 percent of clients in the program were referred by gatekeepers. Clients are also directly referred by relatives, professionals in the medical care system, and other community professionals or agencies.

A high proportion of those identified by gatekeepers were socially isolated, economically disadvantaged, and unlikely to have a personal physician. They tended to be female and received fewer community services than those entering the program via traditional referrals. Gatekeepers were thus able to identify a somewhat distinct population of older adults who particularly needed assistance but who were not visible through other means.

When someone is identified a multidisciplinary team, consisting of psychiatrists, family practice physicians, social workers, nurses, case managers, and other professionals, provides evaluation, diagnosis, and treatment in the home. Clients are thoroughly assessed for evidence of physical illness, psychological disorder, social or economic problems, and support-system deficiencies. The team then develops a comprehensive plan for care and treatment.

Although it is difficult to measure precise outcomes because of the multiplicity of factors involved, there is clear evidence of success. Many individuals learn to function better and are then able to access the services they need. Evidence indicates the suicide rate among the elderly in Spokane county was 15 percent lower than the state average, which may be attributed in part to Elderly Services interventions.

Source: Adapted from Jinks and Raschko, 1990: 974; Florio et al, 1996: 107; Florio and Raschko, 1998: 37.

◆◆◆ MENTAL HEALTH TREATMENT ALTERNATIVES

The goals of mental health treatment are to relieve pain, distress, or illness, while also improving ability to function. Knowledge and understanding about how to meet the goal increased substantially during the 1990s, although much remains to be learned about management of stress, anxiety, loneliness, depression, and dementia. Mental health services for the special problems of older people remain underdeveloped, and insurance programs are inadequate. Consequently, many who could benefit from treatment do not receive services. Moreover, a high proportion of the contemporary older population do not know how to use the mental health system (as noted earlier) and would rather try to hide their illness than be exposed as mentally ill. As they age, the baby boomers are likely to be better informed and have a more open attitude about treatment.[17, 57, 104]

Mental Status Assessment

The first stage of treatment is an assessment process noted earlier that sharpens the diagnosis. Are there clear and definable symptoms of depression, anxiety, memory loss, or other problems? What is the status of prescriptions, over-the-counter drug use, social circumstances, physical health status, and other factors that could be important in defining the problem? Memory loss is especially important since it is often a primary source of concern and an important indicator of mental status.[104]

Comprehensive geriatric assessment may provide a useful initial evaluation by helping to differentiate physical and mental problems while improving the accuracy of diagnosis. Thorough assessment is likely to lead directly to good decisions about possible need for psychotherapy, use of medication, living environment, the role of family members in providing care, and appropriate follow-up.[65]

Types of Treatment Providers

Psychiatrists, clinical psychologists, social workers, and psychiatric nurses are the principle professionally trained providers of treatment, although primary care physicians often identify problems and prescribe medication. A variety of professional settings can serve as treatment centers, including community mental health clinics, in-patient hospital units, out-patient psychiatric offices, private clinical-psychology offices, social-work practices, and nursing homes.[96]

The type of treatment provided will vary depending on the competencies of the specialist providing assistance. For example, depression is likely to be treated most effectively by a psychiatrist or a clinical psychologist using medication and/or psychotherapy. Medication prescribed by a psychiatrist or another physician may be the more important intervention for biological depression, while psychotherapy appears to be more effective with psychological problems. Psychiatrists and other physicians generally tend to place greater dependence on drug treatment than on counseling or psychotherapy because medication is viewed as more effective as well as less expensive. On the other hand, public mental health clinics staffed primarily by psychiatric social workers, psychiatric nurses, or psychologists can be quite effective in treatment of many problems not requiring medication or other forms of physician intervention.[102, 104]

The more specialized fields of geriatric psychiatry and geriatric psychology were initiated in the United Kingdom during the 1960s to help improve treatment of older patients and helping to bring focus to treatment of Alzheimer's disease and other serious problems. The British experience indicates that treatment can be substantially improved through better collaboration between medical specialists. Responsibility of specialists for a patient should be determined by the assessed clinical and care needs, avoiding territoriality among disciplines. From the older patient standpoint specialist mental health services should be unified. Mutual confidence and trust among specialists and with patients can clearly be helpful.[3, 52, 104, 110]

Institutional Treatment of Mental Disorders

As noted above a variety of institutional settings serve as settings for treatment—principally hospitals, nursing homes, and residential homes.

Hospitals. Specialized geriatric assessment and treatment units provide the most comprehensive help for frail and ill patients with neuropsychiatric disorders of various types such as dementia and behavioral disorders. The units can help to relieve emotional stress, diminish disturbed behavior, improve functional abilities, and generally enhance quality of life. Follow-up home health care can often be effective after short- or long-term institutional care, depending on the severity of the case.[17, 77]

Specialized private mental hospitals are a good source for multidisciplinary care in serious cases not amenable to out-patient treatment. Some state public hospitals provide good services, while others have a very poor image. Unfortunately, negative stereotypes cause both private and public hospitals to be viewed by many older people as places to be avoided.

Nursing Homes. The Nursing Home Reform Amendments of the Omnibus Budget Reconciliation Act (OBRA) in 1987 specifically identified mental health as a category of care needing additional regulation and emphasis. The Act requires that upon admission nursing home residents be comprehensively assessed for physical and mental health condition. Until the implementation of the Act, nursing home residents with mental limitations seldom received professional treatment. The assessment results become part of the required *Minimum Data Set* for all residents and serve as the basis for *Resident Assessment and Treatment Protocols*. Patient rights must be kept clearly in mind and a care plan implemented to assure quality of care. The legislation established a basis for improved treatment of mental health problems although research to confirm increased effectiveness remains to be fully implemented. Despite the new requirements, skilled nursing homes are seldom good treatment locations because of insufficient staff training and limited understanding of treatment requirements.[101]

Only a few larger nursing homes have in-house mental health assessment and treatment staff. An individual with a strong advocate, such as an attentive son or daughter, remains more likely to receive treatment than isolated individuals. Evidence indicates that government operated facilities, corporate chain homes, and lower-cost uncertified homes are the least likely to provide accurate diagnosis and appropriate treatment. The most likely ailments to receive attention are depression, schizophrenia, psychoses, or serious behavioral problems, because these cause difficulties for the staff.[90]

Special Care Units. As noted elsewhere, many nursing homes have established special care units for Alzheimer's and other dementia patients. Their purpose is to provide more concentrated attention to serious mental illness. The physical environment is adapted to suit personal and safety needs of patients with serious memory and other cognitive disorders. Staff receive specialized training in management of difficult behavioral problems associated with dementia. They learn how to be helpful to both the patient and the family. Such units are increasing in importance as nursing homes replace state hospitals as the care centers for older mental patients. Evaluation studies indicate that nursing homes are not ideal but can fulfill the treatment function if appropriate standards and training are implemented. However, some evaluative studies suggest that special care units do not appear to slow the rate of functional decline for dementia patients.[43, 76, 77]

Residential Care Facilities. Boarding home residence for older people with mental disorders has increased substantially since the state hospital role has diminished. Such homes do not attempt to offer in-house medical or nursing care and are thus less costly than nursing homes. Consequently, residents receive relatively few mental health or medical services even though many have serious disorders.[39]

Residential homes tend to be somewhat "out-of-sight" from public agencies and service providers in the community. Proprietors may not understand how to use the mental health care system or other programs for their residents. Disabilities may make travel difficult and residents usually have few resources to seek out assistance on their own.[39]

Other Residential Options. Experiments indicate that private apartments for mentally ill individuals require a relatively high level of professional support to be viable. Residents have trouble coping without on-going guidance and support. Yet, their quality of life can be greatly improved if an adequate program is available to meet their medical and support needs, as summarized in Illustration 5–4.[95, 97]

Illustration 5-4
COMMUNITY MENTAL HEALTH CARE AT JEFFERSON TERRACE

Seattle used federal Housing and Urban Development funds to construct the largest high-rise low-income housing project in the Northwest, with nearly 5000 residents including a high proportion of elderly and disabled individuals. A survey indicated that 91 percent had some form of mental disorder, 30 percent had two disorders, and many had a long history of mental problems. The average income level was $473 per month in 1990. Many of the residents had refused to accept help and did not want to leave their apartments for health care. They were isolated, frightened, and did not know how to access the help they needed.

The Community Home Health Care agency received a grant from the National Institute of Mental Health to create a Community Connections program designed to provide assistance with mental and physical health care. The project provided a trained staff (care managers and mental health professionals) to call on residents, gain their confidence, and begin to serve their needs. The health status and mental health condition of many residents improved considerably as a result of education and personal services without necessarily increasing treatment for their mental condition. However, many were willing to accept treatment after getting acquainted with care managers and mental health professionals. The Seattle Housing Authority was sufficiently impressed with the results that permanent funding was provided for ongoing mental health services.

Source: Information from Staebler, 1991: 52-56).

◆◆◆ IMPROVING MENTAL HEALTH SERVICES

Mental health care in the United States and in other countries remains underdeveloped compared to physical health care. Most insurance plans limit or exclude the treatment of mental disorders. The number of visits to mental health professionals is severely limited under most plans, and the payment provided is often less than the usual professional charges, with deductibles as high as 50 percent. Public mental health clinics provide lower-cost treatment in many communities but have limited capacity for long-term assistance to severe cases.[17, 82]

Medicare covers limited mental health care at home and in nursing homes, provided the services are under the supervision of a psychiatrist or a qualified psychiatric nurse. However, the diagnosis must indicate a type of disorder that would ordinarily require treatment in an institution. Depression and other emotional problems may qualify for Medicare coverage if associated with a physical disorder. Support for nursing home mental health care is clearly inadequate in most states, despite the requirements of the 1987 reforms discussed earlier.[59]

Delay in seeking care until very late in progression of a disorder is the norm, largely because of the noted limitations. Consequently serious emergencies such as suicide attempts occur regularly. Poor older people are particularly prone to delay seeking help even though they suffer higher rates of depression than individuals with adequate resources. When delay occurs, care often becomes more difficult and more expensive than might have been the case had treatment begun earlier.[17, 83]

Alternatives for Improving the System

Better information and more education about good mental health practices may be the most important needed change. Systematic educational programs in both community and institutional settings could help raise awareness of mental disorder indicators and sources of needed assistance.[19, 85, 104]

Improving Quality of Care. Quality improvement has received less attention in the mental health care system than in physical health care institutions. Several major changes are needed:[70]

- More widespread licensing requirements of providers to assure minimum levels of competence and greater understanding of quality of care standards.
- Medication reviews to detect misuse of pharmaceuticals in outpatient and institutional settings.
- Standardization of data so that patient outcomes can more readily be measured.
- Improvement of management information systems to increase accessibility and analysis of data.
- Clinical outcomes research to better understand the relationship between diagnoses and consequences of treatment.
- Required advanced training of mental health practitioners.

Trained professionals need to be more readily available in locations accessible to older people without good insurance. A more comprehensive system of services, coupled with more complete insurance coverage, are needed to assure access to appropriate care.[70]

Clinical outcomes research has been widely used in physical health care settings, but has not been adopted to the same degree in mental health care. High quality standardized data is clearly needed for development of patient management information systems. Since medication is a crucial element of treatment for mental disorder, better data on use of medications is of particular importance. Application of such basic principles would help assure consistent diagnosis and treatment.[70]

Services for Rural and Other Underserved Areas. Rural communities have long had a serious shortage of mental health services for older people. Yet, small towns have a much higher proportion of older people than urban areas. Incomes of the older rural population are generally lower than incomes in more urban areas, and access to insurance coverage for treatment of mental disorder is particularly limited.[6, 80]

Most of the available services are provided by professionals who cannot prescribe medications, although many work closely with physicians in securing prescriptions. Very few psychiatrists are available except on an occasional consulting basis, and rural physicians tend to have very limited training in mental health. The situation has been exacerbated by the withdrawal of federal support from community mental health centers and other rural mental health services.[80]

A few states have mounted major efforts to overcome these problems through integration of services and better funding. Retirement and recreation communities in rural locations have done much better than most agricultural or natural resource extraction communities, with access to mental health care equal to, or better than, in urban communities. Attractive residential and recreational opportunities appeal to mental health professionals and their families.

Serving the Most Seriously Ill. Examples of effective mental health programs are available in some locations as Illustration 5–5 indicates.

Illustration 5–5
FLORIDA GULF COAST MENTAL HEALTH SERVICES

The Gulf Coast Jewish Family and Mental Health Services Program in the Tampa Bay region of Florida developed a community-based program with several components :

- A Geriatric Residential Treatment System serves out-patients with serious mental illness.
- Comprehensive assessment, care management, and day treatment are provided for individuals discharged to community settings from residential treatment.
- A Mental Health Overlay program provides professional mental health care to residents of nursing homes (many of whom have been discharged from state mental hospitals) who are physically impaired and have a diagnosed mental disorder.
- A Geriatric Mental Health Support Team provides training in mental health care and provides backup support for professional caregivers and patient families.
- An Alternative Family Program identifies permanent housing in private residences as an alternative to the state mental hospitalization, with supervision by licensed and certified sponsors.
- A professional staff including a psychiatrist, a nurse, a generalist physician, and social workers, provide case management in homes to assure that appropriate care plans are followed.

Source: Data from Bernstein and Hensley, 1993: 201-207)

Evaluations indicate the Florida Gulf Coast program has had considerable success in improving the quality of life for clients while substantially lowering the cost of care compared to state hospital cost.[8]

Relieving Family Caregiver Stress. Caregiver stress is discussed in other sections of this volume, but has special implications for family members who care for someone who has serious mental illness. The burden is particularly heavy because of the long-term and dependent nature of the relationship. For example:[62]

- Seriously mentally ill or demented individuals tend to be economically dependent and unable to fulfill usual family or work roles.
- Household routines are disrupted and must be designed around the care of the dependent person.
- Social activity may be seriously curtailed because of the constant obligation for care.
- Other family members may feel deprived because of resources allocated for caregiving.
- Seeking and securing assistance from the health care system is time-consuming and frustrating.

- Mental health professionals are sometimes reluctant to communicate openly with caregivers about the issues of care.
- The mentally ill or demented older persons may be abusive and hard to manage.
- Feelings of stigmatization may be generated because of attitudes in the community.
- A sense of isolation and burnout is common.

It is obviously very important for a caregiver to function effectively if institutionalization of the dependent person is to be avoided. Although caregiver-support programs have been implemented in many communities, public resources have not been adequate to meet the needs. Home care is an advantage only when it can be viewed as beneficial to both the dependent older person and the caregivers. When the advantage is lost because of severe mental illness or late-stage dementia, transfer to a rehabilitative institution may be appropriate to avoid greatly diminished quality of life for both the older person and the family.[62]

◆◆◆ LEGAL AND ETHICAL ISSUES

The management of ethical and legal issues is a complex problem for many mentally incompetent older individuals and their caretakers. Legal language in the published laws and rules tends to be couched in impersonal and abstract terms that are difficult for the layperson to comprehend. Professional assistance is regularly needed to interpret the rules and requirements.[41]

Informed consent is usually required for mental health treatment. An individual must therefore have the ability to make choices after receiving information. Considerable uncertainty often surrounds decisions about the ability of an ill older adult to reliably provide consent, especially if the individual has limited education and vocabulary.[21, 109]

A major ethical challenge occurs when dependency does not necessarily include mental incompetence or inability to participate in decisions. Families, caretakers, or other parties who are directly affected may take over decisions regarding housing, daily support, and use of resources, for example, which are contrary to the preferences of the older individual. The dependent person may have very little recourse.[41, 109]

Advance Directives: The Living Will and Durable Power of Attorney

A *living will* allows the individual to take the initiative in directing physicians to withhold or withdraw life-sustaining treatment when capability to make decisions no longer exists. Mental disorder, including Alzheimer's disease, is not considered a terminal illness and is not affected by living wills in most states. *Durable power of attorney* is somewhat more flexible and comprehensive than a living will and allows an individual to designate a surrogate, usually a close friend or relative, to make medical decisions if needed. This form of advance directive obviously depends on the integrity and understanding of the person appointed to carry out the decision. Unfortunately, these measures do not always work as perfectly as might be preferred.[109]

Conservators and Guardianship

When very old or seriously ill individuals do not have full capacity to manage their own affairs and do not have family members to look after their daily needs, formal *conservators* or *guardians* must be appointed to manage their resources and help make decisions about personal affairs and medical care. A conservator is responsible in some states for managing the estate, whereas a guardian may handle personal affairs as well as an estate. These services have become a very important issue in every state, particularly for low-income elderly who cannot pay lawyers, bankers, or other professionals in the community for management services.[79, 80, 87]

The process for assigning guardianship or conservatorship is codified in state laws, with considerable variation from one state to another. The determination of need requires a decision by family members or may involve a physician, social workers, social service agencies and possibly an attorney or bank officer. The petitioner(s) must demonstrate that the individual is no longer able to manage personal affairs. The courts will then decide if or when decision capacity of an individual has been lost. A guardian or conservator may then be appointed to serve throughout the life of the individual or until competence returns. However, state rules are not always clear about procedures for determining who needs guardianship, how a guardian should be selected and appointed, specification of the relationship and responsibilities, and a procedure for appropriately terminating the relationship when no longer needed or viable.[87, 93, 109]

The guardianship or conservator decision may be made by a state adult-protective services agency when no responsible family member is available. Legal proceedings and court judgments may be required, especially if an older person who has been judged to be incompetent refuses to accept the guardianship arrangement.[60, 87, 105]

Elder Abuse

Although elder abuse is not strictly a mental health or legal problem, it arises from lack of adequate protection of the personal and legal rights of older individuals. Approximately 1 million older people are affected annually. Most of the cases of abuse occur in home settings rather than within some form of residential care.[68] Abuse includes a wide range of actions summarized in Table 5–4.

Careful screening and identification of an appropriate and honorable guardian is crucial because of the potential for abusive situations. Oppression and exploitation of incompetent older persons occurs regularly when guardians have total and absolute authority with little provision for ongoing oversight by responsible public authorities. It is thus very important that guardianship arrangements be evaluated by legal as well as medical and psychological professionals. A physician who suspects or detects elder abuse has an ethical responsibility to intervene or report the problem to appropriate authorities. Unfortunately, such desirable procedures are not always implemented because of resource shortages and inattention from responsible public agencies.[87, 109]

TABLE 5–4   Types of Abuse with Dependent Elderly

- Physical mistreatment:
  —Hitting.
  —Sexual abuse.
  —Physical restraints improperly used.
- Inadequate living conditions or neglect:
  —Withholding food.
  —Withholding appliances or prostheses such as wheel chairs.
  —Lack of proper sanitation.
  —Inadequate social support.
- Psychological abuse:
  —Name-calling or insulting in other ways.
  —Threatening violence or intimidation.
  —Demeaning the sense of dignity and self-worth.
  —Manipulation.
- Violation of rights:
  —Inappropriately committing to a nursing home or mental hospital.
  —Misusing or stealing financial resources.
  —Improper limitations on mobility.
  —Extortion.

Source: Data from Jarde et al, 1992: 647; Marshall et al, 2000: 47; Perrin, 1993: 162; Quinn and Tomita, 1986: 47.

Elder abuse cuts across ethnic, racial, and social-class boundaries, although the most common circumstance is associated with an older person living with abusive family members. Isolation of the older person from outside contacts increases the risk. The National Elder Abuse Incident Study sponsored by the federal Administration on Aging reported that nearly half a million older persons suffer abuse annually. Women are the most at risk—suffering three-fourths of the cases of psychological abuse and more than 90 percent of financial abuses.[16]

The Select Committee on Aging of the United States Congress estimated that one in every twenty-five older adults was subject to some form of serious abuse. Accurate data are very hard to generate because a high proportion of abuse situations go unreported, whether in private homes, adult family or boarding homes, or nursing homes. Dependent older people tend to be fearful of reporting abuse because of insecurity about residential alternatives. Many do not understand how to secure assistance from public authorities, although most communities have a 24-hour toll free phone service for receiving reports of abuse. Many hospitals and other local agencies have elder-abuse response teams available. States tend not to allocate many resources for protective services to deal with elder abuse, although all states have special statutes making abuse illegal.[16, 75]

Many victims of abuse are identified in emergency departments of local hospitals when they appear seeking assistance. Emergency departments play an active role in working with hospitals, agencies on aging in the community, and other concerned groups that help deal with the problems.[69]

Elder abuse is a true tragedy, often with no acceptable solution because of very limited options, especially when adult children or in-laws are the abusers. The abusing individuals may be designated as beneficiaries in personal wills and be guilty of deliberately withholding needed resources and support so as to enhance their own long-term financial benefits.[50, 79]

◆◆◆ SUMMARY AND CONCLUSIONS

Mental disorders are incorrectly assumed to be part of the aging process. Prevalence of some mental health problems is about the same for younger and older people. Older individuals are particularly subject to depression and dementia. Major depression affects about 5 percent and minor depression affects about 10 percent. Both types are treatable with psychotherapy and/or medication. Dementia affects about 15 percent of the older population, especially those at very advanced ages. Some types of dementia are reversible, but the most severe type, Alzheimer's disease, is not. Alzheimer's is the eighth largest cause of death among the elderly and has a major impact on families because of great difficulty in managing the syndrome and its consequences.

Older individuals are much less likely than younger people to receive mental health treatment. Unfortunately, many mental health professionals prefer not to treat older people. Inadequacy of insurance reimbursement is also a problem. Most forms of insurance, including Medicare, provide only limited reimbursement. Payment for mental health care by insurance companies is generally insufficient to deal with serious and protracted conditions—a great frustration to ill older persons and their families.

Knowledge of, and attention to, mental disorders and their treatment is increasing and should help greatly to diminish the incidence and consequences of such problems in the future. Large numbers of older individuals with mental disorder need access to high-quality mental health services if they are to age optimally. Good quality services are not uniformly available in urban communities and are even less available in smaller rural communities. Treatment of disorders in nursing homes and other institutional settings is particularly inadequate.

Legal documents such as a living will and durable power of attorney can help an older person influence decisions even when they are no longer competent to participate. Guardianship and conservator rules for those who are judged to be incompetent vary widely from state to state, but can help to protect individuals who have lost their mental capacity for decisions. Elder abuse regularly occurs when provisions for protection of dependent individuals are not adequate.

Much remains to be done to make mental health care a consistent contributor to quality of life. Improvements in the system of care are badly needed to improve access, increase quality of services, and expand insurance coverage.

◆◆◆ REFERENCES

1. Abraham, Ivo, Kathleen Coen Buckwalter, Diane G. Snustad, Dianne E. Smullen, Anita H. Thompson-Heisterman, Jane Bryand Neese, and Marianne Smith (1993). Psychogeriatric Outreach to Rural Families: The Iowa and Virginia Models, *International Psychogeriatrics*, 5 (2), 203–11.

2. American Psychiatric Association (1994). *Diagnostic and Statistical Manual of Mental Disorders* (4th ed., Revised). Washington, DC: American Psychiatric Association.

3. Andresen, Elena (1997). Introduction, in Elena Andresen, Barbara Rothenberg, and James G. Zimmer (eds), *Assessing the Health Status of Older Adults*, New York: Springer, xi–xxvi.

4. Andreason, Nancy C., and Donald W. Black (1995). *Introductory Textbook of Psychiatry* (2d ed), Washington, DC: American Psychiatric Press.

5. Ballard, Edna L. (1999). Social Work Perspectives: Issues in Caregiver Research: The Family, *Alzheimer Disease and Associated Disorders,* 13 (Suppl.1), S88–S92.

6. Bane, Share DeCroix, Eloise Rathbone-McCuan, and James M. Galliher (1994). Mental Health Services for the Elderly in Rural America, in John A. Krout (ed), *Providing Community-Based Services to the Rural Elderly,* Thousand Oaks, CA: Sage, 243–66.

7. Bass, Scott A. (1995). *Older and Active: How Americans Over 55 Are Contributing to Society*, New Haven: Yale University Press.

8. Bernstein, Michael A., and Raymond Hensley (1993). Developing Community-Based Program Alternatives for the Seriously and Persistently Mental Ill Elderly, *Journal of Mental Health Administration,* 20, (3), 201–7.

9. Blazer, Dan, Bruce Burchett, Connie Service, and Linda K. George (1991). The Association of Age and Depression Among the Elderly: An Epidemiologic Exploration, *Journal of Gerontology*, 46 (6), M210–15.

10. Boise, Linda, David L. Morgan, Jeffrey Kaye, and Richard Camicioli (1999). Delays in the Diagnosis of Dementia: Perspectives of Family Caregivers, *American Journal of Alzheimer's Disease*, 14 (1), 20–26.

11. Bond, John (1999). Quality of Life for People With Dementia: Approaches to the Challenge of Measurement, *Ageing and Society,* 19 (2), 561–79.

12. Brod, Meryl, Anita L. Stewart, Laura Sands, and Pam Walton (1999). Conceptualization and Measurement of Quality of Life in Dementia: The Dementia Quality of Life Instrument (DQoL), *The Gerontologist,* 39 (1), 25–35.

13. Brodaty, Henry, Rebecca Dresser, Margaret Eisner, Timo Erkunjuntti, Serge Gauthier, Nori Graham, Cees Jonker, Gegory Sachs, and Peter Whitehouse (1999). Alzheimer's Disease International and International Working Group for Harmonization of Dementia Drug Guidelines for Research Involving Human Subjects with Dementia, *Alzheimer Disease and Associated Disorders,* 13 (2), 71–79.

14, Brown, Arnold S. (1996). *The Social Processes of Aging and Old Age*, Upper Saddle River, NJ: Prentice Hall.

15. Bundlie, Scott R. (1998). Sleep in Aging, *Geriatrics*, 53 (Supplement 1), S41–S43.

16. Butler, Robert N. (1999). Warning Signs of Elder Abuse, *Geriatrics*, 54 (3), 3–4.

17. Butler, Robert N., Myrna Lewis, and Trey Sunderland (1991). *Aging and Mental Health: Positive Psychosocial and Biomedical Approaches* (4th ed), New York: Macmillan.

18. Caron, Wayne, and Darryl Ross Goetz (1998). A Biopsychosocial Perspective on Behavior Problems in Alzheimer's Disease, *Geriatrics*, 53 (Supplement 1), S56–S60.

19. Carter, Jimmy (1998). *The Virtues of Aging*, New York: Ballantine Publishing Group.

20. Cheung, T.F., and Vladimir Hachinski (1997). Vascular Factors in Cognitive Decline, chapter 6 in H. M. Fillit and R.N. Butler (eds.) *Cognitive Decline: Strategies for Prevention*, London: Oxford University Press, 53–65.

21. Christensen, Katherine, Ansar Haroun, Lawrence J. Schneiderman, and Dilip V. Jeste (1995). Decision-Making Capacity for Informed Consent in the Older Population, *Bulletin of the American Academy of Psychiatry Law*, 23 (3), 353–65.

22. Cobbs, Elizabeth L., and Anuradha N. Ralapati (1998). Health of Older Women, *Medical Clinics of North America*, 82 (1), 127–44.

23. Cohen-Mansfield, Jiska, and Perla Werner (1999). Outdoor Wandering Parks for Persons with Dementia: A Survey of Characteristics and Use, *Alzheimer's Disease and Associated Disorders*, 13 (2), 109–17.

24. Cotman, Carl W. (1990). The Brain: New Plasticity/New Possibility, in Robert N. Butler, Mia R. Oberlink, and Mal Schechter, *The Promise of Productive Aging: From Biology to Social Policy*, New York: Springer, 70–84.

25. Cox, Carole (1999). Service Needs and Use: A Further Look at the Experiences of African American and White Caregivers Seeking Alzheimer's Assistance, *American Journal of Alzheimer's Disease*, 14 (2), 93–101.

26. Crane, D. Russel (1995). Health Care Reform in the United States: Implications for Training and Practice in Marriage and Family Therapy, *Journal of Marital and Family Therapy*, 21 (2), 115–25.

27. Eastman, Peggy (1999). Helping the Helpers: Alzheimer's Caregivers No Longer Alone, *AARP Bulletin*, 40 (7), 14–17.

28. Ewen, Robet B. (1988). *An Introduction to Theories of Personality* (3d ed), Hillsdale, NJ: Lawrence Erlbaum Associates.

29. Ferguson, Winnie J, and Elenore Goosman (1991). A Foot in the Door: Art Therapy in the Nursing Home, *American Journal of Art Therapy*, 10 (1), 2–3.

30. Filley, Christopher M. (1995). Alzheimer's disease: It's Irreversible but Not Untreatable, *Geriatrics*, 50 (7), 18–23.

31. Fillit, Howard (1997). The Clinical Significance of Normal Cognitive Decline in Late Life, in H. M. Fillit and R. N. Butler (eds), *Cognitive Decline: Strategies for Prevention*, London: Greenwich Medical Media, 1–7.

32. Fleming, Kevin C., Jonathan M. Evans, David C. Weber, and Darryl S. Chutka (1995). Practical Functional Assessment of Elderly Persons: A Primary-Care Approach, *Mayo Clinic Proceedings*, 70 (9), 890–910.

33. Florio, Evelyn R., Todd H. Rockwood, Michael S. Hendryx, Julie E. Jensen, Raymond Raschko, and Dennis G. Dyck (1996). A Model Gatekeeper Program to Find the At-Risk Elderly, *Journal of Case Management*, 5 (3), 106–14.

34. Florio, Evelyn R., and Raymond Raschko (1998). The Gatekeeper Model: Implications for Social Policy, *Journal of Aging and Social Policy*, 10 (1), 37–55.

35. Garrard, Judith, Sharon J. Rolnick, and Nicole M. Nitz (1998). Clinical Detection of Depression Among Community-Based Elderly People with Self-Reported Symptoms of Depression, *Journal of Gerontology: Medical Sciences*, 53A (3), M92–M101.

36. Gatz, Margaret (1998). Toward a Developmentally Informed Theory of Mental Disorder in Older Adults, in Jacob Lomranz (ed), *Handbook of Aging and Mental Health: An Integrative Approach*, New York: Plenum Press, 101–19.

37. Gatz, Margaret, and Michael A. Smyer (1992). The Mental Health System and Older Adults in the 1990s, *American Psychologist*, 47 (6), 741–52.

38. Gilewski, Michael J., Norman L. Farberow, Dolores E. Gallagher, and Larry W. Thompson (1991). Interaction of Depression and Bereavement on Mental Health of the Elderly, *Psychology and Aging*, 6 (1), 67–75.

39. Gottesman, Leonard E., Ellen Peskin, Kathleen Kennedy, and Jana Mossey (1991). Implications of a Mental Health Intervention for Elderly Mentally Ill Residents of Residential Care Facilities, *International Journal of Aging and Human Development*, 32 (3), 229–45.

40. Grant, Leslie A., and Andrew R. Somers (1998). Adapting Living Environments for Persons with Alzheimer's Disease, *Geriatrics*, 53 (Supplement 1), S61–S65.

41. Gromb, Sophie, Gerard Manciet, and Anaud Descamps (1997). Ethics and Law in the Field of Medical Care for the Elderly in France, *Journal of Medical Ethics*, 23 (4), 233–38.

42. Gutman, David (1998). The Psychoimmune System in Later Life: The Problem of Late-Onset Disorders, in Jacob Lomranz (ed), *Handbook of Aging and Mental Health: An Interpretive Approach*, New York: Plenum Press, 281–95.

43. Hampel, Margaret J., and Margaret M. Hastings (1993). Assessing Quality in Nursing Home Dementia Special Care Units: A Pilot Test of the Joint Commission Protocol, *Journal of Mental Health Administration*, 20 (3), 236–46.

44. Hasan, M. Khalid, and Dreama Gail Baker (1993). Competency Assessment in the Elderly, *West Virginia Medical Journal*, 89 (9), 386–88.

45. Hicks, Gail (1998). Personal Communication.

46. Hirst, Clint, Irene M. L. Yee, and Adele D. Sadovnick (1994). Genetic Factors That Protect Against Dementia, *American Journal of Human Genetics,* 55 (3), 588–89.

47. Hurley, Ann C., Ladislav Volicer, Veronica F. Rempulsheski, and Sara T. Fry (1995). Reaching Consensus: The Process of Recommending Treatment Decisions for Alzheimer's Patients, *Advances in Nursing Science,* 18 (2), 33–43.

48. Inouye, Sharon (1997). Delirium and Cognitive Decline: Does Delirium Lead to Dementia, in H. M. Fillit and R. N. Butler (eds), *Cognitive Decline: Strategies for Prevention,* London: Greenwich Medical Media, 85–104.

49. Inouye, Sharon K., Mark J. Schlesinger, and Thomas J. Lydon (1999). Delirium: A Symptom of How Hospital Care is Affecting Older Persons and a Window to Improve Quality of Hospital Care, *American Journal of Medicine,* 106 (5), 565–72.

50. Jarde, O., B. Marc, J. Dwyer, P. Fournier, H. Carlier-Pasquier, and L. Lenoir (1992). Mistreatment of the Aging in the Home Environment in Northern France: A Year Survey, *Medical Law,* 11 (7–8), 641–48.

51. Jinks, Martin J., and Raymond R. Raschko (1990). A Profile of Alcohol and Prescription Drug Abuse in a High-Risk Community-Based Elderly Population, *Annals of Pharmacotherapy,* 24 (10), 971–75.

52. Kafetz, K.M. (1994). In Collaboration with Old Age Psychiatrists, *Age and Ageing,* 23 (3), S34–35.

53. Kane, Michael N. (1999). Mental Health Issues and Alzheimer's Disease, *American Journal of Alzheimer's Disease,* 14 (2), 102–10.

54. Kane, Robert L., Joseph G. Ouslander, and Itamar B. Abrass (1989). *Essentials of Clinical Geriatrics* (2d ed), New York: McGraw-Hill.

55. Katz, Ira R. (1998). Depression as a Pivotal Component in Secondary Aging, in Jacob Lomranz (ed), *Handbook of Aging and Mental Health: An Integrative Approach,* New York: Plenum Press, 463–82.

56. Koenig, Harold G., and Dan G. Blazer (1992). Epidemiology of Geriatric Affective Disorders, *Clinics in Geriatric Medicine,* 8 (2), 235–51.

57. Koff, Theodore H. (1988). *New Approaches to Health Care for An Aging Population,* San Francisco: Jossey-Bass.

58. Kowall, Neil W. (1999). Alzheimer Disease 1999: A Status Report, *Alzheimer's Disease and Associated Disorders,* 13 (Supplement 1), S11–S16.

59. Kozlak, Jeanne, and Marshelle Thobaben (1992). Treating the Elderly Mentally Ill at Home, *Perspectives in Psychiatric Care,* 28 (2), 31–35.

60. Lachs, Mark S., Christianna Williams, Shelley O'Brien, Leslie Hurst, and Ralph Horwitz (1996). Older Adults: An 11-Year Longitudinal Study of Adult Protective Service Use, *Archives of Internal Medicine,* 156 (4), 449–53.

61. Lee, Gary R., Marion C. Willetts, and Karen Seccombe (1998). Widowhood and Depression: Gender Differences, *Research on Aging,* 20 (5), 611–30.

62. Lefley, Harriet P. (1996). *Family Caregiving in Mental Illness,* Thousand Oaks, CA: Sage.

63. Lemme, Barbara Hansen (1995). *Development in Adulthood,* Boston: Allyn and Bacon.

64. Long, Janie (1997). Alzheimer's Disease and the Family: Working with New Realities, in Terry D. Hargrave and Suzanne Midori Hanna (eds), *The Aging Family: New Visions in Theory, Practice, and Reality,* New York: Brunner/Mazel Publishers, 209–34.

65. Lund, Dale A. (1998). Personal Communication.

66. Lund, D. A., M. S. Caserta, and M. F. Dimond (1989). Impact of Spousal Bereavement on the Subjective Well-Being of Older Adults, in D. A. Lund (ed.) *Older Bereaved Spouses: Research with Practical Applications,* New York: Hemisphere, 3–15.

67. Mace, Nancy L., and Peter Robins (1991). *The 36 Hour Day* (Revised ed), Baltimore: Johns Hopkins Press.

68. Marshall, Charles E., Donna Benton, and Joselynn M. Brazier (2000). Elder Abuse: Using Clinical Tools to Identify Clues of Mistreatment, *Geriatrics,* 55 (2), 42–48.

69. McDonald, Alison J. (1999). Social Emergencies in the Elderly, *Emergency Medicine Clinics of North America,* 8 (2), 443–59.

70. Miller, Douglas K., Rodney M. Coe, James C. Romeis, and John E. Morley (1995). Improving Quality of Geriatric Health Care in Four Delivery Sites: Suggestions from Practitioners and Experts, *Journal of the American Geriatrics Society,* 43 (1), 60–65.

71. Molnar, Frank J., and William B. Dalziel (1997). The Pharmacoeconomics of Dementia Therapies, *Drugs and Aging*, 10 (3), 219–33.

72. Moore, Jim (1994). Communities Respond to Common Disease of Aging, *Contemporary Long Term Care*, 17, 3, 32.

73. Mulligan, R., A. Mackinnon, P. Berney, and P. Giannakopoulos (1994). The Reliability and Validity of the French Version of the Canberra Interview for the Elderly, *Acta Psychiatrica Scandanavica*, 89 (4), 268–73.

74. Paymai, Haydeh, Holly Grimslid, Barry Oken, Richard Camicioli, Gary Sexton, Alison Dame, Diane Howieson, and Jeffery Kay (1997). A Prospective Study of Cognitive Health and the Elderly (Oregon Brain Aging Study): Effects of Family History and Apolipoprotein E Genotype, *American Journal of Human Genetics*, 60 (4), 948–56.

75. Perrin, Novella (1993). Elder Abuse: A Rural Perspective, in C. Neil Bull (ed), *Aging in Rural American*, Newbury Park, CA: Sage, 161–70.

76. Philips, Charles D., Philip D. Sloane, Calheine Haues, Gary Koch, Julie Haug, Kathleen Spry, George Deuteman, and Rick Williams (1997). Effects of Residence in Alzheimer's Disease Special Care Units on Functional Outcomes, *Journal of the American Medical Association*, 278 (16), 1340–44.

77. Porello, Peter T., Lynn Madsen, Andrew Futterman, and Gary S. Moak (1995). Description of a Geriatric Medical/Psychiatric Unit in a Small Community General Hospital, *Journal of Mental Health Administration*, 22 (1), 38–48.

78. Powell, Douglas H. (1994). *Profiles in Cognitive Aging*, Cambridge: Harvard University Press.

79. Quinn, Mary Joy, and Susan K. Tomita (1986). *Elder Abuse and Neglect: Causes, Diagnosis and Intervention Strategies*, New York: Springer.

80. Rathbone-McCuan, Eloise (1993). Rural Geriatric Mental Health Care, in C. Neil Bull (ed), *Aging in Rural America*, Newbury Park, CA: Sage, 146–60.

81. Reuben, David B., George T. Grossberg, Lorraine C. Mion, James T. Pacala, Jane F. Potter, and Todd P. Semla (1998). *Geriatrics At Your Fingertips*, Belle Mead, NJ: Excerpta Medica and American Geriatric Society.

82. Rimer, Sara (1999). Gaps Seen in Depression Treatment in Elderly, *New York Times National Sunday Edition*, September 5, 1, 16.

83. Roff, Lucinda Lee, and Charles R. Atherton (1989). *Promoting Successful Aging*, Chicago: Nelson-Hall.

84. Rossen, Eileen Kleinjan, and MaryBeth Tank Buschmann (1995). Mental Illness in Late Life: The Neurobiology of Depression, *Archives of Psychiatric Nursing*, 9 (3), 130–36.

85. Rowe, John W., and Robert L. Kahn (1998). *Successful Aging*, New York: Pantheon Books.

86. Sabat, Steven R., and Michelle Collins (1999). Intact Social, Cognitive Ability, and Selfhood: A Case Study of Alzheimer's Disease, *American Journal of Alzheimer's Disease*, 14 (1), 11–19.

87. Schmidt, Winsor C., Robert Bickel, William Bell, Kent Miller, and Elaine New (1995). Issues in Public Guardianship, in Winsor C. Schmidt (ed), *Guardianship: The Court of Last Resort for the Elderly and Disabled*, Durham, NC: Carolina Academic Press.

88. Schunk, Carol (1999). Psychological and Cognitive Considerations, in Bella J. May (ed), *Home Health and Rehabilitation: Concepts of Care* (2nd ed), Philadelphia: F. A. Davis Company, 220–33.

89. Shaw, Fiona E., and Rose Anne Kenny (1998). Can Falls in Patients with Dementia be Prevented?, *Age and Ageing*, 27 (1), 7–9.

90. Shea, Dennis G., Anrea Streit, and Michael A. Smyer (1994). Determinants of the Use of Specialist Mental Health Services by Nursing Home Residents, *Health Services Research*, 29 (2), 169–85.

91. Simard, Joyce (1999). Making a Positive Difference in the Lives of Nursing Home Residents with Alzheimer's Disease: The Lifestyle Approach, *Alzheimer's Disease and Associated Disorders*, 13 (Supplement 1), S67–S72.

92. Slater, Robert (1995). *The Psychology of Growing Old*, Philadelphia: Open University Press.

93. Smith, George P. (1996). *Legal and Healthcare Ethics for the Elderly*, Washington, DC: Taylor and Francis.

94. Smolak, Linda (1993). *Adult Development*, Upper Saddle River, NJ: Prentice Hall.

95. Sohng, Sung Sil Lee (1996). Supported Housing for the Mentally Ill Elderly: Implementation and Consumer Choice, *Community Mental Health Journal*, 32, 2, 135–48.

96. Solomon, Renee (1996). Coping with Stress: A Physician's Guide to Mental Health in Aging, *Geriatrics*, 51 (7), 46–51.

97. Staebler, Rebecca (1991). Providing Mental Health Services for the Elderly, *Caring Magazine*, 10 (5), 52–56.

98. Stafford, Florence (1992). Differential Assessment of Dementia and Depression in Elderly People, in Florence Safford and George I. Krell (eds), *Gerontology for Health Professionals: A Practical Guide*, Washington, DC: National Association of Social Workers Press, 51–67.

99. Stafford, Florence, and George I. Krell (eds) (1992). *Gerontology for Health Professionals: A Practical Guide*, Washington, DC: National Association of Social Workers Press.

100. Steffens, David C., Christopher M. O'Connor, Wei Jan Jiang, Carl F. Pieper, Maragatha N. Kuchibhatla, Rebekka M. Arias, Adair Look, Chad Davenport, Michael B. Gonzalez, and K. Ranga Rama Krishnan (1999). The Effect of Major Depression on Functional Status in Patients with Coronary Heart Disease, *Journal of the American Geriatric Society*, 47 (3), 319–22.

101. Streim, Joel E., and Ira R. Katz (1994). Federal Regulations and the Care of Patients with Dementia in the Nursing Home, *Medical Clinics of North America*, 78 (4), 895–909.

102. Tannock, Charles, and Cornelius Katona (1995). Minor Depression in the Aged: Concepts, Prevalence, and Optimal Management, *Drugs and Aging*, 6 (4), 278–92.

103. Vaczek, David (1994). How Can Facilities Improve Mental Health Services?, *Contemporary Long Term Care*, 17 (8), 28.

104. VandenBos, Gary R. (1993). Psychology and the Mental Health Needs of the Elderly, in Florence Lieberman and Morris F. Collen (eds), *Aging in Good Health: A Quality Lifestyle for the Later Years*, New York: Plenum Press, 189–212.

105. Veith, Lynn R., Cynthia A. Blair, Nancy V. Leonard, Rayda Bouma, and Holly H. Pazda (1996). Attorney-Case Manager Collaboration in the Conservatorship of Older Adults, *Journal of Case Management*, 5 (3), 115–20.

106. Weiss, Jules C. (1995). Cognitive Therapy and Life Review Therapy: Theoretical and Therapeutic Implications for Mental Health Counselors, *Journal of Mental Health Counseling*, 17 (2), 157–72.

107. Welte, John W., and Amy L. Mirand (1995). Drinking, Problem Drinking, and Life Stressors in the Elderly General Population, *Journal of Studies on Alcohol*, 56 (1), 67–73.

108. Wild, Katherine V., Jeffrey A. Kaye, and Barry S. Oken (1994). Early Noncognitive Change in Alzheimer's Disease and Health Aging, *Journal of Geriatric Psychiatry and Neurology*, 7 (4), 199–205.

109. Williams, Mark E. (1995). *Complete Guide to Aging and Health*, New York: Harmony Books and American Geriatrics Society.

110. Williamson, J. (1994). In the Past, *Age and Ageing*, 23 (3), S9–S11.

111. World Health Organization (1998). Achieving Health Across the Life Span, in B. Vellas, J. L. Albarede, and P.J. Garry (eds), *Women, Aging and Health*, New York: Springer, 11–72.

112. Yaffe, Kristine, Terri Blackwell, Robert Gore, Laura Sands, Victor Reus, and Warren S. Browner (1999). Depressive Symptoms and Cognitive Decline in Nondemented Elderly Women, *Archives of General Psychiatry*, 56 (5), 425–30.

Chapter 6

CHRONIC ILLNESS
AND LONG-TERM CARE

Acute illness — short lived illness. you get it and it goes away.

◆◆◆ INTRODUCTION

This chapter reviews the chronic health conditions that affect the older population and examines the long-term health and personal care system as it responds to chronic illness. Specific topics include:

- Characteristics of chronic illness.
- Goals and types of long-term care.
- Home health care.
- Assisted living services.
- Nursing home care.
- Continuing care retirement communities.
- The hospice.
- Measuring and improving effectiveness.

long-term repetitive care.

Chronic illnesses are prolonged health conditions or disabilities not readily subject to cure. Not all chronic illnesses are necessarily debilitating. However, when the condition becomes severe, some form of long-term care may be necessary to alleviate pain and suffering, treat symptoms, and provide social support—at home, in the immediate community, and/or in a variety of institutional settings.[140]

Fortunately, the incidence of many serious chronic conditions—hypertension, heart disease, arthritis, and emphysema, for example—has declined in the United

132

States and other economically advanced countries during recent decades, thus decreasing the proportion of older individuals who need nursing home care. Moreover, an increasing number of older people with disabilities are able to manage in their home or in an assisted living apartment with home health care—alternatives that mean less dependence on the formal system of long-term health care.[9]

◆◆◆ CHARACTERISTICS OF CHRONIC ILLNESS

Chronic illnesses have several distinctive characteristics:[90]

- An uncertain prognosis, resulting in a need for continuous monitoring.
- Limitations in ability to function at home and in the community.
- Several concurrent conditions may interact and be additive in lowering functional capacity.
- A requirement for continuing health care, personal care and social services in severe cases.
- Possible need for palliative care including pain control and alleviation of discomfort.
- Possible social isolation.

The complexity of care implied by these characteristics means that coordination among care providers is highly important. Until recent decades institutionalization was viewed as the best means of achieving both coordination and a continuum of care. However, such assumptions were eventually challenged because of the high cost and the realization that many patients do not need the intensive services characteristic of nursing homes. Improved provision of ambulatory and home care has replaced many of the functions that were formerly exclusive to nursing homes and hospitals.[90]

Causes of Chronic Disease and Disability

The likelihood of chronic illness and disability varies depending on occupation, social class, education, and individual proclivity to practice preventive health care. For example:[53, 113]

- Older blue-collar workers or laborers are more likely to suffer physical disability than older white collar or professional workers because working conditions are more difficult and dangerous.
- Lower-income older people are more likely than the more affluent to have serious chronic illnesses as a consequence of less adequate housing, poorer nutrition, more difficult social conditions, and less access to good medical care.
- Older individuals with less education are likely to have higher rates of disability than are the more educated because they have less knowledge about prevention and a lower likelihood of engaging in good health practices.

- Older women are more likely than men to have chronic illness and disability because they have lower average incomes and tend to live longer.
- Individuals who do not practice preventive behaviors are more likely to incur chronic illness than those who do.

Hence, the incidence of chronic illness and need for long-term care is highest for older blue-collar workers, older individuals with lower incomes, those with less education, women, and others who do not practice preventive behaviors, although other groups will also need long term at somewhat lower rates. Severe chronic illness leads to a need for health care and assistance with activities of daily living.[9, 79, 145]

◆◆◆ GOALS AND TYPES OF LONG-TERM CARE

High-quality long-term care pursues several primary goals summarized in Table 6–1.

TABLE 6–1   Goals of Long-Term Care

- Fostering as much independence, autonomy, dignity, and self-respect as possible with the fewest restrictions.
- Encouraging self-care to the degree possible.
- Preventing or avoiding physical and mental deterioration when possible.
- Improving functional status through rehabilitation.
- Providing a "continuum of care" to meet changing needs.
- Protecting from physical and mental harm.
- Prolonging life for as long as possible without artificial life support.

Source: Adapted from Koff, 1988: 33; Konrad, 1998: 9.

The goals listed in Table 6–1 can be largely achieved through high-quality home care, day care, assisted living, and nursing home care. Unfortunately, they are not achieved in many situations because of poor quality standards, shortage of resources, limited caregiver knowledge of appropriate care, and other missing ingredients.[17]

Types and Intensity of Care

The degree of appropriate care obviously varies depending on the condition of the patient. At the minimal level, self-care and informal family care are sufficient. At the maximum, skilled nursing, hospitalization, or hospice care are needed. The various settings and levels of intensity are summarized in Table 6–2.

◆◆◆ HOME HEALTH CARE

Formal home support services increased by 25 percent per year in the early 1990s, although cutbacks in federal funds, as well as tightened regulations, slowed down the growth later in the decade. The surge in demand led to a four-fold increase in expenditures during the eleven-year period from 1985 to 1996. More than 7 million individuals received health care at home through at least 17,500 providers in 1995.

TABLE 6–2   Types and Intensity of Long-Term Health Care

Settings	Intensity and Types of Services
Private home, informal	Self-care, family care
Private home, informal and formal	Personal care plus professional home care
Adult day center, formal care	Daytime health services, nutrition, and social support
Assisted living or group home	Personal care and home health care
Nursing home	Skilled nursing, rehabilitation, subacute care, and personal care
Continuing care retirement community	Skilled nursing, rehabilitation, medical care, personal care, and long-term housing
Hospital	Acute care, skilled nursing, rehabilitation, personal care, specialized medical care
Hospice — *last stages of life* (*next stop: mortuary*)	Palliative services, including pain control, skilled nursing, and social support

Source: Data from Kaye, 1995: 4; Konrad, 1998: 11; Snider, 1995: 4–5; Sherwood et al, 1997: 1–2; Stuart, 1997: 30.

Home health care costs went from about $2 billion in 1985 to $4 billion in 1996. Home visits increased from 40 million to 258 million. Seventy-two percent of the recipients were age 65 or older, and more than 70 percent were women. Skilled nursing was the most used service by 83 percent of patients, followed by personal care by 59 percent; homemaker or companion services were used by 19 percent; physical therapy by 18 percent; and social services by 12 percent.[49, 50, 73, 147]

Professional home care is clearly viewed as highly desirable by most disabled older persons and their informal caregivers, especially as an alternative to entering any form of institutional facility. As the number of very old individuals increases, home health care will clearly play a key role in helping older people remain in a private home as long as possible.[73]

The "home" is defined under Medicare rules as any residential setting that is outside a formal medical establishment. It can thus mean a detached house, apartment, a unit in a congregate or assisted living complex, or a boarding home. Eligibility rules for at-home services require confinement to the home and physician certification of disability. A certified home health agency must be available to provide the care under a plan arranged with physician direction.[32, 135]

Informal Caregiving: The Family Role

Most home care is provided informally by a spouse and/or adult children. Approximately one in four (2.4 million) American households provided care to an older family member in 1997. More than 25 million family members participate in some form of care for other family members. About three-quarters of the severely disabled elderly in the United States relied almost entirely on self-care and assistance of family members or other unpaid caregivers in 1997. This is the clear preference of most older individuals because it can preserve private personal space and independence, especially in the presence of a protective and loving family. An older individual is more likely to maintain a positive self-concept, self-respect, and a strong sense of personhood among family and friends. When individuals with disabilities, either physical or mental, must leave home because of their condition, they often feel home*less*.[24, 66, 133]

A high proportion of caregivers are themselves elderly spouses, or post age 65 daughters, daughters-in-law, or other older family members. Seventy-three percent of caregivers are female. Daughters are more likely to provide care than are sons. Fully 64 percent are full- or part-time workers. Family caregivers have learned to perform many tasks formerly reserved to professional medical practitioners, even including home dialysis, injections, tube feeding, administering oxygen, and managing incontinence.[24, 66, 69, 83, 95, 106]

When more than one daughter or son is close at hand, caregiving is often shared and responsibilities divided. It should be noted that caregiving may significantly *increase* the closeness and strength of family ties, although it can also sometimes lead to conflict.[93, 104, 159]

Siblings play a very important emotional and companionship support role but are clearly secondary to spouses and adult children as caregivers. Siblings seldom exchange significant material support with each other. More distant kin such as cousins, nieces, and nephews may similarly provide emotional support but seldom get directly involved.[20]

Variations in Responsibility. The care-giving relationship is quite diverse, ranging from simply managing the care plan to providing ongoing personal care. The possibilities include routine assistance and management of care, backup assistance to supplement routine care in times of special need or emergency, predefined or occasional assistance at family members' convenience, and limited responsibility or sporadic assistance that is not predictable or dependable, as in the case of an adult child living at some distance from the disabled parent.[43]

Although most spouses and adult children are quite willing to assume responsibility for routine or backup assistance to a husband, wife or parent, it is not unusual for one or more adult children to take a predefined or sporadic role—because of professional work demands, distance from the location, or in rare cases because they are unwilling to assume any responsibility. In the latter instance family conflict may be either a cause or consequence of the lack of shared responsibility, as discussed in illustration 6–1.

Illustration 6–1
CONSEQUENCES OF FAMILY CONFLICT

Ed and Betty had six adult children who generally got along quite well. Four of them remained in nearby communities, whereas two moved to other states. When Ed suffered a massive stroke and entirely lost his ability to manage his personal and family responsibilities, Betty assumed routine care responsibility for him, with regular backup assistance from two daughters and a son who lived nearby. The other children were available for only sporadic visits and minimal caregiving assistance. Within a relatively short time, Betty was diagnosed with cancer and was unable to provide the needed home care for her husband.

One of the daughters moved into the household and began to assume primary responsibility for routine care of both parents. It was at this point that serious family conflict arose. The caretaking daughter thought she should take full responsibility for managing both personal and financial affairs of her parents, convincing her mother to sign over management duties—even though the nearby son had earlier been given much of the responsibility. He was accused of mismanaging the family property because it did not generate as much income as the sister felt was needed to pay for the costs of care. She was unwilling to share most of the tasks with her other sisters or brothers and essentially predefined their participation for her convenience. Yet, she also felt they were not doing their part. They wanted to provide more support but were limited to sporadic assistance by their sister's attitude. The two out-of-state children were largely isolated from participation except for occasional visits. The relationship degenerated to the point that some of the adult children were no longer on speaking terms.

When the cancer overcame Betty, the situation only got worse. The sister providing routine care to her father became seriously alienated from all but two sisters, essentially refusing to allow participation by the other siblings. Upon Ed's death, the conflict continued over disposition of the home and other family resources.

Family Caregiver Stress. Disability can gradually transform an interdependent family relationship into one of deep dependence as in the illustration—and it can become quite traumatic for all concerned. The most difficult commitment occurs when there is need for constant support for activities of daily living. In some instances, the caregiving spouse or an adult child may also be partially disabled and yet must try to cope with management of financial and legal affairs as well as personal care. The stress of the required work may mean that caregivers incur serious physical or mental problems. Spouses and other caregivers have been referred to as "hidden patients" because of the stresses they often undergo, such as:[10, 94, 149]

- Less time for social interaction with peers.
- Conflict with a spouse (or adult siblings) who may not share the commitment.
- Financial problems because of required costs or a need to give up a job.
- Poor physical health.
- Depression and unhappiness.

Fortunately, negative effects on caregivers appear to be temporary. Stress tends to diminish or disappear when the aged parent or relative dies.[30, 77]

The stresses are very similar to those noted earlier for caregivers of Alzheimer's victims. Studies indicate, however, that only about 5 percent of caregivers entirely abandon the responsibility. They sometimes feel abandoned by the health care system because of great difficulty in securing resources to help with caregiver tasks. Close friends may not help directly, but can provide very important emotional support that helps alleviate the burden. Fortunately, caregiver support programs have been developed in many communities to help cope with the physical and emotional stress. The national Alzheimer's Association has sponsored many such efforts throughout the country, as have local groups. The goal is to prevent social isolation and share information with others who have similar challenges.[19, 58, 85, 89, 106, 115]

Satisfaction and Reward. Many caregivers do not view the work as unreasonably burdensome. About 90 percent of female and 58 percent of male caregivers reported (in a 1991 U. S. national survey) considerable satisfaction and reward from their role—especially spouses, although husbands reported more reluctance than wives to provide personal care (particularly bathing, dressing, and other intimate care). Many caregivers derive enough reward from the role that they continue many of the same kinds of support after a move to a nursing home.[51, 77, 82]

In sum, family caregiving is a highly varied arrangement. The predominant attitude is strong commitment by family members to successfully manage informal care with little outside help. However, supplemental formal assistance is usually welcomed when available at reasonable cost. In some states public funds are used to assist family caretakers through Medicaid (i.e., California, Oregon, and Wisconsin for example). Adult Foster Care funds are available in Oregon when the older person is cared for in the home of a qualified relative. Several European countries routinely compensate families for providing care. Family physicians in Canada are strongly encouraged to provide support not only to disabled patients at home but also to family caregivers.[10, 40, 66, 89]

Changes in long-term care policy at the national level suggest a growing emphasis on even greater involvement of family members. Earlier discharges from hospitals, coupled with fewer public resources for formal home care and nursing home care, may mean that families will have to shoulder more of the burden in the future. If families do not provide most of the needed care, the demand for professional home care, assisted living accommodations, and nursing home space will greatly increase.[82]

Formal Home Care: Professional Roles

Nurses, nurses aides, social workers, therapists, and occasionally physicians, pharmacists and clinical psychologists, are the primary providers of home care. The types of services available in many communities include activities funded through Area Agencies on Aging, Medicare, Medicaid, state agencies, by local governments, and privately. Options include: information and referral, telephone assistance and reassurance, emergency messaging, telemedicine, computerized alert and e-mail messaging, visiting nurses and home health aides, physical therapy, occupational therapy, speech therapy, nutrition programs such as "meals-on-wheels," mental health care, pharmacy services and prescription-by-mail programs, subacute care, and provision of durable medical equipment. Availability of each type of service varies widely by location, with urban areas generally much more likely to have a full range of options.

Formal home health services and other forms of assistance are designed primarily to supplement family support, but may assume a larger role when a disabled person does not have access to family care. The amount of paid formal home care received does not appear to substitute for or reduce informal care, although disabled individuals with both types certainly receive more overall care. The informal caregiver burden may not be diminished but involve somewhat less stress.[70, 153]

Information and Communication Assistance. Telephone services provide ongoing contact with family and service providers for anyone able to use the phone. Electronic emergency response systems have been widely adopted in the United States and other countries with a basic goal of enabling individuals who suffer a fall or other crisis to immediately call for help without necessarily speaking on the telephone. Emergency messaging usually includes electronic push buttons for automatic calls for help. Portable radio medical alert devices or alarms for fire or medical emergencies are among other available technologies. Such monitoring services usually require a monthly fee.[132]

The Lifeline System is the most used personal response mechanism with more than 65 percent of the U.S. market, usually with the nearest hospital as the response center. The systems offer peace of mind for both the older person and family members. However, the relatively high cost has limited implementation among individuals with lower incomes.[107]

Emergency response systems have resulted in decreased use of in-patient care and substantial cost savings for home care. Most users are older women (average age 76 in one study) with serious chronic health problems. Evaluation studies indicate that most are very satisfied with their system. Emergency response appears to be a viable alternative to more expensive daily surveillance by a family member or home health aid.[78]

Videotelephones with telecare services have been introduced experimentally in Germany as devices for enabling visual assessment of a client from a distance. The possibility for visual contact has special advantages for caretakers who need help in solving a problem. Videophones thus serve a social-support function as well as enhanced emergency contact. The new services have the potential to lower costs of home care and long-term care as the cost of the technology declines.[54]

Computerization, miniaturization, phone alarm systems, and mobility of products have made home care much more technologically sophisticated than in previous decades. Many treatments, such as kidney dialysis, medication monitoring, and cancer therapy can now be performed cost effectively in the home. Rehabilitation is increasingly possible for such conditions as cardiac recovery. Advanced technologies such as telemedicine, teleconsulting and teleradiology are widely used in some regions of the United States, albeit sometimes on a subsidized basis with outside grant funds because of the relatively high cost. Barriers are sometimes presented by such problems as outdated local telephone systems, excessive rates, licensure issues for out-of-state physicians, software and hardware incompatibility, lack of standards, and reimbursement difficulties.[4, 21, 102]

Current computer technology offers the potential for communication through e-mail messaging, programmed check-in with a message center, and emergency contact in times of crisis. These more complex systems are becoming less costly year by year. Use of the computer has clearly enhanced quality of life for many older people through access to the Internet for e-mail and many other services.

Health Care Services. Visiting nurses provide assurance that basic health care needs are met. Nurse aides provide routine care for medical problems such as incontinence or medication needs. In some locations physician visits are available for physical checkups or emergencies. Hot meal programs provide a healthy nutritional diet without requiring the older person to do extensive cooking and cleanup.

Comprehensive subacute home care is available in some locations to help rehabilitate patients who have been discharged from a hospital. The goal is to facilitate optimal recovery while avoiding the need for institutional care. Evidence from the National Long-Term Care Channeling Demonstration Project indicates such efforts have been quite successful. Patients are able to improve functional levels more quickly than if rehabilitation took place in an institutional setting.[65, 124]

Other Support Services. A number of supplementary programs help with household support, such as:

- Home maintenance services for cleaning, repairs, and yard care.
- Chore assistance such as grocery purchasing, securing other supplies, and errands.
- Social support such as respite care and friendly visitors.
- Transportation using van services and taxis.
- Adult day-care center services such as group meals, recreation, and supervision.
- Multipurpose senior centers provide health education and screening.
- Moving and assistance with household relocation.
- Legal and protective services.
- Case management.
- Hospice care.

The Senior Companion Program and the Retired Senior Volunteer Program (both authorized by the Domestic Volunteer Service Act of 1973) are federally sponsored and involve older volunteers in the provision of in-home services. Stipends provide an incentive to lower-income older individuals. Friendly Visitors is a volunteer program to provide social contact in the home and is often organized by Area Agencies on Aging or other local organizations. It helps avoid isolation by assuring regular visits and companionship from someone in the community. These programs provide valuable support for many families, but they represent a relatively small part of the home care workforce.[92]

Licensing and Certification Requirements. Licensing and certification of home health agencies must usually be approved by a state agency responsible for long-term care services. Four types of certification schemes are available: through Medicare, through Medicaid, state licensing, or private licensing boards. In the latter case, payment for care must come from private insurance or be privately paid. Most full-service home health agencies are Medicare and Medicaid certified.[131]

Performance of many services is restricted to individuals who have formally demonstrated their competence through education, training, passing a test, or other procedure leading to a medical, nursing, therapy, social work, or other license. Physicians may also need special licensing in formal care management which allows them to provide advice to families and home care providers regarding application and use of home health procedures.[83]

Important professional characteristics include:[25, 50, 69]

- Training in insurance programs, medical issues associated with home care, caregiver stresses, medical ethics, legal issues, and rehabilitation.
- Flexibility and compassion.
- Effectiveness as communicators, educators and team players.
- Sensitivity to the care environment.

These attributes are critical because of the unique features of care in a private domicile. Professional interest, understanding, and support for home care has a very positive effect on the quality and scope of services.[25]

The Providers of Care

Nurses. Nurse-practitioners and nurses' aides form the backbone of the system. Visiting Nurses Associations pioneered home health care, but have now been joined by a wide variety of other agencies. As of 1996, 47 percent of home care visits were by nurses or nurses' aides, 9 percent by physical therapists, 1 percent each by occupational and speech therapists, and about 1 percent by social workers. The remainder were nonhealth care support personnel. Nurses also provide the majority of the supervision, often having responsibility for as many as 60 to 100 patients at one time. Much of their responsibility is for acute episodes of illness.[2, 25]

Physicians. Physicians play a crucial (if limited) role as the senior and responsible medical provider. Only the physician can prescribe medications, undertake procedures such as injecting an arthritic knee, treat unrecognized depression, arrange for geriatric evaluation, and initiate other medical actions not formally within the capacity of other home health care workers. Physicians do not necessarily make many home visits themselves, nor do they usually receive training in the special characteristics of home health care. However, the American Medical Association has strongly encouraged greater physician involvement.[25, 124]

Physicians have generally felt that home care is somewhat inefficient, poorly reimbursed, overly regulated, and not interesting work. However, interest has been growing and has led to the creation of a professional organization referred to as the American Academy of Home Care Physicians. The home care physician is often trained as a geriatrician since a high proportion of the work is with older patients. A physician can be particularly important to understanding and supporting the caregiver function, sometimes forestalling decisions to initiate institutional care.[25]

Therapists. Physical therapists, occupational therapists, speech therapists, psychologists, psychiatrists, and social workers play important supporting roles. As noted earlier, equipment innovations for many procedures have increased mobility and effectiveness in the home setting. However, many of these services have not been widely used because of relatively high cost, strict constraints, and limited insurance reimbursement.

Securing mental health services from psychiatrists and psychologists has been particularly difficult. Yet, many nurses and social workers may not be adequately trained in mental health. Managed care organizations are increasing their emphasis on home mental health care, although the quality of results remains to be fully documented.[25, 35, 68]

Respite Care Providers. Respite care is among the elements of home health care that may be most valuable to the at-home caregiver. Studies indicate that most would benefit greatly from occasional breaks and vacations. Respite care provides time for caregivers to handle other chores, including their own medical care. Respite providers can help the caregivers maintain their own physical and emotional strength, and may help prevent decisions to move patients to assisted living or nursing home facilities. Respite is particularly important in the case of dementia. If well managed, respite care is usually a much more acceptable solution than a move to an assisted living or a nursing home.[74, 98, 116]

Adult day care is an alternative in some communities and is especially useful to caregivers who must work during the day. Volunteers provide much of the assistance to individuals with limited income. For example, the Senior Companion Program worked with the Visiting Nurses Association of America in several demonstration projects to test alternative respite approaches. A formal assessment revealed a high level of satisfaction with the volunteer role in helping to meet personal care needs.[34]

Case Managers and Geriatric Care Managers. Case managers, care managers, and geriatric manager roles have all been created to serve as linkages between dependent individuals and the array of public and private agencies in the community. Case managers are trained to monitor individual care plans and help secure services. They may be employed in public agencies or, when private funds are available, may be hired by an individual or family. The downside is that the elderly individuals may become very dependent on the case manager for assistance and feel a serious loss when "their" manager changes or the service is withdrawn.[26, 66]

Case managers may occasionally feel torn when the wishes of the older person as client differs from the expectations, regulations, and legal requirements of their sponsoring agency. Autonomy and self-determination may be the goal for the older person, but eligibility criteria and reimbursement rules may take precedence for the professional worker. The rules may exclude what the client wants or needs most—even though the manager may feel a stronger commitment to the older person.[39, 66]

Gatekeepers. The gatekeeper role is defined somewhat differently than case or geriatric care manager functions. As discussed in the previous chapter, gatekeepers can be lay individuals who help identify older individuals with medical or mental problems. In other instances they are professional workers in public agencies or private institutions who, after collecting information and assessing needs, have responsibility for decisions about allocation of appropriate services. The role is sometimes filled by a personal physician who assesses the status of an older individual and certifies the medical and personal services needed. This process has been termed "medicalization" of services that do not necessarily have a specific medical purpose.[26]

The concepts of case management and gatekeeping pose major ethical dilemmas for the professional who takes responsibility for decisions about disabled and somewhat dependent older individuals. Their goal must be to "do no harm" to their client, protect their autonomy, and assure their safety, as well as help them with care needs. A problem can sometimes arise if the client is mentally incompetent and is represented by a surrogate family member. Both the client and surrogate must be fully involved in the care effort. Yet the information available for decisions may be limited and uncertain without clear choices. When errors are made, providers of care may be held legally responsible if their decisions result in harm to the client.[12, 143]

Accessibility and Utility of Home Care

Home care is inaccessible or very limited in some smaller communities, inner cities, and in some minority communities. Long distances between residences mean high costs per visit, diminishing the willingness of providers to offer services. Inept staff regularly fail to offer good care. Services are occasionally provided to enhance the income of providers rather than for the well-being of clients. Patients and caregivers also occasionally manipulate the system, generating extra costs.[25]

Efficiency and cost control have been increased via the "cluster care" concept—initiated in Sweden. A neighborhood becomes the focus rather than just the individual home. Instead of independent visits to homes, teams of service workers are employed to serve groups of older people. Team members prepare meals for groups rather than for each home. Shopping is undertaken for several individuals by one chore aide. Nurses will visit several households in one trip. The cost of providing services to each home is thus lowered while maintaining wide access.[14, 44]

Federal Cutbacks. Evidence of operational problems, coupled with efforts to economize on Medicare costs, led to major cuts in federal allocations for home care beginning in 1997. The cutbacks seriously compromised access for some 700,000 older individuals who had come to depend on the services. Many home health care providers went out of business; for example, in some states (i.e., Utah), half of the home health providers were eliminated in the two-year period from 1997 until 1999. Many of the cuts were restored in 1999 when it became clear that serious damage was being done to the home care system.[164]

◆◆◆ ASSISTED LIVING SERVICES

Assisted living developed very rapidly during the 1990s—with many new jobs for health aides, kitchen staff, housekeepers, administrators, and other workers who provide the basic services. Older individuals and their families have recognized the value of a well-organized and appealing housing and personal care arrangement with privacy, meals, and social services available at lower cost than in nursing homes.

However, most assisted living homes do not provide on-site health care except for a part-time nurse or nurse aid. The focus is on support for activities of daily living. Acute or chronic health care problems require home health services or travel to nearby medical facilities. Projections suggest that as assisted living becomes more developed many residents will have some level of mental impairment, some degree of incontinence, and most will have one or more other chronic conditions requiring personal care.[56, 98, 126]

Payment comes from private resources, insurance, Medicare, or Medicaid, depending on the circumstances of the individual. Until the late 1990s, services were almost entirely paid privately through monthly fees. However, the federal Frail Elderly Act (1991) provided for increased Medicaid payments for lower-income individuals who required support for activities of daily living without necessarily needing daily skilled nursing care. The Act requires case management and state licensing of participating facilities, as well as direct inspections by state staff. The states are not required to participate except at their own initiative.[125]

Assisted living in some European countries is generally more integrated with health services than in the United States. An on-site clinic, adult day care, a public restaurant, information services, and the headquarters for an emergency alarm system are all common features. The services are usually accessible to other older individuals in the community as well as residents of the facility.[126]

Group homes or adult foster homes are generally smaller and less expensive forms of assisted living with fewer services. Most are operated by families who open their private homes to older individuals needing housing and meals but limited personal care. More than 5000 older people in Oregon live in foster homes—at cost-savings of 50 percent when compared to nursing home care. The homes are inspected occasionally by a responsible state agency, and operators must undergo a short period of training in personal care. The range of quality and services is enormous with relatively little regulatory oversight in many states.[22]

Assisted living homes are discussed further in the following chapter on housing.

◆◆◆ NURSING HOME CARE

Nursing homes serve the needs of disabled older and younger individuals who are unable to function independently and who will benefit from 24-hour access to both personal care and skilled nursing assistance. The staff includes full-time registered nurses, nurse aides, rehabilitation therapists, and other support personnel who provide a relatively intensive level of continuing health care.

As of 1996 about 4.2 percent (about 1.4 million) of older people in the United States were residents of nursing homes—a decline from 4.6 percent in 1985. Nonetheless, the actual number of residents grew by 4 percent because of population growth. Seventy percent of residents were women. About two-thirds were supported by Medicaid.[5, 17, 24, 73, 146]

Basis for Entry

Table 6–3 summarizes the primary medical reasons for entering a nursing home, care needs and likely duration of residence.

Roughly 25 percent of residents are of short-term duration; they receive various forms of rehabilitation therapy or are simply convalescing from surgery or serious illness. Another 25 percent are terminally ill and usually remain for less than six months before death. The remainder suffer from serious chronic conditions accompanied by mental or physical disabilities and usually remain for longer periods. Stroke, heart disease, cancer, and Alzheimer's are among the primary medical conditions; as many as 40 percent or more suffer from some form of dementia or other mental illness. Most current residents have two or more chronic conditions and are unable to perform two or more of the basic activities of daily living. Roughly 90 percent of institutionalized older individuals are in nursing homes; the remaining 10 percent are either in mental institutions or hospitals.[81, 166]

During the decade of the 1990s the average age of residents in nursing homes has increased, and they have become more chronically ill. The increase in age and illness has occurred as the proportion of older people in nursing homes has declined—in part as a consequence of the improved health conditions for the younger cohorts. The abundance of new alternatives for assisted living can meet the needs of many individuals who might formerly have had no choice but a move to skilled nursing care.[166]

TABLE 6–3   Types of Medical Conditions, Care Needs, and Likely Duration of Nursing Home Residence

Condition	Care Needs	Likely Duration
Convalescence	Personal care Monitoring	Short
Rehabilitation	Personal care Therapies	Usually short
Chronic condition:		
Disabled but mentally alert	Personal care Monitoring	Long
Cognitively impaired	Personal care Supervision Treatment as needed	Long
Comatose	Personal care Monitoring	Uncertain
Terminal illness	Pain control Symptom management Personal care	Short

Source: Author observations and data from Kane, 1996: 97.

Illustration 6–2 describes Covenant House in North Dayton, Ohio, a typical contemporary high-quality nursing home.

Illustration 6–2
COVENANT HOUSE IN NORTH DAYTON, OHIO

Covenant House is a full-service nursing home with space for 67 residents in an attractive building situated in a park-like location on the northern edge of the city of Dayton. It is a division of the Jewish Federation of Greater Dayton, with some funding support from the United Jewish Campaign. Physical, occupational, respiratory, speech, and art therapies are available to help improve quality of life and recovery from illness. An extensive activities program is available with support from professional staff and volunteers.

Many residents are short-term, recovering from hospitalization or are there for temporary respite. The average age is the mid-80s, and they run the gamut of physical and mental disabilities. A high proportion have some form of dementia. The Arthur Boonshoft Pavilion is a special secured section for Alzheimer's and other cognitively disabled residents. A spacious multipurpose room with exterior views of trees, birds, and outdoor activities is available for special activities particularly appropriate for 11 Pavilion residents. A fenced patio allows them to have regular and safe outdoor experiences. A consistent attempt is made to create a soothing and supportive environment with somewhat greater attention to their needs than is available to other residents. Staff have received training specific to the problems of Alzheimer's disease.

Dr. Arthur Cohn, administrator, indicates that the primary challenges are (1) maintaining staffing levels and quality of personnel, and (2) securing adequate reimbursement from public and private payment sources. There is a shortage of potential employees in the Dayton area (and nationally) who are qualified with adequate knowledge, skills, and caring attitudes. Turnover is high and a constant training program is needed to enhance the capacity of new and current staff. The longest serving staff members are the administrator and activity director who have been there for 20 years.

Payment rates are generally good in Ohio compared to other states, but subsidies from donated gifts are still needed to maintain the facility and provide the range of services currently available to residents. About half of the residents are supported by Medicaid. Medicare is available for short-term medical care depending on the status and condition of the resident.

Consultation and assessment are provided to people in the community who may be considering the need for nursing home residence. The home is part of a larger complex that also includes a community center and day care center for community residents and employee's children.

Sources: Authors' observations, interviews with staff and administrators, Covenant House brochure, 1999.

Changes in Nursing Home Use

Table 6–4 summarizes the changes between 1975 and 1997 for major age categories and by gender.

Nursing home residence has declined steadily in all age categories since 1975 as indicated in the table. As age increases the proportion in nursing care increases, from 1 percent of those 65-74 in 1995, to 4.6 percent of those between ages 75-85, to nearly 20 percent for those over age 85. Men were much less likely than women to live in nursing homes. In 1997 2.6 percent of men and 5.4 percent of women of all ages were in nursing homes. The gender difference is particularly noticeable after age 85, when 22.5 percent of women were in nursing homes compared to only 13.1 percent of men. The proportion of older people in nursing homes has continued to drop since 1995.[113]

These trends suggest that we can continue to expect the *proportion* of older people needing nursing care to decline somewhat but the *numbers* will continue to increase because of the greater population of very old individuals. As noted in Table 6–4, the nursing home population is heavily women, most of whom do not have sufficient income to pay their way and need public support if they are to be adequately cared for.

Projections indicate that between 35 percent and 43 percent (depending on the source of the estimate) of all individuals over age 65 are likely to need some form of nursing home care during their remaining lifetime, despite the small proportion who are residents at a given time. Married individuals are only half as likely to enter nursing homes as single persons. Approximately half of those who enter nursing care will stay three months or less; roughly 25 percent will return home; and 25 percent will die without returning home. Approximately 20 percent to 25 percent will remain residents for 3 or more years. The proportion needing Medicaid assistance increases greatly after age 85.[6, 118, 168]

TABLE 6–4 Proportion of Older Age Categories Who Were Nursing Home Residents, 1975–1995

Age	1975 (percentage)	1985 (percentage)	1995 (percentage)
65 and older	4.5	4.6	4.2
65-74	1.2	1.3	1.0
75-84	5.8	5.8	4.6
85+	25.7	22.0	19.9
Gender Differences: 1997			
Men:	65 and older	2.6	
	85+	13.1	
Women:	65 and older	5.4	
	85+	22.5	

Source: National Center for Health Statistics, 1998: 317.

The Regulatory Environment

Every nursing home in the United States must meet federal and state criteria if it is to receive Medicare and Medicaid reimbursement. The general requirements include: a governing board, a licensed administrator, and specified levels of skilled nursing and support staff as defined by state rules. Infection and sanitation controls are monitored by the state, as are fire and safety rules. Other basic nursing home requirements include: rooms that meet state-defined standards, dietary and nutrition services, medical and dental care, pharmacy services, rehabilitation services, social services, recreation, and laundry. Utilization reviews are required to regularly track residents and services.[112]

Adherence to a list of resident rights is required. All residents are to be fully informed of their right to a dignified existence and opportunity for communication with any chosen individuals and representatives. The specific rights also include protection of funds, free choice of physician, privacy, ability to express any grievances, to receive visitors, and to inspect and secure copies of any personal records held by the facility.[5]

Administrative and Staff Responsibilities

In addition to a full-time licensed administrator, most nursing homes have a part-time medical director who has responsibility for an initial physical assessment of new residents to identify and stabilize acute and chronic illnesses. The goal is to delay progression of disabilities by treating any diagnosed symptoms. The medical director or a personal physician is expected to evaluate patients every 30 to 60 days, although relatively few physicians are willing to provide this level of service. Several disincentives discourage greater physician involvement:[121]

1. Reimbursement from Medicare, Medicaid and other insurance is relatively modest.
2. Cures for chronic conditions are generally not possible; good outcomes from medical care are minimal.
3. Regulations require extensive paperwork and other red tape.
4. Most physicians do not have adequate training for effective nursing home practice.

Because of these disincentives many nursing homes have great difficulty securing qualified and consistent physician services, although the larger and better-funded homes are able to employ a part-time salaried medical director with training in geriatric medicine. In most situations family practitioners from the community provide the required medical care, usually with close assistance and management by directors of nursing, nurse-practitioners or physician assistants who perform on-going assessment and monitoring.[42]

Improved physician practice in nursing homes is facilitated by a technique called "physician practice agreements." These arrangements give physicians a more formal affiliation with the institution, often including a fee schedule assuring adequate compensation. The agreements also require physicians to abide by accepted nursing home practices.[108]

Nursing Services. A director of nursing is responsible for implementing health care activities under the general guidance of the administrator and medical director. Managed care organizations have in some instances formed teams of nurse-practitioners and physicians. A demonstration project in Massachusetts found use of nurse-practitioners to replace many physician services led to good results with 26 percent lower costs and more service to patients.[29]

Many nursing homes have difficulty hiring a sufficient number of well-qualified nurses because of work difficulty and lower pay than in hospitals. This often means that less trained licensed practical nurses (LPNs), licensed vocational nurses (LVNs), and personal care aides do the majority of the work with residents under general supervision from registered nurses. Nurse staffing levels in a high proportion of nursing homes are lower than recommended by the federal Institute of Medicine, varying widely from state to state and from facility to facility within states.[6, 71]

Personal Care Staff. The personal care staff provides up to 80 percent of the direct care to residents and also plays a key role in resident satisfaction and quality of life. Many nursing homes also have great difficulty in maintaining adequate numbers and quality of personal care employees. Wage rates tend to be relatively low and the work is very difficult.[41]

Effective communication with, and care of, residents requires careful in-service training—a continuing challenge given the high turnover rates. If staff members do not understand the needs of residents and do not have the time needed to observe and listen, they are unlikely to provide support for the emotional and physical needs of those in their care. If a nursing home serves Medicaid-funded residents primarily, with relatively low state reimbursements, the quality of staff is likely to be lower than in homes which primarily serve self-pay, privately insured, or Medicare patients.[86, 105]

Mental Health Staff. As noted earlier, the Nursing Home Reform Act (1987) requires that nursing homes with federal funding screen and assess all new admissions and other residents for mental health status and treat those who have some form of mental illness. However, medical directors, nursing directors, and support staff do not usually have mental health training, although some homes employ part-time mental health professionals. Low fees from Medicaid and Medicare are a disincentive for psychiatrists and other mental health professionals to get involved. Inattention to mental health problems because of staff shortages or lack of appropriate training is among the most serious nursing home problems.[3, 97, 139, 141, 155]

As noted earlier, special care units are designed for individuals with serious mental conditions such as Alzheimer's. Nursing homes with such units often have professional staff available who are trained to deal with mental disorders—a critical element in dealing with the unique needs of these residents.[119, 155]

Care Management. Many nursing homes have adopted the care manager concept in which the responsible manager for a resident works with members of the care team—family members, doctors, nurses, administrators, and other professionals—to consider all of the available resources that might help optimize quality of life. In some locations, care management is targeted only to individuals with complex medical and social needs who do not have family or other forms of immediate social support.[11, 98]

Dilemmas for Administrators and Staff

Managing the lives of residents in nursing homes is a major professional challenge for all concerned. The needs of the residents must constantly be balanced against institutional requirements, limitations of resources, and the personal priorities of the staff. Effective training in the knowledge, skills, and values of the care system is essential for effective teamwork—given the potential conflicts over use of resources.

Role Conflicts. There is always a danger that decisions will be made for institutional convenience, or to minimize costs, rather than in the best interests of the resident. Staff members are regularly faced with conflicts between advocacy for the older person, on the one hand, and responsibility to meet institutional priorities and conserve public or private resources, on the other.[39]

High Turnover. Turnover is the primary staff problem in most institutions, as noted earlier. Finding enough personal care aides and nurses is especially challenging. A high proportion of aides come from poor social circumstances where they have usually earned near the minimum wage. The work often leads to frustration and anger, especially when the daily schedule does not go smoothly, perhaps with very detrimental effects on the well-being of residents. Aides tend to have low morale and low job satisfaction. Under these circumstances, meeting state and federal staffing requirements is very difficult for administrators.[156]

Staff Roles and Resident Rights. Staff mistreatment of residents has been a perennial problem in many facilities as a direct result of the problems noted above. The individual rights developed as part of Nursing Home Reform Act of 1987 mandated respect for and protection of residents. Yet about 40 percent of nursing homes were not in full compliance in 1998. Consequently, tougher new rules were initiated by the Health Care Financing Administration in 1999—including fines for violation of resident rights. Unfortunately, the rules are not always fully enforced by short-staffed state regulatory agencies.[17, 32, 36]

Use of restraints is one of the major issues. Restraint may be justified by the need to protect residents from falling, wandering inappropriately, or harming other residents. However, a definite correlation has been detected between low staffing levels and higher use of restraints—even though the federal Act gave residents the right to be free of physical and chemical restraints imposed purely for staff convenience. Although use of restraints has dropped since 1990 and the quality of care has improved, serious problems continue in lower-quality facilities.[17, 36, 96]

Admissions Process and Issues

The prospect of admission to a nursing home is likely to be a traumatic and stressful experience for the new resident and family. The older person may feel a great sense of loss at leaving a beloved home, family, and neighborhood. The family may feel they are abandoning one of their own. Feelings of guilt and uncertainty are very common. Moreover, the financial requirements, regulations, and adjustment to the unique structure of nursing homes are likely to be frustrating. There may be a multitude of practical and ethical issues as well, especially if the move is resisted by the older person.[137, 157, 163]

On the other hand, the decision to enter a nursing home is sometimes viewed positively, especially when based on a conscious affirmative choice because the move is a better alternative than the previous situation. In some cases, the home experience has not been supportive. The disability can usually be better managed in the nursing home setting while the secure nurturing environment may be a net gain in quality of life.[67]

In situations where a major health crisis occurs without warning, family members may be forced to quickly search for an available space—whether or not it perfectly suits the needs of the older person. The family may not have time to research availability and ratings of alternative homes, although such information is usually accessible from Area Agencies on Aging or offices of state departments of health and social services. Immediate medical needs, availability of bed space, and financial capacity may dictate the choice, rather than longer-term considerations. A second move is thus often required after greater deliberation and better understanding of what might work best.[101, 103, 157]

Advance planning for entry to a nursing home is certainly the most desirable approach with the best outcome. A decision to enter a continuing care community or some form of assisted living in advance of a major crisis is often appropriate when there is evidence of a debilitating disability—thus avoiding or delaying the need for nursing home care.[16, 101]

Adjustment to Nursing Home Life

Life in a nursing home has all of the dynamics of other social institutions, albeit with some unique features. Many individuals make an easy adjustment and enjoy participating fully in the social life of the new home. They maintain good humor despite the difficulties associated with their disability and dependence. Many residents have inner strength and enormous resources that have enabled them to survive to an advanced age. With reasonable support, medical care, and a pleasant environment, they can learn to function quite well in the new setting.[67]

Other residents may guard their personal space carefully and may be constantly on the lookout for infringements by other residents or staff. They want freedom and privacy to do what they wish and expect other people to have good manners such as knocking when entering and keeping their distance. They insist on being respected as individuals.[67]

Nursing home life can also mean very limited physical and social activity, leading to further decline in function. Maintaining a pattern of vigorous activity is likely to promote a good adjustment while maintaining the optimum level of health within the range of possibilities. Consequently, many nursing homes have instituted formal exercise programs, including regular walking and other forms of bodily movement, as part of a wide range of supportive activities.[100]

Adjusting to a Wheelchair. The treatment of functional disability by family and medical professionals can make a great deal of difference to self-perceptions and satisfaction of an older person. For example, requiring the use of a wheelchair or walker can be viewed as either a major loss of freedom or a major gain that facilitates better control over social and physical space. A wheelchair can produce a sense of confinement, or it can become a somewhat natural and acceptable extension of the physical self.[144] Illustration 6–3 makes the point.

Illustration 6–3
JENNIFER'S LIBERATION

Jennifer, age 91, had struggled for years with arthritis, bad knees, and an inability to do many of her favorite activities. She reluctantly began living with her son and his wife when she could no longer drive or take care of her own home. A walker became a necessity for getting around the house, to the bathroom, and to the kitchen.

She finally decided it would be preferable to move to an assisted living home with some personal care available. She had a very comfortable room with her own furniture, pictures, TV, and other amenities. However, the dining room, library, recreation room, and many other services were some distance away through long hallways.

After having rejected the idea for years, she reluctantly decided a wheelchair would be easier than trying to navigate with a walker. Her son helped her find a good quality motorized model. She was suddenly able to enjoy the amenities of her larger "home" with much less difficulty, motoring to the library to read the latest magazines, to the dining room to visit with her friends over meals, to the patio where she could enjoy the outdoors, and to entertainment in the recreation area. The wheelchair opened her life to a range of new opportunities that had not been available even at home.

As the illustration indicates, a wheelchair can become the primary device for mobility and may in some sense replace the automobile as a symbol of individual autonomy and control. Owning or having control of a good wheel chair can provide social status and power to the user. However, wheelchairs can also serve as a basis for staff control of residents, as tools to enforce relative immobility, confinement, and dependence, if their use is restricted or the wheels are locked to constrain mobility. Thus, the wheelchair experience can be liberating or confining, depending on the degree of resident disability, resources, and initiative.[144]

The Continuing Family Role. Most nursing homes emphasize the important role of the family in continuing care, sponsoring meetings between the family, resident, and staff, or deliberately defining a specific family responsibility. On the other hand, staff members may inform family members of issues important to the institution but not allow any real opportunity for input. The language of the meetings may tend to be technical, based on nursing home jargon, and may be hard for family members to appreciate. The family may in effect be marginalized and have little influence on the care of their loved one. In these instances, family members and staff may become adversarial, with distrust and dissatisfaction on both sides and with negative effects on care of the resident. There is evidence that involvement of family members tends to shorten the length of stay for many residents.[59]

Unfortunately, some families essentially abandon nursing home residents and avoid visiting what they perceive as a stressful environment. Even though the older person may be sufficiently mobile to attend family holiday gatherings, they may not be informed or invited. Substantial numbers of nursing home residents receive very few visitors and have little interaction with family members

Subacute Care and Rehabilitation

Many nursing homes with subacute care units have medical school affiliations and are associated with geriatric health centers. The goal is to provide both physician training and comprehensive care for frail elderly patients, as described in Illustration 6–4:[1, 31]

Illustration 6–4

VETERANS AFFAIRS GERIATRIC AND EXTENDED CARE CENTER, TUCSON, ARIZONA

The Veterans Affairs Geriatric and Extended Care Center in Tucson was constructed in 1991 to meet the expanding needs of older veterans in the southwestern United States. The purpose is to rehabilitate patients and return them to the community with home care support. The Center provides comprehensive geriatric services, rehabilitation, skilled nursing, adult day health care, home health aide and homemaker services, community residential services, and counseling in homes or at the institution, depending on individual capacities and needs. Planning and coordination are provided by an interdisciplinary team of physicians, nurses, administrators, and student interns.

A high incidence of pneumonia and other pulmonary diseases associated with a very high prevalence of smoking are among the major health problems. Many veterans arrive at the institution in a seriously debilitated state and die within two years after an episode of pneumonia. Others can be rehabilitated quite successfully and enjoy a great improvement in quality of life.

A strong focus on quality of services at this Center led to an excellent evaluation (99 of 100 points) by the Joint Commission on Accreditation of Health Care Organizations and the 1995 Order of Excellence award from the Veteran's Administration for innovative design and programs.

Source: Data from Brunk, 1995: 39–40; Muder et al, 1996: 2365.

Access Problems in Nursing Homes

Availability of space varies widely from state to state. For example, 22 beds were available per 1000 people over age 65 in Florida, whereas Minnesota had 91 beds per 1000 in 1995. Waiting for space was common for individuals wanting to enter nonprofit or public facilities, but for-profit chains usually had openings. Occupancy rates were generally highest in rural communities, where locally sponsored nonprofit facilities are the norm.[46, 73, 88, 152]

Racial and Ethnic Variations. African Americans and Hispanic Americans have a higher incidence of chronic disease and disability, but use nursing homes less than European Americans. One national study indicated that 34 percent of older African Americans with dependency in three to five activities of daily living were nursing home residents, whereas the proportion was 53 percent for European Americans. Elderly Hispanics had higher rates of need for nursing home care but were also admitted to nursing homes at a lower rate than European Americans. It was not clear whether these differences were a consequence of inequity of access, discrimination, cultural preferences, or differences in financial capability. It is clear that culture plays a strong role in use of home care among Hispanics.[8, 161]

A much higher proportion (80 percent) of African Americans were dependent on Medicaid to pay for long-term care costs in 1997, as compared to European Americans (32 percent). African Americans generally have higher dependence on public programs for formal home care as well. They are also much less likely to enter higher-cost facilities such as continuing care retirement communities.[160]

Nursing Home Reform

The United States Congress concluded in 1997 that nursing home costs were rising too fast, with substantial costs associated with ancillary services. Legislation was approved to limit Medicare cost increases and change the incentive system for nursing homes. A prospective payment system was instituted that included all costs—replacing an arrangement that allowed payment for charges as billed. The change had the effect of lowering average revenue per resident as much as 20 percent for some nursing homes. The revenue loss was substantial for large nursing home companies, with potential for lowering the quality of care for residents. Several large nursing home chains went bankrupt. As a consequence, the rules were again changed in 1999 to increase compensation.[76, 162]

It is noteworthy that a recent international study could not identify any relationship between expenditure of funds on health care and proportion of older people in nursing homes, quality of outcomes for nursing home residents, or length of life. Apparently, local culture, policies, and practices in management of nursing home care are more significant than expenditures.[33]

Hospitals and Long-Term Nursing Care

Many hospitals serve a long-term care function, especially in smaller communities where there is no nursing home or occupancy is at the maximum. Skilled nursing services and subacute care are provided within the hospital setting. Use of hospitals as long-term care institutions is common in some other countries such as Japan, where nursing homes are in short supply.

The most common form of hospital long-term care in the United States is the "swing bed" arrangement. A group of hospital beds is set aside for long-term care patients, some of whom may have exhausted their Medicare allocation. Less intensive and less costly support is provided to swing bed patients than is applied in the standard acute care hospital situation.

In other instances, older patients remain in the hospital until space becomes available in a nursing home. When hospital costs are paid privately, the patient or family may choose to continue hospital residency as a preferred alternative over nursing home placement.

◆◆◆ CONTINUING CARE RETIREMENT COMMUNITIES

Comprehensive continuing care retirement communities (referred to as CCRCs) combine all of the long-term care options discussed above in one setting. In the most developed complexes it is possible to purchase a home or condominium and have ready access to home health care, primary care, assisted living, skilled nursing, and hospice care—all integrated in one financing scheme.[140]

Efficiencies are achieved through use of on-site medical, nursing, and support staff for the full range of services. The availability of personal care in a private living unit tends to reduce the use of more expensive nursing home care. More time is spent under nursing care at home rather than in the nursing home setting. Less time spent in the hospital compared to older individuals living in private homes during the last year of life is another positive outcome.[134]

Although CCRCs have existed for a century they have some of the features of contemporary managed care health insurance plans. Three general types of contracts are common:[140, 142]

1. A prepaid lump-sum fee initiates a contract covering housing and health services, with a monthly fee paid for on-going care.
2. Housing and a limited amount of health and nursing care are purchased, with additional fees for any services beyond the contracted amount.
3. Payment on a monthly basis for all services needed.

Communities vary considerably with respect to contract details and services offered. Some have many more housing choices and amenities than others, as discussed in greater detail in the following chapter.

Social Health Maintenance Organizations. The Social/HMO concept is a variation on the continuing care retirement community and was implemented through a national research and demonstration project beginning in 1985. The original goal was to examine whether institutional and noninstitutional long-term care are insurable and cost-effective under a managed care approach and whether or not a model could be constructed that would improve quality of life for older lower-income disabled individuals.

Evaluations indicate the utility of the social HMO depends heavily on selection of participants. One of the studies found that costs are high when a broad range of clients are accepted. If eligibility is restricted so that high-cost patients are excluded, costs are more reasonable. Oregon is attempting to use the Social HMO concept to reduce costs for Medicaid recipients while improving or at least maintaining quality of life, apparently with considerable success, as indicated in Illustration 6–4.[99, 142]

Illustration 6–5
PROVIDENCE ELDERPLACE, PORTLAND, OREGON

Providence Elderplace is a form of continuing care health maintenance organization. The primary goal is to help frail elderly individuals remain independent in their homes as long as possible by merging acute and long-term care. The program is financed through a capitated and integrated funding pool—including resources from Medicare, Medicaid, and private payments. Participants averaged 79 years of age in 1993. About 68 percent were diagnosed as cognitively impaired.

Participants must be in need of long-term care but still be able to live in the community with some home care support. Providence provides community-based health care and long-term care support services through an adult day health center visited by participants three times per week. Services include physician consultations, preventive care, prescriptions, rehabilitation therapies, nutrition education, inpatient care, home care, social services, respite care, hospice care, nursing home care, care management, and transportation.

The functional capacity of prospective participants is initially evaluated by a care manager who recommends a needed level of care. Eligibility for Medicaid-financed nursing home care is available to anyone over age 55 with disabilities restricting three or more activities of daily living.

In addition to health care and long-term care, Providence developed low-income housing with federal HUD funding. Elderplace home care staff provide services to residents. The monthly rate for long-term care was $1349 in 1993, less than half of the state average of $3000.

The demonstration was judged to be quite successful. However, there were some downsides. Geriatric physicians were not consistently involved and primary care physicians were not well informed about the range of services available. Communication between staff and local medical providers was thus somewhat less than ideal. As a consequence, available options were not always pursued for each client.

Source: Data from Gorshe, 1993: 57–59; Newcomer, Harrington, and Kane, 1997: 20.

The Arizona Long-Term Care System (ALTCS). Arizona was the first to create a statewide managed continuing care program for low-income older residents. The system is fully capitated and available for all elderly Medicaid recipients in the state. They must obtain all services through one of fourteen health plans under state contract. (The cost-saving potential of the program is discussed in Chapter 8.)[80]

◆◆◆ THE HOSPICE

The primary goal of a hospice is to allow people diagnosed as terminally ill to die peacefully and without pain while enjoying the highest possible quality of life—at home if possible. Hospice care can be requested by patients, their families, or a physician, when an individual is diagnosed as having six months or less to live. Care may be provided at home, in assisted living homes, in nursing homes, in the hospital or elsewhere. Hospice care incorporates one or more of the other levels of care discussed above, depending on health condition and resources available to the patient.[122]

The first recorded American hospice began at Calvary Hospital in New York in 1899—inspired in part by Our Lady's Hospice of Dublin, Ireland, initiated in 1879. The more contemporary concept was developed in the United Kingdom as a response to the overzealous high technology treatment of dying patients in hospitals and nursing homes. St. Christopher's Hospice in London became the international model for more humane and appropriate support of dying individuals.[136]

A well-known book, *On Death and Dying*, by Elizabeth Kubler-Ross (1969), had a profound impact on public attitudes toward treatment of dying individuals and their families in the United States and elsewhere and served as a major incentive for expansion of hospices. Kubler-Ross emphasized that dying is a normal and acceptable part of life. Other research and education related to hospice operation has become widespread since the 1960s.[52]

Types of Services

The primary activities include routine and continuous home care, inpatient acute and respite care in hospitals or nursing homes, physician and skilled nursing care, symptom control, pain control through prescription of appropriate drugs, medical appliances, physical and occupational therapy to improve function, personal counseling for patients and families, supportive social services, support from home health aides and homemaker services, support for the family, bereavement follow-up with family, as well as research, evaluation, education, and training.[61, 128]

Free-standing hospices are the most common in the United States whereas hospital-based services are more common in Europe. Nursing homes are rapidly adding hospice specialty care services and tend to be relatively expensive compared to hospitals, home health agencies, and free-standing hospices. Hospice services are relatively well compensated by Medicare and thus serve as an added source of revenue for sponsoring agencies. Minority older people are more likely to be served by hospital-based hospices than in nursing homes.[15, 122, 167]

Most hospice agencies (53 percent in 1994) are relatively small, serving 30 or fewer patients at any one time. Only 20 percent of the agencies had 100 or more individuals under their care. Roughly 80 percent of patients were served by voluntary nonprofit groups. Thirty-three percent of patients received services from an organization affiliated with a hospital.[72]

Evolution of Palliative Care

Palliative medicine is defined as total care of the body, mind, and spirit, including the evaluation and management of individuals with progressive and advanced disease. The control of pain is a major focus, as is control of other disease symptoms. Psychological, social, and spiritual care is an important part of the responsibility. An interdisciplinary team is viewed as the ideal approach to provision of services.[47]

As hospices evolved it became obvious that professional training was needed to help guide and supervise care in the home, hospital, or nursing home. The physician specialty in palliative care has grown directly from experience with the hospice movement. Most referrals to the hospice are by physicians.[52, 136]

Once a referral is made the core team usually includes a physician, nurse, social worker, chaplain, the family, the patient, and volunteers. Occasional team members can include a physiotherapist, an occupational therapist, a music therapist, an art therapist, a dietitian, a pharmacist, or a dentist. Rehabilitation through therapy helps to keep the patient functioning at a maximum possible level mentally and physically, given their medical condition.[38, 47, 60]

Public Support

The federal Health Care Financing Administration determined that treatment of dying individuals under hospice sponsorship considerably improved patient well-being without increasing cost. In fact, some evidence indicated that costs could be decreased through less aggressive and less intensive end-of-life care than in hospitals. Medicare thus began financing palliative care in 1982. More than half of patients were supported by Medicare in 1996—some 220,000 of the 450,000 patients served. Congress added hospice benefits to Medicaid insurance coverage in 1986 and included patients in nursing homes. Payment had previously come largely from donations, private payment, grants, and other local sources. In 1989 a 210-day limit was repealed, allowing hospices to accept a broader range of patients.[15]

In 1998 the median survival period after enrollment in a hospice was 36 days, although 15 percent lived longer than six months. Approximately 57 percent of patients had cancer in 1994, while 9 percent had heart disease, and the remainder had other illnesses. Approximately 84 percent were receiving services in private residences, 11 percent were within in-patient facilities, and 5 percent were in other types of homes.[61, 72]

A national poll in 1996 indicated that nine out of ten Americans would rather die at home than in a hospital. Yet, nearly 75 percent of deaths still occurred in hospitals or nursing homes without hospice services. By 1998 about 3000 hospices had been established throughout the United States, making them widely accessible although certainly not in every community.[38]

The increasing rate of Alzheimer's disease means that more families are likely to select hospice care. Roughly 70 percent of Alzheimer's patients remain at home until death. Respite for caregivers of these patients has become one of the primary hospice services.[13]

Hospice care has added a great deal of compassion to the end-of-life experience and has made death much more personalized, dignified, and acceptable as compared to high technology intensive care in hospitals. The quality of life of the patient is enhanced and heroic efforts to maintain life are minimized.[61]

Medical costs for hospitalization during the final six months of life averaged $16,571 in New York City during 1997, while it was only $6000 in Oregon where hospice care is widespread. The national average was $9,000. Studies have demonstrated that Medicare saves an estimated $1.52 for every $1.00 spent. Hospices have been widely adopted as a "product line" by managed care organizations and large integrated health care systems.[7,23]

Integration with Health Care. Some states such as Oregon and Arizona have begun to integrate acute and long-term care programs, with hospices as the end-part of the continuum. The Arizona Long-Term Care System, discussed earlier, served approximately 10,300 elderly participants in 1995, all of whom could receive hospice care. Evaluative evidence suggests the program operates effectively, assures quality, and creates incentives for cost-effectiveness.[130]

Despite the advantages of hospice care noted above, the issue of using addictive drugs for pain control is not fully resolved. Many physicians hesitate to write the prescriptions because such drugs are generally not considered appropriate on a long-term basis except with terminal illnesses.[150]

Many of the values underlying the hospice have much broader application to health care. Comfort and happiness are important to every older person as is willingness of health care professionals to provide care even without a likelihood of recovery. Each individual is treated as a unique personality and care plans are adjusted as patient circumstances change.[62]

◆◆◆ MEASURING AND IMPROVING EFFECTIVENESS

Research has provided the basis for a much improved understanding of long-term care practices—contributing directly to better decisions. Efforts have also expanded to improve information available to the public.

Increasing the Quality of Home Health Care

Measurement of outcomes in home health care is a major challenge. The nature of care makes it difficult to precisely monitor services and overall quality. A measurement and management system has been developed by the national Home Health Quality Assurance Improvement Demonstration project—including an emphasis on most of the major relevant factors.[138]

Standardized use of specific measurements serve as the basis for better comparative judgments about process, outcomes, and overall quality of care. Studies in single locations using variations of these measures have indicated, for example, that fee-for-service home health care appears to achieve better outcomes than managed or capitated home care.[138]

Other studies indicate weaknesses of home care, such as fragmented public policies, uncertain and intermittent financing, inadequate training of personnel, insufficient use of health care technology, and wide variation in quality and completeness of service delivery within and between communities. These findings suggest that quality of home care can be improved through clarification of public policies, more stable and adequate financing, better training of personnel, greater coordination and integration of services, greater use of technology, improved access for those in need and wider uniformity of services among communities. Formal home care can be better blended with greater support for family caregivers, relieving much of the strain from caregiving.[57, 75]

The Family and Medical Leave Act of 1993 was viewed by many advocates as a step in the appropriate direction, providing for greater family involvement in health crises of older family members. The Act provides for up to 12 weeks of unpaid leave each year for care of parents or other close relatives while assuring that the job and benefits will not be lost.

Nursing Home Evaluation

The initial evaluation of new residents in nursing homes requires a so-called "Minimum Data Set" which must be completed within 14 days of admission. If any of the Minimum Data Set assessments indicate a need for further medical or other follow-up, a Resident Assessment Protocol is implemented to further examine the patient and treat the problems.[169]

Quality Improvement. One of the purposes of the Medicare and Medicaid minimum data requirements is to provide for quality assessment of care. State agency measurements and inspections are the primary mode to ensure that the requirements are fully met. Some nursing homes also use the collected data for securing accreditation from the Joint Commission for the Accreditation of Health Organizations (JCAHO).[169]

Indicators are quantified and systematically used to measure nursing home status and progress over time. When combined with the Minimum Data Set, the measures encourage systematic tracking of the condition and care of each patient and the population of patients, thus serving as the foundation of an ongoing quality assessment program for the individual nursing homes, state-wide norms, and national summary data.[64, 84]

Resident Assessments. The American Health Care Association (a trade association for nursing homes) has developed survey instruments to measure satisfaction with long-term care services from the resident viewpoint and from the family perspective. The questions include safety issues, relationships within the care unit, staff behavior, toileting responsiveness, management of the facility, and other important issues which collectively provide feedback into decisions about continuing improvement of resident care.[158]

Admission Assessment. Accurate initial assessment is among the most important ingredients in decisions about transfers from home or assisted living to nursing homes. If careful and comprehensive assessment indicates that adaptation of the home, or a move to an assisted living environment, can avoid nursing home placement, many entries to nursing homes would be unnecessary or delayed, thus saving major stress and cost. Similarly, evidence indicates that transfers from nursing homes to hospitals can be lessened by better assessment without increases in mortality.[37, 120]

Furthermore, recent studies suggest that the number of people using nursing homes could be reduced by at least 15 percent in the United States—a strategy that has already become the pattern in several European countries such as the Netherlands, Sweden, and the United Kingdom. The demonstration projects described earlier suggest that tightly managed home care can substitute for institutional care of many people, while lowering overall costs.[148]

However, some caution is necessary. A recent study in ten countries indicated little consistency between assessment results and nursing home placement. Rather, institutionalization rates appeared to be a result of (1) differences in organization and financing of long-term care services, (2) the amount of responsibility assumed by families, and (3) the availability of nursing home beds. Countries with great financing tended to have more people in nursing homes. If more nursing home beds are available, they tend to be filled. When families assume greater responsibility, fewer people are in nursing homes.[129]

Enhancing Care Management

Evaluation of the care management concept was undertaken as part of the Medicare funded National Long-Term Care Demonstration in twelve sites around the country. The demonstrations focused on the broad population of older people rather than simply those with the greatest needs. Evidence indicated that application of care management led to improved quality of life for participants but resulted in relatively few cost savings. Evaluations in several European countries have more forcefully revealed that care management can achieve important gains in the well-being of clients while also cutting the overall costs. The use of this management technique thus seems clearly beneficial to the long-term care process.[118, 165]

Humanizing the Institutional Environment

Studies indicate that greater care can be exercised to assure the "human touch" that maintains individuality and integrity. Institutions can become very humane and supportive environments if both administrators and staff are willing to adopt the appropriate values. Direct involvement by staff and able residents in designing an appropriate environment has proven beneficial. Resident and family councils have been formed with assured power to influence outcomes. Administrators help make changes effective by demonstrating their support. This kind of participation can of course become a threat to insecure managers and staff who may resist giving up any of their control.[27]

Abundant evidence indicates that involvement in meaningful activities is necessary to preservation of the self-concept and sustaining some control over life. Satisfaction with life can usually be maintained if enjoyment of preferred experiences can be continued at some level.[154]

Diminishing Inequity and Discrimination

As noted elsewhere, Medicaid reimbursement rates are usually lower than for private-pay or privately insured residents in nursing homes. Nursing homes therefore tend to give preference to private-pay patients when spaces are limited and refuse accommodation to lower-income individuals who require public funding. Since Medicaid continues to be the primary source of funds for nursing home care, a strong argument can be made that payment levels should be increased to cover costs for high-quality care, thus allowing equal access to lower-income applicants. However, some critics argue that this would simply increase the profits of private nursing home operators.[55, 127]

Access to appropriate services would clearly be improved if better information were available. Guidebooks have been published in many communities describing the available choices for long-term home care and nursing home care. For example, the American Association of Homes and Services for the Aged, The National Council on Aging, The American Association of Retired Persons, and the Eldercare Locator publish manuals and directories that can be accessed by mail or on the Internet.

Improving Confidentiality and Ethical Treatment

Professionals in long-term care do not always maintain confidences nor treat patients with dignity and respect. Yet, most patients prefer strict privacy about their medical status. Ethical and confidential behavior can be particularly infringed when care is provided by volunteers who may not have had appropriate training.[48]

The General Accounting Office reported in 1999 that one in four nursing homes had serious deficiencies that harm residents. Many are repeat offenders. The number of formal complaints rose 14 percent over the three year period from 1995 to 1997. A court ruling in 1998 levied a $95-million fine against a major nursing home company for negligence in the care of one elderly resident. A series of other lawsuits have taken the industry to task for failing to provide adequate care. Partly as a consequence, many states have passed requirements that nursing home employees be given background checks to detect criminal or abusive records.[18, 109, 110]

Professional Training Improvement

Training of staff is central to improving knowledge, skills, and positive values about long-term care. Many of the noted problems in home care and in nursing homes could be alleviated by qualified administrators and staff. The ever-growing body of research and experience means that continuous in-service learning and skill-building of staff in any long-term care enterprise are critical to effective work in the field.

Because of the increase in the population of older individuals requiring some form of long-term care, many medical, nursing, pharmacy, and other health education institutions are using nursing homes as locations for internships and residencies. The American Board of Family Practice has taken leadership in encouraging such training for family physicians.[42]

Changing Public and Private Responsibilities

The United States and some other advanced countries have been slow to provide comprehensive support for long-term care. As we have indicated, many short-comings remain. For example, the requirement of impoverishment to secure Medicaid funding for institutional care may not be good public policy, if respect for personal dignity of older individuals is an important value. Despite the effort to develop home care and assisted living alternatives which encourage greater autonomy, the proportion of long-term care expenditures going to nursing home services continues to be near 90 percent in most states.[117, 123]

It should be noted that the quality of services and facilities for long-term care vary widely within and among American states. Many states have upgraded standards and maintain ongoing inspection programs to assure that the level of quality meets Medicare, Medicaid, and state-defined standards.[32]

Overall, a more constructive set of policies and funding arrangements would assure more adequate quality of later life for all older people. Actions are needed in the states and at the national level to improve every dimension of long-term care.

◆◆◆ SUMMARY AND CONCLUSIONS

Chronic illnesses and disability are likely to increase as the number of very old individuals increases, leading to greater need for long-term care. The range of alternatives for home care, assisted living, day care, continuing care retirement communities, and hospices has increased substantially in recent decades, as has the number of spaces needed in nursing homes.

Families carry the primary long-term care responsibility although expanded home care services and technology have somewhat diminished the stress and financial burden. Increased support for the role of the family can help optimize the comfort and satisfaction of disabled older relatives while keeping costs for outside assistance somewhat lower. High-quality public forms of support will continue to be needed for those older individuals without family support and/or personal resources—especially for the very large number of older women who make up some 70 percent of the disabled older population.

Serious attention must be given to providing more humane and hospitable nursing home environments for cognitively disabled individuals who cannot manage without institutional care. Increased quality of care is gradually evolving, as indicated by studies of home health care and nursing homes. However, quality ultimately rests on the capacities and values of the professional staff responsible for the care. Improved training, better management, and high-quality information systems are among the primary elements in assuring that effective professional work is achieved.

Preparation for the end of life is an important consideration for older individuals, their family, and friends. The promise of good treatment during terminal illness, through hospice and other supportive programs, can greatly improve the outlook on life for the terminally ill and their families when no hope remains for successful treatment.

Careful attention to all dimensions of the long-term care continuum will mean that fewer of our older citizens are likely to suffer neglect and isolation at this crucial period of their lives. Public policy makers at the federal and state levels have the responsibility to provide guidelines and resources to assure ethical and humane long-term care.

◆◆◆ REFERENCES

1. Aaronson, William E., Jacqueline S. Zinn, and Michael D. Rosko (1995). Subacute Care, Medicare Benefits, and Nursing Home Behavior, *Medical Care Research and Review*, 52, 3, 364–88.
2. Abbey, Carol, Judy Didion, Mary Beth Durbin, Kathy Perzynski, and Rebecca Zechman (1994). Neighborhood Wellness Centers: Collaboration Between Home Care and Nursing Education, *Caring Magazine*, 13 (11), 26–31.
3. Abrams, Robert C., Jeanne A. Teresi, and Danielle N. Butin (1992). Depression in Nursing Home Residents, *Clinics in Geriatric Medicine*, 8 (2), 309–22.
4. Adams, Diane L., Kenneth L. Seymens, Gloria Rookard, and Brenda A. Leath (1997). Home Healthcare: A New Venue for Telemedicine, in Brian Kellock (ed), *World Medical Technology Update 1997/1998*, London: Kensington Publications, Ltd., 226–28.
5. Administration on Aging (2000). *Nursing Home Residents' Rights in the United States,* Online at www.aoa.gov/international/principles/usnurshm.html.
6. Agency for Health Care Policy and Research (1997). AHCPR Research on Long-Term Care, *AHCPR Program Note 4*, AHCPR Publication No. 97-0054, Rockville, MD: U.S. Public Health Service.
7. Anders, George (1997). ZIP Code Is a Key to Course of Terminal Care, *Wall Street Journal*, October 15, B1.
8. Angel, Jacqueline L., Ronald J. Angel, Judi L. McClellan, and Kyriakos S. Markides (1996). Nativity, Declining Health, and Preferences in Living Arrangements Among Elderly Mexican Americans: Implications for Long-term Care, *The Gerontologist*, 36 (4), 464–473.
9. Angel, Ronald J., and Jacqueline L. Angel (1997). *Who Will Care for Us? Aging and Long-Term Care in Multicultural America*, New York: New York University Press.
10. Antonucci, Toni C. (1990). Social Support and Social Relationships, in Robert H. Binstock and Linda K. George (eds), *Handbook of Aging and the Social Sciences* (3d ed), San Diego: Academic Press, 205–26.
11. Atchley, Robert C. (1988). *Social Forces and Aging: An Introduction to Social Gerontology* (5th ed), Belmont, CA: Wadsworth.
12. Aulisio, Mark P., Thomas May, and Mary S. Aulisio (1998). Vulnerabilities of Clients and Caregivers in the Homecare Setting, *Generations*, 22 (3), 58–63.
13. Austin, Barbara, and Pam Melbourne (1990). Hospice Services for the Terminal Alzheimer's Patient, *Caring*, 9 (11), 60–62.
14. Balinsky, Warren, and James F. LaPolla (1993). The New York City Shared Aide Program (Cluster Care): A Model for the Future, *Home Health Services Quarterly*, 14 (1), 41–54.
15. Banaszak-Holl, Jane, and Vincent Mor (1996). Differences in Patient Demographics and Expenditures Among Medicare Hospice Providers, *The Hospice Journal*, 11, 3, 1–19.
16. Barnhill, William (1997). I Was Just Passing By, *AARP Bulletin*, 38 (9), 2, 10.
17. Barry, Patricia (1999). Senate Panel Pushes Reform, *AARP Bulletin*, 40 (5), 7, 25.
18. Bates, Steve (1999). Nursing Home Horrors, *AARP Bulletin*, 40 (8), 9–11.
19. Baumgarten, Mona, Renaldo N. Battista, Claire Infante-Rivard, James A. Hanely, Rubin Becker, and Serge Gauthier (1992). The Psychological and Physical Health of Family Members Caring for an Elderly Person with Dementia, *Journal of Clinical Epidemiology*, 45 (1), 61–70.
20. Bengtson, Vern, Carolyn Rosenthal, and Linda Burton (1990). Familes and Aging: Diversity and Heterogeneity, in Robert H. Binstock and Linda K. George (eds), *Handbook of Aging and the Social Sciences* (3d ed.), San Diego: Academic Press, 263–87.
21. Benjamin, A. E. (1992). An Overview of In-Home Health and Supportive Services for Older Pesons,

in Marcia G. Ory and Alfred P. Duncker (eds), *In-Home Care for Older People: Health and Supportive Services,* Newbury Park: Sage Publications, 9–52.

22. Bennet, James (1999). Foster Seniors, *New York Times Magazine,* August 29, 36–39.

23. Beresford, Larry (1997). The Future of Hospice in a Reformed American Health Care System: What Are the Real Questions? *Hospice Journal,* 12 (2), 85–91.

24. Blair, Cornelia, Mark A. Siegel, and Jacquelyn Quiram (1998). *Growing Old in America,* Wylie, TX: Information Plus.

25. Boling, Peter A. (1997). *The Physician's Role in Home Health Care,* New York: Springer.

26. Bould, Sally, Beverly Sanborn, and Laura Reif (1989). *Eighty-Five Plus: The Oldest Old,* Belmont, CA: Wadsworth.

27. Brown, Roy S., and Michael Spiers (1992). Thoughts on Reform in Long-Term Care, *Leadership in Health Services,* 1 (5), 12–15.

28. Brunk, Doug (1995). Honoring Long Term Care's Order of Excellence, *Contemporary Long Term Care* 18 (12), 34–40.

29. Burl, Jeffrey B., Alice Bonner, and Maithili Rao (1994). Demonstration of the Cost-Effectiveness of a Nurse Practitioner/Physician Team in Long-Term Care Facilities, *HMO Practice,* 8 (4), 157–61.

30. Burnley, Cynthia S. (1992). Caregiving: The Impact of Emotional Support for Single Women, in Jaber F. Gubrium and Kathy Charmaz (eds), *Aging, Self, and Community,* Greenwich, CT: JAI Press, 117–28.

31. Burton, John R. (1994). The Evolution of Nursing Homes Into Comprehensive Geriatric Centers: A Perspective, *Journal of the American Geriatric Society,* 42, 7, 794–96.

32. Butler, Robert N., Myrna Lewis, and Trey Sunderland (1991). *Aging and Mental Health: Positive Psychosocial and Biomedical Approaches* (4th ed), New York: Macmillan.

33. Carpenter, G. I., J. P. Hirdes, M. W. Ribbe, N. Ikegami, D. Challis, K. Steel, and R. Bernabei (1999). Targeting and Quality of Nursing Home Care: A Five Nation Study, *Aging Clinical Experimental Research,* 11 (2), 83–89.

34. Carroccio, Jean, Laura Wilson, Jeff Pryor, Lori N. Marks, and J. Kelly Nippes (1996). A Senior Volunteer/Home Care Agency National Collaboration: Assessment of the Partnership, *Journal of Volunteer Administration,* 14 (4), 29–37.

35. Carson, Verna Benner (1996). Psychiatric Home Care: Evaluating the Present, Envisioning the Future, *Caring Magazine,* 15 (12), 34–39.

36. Castle, Nicholas G., Barry Fogel, and Vincent Mor (1997). Risk Factors for Physical Restraint in Nursing Homes: Pre- and Post-Implementation of the Nursing Home Reform Act, *The Gerontologist,* 37 (6), 737–47.

37. CD Publications (1997). Hospital Rates Drop for Frail Aged Without a Resulting Rise in Deaths, *Senior Health Digest,* September, 4.

38. Christakis, Nicholas A., and Jose J. Escarce (1996). Survival of Medicare Patients After Enrollment in Hospice Programs, *New England Journal of Medicine,* 335 (3), 172–78.

39. Clemens, Elizabeth, Terrie Wetle, Michael Feltes, Benjamin Crabtree, and Deborah Dubitzky (1994). Contradictions in Case Management, *Journal of Aging and Health,* 6 (1), 70–88.

40. Cohen, Carole A. (2000). Caregivers for People with Dementia: What is the Family Physician's Role?, *Canadian Family Physician,* 46 (February), 376–89.

41. Cohen, Joel W., and William D. Spector (1996). The Effect of Medicaid Reimbursement on Quality of Care in Nursing Homes, *Journal of Health Economics,* 15, 1, 23–48.

42. Coll, Patrick (1993). Nursing Home Care in 2001, *Journal of Family Practice,* 36 (4), 431–35.

43. Conner, Karen A. (1992). *Aging America: Issues Facing an Aging Society,* Upper Saddle River, NJ: Prentice Hall.

44. Corbin, Juliet M., and Anselm Strauss (1990). Making Arrangements: The Key to Home Care, in Jaber F. Gubrium and Andrea Sankar, *The Home Care Experience: Ethnography and Policy,* Newbury Park, CA: Sage, 59–74.

45. Covenant House Brochure, 1999.

46. Coward, Raymond T., Claydell Horne, and Chuck W. Peek (1996). Predicting Nursing Home Admissions Among Incontinent Older Adults: A Comparison of Residential Differences Across Six Years, *The Gerontologist,* 35, 6, 732–43.

47. Cummings, Ina (1998). The Interdisciplinary Team, in Derek Doyle, Geoffrey W. C. Hanks and Neil MacDonald (eds.), *Oxford Textbook of Palliative Medicine* (2d ed), Oxford, England: Oxford University Press, 19–30.

48. Dellinger, Anne M. (1997). Legal Requirements for Confidentiality in Hospice Care, *Hospital Journal,* 12 (2), 43–48.

49. Dey, Achintya N. (1996a). Characteristics of Elderly Home Health Care Users, *Advance Data from Vital and Health Statistics,* Hyattsville, MD: National Center for Health Statistics, Bulletin 272.

50. Dey, Achintya N. (1996b) Characteristics of Elderly Home Health Care Users: Data From the 1994 National Home and Hospice Care Survey, *Advance Data,* Issue 279, 1–12.

51. Doty, Pamela (1995). Older Caregivers and the Future of Informal Caregiving, chapter 5 in Scott A. Bass (ed.), *Older and Active: How Americans over 55 Are Contributing to Society,* New Haven, CT: Yale University Press, 115–21.

52. Doyle, Derek, Geoffrey W. C. Hanks and Neil MacDonald (eds.) (1998). Introduction to *Oxford Textbook of Palliative Medicine* (2d ed), Oxford, England: Oxford University Press, 3–8.

53. Edvartsen, Trond O. (1996). Possibilities and Problems in Cross-Country Comparative Analysis of Long-Term Care Systems, in Roland Eisen and Frank A. Sloan (eds), *Long-Term Care: Economic Issues and Policy Solutions,* Boston: Kluwer Academic Publishers, 25–44.

54. Erkert, Thomas (1997). High-Quality Television Links for Home-Based Support for the Elderly, *Journal of Telemedicine and Telecare,* 3 (S1), 26–28.

55. Ettner, Susan L. (1993). Do Elderly Medicaid Patients Experience Reduced Access to Nursing Home Care? *Journal of Health Economics,* 11, 3, 259–80.

56. Fisher, Christy (1996). Spoke Services Expand the Field, *Provider,* 22 (4), 32–39.

57. Ford, Doris E. Dinkins (1994). Home is Not Where the Heart Is: Looming Problems of the Home Care Industry, *Journal of Health and Human Services Administration,* 17, 2, 227–42.

58. Forde, O. Ted, and Sholom Perlman (1999). Breakaway: A Social Supplement to Caregivers' Support Groups, *American Journal of Alzheimer's Disease,* 14 (2), 120–25.

59. Freedman, Vicki A. (1993). Kin and Nursing Home Lengths of Stay: A Backward Recurrence Time Approach, *Journal of Health and Social Behavior,* 34 (June), 138–52.

60. Fulton, Colette L., and Rhona Else (1998). Physiotherapy, in Derek Doyle, Geoffrey W. C. Hanks and Neil MacDonald (eds.), *Oxford Textbook of Palliative Medicine* (2d ed), Oxford, England: Oxford University Press, 819–28.

61. Glasheen, Leah K., and Susan L. Crowley (1998). A Family Affair: Hospice Eases the Way at Life's End, *AARP Bulletin,* 39 (5), 2.

62. Goodwin, James S. (1999). Geriatrics and the Limits of Modern Medicine, *New England Journal of Medicine,* 340 (16), 1283–85.

63. Gorshe, Nancy (1993). An Effective, Efficient Elder Care Program, *Health Progress,* 74, 3, 57–59.

64. Graber, David R., and Patrick M. Sobczak (1995). Nursing Homes in an Era of Health Reform: Implications for the Future, *Journal of Health and Human Services Administration,* 18 (2), 131–42.

65. Greene, Vernon L., Mary E. Lovely, Mark D. Miller, and Jan I. Ondrich (1995). Reducing Nursing Home Use Through Community Long-Term Care: An Optimization Analysis, *Journal of Gerontology,* 50B, 4, S259–S268.

66. Greider, Linda (1999). Caring for Parents from Faraway, *AARP Bulletin,* 40 (9), 14–16.

67. Gubrium, Jaber F. (1993). *Speaking of Life: Horizons of Meaning in Nursing Home Residents,* New York: Aldine de Gruyter.

68. Haight, Barbara K., and L. Julia Ball (1995). Geropsychiatric Nursing Knowledge: A Need in Home Care, *Caring,* 14, 7, 56–59.

69. Halamandaris, Val J. (1995). *Basic Statistics About Home Care 1995,* Washington, DC: National Association for Home Care.

70. Hanley, Raymond J., Joshua M. Wiener, and Katherine M. Harris (1991). Will Paid Home Care Erode Informal Support? *Journal of Health Politics, Policy and Law,* 16 (3), 507–21.

71. Harrington, Charlene, Helen Carrillo, Joseph Mullan, and James H. Swan (1998). Nursing Facility Staffing in the States: The 1991 to 1995 Period, *Medical Care Research and Review,* 55 (3), 334–63.

72. Haupt, Barbara J. (1997). Characteristics of Patients Receiving Hospice Care Services: United States, 1994, *Advance Data,* National Center for Health Statistics, Issue # 282, 1–14.

73. Havemann, Judith (1997). Independently Elderly, *Washington Post National Weekly Edition*, February 3, 35.

74. Heery, Kathleen (1991). The Challenge of the '90s, *Caring Magazine*, 10 (5), 62–66.

75. Hermanova, Hana (1997). New Challenges in Ageing: Home Care, *Disability and Rehabilitation*, 19 (4), 142–46.

76. Hilzenrath, David S. (1999). Nursing Homes Are On The Critical List, *Washington Post National Weekly Edition*, 16 (35), 29.

77. Hogan, Dennis P., David J. Eggebeen, and Sean M. Snaith (1996). The Well-Being of Aging Americans with Very Old Parents, in Tamara K. Hareven (ed), *Aging and Generational Relations Over the Life Course: A Historical and Cross-Cultural Perspective*, New York: Walter de Gruyter, 327–37.

78. Hyer, Kathryn, and Lina Rudick (1994). The Effectiveness of Personal Emergency Response Systems in Meeting the Safety Needs of Home Care Clients, *Journal of Nursing Administration*, 24 (6), 39–44.

79. Imai, Kaori (1998). Bed-Ridden Elderly in Japan: Social Progress and Care for the Elderly, *International Journal of Aging and Human Development*, 46 (2), 157–70.

80. Johnson, J. Russell (1997). State and Local Approaches to Long-Term Care, in Robert J. Newcomer and Ann M. Wilkinson (eds), Focus on Managed Care and Quality Assurance, *Annual Review of Gerontology and Geriatrics*, Vol. 16, New York: Springer Publishing Company, 112–39.

81. Kane, Rosalie A. (1996). The Future of Group Residential Care, in Organization for Economic Cooperation and Development, *Caring for Frail Elderly People: Policies in Evolution*, Paris: OECD, 93–105.

82. Kane, Rosalie, James Reinhardy, Joan D. Penrod, and Shirley Huck (1999). After the Hospitalization Is Over: A Different Perspective on Family Care of Older People, *Journal of Gerontological Social Work*, 31 (1/2), 119–41.

83. Kapp, Marshall (1995). Family Caregiving for Older Persons in the Home: Medical-Legal Implications, *Journal of Legal Medicine*, 16 (1), 1–31.

84. Karon, Sarita L., and David R. Zimmerman (1996). Using Indicators to Structure Quality Improvement Initiatives in Long-Term Care, *Quality Management in Health Care*, 4, 3, 54–66.

85. Kasper, Judith D., Ulrike Steinbach, and Jane Andrews (1994). Caregiver Role Appraisal and Caregiver Tasks as Factors in Ending Caregiving, *Journal of Aging and Health*, 6 (3), 397–414.

86. Kato, Jill, Louise Hickson, and Linda Worral (1996). Communication Difficulties of Nursing Home Residents, *Journal of Gerontological Nursing*, 22 (5), 26–31.

87. Kaye, Lenard W. (ed) (1995). *New Developments in Home Care Services for the Elderly*, Binghamton, NY: The Haworth Press.

88. Kenney, Genevieve (1993). How Access to Long-Term Care Affects Home Health Transfers, *Journal of Health Politics, Policy and Law*, 18 (4), 937–65.

89. Knapp, Marshal B. (1991). Legal and Ethical Issue in Family Caregiving and the Role of Public Policy, *Home Health Services Quarterly*, 12 (4), 5–28.

90. Koff, Theodore H. (1988). *New Approaches to Health Care for An Aging Population*, San Francisco: Jossey-Bass.

91. Konrad, Thomas R. (1998). The Patterns of Self-Care Among Older Adults in Western Industrialized Societies, in Maria G. Ory and Gordon H. DeFriese (eds), *Self-Care in Later Life: Research, Program, and Policy Issues*, New York: Springer, 11.

92. Lee, Che-Fu, and Lois C. Gray (1992). Respite Service to Family Caregivers by the Senior Companion Program: An Urban-Rural Comparison, *The Journal of Applied Gerontology*, 11 (4), 395–406.

93. Lee, Gary R., Jeffrey W. Dwyer, and Raymond T. Coward (1993). Gender Differences in Parent Care: Demographic Factors and Same-Gender Preferences, *Journal of Gerontology*, 48 (1), S9–S16.

94. Levine, Carol (1999). The Loneliness of the Long Term Care Giver, *New England Journal of Medicine*, 340 (20), 1587–90.

95. Levine, Susan (1997). To Grandmother's House We Go, *The Washington Post National Weekly Edition*, 14 (22), 35.

96. Ljunggren, Gunnar, Charles D. Phillips, and Antonio Sgadari (1997). Comparisons of Restraint Use in Nursing Homes in Eight Countries, *Age and Ageing*, 26 (S2), 43–47.

97. Lombardo, Nancy Emerson (1995). Mental Health Breakthroughs, *Contemporary Long Term Care*, 18 (10), 52–56.

98. Lund, Dale A. (1998). Personal Communication.

99. MacAdam, Margaret, Jay Greenberg, Merwyn Greenlick, Leonard Gruenberg, and Joelyn (1991). Targeting Long-Term Care for the Frail Elderly: Models From the Social/HMO Demonstration, *Journal of Applied Gerontology*, 10, 4, 389–405.

100. MacRae, Priscilla G., Leslie A. Asplund, John F. Schnelle, Joseph G. Ousland, Allan Abrahamse, and Celee Morris (1996). A Walking Program for Nursing Home Residents: Effects on Walk Endurance, Physicial Activity, Mobility, and Quality of Life, *Journal of the American Geriatrics Society*, 44 (2), 175–80.

101. Maloney, Susan K., Jeffrey Flinn, Diane L. Bloom, and Julie Andreson (1996). Personal Decision-making Styles and Long-Term Care Choices, *Health Care Financing Review*, 18 (1), 141–55.

102. Martin, Karen, Gary Leak, and Cathy Aden (1992). The Omaha System: A Research-based Model for Decision Making, *Journal of the Omaha Nursing Association*, 22, 11, 47–52.

103. Mastrian, Kathleen Garver, and Cheryl Dellasega (1996). Helping Families With Long-Term Care Decisions, *Caring Magazine*, 15 (2), 71–72.

104. Matthews, Anne Martin, and Lori D. Campbell (1995). Gender Roles Employment and Informal Care, in Sara Arber and Joy Ginn (eds), *Connecting Gender and Aging: A Sociological Approach*, Philadelphia: Open Unversity Press, 129–43.

105. Mattiasson, Anne-Cathrine, Lars Andersson, Larry C. Mullins, and Linda Moody (1997). A Comparative Empirical Study of Autonomy in Nursing Homes in Sweden and Florida, USA, *Journal of Corss-Cultural Gerontology*, 12 (1), 299–316.

106. Mellins, Claude A., Mindy J. Blum, Sandra L. Boyd-Davis, and Margaret Gatz (1993). Family Network Perspectives on Caregiving, *Gennerations*, 17 (1), 21–24.

107. Montgomery, Christina (1992). Personal Response Systems in the United States, *Home Health Services Quarterly*, 13 (3–4), 201–22.

108. Morris, Robert L. (1995). Physician Agreements in Long Term Care, *Provider*, 21 (10), 123–24.

109. Moss, Michael (1998a). Many Elders Receive Care at Criminals' Hands, *Wall Street Journal*, February 18, 1998, B1, B7.

110. Moss, Michael (1998b). Nursing Homes Get Punished by Irate Jurors, *Wall Street Journal*, March 6, 1998, B1.

111. Muder, Robert, Carole Brennen, David L. Swenson, and Marilyn Wagener (1996). Pneumonia in a Long-term Care Facility, *Archives of Internal Medicine*, 156 (20), 2365–70.

112. Mullins, Larry C., Mary F. Mushel, and Odette Hermans (1994). Nursing Homes in the United States: An Historical View and Contemporary Description of Facilities and Residents, *Journal of Health and Human Services, Administration*, 17 (2), 136–47.

113. National Center for Health Statistics (1998), *Health United States 1998*, Washington, DC: U.S. Government Printing Office.

114. Newcomer, Robert J., Charlene Harrington, and Robert Kane (1997). Managed Care in Acute and Primary Care Settings, in Robert J. Newcomer and Ann M. Wilkinson (eds), *Managed Care and Quality Assurance*, Annual Review of Gerontology and Geriatrics, Vol. 16, New York: Springer, 1–36.

115. Norris, Joan E., and Joseph A. Tindale (1994). *Among Generations: The Cycle of Adult Relationships*, New York: W. H. Freeman.

116. Noyes, Line E. (1996). Making a Respite Stay Comfortable, *Provider*, 22 (3), 85–86.

117. Olson, Laura Katz (1994). Public Policy and Privatization: Long Term Care in the United States, in Laura Katz Olson (ed), *The Graying of the World: Who Will Care for the Frail Elderly?* New York: Haworth Press, 25–58.

118. Organization for Economic Cooperation and Development (OECD) (1994). *Caring for Frail Elderly People*, Paris: OECD.

119. Orr-Rainey, Nancy (1994). The Evolution of Special Care Units: The Nursing Home Industry's Perspective, *Alzheimer Disease and Associated Disorders*, 8 (Suppl. 1), S139–S143.

120. Osterweil, Dan, Marla Martin, and Karl Syndulko (1995). Predictors of Skilled Nursing Placement in a Multilevel Long-Term-Care Facility, *Journal of the American Geriatric Society*, 43 (2), 108–12.

121. Ouslander, Joseph G., and Dan Osterweil (1994). Physician Evaluation and Management of Nursing Home Residents, *Annals of Internal Medicine*, 120 (7), 584–92.

122. Petrisek, Ann C., and Vincent Mor (1999). Hospice in Nursing Homes: A Facility-Level Analysis of the Distribution of Hospice Beneficiaries, *The Gerontologist*, 39 (3), 279–90.

123. Polivka, Larry (1998). The Science and Ethics of Long-Term Care, *Generations*, 22 (3), 21–25.

124. Portnow, Jay, Thomas Kline, Marilyn A. Daly, Susan Maria Peltier, Carol Chin, and Jessica Robins Miller (1991). Multidisciplinary Home Rehabilitation: A Practical Model, *Clinics in Geriatric Medicine*, 7 (4), 695–708.

125. Pristic, Susan (1991). Assisted Living in the Spotlight, *Contemporary Long-Term Care*, 14, 2, 40–42.

126. Regnier, Victor (1996). Long Term Care Design: Strategies for Planning the Next Generation of Assisted Living Facilities, *Journal of Health Care Design*, 8 (1), 47–51.

127. Reschovsky, James D. (1996). Demand for and Access to Institutional Long-Term Care: The Role of Medicaid in Nursing Home Markets, *Inquiry*, 33, 1, 15–29.

128. Rhymes, Jill A. (1991). Home Hospice Care, *Clinics in Geriatric Medicine*, 7, 4, 803–16.

129. Ribbe, Miel W., Gunnar Ljunggren, Knight Steel, Eva Topinkova, Catherine Hawes, Naoki Ikegami, Jean-Claude Henrard, and Palmi V. Jonnson (1997). Nursing Homes in 10 Nations: A Comparison Between Countries and Settings, *Age and Ageing*, 26 (S2), 3–12.

130. Riley, Trish, and Robert L. Mollica (1996). The Arizona Long Term Care System, *Journal of Case Management*, 5, 2, 78–82.

131. Rodebush, Peggy, and Kevin Cornish (1995). Subacute Opens Arms to Home Care, *Provider*, 21 (10), 48–50.

132. Rodriguez, Luis (1992). Emergency Response Systems—The Canadian Perspective, *Home Health Care Services Quarterly*, 13, 3–4, 5–22.

133. Rubinstein, Robert L. (1990). Culture and Disorder in the Home Care Experience, in Jaber F. Gubrium and Andrea Sankar, *The Home Care Experience: Ethnography and Policy*, Newbury Park, CA: Sage, 37–58.

134. Ruchlin, Hirsch S., Shirley Morris, and John N. Morris (1993). Resident Medical Care Utilization Patterns in Continuing Care Retirement Communities, *Health Care Financing Review*, 14, 4, 151–68.

135. St. Pierre, Mary (1996). Diversity in Delivery: The Medicare Home Health Benefit, *Caring Magazine*, 15, 2, 10–14.

136. Saunders, Cicely (1998). Foreword, in Derek Doyle, Geoffrey W. C. Hanks and Neil MacDonald (eds.), *Oxford Textbook of Palliative Medicine* (2d ed), Oxford: Oxford University Press, v–ix.

137. Schneider, Robert L., and Nancy P. Kropf (1996). The Admission Process in Nursing Homes: A Clinical Model for Ethical Decision-Making, *Journal of Long-term Home Health Care*, 15, 3, 39–46.

138. Shaughnessy, Peter W., Robert E. Schlenker, Kathryn S. Crisler, Angela G. Arnold, Martha C. Powell, and James M. Beaudry (1996). Home Care: Moving Forward with Continuous Quality Improvement, in Marie E. Cowart and Jill Quadagno (eds), *From Nursing Homes to Home Care*, Binghamton, NY: Haworth Press, 149–68.

139. Shea, Dennis G., Michael A. Smyer, and Andrea Streit (1993). Mental Health Services for Nursing Home Residents: What Will it Cost? *Mental Health Administration*, 20 (3), 223–35.

140. Sherwood, Sylvia, Hirsch S. Ruchlin, Clarence C. Sherwood (1997). *Continuing Care Retirement Communities*, Baltimore: Johns Hopkins University Press.

141. Sloan, Frank A., Thomas J. Hoerger, and Gabriel Picone (1996). Effects of Strategic Behavior and Public Subsidies on Families' Savings and Long-Term Care Decisions, in Roland Eisen and Frank A. Sloan (eds), *Long-Term Care: Economic Issues and Policy Solutions*, Boston: Kluwer Academic Publishers, 45–78.

142. Sloan, Frank A., May W. Shayne, and Christopher J. Conover (1995). Continuing Care Retirement Communities: Prospects for Reducing Institutional Long-Term Care, *Journal of Health Politics, Policy and Law*, 20 (1), 75–98.

143. Smith, George D. (1996). *Legal and Healthcare Ethics for the Elderly*, Washington, DC: Taylor and Francis.

144. Smithers, Janice C. (1992). A Wheelchair Society: The Nursing Home Scene, in Jaber F. Gubrium and Kathy Charmaz, *Aging, Self, and Community*, Greenwich, Connecticut: JAI Press, 237–51.

145. Snider, S. (1995). Long-Term Care and the Private Insurance Market, *Employee Benefit Research Institute Issue Brief*, No. 163, July, 1–23.

146. Spector, Willam D., James D. Reschovsky, and Joel W. Cohen (1996). Appropriate Placement of Nursing Home Residents in Lower Levels of Care, *The Milbank Quarterly*, 74, March, 139–60.

147. Stanfield, Rochelle L. (1996). The Aging of America, *National Journal*, 28 (29–30), 1578–83.

148. Steel, Knight, Alan Rosenfeld, Anna Bissonnette, Marilyn Pajk, and Eileen O'Brien (1992). Home Care as an Effective Option to Institutional Care for the Medicaid-Eligible Elderly Population: A Pilot Study of Cost and Operations, *Pride Institute Journal of Long Term Home Health Care*, 11 (4), 11–17.

149. Sterneck, Joy Gardner (1990). Family Care Giving: What Price Love? *Journal of Long Term Care Administration,* 18 (2), 16–21.
150. Stjernsward, Jan (1997). The International Hospice Movement From the Perspective of the World Health Organization, in Dame Cicely Saunders and Robert Kastenbaum (eds), *Hospice Care on the International Scene,* New York: Springer, 13–20.
151. Stuart, Lettice (1997). *Making the Move: A Practical Guide to Senior Residential Communities,* New York: Avon Books.
152. Swan, James H., Carroll Estes, and Charlene Harrington (1995). Nursing Home Waits for Admission in an Era of Change, *Journal of Health and Social Policy,* 7, 2, 33–45.
153. Tennstedt, Sharon L., Sybil L. Crawford, and John B. McKinlay (1993). Is Family Care on the Decline? A Longitudinal Investigation of the Substitution of Formal Long-Term Care Services for Informal Care, *The Milbank Quarterly,* 71 (4), 601–24.
154. Tobin, Sheldon S. (1999). *Preservation of the Self in the Oldest Years.* New York: Springer.
155. Van Nostrand, Joan F., Baila Miller, and Sylvia E. Furner (1993). Selected Issues In Long-Term Care: Profile of Cognitive Disability of Nursing Home Residents and the Use of Informal and Formal Care by Elderly in the Community, *Vital Health Statistics,* 27 (January), 143–85.
156. Vitez, Michael (1998). Critics: Nursing Home Proposal All Talk, *The Spokesman Review* (Spokane, Washington), August 2, A4.
157. Wackerbarth, Sarah (1999). What Decisions Are Made By Family Caregivers, *American Journal of Alzheimer's Disease,* 14 (2), 111–19.
158. Wagner, Lynn (1995). Key to Quality, *Provider,* 21 (11), 48–52.
159. Walker, Alan, and Tony Maltby (1997). *Ageing Europe,* Philadelphia: Open University Press.
160. Wallace, S. P., L. Levy-Storms, R. M. Andersen, and R. S. Kington (1997). The Impact by Race of Changing Long-Term Care Policy, *Journal of Aging and Social Policy,* 9 (3), 1–20.
161. Wallace, S. P., L. Levy-Storms, R. S. Kington, and R. M. Andersen (1998). The Persistence of Race and Ethnicity in the Use of Long-term Care, *Journal of Gerontology: Social Sciences,* 53B (2), S104–S112.
162. Weaver, Peter (2000). Nursing Home residents Buffeted by Bankruptcies, *AARP Bulletin,* 41 (5), 9, 13.
163. Weiss, Jules C. (1995). Cognitive Therapy and Life Review Therapy: Theoretical and Therapeutic Implications for Mental Health Counselors, *Journal of Mental Health Counseling,* 17 (2), 157–72.
164. Wheeler, Larry (1999). Lawmakers Scrambling to Fix Medicare, *Salt Lake Tribune,* April 4, A16.
165. Williams, Judith K. (1993). Case Management: Opportunities for Service Providers, *Home Health Care Services Quarterly,* 14 (1), 5–40.
166. Williams, Mark E. (1995). *Complete Guide to Health and Aging,* New York: Harmony Books and American Geriatrics Society.
167. Wilson, Marilyn, and Robert Kastenbaum (1997). Worldwide Developments in Hospice Care: Survey Results, in Dame Cicely Saunders and Robert Kastenbaum (eds), *Hospice Care on the International Scene,* New York: Springer, 21–38.
168. Wise, David A. (1994). Introduction, in David A. Wise (ed), *Studies in the Economics of Aging,* Chicago: University of Chicago Press, 1–9.
169. Zinn, Jacqueline S., William E. Aaronson, and Michael D. Rosko (1993). The Use of Standarized Indicators as Quality Improvement Tools: An Application in Pennsylvania Nursing Homes, *American Journal of Medical Quality,* 8 (2), 72–78.

Chapter 7

THE RESIDENTIAL ENVIRONMENT
Neighborhood, Community, and Home

◆◆◆ INTRODUCTION

This chapter examines the effects on older people of the residential environment: the home, neighborhood, community, and local services. Specific topics include:

- Community and service preferences.
- Alternative home arrangements.
- Personal care and/or board and care homes.
- Assisted living and congregate homes.
- Continuing care retirement communities.
- Specialized senior citizen communities.
- The public role.
- Housing and community issues.

As mobility declines, the immediate environment is of enormous importance to older individuals. The home and neighborhood become more of a primary source for basic needs, social life, and recreation. A private home or a group housing alternative should not only meet the need for living space but should have other attributes that fulfill individual personality preferences and contribute to a high quality home life. Adaptation of the dwelling to make disabilities manageable is very important. Services needed on a daily or weekly basis should be available in the immediate neighborhood or accessible larger community.[60]

◆◆◆ COMMUNITY AND SERVICE PREFERENCES

Preferences of retirees have served as primary bases for ratings of desirable community locations. National publications such as *Money Magazine*'s "Best Places to Live in America" and *Retirement Places Rated,* for example, describe the enormous diversity among communities in job opportunities, educational options, recreational choices, social services, health care services, and cultural outlets. The number and quality of services needed by older people vary dramatically from one community to another.[65]

Important qualities of communities are summarized in Table 7–1.

Older people interested in moving to a new location look for communities with good ratings on most of these attributes, although each individual or couple gives greater weight to some categories that particularly meet their lifestyle preferences. For example, those who strongly prefer warmer weather may be more satisfied, at least for part of the year, with a small space in an RV park, condominium, or apartment in southern Arizona than with a much larger home located in a colder northern climate. Those who must (or want to) continue working will try to locate where there are good job opportunities for older citizens.

Preferred Residential Area Characteristics

Many older individuals give priority to specific community and neighborhood features, such as: a well-managed neighborhood and community government, easy access to social and recreational activities, close proximity to shopping, easy access to transportation, availability of resources for maintenance and repair of the home, safety in terms of weather and personal security, and ready access to family and friends.[9, 41, 42]

Other senior citizens benefit from services tailored specifically to their concerns, such as:[20, 31]

- Adjustment and integrative services including senior services programs, structured recreation, retirement counseling, and opportunities for blending with the community.

TABLE 7–1 Criteria for Rating Retirement Communities

- Environmental factors such as natural beauty, clean air, clean water, and access to parks, lakes, and streams.
- Climate, including average temperature, rainfall, snow, and seasonal variations.
- Population size and density.
- Economic status in terms of income levels, cost of living, earning possibilities, insurance rates, and tax rates.
- Housing availability—cost and choices.
- Personal safety issues such as crime rates.
- Services such as health care, education, libraries, and transportation.
- Leisure opportunities such as visual or performance arts, sports, and other outdoor activities.
- Volunteer possibilities.

Source: Data from Fried, Marable, and Nance-Nash, 1996: 66; Savageau, 1995: 12.

- Educational opportunities like Elderhostel and other noncredit continuing education courses, special lectures, and opportunities for personal development.
- Protective services designed to provide security and ethical treatment, especially in the event of disability and limited competence to manage their own affairs.

Geographic Preferences

In a 1997 survey, about 48 percent of older people in the United States chose to live in the *suburbs* of large cities; 29 percent lived in *central* or *smaller* cities; and 23 percent lived in *small towns* or rural communities. This contrasts with younger age groups: 81 percent of those under age 65 live in suburbs and central cities and only 19 percent in small towns and rural areas. The elderly have tended to remain in small towns and rural communities while younger people have departed in large numbers.[3, 23, 71]

Preferred Environments. Clean air and water, green space, and other elements of the environment are very important to good health and longer life expectancy. A built environment (houses, streets, commercial buildings, decoration, etc.) that blends pleasantly with the landscape creates a community and home atmosphere that is satisfying to the senses of older people. This principle holds for interior spaces as well as the outdoors. Assisted living residences, nursing homes, and private homes or apartments with well coordinated plants, interior landscaped courtyards, and even birds or other animals, can help lift spirits and make life more enjoyable for residents.[61]

Aging in Place. "Aging in place" was the clear preference for 85 percent of the older population interviewed in a 1990 national survey sponsored by the American Association for Retired Persons. A U.S. Census survey in 1991 also indicated that 76 percent were satisfied with their present community, and 86 percent preferred to remain in their home community after retirement. Staying in a community of long-term residence usually provides the most independence and social support. Moreover, familiar homes and neighborhoods hold memories of family and personal history. Living in close proximity to family and friends is considered by a high proportion of older people the best means to achieve quality of life.[14, 15, 47, 57]

The Mobility Preference

A change of home is the strong preference for the relatively small proportion of older individuals or couples who place a high priority on travel, better climate, or simply a new environment. Generally speaking, the movers tend to be more affluent, better educated, and healthier than those who remain in the home community. They are comfortable with new environments perhaps because of past travel experiences. Many move seasonally or permanently to a different state or even overseas and view change as desirable and life-enhancing.[20, 30]

The American states vary considerably in attractiveness to older people. The greatest migration has been to the South and Southwest, where the total increases were 14 percent or more in several states between 1990 and 1997. The biggest increases were 49 percent in Nevada, 25 percent in Arizona, 19 percent in Utah, 19 percent in Colorado, 18 percent in New Mexico, 18 percent in Tennessee, 15 percent in North Carolina, 14 percent in South Carolina, 14 percent in Florida, and 14 percent in Texas. There were substantial increases also in Alaska (43 percent), Hawaii (25 percent), and Wyoming (15 percent). Among the northeastern states only Delaware (17 percent increase) was a strongly preferred destination.[3]

Special Retirement Communities. Many older people live in communities designed especially for retirement. Although most of these locations are in the milder climates of the southeast and southwest, nearly every state has some special retirement locations. The construction of such communities has become a major industry in Arizona, Florida, Texas, California, and several other states.[30]

New retirement communities are usually built around or include recreational amenities, such as golf courses, lakes and streams, forests, or parks. Some have been planned to meet the social, economic, recreation, leisure and other lifestyle preferences of particular categories of the older population—such as recreational vehicle owners who move from one location to another during the year (so-called "snowbirds" are one example).[24] In 1998 roughly 1½ million retired people traveled and lived essentially full-time in well-appointed motorhomes, fifth wheel units which attach to trucks, or trailers pulled by cars or pickups.

One example of such a community is described in Illustration 7–1.

Illustration 7–1
THE BIG RIG RV RESORT

Crystal Lakes near Naples, Florida, offers 30 by 60 feet recreational vehicle lots located next to an artificial pond stocked with fish. The lots sold for $25,000 in 1995 but rose quickly to $75,000 in 1998 because of their popularity. Palm trees, tropical bushes, and acres of grass decorate the landscape. A golf course is located nearby; tennis courts and shuffleboard are available on the premises. The Gulf of Mexico is about 20 minutes away.

Most of the owners at Crystal Lakes were from northern states or Canada and live there for all or part of the winter season in motorhomes that ranged upward in price from $100,000—many costing $500,000 or more. In some instances several families who were long-time friends purchase lots close together, transplanting their neighborhood social gatherings, along with their golf or tennis partners.

Crystal Lakes is only one of many new RV communities in the Naples region. Others catering to the diverse lifestyle preferences of Canadians and Americans are located throughout the coastal and interior areas of south Florida. Each is designed for the special recreational interests of a subgroup such as trailer owners, fifth wheel owners, or various motorhome sizes and types. Developments may have lots for sale or rent spaces on a long- or short-term basis.

With few exceptions these snowbirds feel they are living an optimal lifestyle. They love the mobility of motorhome travel, enjoy making new friends, and are delighted to be out of the winter climate up north.

As the illustration suggests, retirement communities tend to be relatively homogeneous, with most residents of similar age, comparable income, and in relatively good health. The environment of planned communities or neighborhoods may appear artificial, compared to most traditional communities, but careful design considerations usually assure that most of the needs and interests of residents are met.

Whether planned or unplanned, retirement communities are self-governing to some degree. Residents work hard at satisfying their social, economic, medical, and recreational needs. They deliberately try to recruit additional residents to advance the local economy and community services. Residents tend to volunteer in large numbers for community enhancement activities, often providing important leadership.

Rural Retirement Communities. Rural communities with high environmental and recreational amenities serve as the destination of retirees who migrate from urban locations specifically to gain access to fishing, other water recreation, golf, mountain or water views, or good climates.[17, 57]

Jackson Hole, Wyoming, near Grand Teton National Park, is a classic example of a high-amenity retirement locale, with outdoor recreation in summer and skiing or snowmobiling in winter, as summarized in Illustration 7–2.

Illustration 7–2
A HIGH–AMENITY RURAL COMMUNITY AS A RETIREMENT DESTINATION

Jackson Hole is the location of Grand Teton National Park and among the most environmentally rich and scenic locations in the world. The mountains and lakes are spectacular, the plant life is abundant and diverse, and a great array of wildlife is readily visible. Two major ski areas are among the best in the West. Consequently, it is a favorite summer and winter spot for hundreds of retirees who love the outdoors summer and winter.

Housing prices in Jackson, Teton Village, and many other locations around the valley have increased dramatically, making it necessary for many less affluent retirees—and service workers—to live across the border in Idaho (over a 10,000 foot mountain pass). Prices are much lower and the scenery is almost as beautiful. Although health care services and the local hospital have improved over the years, highly specialized and high technology medical care is 270 miles away in Salt Lake City, Utah, or elsewhere at a greater distance from Jackson. Nonetheless, the Jackson Hole area is a prime example of a rural retirement living at its finest.

Changing and Reorganizing Communities

Jackson Hole has been strongly impacted by the retirement population. While it began with few of the attributes for retirement living discussed earlier in the chapter, it has gone through a development process based in part on the demands of visiting retirees.

Retirement communities regularly undertake considerable effort to increase the quality and supportive services demanded by their new populations. A formal process has been developed to enhance community problem-solving and develop leadership skills, often with support from one or more outside consultants. Surveys or community focus-group meetings identify needs. These serve as the basis for planning and development that attempt to improve services or enhance the community social and physical environment.

However, other retirement communities do not attempt to provide all services locally. They leave it to the retirees to discover and locate what they need. Many services and vast amounts of information are now available via the Internet and other sources. State and national resources are also well-used, such as the National Park Service facilities near Jackson. Concession services in public land areas diminish the responsibility of local communities. Local government-provided services can be limited and still attract large numbers of older people.

Transportation

Transportation becomes a major issue when disability develops. The capacity to drive safely declines in older age meaning serious loss of mobility, especially if no alternate travel options are available from family or friends. Lack of ready transportation restricts lifestyle choices, reduces interaction with friends and family, and diminishes opportunities for entertainment and recreation. Older people can become essentially trapped in their homes. Many communities, often with state and federal government support, have acted to increase public transportation access for those who remain mobile. Even where available, public bus transportation as the primary means of mobility is not considered satisfactory by many older people. Good transportation is among the most important attributes of retirement communities.[71]

◆◆◆ ALTERNATIVE HOME ARRANGEMENTS

The features and comfort of home influence the sense of personal autonomy, independence, association with family, interactions with friends, and assistance from outside helpers. The 1991 White House Conference on Aging concluded that access to appropriate housing was among the two or three most important elements in quality of life.[6, 7, 22, 41, 42, 58]

The Diversity of Housing Arrangements

The primary options and opportunities include: (1) traditional independent alternatives such as detached owned or rented houses, owned condominiums or town houses, rented apartments, mobile homes or other manufactured homes, rooming houses or hotels, and space in the home, or adjacent to the home, of a close relative; (2) group options such as specially designed detached houses, specially designed condominiums or town houses, congregate rental apartments, age-based mobile home or manufactured home parks, or recreational vehicles located in age-segregated parks; and (3) institutional housing with formal support, such as adult family or personal care homes, boarding and foster care homes, assisted living apartments, nursing homes, and continuing care retirement communities.[2]

A wide range of options is thus available to meet a spectrum of needs, although all of the categories and subcategories may not be available in every community. About 79 percent of the older population owned their own homes in 1997; the remaining 21 percent were renters. Seventy-seven percent of owners had paid off their mortgages. About 84 percent of the owned units are single-family detached houses; the remainder include attached units such as duplexes or condominiums. Ownership varies somewhat by age level: 81 percent for those 65 to 69; 82 percent for those 70-74; and 76 percent for those 75 and older. Roughly 31 percent of older renters lived in publicly owned or subsidized apartments (compared to 14 percent of the younger population). On average, housing costs and maintenance consumed more than one-fourth of incomes for 37 percent of older Americans (compared to 30 percent for the younger population). Costs for renters averaged considerably higher than for owners.[1, 3, 56, 58]

Thirty-one percent of the older population lived alone in 1998. The rate for women was 41 percent, with the proportion rising to 53 percent for women who are 75 or older and 60 percent for those over age 85. The rate for men was 17 percent, rising to 23 percent for those over age 75. The proportions living alone have increased considerably since 1980.[12, 74]

Home Ownership Issues

Owners may have major financial equity associated with homes but at the same time have insufficient income for on-going maintenance and expenses. About 59 percent of average net worth for older people in 1993 was based on the value of their home.[45] Illustration 7–3 is an example.

Illustration 7–3
THE HOME AS HAVEN AND PROBLEM

Sarah is widowed and lives in her owned and mortgage-free home in a small southern city. She worked at low-paying jobs for most of her life and has minimal Social Security income—barely sufficient for food, clothing, utilities, expenses for her car, and other immediate costs of daily life. Home repairs, auto repairs, supplemental medical insurance costs, homeowners insurance and property taxes are dreaded because she has great difficulty paying for them. Fortunately, her children and friends can be relied upon to help with minor repairs but are generally unable to undertake major repairs. Consequently, she is always struggling to keep her financial house in order.

She knows about the potential for a home equity loan, but wants to live many more years in the house without any risk of losing it. She prefers to avoid a mortgage and leave the value of the home as part of an estate for her three children. She fears the day when a major illness, house repair, or an auto breakdown will force her to give up her home and her independence.

A home can sometimes become a burden because of size and the resources required for upkeep, as Sarah's circumstance illustrates. Older homes may be in poor physical condition because they have not been maintained. They may be poorly insulated and expensive to heat or cool. Electrical wiring and plumbing are often out-of-date and even hazardous to health and safety.[46]

Modifications of the home may be possible to improve safety and comfort. Personal emergency response systems, hand-rails, ramps and wider doorways for wheel chair access can be added but such modifications are often quite expensive and not affordable for lower-income individuals. Furthermore, utility costs and property taxes are a major drain on income—although some states have special programs (the "homestead exemption," for example) to help relieve the stress.[29, 71]

Using the Equity. A home equity loan or reverse mortgage may be a potential solution for many older people. Such loans are designed to increase flexibility through transfer of assets from property to pay for repairs or generate a flow of income. A financial institution loans money in a lump sum or on a monthly basis—with the home as collateral. When the owner dies or the home is eventually sold the loan must be repaid with interest, but in the meantime the owner has supplemented his or her income from the home equity.[37, 62]

Special Issues for Rural and Minority Elderly. A higher proportion of rural older people own their homes free and clear of mortgage than urban residents, although the average value is lower. Older and poorly maintained homes are a significant problem in many smaller rural communities. Few alternatives may be available locally, although housing authorities in many small communities have been organized to construct senior housing, sometimes with the help of federal or state grants or long-term low-interest loans.[48, 54]

Home ownership and equity vary considerably by racial and ethnic status. For example, in the United States the value of home equity in 1992 was nearly twice as high for European-American families as compared to African Americans or Hispanic Americans. The quality of housing for minority elderly is generally much lower than for the majority.[5, 57]

Home Rental Issues

The oldest age groups are most likely to need rental housing. Many lower income individuals and couples are seeking space in a very limited number of subsidized apartments—a situation that is likely to get worse as numbers increase. The choices are particularly limited for lower-income elderly in the face of rising prices. More than 40 percent of subsidized public rental units in the United States are already occupied by the elderly.[10, 12, 36]

Subsidized housing is much more extensive in most European countries, in part because housing costs tend to be even higher than in the United States and incomes are not adequate to cover housing and other necessities. The later country chapters provide greater detail.

Residence with a Relative or Friend

As noted elsewhere, a small proportion of older individuals or couples live in the home of a daughter, son, or other relative. In some instances the older person with a home invites a relative to join him or her. These patterns are more common among African American, Hispanic American, and Asian American families than with European Americans, and more commonplace in Japan and Eastern Europe than in the United States or Western Europe.[15, 19, 75]

Adjacent Housing. An accessory apartment or so-called "granny flat" (an Australian concept) is one variation. A small house or mobile home is sometimes located adjacent to a larger family home. The Elder Cottage Housing Opportunity (ECHO) is an example of a living unit specifically manufactured for placement in proximity to a family member home. The older person may live with relative independence or may regularly share meals and social life with the family. The family may or may not provide daily personal assistance. Zoning laws in some communities prohibit accessory units if they are detached from the main house. The adjacent housing concept is widely used in other countries, particularly Japan, the United Kingdom, Australia, and to a lesser extent in Canada.[8, 15, 43]

Home Sharing. Formalized home sharing among non-related adults is quite common, particularly for single women. Household expenses and responsibilities are shared, contributing to a sense of control by the individuals involved. This option is encouraged by the National Shared Housing Resource Center, a provider of information and assistance to interested parties. The usual procedure is for individuals who have extra home space to volunteer for participation. Home sharing can provide informal support of disabled individuals with minimal family involvement. However, compatibility can sometimes be a major problem for two people who do not share basic values and preferences.[15]

◆◆◆ PERSONAL CARE OR BOARD AND CARE HOMES

The adult family home or personal care home is the least formal and most abundant type of residence for modest income and dependent older individuals, as noted in the previous chapter. The usual arrangement is for a family with a house and several bedrooms to care for older individuals or couples who need assistance with food preparation and self-care. Privacy and flexibility are somewhat greater than in a nursing home. The majority of residents are single women or men who do not have immediate family able to provide for them. Most states require a license and uniform standards, although direct supervision by state inspectors is usually minimal. Well-managed homes provide a comfortable setting for individuals who would otherwise have very limited options. Unfortunately, examples of poor management and inadequate care have been widely documented. The costs vary substantially depending on quality of space and services—ranging upward from approximately $6,000 per year.[57]

Boarding and foster care homes are a variation of the personal care home. They often house very low-income elderly on welfare who do not need daily nursing or mental health care. The proprietors usually provide assistance with transportation, shopping, medications, medical services, social services, and activities of daily living. Foster care implies that an older person has been somewhat neglected and is dependent on public support for housing and sustenance. Residents may suffer from dementia or other mental disorders and have limited ability to perform daily living tasks. At least 34,000 boarding and foster care homes were licensed in the United States as of 1990, and many more operated without a license. Roughly ½ million elderly lived in licensed homes in 1996 and approximately 1 million lived in unlicensed homes.[15, 53, 70]

Administration of prescription drugs is among the key problems. Most residents take one or more medications—for depression, diabetes, hypertension, Parkinson's disease, and other chronic illnesses. The drugs are stored in the home and unskilled or poorly trained staff may be responsible for assuring that residents take the medications. Legal provisions are not usually in place to require review by a pharmacist or physician. Even licensed homes are often not closely regulated and may sometimes not be particularly safe.[70]

Nonetheless, board, care, and foster homes are a viable and low cost option for many individuals who might not otherwise have adequate care. The option is much more widely used in some states (Oregon has more than 1450 licensed homes) than in others. Licensing and close public supervision appear to be critical to a successful and safe operation.[49]

◆◆◆ ASSISTED LIVING AND CONGREGATE HOUSING

Assisted living and congregate housing are similar in terms of available services, although different in sponsorship, amenities, and clientele. Both tend to be much larger with more services than personal care or board and care homes.

Congregate Housing

Congregate accommodations are usually publicly financed, targeted to lower income elderly, and consist of large blocks of apartments with support services. They are sometimes referred to as "sheltered" homes because special provisions are made for meeting the needs of disabled older residents. Most are in urban areas. Some of the larger developments are a type of planned neighborhood consisting of high rise buildings. The goal is usually to combine some of the homelike attributes of a retirement community with support services needed by partially disabled individuals.[2, 14]

Most apartments or studios have small kitchens although congregate meals may also be available. Residents can use their personal furnishings and have as much privacy as they prefer. Although they may receive assistance with activities of daily living, 24-hour nursing care is usually not available on the premises. Housekeeping, laundry service, home health care, beauty/barber shops, laundry, activity centers, a library, transportation and other services may be available. Residents can usually come and go as they please.[25]

Most residents are women with an average age of 80 or older. As length of life has increased, the average age in congregate housing communities has been rising, sometimes causing administrators to adjust the types of services to include a higher level of ongoing personal support. As the health of residents begins to deteriorate, an array of home health services is needed if they are to remain in the unit. Many are eventually forced to move to a nursing home. Nonetheless, congregate housing residents exhibit a somewhat lower level of disability than residents of private assisted living accommodations.[16, 50]

Assisted Living Homes

Most assisted living homes are privately financed and are targeted to somewhat more affluent clientele than those in congregate housing. As noted earlier, assisted living is rather sharply distinguished from nursing homes because the level of health care is much less intensive. The emphasis is on a residential atmosphere in which occupants can remain largely independent, with personal support as needed for activities of daily living. Assisted living enterprises are not subject to as much financial and regulatory restrictions as nursing homes, which gives them an advantage in cost and flexibility of operation. Complexes are often built in conjunction with, or adjacent to, independent living apartments to take advantage of economies of shared spaces such as dining rooms, common recreation areas, laundry services, and a landscaped campus.[11, 56, 59]

Proprietors of assisted living homes emphasize that they can provide a private, permanent, and complete apartment for most residents until death, except for possible episodes of required hospitalization for acute illness. This is considered especially desirable for couples when one of them may be more disabled and in need of greater assistance than the other. Health maintenance, physical movement, and mental stimulation are emphasized. Families are strongly encouraged to engage with the residents and staff on a regular basis at meal time and otherwise, and are welcomed wholeheartedly as participants in caregiving, with freedom to visit as they wish.[59]

Successful facilities do their best to give residents as much independence, individuality, privacy, and control as possible. Creation of a sense of neighborliness and community spirit, as well as mental and physical stimulation, are emphasized. A high proportion of residents in well-managed facilities feel content and very much at home, as in Illustration 7–4.[40, 44, 61]

Illustration 7–4
LIFE AT MISSION RIDGE, SPOKANE, WASHINGTON

Mission Ridge Assisted Living was constructed in 1996 with 56 apartments. It was designed for older individuals who needed assistance with activities of daily living but did not require skilled nursing care. The first administrator had a Master's degree in psychology and placed great emphasis on meeting the social and mental health needs of residents and their families.

The apartments consist of either two rooms (usually occupied by a couple) or one large room, each with private bath, kitchenette, and personal furnishings. All meals are served in a dining room under the management of a professional chef. The facility has an extensive and comfortable library, large living room area, exercise facilities, physical rehabilitation room, recreation and crafts room, laundry room, and a large landscaped outdoor patio. A bus is available to transport residents to shopping, cultural events in the city, and for excursions to nearby recreational areas.

In addition to the administrator and chef, the staff includes a marketing specialist, a social activities coordinator, several personal care aides, a kitchen staff, a part-time nurse, and a maintenance person. Physical therapists, occupational therapists, speech therapists, and home health specialists are available on call as needed.

Rehabilitation to improve functional ability is encouraged whenever possible. Maintenance of connections and contacts with the outside community are strongly supported. The social activities director helps organize activities that foster interaction, enjoyment, friendships, and satisfaction with the environment. Residents have a very positive attitude about their home.

A national television network program (*48 Hours* on CBS) did a special segment on Mission Ridge in 1998—because it represents an advanced concept in assisted living. The private sector has been responding to a strong demand and has been able to secure financing for rapid expansion of facilities. For-profit companies managed 80 percent of the available units in 1996. The remaining homes are voluntary and nonprofit, often church sponsored. Financing has come primarily from banks, real estate investment trusts, pension funds, the Housing and Urban Development 232 program, and stock market sales.[18, 27, 50, 71]

Oregon has been somewhat of a pioneer in identifying older individuals living in nursing homes who could function with relative independence in assisted living apartments if given the opportunity—using Medicaid funds for payment. The state was thus able to conserve resources by making better use of lower-cost facilities—saving 25 to 30 percent per move in 1996. The state Medicaid program has begun official certification of assisted living facilities with less rigorous requirements than nursing homes.[40, 61]

Design and Management Principles. Considerable effort is made in the design of new facilities to take full account of the sensual and physical declines that accompany older age. For example, red, orange, and yellow colors are used frequently because they are more readily visible to individuals who have lost some visual acuity. Lights are bright for ease of seeing in rooms and hallways and for reading. Halls are designed for easy walking and wheel chair access. Windows with an exterior view are low enough so wheelchair bound elderly can see out easily. Multilevel buildings with elevators are common in urban areas whereas single-level units are more usual in less dense communities. Most have no more than 40 to 80 units per building.[33]

The Marriott Corporation has used its expertise in hotel and restaurant management to develop a chain of assisted living homes throughout the United States and overseas. The Senior Services Division in Bethesda, Maryland, supports Brighton Gardens University in Florida as a training unit for employees.[11]

Illustration 7–5 summarizes the features of a facility in Chevy Chase, Maryland.

Illustration 7–5
BRIGHTON GARDENS IN CHEVY CHASE, MARYLAND

The complex occupies a six-story building in Friendship Square, a prime shopping center and residential area. The services include three meals per day, all utilities, regular health and wellness assessments, round-the-clock emergency response, weekly housekeeping, active social and cultural activities, and local transportation. In addition, various levels of personal assistance are available, including support for activities of daily living such as bathing, dressing, medications, eating, moving about, and incontinence.

Residents have access to a library, living room, dining room, an activities and crafts room, a full-service beauty and barber shop, and a landscaped courtyard for outdoor enjoyment. A Special Care Center is available with secured residential units for individuals with Alzheimer's and related dementia or mental health problems.

The staff is carefully selected for knowledge, skills, values, and attitudes that are positive and supportive of older people. The general atmosphere is upbeat and the staff attempts to create an environment that is comfortable and secure. Senior staff attend regular training seminars at Brighton Gardens University and elsewhere, where they learn about the company philosophy and basic skills needed for effective management.

Brighton Gardens is a relatively upscale and expensive accommodation, although it is by no means the most costly. Many larger complexes have a range of units with varied quality and prices. Most exclude applicants who suffer from the most serious mental disorders or who have other chronic ailments that require continuous nursing care. They do not attempt to compete with skilled nursing facilities in this respect.[18]

However, increased emphasis has been focused on accommodating individuals with mental disabilities when they do not need daily skilled nursing care. In the more specialized facilities, support staff may include case managers, resident counselors, psychiatric nurses, and psychiatrists who play a crucial role in enabling residents to remain in supported apartments. Although the level of required support is relatively high and expensive, it provides a higher level of choice and greater freedom for residents than would be the case in nursing homes or psychiatric hospitals.[67]

Quality Control. The American Health Care Association (AHCA), a professional association of assisted living facilities, established a Quality Initiative for Assisted Living in 1996. The goal is to measure specific outcomes and customer satisfaction levels as devices for establishing quality standards. The Association would prefer to self-regulate quality levels and avoid public regulation as much as possible.[28]

◆◆◆ CONTINUING CARE RETIREMENT COMMUNITIES

Continuing Care Retirement Communities (CCRCs) attempt to incorporate the full range of housing needs for older people in one comprehensive grouping of residences: (1) independent living apartments or condominiums for minimally disabled couples or individuals, with available maintenance, home care, and dining services; (2) assisted living units for those who need some regular assistance with daily living, accompanied by maintenance, recreation, social services, and dining services; (3) skilled nursing units for those who are disabled enough to need various degrees of daily health care support; (4) comprehensive rehabilitation facilities and home health services; (5) on-site medical clinics with part-time staff; and occasionally (6) on-site training and/or research programs undertaken in association with a nearby university.[52, 66]

The spectrum of services is tailored to meet changing resident needs. Community members can move from one form of housing to another as their health status and mobility change over time. Dining services, household maintenance, personal care, recreation, rehabilitation, and social services are accessible in most communities. Physician and hospital services are separately provided under contracts with nearby clinics and hospitals except in large complexes that may have an on-site medical director. The arrangement provides a reasonably comprehensive form of managed housing and managed health care in one package.[26, 66, 68]

Residents of CCRC communities are clearly better educated and more affluent than average. Nonetheless, substantial numbers of elderly Americans can afford the costs and prefer the security of a continuing care arrangement.[15, 68]

Contractual Agreements

The early continuing care retirement communities were distinguished by a long-term contractual agreement between the older person or couple and the sponsoring organization. The contract usually guaranteed accommodations, health care, and support services until the end of life in exchange for an entrance fee and monthly payments. As noted in the previous chapter, contracts vary considerably, from a guarantee of housing and health care for life under any health circumstances, or full housing and a guarantee of health care up to a defined limit, or monthly rental fees for housing and a monthly health insurance fee.[68]

The advance fee arrangements are referred to variously as "lifecare contracts," "life lease contracts," or "self-insurance for life." The initial fee implements the contract, varying in value by the size and amenities of the living space as well as life expectancy. Restrictions on who will be accepted are common. Individuals who apply for admission at very advanced ages or with poor health, for example, may be excluded.[63, 68]

The risk is obviously lower for the facility when the contract is based only on required monthly payments; the risk is transferred from the proprietor to the resident. This allows fees to be increased as costs for housing and health care rise—an arrangement much like assisted living. The elderly person retains the funds that would otherwise go to pay the advance fee, and thus has more long-term flexibility in the event the continuing care arrangement is not satisfactory. This lower-risk option has become much more popular in the 1990s since it provides greater freedom and less risk to both the sponsoring organization and the resident.[38]

Regulation

Legal standards and requirements are not uniform among states, although the skilled nursing component is usually regulated by the same state unit responsible for other nursing homes. The communities are represented at the national level by the American Association of Homes and Services for the Aging (AAHSA)—which prepares directories (i.e., *National Continuing Care Directory*), consumer guides, model regulations, and accreditation standards.[66, 69]

Illustration 7–6 describes two continuing care retirement communities.

Illustration 7–6
CONTINUING CARE RETIREMENT COMMUNITIES IN CHARLOTTESVILLE, VIRGINIA

Charlottesville (population 42,400 in 1998) is one of the preferred retirement communities in the mid-Atlantic region and is the home of the University of Virginia as well as many high-tech private companies. Several major retirement developments are located here.

University Village. The village consists of 97 upscale condominiums in a six-story building that opened in 1991 with sponsorship by the Holiday Retirement Corporation. Life Care Retirement Corporation was responsible for design of health care services. A second wing was added in 1993. Residents are expected to be age 62 or older, although some units are owned by younger individuals. The building overlooks the city to the east and the mountains to the West—with a truly spectacular setting. Many amenities are immediately available, including a large indoor swimming pool, large dining room, spacious library, medical clinic, and spacious lounge areas. The building and service system are designed to optimize independence.

Each unit has an electric call button and electronic motion monitor as emergency devices to call for help. An in-house registered nurse responds to daily medical needs, and a certified nursing assistant is available to help with activities of daily living. Weekly visits by a staff physician from the University of Virginia enable residents to secure primary medical care on-site.

All services are covered by monthly fees that vary depending on size of living unit. The fee includes all utilities and maintenance. Guest bedrooms are available for visitors. The Village is self-governing with unit owners elected to the board of directors. A finance committee is responsible for the economic viability of the community. A Manor House assisted living facility was recently constructed next door to provide adult day care, an Alzheimer's wing, and other support services for residents who need assistance not available in the condominium building.

Residents are generally a very sophisticated group, many with graduate degrees. Authors and artists abound. They take a very active part in organizing and participating in activities within the neighborhood and in the larger community of Charlottesville.

The Colonnades. The University of Virginia Foundation has created a Senior Living Community in the form of a 59-acre planned-unit development at the edge of the city—managed by Marriott Senior Living Services. The community has a full range of continuing care services, ranging from independent living apartments (180 in 1997), cottages (49), assisted living apartments (44), skilled nursing beds (54), and a primary health care clinic with full medical services.

The Marriott philosophy is to maintain maximum independence and dignity for each resident by encouraging good health practices, good nutrition, physical and social activity, and rehabilitation for anyone who suffers from disabilities. The staff attempts to make each resident feel secure and well cared for—with freedom of choice, privacy, personal security, comfort, convenience, and personalized attention.

Residents receive complete maintenance services for their cottage or apartment, daily meals if they choose, local transportation, financial services, cultural events, medical care, and access to social activities. A program of social and educational events is available to all residents. An extensive library provides books, magazines, and other reading material. There is an arts and crafts room, a swimming pool, walking trails, and an exercise room.

In-home personal and health care services are provided to all residents of the independent living apartments and cottages—including nurse assessments, medication assistance, blood pressure checks, help with daily activities like bathing, dressing, bed making, shopping, errands, meal preparation, housekeeping, and even companionship. When independent living is no longer possible, residents can move to the assisted living or skilled nursing units for more intensive assistance.

A secured Special Care Center serves the needs of residents with dementia and their families. An effort is made to compensate for the mental and physical losses by providing a homelike setting that minimizes the possibility for confusion and anxiety. Staff is specially trained to work with Alzheimer's patients and families.

Continuing care retirement communities have proven sufficiently successful to be widely adopted as a solution to housing problems of the disabled elderly. Individuals or couples can age in place. Most residents appear to be quite satisfied with the experience.[66]

Individuals and families attracted to continuing care communities are likely to have serious health problems at the time of entry. Many healthy older individuals do not like the idea of establishing permanent residence in a community of mostly elderly and disabled residents. Others strongly prefer daily contact with a range of ages and may not find such communities appealing.[32, 38, 68, 69]

The financial commitment necessary to join a continuing care community with a substantial up-front fee requires confidence in long-term viability of the arrangement. The fee "guarantees" the contracted services but does not assure the financial viability of the company nor necessarily provide for any refundable equity when costs are greater than anticipated or management is inadequate. Occasionally adequate quality control has been a problem.[66]

◆◆◆ NURSING HOMES

Although nursing homes are not usually considered to be "housing" as much as health care facilities, they were the permanent or temporary residence for about 4.1 percent of the older population in 1998. Many public and private proprietors work very hard to make them as homelike as possible under the circumstances. As noted in Chapter 6, nursing homes vary in size, quality, and complexity—with resident costs changing accordingly.[1]

◆◆◆ SPECIALIZED SENIOR CITIZEN COMMUNITIES

A great variety of specialized housing for older citizens has evolved over recent years, including condominiums, cooperative apartments, real estate developments in nearly every state, and innumerable other variations. Charleston, South Carolina, has initiated an interesting approach combining downtown renovation with creation of senior apartments and condominiums.[57] Illustration 7–7 offers one example.

Illustration 7–7
SENIOR HOUSING IN CHARLESTON

Charleston, South Carolina, is a beautiful old southern city by the bay. It has become a major retirement destination for northerners from other states and southerners from other parts of South Carolina. In the interest of managing the growth, while preserving classical older buildings, the city government has encouraged various forms of planned housing under the auspices of a public nonprofit organization, the Charleston Affordable Housing Corporation. The Corporation sponsored several groups of new duplexes, specifically for older people, in areas of the city where there was vacant land. They are also converting existing older buildings, including nineteenth century mansions near the bay, to rental apartments. Ten sites with cottages were under development in 1998 for low-income elderly.

Source: Selected data from Editors, 1994: 66, 83.

Cooperative Housing

Cooperative homes are privately owned but may be developed with public sponsorship. Ownership rights and responsibilities are defined through formal agreements. In the best of circumstances this provides for a democratic approach to decisions and a strong community spirit—assuming reasonable compatibility among participating members. Cooperative apartment complexes can be very modest or quite upscale.[43]

Planned Retirement Communities

Many of the nations largest housing development organizations are targeting the active older population by designing and building large communities specifically to suit retirement preferences. Although communities may be planned, they are highly varied, from upscale golf and tennis developments, to more modest mobile home or manufactured home parks. Tremendous choice is available in amenities and cost. Prices can be considerably lower in warm-weather mobile home parks, where insulation and heating are less needed, than in northern climates with cold winter weather. The lower costs in southern climates are among the reasons for migration from the north.[64, 72]

The degree of advanced planning ranges from simple grouping of houses, condominiums or apartments in an urban or rural neighborhood designated for ages 55 and over—with no special recreational or service arrangements—to complete communities with varied housing for several income levels and most needed local services deliberately constructed adjacent to residences. The larger developments are essentially self-contained.

Private Corporate Developments. Corporate retirement communities have been growing at an annual rate of 13 percent. Many of the new communities provide on-site access to a wide variety of daily service needs, including home care, cleaning, and maintenance services, and are in close proximity to senior-oriented health services. For example, The Vineyards, a major planned unit development near Naples, Florida, has services available for full maintenance of houses or condominiums. A unit of the Cleveland Clinic is located adjacent to the property—with a wide range of health services specifically designed for elderly needs. Other planned developments are located nearby and have convenient access to the Clinic.

Many older couples who occupy retirement communities or recreational vehicle parks are using the income from sale of homes to help finance their new homes or high-quality RVs and their comfortable lifestyles in new locations. A substantial proportion of the new residents in the southern United States also maintain a home in a northern community.[72]

Mobile Homes. Pre-manufactured homes with some degree of portability have become increasingly popular—some on fixed sites and others fully capable of being moved at will. Mobile home or manufactured home communities with predominantly older populations have become a popular alternative throughout the United States. They cost considerably less than individually constructed homes or condominiums but still have the virtue of independent living. The disadvantages of assembly-line construction have been overcome to some degree by advanced designs and improved quality control, although quality problems certainly continue.

A wide range of quality and price means abundant choices are available. Some mobile home parks are very well designed and managed, with private ownership of sites; others are of course less desirable. Unfortunately, run-down and tacky mobile home communities largely occupied by older people are all too common.

Manufactured Homes. Manufactured home developments are similarly varied. However, homes and lots are usually owned and maintained by the residents, contributing to greater pride, quality of homes, and attractive neighborhoods. A high-quality development near Spokane, Washington, is described in Illustration 7–8.

Illustration 7–8
COTTAGE HOMES AT THE RESORT

Cottage Homes at the Resort is a 73 unit manufactured home community located in a beautiful ponderosa pine grove near the western edge of Spokane, Washington. An adjacent RV park has permanent sites for year-around living including camping cabins and abundant recreation, including a mini-golf course, indoor swimming pool, playgrounds, games, a large recreation building for indoor activities, and an 18-hole public golf course next door.

The manufactured home park is designed for middle-income retired individuals or couples who have full access to the RV park facilities and golf course. It is secluded, yet only 5 minutes from a freeway and 15 minutes from abundant shopping, entertainment, two major medical centers, and other services and has the benefits of rural living with easy access to urban amenities.

Recreational Vehicles. The number of retired full-time recreational vehicle users is increasing rapidly, estimated at 1½ million in 1998. Cost and size of RVs varies widely, from small vans to 45-foot deluxe motorhomes with great lifestyle diversity. Many couples and single individuals travel in the southern states in winter and in the northern states during the summer. Others have a headquarters in the north or south or both and spend most of their time in one or the other of these locations with relatively little on-going travel. RV parks designed for each of these choices are springing up in desirable locations throughout the north and south. (Such lifestyle alternatives are discussed further in Chapter 9).

Hotel Living

Hotels are an option for older couples or individuals who are comfortable in a single room or small apartment. Most are renovated older buildings in downtown areas that appeal to renters who find an inner-city or small-town lifestyle desirable. Old hotels in high-cost real estate areas have been converted to very desirable condominiums.

Modest hotels with limited renovation (sometimes referred to as Single Room Occupancy hotels) in small towns and urban centers are usually low-cost and often somewhat run-down. A high proportion of residents are single low-income older men or women, many on welfare or minimal Social Security. The building residents sometimes include drug addicts, alcoholics, mentally ill younger men or women, and others whose behavior can be very disruptive. Rooms may have minimal kitchen facilities and shared bathrooms.

Nonetheless, poor and sometimes mentally ill older people would be at risk for homelessness without access to these types of accommodations. A substantial proportion of residents choose to stay in these buildings even if offered a better alternative. They like the familiarity of the location, closeness to services, and the friends among their neighbors.[7, 62]

◆◆◆ THE PUBLIC ROLE IN HOUSING

Most federal, state, and local public housing programs focus primarily on individuals with special needs, through a series of important federal initiatives. Although the 1937 Housing Act established the concept of federally sponsored public housing, a 1959 National Housing Act expanded the options, including: Section 202 creating a direct-loan program for private developers of rental housing for the elderly (suspended in 1969 and reinstated in 1974); Section 231 creating mortgage insurance for subsidized and unsubsidized rental housing; Section 232 providing insurance for loans to construct or rehabilitate nursing homes and other long-term care units.[56]

In 1962 Congress authorized the Farmers Home Administration to initiate Section 515 for rural and small town cooperative and rental housing projects, many for older people. The 1974 Housing and Community Development Act reinstated Section 202 to encourage independent living by providing direct loans for construction and operation of nonprofit multifamily housing projects. Section 8 provided housing subsidies to lower income elderly who qualify.[7]

The 1978 Amendments to the Housing and Community Development Act provided for Congregate Housing Services Programs as well as repair and rehabilitation of existing private homes. In 1987 Congress made congregate housing for the elderly a permanent federal program, but with modest funding of $5.4 million in 1989. By

1987 when the congregate housing act was passed, about 44 percent of all public housing units were occupied by the elderly. The National Affordable Housing Act was passed in 1990 with the goal of assuring a decent home for every older American family.[7]

The federal role diminished in the 1990s as responsibilities were shifted to the states and private enterprise. Federal support of new nonprofit providers of housing has been cut to one-third of the level in the 1970s. Rental subsidies have not increased. Funds for public housing have increased in some states and localities.[58]

Federal, State, and Local Cooperation. As a partial result of Federal actions, most state and local governments have taken an active housing role. Federal block grants have helped to decentralize and consolidate responsibility for public service delivery at the community level, thus improving local capacity for housing projects while increasing the legitimacy of public programs.[58]

National, state, and local policies support mortgage guarantees and tax incentives for home ownership by older individuals who are able to pay their own way. Many communities have organized housing projects with federal and state support. Local housing corporations have designed and built modestly priced housing with special adaptations for the disabled low-income elderly.[42, 56]

Construction Subsidies. Subsidies are sometimes provided to builders who construct apartments or houses that can be sold or rented at lower than going market rates. Rent supplements and interest reductions make monthly costs manageable for individuals or couples who would not otherwise be able to make payments, as in Illustration 7–9.

Illustration 7–9
LOW INCOME RENTAL HOUSING IN A SMALL COMMUNITY

Winifred is retired and is receiving very modest social security payments. Her ability to manage is facilitated greatly by an apartment in a downtown community-sponsored housing complex for the elderly. The apartments are in a remodeled older building—with businesses on the lower level and living units above with elevator access for those unable to navigate stairs. Residents have ready access to the social activities and services of downtown.

The apartments were built by the local housing authority with federal and state support. Since original remodeling costs were subsidized, resident rental payments cover only the costs of management and maintenance. Winifred is part-time resident manager and pays only about $140 per month (in 2000) for rent and all utilities except telephone.

Other state and federal programs provide for property-tax relief, subsidies for heating and cooling, and home equity loans. High demand with consequent increases in housing prices makes it difficult to sustain low rental rates for private housing.[36]

◆◆◆ HOUSING AND COMMUNITY ISSUES

Re-Defining the Federal Role

Despite the noted public efforts, critics such as the American Association of Retired Persons argue that much more government action is needed to assure a supply of adequate housing for lower-income older families. The number of applicants for public housing is much greater than the supply. Public policy in the United States related to housing has not generally been consistent and sustained, particularly when contrasted with such countries as the Netherlands, Sweden, and the United Kingdom where housing and related social services are considered integral dimensions of the larger social support system. Federal housing support in the United States has been considered supplementary to private efforts or local and state programs, rather than part of a comprehensive set of national housing goals.[56]

Regulation of Housing Facilities

Institutional housing is faced with numerous standards and regulations imposed by states and the federal Health Care Financing Administration for Medicaid and Medicare recipients. Facilities must meet state accreditation standards to remain open. Some requirements are very costly to meet despite their worthy intent. Institutional facilities can apply for national accreditation by the Joint Commission on Accreditation of Healthcare Organizations or the Accreditation Council for Long Term Care Facilities—also with costly performance standards.[15]

Appropriateness and cost-effectiveness of regulations are major concerns of administrators and staff. Many required building codes and performance standards are not viewed as having worthwhile purposes or value to residents, but nonetheless raise costs, increase the burden to staff, and make many institutions less financially viable.

Regulation of private housing for the elderly is minimal in the United States compared to many other economically advanced countries. Developers are generally quite free to construct housing complexes as they wish, within the parameters of local building codes. The market is the primary regulator of housing types.[2]

Home Design and Modification

The physical design of residential facilities is sometimes not conducive to easy mobility of residents. This is particularly the case in older multiple-level units where elevators and hallway systems are not well designed for wheelchairs or walkers. Fortunately, many newer private and institutional homes have been specifically planned for maximal comfort and mobility. Several of the major skilled nursing home chains have invested heavily in architectural and landscape designs to optimize indoor and outdoor mobility, recreational opportunities, and aesthetic pleasure—especially for the needs of mentally confused or demented patients.[4, 73]

Much housing was designed for younger families and is now occupied by older people and not suitable for someone who is physically disabled. Modifications may be needed, such as sloping entryways, wide hallways and doors large enough to allow access by wheelchairs, protective railings, foors with dull surfaces to reduce the possibility of falls, and cabinets low enough for easy access.

Staff Shortages for Assisted Living and Nursing Homes

Recruitment of adequately trained and experienced administrators and staff has been a major challenge and an obstacle to high-quality facilities. A special kind of value orientation and unique skills are needed for success in this kind of work. Relatively low wages for nursing assistants and aides is a primary reason for inability to attract and retain the numbers and quality of needed personnel.

Annual turnover rates have been as high as 60 percent to 80 percent in assisted living and nursing homes. Most food service workers, housekeepers, and aides come with minimal training, even though the nature of the work requires considerable skill and is accompanied by high stress and long hours on weekends and evenings. Managers are being forced to improve working conditions and increase benefits such as health care and retirement plans, ultimately increasing costs to residents.[35, 55]

Housing Demented Individuals

Housing individuals with dementia is a major challenge to both assisted living facilities and nursing homes. Buildings must be designed to accommodate memory loss, wandering, and other consequences of dementia. Creation of a homelike atmosphere with easy and safe access to services is one critical requirement. However, complete segregation of residents with dementia is also a problem because of the "stigma" associated with locked units.[60]

Issues Specific to Retirement Communities

A series of issues have arisen to challenge the conventional wisdom about the desirability of older age-concentration in retirement communities. Segregation would obviously not occur, however, if it were not deemed desirable by large numbers of older people. Surveys indicate that most residents of the new communities prefer interacting primarily with their age peers. Age-concentration does not appear to damage older residents or interfere with family relationships.[64]

Older African American and Hispanic populations are underrepresented in most of the special housing categories described above. Most residents of Continuing Care Retirement Communities, for example, are European American women. Income levels obviously play a major role. The incidence of poverty is nearly 2.5 times higher for African American elderly than for European Americans. Beyond that, it is not entirely clear whether minority elderly are underrepresented because of racial discrimination or cultural preference.[13, 34]

Research and Education

Research and education on communities and housing for the elderly are somewhat limited. There is clearly a need for better information. Some institutions such as the University of Florida have purchased nearby facilities as experimental research and teaching institutions. Most of the design disciplines are studying facility and housing needs for older people and have generated excellent ideas and designs.[15, 21]

Further research is called for on the various technologies that can help support aging in place. Many improvements have been made to increase convenience, safety, and communication, and more improvements will come after more experiments are conducted in prototype homes for older people.[39, 73]

The World Wide Web is greatly increasing accessibility of research results for anyone with Internet access. For example, ElderConnect (www.elderconnect.com) offers a database on more than 33,000 housing alternatives, including most of the variations described in this chapter. Similarly, the American Association of Retired Persons has a website (WWW.aarp.org) that includes a guide to retirement housing and communities.[39]

Numerous books, magazine articles, journals, and other sources of information are available in bookstores and libraries (many identified in the reference sections of this volume), and new information is generated each year. Continuing research and development will lead to more abundant and better housing choices for the older population.

◆◆◆ SUMMARY AND CONCLUSIONS

Most older people reside in a community of long-time residence and live in a home which they own. However, the home is sometimes not suitable as they age and one or more disabilities may limit ability to undertake activities of daily living. Major costs may be incurred to accommodate disability and for continuing home maintenance.

Modern facilities and communication systems coupled with home health and help services have made aging in place more plausible than in earlier decades. New forms of housing as alternatives to a private home, such as assisted living and planned retirement communities, grew rapidly in the 1990s, providing a workable and even desirable alternative to both private homes and nursing homes. The quality of nursing homes has also improved considerably, making them much more attractive as places to live.

Greater understanding of the characteristics of frail elderly people has helped with design of housing and community settings to meet capacities and special needs. Affordability, suitability, resources for maintenance, safety, security, and environmental quality are of primary importance. The home is increasingly augmented by a community service system that links individuals to the help they need—when they have resources to pay the costs. Continuing care and specialized retirement communities are widely available in most parts of the United States, especially in regions with milder climates. However, lower-income older people continue to be at a distinct disadvantage with respect to adequate housing and support services.

Public policy in the United States has not consistently supported programs that would solve the housing inadequacies. Federal financial support for housing programs declined in the 1990s. States, localities, and individuals have taken the initiative to fill some of the gaps but shortages of appropriate and affordable housing remain. The future challenge is to strengthen neighborhood, community, state, and federal capacity to provide the housing, environmental standards, and resources that not only meet basic needs but also contribute to an optimal quality of life for older citizens.

◆◆◆ REFERENCES

1. Administration on Aging (1999). *Profile of Older Americans*, Online at www.aoa.gov/aoa/stats/profile/default.htm.
2. Alexander, Ernest R. (1997). Regulation and Evaluation Criteria for Housing for the Elderly: An International Comparison, *Journal of Housing for the Elderly*, 12 (1/2), 147–68.
3. American Association of Retired Persons (AARP) (1998). *A Profile of Older Americans*, Washington, DC: AARP.
4. Anderson, Steve (1996). Administrator of Beverly Health and Rehabilitation Center, Spokane, WA, in a presentation to a Washington State University class on Aging and Long-term Care Administration.
5. Angel, Ronald J., and Jacqueline L. Angel (1997). *Who Will Care for Us? Aging and Long-Term Care in Multicultural America*, New York: New York University Press.
6. Arber, Sara, and Maria Evandrou (eds) (1993). *Ageing, Independence and the Life Course*, London: Jessica Kingsley Publishers.
7. Barausch, Amanda (1994). *Older Women in Poverty: Private Lives and Public Policy*, New York: Springer.
8. Barrow, Georgia M. (1996). *Aging, the Individual and Society* (6th ed). Minneapolis/St. Paul: West Publishing.
9. Bartel, Frank (1998). Elders Resent Housing That Imprisons, *Spokesman-Review* (Spokane, WA), February 8, A16.
10. Bartel, Frank (1997). Senior Housing Rental Rates Skyrocketing, *Spokesman- Review*, December 7, 1997, A12.
11. Bergsman, Steven (1998). Into the Sunset for Assisted Living? *Barron's*, February 16, 35–36.
12. Blair, Cornelia, Mark A. Siegel, and Jacquelyn Quiram (1998). *Growing Old in America*, Wylie, TX: Information Plus.
13. Brooks, Steve (1996). Separate and Unequal, *Contemporary Long Term Care*, 19 (6), 40–49.
14. Brown, Arnold J. (1996). *The Social Processes of Aging and Old Age*, Upper Saddle River, NJ: Prentice Hall.
15. Butler, Robert J., Myrna Lewis, and Trey Sunderland (1991). *Aging and Mental Health: Positive Psychosocial and Biomedical Approaches* (4th ed), New York: Merrill.
16. Cinelli, Daniel J. (1996). Long-Term Care Design: A Revolutionary Prototype for Assisted Living, *Journal of Healthcare Design*, 8, 53–57.
17. Clark, D.O. (1993). Volume and Distribution of AAA Sponsored Services and Service Use by Disabled Older Adults, *Home Health Care Services Quarterly*, 14 (2–3), 175–98.
18. Clark, Dwayne (1996). The Right Stuff, *Contemporary Long Term Care*, 19 (6), 50–55.
19. Clarke, Clifford J., and Lisa J. Neidert (1992). Living Arrangements of the Elderly: An Examination of Differences According to Ancestry and Generation, *The Gerontologist*, 32 (6), 796–804.
20. Conner, Karen A. (1992). *Aging America: Issues Facing an Aging Society*, Upper Saddle River, NJ: Prentice Hall.
21. Coward, Raymond (1997). Director, Institute for Gerontology, University of Florida, Gainesville. Interview with the authors on April 2, 1997.
22. Coward, Raymond T., Chuck W. Peek, and John C. Henretta (1997. Race Differences in the Health of Elders Who Live Alone, *Journal of Aging and Health*, 9 (2), 147–170.

23. Coward, Raymond T., and John A. Krout (1998). *Aging in Rural Settings: Life Circumstances and Distinctive Features*, New York: Springer.

24. Cox, Harold G. (1996). *Later Life: The Realities of Aging* (4th ed), Upper Saddle River, NJ: Prentice Hall.

25. Doyle, Michael J. (1991). Hybrid Approach Offers Option for Long Term Older Adult Care, *Health Care Strategic Management*, 9 (4), 15–17.

26. Editors (1994). Housing Innovations, *Architecture*, 83 (10), 82–87.

27. Fisher, Christy (1996). The Outlook for 1996, *Provider*, 22 (1), 36–42.

28. Fisher, Christy (1997). The Road Ahead, *Provider*, 23 (1), 26–32.

29. Fox, P. L. (1995). Environmental Modifications in the Homes of Elderly Canadians with Disabilities, *Disability and Rehabilitation*, 17 (1), 43–49.

30. Freundlich, Deborah (1998). *Retirement Living Communities*, New York: Macmillan.

31. Fried, Carla, Leslie M. Marable, and Sheryl Nance-Nash (1996). Best Places to Live In America, *Money*, July, 66–94.

32. Fromhart, Stephen G., editor (1995). Which Works Better: A Freestanding Assisted Living Facility or One on a Nursing Home Campus?, *Contemporary Long Term Care*, 18 (3), 33.

33. Godfrey-June, Jean (1992). What Do the Aging Want? *HealthStar*, 34 (3), 55–57.

34. Goldstein, Arnold A., and Carolyn C. Rogers (1993). Minority Population, in National Center for Health Statistics (ed), Common Beliefs About the Rural Elderly: What Do National Data Tell Us? *Vital Health Statistics*, 3 (28), 21–24.

35. Grape, Thomas (1993). Different Philosophies, Services Integral to Assisted Living, *Provider*, April, 55.

36. Grunwald, Michael (1999). 1 BR, No A/C, No Heat: $460/Mo., *Washington Post National Weekly Edition*, 16 (51), 32.

37. Haslebacher, Al (1998). Home Ownership Offers Wealth-Building Advantages, *Spokesman Review* (Spokane, WA), January 11, F3.

38. Higgins, David P. (1992). Continuum of Care Retirement Facilities: Perspectives on Advance Fee Arrangements, *Journal of Housing for the Elderly*, 10 (1/2), 77–92.

39. Howell, Sandra C. (1994). The Potential Environment: Home, Technology, and Future Aging, *Experimental Aging Research*, 20 (4), 285–90.

40. Jacobsen, Ryan (1996). Program Director, Assisted Living Facility in Hayden Lake, Idaho, in a presentation to a Washington State University class on Aging and Long-term Care Administration.

41. Klein, Helen Altman (1994). Aging in Place: Adjusting to Late Life Changes, in Dunn, D. S. (ed.), Psychosocial Perspectives on Disability [Special Issue], *Journal of Social Behavior and Personality*, 9 (5), 153–68.

42. Lawton, M. Powell (1995). Forward, in Jon Pynoos and Phoebe S. Liebig (eds), *Housing Frail Elders: International Policies, Perspectives, and Prospects*, Baltimore: Johns Hopkins University Press, ix–xi.

43. Lucksinger, Melissa K. (1994). Community and the Elderly, *Journal of Housing and the Elderly*, 11 (1), 11–78.

44. Macedonia, Dick (1994). A Time For Transition, *Provider*, 20 (10), 97–98.

45. Malveaux, Julianne (1993). Race, Poverty, and Women's Aging, in Jessie Allen and Alan Pifer (eds), *Women on the Front Lines*, Washington, DC: The Urban Institute, 167–90.

46. Markham, John, and John I. Gilderbloom (1998). Housing Quality Among the Elderly: A Decade of Changes, in *International Journal of Aging and Human Development*, 46 (1), 71–90.

47. McFadden, Daniel L. (1994). Problems of Housing the Elderly in the United States and Japan, in Yukio Noguchi and David A. Wise (eds), *Aging in the U. S. and Japan*, Chicago: University of Chicago Press, 109–37.

48. McGough, Duane (1993). Housing, Chapter 5 in Common Beliefs About the Rural Elderly: What Do National Data Tell Us? *Vital and Health Statistics*, Hyattsville, MD: National Center for Health Statistics, U.S. Public Health Service, 33–36.

49. Mehrotra, Chandra M. N., and Karl Kosloski (1991). Foster Care for Older Adults: Issues and Evaluations, *Home Health Care Services Quarterly*, 12 (1), 115–36.

50. Moore, Jim (1993a). Human Drama Carries Enormous Impact: Consequences of Aging in Place, *Contemporary Long Term Care*, 16 (5), 24.

51. Moore, Jim (1993b). Small Scale Retirement Communities Work: Untapped Opportunities in Non-Metro Markets, *Contemporary Long Term Care*, 16 (4), 76.

52. Newcomer, Robert, Steven Preston, Sue Schock Roderick (1995). Assisted-Living and Nursing Unit Use Among Continuing Care Retirement Community Residents, *Research on Aging*, 17 (2), 149–67.

53. Newcomer, Robert, Karen Brown Wilson, and Paul Lee (1997). Residential Care for the Frail Elderly: State Innovations in Placement, Financing and Governance, in Robert J. Newcomer and Anne M. Wilkinson (eds), Focus on Managed Care and Quality Assurance, *Annual Review of Gerontology and Geriatrics*, Vol. 16, 140–62.

54. Norris-Baker, Carolyn, and Rick J. Scheidt (1994). From 'Our Town' to 'Ghost Town'?: The Changing Context for Rural Elders, *International Journal of Aging and Human Development*, 38 (3), 181–202.

55. Packer-Tursman, Judy (1996). Reversing the Revolving Door Syndrome, *Provider*, February, 50–54.

56. Pynoos, Jon, and Phoebe S. Liebig (1995). Housing Policy for Frail Elders: Trends and Implications for Long Term Care, in Jon Pynoss and Phoebe S. Liebig (eds), *Housing Frail Elders: International Policies, Perspectives, and Prospects*, Baltimore: Johns Hopkins University Press, 3–16

57. Pynoos, Jon, and Stephen Golant (1996). Housing and Living Arrangements for the Elderly, in Robert H. Binstock and Linda K. George (eds), *Handbook of Aging and the Social Sciences* (4th ed), New York: Academic Press, 303–24.

58. Redfoot, Donald, and Jeremy Citro (1998). Independence and Dignity: Housing Directions for Older Persons, *Innovations in Aging*, 27 (2), 24–26.

59. Regnier, Victor (1994). *Assisted Living Housing for the Elderly: Design Innovations from the United States and Europe*, New York: Van Nostrand Reinhold.

60. Regnier, Victor (1997). Design for Assisted Living, *Contemporary Long Term Care*, 20 (2), 50–56.

61. Regnier, Victor (1996). Long-Term Care Design: Strategies for Planning the Next Generation of Assisted Living Facilities, *Journal of Healthcare Design*, 8, 47–51.

62. Roff, Lucinda Lee, and Charles R. Atherton (1989). *Promoting Successful Aging*, Chicago: Nelson-Hall.

63. Ruchlin, Hirsch S., Shirley Morris, and John Morris (1993). Resident Medical Care Utilization Patterns in Continuing Care Retirement Communities, *Health Care Financing Review*, 14 (4), 151–68.

64. Rushlo, Michelle (1998). Builders Target Active Retirees, *Spokesman-Review*, October 18, A16.

65. Savageau, David (1995). *Retirement Places Rated* (4th ed), New York: Macmillan.

66. Sherwood, Sylvia, Hirsch S. Ruchlin, Clarence C. Sherwood, and Shirley A. Morris (1997). *Continuing Care Retirement Communities*, Baltimore: Johns Hopkins University Press.

67. Sohng, Sung Sil Lee (1996). Supported Housing for the Mentally Ill Elderly: Implementation and Consumer Choice, *Community Mental Health Journal*, 32 (2), 135–48.

68. Somers, Anne R. (1993). "Lifecare:" A Viable Option for Long-Term Care for the Elderly, *Journal of the American Geriatric Society*, 41 (2), 188–91.

69. Somers, Anne R., and Winifred S. Livengood (1992). Long Term Care for the Elderly: Major Developments of the Last Ten Years, *Journal of Long Term Home Health Care* (PRIDC Institute), 11 (1), 6–18.

70. Spore, Diana, Vincent Mor, and Jeffrey Hiris (1995). Psychotropic Use Among Older Residents of Board and Care Homes, *Journal of the American Geriatrics Society*, 43, December, 1403–9.

71. Stanfield, Rochelle L. (1996). The Aging of America, *National Journal*, 28 (29–30), 1578–83.

72. Steinnes, Donald N., and Timothy D. Hogan (1992). Take the Money and Sun: Elderly Migration as a Consequence of Gains in Unaffordable Housing Markets, *Journal of Gerontology*, 47 (4), S197–203.

73. Thompson, Ian (1994). Woldeberg Village: An Illustration of Supportive Design for Older Adults, *Experimental Aging Research*, 20 (3), 239–44.

74. United States Bureau of the Census (1998). *National Data Book*, Washington, DC: U.S. Government Printing Office.

75. Wenger, G. Clare (1997). Review of Findings on Support Networks of Older Europeans, *Journal of Cross-Cultural Gerontology*, 12 (1), 1–21.

Chapter 8

ECONOMIC AND FINANCIAL CONDITIONS

◆◆◆ INTRODUCTION

This chapter identifies and analyzes the major economic conditions encountered by the older population and the financial challenges faced by nations as the numbers of elderly people increase. Topics include:

- Economic implications of demographic changes.
- Financial security in retirement.
- Health insurance and expenditures.
- Long-term care issues and expenditures.
- Impact of cost control efforts.
- Impact of fraud and abuse.
- Economic and financial policy issues.

Governments of most of the economically advanced nations have been assuming that retirement at a relatively early age (usually between 55 and 65) was good politics and good policy. Social security, pension systems, health care insurance, and long-term care policies were structured on this assumption. The substantial increases in life expectancy, lowered birthrates, and increases in the older population were not widely understood or anticipated until recently. Consequently, the necessary policy changes in response to the demographic imperatives remain incomplete in the United States and in other countries.[28, 92]

◆◆◆ ECONOMIC IMPLICATIONS OF DEMOGRAPHIC CHANGES

The older population numbers in 1997, plus projected increases by 2030 and 2050 for the United States, are summarized in Table 8–1.

The number of older people will more than double in 30 years. The large projected increases in the oldest and most fragile group, as noted in the table, obviously have great economic significance. Most of those beyond age 85 are women, as noted earlier, many without adequate pensions or supplementary health insurance. About 83 percent of centenarians are women; only 39 men per 100 women have survived past age 85. A high proportion of older women must therefore depend on public support. The demographic shift has already directly affected the size and distribution of public expenditures, with further increases likely early in the twenty-first century.[68, 94]

The high rate of increase in the older population has a number of specific economic effects:

- The income support needed by an increased number of older people will rise substantially.
- Health care and long term care costs will rise significantly.
- The need for various forms of special housing to accommodate disabilities, heretofore supported in part by public financing, is likely to increase.
- The proportion of people at work who contribute to payroll taxes will decline relative to retirees, especially if the early retirement pattern continues, requiring rate increases in payroll taxes to generate the needed revenue.
- Production of goods and services will change in accord with the needs and preferences of an older population.
- Public spending at local, state, and national levels will increase substantially to meet needs that cannot be financed privately.

Increasing Public Expenditures

Payroll cost projections for major federal programs are summarized in Table 8–2.

The projected growth of per capita payments for income support, Medicare, and Medicaid—i.e., payroll and other taxes—is expected to nearly double between

TABLE 8–1   Projected Changes in Older American Age Distributions (in millions)

Age Category	Time Period		
	1997	2030	2050
Over age 65	34.2	69.4	78.9
65-84	30.3	60.9	60.6
85 and older	4.0	8.5	18.2

Source: United States Census Bureau, 1998.

TABLE 8–2   Projected per Worker Costs for Major Federal Programs (in U.S. dollars)

Program	Year			
	1990	2000	2020	2040
Social Security	1340	1388	1862	2316
Medicare	513	544	710	985
Medicaid	333	351	383	485
Total	2186	2283	2955	3786

Source: Selected data excerpt of Table 1.6 from Shoren, Topper & Wise, in Wise, ed., STUDIES IN THE ECONOMICS OF AGING, pp. 25–26. Copyright © The University of Chicago Press. Used with permission of the publisher.

1990 ($2,186) and 2040 ($3,786)—with particularly dramatic growth in Medicare. The increase may be quite manageable if economic growth continues and if longevity does not greatly increase. However, if economic growth declines or turns negative because of a recession, and wages do not rise, the burden on workers could be very substantial.[21, 24]

The federal Administration on Aging direct service programs under the Older Americans Act are likely to increase significantly as well, requiring additional federal taxes. The Department of Housing and Urban Development housing assistance program for the low-income elderly could also rise, as could programs of other federal and state administrative units. The potential thus exists for major growth even if additional benefits—such as further alleviation of poverty and prescription benefits under Medicare—are not added.[24, 60]

Labor Force Effects

About 3.3 people were at work for every retiree in 1998. By 2010 the ratio is expected to drop to 2.9 and may be as low as 2 by 2030. The projected changes thus have the clear potential to significantly increase required payroll and other taxes for older and younger members of the population.[46, 105]

Take-home pay may level off or diminish as has already been the case in many European countries—as more and more resources are devoted to retirement-income support, health care, long-term care, and housing. Upward adjustments in retirement ages and downward trends in benefit levels are already underway in some countries. Tax-based programs intended to provide for elderly populations are in danger of bankruptcy if policy changes are not made. Yet, some economists insist it is quite possible to make the needed policy and program adjustments without undue damage to workers or the economy. Doomsday is by no means upon us, as several of the European countries with older populations than the United States have already demonstrated. However, substantial modifications in public attitudes and values will be necessary.[24, 92, 113]

◆◆◆ FINANCIAL SECURITY IN RETIREMENT

Retirement income trends have been changing steadily over recent decades. For example:[34, 109, 114]

- Standards of living have been rising, especially among those 65 to 75 years old.
- Poverty has persisted for a minority (mostly women) who have earned low incomes or have not worked and did not participate in a retirement benefit scheme.
- Substantial and increasing inequities in retirement incomes are evident.
- Private pensions increased steadily after World War II until the mid-1990s, with considerable benefit to higher-wage workers. The trend has been somewhat stalemated as lower paid service occupations have increased, unions have become less influential, and international competition has increased.

Median income for families headed by an individual age 65 and over rose by 57 percent between 1969 and 1996. Single older people did somewhat better with a median increase of 63 percent during the same period. Gender differences were pronounced: the median income for older single men was $18,166 and for women was $10,504 in 1998. Household median income was $31,568 for families headed by someone 65 or older in 1998, compared to $51,921 for younger families. The median income for all families was $35,172. Only about 10 percent of the elderly are considered high income (more than $75,000 annually), while 17 percent of all families fall into higher-income categories. Approximately 14 percent of older families had annual incomes of less than $15,000.[3, 104, 113]

The sources of income have changed somewhat since 1967—from heavy reliance on current earnings to greater dependence on social security, private pensions, and savings, as illustrated for 1967, 1986, 1992, and 1996 in Table 8–3.[82, 95]

TABLE 8–3   Changes in Sources of Retirement Income (in percentages)

Source	Year			
	1967	1986	1992	1996
Social Security	34	38	41	40
Pensions & annuities	16	16	22	18
Savings and investments	15	26	21	18
Earnings	29	17	13	20
Other (including Supplemental Social Security)	4	3	3	4

Sources: Data from Administration on Aging, 2000; Schwenk, 1993: 20; Ward and Stone, 1996: 269; Yakoboski and Silverman, 1994: 11.

F
I
C
A

Social Security Income

The Social Security system was initiated in 1935 and was expanded to most of the working population by 1965. Payments had increased sufficiently by 1972 to raise most of the elderly above the poverty level—*if they had contributed* to the Social Security system. However, a sizeable proportion of older workers were not employed in positions with Social Security benefits. Participation is considerably lower among ethnic minorities than for the majority population in the United States. For example, only 80 percent of older Hispanics and 88 percent of older African Americans received Social Security payments in 1995—compared to 91 percent of all older people.[1, 3, 34]

The several sources of income noted in Table 8–3 enable the average middle income American couple to retire with 70 to 90 percent of their preretirement income with only 20 percent coming from social security. For lower-income individuals 70 to 80 percent of their retirement income comes from Social Security—often much less than they earned while working. Social Security was on average about 40 percent of total income for retirees in 1996, a considerable increase from earlier decades when many more older individuals had to continue working for survival.[3, 34]

About one-fifth of older Americans relied entirely on Social Security for their livelihood in 1995; it is the *primary* source of income for two-thirds of retirees, with pensions and savings playing only a relatively small part. However, social security is only about 20 percent of average preretirement income for American workers while in European countries public pensions replace nearly half of preretirement income.[80, 117, 119]

Test Question → As the number of older people increases, the proportion of GDP required for Social Security is expected to rise by 50 percent—to 6 percent of GDP by the year 2020. Medicare absorbed approximately 3 percent of GDP and Medicaid 1 percent in 1998. Both are expected to grow steadily to 5 percent for Medicare and 2 percent for Medicaid by 2020. The overall growth for the three major social protection programs—Social Security, Medicare, and Medicaid—would change from 8 percent of GDP in 1998 to 13 percent in 2020, if projections hold. The three programs used one-third of the federal budget in 1998 and could absorb much more in the years ahead if no changes are made. However, the rapidly growing economy, with greater tax revenues, was having a beneficial effect on all of these programs as the new century began.[25, 90, 91]

Contribution Levels. The payroll and other tax costs for workers are summarized in Table 8–4.

Self-employed individuals must pay their own way at twice the 7.65 percent rate paid by employees. Both employees and the self-employed paid from income up to $76,600 annually in 1998. Recipients of Medicare pay $45 per month (in year 2000) or $546 annually to enroll in Part B Medicare, for physician costs and some other costs outside the hospital.

Benefit Levels. Social Security benefits are still very modest as an only source of income, as illustrated in Table 8–5.

The benefit levels displayed in Table 8–5 barely rose above the official poverty level in each case during 1999, and fail to reach above poverty for individuals and

TABLE 8–4   Social Security and Medicare Tax Costs, 1999

Payroll tax rate for employees	7.65%
Social Security segment	6.20
Medicare segment	1.45
Tax rate for the self-employed	15.30
Maximum taxable payroll earnings	$76,600
Annual Medicare Part B premium	546

Source: Data from AARP Bulletin, 1999: 8.

on test ↓

TABLE 8–5   Benefit Levels from Social Security, 2000

Type of Recipient	Monthly Income	Annual Income
Average annual payment to an individual	$804	$9,648
Average for an elderly widow or widower living alone	775	9,300
Average for a retired couple	1,348	16,176
Maximum individual benefit	1,433	17,196
Maximum Supplemental Social Security for individuals	512	6,144
Maximum Supplemental Social Security for a couple	769	9,228

Source: Data from Social Security Administration, 1999; AARP Bulletin, 1999: 13.

couples who must rely on Supplemental Social Security (allocated to those who do not otherwise qualify for Social Security because of insufficient workforce participation). Supplementary Social Security is clearly a poverty income, requiring *less than $2000 in assets* for qualification. Food stamps or other forms of additional assistance are needed to sustain someone who has no other source of income.

Anyone who has worked at low wages, often with companies not paying pension benefits, thus has very low benefits. There is a question of fairness to older men or women who have, for reasons beyond their control, not worked for employers that pay Social Security benefits, as Illustration 8–1 illuminates.

Illustration 8–1
LIFE AFTER MOTHERHOOD AND LOW–INCOME WORK

Joan was married at age 19 shortly after completing high school. She did not work except occasionally for 25 years while she raised five children. Her husband had a manager's job with a major supermarket chain, and he provided generally good support for the family. However, he turned to alcoholism, became abusive, and eventually the marriage ended in divorce.

Since she had maintained few employment skills while raising her children, and had few job alternatives, she worked as a waitress in local restaurants—her primary means of livelihood until health problems forced her to retire at age 62. She had no health insurance, little savings, and Social Security Income of $470 per month—barely enough to buy food and pay rent for a modest apartment. Paying medical bills, maintaining a car, and buying Christmas presents for her numerous grandchildren were largely impossible. She neglected health care until reaching Medicare age, and in process developed several untreated chronic diseases. Without continuing assistance from her family she would have been unable to pay her expenses and would undoubtedly have shortened her life considerably—less than optimal aging for someone responsible for the upbringing of five children.

Joan's situation illustrates one of the major problems for older women who have stayed at home and raised families without acquiring skills or doing professional work with good wages. They have few options if their marriage ends in divorce or their husband dies without a good pension, and they must either continue to work or become very dependent on family support. It should be noted that a divorced wife or husband can receive one-half of a former spouse's benefits if the marriage lasted 10 years or more, with no disadvantage to him, her, or a new spouse.[22, 86, 94]

When this is not possible, Supplemental Social Security may be the only alternative, which explains in part why 20 percent of single older people (40 percent of women) live below the poverty level ($7,755 for individuals and $9,780 for couples in 1997); 58 percent of women older than age 85 are in poverty.[68]

Incentives for Continued Work. The Social Security system encourages work beyond age 65 by increasing benefits at a rate of 4 percent per year up to age 70. However, the rules for working between age 62 and 69 while drawing benefits were somewhat perverse until the United States Congress changed the law in early 2000. A reduction of Social Security income of one dollar for every three dollars earned was required if outside income was over a specified amount—$17,000 in 2000 for those age 65 to 69, and $10,080 from age 62 to 65. After age 70 there was no penalty. Congressional action eliminated the earnings test altogether. However, relatively few older individuals are affected because only a small number reached the income limit. The relatively affluent will benefit most from the change.[9, 78, 83]

Inequities. It is possible for a retired two-earner couple to receive lower Social Security payments than a single-earner couple when all earnings are based on the husband's income. There is little retirement-income advantage for a spouse to work at low wages. A long-term disadvantage occurs for wives who outlive their husbands—as most of them do.[35, 68, 94]

Pensions and Annuities

Pensions account for about 20 percent of the average retirement income. Participation in private pension plans expanded considerably to 55 percent of all workers in 1984 but has not improved since. Participation rates are much higher for mature workers than younger workers. Participation of female workers has improved whereas male participation has declined slightly.[38, 112, 119]

Support for pension and annuity benefits varies widely depending on the industry and occupation. Differences exist in size of benefit and form of contribution. "Defined benefit" means that retirees are guaranteed a fixed benefit depending on years of service and average earnings. "Defined contribution" means that a specified level of deductions are made by the employee and worker, with precise returns dependent on earnings from the total volume of contributions.[112]

In general, increases in pension support by employers has had the effect of increasing inequity of income among retirees in the United States. However, pensions helped to decrease inequities in the Netherlands, Sweden, Germany and other European countries because of much greater public sponsorship and universality.[112]

When an employer encounters financial difficulty in the United States, or the national economy declines, retirement funds may become threatened or are terminated—with workers unable to collect full benefits. Many companies in the late-1990s were considering a change to "cash-balance" plans based on defined contributions over time that can be received in a lump-sum payment with job changes or at retirement. Older workers who had been on a defined benefit plan would be somewhat disadvantaged by the change.[15, 93]

Personal Savings and Investments

Individual Retirement Accounts (IRAs) have become commonplace, giving workers somewhat more control over allocation of the accumulation than with employer-managed pension funds. IRAs are tax free until used. Supplemental Retirement Accounts (SRAs) are voluntary and are taxable prior to deposit of funds into the accounts by the employer.[93]

The overall savings rate among Americans has remained very low by international standards. Retirement income from savings and investments averages little more than 20 percent. Consequently, most families do not have a large pool of savings for retirement or emergencies such as unexpected long-term care requirements. As noted earlier, the primary investment for most older families is their owned home or other real estate, although ownership of stocks and bonds has become quite common among middle- and upper-income groups. Home care or nursing home costs can thus deplete savings very quickly.[47]

Full- or Part-time Work

Approximately 70 percent of men age 65 or older were working in 1900. By 1997 the proportion had dropped to less than 16.5 percent for men and 8.3 percent for women, as indicated in Table 8–6.

As of 1997 about half of those age 65 and over who worked were part-time—many self-employed. The proportion of working older women has increased somewhat since 1980 from 7.8 percent to 8.3 percent. By age 70 the proportion drops to 10 percent for men and 5 percent for women. Among the 4 percent who continued to work after age 75 in 1998, two-thirds were women.[8, 78, 109]

TABLE 8–6   Changing Participation in the Labor Force from 1980 to 1997

Year	Proportion of Employed Older Individuals		
	Total (%)	Men (%)	Women (%)
1980	12.2	18.4	7.8
1990	11.5	15.9	8.4
1997	11.8	16.5	8.3

Source: U.S. Bureau of the Census, 1998: 50.

About one-third of individuals who retire at age 65, or before, eventually return to work for some period of time before full retirement at a later age. Many retirees stopped working as a consequence of incentives, negative or positive, from their employers and found they did not have enough income to afford full retirement. Others simply want something productive to do.[72]

Other Contributors to Financial Well-Being

Measuring economic well-being strictly on the basis of personal income can be very misleading. A complete view of economic status should include the several categories shown in Table 8–7 as well.[93, 119]

The combination of resources summarized in Table 8–7 explains in part why economic status and well being have improved more than revealed by income statistics alone. Wealth plays a major role in financial status but may not be fully reflected in annual income. If a residence is fully paid for—the case for most older homeown-

TABLE 8–7   Sources of Financial Support in Addition to Social Security, Pensions, Savings, and Investments

For Those with Low Incomes
- Public cash benefits or social assistance.
- Benefits from mutual aid societies established by labor unions or other voluntary organizations.
- In-kind or non-cash public benefits such as homemaker services, meals-on-wheels or congregate meals, home maintenance services, adult day care, and transportation services.
- Subsidized public housing.
- Non-cash transfer payments such as Medicare and Medicaid.

For Those with Higher Incomes
- Employer-financed health insurance that continues into retirement.
- Capital gains from asset ownership.
- Potential rent from owner-occupied housing.
- Interest and dividends from investments.

Source: Data from Schulz and Myles, 1990: 399; Yakoboski and Silverman, 1994: 13.

ers—the amount of income needed for ongoing living expenses is obviously reduced. Interest and dividends also contribute to economic well-being for many families but may not be counted as part of regular income. In addition to direct income and wealth, Medicare, Medicaid, and public housing programs have considerably improved economic status for many older individuals. In fact, census data suggest that if the full value of assets is considered the poverty rate among the older population would have been only 5.6 percent in 1997 rather than 10.5 percent as discussed below.[20, 47]

The Continuing Poverty Problem.

The changes in poverty rates among older people are summarized in Table 8–8.

Poverty among older Americans declined from 29 percent in 1966 to 10.5 percent in 1998 (the same as for the younger population), according to federal standards, but is still much greater than in most countries. Women are almost twice as likely to be poor (12.8 percent) as men (7.2 percent). Two-thirds of older individuals below the poverty level are women who are widowed, divorced, or were never married. Older African Americans (26.4 percent) and Hispanics (21 percent) were much more likely to be poor than older European Americans (8.9 percent). Older persons living alone were the poorest (20.4 percent), especially when compared to those living with families (6.4 percent). Nine percent of older women received Supplementary Social Security Benefits.[3, 66, 77, 78, 98, 113]

Many middle-income older women become impoverished in later life because of widowhood and loss of a husband's income, divorce, the high costs of housing, nursing home care in the event of disability, or simply running out of resources during a long life. They have not tended to benefit as much from public policies as older men; dependence on Medicaid and Medicare is much more likely.[68]

The major income gap between men and women was exacerbated by policy changes made in the 1980s, negatively affecting elderly women. Income improvements went largely to upper-income levels of the population. Increased ability to purchase supplemental health care insurance did little to meet the needs of older women because they could not afford the cost.[14, 115, 119]

Further public policy changes may be needed if the nation is to overcome the continuing income deficits of older individuals, particularly women, who do not adequately benefit from current retirement resources. Many countries have established an income floor, a minimum social security benefit above the poverty level regardless of prior work history beneath which no one is allowed go. Supplemental Social Secu-

TABLE 8–8   Changing Poverty Rates Among the Elderly

Year	Total (%)	Male (%)	Female (%)
1980	15.2	11.1	17.9
1990	11.4	7.8	13.9
1998	10.5	7.2	12.8

Source: Data from Administration on Aging, 2000; American Association of Retired Persons, 1998: 10; Pressley, 1998: 30; U.S. Bureau of the Census, 1998.

rity in the United States was originally intended to provide such a base but is woefully inadequate. A higher floor could largely eliminate poverty.[17, 68]

◆◆◆ HEALTH INSURANCE AND EXPENDITURES

The sources of funds for health care are summarized in Table 8–9.

Public financing of health care is increasing steadily as noted earlier, with federal and state government expenditures accounting for 46 percent of all health care costs in 1997. Private or employer-financed health insurance and other private payments continue to be the largest single sources of financing, despite the growth in public programs. However, employer-sponsored health insurance that covers retirees has been steadily declining—from 40 percent of retirees in 1990 to 31 percent in 1997—forcing retirees to pay the costs for individual insurance or a group plan. Further decline in employer coverage is expected because of the increasing cost, which averaged $3,924 per retiree in 1997. As of 1996, 72 percent of the elderly had supplementary private insurance.[22, 67, 75, 110]

As a consequence, personal expenditures on health care rose to an average of $2,855 annually in 1997, a 35 percent increase since 1990. The typical older person between the ages of 65 and 74 spent 12 percent of their income for health care; after age 75 the individual spent 14.4 percent of their income. Expenditures for health care average 53 percent for supplemental health insurance, 19 percent for physician and hospital care, 22 percent for prescription drugs, and 5 percent for medical supplies. Of the total, an average of $1,523 was for supplementary health insurance and $637 was for prescription drugs.[3, 45, 63, 109]

Medicaid has partially filled the gap for lower-income individuals but is of no help for most of the population. Older citizens are thus experiencing an increasing burden from rising health care costs, in part because of the decrease in proportion of costs paid by Medicare and Medicaid, as federal and state governments restrict spending.[95, 114]

Basis for Cost Increases. It should be emphasized that increases in health care costs do not simply reflect greater numbers of older people. Estimates indicate the *rise*

TABLE 8–9   Sources of Funds for Health Care (1997)

Sources	Proportion (%)
Private health insurance	31
Out-of-pocket payment	19
Medicare	19
Medicaid	14
Other government programs (e.g., military)	13
Other private programs	4
Individual medical savings accounts	<1
(Uninsured)	(14)

Source: Data from National Center for Health Care Statistics, 1998.

TABLE 8–10   Distribution of Health Care Expenditures in 1998

Type of Expenditure	Proportion (%)
Hospital care	33.4
Physician care	19.3
Drugs and medical nondurable goods	9.3
Nursing homes	7.6
Health program administration	6.5
Dental care	4.7
Government public health services	3.6
Research and construction	2.9
Home health care	2.9
Vision care and other durable products	1.2
Other health services	8.6

Source: Data from Iglehart, 1999a: 74; National Center for Health Care Statistics, 1998: 346.

in costs per individual older person represents two-thirds of the increase, whereas the increasing elderly population contributes about one-third. The growth in costs is also a consequence of: (1) escalation in medical costs beyond general inflation; (2) rising average use of health services; and (3) greater application of technology, with accompanying intensity of health care. The combination of these factors has led to continuing increases in the proportion of Gross National Product allocated to health care in most countries, especially in the United States.[1, 97]

Distribution of Costs

The overall distribution of health care costs for the entire population in 1996 is summarized in Table 8–10.

The majority of expenditures go for hospital care (33.4 percent) and physician care (19.3 percent), followed by drugs and durable medical supports (9.3 percent). Nursing home care consumed about 7.6 percent of national health care costs in 1998. Long-term care provided through home health agencies was 2.9 percent. Medicare provided about one-third of the funding for home care in 1995, while Medicaid, the Older Americans Act, Social Services Block Grants, and veterans programs provided the bulk of the other public funding. The elderly accounted for 68 percent of Medicaid expenditures in 1994, largely for nursing home care, although they represented only 12 percent of the beneficiaries.[39, 75, 87, 99]

Approximately 36 percent of all hospitalizations in 1997 and 49 percent of all days of care in hospitals were for the elderly. The average length of stay was 6.8 days, compared to 5.5 days for younger people. Furthermore, older people had more than twice as many visits to physicians (average 11.7) as did younger people (4.9) annually.[3]

The Medicare System

Medicare was initiated in 1965 and is administered by the Health Care Financing Administration in the U.S. Department of Health and Human Services. The program has two primary components:[55]

- Part A hospital coverage for everyone over age 65.
- Optional Part B for physician services and several other costs not covered by Part A. Participation requires a monthly premium, usually deducted from Social Security benefits; 97 percent of older people participate.

Table 8–11 summarizes the benefits from Medicare and Medicaid. Part B received about 25 percent of resources from premiums, with the balance coming from federal revenues. Overall, about 89 percent of Medicare resources came from payroll deductions in 1998, whereas 11 percent came from monthly premiums for Part B. The allocation of these funds is highly efficient by health insurance standards. Administrative expenses were only 1 percent for Part A and 2 percent for Part B.[55, 57]

Exclusions. Neither Part A nor Part B of Medicare cover many basic health care needs, such as outpatient prescriptions or over-the-counter drugs, eye examinations and glasses, hearing examinations and aids, dental care or dentures, most immunizations, physical examinations, out-patient mental health care, routine foot

TABLE 8–11   Primary Medicare and Medicaid Benefits, 1998

Type of Coverage	Benefits
MEDICARE: Part A: Available to all Social Security recipients at age 65	80% of hospital costs, up to 90 days per illness episode *plus* 60 days during a lifetime.
	Direct costs to patient: $768 deductible required for first 60 days; plus a copayment of $192/day for 61-90 days.
	80 percent of nursing home and rehabilitation costs for up to 100 days, but only after 3 days of hospitalization. First 20 days fully paid, then $96/day co-payment for 21-100 days.
Part B: Monthly premium required of $45.50/month (in 2000)	80% of physician costs, therapy, diagnostic tests, ambulance, home health care, prostheses, surgery, some supplemental hospital costs not covered by Part A.
	Cost to Patient: $100 deductible per episode of illness.
MEDICAID: Available to low–income citizens who meet poverty standards.	100% of negotiated Medicaid rate for hospitalization, physician care, drugs, ambulance, home health care, prostheses, surgery. *and* 100% of negotiated nursing home rate, depending on access to other resources.

Source: AARP Bulletin, 1999: 8; Health Care Financing Administration, 1997.

care, nursing home care for more than 100 days, and physician or hospital charges which exceed the allowable Medicare limits.[45]

The noncovered costs are the principle reason that out-of-pocket costs have placed a heavy burden on many older people. Lower-income individuals who cannot afford supplementary insurance must apply for the Qualified Medical Beneficiary program administered through Medicaid by states. Those who do not qualify for Social Security or Medicare, because of their limited work history, can apply for Supplemental Social Security, which also makes them eligible for the Qualified Medical Beneficiary alternative. The inadequacies of Medicare are most pronounced for lower-income elderly who do not qualify for Medicaid but still cannot afford supplementary insurance.[12, 114]

Medigap Insurance

Supplementary insurance can be quite expensive if it covers all Medicare deficiencies. For example, The American Association of Retired Persons (AARP) offered a supplemental coverage plan in 1997 with costs varying from $39.50 per month for basic benefits to $150 per month for comprehensive coverage. Other plans have monthly prices in the same range. Costs have been increasing at roughly 8 percent per year for most medigap insurance plans.[7]

Medicare has a regressive health care financing structure, even though it is intended to assure health care for all older individuals. Since lower-income older people who are less healthy must spend a higher proportion of their income for health care, they become even less well off compared to the more wealthy and healthy.[41]

The Pattern of Cost Increases

The pattern of increased public expenditures for both Medicare and Medicaid is quite dramatic. Medicaid is the single fastest growing part of state government expenditures, growing to an average of 20 percent in 1998. Consequently, many states have chosen to sharply limit qualification for benefits and have increased co-payments.[65, 71, 73]

◆◆◆ LONG-TERM CARE ISSUES AND EXPENDITURES

Sources of funding for nursing homes and home health care are summarized in Table 8–12. As the table indicates, government programs collectively pay well over half of both overall costs and nursing home costs, although private resources continue to pay for a substantial proportion. It should be noted that the distributions indicated in Table 8–12 vary considerably from one part of the country to another. Furthermore, the substitution of home care for nursing home care varies widely depending on accessibility of home health agencies. As noted earlier, evaluative studies in Oregon, Washington, and Wisconsin suggest achievement of major savings when home care or assisted living is substituted for nursing home care whenever possible.

TABLE 8–12   Sources of Long Term Care Funding, 1997

Source	Percentage
Long–Term Care Overall	
Privately paid	42
Medicaid	35
Medicare	18
Other government programs	4
Private insurance	1
Nursing Home Care	
Privately paid	33
Medicaid	52
Medicare	9
Other government programs	4
Private insurance and other	2

Sources: Data from Lewis, 1997: 111; Teachers Insurance and Annuity Company, 1998: 3.

Partially as a consequence, nursing home utilization dropped from 4.6 percent of older people in 1985 to 4.1 percent in 1995, whereas use of home health care increased steadily.[26, 71]

Home Health Care Expenditures

Home health care costs grew from 0.8 percent of all health expenditures in 1980 to nearly 3 percent in 1996. Average annual costs for home care were estimated at about $12,000 per year in 1998. Although home care has been provided largely by non-profit visiting nurses and home care agencies, for-profit firms became very competitive in the early 1990s, until imposition of limitations in 1997.[64, 75]

The limitations capped and considerably reduced payments per individual recipient, causing many older individuals to lose benefits. Visits by agency staff to home health patients declined substantially. It was more difficult for the sickest and most costly patients, with the greatest needs, to secure care because agencies indicated they could not afford to provide care. The annual growth rate of 25 percent was slowed dramatically. Fraud and excesses in the system were also lowered significantly. About 14 percent of the home health agencies withdrew their services by December of 1998. The net effect was that much of the incentive to provide home health services has been removed. However, a General Accounting Office study published in mid-1999 indicated that access to home health care had not been significantly impaired.[13, 89]

Assisted Living Costs

Assisted living prices are roughly two-thirds those of nursing homes, depending on location and on the amenities in either type of facility. The average income of assisted living residents nationwide was estimated to be about $28,000 in 1997, plus $192,000 in assets. The average length of residency was 2.5 years. Private payment remains predominant but Medicaid is covering costs under some conditions in several states. As the Oregon experiment discussed earlier indicates, as many as 15 percent of nursing home patients could function quite well in an assisted living environment—at considerable cost saving to states and to the federal government. Consequently, more federal Medicaid waivers for this option are likely to be forthcoming.[76]

Nursing Home Expenditures

Average monthly payments by Medicaid to nursing homes were considerably less than private pay and half the amount paid by Medicare. This differential is largely a result of state-negotiated Medicaid contracts dictating nursing home charges. Many nursing home administrators indicate Medicaid rates are insufficient to pay costs, which must be made up by charging more for Medicare and private pay residents. When Medicare rates were restricted in 1997, this transfer of resources became less possible and was a primary reason for the marginal status, and even closure, of many nursing homes in the late 1990s.[11, 29, 69]

Two-thirds of nursing home residents in the United States live in private for-profit facilities; the remainder live in homes operated by nonprofit organizations or various forms of government-sponsored accommodations. Average charges in proprietary homes are somewhat smaller for Medicaid-supported residents but are higher for private pay and Medicare residents as compared to nonprofit or government facilities. Nonprofit and government facilities have a higher average charge in part because residents tend to have greater health problems and are older than residents of private for-profit homes. The highest charges occur when Medicaid-dependent residents need expensive health care paid for by Medicare. This is often the case with very old residents who have several acute and chronic conditions.[75]

The average annual cost for nursing home care was $37,620 in 1995, increasing to approximately $40,000 in 1998—depending on the location. Estimates suggest we can expect increases to as much as $53,600 annually by 2003. Costs vary widely among states and communities: $46,848 ($3,904 per month) in the Northeast in 1995; $44,520 ($3,710 per month) in the West; $33,024 ($2,752 per month) in the South; and $32,448 ($2,704 per month) in the Midwest. The average daily cost for nursing home care ranged from a low of $63 in Arkansas to $145 in New York in 1993. These differences reflect variations in wage and real estate costs—higher in the Northeast and West than in the South and Midwest.[4, 65, 75, 85, 101, 106]

Nursing home fees also vary widely among facilities. A "case-mix-related reimbursement" system has been adopted by many states to take account of variations in the needs and requirements of residents. This enables nursing homes to charge more for postsurgical and other types of subacute patients. However, the 1997 Congressional changes placed limits on rehabilitation services and thus diminished reimbursement.[37, 44, 80]

Most states attempt to recover funds from the estates of Medicaid recipients upon their death, primarily through sale of private homes which residents were allowed to retain in the event they were able to return home or when a spouse was using the home. However, this recovery effort does little to lower the overall cost of long-term care expenditures paid for by Medicaid.[80]

Board and Care Home Costs

Board and care homes have fewer services than nursing homes and are thus less costly. Payment is made from Social Security, Supplementary Social Security, state supplementary payments, pensions, or other income. Medicaid will pay for personal care and Medicare will pay for medical services for residents of licensed facilities.[80]

Public Policy and Insurance Issues

Publicly provided insurance for nursing home care leads to "moral hazard." When care is made available at public cost, the tendency to use it increases, potentially decreasing care provided by families or through other voluntary charitable measures. Greater access to nursing care may result if Medicaid payment rates increase to more adequately reimburse nursing homes. Government policies can thus have a substantial negative or positive impact on access to and use of nursing home and home health care services.[36, 99]

The Kassebaum-Kennedy legislation of 1996 is an example—allowing a tax deduction of up to $2500 for "qualified" long-term care insurance plans and placing long-term care insurance in the same category as other health care insurance. Employers can deduct the costs of providing coverage for employees. Individuals can get a deduction if the total cost of medical care and long-term care premiums exceeds 7.5 percent of income. (Very few taxpayers qualify, however, because only about 6 percent were able to take health care cost deductions in 1994.) The Act levies a fine of up to $25,000 and 1 to 5 years in jail for shifting assets to other family members through "estate planning" as a means of qualifying for Medicaid. The new federal rules, coupled with restrictive state policies, have thus impeded the use of Medicaid by many moderate income families.[50]

◆◆◆ IMPACT OF COST CONTROL EFFORTS

Diagnosis Related Groups (DRGs) were introduced for Medicare recipients in 1983 as a method of classifying illnesses and setting average cost limits for hospital treatment. Prospective payment rates are established prior to the provision of care as an incentive to conserve application of medical resources. Patients are admitted after diagnosis in one or more of 495 categories (in 1995). Since the system was introduced, it has had a clear cost-controlling effect and at least temporarily diminished the possible overuse of technology. However, the new system was not sufficient by itself to stop the rapid growth in overall Medicare expenditures.[6, 45]

DRGs have also caused earlier discharges, placing increased demand on families, home health care providers, and long-term care facilities that provide post-hospital care. Patients who remain hospitalized or in nursing homes are generally sicker and more fragile than before the advent of DRGs. The healthier patients are at home or have entered some form of assisted living that does not require daily medical care.[45]

Cost shifting between payment sources has been one of the unanticipated effects. Uncompensated or undercompensated care costs are shifted to other patients who have higher paying insurance. For example, since Medicare paid only an average of 89 percent of a hospitals' computed patient cost in 1993, and Medicaid paid 93 percent, costs where shifted to patients with private insurance which paid 129 percent of costs. Rather than saving overall costs, the cost burden was simply shifted internally to payment sources that were not rigidly controlled.[6, 45]

Effects on Hospitals

Hospital use as a proportion of the total Medicare budget fell from 70 percent in 1982, before DRGs, to 33 percent in 1998. Most hospitals were forced to reduce expenditures and many eventually downsized because of fewer older patients. Some of the payment shift went to Medical Specialty Units or subacute care sections in nursing homes, significantly increasing their revenues because they are able to provide the services at lower cost than similar services in hospitals.[45, 55, 81]

Although the cost-saving benefits are clear, the DRG payment system has had the further effect of forcing health professionals to respond to what Medicare will pay for, whether or not it meets the primary patient need. This means that diagnosis, evaluation, and treatment are often short-changed. Older patients are sometimes shifted to treatment that is less beneficial than needed simply to stay within payment guidelines. However, the DRG system has been deemed quite successful and has been widely adopted, and adapted, by other countries.[40]

Nonetheless, per capita Medicare expenditures have continued to rise. The DRG-generated Prospective Payment System did not substantially alter the underlying basis for high costs of hospitalization, physician care, and long term care.[45]

Effects on Physicians

A Medicare payment system for physicians—the Resource Based Relative Value Scale (RBRVS) introduced in 1992—is somewhat comparable to DRGs for hospitals. The scale restructured fees so as to lower payments to higher-cost specialists while increasing payments to lower-cost primary care providers. Overall costs for physician care were also somewhat lowered. The change caused great concern, uncertainty, and some conflict among family practice, generalist, and other specialist physicians. They feel that the quality of care for older patients may have been lowered as a result of the controls on fees.[45, 57]

Impact on Pharmaceuticals

Pharmaceutical companies have in large part been able to resist cost-cutting efforts (at least until the end of the twentieth century). The prices of medications have risen steadily and the profitability of drug companies has remained very strong. Medicare and Medicaid have not been granted major discounts, nor have other institutional purchasers. Managed care companies have widely varying prescription drug policies, ranging from full coverage to no coverage. They have generally attempted to limit full payment for drugs to those included in an established formulary containing largely generic drugs.[64, 107]

Medicaid Cost-Saving Effects

Medicaid has become the largest health insurer in the country, covering roughly 41 million lower income individuals in 1997. Some states have deliberately attempted to limit growth in Medicaid expenditures for nursing homes by using the Certificate-of-Need process and other restrictions to limit growth of new facilities or expansion of existing homes. Certificate-of-Need requirements can limit capital expenditure for space and equipment to avoid excess capacity or unnecessary duplication of facilities. Nevertheless, the demand for space and overall incentives to for-profit nursing homes have caused the number of nursing homes and beds to increase steadily.[6, 45, 56]

Medicaid has become the dominant low-cost third-party payer for long-term care. This is particularly a challenge for small hospitals with swing beds or nursing homes with a high proportion of low-income elderly patients. It makes financial viability very difficult, resulting in a significant decline in availability of smaller facilities. The result is limited access to needed health care and nursing home care in many locations.[99, 101]

Medicaid's original mandate was to pay for health care. It has become the vehicle to provide subsidized housing, sustenance, and nursing care for disabled elderly because no other source of payment was available. The deep dependence on public subsidy for non-medical nursing home care is one of the major reasons for the rapidly increasing public costs of Medicaid, Medicare, and overall health care costs.

Managed Care And Integrated Networks

Roughly 65 percent of privately insured Americans were enrolled under managed care plans in 1997, including 15 percent of Medicare beneficiaries and most Medicaid recipients. State Medicaid programs and most employers have adopted managed care as a mechanism for controlling costs, generating the primary integrating mechanism for provision of health insurance. Capitation (flat monthly payments per enrollee) is used to pay hospitals, primary and specialty care physicians, and nursing homes—with strict controls on the use of medical services.[56, 59, 62]

Several managed care options are summarized in Table 8–13. The Health Care Financing Administration (HCFA) encourages Medicare beneficiaries to select one of the options listed in Table 8–13. The specific coverage varies depending on the provider organization. Prescription drugs, eye glasses, and hearing aids are sometimes included as part of managed care benefits.[88]

HCFA pays managed care plans 95 percent of the usual fee-for-service charges in the geographic area of the beneficiary, with adjustments for age, sex, and disability. Private for-profit or nonprofit managed care companies contract with federal and state governments to provide services to Medicare and Medicaid patients. The quality and completeness of the care provided varies considerably between companies,

TABLE 8–13 Forms of Integration and Care Management

- *Health Maintenance Organizations* (HMOs) operated by a single nonprofit or for-profit company have been the prototype managed care system. The employer or subscriber pays a fixed fee per month. Service is provided by physicians groups, hospitals, pharmacies, home health care agencies, and nursing homes, owned by, or under contract to, the HMO.
- *Point of Service Organizations* are HMOs with a fee-for-service option that allows enrollees to seek care outside the provider network. Permission must be secured if an enrollee is to be reimbursed.
- *Preferred Provider Organizations* (PPOs) provide discounted fee-for-service payment to a network of contracting private physicians, hospitals, pharmacies, home health agencies, and nursing homes. Greater freedom is available for subscribers to select providers than in HMOs.
- *Provider Sponsored Organizations* (PSOs) are integrated insurance networks of physicians, hospitals, pharmacies, home health agencies, nursing homes, and a variety of other health service providers. Providers collaboratively design a care system, sometimes referred to as Physician, Hospital, Community Organizations (PHCOs), with varying characteristics and payment arrangements.
- *Medicare+Choice* is a relatively new managed care alternative (as of 1997). The advantage of the new arrangement is somewhat greater choice and coverage of all health care costs, without the need for separate and increasingly expensive Medigap policies.

Source: Data from Alpha Center, 1999: 4–5; Kane and Baker, 1996; Health Care Financing Administration, 1998.

communities, and states, depending on the local rules and oversight mechanisms. Some emphasize preventive care and wellness, while others concentrate on acute and chronic care. Nearly all companies attempt to deemphasize expensive hospital care and rely heavily on primary care through local physicians or mid-level practitioners (physician assistants and nurse practitioners) who serve as gatekeepers to specialized and hospital care.[26, 65]

Some assisted living facilities have begun to accept Medicaid supported residents under managed care contracts as a lower-cost alternative to nursing homes in states allowing this arrangement. There may be distinct advantages for the older person, if their health is good enough to be adequately cared for in the assisted living environment.[37]

Home health care is also available through managed care organizations and is often contracted to local home health care agencies. However, reimbursement to the agency may be equal to or lower than their cost and lead to losses. One estimate indicated that as many as 85 percent of home health agencies that contracted with HMOs lost money in early 1990s.[42]

Medicare+Choice. The Balanced Budget Act of 1997 created the new alternative referred to as Medicare+Choice. It was designed to further increase the attractiveness of managed care by encouraging a wider range of choices, such as the PPOs and PSOs described above. The legislation increased fees in low-fee areas and decreased them in high-fee areas. Freedom to switch from one plan to another was increased. The goal was to shift even more of the elderly to managed care in an attempt to slow the rate of cost increases. However, many older people and their special interest groups, such as the American Association for Retired People, resisted the new option.[30, 88]

Coordinated Care. Managed care programs purport to create cost efficiencies by coordinating all health care for their members, while also providing education and assistance with preventive care and health maintenance. Paperwork for billing is considerably less than with fee-for-service financing, and most services can be obtained at one location. The down side is that permission is required to see physician specialists and for hospitalization, although some managed care plans began dropping this requirement in 1999. The Medicare beneficiary must use providers who are associated with the managed care plan in the local area. Choices are restricted when traveling outside the service area.[88]

Monitoring Resource Use. Cost-effectiveness is a paramount objective of most managed care plans, accompanied by close monitoring of payments to physicians, of the use of specialists, and of admissions to hospitals. Many for-profit companies achieved substantial profits in the short-term by deliberately serving only relatively healthy Medicare enrollees and avoiding or providing less service to less healthy members. This practice has been curtailed by federal rule changes.[5, 87]

Subcontracting. Managed care companies often contract with fee-for-service organizations to provide specific services. For example, an HMO is likely to negotiate with a home health agency for the lowest possible home health care rate as noted above. The subcontract rate may be lower than the cost to the managed care company for providing the care through an internal subdivision.[26, 42]

Medicaid Managed Care and the States. The rapid shift to managed care as an insurance mode for long-term care has had a major impact in many states. New administrative and operational skills are required. In most instances Medicare and Medicaid payments must be appropriately integrated so that one form of payment does not subsidize the other, as described in Illustration 8–2.[30, 58, 88]

Illustration 8–2
INTEGRATED FINANCING AND CARE IN ARIZONA

Arizona received a waiver in 1989 to use Federal Medicaid funds for operation of a managed care health insurance and long-term care program. More than 450,000 low-income patients were enrolled by 1995. The state managed care structure has created a data system that systematically tracks patient information, including costs and outcomes. Estimates indicate that savings are 7 percent a year for acute care and 16 percent for long-term care when compared to other state Medicaid programs. This is partly a result of highly competitive bidding among health care companies for state contracts.

Capitation rates for nursing care are substantially below the average cost of care in nursing homes, resulting in major cost savings. Basic medical care and long-term care are provided under separate funding arrangements through Medicare and Medicaid. The program has stringent preadmission standards for eligibility; applicants must be at high risk for institutionalization.

Independent evaluations indicate that quality of care may be a problem. The state is establishing formal indicators of quality. Contractors who manage the care programs are under pressure to keep costs down and place patients in community settings, such as adult foster homes or assisted living residences rather than nursing homes. The average cost of community-based care was $800 per month in 1995, whereas nursing home care averaged $3000.

The program has matured and is now viewed by state officials as generally successful despite the uncertainty about quality of care.

Sources: Data from Alpha Center, 1999: 15; Gleick, 1995: 32; Hawryluk, 1996: 23-24; Johnson, 1997: 127-128; Serafini, 1995: 2803-2806.

Managed Mental Health Care. Most indemnity insurance programs severely limit coverage of mental illness for the elderly. High co-payments, service restrictions, and lifetime benefit limitations are usually the rule when coverage is provided. Managed care organizations have also traditionally limited their services, excluding the seriously mentally ill from coverage. When private benefits terminate patients must turn to public programs. As a consequence, roughly 54 percent of mental health care costs in 1996 were the responsibility of federal, state, and local governments, via Medicare, Medicaid, Veteran's Affairs, and other public programs. Most states have now adopted managed care as the primary mechanism for offering mental health services to low-income clients.[27]

Continuing Care Retirement Communities. Continuing care retirement communities have a long history of managing health care for the elderly, although quite differently than through contemporary managed care programs. Studies of the cost-effectiveness of continuing care communities suggests, among other results, that provision of home services in the independent living and assisted living units does reduce the need and cost for nursing care. Proximity and timeliness of services when needed is clearly an advantage of the continuing care approach, as contrasted with the need to travel to service providers or wait for services from off-site home health agencies.[100]

CCRCs are in a better position than fee-for-service acute care providers to prevent or at least postpone moves to the nursing home setting. They are also able to screen applicants on the basis of health status and may not accept severely ill or disabled individuals. Widespread use of the CCRC concept for low-income older people requires some form of public subsidization through Medicaid, Medicare, or other public programs, as in the Oregon experience discussed earlier.[100]

Challenges with Managed Care. A big advantage of managed care companies (as advertised) was full coverage without the need for supplementary medigap insurance. Supplemental services often included well-adult physicals, prescription drugs, and dental care. These features are rapidly disappearing, however, because of increasing costs. Most of the companies offering plans for Medicare beneficiaries have had to continually increase rates or leave the market. The additional costs have since been largely shifted to beneficiaries or services are no longer available except with an additional charge.[59, 62, 88]

Private Long-Term Care Insurance

Only about 2 percent of nursing home costs were paid through private insurance in 1996. Fewer than 5 percent of the age 65 and over population had any form of long-term care insurance in 1995. Nonetheless, a larger market for long-term care insurance appears to be evolving, in part as a form of asset protection for individuals with substantial resources.[31, 43, 108]

For those who qualify, private long-term care options include:

- Direct purchase of long-term care insurance policies through private companies or professional associations, widely available but at relatively high cost.
- Social health organizations, which offer community-based and institutional long-term care policies. Relatively high cost and limited access have so far constrained widespread use.
- Individual medical accounts, affordable only to middle- and upper-income elderly with very limited adoption.
- Home equity conversions or loans that provide resources for long-term care. This option would provide significant funding only for homeowners with substantial equity or expensive homes.
- Continuing care retirement communities, as described above, which are also costly and affordable only to middle- and upper-income elderly.

The private options have increased considerably in recent years but continue to cover relatively few older individuals because of the high cost. Approximately 23 percent of individuals age 65 and over are excluded from private insurance because their health condition represents a greater risk than insurers are prepared to cover. The exclusions include individuals who cannot perform basic activities of daily living, have dementia, cancer, diabetes, or obesity, have had a stroke or a heart attack or chronic obstructive pulmonary disease, or who consume alcohol heavily.[74, 101, 116]

Policies are usually very legalistic, written in technical language, and very difficult for the average person to understand. Insurance agents may attempt to sell policies to individuals and couples that may not serve them well. Sales efforts are sometimes characterized by misinformation or misleading claims. Coverage is often much less than the purchaser expects and rate increases can quickly make costs much greater than anticipated. Insurance companies are likely to try to avoid clients deemed to be bad risks. Many insurers exclude anyone over age 84. Some form of high risk government sponsored insurance appears to be the only means of insuring these individuals.[31, 61]

Very few large private companies include long-term care coverage as part of employee benefits, although availability is gradually increasing and usually at the employee's expense. Smaller companies are less likely to provide insurance. However, individuals with appropriate affiliations are able to purchase coverage at group rates through plans offered by nonprofit associations. The provisions and degree of coverage vary widely.[16, 101]

A reliable insurance carrier with substantial experience and sufficient capital to pay benefits in later years, is crucial to the purchaser of long-term care insurance. Insurance rating services such as Moody's, A. M. Best, or Standard and Poor's can be very helpful in evaluating companies.[70]

◆◆◆ IMPACT OF FRAUD AND ABUSE

The Health Care Financing Administration estimated that $23.2 billion dollars was lost to fraud in 1996—14 percent of total Medicare expenditures. As the second most important investigative priority after violent crime, the FBI investigated 2200 fraud cases in 1996. Civil fraud investigations totaled 2488 cases, and the number of cases has increased dramatically from year to year.[18]

As a consequence, the Health Care Financing Administration has become increasingly stringent with provider payments. Nursing homes and attending physicians are expected to pay close attention to use of the Minimum Data Set, for example, to assure that the health condition of residents is carefully tracked as required. Physician specialists in geriatrics have received special training in Medicare fraud and abuse avoidance, under the auspices of the American Geriatrics Society, so as to minimize the risk of inadvertent errors.[10]

Funds for payment of health care expenses would be greater if providers did not defraud the system. Up-coding of DRGs has been used, for example, to collect payments for a more expensive level of care than is needed. Claims are sometimes falsified deliberately. Bills are occasionally submitted for nonexistent patients. Columbia Health Care, one of the largest providers of hospital care and other health care services in the United States, was taken to court and forced to admit liability for major fraudulent claims of this type.

The "Spending Down" Phenomena

All income of a nursing home resident, except $30-50 per month, must go toward nursing care before public funds are used. The individual must spend any net worth except for about $2000, but can keep a primary residence and furnishings, a car, a burial plot, funeral costs, a small life insurance policy, and personal belongings. An allowance for home maintenance may also be retained but the house must usually be sold after death for reimbursement of Medicaid. In nineteen states Medicaid cannot be obtained if monthly income is more than about $1450, although that amount is insufficient to pay for nursing home costs in those states.[32]

The spouse of a nursing home resident on Medicaid may keep only $1327 to $1976 (in 1997, and depending on the state) per month of joint income—but may keep all income that is entirely in his or her name including savings and investments up to $79,000 (again depending on the state). Women without independent income whose husbands are confined to a nursing home must attempt to live on the remaining resources. Husbands who stay at home may be better off because their continuing independent income is likely to be higher.[32]

The high cost of nursing home care is clearly a major issue for lower- and middle-income disabled older individuals and their families. Since no good financing alternatives exist except Medicaid or long-term care insurance, many families feel justified in transferring assets so as to avoid spending the entire family treasure as required by Medicaid rules.

"Estate" Planning. The rigid rules outlined above have led to a special kind of legal process which helps disabled older individuals and their families to plan their estates by sheltering, divesting, or transferring assets to family members. Eldercare attorneys specialize in advising families about how to meet legal requirements for transferring assets between spouses, transferring funds into ownership that is not counted in computing eligibility, or setting up trust accounts that are exempt from consideration. For example, establishing an irrevocable trust can help retain assets in some states if completed more than three (five in some states) years before applying for Medicaid. The U.S. Congress has enacted laws to constrain the practice, but legal loopholes remain available.[2, 32, 84]

The practice of estate planning is a direct result of the lack of good alternatives. Although the practice may help retain family wealth, the impoverishing effect of asset transfers is often emotionally difficult for the self-image of disabled individuals who must enter a nursing home. They simultaneously lose both their freedom and control of their resources.[2, 73, 84, 99]

The legal provision that allows retention of a house by nursing home residents may be somewhat costly to Medicaid. The average value of owned homes would have paid for approximately two years of care. It is not clear how much would be saved if the sale of the home were required in advance to help pay for the cost of care.[99]

◆◆◆ ECONOMIC AND FINANCIAL POLICY ISSUES

Major economic and financial policy adjustments may be needed to adequately respond to the changing and expanding older populations. A summary of several important issues is presented below.

Social Security and Pensions

The solutions under formal consideration to resolve potential shortages in the Social Security system include: benefit reductions, higher retirement ages, greater personal savings or pensions imposed by public policy, increases in social security taxes, greater advance funding of the system, and/or privatization of pension systems. Imposition of a higher retirement age, to 67 by the year 2020, for receiving Social Security is already gradually underway.

Local, state, and federal governments, many corporations, and most universities and colleges, already impose retirement savings through payroll deductions in addition to Social Security. Government action could make this requirement universal. Expansion of 401 (k) retirement funds is among privatization options, but other possibilities are available as well.[24, 79]

A bi-partisan National Commission on Retirement Policy has offered several recommendations. They would add investment in individual retirement accounts as a requirement by using 2 percentage points of the 12.4 percent payroll tax. They recommended increasing the minimum level Social Security benefit as a means of protecting lower-income recipients. The retirement age would be raised to 70 by 2029. Finally, the earnings limit for people receiving Social Security benefits would be eliminated, allowing retirees to earn whatever they can. This latter recommendation was adopted by the U.S. Congress in 2000.[49]

Public Long-Term Care Insurance Options

A variety of measures have been proposed to help alleviate problems with access to long-term care:[116]

- Universal public payment for long-term care through Medicaid, including home care. Partial use of this concept in a few states is the basis for greatly increased home health care services as an alternative to nursing home care.
- Public long-term care insurance through expansion of Medicare or new insurance to achieve universal coverage of long-term care. This could considerably increase Medicare costs but would presumably decrease Medicaid expenditures. Germany initiated a variation of this approach in the early 1990s.
- Increases in income taxes, payroll taxes, sales taxes (or value added tax), or estate and gift taxes to directly fund public payment for long-term care. Sweden, the Netherlands, and the United Kingdom have implemented variations of this approach.
- Reliance on assessment of families who have resources, or imposition of a legal requirement on immediate family members with resources to pay long-term care costs directly. Japan has been operating under this approach but has now expanded the public role. The approach is costly to implement and monitor and has not worked well in Japan or in American states where it has been tried.

Creating a More Prowork Environment

The earnings penalty described earlier created a disincentive for highly skilled workers to continue work after age 65. The new 2000 law eliminating the penalty should increase employment of older people in both full- or part-time jobs.[19, 118]

A delayed retirement credit is available to individuals who postpone Social Security benefits after age 65, with gradually increasing benefits to age 70. Speeding up the credits would provide a greater incentive for continued work and would lower the burden on the Social Security system. As the law is currently written, the higher benefits go largely to higher-income individuals who depend less on Social Security.[19]

Health Insurance as an Incentive. Health insurance is a major issue in the employment of older workers, especially for self-insuring companies. As noted earlier, the health care costs for older individuals are clearly higher than for younger workers. At present, a company employing an older worker is the first-payer of health insurance coverage, while Medicare is the second payer. If this were reversed, the cost of employing older workers would be diminished.[19]

Changing the Work Environment. As noted earlier, many older employees want to work part-time and with greater flexibility of schedule than was possible in their younger years. Such changed work settings may in fact be critical to the continuing prosperity of the United States economy, given the chronic shortage of workers in some locations and industries during the late 1990s. Shortages were particularly acute in high-skill professional fields, technical fields, and service industries from which many older workers have retired. The very good job-performance record of older workers represents a valuable source of skill, knowledge, and energy that the United States and other countries can no longer afford to dismiss.[19, 33]

Early Retirement Policies. In 1998 approximately 58 percent of workers had retired by age 62 in the United States and 94 percent had retired by age 66. Policies that encourage early retirement may need reexamination. Pension benefits are reduced for anyone who continues to work after age 65 in some companies. Elimination of such disincentives would encourage continuation of work. Similarly, greater opportunities for part-time work would quite likely increase the incentive for many older workers to continue.[19, 67]

Improving Incentives for Lower-Income Workers. Forty percent of working Americans aged 51 to 60 had no potential pension income other than Social Security in 1995. Twenty percent had no assets such as a house, investments, or savings. Fourteen percent had no health insurance. Many of these individuals may have difficulty remaining in the workforce in the face of age discrimination and inadequate preparation for available jobs. Greater incentives and job training are needed to further encourage continued employment.[19, 103]

Financing Needed Elderly Housing

As indicated in Chapter Seven, major initiatives may be needed to provide sufficient housing for older Americans. Although the rate of home ownership is likely to continue to be high, a substantial segment of lower-income elderly must pay rent at increasingly high rates because of high demand and short supply. Further public action may be needed to assure the construction of additional lower-cost units.

Another problem is among older individuals or families with modest incomes who are disabled and need special forms of barrier free housing. The increases in rental prices has the potential to create serious shortages unless policies are improved to assist those who are unable to manage under market or current public housing policy conditions.

Recent Policy Initiatives

The U.S. Congress has been steadily increasing resources for research on aging and public programs for the older population. For example, in 1998 the appropriation for the National Institute on Aging rose to $596 million annually, a $78 million increase from 1997. The Department of Veterans Affairs, the largest supporter of geriatric medicine, received a 15 percent budget increase for medical research, to $316 million annually, in part to support several new Geriatric Research, Education, and Clinical Centers around the country. Congress also reauthorized geriatric faculty fellowships and geriatric education centers to support multidisciplinary training in geriatrics.[51]

◆◆◆ SUMMARY AND CONCLUSIONS

Policies on financial security, health care, long-term care, and housing for the older population have improved substantially during recent decades. Social Security and pension programs have helped raise a high proportion of older people above the poverty level. Medicare has provided universal, if incomplete, health care. Medicaid has provided a long-term care safety-net for lower-income people. Federal, state and local housing programs have facilitated the construction or remodeling of homes for many older families and individuals.

However, the Social Security system was designed for workers in an earlier era when women tended not to work and families were more likely to remain intact. It clearly does not currently meet the needs of large numbers of older single women, nor are the benefits by themselves sufficient to support a good standard of living for an older family. Single, divorced or widowed women are more at risk than men because they often have not worked, or earned less income, and they live longer.

Impoverishment of many older individuals because of major medical expenses is inevitable under current conditions. Medicare covers only part of acute care health costs and medications are not reimbursed. A choice must regularly be made between medical care and other necessary expenses. Middle- and lower-income people must worry about the potential for losing their assets to long-term care costs before support from Medicaid is available. Inadequacy of payments from Medicaid is a great frustration to beneficiaries and health care providers who serve the lower-income older population and who often have trouble securing sufficient compensation to cover expenses.

As the population ages, the need for increased long-term care options will undoubtedly increase. Private insurance programs are not generally affordable by middle- and lower-income older people. Coverage is only partial under most policies, varies substantially from state to state, and does not appear to be a good solution for most people. An improved public program seems essential as a replacement for the current Medicaid-financed approach.

It may become increasingly appropriate for older workers to continue employment. Opportunities were certainly improving in the late 1990s. Many are perfectly capable, and willing, to work full-time or part-time to earn enough for a basic liveli-hood while responding to the need for additional workers. The additional taxes paid by older workers can help support the growing number of very old citizens who are disabled and unable to work.

It seems clear that the American economy is capable of providing adequate support for the older population. New policies and incentives will be required to fill the gaps in programs of income support, physical health care, mental health care, long-term care, and housing to create an environment providing a reasonable quality of life in older age.

◆◆◆ REFERENCES

1. Aaron, Henry J. (1996). Is a Crisis Really Coming? *Newsweek*, December, 31.
2. Adams, E. Kathleen, Mark R. Meiners, and Brian O. Burwell (1993). Asset Spend-down in Nursing Homes, *Medical Care*, 31, 1, 1–23.
3. Administration on Aging (2000). *Profile of Older Americans,* Online at www.aoa.gov/aoa/stats/profile/default.htm.
4. Agency for Health Care Policy and Research (1997). *Meeting Medicaid's Cost and Quality Challenges: The Role of AHCPR Research*, AHCPR Publication No. 97–0044, Rockville, MD: Agency for Health Care Policy and Research.
5. Agency for Health Care Policy and Research (1996). Study Links Decline in Physician's Income to Managed Care, *Research Activities*, 199 (December), 5.
6. Alpha Center (1999). *Purchasing Pathfinders*, Washington, DC, Alpha Center.
7. American Association of Retired Persons (1997). AARP Group Health Insurance Program, Allentown, PA: Prudential Insurance Company of America.
8. American Association of Retired Persons (1998). *A Profile of Older Americans*, Washington, DC: AARP.
9. American Association of Retired Persons (1999). Social Security and Medicare Changes: 2000 Benefits and Changes, *AARP Bulletin*, 40 (2), 8, 13.
10. American Geriatric Society (1998). AGS Explores Medicare Fraud and Abuse, *AGS Newsletter*, 27 (3), 1.
11. Anderson, Steve (1996, 1998). Administrator, Beverly Health and Rehabilitation Center, Spokane, WA. Presentations to a Washington State University class on "Aging and Long Term Care Administration."
12. Angel, Ronald J., and Jacqueline L. Angel (1997). *Who Will Care For Us? Aging and Long Term Care in Multi-Cultural America*, New York: New York University Press.
13. Appleby, Julie (1999). GAO: Cuts Help Health Plan, *USA Today*, 17 (180) May 27, 3B.
14. Arendell, Terry, and Carroll L. Estes (1991). Older Women in the Post-Reagan Era, *International Journal of Health Services Research*, 21 (1), 59–73.
15. Armour, Stephanie (1999). Pension Debate Is Heating Up, *USA Today*, September 21, B1.
16. Ball, Robert M. (1990). Public-Private Solution to Protection Against the Cost of Long-Term Care, *Journal of the American Geriatric Society*, 38 (2), 156–63.
17. Barausch, Amanda Smith (1994). *Older Women in Poverty: Private Lives and Public Policy*, New York: Springer.
18. Barker, Kim (1997). Sheer Number of Claims Opens Door to Billing Fraud, *The Spokesman-Review*, October 26, A-12.
19. Barth, Michael C., William McNaught, and Philip Rizzi (1995). Older Americans as Workers, in Scott A. Bass (ed), *Older and Active: How Americans over 55 Are Contributing to Society*, New Haven: Yale University Press, 35–70.
20. Besharov, Douglas J., and Keith W. Smith (1999). Neglecting the "Oldest Old," *The Washington Post National Weekly Edition*, 16 (34), 23.

21. Binstock, Robert H. (1994). Changing Criteria in Old-Age Programs: The Introduction of Economic Status and Need for Services, *The Gerontologist*, 34 (6), 726–30.

22. Blair, Cornelia, Mark A. Siegel, and Jacquelyn Quiram (1998). *Growing Old in America*, Wylie, TX: Information Plus.

23. Bosworth, Barry, and Gary Burtless (1997). Budget Crunch: Population Aging in Rich Countries, *The Brookings Review*, 15 (3), 10-15.

24. Bosworth Barry, and Gary Burtless (1998). Population Aging and Economic Performance, in Barry Bosworth and Gary Burtless (eds), *Aging Societies: The Global Dimension*, Washington, DC: Brookings Institution Press, 1–27.

25. Carlson, Elliot (2000). New Forecast Adds Life to Social Security and Medicare, *AARP Bulletin*, 41 (5), 8.

26. Carr, Margaret N. (1999). Reimbursement, in Bella J. May. *Home Health and Rehabilitation: Concepts of Care* (2nd ed.), Philadelphia: F.A. Davis Company, 321–35.

27. Carson, Verna Benner (1996). Psychiatric Home Care: Evaluating the Present, Envisioning the Future, *Caring Magazine*, 15 (12), 34–39.

28. Carter, Marshall N., and William G. Shipman (1996). The Coming Global Pension Crisis, *Foreign Affairs*, 75 (6), S1-S10.

29. Cohn, Arthur (1999). Administrator, Covenant House, Dayton, Ohio. Personal Conversation.

30. Coile, Russ (1995). Age Wave: Organizing Integrated Care Networks for an Aging Society, *Health Trends*, 7 (6), 1–8.

31. Consumer Reports (1997a). How to Judge a Policy, *Consumer Reports*, October, 40–50.

32. Consumer Reports (1997b). What to Expect from Medicaid, *Consumer Reports*, October, 36–39.

33. Coon, Dennis (1989). *Introduction to Psychology* (5th ed), New York: West.

34. Cooper, Glenn, and Peter Scherer (1998). Can We Afford to Grow Old, *OECD Observer*, June/July (Issue 212), 20–22.

35. Crenshaw, Albert B. (1998). Women and Social Security: A Special Special Interest, *Washington Post National Weekly Edition*, August 17, 12.

36. Cutler, David M., and Louise M. Sheiner (1994). Policy Options for Long-Term Care, in David A. Wise (ed), *Studies in the Economics of Aging*, Chicago: The University of Chicago Press, 395–442.

37. Daus, Carol (1997). NASL: An Advocate for Long-Term Care Providers, *REHAB Management*, 10 (1), 13, 114.

38. Deets, Horace B. (1998). Pension Reforms Would Boost Income Security, *AARP Bulletin*, 39 (4), 3.

39. Dey, Achintya N. (1996). Characteristics of Elderly Home Health Care Users, *Advance Data from Vital and Health Statistics*, Bulletin 272, Hyattsville, MD: National Center for Health Statistics.

40. Dittbrenner, Heather (1996). Building Bridges to Wellness: Changing the Medicare System, *Caring Magazine*, January, 30–33.

41. Evans, Robert G. (1997). Going for the Gold: The Redistributive Agenda Behind Market-Based Health Care Reform, *Journal of Health Politics, Policy and Law*, 22 (2), 427–65).

42. Fischer, Lucy Rose, Marcie Parker, Cynthia L. Polich, William Pastor, and Laura Pitt (1991). How Does An HMO Decide Whether to Create Its Own Home Health Care Agency or Contract Out for Services? *Health Care Supervisor*, 9 (3), 39–50.

43. Fisher, Christy (1996). The Outlook for 1996, *Provider*, 22 (1), 36–42.

44. Fisher, Christy (1997). The Road Ahead, *Provider*, 23 (1), 26–32.

45. Folland, Sherman, Allen C. Goodman, and Miron Stano (1997). *The Economics of Health and Health Care*, Upper Saddle River, NJ: Prentice Hall.

46. Friedland, Robert B. (1996). Demographic, Economic, and Health Factors Likely to Affect Public Policy, *Journal of Long Term Home Health Care*, 15 (4), 24–37.

47. Genovese, Rosalie G. (1997). *Americans at Midlife: Caught Between Generations*, Westport, Connecticut: Bergin & Garvey.

48. Gleick, Elizabeth (1995). A Tale of Two States, *Time*, 146 (25), 31–36.

49. Gregg, Judd, John Breaux, Jim Kolbe, and Charles W. Stenholm (1998). A Unanimous Proposal From a Bipartisan Commission, *Washington Post National Weekly Edition*, August 17, 9–10.

50. Haas, Jane Glenn (1996). 'Spend Down' Law A Scare for Seniors, *The Orange County Register*, December 16, 1, 6.

51. Halter, Jeffrey B. (1998). From the President: Jeffrey B. Halter, MD, *American Geriatric Society Newsletter*, 27 (4), 2.

52. Hawryluk, Markian (1996). Lessons From Arizona on Managing Costs, *Provider*, 22 (7), 23–24.

53. Health Care Financing Administration (1997, 1998). Online at www.hcfa.gov.

54. Hurd, Michael D. (1990). Research on the Elderly: Economic Status, Retirement, and Consumption and Saving, *Journal of Economic Literature*, 28, June, 565–637.

55. Iglehart, John H. (1999a). The American Health Care System: Expenditures, *New England Journal of Medicine*, 340 (11), 70–76.

56. Iglehart, John H. (1999b). The American Health Care System: Medicaid, *New England Journal of Medicine*, 340 (5), 403–8.

57. Iglehart, John H. (1999c). The American Health Care System: Medicare, *New England Journal of Medicine*, 340 (4), 327–32.

58. Johnson, Russell J. (1997). State and Local Approaches to Long-Term Care, in Robert J. Newcomer and Ann M. Wilkinson (eds), Focus on Managed Care and Quality Assurance, *Annual Review of Gerontology and Geriatrics*, Vol. 16, New York: Springer, 112–39.

59. Kane, Rosalie A., and Mary Olsen Baker (1996). Emerging Trends in Managed Care, presentation to a conference on *Managed Care Issues and Themes: What Next for the Aging Network?* Sponsored by the Administration on Aging, Department of Health and Human Services, Washington, DC.

60. Koff, Theodore H. (1988). *New Approaches to Health Care for An Aging Population*, San Francisco: Jossey-Bass.

61. Kolb, Deborah S., Petr J. Veysey, and Joseph L. Gocke (1991). Private Long-Term Care Insurance: Will It Work? *Topics in Health Care Financing*, 17 (4), 9–21.

62. Kuttner, Robert (1999a). The American Health Care System: Employer-Sponsored Health Coverage, *New England Journal of Medicine*, 340 (3), 248–52.

63. Kuttner, Robert (1999b). The American Health Care System: Health Insurance Coverage, *New England Journal of Medicine*, 340 (2), 163–67.

64. Kuttner, Robert (1999c). The American Health Care System: Wall Street and Health Care, *New England Journal of Medicine*, 350 (8), 664–68.

65. Lew, Nancy De, George Greenberg, and Kraig Kinchen (1992). A Layman's Guide to the U.S. Health Care System, *Health Care Financing Review*, 14 (1), 151–68.

66. Lewis, Robert (1998a). New Pension Break for Women? *AARP Bulletin*, 39 (11), 6.

67. Lewis, Robert (1998b). Retirement Age: No Easy Answer, *AARP Bulletin*, 39 (8), 1, 11.

68. Lewis, Myrna I. (1997). An Economic Profile of American Older Women, *Journal of the American Medical Women's Association*, 52 (3), 107–12.

69. Love, Alice Ann (1998). Nursing Homes: Who Pays?, *Spokesman-Review* (Spokane, WA), 115(340), A1, A9.

70. Marlowe, Joseph F. (1996). Long-Term Care Insurance: A Private Sector Challenge, *Employee Benefits Journal*, 21 (4), 8–12.

71. McDonald, Ingrid (1998), The Cost of Home- and Community-Based Care, *Innovations*, 27 (1), 25–27.

72. Mergenhagen, Paula (1994). Rethinking Retirement, *American Demographics*, June, 28–34.

73. Moody, Harry R. (1994). *Aging: Concepts and Controversies*, Thousand Oaks, CA: Pine Forge Press.

74. Murtaugh, Christopher, Peter Kemper, and Brenda C. Spillman (1995). Risky Business: Long-Term Care Insurance Underwriting, *Inquiry*, 32, Fall, 271–84.

75. National Center for Health Care Statistics (1998). *Health United States 1998*, Washington, DC: U.S. Government Printing Office.

76. Neely, Jamie Tobias (1997). Home Improvement, *The Spokesman Review* (Spokane, WA), September 7, E1, E7.

77. Organization for Economic Cooperation and Development (OECD) (1994). *Caring for Frail Elderly People*, Paris: OECD.

78. Organization for Economic Cooperation and Development (OECD) (1995). *The Labour Market and Older Workers*, Paris: OECD.

79. Organization for Economic Cooperation and Development (OECD) (1996a). *Ageing in OECD Countries: A Critical Policy Challenge*, Paris: OECD.

80. Organization for Economic Cooperation and Development (OECD) (1996b). *Caring for Frail Elderly People: Policies in Evolution*, Paris: OECD.

81. Pallarito, Karen (1991). Integrated Health Services Finds Profitable Niche in Geriatric Medical Care, *Modern Healthcare*, 21 (32), 44–45.

82. Pressley, Sue Anne (1998). Taxation for Education Hits Gray Area, *The Washington Post National Weekly Edition*, 15 (12), January 19, 30.

83. Protulis, Steve (1999). No: Only the Well-Off Would Benefit, *AARP Bulletin*, 40 (9), 29.

84. Regan, Shawn Patrick (1996). Medicaid Estate Planning: Congress' Ersatz Solution for Long-Term Health Care, *Catholic University Law Review* (Specialty Law Digest: Health Care Law), 213, 9–59.

85. Rich, Spencer (1997). Curing Disabilities Might Save Medicare, *The Washington Post National Weekly Edition*, 14 (21), 35.

86. Rix, Sara E. (1994). Retirement and the American Woman, in Abraham Monk (ed), *The Columbia Retirement Handbook*, New York: Columbia University Press, 433–47.

87. Rodat, Carol, and Jim Zadoorian (1996). Societies Abandonment of the Frail Elderly: True or False? *Journal of Long Term Home Health Care*, 15 (1), 30–46.

88. Rovner, Julie (1997). Managed Care Medicare, *Modern Maturity*, 40 (6), 4, 35–43, 75–77.

89. Rundle, Rhonda L., and Laurie McGinley (1998). Medicare Cuts Draw Blood In Home-Care Industry, *Wall Street Journal*, May 1, B1, B4.

90. Samuelson, Robert J. (1998). Redefining Elderly, *The Washington Post National Weekly Edition*, 16 (2), 26.

91. Samuelson, Robert J. (1999). The Seduction of Surpluses, *Newsweek*, 134 (2), 74.

92. Schulz, James H., Alan Borowski, and William H. Crown (1991). *Economics of Population Aging: The "Graying" of Australia, Japan, and the United States*, New York: Auburn House.

93. Schulz, James H., and John Myles (1990). Old Age Pensions: A Comparative Perspective, Chapter 21 in Robert H. Binstock and Linda K. George (eds.) *Handbook of Aging and the Social Sciences* (3rd ed.), San Diego, CA: Academic Press, 398–414.

94. Schulz, James H., Linda Rosenman, and Sara E. Rix (1999). International Developments in Social Security Privatization: What Risk to Women?, *Journal of Cross-Cultural Gerontology*, 14 (1), 25–42.

95. Schwenk, F. N. (1993). Changes in the Economic Status of America's Elderly Population During the Last 50 Years, *Family Economics Review*, 6 (1), 18–27.

96. Serafini, Marilyn Werber (1995). Praising Arizona, *National Journal*, 27 (45), 2803–6.

97. Shoven, John B., Michael D. Topper, and David A. Wise (1994). The Impact of Demographic Transition on Government Spending, in David A. Wise (ed), *Studies in the Economics of Aging*, Chicago: The University of Chicago Press, 13–40.

98. Siegenthaler, Jurg K. (1996). Poverty Among Single Elderly Women Under Different Systems of Old Age Security: A Comparative Review, *Social Security Bulletin*, 59 (3), 31–44.

99. Sloan, Frank A., and May W. Shayne (1993). Long-Term Care, Medicaid, and Improverishment of the Elderly, *Inquiry*, 71 (4), 575–99.

100. Sloan, Frank A., May W. Shayne, and Christopher J. Conover (1995). Continuing Care Retirement Communities: Prospects for Reducing Institutional Long-Term Care, *Journal of Health Politics, Policy, and Law*, 20 (1), 75–98.

101. Snider, Sara (1995). Long-Term Care and the Private Insurance Market, *Employee Benefit Research Institute Issue Brief*, Number 163, July.

102. Social Security Administration (1999). *Social Security Programs Around the World*, Washington, DC: U.S. Government Printing Office.

103. Sterns, Harvey L., and Anthony A. Sterns (1995). Health and the Employment Capability of Older Americans, in Scott A. Bass (ed), *Older and Active: How Americans over 55 Are Contributing to Society*, New Haven: Yale University Press, 10–34.

104. Stevens, Roseman A. (1999). Let's Figure Out How to Pay for Medicare, *Washington Post National Weekly Edition*, April 12, 23.

105. Tanner, Michael (1998). Re-Thinking Social Security, *The Washington Post Weekly Edition*, August 17, 8.

106. Teachers Insurance and Annuity Association (1998), Long-Term Care Alternatives, *TIAA-CREF Bulletin: Special 1998 Update*, Winter.

107. Toner, Robin (1999). Wide Variance Is Found in HMO Drug Benefits for Elderly, *The New York Times*, August 22, 19.

108. Travis, Shirley, and William J. McAuley (1994). Conceptions of Long-Term Care Risk, Costs, and Reimbursement Among Middle-Aged and Elderly People, *Journal of Health and Human Services*, 17 (2), 146–61.

109. United States Bureau of the Census (1998). *National Data Book*, Washington, DC: U.S. Government Printing Office.

110. USA Today (1998). Health Costs, *USA Today*, January 20, 1.

111. Vobejda, Barbara (1998). The Rich Get Richer, and So Do the Old, *Washington Post National Weekly Edition*, 15 (45), 34.

112. Walker, Alan, Jens Alber and Anne-Marie Guillemard (1993). *Older People in Europe: Social and Economic Policies*, Brussels: European Observatory, Commission of the European Community.

113. Walker, Alan, and Tony Maltby (1997). *Ageing Europe*, Philadelphia: Open University Press.

114. Wall Street Journal (1998). Medicare Beneficiaries, *Wall Street Journal*, March 5, 1.

115. Ward, David A., and Lorene H. Stone (1996). *Sociology*, Minneapolis/St. Paul: West.

116. Wimberly, Edward T. (1993). Public and Private Strategies for Reforming Long-Term Care, *Journal of Human Resources Administration*, 16 (2), 157–70.

117. Wise, David A. (1997). Retirement Against the Demographic Trend: More Older People Living Longer, Working Less, and Saving Less, *Demography*, 34 (1), 83–95.

118. Wright, Jim (1997). Older Workers Essential for Economy, *Spokesman-Review* (Spokane, WA), 115 (154), B10.

119. Yakoboski, Paul, and Celia Silverman (1994). Baby Boomers in Retirement: What Are Their Prospects? *Employee Benefit Research Institute Issue Brief Number 151*, July 1994.

Chapter 9

LIFESTYLES
Work, Retirement, and Leisure

 INTRODUCTION

This chapter examines some lifestyle types, work patterns, retirement preferences, and leisure options of older people. Specific topics include:

- Work and retirement history.
- Continuing work.
- Characteristics of retirement.
- Major retirement activities.
- Lifestyle change alternatives.

The lifestyle choices are abundant and the variation enormous. Consequently, we have selected and characterized only a few of the predominant patterns. Lifestyles gradually evolve for most people as they age and radical change is the exception rather than the rule. Adaptations are made as new knowledge and experience are gained or as choice is limited by declining health. Individuals who make thoughtful advance preparations will generally manage the transitions better than those who do not, as former President Carter emphasized in his book, *Virtues of Aging.*[21, 67, 90]

Popular media images sometimes suggest that a high proportion of older people lead a leisurely life with declining social involvement, limited responsibility, eventual dependence, and declining contributions to society. Although these images do fit some people, active and productive lifestyles are more typical. Most older people continue to make very substantial contributions to family life, their communities, volunteer activities, politics, and public policy.

◆◆◆ WORK AND RETIREMENT HISTORY

The pattern of retirement was structured early in American history through union contracts in American auto companies and other industries. The option of separation at age 55 after 30 years of service was common. Blue-collar workers were much more likely to retire earlier and more voluntarily than professionals, managers, or white-collar workers. When Social Security retirement age was set at age 65, with partial benefits available at age 62, a high proportion of workers left the workforce in their early 60s because the resources were available to live reasonably well. Medicare benefits were added in 1965 making retirement even more financially feasible.[43]

A similar pattern developed in Europe, although the retirement age was set somewhat younger (55 to 60) in many countries to open positions for younger workers. Benefits for retirees were generally somewhat more generous, as were health care benefits. However, in Japan retirement is often delayed to a much later age, in part because the pension benefits are not as generous as in Europe or the United States and retirees must depend on family support.

When the federal government in the United States began to require that private corporations count their retirement obligations as debits in annual accounting reports, net worth was lowered and corporate interest in early retirement pension benefits began to diminish. This was among the factors that decreased contributions to employee pension benefits in the 1990s, making early retirement less possible.[43]

Public employers such as the United States Department of Defense offer early retirement to military personal. Other federal departments allow employees to retire after 35 years of service. State and local government retirement systems also have provisions for early retirement of police, fire fighters, and other employees in high stress positions. To some extent Social Security also encourages early retirement by making benefits available beginning at age 62, albeit at somewhat lower levels than at age 65 or older. This has helped to make 62 more common as a retirement age than age 65.[43, 70]

Retirees have traditionally tended to continue a lifestyle developed over many years in the same community. Most people remain in the same home in the same neighborhood throughout retirement. For example, in 1997 only about 5 percent of older people moved at all, compared to 18 percent of the population under age 65. Roughly 2 percent of the moves were to another home within the community; 2 percent moved within the same county; and only 1 percent moved out of state.[3, 96]

A small proportion of older people do not retire, but remain very busy continuing a first career or pursuing a second or third career or vocation. A vigorous routine is obviously more possible for some older people than others; physical health, mental condition, family support, adequacy of income, and other life conditions may limit choices.[60, 85]

General Lifestyle Types

We define lifestyle as a general pattern of behavior, activities, and leisure developed over a lifetime. An individual's "style" is influenced by personal values, experience, community traditions, and larger cultural expectations. Lifestyle depends heavily on social class, as discussed earlier, and the potential for choice dictated by income level, education, occupation, and other dimensions of personal background.

The Upper Class. Upper-class status is limited to an estimated 10 percent or less of the older population in the higher-income, greater education, and more prestigious occupational categories. For them, optimal aging and high quality of life are readily possible, although not always realized. Upper-class individuals and couples are likely to have substantial resources available—financial security, knowledge, skills, and personal influence. Many continue working because they like what they do. Relatively good health into older age is the norm. National and international travel is a common experience, as are moves from a home community to seek a leisurely lifestyle in deluxe retirement communities.[57]

Communities surrounding a golf course represent one example of upper-class retirement choice. Residents tend to design their lives around golf and the opportunities afforded by a relatively affluent environment. They choose the golf club atmosphere in part because it gives them the freedom to do as they like—outdoor activity, enjoyment of the natural and constructed beauty of the environment, and social activities with friends of similar background.

The Middle Class. The great majority of middle-class older people retire in the community of long-term residence. High value is placed on staying in touch with a circle of long-time friends, maintaining a house and yard, being of service to the community, going to local clubs, gathering with family on holidays, and generally enjoying the neighborhood ambiance. A certain proportion have sufficient resources for leisurely travel, visiting children or friends, and even spending part of the year in other locations around the country. Very few continue to work after age 65. A retirement lifestyle is typically supported from several sources: Social Security, a pension, savings and homeownership. Lifestyles are highly diverse and thus difficult to precisely characterize.

The Lower Class. Limited resources and limited options characterize lower social class lifestyles. Many must manage in relative poverty without the amenities usually associated with a good quality of life. Housing may be modest. Health care and mental health care are often inaccessible because of limited knowledge and lack of private health insurance; Medicare and supplemental Medicaid may be the only options available. Recreation may be largely limited to activities in the home and immediate neighborhood.[66]

Because of relatively low retirement income, continued work may be necessary at lower paying jobs. Chronic disease and disability are common—in part because of poor health maintenance practices and limited access to high-quality health care.

A high proportion of older women are poor because a spouse has not survived to older age and insufficient retirement resources were in place. Life is nearly always something of a struggle. Aging may not be optimal and quality of life may be marginal. Nonetheless, many individuals function very well within their limited resources.

The characterizations of upper, middle, and lower social classes described above are intended to portray a general image. Clearly, there are enormous variations within each social class level. Ability to function independently is a key factor in lifestyle regardless of social class; major disability diminishes options for everyone but need not always destroy quality of life.[83]

◆◆◆ CONTINUING WORK

The tendency to retire early has increased significantly during recent decades in the United States and other countries, as summarized in Table 9–1, for men ages 55 to 64 in several countries.

The countries listed in the table have experienced significant employment declines between 1970 and 1990 for individuals age 55 to 64, especially notable in the Netherlands, Germany, and France, and somewhat less so only in Sweden. In Europe many of those not employed were receiving some form of disability payments or unemployment benefits as a substitute for social security income. Consequently, costs for such benefits rose rather substantially, and were largely ended during the 1990s. Efforts are now underway in most countries to encourage continued work to later ages.[41]

Although overall employment of older workers has decreased, part-time work has actually increased in the United States. Full- or part-time employment patterns include:[41]

1. Continuing to work to cover expenses.
2. Wanting to remain productively occupied but with greater leisure.
3. Needing to work following retirement under duress because of organizational policy or disability.

TABLE 9–1   Employment Status of Men Between Ages 55 and 64 (percentages employed)

Country	1970	1980	1990
United States	78	69	64
United Kingdom	87	74	63
Netherlands	77	61	44
Germany	79	64	52
Sweden	84	77	75
France	74	65	43

Source: Selected data from OECD as reported in Guillemard, 1996: 224.

4. Wanting to maintain work-related social relationships and social status.
5. Having high-demand knowledge and/or skills and being willing to receive less pay than younger workers and receive fewer benefits.
6. Enjoying the flexibility of temporary positions or helping out in particularly busy seasons.

Higher-paid professional workers holding jobs with considerable autonomy, intellectual challenge, and minimal physical demands are especially likely to continue working past the usual retirement age. A high proportion of the baby boom generation believe that continued work is desirable or necessary, as revealed in a 1998 survey by the American Association of Retired Persons: roughly 80 percent intend to continue full- or part-time. About 70 percent are saving and investing to prepare for retirement but are not sure it will be sufficient; they distrust the continuing viability of Social Security and Medicare. A 1991 Commonwealth Fund national survey indicated work at older ages is related to satisfaction with life: 67 percent said they were very satisfied.[9, 33, 59, 83]

Reentry to the Work Force After Retirement

A national study indicated that nearly one-third of retirees reenter the work force, most within one year—although only 12 percent were working in 1998 of whom more than half were part-time. They may have misjudged their retirement resource needs or realized the purchasing power of retirement income was insufficient. Some become bored with *too much* leisure. However, for many people major disadvantages result from a return to full-time work. A new job may not fit skills that were appropriate in previous employment; compensation may not be comparable; or experience with managers and co-workers may not be satisfying. A substantial decline in wages is commonplace in postretirement jobs.[1, 47]

Gender Differences

More older men were at work (16 percent) in 1998 than older women (8 percent). However, shortage of retirement resources means that more widowed or divorced women than men must work; more women over age 75 are at work than men of the same age, although the numbers are relatively small. Many younger women continue to work after an older husband retires, sometimes until they are independently eligible for a pension or social security. Others work because the husband's retirement resources are considered insufficient for their preferred lifestyle. On the plus side, employed women in the United States over age 25 were nearly as likely as men to be covered by pension plans by the mid-1990s—although pensions are generally smaller because of lower average wages in the workplace.[1, 35, 70, 91]

Women tend to have more positive attitudes toward older age and retirement than men and are more likely to retire early, sometimes as caretakers for a parent or a spouse who is ill. They experience less role change since they are more likely than men to continue many tasks and relationships experienced throughout their lives.[42]

Demands and Opportunities

The experience and skills of older workers become more valuable in times of low unemployment, as was the case in the late 1990s. Many older workers have well-developed competencies at problem-solving. Abundant opportunities were available for those who wanted to work, especially in the service sector. The new "information age" jobs have become more dependent on mental rather than physical capacity, which gives certain advantages to healthy older workers with the appropriate knowledge and skills. Trained individuals in highly technical fields, such as computer operation, nursing, medicine, teaching, law, or accounting, can maintain much of their learning ability and skills well into advanced age. They are likely to be very responsible workers, thus diminishing the employer need and expense for hiring and training new workers.[93]

Older workers also have an advantage in jobs that require interaction with other older people, whether in retail establishments, health care, recreation, or other domains. Good relationships with co-workers and social participation through group activities are on average considered more important by older than younger workers. On the downside, older workers who have stayed in one job for a long time are likely to have seniority and be paid more, thus generating high labor costs for an employer.[93]

Age Discrimination and Its Consequences

The formal expectation of retirement at the chronological age of 65 often puts mentally and physically fit older individuals at a substantial disadvantage if they want to continue working. Evidence of discrimination against older workers led to anti-age discrimination laws such as the Age Discrimination in Employment Act of 1967, passed by Congress to eliminate mandatory retirement requirements in both private and public organizations. The law was intended to counter ageism attitudes of employers that seriously limited opportunities for older workers.[72, 76]

Independent professionals and other highly trained workers want the freedom to continue as long as they like. A survey in three countries (The United States, the United Kingdom, and Germany) indicated that individuals with higher levels of education and self-employed workers tend to oppose mandatory retirement more vigorously than those with less education who work for wages. This is among the reasons that Sweden has taken the lead in supporting gradual retirement and encouraging opportunities for older workers to continue on a part-time basis. Japan has also encouraged continued work.[11, 44]

Many employers in the United States are unwilling to invest in older worker training, continuing education, or retirement planning. Unequal treatment with respect to salary increases, promotions, and performance evaluation may mean loss of status and ill feelings of older workers toward the employer.[2, 9, 17] Consequently, continued productive work may be very difficult, as suggested in Illustration 9–1.

Illustration 9–1
AGE DISCRIMINATION AND UNEQUAL TREATMENT IN ACADEMIA

After 20 years at a western university and at age 59, Professor Raymond was appointed director of a new graduate program. Among his new roles was hiring of faculty. The best candidates were relatively young and somewhat inexperienced, but they were in high demand and would only accept the positions at base salaries that were 10 percent higher than Professor Raymond himself was paid. Administrators felt forced to pay the higher salaries to fill the positions—a common dilemma within academic institutions.

Higher administrators were unwilling to increase Professor Raymond's salary to a level above salaries of the new faculty, despite his much greater experience, evidence of high productivity over many years, and institutional rules against inequity and age discrimination. They resisted in part because it would have been very expensive to upgrade the salaries of all senior faculty to make them equitable with new and younger faculty. Professor Raymond felt considerable anger and resentment over the inequity involved.

A few years later, when Raymond announced his intention to retire, a new program director who was fifteen years younger, with much less experience and prestige, was hired at a salary 37 percent higher than Raymond's. After the threat of a law suit the University finally agreed to somewhat redress the inequity, but not without ill feeling and considerable discomfort among administrators who professed to believe in equitable treatment.

Discrimination and inequity occur even in the most enlightened organization settings, despite formal policies to the contrary. Incentives for productivity in later years become negative when younger employees receive higher rewards for equal work. Efforts to further enhance opportunities for older workers have been vigorously pursued by such organizations as the American Association of Retired Persons and some corporations. Deliberate efforts are made to increase positive images of older individuals.[8]

The initiatives seem to have had positive effects on attitudes of employers. For example, the Travelers Companies (insurance and financial services) encouraged retired employees to come back to work on salary for 120 days each year without cutting their pensions. IBM rehired many of the skilled employees who were laid off during the downsizing of the early 1990s and designed a mentoring system that pairs senior employees with newly hired college graduates, as an incentive and training device. The opportunities for older workers have clearly improved and may get better as younger workers become scarce (increases of only 1 percent per year in younger workers are projected for the first decade of the twenty-first century).[27, 39, 61, 93, 99, 101]

Alternative Working Lifestyles

Increasing numbers of older individuals work part of the year in national, state, and other parks—as hosts, maintenance personnel, or in commercial store outlets. In return for the work, they receive a free campsite, have water and electricity provided, and are also paid a modest salary. Park rangers are responsible for managing any major problems with campers or wildlife. Such seasonal work with minimal benefits is viewed as desirable by both employers and employees. Because they are already drawing retirement income, and are covered by Medicare and/or supplementary insurance, they don't feel a need for the extra benefits. It would be difficult to keep some national forests and parks, and state parks, functioning without part-time older workers.

Older campground hosts often voluntarily do much more work than is required because they enjoy the setting, appreciate the interaction with visitors, and want the area for which they are responsible to be in top condition. Most hosts enjoy the experience, having been active users of the parks for many years.[6, 40] Illustration 9–2 describes one such experience.

Illustration 9-2
PART-TIME WORK IN A CAMPGROUND

George and Emma from southern Missouri were hosts for the summer of 1998 at Luby Bay National Forest campground at the edge of Priest Lake in the Idaho panhandle—surely among the most magnificent retirement locations in the northern United States. They collected fees, cleaned campsites and rest rooms, and helped keep track of the numerous black bears that were constantly invading the campground, as were less troublesome deer, elk, moose, and innumerable smaller animals and birds.

They worked for a private contractor employed by the U.S. Forest Service to manage campgrounds in the region. They received a small salary, a camping space, a phone, water, sewer, and electrical hookups in return for their work. Most campers were easy to deal with and even became good friends. Only a few caused major problems requiring intervention by the full-time park rangers.

Overall, they were delighted with the experience, although it was hard work. They took great pride in maintaining the beautiful setting and considered their work as a personal contribution to maintenance and enhancement of valuable public resources.

◆◆◆ CHARACTERISTICS OF RETIREMENT

Strong emotions are associated with a retirement decision since it represents a major change in lifestyle for many individuals who have worked eight hours or more per day for most of their adult lives. Uncertainty about the decision, fear of the unknown, hope, excitement, happiness, and other such feelings are common.[100]

The Meaning of Retirement

The primary societal goals for retirement are to: (1) shift individuals from full-time work to part-time or nonworking status so as to open opportunities for younger workers, and (2) to honor older individuals with the opportunity for leisure and fulfillment in their final years. The first goal is the primary basis for public policy in the United States and abroad, especially in times of high unemployment—characteristic of many European countries in recent decades. The goals are in flux in the early twentyfirst century as many countries rethink their retirement policies.[78]

Retirement status as a social role is in many respects ambiguous, with no clear cultural delineation of behavioral expectations. Individual goals or expectations vary greatly depending on what is socially permissible and whether or not retirement income is adequate. How to make use of the new free time is among the primary challenges for the retiree. The requirements of full-time work are gone and a new routine must replace the old one, with new ways of measuring accomplishments and contributions.[5, 34, 45]

Effects on the Family. Retirement of older parents can be positive or negative for adult children. On the one hand, it frees up time for greater family support, such as caring for children, providing transportation, and offering other forms of support. Retired couples have more time to do things together and tend to share household decision making more than in preretirement years. A high proportion of older couples indicate their marriages are happier after retirement than before. The freedom to travel may increase contact with children and grandchildren. On the other hand, additional time for family may be perceived as infringing on adult children's opportunity to concentrate on their own careers and nuclear family relationships.[31, 95]

Types of Retirees and Alternative Meanings. Four general types of retirees have been identified (although there are many subcategories) with these approaches to retirement:[42]

1. A desire to "wind down," fulfilling a preference for less structure, fewer daily requirements, and time for preferred leisure activities.
2. The primary focus of life shifting to opportunities for new experiences and revitalization; individuals remaining active without necessarily diminishing overall workload.
3. Experiencing no particular transition, challenge, or opportunity; part-time or new full-time work is initiated and preferred leisure activities are largely continued.
4. Experiencing a loss of a part of personal identity; often a new focus is difficult to achieve because of forced retirement or as a consequence of poor health.

The mode of adaptation is quite different for individuals in each of the general categories. Members of the first two groupings feel emancipated from control by an organization and like the opportunity to pursue a more fulfilling life. The third type experiences no major change. Self-employed workers tend to fall heavily into the third grouping with relatively little real transition at retirement age—depending in part on their economic status. They quite often continue with full- or part-time work. The first three types are likely to have a successful retirement, whereas the fourth may not, as Illustration 9–3 suggests.

Illustration 9–3
HANGING ON WITH PROFESSOR JONES

Professor Jones had been a pillar of the university for many years, as a department chairperson, director of a research center, member of many university committees, and as a very successful researcher with numerous major grants for investigation in his field. He had devoted his whole life to success in the university environment, with few other satisfying outlets.

Although he was well prepared financially, when time for retirement came at age 65 he did not want to give up his power and influence. Rather, his preference was to continue working in his campus office, going to faculty meetings, and exercising his influence, despite the fact that younger faculty were not happy with his participation. He wanted to continue controlling research projects even though he was no longer securing large research grants.

His involvement was eventually rejected by faculty, and he was advised by the new and younger department chair that he could not continue to represent the department on campus nor control research projects. He became upset for what he considered to be lack of respect for his accomplishments. He felt mistreated because of his age. Fortunately, he was eventually able to identify productive retirement alternatives, but not without considerable pain.

The Professor Jones case illustrates that not all professionals find it easy to make the transition from work to retirement. Negative consequences may occur when an individual who has been successful fails to prepare for an alternative future. Many senior executives who have worked hard and been in the limelight much of their lives find retirement boring; they often return to some form of professional work in a new environment that gives them a sense of achievement and responsibility.[34]

Individuals in nonprofessional and physically demanding jobs with little autonomy tend also to have some difficulty with retirement. They may retire early because of physical disability. They are more likely to have experienced unemployment and may have few resources for retirement. In some instances their predicament is a result of "career unraveling" in the sense that they suffer job loss or downward mobility prior to retirement. Studies indicate that older African American males often find themselves in this situation. Overall, they are less likely to have had higher education than European American males, and thus less opportunity for good retirement pensions. They are more likely to be disabled. If not, they must usually continue to work for sustenance until very late in life with little opportunity for leisure.[45, 46]

Socioeconomic background is clearly not the only important factor in retirement satisfaction. For example, single men and women who have never married may have difficulty adjusting to a nonworking life unless they have close and intimate friends or companions.[45, 84]

The Bases for Retirement Decisions

The ideal retirement occurs when it is entirely voluntary and based on personal choice, with positive new alternatives available. Most individuals want to visualize a secure future and have confidence about income, health care, and projected activities before deciding to give up work. However, it is difficult for many lower-income older workers to predict the return on modest savings or investments or the adequacy of private pensions. The news media are replete with stories about possible cutbacks in Social Security, Medicare, and other benefits to older workers. The family retirement decision is somewhat more complicated when the spouse is also working.[53, 95, 100]

Retirement Preparation

The best preparation involves careful financial planning, experimenting, and trying out several alternative lifestyles well before the retirement date. Husbands and wives should discuss the topic well in advance, with each having considerable influence in the discussions—especially when both are working.[21, 25, 47, 92, 94]

However, adequate preparation is easier said than done. For example, physicians are in a highly prestigious profession, and retirement is often difficult to contemplate because of the huge change required when shifting from a busy medical practice to a leisurely lifestyle. Some of the more difficult issues faced by professionals like physicians are summarized in Illustration 9–4.

Illustration 9–4
PHYSICIANS AND RETIREMENT

Most physicians believe retirement should be a time of reflection and personal enhancement while they continue to make important contributions to society. They would like to continue being active, healthy, and financially secure. However, having a sound mind, body, and abundant resources guarantees nothing about adjustment to aging or retirement.

A high proportion of older doctors have devoted their lives to a very busy schedule of seeing patients and managing health care in an office or hospital setting, with little time spent on outside activities that prepare them for the required major lifestyle adjustments. The stress of daily professional commitments may have limited close ties with family and precluded development of fulfilling hobbies or other personal interests. The so-called golden years may simply not be welcome. (Such reactions, incidentally, tend to be more the case with male than female physicians, who have more often developed other leisure interests.)

For some male physicians, liberation from the daily medical practice is like becoming unshackled from a burdensome daily routine. For others the contemplation of freedom brings fear and uncertainty because they do not have a range of options in mind and are not prepared to enjoy the liberation. Retirement is viewed as unemployment would be, with no ready stimulating alternatives. A huge sense of loss is often felt even though the pressure from colleagues to retire, or the loss of patients, may make continuing practice untenable or intolerable. Prestige and a meaningful position are gone with nothing to replace them.

Many physicians admit they need considerable assistance in thinking about and planning their retirement. Although, they might like to volunteer some of their time, they have difficulty identifying worthwhile and stimulating volunteer tasks, given their backgrounds. The retired physician is not in great demand for part-time work or other medical contributions at a time when highly qualified younger physicians are available in abundance. Most volunteer jobs are viewed as being without challenge, dignity, or sufficient reward. They must find something they believe in and feel is worth the effort—a major challenge involving identification of their personal values and preferred pathways in retirement.

Source: Information adapted from Weisman, 1996: 298–306. Used with permission of Guilford Press.

Numerous books and computer software systems are available to help the retirement planning process. The American Association of Retired Persons offers an extensive list of booklets and guidelines. Computer software manufacturers also offer a variety of tools, such as Quicken Financial Planner, Vanguard Retirement Planner, and the Charles Schwab Fund-Map. The Teachers Annuity and Insurance Association has designed a specific planning process with accompanying booklets that helps individuals to think through what resources they need and what they would most like to do in retirement. Important recommendations include:[25]

- Identify basic personal needs and desires: What values and experiences are most important and must be satisfied to have long-term satisfaction?
- Establish goals that explicitly define central interests: What achievements or outcomes will be challenging and likely to remain of high priority over many years?
- Identify specific preferred activities: What activities will have continuity and can be enjoyed and built upon over time?
- Plan for continued growth and personal development: What will stimulate the mind and body and continually enhance self-esteem?
- Replace work with creative alternatives: What products or activities will provide a sense of ongoing accomplishment?

Spending some time with pencil and paper systematically ranking goals and alternatives for reaching them, can help sort out and establish priorities.[54]

Some individuals set goals that turn out to be major challenges and lead to truly spectacular achievements, as described in Illustration 9–5.

Illustration 9–5
GOING FOR A HIKE

Earl Shaffer, a contractor and antique dealer before retirement in York Springs, Pennsylvania, was the first person to hike the Appalachian Trail from Springer Mountain, Georgia, to Millinocket, Maine—a distance of approximately 2,150 miles. He did it in 1948 when he was 29 years old, and again for the second time in 1965, going from Maine to Georgia in 99 days. He hiked it for the third time in 1998 when he was 79 years old, celebrating the fiftieth anniversary of the first trip! It took him a little longer, 173 days, but was an example of remarkable endurance and discipline.

Source: Data from Sharp, 1998: A16.

Retirement tends to be more a matter of building on previous foundations than striking out in radically new directions. Great retirements are largely a consequence of recognizing and pursuing opportunities for stimulation and fulfillment that coincide with one's preferred lifestyle.[55]

◆◆◆ MAJOR RETIREMENT ACTIVITIES

Possible retirement activities are innumerable. Several magazines and many books are available outlining options.[30]

Continuing Education

A high proportion of retired individuals are stimulated by continued learning and new experience. A few take formal classes in college or university settings, but informal education is even more popular. The National Center for Education Statistics reported that 38 percent of the older population participate in some form of adult education. Older adults are as able to learn how to use computers and search the World Wide Web as are younger people and have become actively involved in the use of information technology.[14, 56]

An analysis of students attending Open University classes in the United Kingdom indicated that older students age 60 to 64 were the overall best performers of any age group. Furthermore, comparisons with older students in other parts of Europe suggested that the British group was reasonably representative of older students in general. This is encouraging evidence for those who want to pursue intellectual opportunities as they age.[90]

Elderhostel. Elderhostel is among the most popular informal educational programs. It was created at the University of New Hampshire in 1975 especially for people age 55 and older. The courses last one or two weeks. Meals are included, as are field trips to regional attractions. More than 300 special Elderhostel experiences were available to recreational vehicle travelers in 1998. Costs ranged from $250 to $400 for a package including meals, instruction, field trips, admissions, and printed course materials.[79]

Opportunities for travel and study with Elderhostel are currently available throughout the United States, Canada and Europe. A quarterly catalog is published listing locations and available courses (75 Federal Street, Boston, MA 02110). Many course locations are conducted at colleges and universities where dormitory rooms are available at relatively low cost. Most classes focus on the unique qualities of the region and feature instructors who are local experts. More than 300,000 individuals participated in 1997, some attending several programs during the year.[79]

The Chautauqua Institute. The Chautauqua Institute in western New York has been influential as a learning opportunity since 1874. It has hosted many distinguished speakers (including most American presidents) in a Victorian village on 856 acres in a beautiful area. Weekend and week-long educational programs are offered in the arts, religion, recreation, and other fields.[34]

Senior College. The University of Southern Maine sponsors a college opportunity for senior citizens. The goal is to provide a curriculum of intellectual opportunities and special activities that addresses crucial aspects of living in older age while stimulating the mind, body, and spirit. The majority of courses are taught by older persons with training or experience in subjects of interest to other older individuals. Community forums are also available on issues of current interest. Social, leisure, and recreational opportunities include field trips, international learning opportunities, and regular luncheons.[86]

Participants pay a membership fee of $25, entitling them to ongoing information from the Senior College and the wider University. Membership totaled 496 for the 1998-99 academic year. Fees were $50 for one course or $75 for two courses per semester. The program is affiliated with the Elderhostel Institute Network and administered by the University Center for Extended Academic Programs.[4]

These are just a few examples of innumerable special education programs for retirees. Continuing education has already become a lifelong process for a substantial proportion of the older population. They have learned that maintaining and enhancing knowledge and skills, while adapting to the rapid changes of the information age, requires constant learning and adaptation.[77]

Volunteering for Community Service

A 1991 survey by the Commonwealth Fund, described earlier, indicated that 44 percent of older people had volunteered in community activities. The median time spent per week was 6.5 hours (an average of 4 hours per week was reported in a Marriott sponsored Senior Volunteerism study). Church-related activity is by far the most common form of participation, followed by service in hospitals, nursing homes, hospices, or other health care settings. Involvement in civic organizations and senior citizen centers are also common. Most volunteer activity was viewed as fulfilling rather than a burden.[10, 14, 20, 80, 98]

Public policy directly supports volunteer activity, through funding of programs that target older people, such as the Senior Volunteer Program described elsewhere. Social participation in communities, nationally and internationally, is subsidized to encourage productive and worthwhile work. Many local governments sponsor volunteer programs that appeal to older citizens.[7]

Communities are heavily dependent on older citizens—especially in small towns where there may be a shortage of younger people. Volunteerism is very popular in retirement communities where most of the social and cultural life is locally organized. A study of volunteers and nonvolunteers in one Arizona retirement community revealed that 58 percent had volunteered for at least one service activity in the past year. People with higher education and/or professional or technical skills tend to volunteer more than those with less education and fewer skills. Higher incomes, good health, being married, and religious activism contribute to volunteerism.[73]

Direct service, tutoring, advising, coaching, or directly helping other individuals, is viewed as the most fulfilling and is the most usual type of activity. Volunteers are especially motivated by the possibility of making an important impact that will be appreciated by the individual or organization served. Physical work such as cleaning or environmental maintenance, fundraising for church, supporting political candidates, and serving on boards or committees are also popular. Volunteering is more common among women than men.[20]

Older individuals want to feel that their work is significant and worthwhile. Receiving a small stipend for such programs as Senior Companions (who assist disabled elderly in their home) or Foster Grandparents is attractive to retirees with lower incomes who need additional resources to live comfortably.[20]

A much larger group volunteer for causes that affect their own self-interest. Older citizens have become a very strong force in American politics through activism in political parties and special interest organizations, such as the National Council of Senior Citizens, the National Committee to Preserve Social Security and Medicare, Gray Panthers, the Older Women's League, the Seniors Coalition, the United seniors Association, the 60/Plus Association, and, by far the largest, the American Association of Retired People (AARP). All of these organizations have taken an active role in state and national policy formation efforts related to the older population and involve thousands of older people in direct lobbying, phone calls, or letter-writing to influence legislation that affects the well-being of their age peers. However, the various groups are by no means united in their viewpoints; they vary across the political spectrum from very conservative to very liberal.[26, 65]

Older individuals vote at a much higher rate than the younger population, for example, 67 percent versus 54 percent in 1996 presidential elections. Many are active in political parties and in special interest groups such as the American Association of Retired Persons. Age-based groups have gained a great deal of power and credibility with political leaders. Political activity in community governance tends also to be popular. Politicians usually cater to groups of older people and are happy to have volunteers for fund-raising and get-out-the-vote efforts.[13, 14]

Knowledge and Skill Sharing

Especially knowledgeable and skilled members of the older population represent a rich resource that can enhance the well-being of families, communities, and nations, through a great variety of consulting and teaching activities.[16, 29]

Consulting and Freelancing. Many individuals consult on a part-time basis to share their knowledge or skills with private firms and/or community, state or national organizations. Private consulting groups hire skilled retirees for temporary work with short-term projects—an alternative that is particularly attractive to individuals who like to travel in the United States or overseas. As an example, the International Executive Service Corps (P.O. Box 10005, Stamford, CT 06904-2005) was established in 1964 by a group of American business people to transfer managerial and technical skills to less-developed countries. The program operates in more than 50 nations with partial support from the U.S. Agency for International Development. Consultants provide technical assistance, help solve environmental problems, help reform economies, and promote small business development.[34]

The Service Corps of Retired Executives is a similar type of opportunity that offers services only within the United States. Participants assist small businesses and public organizations with resolution of management problems, usually receiving out-of-pocket expenses but no salary. A wide variety of comparable volunteer opportunities are available, such as the Peace Corps, Foster Grandparent Program, and the Retired Senior Volunteer Program.[2]

Part-time work by retirees has helped to alleviate the shortage of skilled individuals in such fields as computer programming, teaching, engineering, and other high demand occupations. Temporary employment firms such as Manpower, Incorporated, occasionally hire retired individuals. Eldertemps in Potomac, Maryland, specializes in placing older workers in short-term jobs.[34]

Domestic and International Travel

Travel is a very popular retirement pursuit, particularly to visit friends and relatives, but also to state and national parks and most other tourist destinations.[15]

A combination of travel and work is described in Illustration 9–6.

Illustration 9–6
TRAVEL AND ENTREPRENEURSHIP AT QUARTZITE, AZ

The largest Flea Market in the world is located at Quartzite, Arizona. More than a million visitors pass through there during the winter months each year. Hundreds of older (and younger) entrepreneurs set up booths and conduct business from December through March, selling everything from handmade bird feeders to elaborate handcrafted leather goods from South America. A wide variety of retirees are involved. An annual nine-day Sports, Vacation, and RV Show attracts as many as

125,000 people to see the products of 270 exhibitors in a 37,000 square foot tent. The annual Hobby, Craft, and Gem Show is similarly popular. Visitors come from throughout the United States, Canada, and other parts of the world. It is a truly "cosmopolitan" meeting and marketing place.

Source: Author observations; McBride, 1999: 37.

Religious Participation

About 60 percent of older people are active in church-related groups. A high proportion indicate they believe in God, immortality, and feel religion is important in their lives. They are more likely than younger people to engage in private prayer. Church participants identify themselves as happier, better adjusted, and healthier than non-churchgoers. Church attendance increases slightly after age 54, and remains relatively stable until age 80 when it declines somewhat, perhaps because of health problems.[23, 71]

Church activities provide important roles for older people after retirement, reducing isolation and loneliness. There are always volunteer opportunities for reaching out to the community, counseling younger people, teaching Sunday school, maintaining church property, visiting the sick, and assisting with recreation and social functions. These activities can contribute directly to quality of life. Religious involvement also has the potential to reduce stress, providing a sense of coherence and meaning while enhancing feelings of self-esteem.[23, 71]

On the other hand, not all religious involvement has been positive. Participation in some settings can create a sense of guilt and failure, leading to greater stress, lack of coherence, and lowered sense of self-worth. A few churches neglect or even mistreat older members, leading to a sense of social isolation and alienation. Other church groups actually victimize older adults by seeking their financial contributions while offering little in return. There have been studies of ill older people who reported strong religious commitment and received relatively little assistance from the church during recovery.[22, 58, 71]

The Use of Leisure

Summing up, well-used leisure can lead to novelty and diversity of experience, satisfying interaction with interesting people, a sense of freedom and control, pleasure and satisfaction. A feeling of productivity is among the primary factors in psychological well-being, contentment, successful aging, and quality of life.[66, 89]

◆◆◆ LIFESTYLE CHANGE ALTERNATIVES

As noted earlier, the great majority of retirees choose to remain in their home communities and engage in the same types of activities preferred in younger days. However, others want to make changes.

Migration to a New Location

About 1 percent of older couples make a long distance move each year and many more make local moves. A significant proportion have been planning a change for many years and have visited potential locations several times before moving. Major moves are usually based on attraction to a new location, although occasionally negative features of the previous residence encourage a change—such as the high cost of living, fear of crime, population pressure, environmental deterioration, lack of access to good health care, high taxes, a cold and snowy climate, or departure of children to a new place. In the new community a better quality of life is anticipated and may include additional recreation or cultural opportunities.[19]

Mobility appears to increase with retirement, assuming good health and relative affluence. Some retirees want to scale back responsibilities and diminish living space in a new location. Because of the long retirement period for healthy individuals, the likelihood of more than one move before the end of life is increasing, sometimes to accommodate health decline and disability.[36, 37]

Two primary types of older "migrants" have been identified, based on the degree of integration into a new community: (1) those who are attracted to the new community because of its location and general appeal, and who fully join in the social life and culture, enjoying the new local neighbors as well as the larger community and state, and (2) those who are attracted to specific lifestyle amenities, including recreation options such as golf, and who prefer to interact primarily with other similar types in a retirement "enclave" rather than fully joining the wider community. While there are many variations of these two classifications, the primary distinction here is the degree to which migrants become active citizens, making productive contributions to civic life, or whether they are interested primarily in their own personal enjoyment. Some critics believe the latter attitude results in a loss to society because the knowledge and skills of able older individuals are not applied to useful social purposes.[19, 62]

Some preferred destinations identified in national studies are:[19, 24]

- The so-called sunbelt states: Arizona, California, Florida, New Mexico, Texas, the South Atlantic and the Gulf Coasts.
- Coastal New England and New Jersey.
- Selected interior communities such as Asheville, NC, and the Appalachian region between Pennsylvania and Georgia.
- The mountainous Ozark region in Arkansas and Missouri.
- Resort regions of Nevada, especially Las Vegas.
- The Washington and Oregon coastal regions.

In addition, Montana, Wyoming, Idaho, and Utah attract retirees who like the natural beauty of mountains and outdoor recreation such as skiing, hiking, and fishing. Much of the migration is actually within states or between adjacent states. Retirees have caused major population growth in sunbelt states like Arizona, California, and Florida.

A smaller number migrate to Mexico, Costa Rica, or other foreign locations, where the cost of living is often much lower, local residents respect older people, and it is often possible to employ a full- or part-time maid and gardener at low cost. Language can of course be a significant barrier unless they become fluent in the local language.[75, 82]

The most desirable locations for many retirees are within relatively easy travel distance to a previous permanent home, as described in Illustration 9–7.

Illustration 9–7
LIVING THE GOOD LIFE ON CAPE COD

Cape Cod, Massachusetts, is characterized by many of the amenities attractive to retirees: the Atlantic Ocean, beaches, a temperate climate, nature trails, unique towns, and golf courses. Boston and Providence, Rhode Island, with all of their cultural opportunities, are only two hours away.

More than 21 percent of the population of Barnstable County (which encompasses much of the Cape) was over age 65 in 1990. Most retirees had visited the Cape more than once before retirement and were from elsewhere in New England. They tended to be within relatively easy travel distance to their children, grandchildren, or older parents. It is obviously a place where family and friends might like to visit.

Source: Data in part from Cuba and Longino, 1991: S36.

Lifestyle Options in Planned Retirement Communities

In planned communities, residents are able to retain power and control over their lives, even though they relinquish some responsibilities and freedoms.[37] Much of the home and yard maintenance, for example, is performed by professional staff in many retirement communities.

Recreation Resorts. Many new developments deliberately create an environment for the active lifestyle preferred by relatively affluent couples or individuals who enjoy golfing, swimming, tennis, skiing, fishing, and other recreational activities. Some of the communities have themes or amenities that appeal to the aesthetic interests of retirees. Golf club communities are pervasive in California, Arizona, Texas, Florida and many other states. Marina clubs are very popular in locations close to lakes or the ocean. Skiers may locate at least part of the year near ski resorts such as Sun Valley, Idaho, Aspen, Colorado, or Park City, Utah. Other resorts appeal to middle or modest income couples or individuals who can live rather inexpensively in an apartment, mobile home, manufactured home, or recreational vehicle for all or part of the year.

Recreational Vehicle Parks. About 44 percent of RV owners are age 55 or older—many migrating to a Sunbelt recreational vehicle park during the colder months, or from the south to northern parks in the warmer months. RVers have been credited with building "instant communities" because of their common inter-est in travel and in each other. They find it easy to make friends with others who share the lifestyle.[48, 49, 51]

Tucson, Arizona, enjoys a population increase of more than 100,000 people during the winter months—most retired and temporary residents. Part-time job opportunities for those who wish to work are abundant as hosts and service providers in RV parks and other tourist facilities that serve retirees.[48, 68]

College or University Affiliated Communities. "Life-long learning" is a theme for many retirement complexes located near college campuses. The special appeal by developers is to alumni and faculty retirees, but most of these communities are open to others as well. College campuses provide access to cultural amenities, sports activ-ities, and libraries. The communities are usually stable and relatively safe.[38, 63, 88]

Life-long learning communities sometimes provide opportunity for students to learn about aging through formalized interaction with the retirement community members. This helps to break down stereotypes of the elderly and enriches both young people and older people at the same time. For example, the University of Ari-zona is associated with a Senior Academy for life-long learning. A retirement com-munity, Academy Village, provides permanent residence for couples and individuals interested in the intellectual and cultural life of the University and community. Stu-dents interested in aging issues can learn from residents as part of their university experiences.[28, 63, 64, 76]

Retirement as an Economic Development Enterprise

Although many states cater to retirees, Florida has been the most successful in attract-ing large numbers, as the most favored destination for older individuals from the eastern states and Canada. Partially as a consequence, nearly 25 percent of the Florida's population was over age 65 in 1997, by far the highest among the states. Only one-third of the population was native born. A relatively mild climate, housing at reasonable prices, generally low cost of living, and receptive state and local gov-ernments appeals to potential migrants.

Older people are considered an "industry" by the state government and pri-vate entrepreneurs. A department of state government with a $200 million budget (in 1996) promotes and supports retirement opportunities. Services include a newspaper called *Elder Update,* which offers advice and information to the older population.

Both affluent and the modest income retirees can find comfortable places to live, whether in one of the deluxe gated communities with a golf course, or in an RV, a mobile home, or a manufactured home park. However, careful planning by the state has been needed to assure a positive and sustainable lifestyle can be achieved by both older and younger citizens. Florida serves as something of a prototype for other states whose populations are rapidly aging.

The downside for the state is the high cost of building infrastructure, devel-oping nursing homes, and providing other forms of support for an increasingly very old population. Some migrants eventually run out of money and must be supported by Medicaid home or nursing home services.[12]

Many other states have active retiree recruitment efforts underway, notably the Gulf Coast states of Alabama, Mississippi, and Louisiana, and other southern states such as South Carolina and Georgia, Washington, Oregon, Maine, New Hampshire and Vermont have formal state programs to encourage migration for retirement. The rationale is that retirees are a relatively low cost in overall state budgets but they bring substantial incomes and purchasing power with them.[50]

Widowhood

Widows and widowers sometimes have trouble remaining integrated in retirement communities after the death of their husband or wife. Furthermore, as a retirement community matures and the average age of residents increases, the proportion of widows rises, creating challenges for both the individuals and the community. The problem is more pronounced for women because men are more likely to remarry after a period of bereavement. Community activities are often couple-oriented which means that a surviving spouse tends to discontinue regular relationships with other couples. Although couples may occasionally invite widows to dinner or other events, it is generally problematic for the community to provide social support to large numbers of widows. Fortunately, older women tend to make close friends and build their own social networks.[52]

Despite these drawbacks, a high proportion of widows and other older individuals defy expectations. They thrive as they age, adapt to disability, and are highly productive—often with modest income and declining health. A recent survey of older Americans indicated that 61 percent believe in being active and involved, setting new goals, and initiating new activities. Only 32 percent prefer taking it easy, resting, enjoying leisure, and looking only after themselves.[18, 81]

This phenomena has been characterized by the French as the "third age" since it appears to add a major dimension to older age. The later period of life is a time when intergenerational ties can be forged more strongly, when self-knowledge and understanding can be greater, and personal experience can be much enhanced. Individuals can come to terms with themselves and develop self-respect for their achievements.[32, 67]

◆◆◆ SUMMARY AND CONCLUSIONS

The lifestyle available to older individuals is in part a consequence of social class. Upper-class individuals have considerably more freedom than middle- and lower-classes to choose where they want to live and what they want to do in older age. Lower-class older people may be particularly constrained because of income limits and a higher likelihood of illness and disability.

Although the trend over many decades has been for fewer and fewer older individuals to continue working beyond age 65, better health, greater vigor, and demand for workers is somewhat reversing the trend. Part-time work is especially attractive to those who want to remain active while supplementing limited income.

The great majority of retirees remain in their community of long term residence, volunteering for good causes, and helping to sustain community viability. Their lifestyle is likely to vary little from the patterns developed over a lifetime. Those who are sufficiently affluent may travel or move to other locations—to rural retirement havens or to new communities especially designed for active older adults.

Every state encourages in-migration of retirees. The retirement market is an economic development goal for many states, especially in the southern United States, where a boom in specialized new retirement communities has been documented. College towns have recognized the opportunity to provide residential opportunities for older alumni, faculty, and others who want to enjoy the culture, sports, and educational opportunities of a college-related environment.

Older Americans are thus characterized by highly diverse retirement lifestyles. Continuing improvements in health status, length of life, and affluence are likely to increase diversity and opportunity even more. The French concept of the third age has been introduced to highlight the considerable potential for increasing the quality of life in older age for those who maintain their health, vigor, and intellectual curiosity.

◆◆◆ REFERENCES

1. Administration on Aging (2000). *Profile of Older Americans:1999*, Online at www.aoa.gov/aoa/stats/profile/default.htm.
2. Aiken, Lewis R. (1995). *Aging: An Introduction to Gerontology*, Thousand Oaks, CA: Sage.
3. American Association of Retired Persons (AARP) (1998), *A Profile of Older Americans*, Washington, D.C.: AARP.
4. Annual Report (1999). Senior College, University of Southern Maine, Portland, ME.
5. Atchley, Robert C. (1993). Critical Perspectives on Retirement, in Thomas R. Cole, W. Andrew Achenbaum, Patricia L. Jakobi, and Robert Kastenbaum (eds), *Voices and Visions of Aging: Toward a Critical Gerontology*, New York: Springer, 3–19.
6. Baker, Beth (1998). Home Away From Home, *AARP Bulletin*, 39 (8), 12–14.
7. Baldock, Cora Vellekoop (1999). Seniors as Volunteers: An International Perspective on Policy, *Ageing and Society*, 19 (4), 581–602.
8. Bartel, Frank (1998). Retirees Have Major Impact on Workplace, *The Spokesman Review* (Spokane, Washington), January 18, A16.
9. Barth, Michael C., William McNaught, and Philip Rizzi (1995). Older Americans as Workers, in Scott A. Bass (ed), *Older and Active: How Americans Over Age 65 Are Contributing to Society*, New Haven: Yale University Press, 35–70.
10. Bass, Scott A. (ed) (1995). *Older and Active: How Americans Over Age 65 Are Contributing to Society*, New Haven: Yale University Press.
11. Beck, Barbara (1996a). A Gradual Goodbye, *The Economist*, 338 (7950) January 27, S5.
12. Beck, Barbara (1996b). The Luxury of Longer Life, *The Economist*, 338 (7950), January 27, 3–16.
13. Binstock, Robert H., and Christine L. Day (1996). *Aging and Politics*, in Robert H. Binstock and Linda K. George (eds), *Handbook of Aging and the Social Sciences* (4th ed), New York: Academic Press, 362–81.
14. Blair, Cornelia, Mark A. Siegel, and Jacquelyn Quiram (1998). *Growing Old in America*, Wylie, TX: Information Plus.
15. Blazey, Michael A. (1992). Travel and Retirement Status, *Annals of Tourism, Research*, 19, 771–83.
16. Butler, Robert N., Mia R. Oberlink, and Mal Schechter (eds) (1990). *The Promise of Productive Aging: From Biology to Social Policy*, New York: Springer.
17. Bytheway, Bill (1995). *Ageism*, Philadelphia: Open University Press.

18. Carlson, Elliot (1998). Aging Gracefully: Dr. John Rowe Tells Us How, *AARP Bulletin*, 39 (8), 24, 15.
19. Carlson, John E., Virginia W. Junk, Linda Kirk Fox, Gundars Rudzitis, and Sandra E. Cann (1998). Factors Affecting Retirement Migration to Idaho: An Adaptation of the Amenity Migration Model, *The Gerontologist*, 38 (1), 18–24.
20. Caro, Francis G., and Scott A. Bass (1995). Increasing Volunteering Among Older People, in Scott A. Bass (ed), *Older and Active: How Americans Over 55 Are Contributing to Society*, New Haven: Yale University Press, 71–96.
21. Carter, Jimmy (1998). *The Virtues of Aging*, New York: Ballantine Publishing Group.
22. Chadiha, Letha A., Enola K. Proctor, Nancy Morrow-Howell, Osei K. Darkwa, and Peter Dore (1996). Religiosity and Church-Based Assistance Among Chronically Ill African-American and White Elderly, *Journal of Religious Gerontology*, 10 (1), 17–36.
23. Cox, Harold, and Andre Hammonds (1988). Religiousity, Aging, and Life Satisfaction, *Journal of Religion and Aging*, 5 (1/2), 45–51.
24. Cuba, Lee, and Charles F. Longino, Jr. (1991). Regional Retirement Migration: The Case of Cape Cod, *Journal of Gerontology: SOCIAL SCIENCES*, 46 (1), S33–42.
25. Davidhizar, Ruth (1998). It's Never Too Early to Plan for Retirement, *Health Care Supervisor*, 16 (3), 9–16.
26. Day, Christine (1998). Old-Age Interest Groups in the 1990s: Coalition, Competition, and Strategy, Chapter 8 in Janie S. Stechenrider and Tonya M. Parrott(eds.), *New Directions in Old Age Policies*, Albany: State University of New York Press, 131–48.
27. Dym, Barry (1998). Retire? No Way, *Boston Globe*, September 20, F1.
28. Editors (1994). Housing Innovations, *Architecture*, 83 (10), 82–87.
29. Elder, Jean K. (1990). Productivity and the Role of Public Policy, in Robert N. Butler, Mia R. Oberlink, and Mal Schechter (eds), *The Promise of Productive Aging: From Biology to Social Policy*, New York: Springer, 123–24.
30. Eldridge, William D. (1995). *The Challenge of Maturity*, New York: University Press of America.
31. Erlanger, Mary A. (1997). Changing Roles and Life-Cycle Transitions, in Terry D. Hargrave and Suzanne Midori Hanna (eds), *The Aging Family: New Visions in Theory, Practice, and Reality*, New York: Brunner/Mazel Publishers, 163–77.
32. Fahey, Charles J., and Martha Holsetin (1993). Toward a Philosophy of the Third Age, in Thomas R. Cole, W. Andrew Achenbaum, Patricia L. Jakobi, and Robert Kastenbaum (eds), *Voices and Visions of Aging: Toward a Critical Gerontology*, New York: Springer, 241–56.
33. Falk, Ursula, and Gerhard Falk (1997). *Ageism, The Aged, and Aging in America*, Springfield: Charles C Thomas Publishers.
34. Fetridge, Guild A. (1994). *The Adventure of Retirement*, Amherst, NY: Prometheus Books.
35. Feuerbach, Eileen J., and Carol J. Erdwins (1994). Women's Retirement: The Influence of Work History, *Journal of Women and Aging*, 6 (3), 69–85.
36. Fletcher, June (1997). Retirees Say No to Parents' Communities, *Wall Street Journal*, November 14, B16.
37. Free, Mary Moore (1995). *The Private World of the Hermitage: Lifestyles of the Rich and Old in an Elite Retirement Home*, Westport, CT: Bergin & Garvey.
38. Gajilan, Arlyn Tobias (1998). A Golden Age on Campus, *Newsweek*, November 9, 80.
39. George, Linda K. (1990). Social Structure, Social Processes, and Social-Psychological States, in Robert H. Binstock and Linda K. George (eds), *Handbook of Aging and the Social Sciences* (3d ed.), San Diego: Academic Press, 186–200.
40. Grimsely, Kirstin Downey (1999). An Experienced Work Force, *Washington Post National Weekly Edition*, 16 (46), 18.
41. Guillemard, Anne-Marie (1996). Equity Between Generations in Aging Societies: The Problem of Assessing Public Policies, in Tamara K. Hareven (ed), *Aging and Generational Relations Over the Life Course*, New York: Walter de Gruyter.
42. Hanson, Kaaren, and Seymour Wapner (1994). Transition to Retirement: Gender Differences, *International Journal of Aging and Human Development*, 39 (3), 189–208.
43. Hardy, Melissa A., and Jill Quadagno (1995). Satisfaction with Early Retirement: Making Choices in the Auto Industry, *Journal of Gerontology: SOCIAL SCIENCES*, 50B (4), S217–S228.

44. Hayes, Bernadette C., and Audrey Vandenheuvel (1994). Attitudes Toward Mandatory Retirement: An International Comparison, *International Journal of Aging and Human Development*, 39 (3), 209–31.

45. Hayward, Mark D., Samantha Friedman, and Hsinmu Chen (1998). Career Trajectories and Older Men's Retirement, *Journal of Gerontology: SOCIAL SCIENCES*, 53B (2), S91–S103.

46. Hayward, Mark D., Samantha Friedman, and Hsinum Chen (1996). Race Inequities in Men's Retirement, *Journal of Gerontology: SOCIAL SCIENCES*, 51B (1), S1–S10.

47. Hayward, Mark D., Melissa A. Hardy, and Mei-Chun Liu (1994). Work After Retirement: The Experiences of Older Men in the United States, *Social Science Research*, 23 (1), 82–107.

48. Henry, Bonnie (1997). Roamin Empire, *Arizona Daily Star* (Tucson, AZ), February 16.

49. Highways Editors (1998), *Highways*, March, 13.

50. Hoffman, Ellen (1999). States' New Cash Crop: Recent Retirees, *AARP Bulletin*, 40 (5), 9, 11.

51. Holmes, Ellen Rhoads, and Lowell D. Holmes (1995), *Other Cultures, Elder Years* (2nd ed), Thousand Oaks, CA: Sage Publications.

52. Hoonaard, Deborah Kestin Van Den (1994). Paradise Lost: Widowhood in a Florida Retirement Community, *Journal of Aging Studies*, 8 (2), 121–32.

53. Johnson, Hans, Gary Kielhofner, and Lena Borell (1997). Anticipating Retirement: The Formation of Narratives Concerning an Occupational Transition, *American Journal of Occupational Therapy*. 51 (1), 49–56.

54. Keating, Peter (1996). Planning for the Lifestyle You Want, *Money Magazine*, October 1996, 95–99.

55. Kelly, John R. (1994). Recreation and Leisure, in Abraham Monk (ed), *The Columbia Retirement Handbook*, New York: Columbia University Press, 489–508.

56. Kubeck, Jean E., Sally A. Miller-Albrecht, and Martin D. Murphy (1999). Finding Information on the Web: Exploring Older Adults Exploration, *Educational Gerontology*, 25 (2), 167–83.

57. Lenzer, Anthony (1998). Retirement Orientations: A Conceptual Overview, in David E. Redburn and Robert P. McNamara (eds), *Social Gerontology*, Wesport, CA: Auburn House, 183–93.

58. Levin, Jeffrey S. (1997). Religious Research in Gerontology, 1980–1994: A Systematic Review, *Journal of Religious Gerontology*, 10 (3), 3–31.

59. Lewis, Robert (1998). Boomers May Spend Their Retirement—Working, *AARP Bulletin*, 39 (8), 7.

60. Lewis, Robert (1999a). Older Workers Vow To Stay On The Job, *AARP Bulletin*, 40 (9), 4.

61. Lewis, Robert (1999b). Suddenly, Older Workers Find They're in Demand, *AARP Bulletin*, 40 (10), 22.

62. Longino, Charles F., Jr. (1992). The Forest and the Trees: Micro-Level Considerations in the Study of Geographic Mobility in Old Age, in Andrei Rogers (ed), *Elderly Migration and Population Distribution*, London: Belhaven Press, 23–34.

63. Loose, Cindy (1998). Going Back for Post-Graduate Studies, *The Washington Post National Weekly Edition*, 16 (3), 29.

64. Lucksinger, Melissa K. (1994). Community and the Elderly, *Journal of Housing and the Elderly*, 11 (1), 11–78.

65. Macmanus, Susan, and Kathryn Dunn Tenpas (1998). The Political Activism Patterns of Older Americans: "Don't Throw Dirt Over Us Yet," Chapter 7 in Janie S. Stechenrider and Tonya M. Parrott (eds.), *New Directions in Old Age Policies*, Albany: State University of New York Press, 111–30.

66. Mancini, Jay A., and Dan M. Sandifer (1995). Family Dynamics and the Leisure Experiences of Older Adults: Theoretical Viewpoints, in Rosemay Blieszner and Victoria Hilkevitch Bedford (eds), *Handbook of Aging and the Family*, Westport, CT: Greenwood Press, 132–45.

67. Manheimer, Ronald J. (ed) (1997). *Older Americans Almanac*, Detroit: Gale Research Inc.

68. Maxwell, Gaylord (1998). The Baby-Boomer Effect, *Motorhome*, 35 (6), 28.

69. McBride, Sherry (1999). Crossroads, *Motorhome*, 36 (5), 37.

70. Mergenhagen, Paula (1994). Rethinking Retirement, *American Demographics*, June, 28–34.

71. Morris, David C. (1997). Health, Finances, Religious Involvement, and Life Satisfaction of Older Adults, *Journal of Religious Gerontology*, 10 (2), 3–17.

72. Newman, Sally, Christopher R. Ward, Thomas B. Smith, Janet O. Wilson, and James M. McCrea (1997), *Intergenerational Programs: Past, Present, and Future*, London, UK: Taylor and Francis.

73. Okun, Morris A. (1993). Predictors of Volunteer Status in a Retirement Community, *International Journal of Aging and Human Development*, 36 (1), 57–74.

74. Organization for Economic Cooperation and Development (1995). *The Transition from Work to Retirement*, Paris: Organization for Economic Cooperation and Development.

75. Otero, Lorena Melton Young (1997). U.S. Retired Persons in Mexico, *The American Behavioral Scientist*, 40 (7), 914–22.

76. Palmore, Erdman B. (1999). *Ageism*, New York: Springer.

77. Peterson, David A., and Pamela F. Wendt (1995). Training and Education of Older Americans as Workers and Volunteers, in Scott A. Bass (ed), *Older and Active: How Americans Over 55 Are Contributing to Society*, New Haven: Yale University Press, 217–36.

78. Phillipson, Chris (1998). *Reconstructing Old Age: New Agendas in Social Theory and Practice*, Thousand Oaks, CA: Sage Publications.

79. Prange, Betty (1998). Adventures in Learning, *Motorhome*, 35 (6), 84–90.

80. Rein, Martin, and Harold Salzman (1995). Social Integration, Participation, and Exchange in Five Industrial Countries, in Scott A. Bass (ed), *Older and Active: How Americans Over 55 Are Contributing to Society*, New Haven: Yale University Press, 237–62.

81. Rimer, Sara (1999). Older People Want to Work in Retirement Survey Says, *New York Times*, September 2, A10.

82. Rogers, Andrei (1992). Elderly Migration in the U. S., in Andrei Rogers (ed), *Elderly Migration and Population Redistribution*, London: Belhaven Press, 226–48.

83. Rones, Philip L. (1994). The Job Market After Retirement, in Abraham Monk (ed), *The Columbia Retirement Handbook*, New York: Columbia University Press, 153–70.

84. Rubinstein, Robert L. (1994). Adaptation to Retirement Among the Never Married, Childless, Divorced, Gay and Lesbian, and Widowed, in Abraham Monk (ed), *The Columbia Retirement Handbook*, New York: Columbia University Press, 448–62.

85. Schwartz, Pepper (1999). Quality of Life in the Coming Decades, *Society*, 36 (2), 55–59.

86. Senior College (1999). Center for Extended Academic Programs, University of Southern Maine, Portland, ME.

87. Sharp, David (1998). First to Complete Appalachian Trail Does It Again 50 Years Later, *Spokesman-Review* (Spokane, WA), October 22, 1998, A16.

88. Shuman, Sue Kovach (1999). Back to School, *AARP Bulletin*, 40 (10), 9–10.

89. Siegenthaler, K. L. (1996). Leisure and the Elderly, *Parks and Recreation*, 31 (1), 18.

90. Slater, Robert (1995). *The Psychology of Growing Old: Looking Forward*, Buckingham, UK: Open University Press.

91. Slevin, Kathleen F., and C. Ray Wingrove (1995). Women in Retirement: A Review and Critique of Empirical Research Since 1976, *Sociological Inquiry*, 65 (1), 1–21.

92. Smith, Deborah B., and Phyllis Moen (1998). Spousal Influence on Retirement: His, Her, and Their Perceptions, *Journal of Marriage and the Family*, 60 (3), 734–44.

93. Sterns, Harvey L., and Anthony A. Sterns (1995). Health and the Employment Capability of Older Americans, in Scott A. Bass (ed), *Older and Active: How Americans Over 55 Are Contributing to Society*, New Haven: Yale University Press, 10–34.

94. Taylor, Mary Anne, and Lynn McFarlane Shore (1995). Predictors of Planned Retirement Age: An Application of Beehr's Model, *Psychology and Aging*, 10 (1), 76–83.

95. Treas, Judith, and Michele Spence (1994). Family Life in Retirement, in Abraham Monk (ed), *The Columbia Retirement Handbook*, New York: Columbia University Press, 419–32.

96. United States Bureau of the Census (1998). *National Data Book: Statistical Abstract of the United States*, Washington, D.C.: U.S. Government Printing Office.

97. Weisman, Avery D. (1996). The Physician in Retirement: Transition and Opportunity, *Psychiatry*, 59 (3), 298–306.

98. Wheeler, Judith A., Kevin M. Gorey, and Bernard Greenblatt (1998). The Beneficial Effects of Volunteering for Older Volunteers and the People They Serve: A Meta-Analysis, *International Journal of Aging and Human Development*, 47 (1), 69–79.

99. Williams, Larry (1997). Older Workers Staying on the Job, *The Spokesman Review* (Spokane, Washington), 115 (155), A1–A2.
100. Williamson, Robert C., Alice Duffy Rinehart, and Thomas O. Blank (1992). *Early Retirement: Promises and Pitfalls*, New York: Plenum Press.
101. Wright, Jim (1997). Older Workers Essential for Economy, *The Spokesman Review*, 115 (154), B10.

Part III

AN INTERNATIONAL PERSPECTIVE

The goals of Part III are to examine demographic change, important historical background events, public policies, programs, noteworthy achievements, major unresolved issues, and implications for quality of life for older people in a selection of countries. The seven nations (Canada, Japan, the United Kingdom, the Netherlands, Germany, Sweden, and France) were deliberately chosen because they have collectively confronted some of the most challenging problems and illustrate effective responses.

Most of the countries have larger proportions of older people than the United States (Canada is the exception). All have universal health care available for the older and younger populations at modest cost to the individual. A few have reasonably good mental health treatment programs, although actions have been slower in this area. Adequate care has yet to be realized in most countries. Several countries have universal long-term care insurance and have achieved high quality long-term care programs. Several have excellent housing programs and adequate income support for all of the older population.

We should emphasize that the countries considered are among the most economically advanced in the world. They were selected as illustrations of both the problems associated with increasing numbers of older people and possible policies and programs to optimize quality of life. No attempt is made to comprehensively consider the less-developed countries or all of the advanced countries.

The specific topics covered for each country (all included in the previous nine chapters for the United States) include:

- A summary of country characteristics.

- Demographic characteristics of the older population.
- A historical perspective.
- The social support system.
- Health care, mental health care, and long-term care.
- The residential environment.
- Economic and financial conditions.
- Lifestyles: work, retirement, and leisure.
- Noteworthy achievements and major challenges.

The data and analysis for each country provides the basis for comparisons among all countries—undertaken in Part IV.

Cont 316

* Official retirement age?
* UK's position on social support w/ their family?
  UK's position on what is a healthy lifestyle?
  Lifestyle is the product of culture.

Chapter 10

CANADA
Seeking Equity and Universality

◆◆◆ INTRODUCTION

Canada has the largest land area in the Western Hemisphere and is the second largest country in the world, with about 31 million people in 2000. Roughly 87 percent of the population lives within 200 miles of the U.S. border. The southern regions of Ontario, Quebec, and British Columbia contain about three-quarters of the total. The prairie provinces, the northern territories, and northern parts of Ontario, Quebec, and British Columbia are all sparsely settled except for a few large urban centers.[74, 93]

The central government collects and redistributes most taxes, allocating funds so that services are somewhat comparable across the 10 provinces and two territories. Most of the responsibility for providing programs for older people is delegated to the provinces and territories. Local governments function as administrative subdivisions of provinces without much independent responsibility.

In the decades of the 1980s and 1990s the federal government emphasized decentralization, further delegating the responsibility and financing of programs to provinces. Thus, authority, power, and resources are shared between federal, provincial, and local governments, with considerable variation between the provinces in the mode of policy implementation for programs on aging, health care, and long-term care.[58]

Demographic Characteristics

The nation is both multicultural and multilingual with about 63 percent of the population primarily English speaking; 25 percent speak mostly French; and the remainder speak Italian, Chinese, German, Spanish, native American, or other languages. Canada continues to be characterized by high levels of immigration from other countries, in part because of its longstanding reputation for social equity, strong programs of social support, and a generally hospitable environment for minorities. Sixteen percent of the population are recent immigrants; more than 22 percent of the group aged 65 to 74 were born abroad as were 35 percent of those over age 75. Per capita income was $24,468 in 1998—seventh highest in the world.[63, 74]

In the year 2000, approximately 12.5 percent of the population was age 65 or older but low birthrates and increased life expectancy mean this proportion could rise to 25 percent by 2036—among the highest rates of increase in the world along with Japan. Average life expectancy was 79.4 years in 2000, second only to Japan. The population pyramid in Figure 10–1 indicates the higher prevalence of women in the older population; the potential increase in future older population is indicated by the bulge in numbers for age categories from 35 to 59.[53, 93, 96]

The post World War II "baby-boom" phenomenon plus increasing length of life will require new government policies as this large population group causes the number of retirees to rise. The national and provincial governments have begun to reshape policies accordingly.[37]

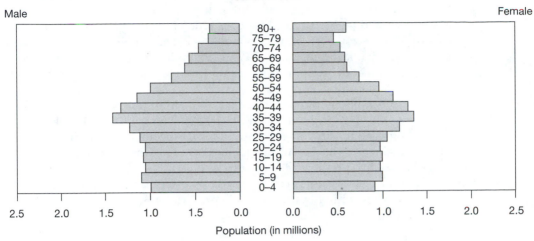

Canada: 1999

Male   Female

| 80+ |
| 75–79 |
| 70–74 |
| 65–69 |
| 60–64 |
| 55–59 |
| 50–54 |
| 45–49 |
| 40–44 |
| 35–39 |
| 30–34 |
| 25–29 |
| 20–24 |
| 15–19 |
| 10–14 |
| 5–9 |
| 0–4 |

2.5   2.0   1.5   1.0   1.5   0.0   0.0   0.5   1.0   1.5   2.0   2.5

Population (in millions)

FIGURE 10–1   Population Pyramids for Canada
Source: U.S. Census Bureau, *International Data Base,* 2000.

◆◆◆ HISTORICAL PERSPECTIVE

The nation enjoyed a long period of prosperity and progress during most of the late twentieth century. Social programs and health care flourished. International rankings by United Nations agencies in 1990 indicated that Canada had the best socioeconomic conditions, population health status, and quality of life among nations of the world—based on international measures. More recent evaluations by the World Health Organization have been less generous however. Aging has been defined as a social issue requiring collective public responses. The family, community, provincial governments, and the federal government are expected to work together to solve the social problems related to aging.[26, 57, 70]

However, prosperity was somewhat threatened as the national economy entered a state of severe recession during the late 1980s and early 1990s. The overall unemployment rate reached about 12 percent (since lowered considerably), not counting discouraged workers who were not trying to find work. The baby boom generations appear to be concerned, as elsewhere, that health care and other services will not be fully available when they retire. Taxes remain high even though services have declined—a very upsetting course of events to many citizens. Canadians have generally taken great pride in the stability of services and security of health care.[32]

Publicly provided health insurance has been available since 1961 when hospital coverage was provided to all residents. Physician insurance coverage followed in 1968 with the National Medical Care Insurance Act, after considerable controversy including a national physician strike. The Act essentially eliminated financial barriers to health care, allowed for freedom of choice in selection of physician and hospitals, generally maintained physician freedom of practice location and patient scheduling, and provided negotiation of fee schedules between medical associations and the various provincial health plans. In 1977 the Extended Health Care Services Program provided additional support for nursing home care, adult residential care, home care, and other ambulatory health services.[73]

Home care has a long tradition in Canada, with examples dating to more than 100 years ago when the first public health nurses (the Victorian Order of Nurses) began providing care in the home. Government involvement began in the 1960s when the provincial governments of Alberta and other provinces provided grants to a variety of home care programs. Home care evolved so that all provinces except Newfoundland now provide universal access to home care for eligible older people. Need must be demonstrated by serious acute or chronic medical problems resulting in some level of disability.[76, 79, 82]

During the decade of the 1990s, the population appeared to develop a sense of insecurity about the future. Baby boomers were taking a more active role in politics in an effort to change the situation. Fortunately, conditions began to improve after 1995. The economy rebounded and unemployment declined. Optimism was returning at the beginning of the new millennium.[27, 32]

Policy changes underway in the 1990s shifted toward greater individual initiative, more private enterprise in health care and long-term care, and expanded community responsibility for services. The earlier emphasis on publicly sponsored medical and social care was diminishing. Consequences of these changes for the well-being of the older population remain unclear although great concern about negative consequences has been expressed in the media. Despite the changes, Canada continues to have among the most comprehensive and supportive aging policies of any country.[27, 63]

◆◆◆ SOCIAL-SUPPORT SYSTEMS

Nationally articulated values emphasize individual responsibility and independence of the older population: personal independence, community residence for the disabled whenever possible, convenient service access, affordability of services, local management, individualization of services, and informal caregiver support if needed. These principles have been coupled with a public support system for older citizens requiring relatively few financial risks. A combination of social security, other supplementary-income programs, health insurance, long-term care support, and a range of housing choices are available to citizens regardless of income or social status. The Canadian Association of Gerontology plays a role as a national scientific and educational association representing the interests of professionals who serve the older population. Several major universities support research and service programs in gerontology.[5, 13, 46]

The Family Role

Families take primary responsibility for care of older members here as elsewhere, and suffer the same stresses in times of crisis. A study in Quebec revealed that 37 percent of a sample of caregivers suffered stress, depression, guilt, and isolation. They made relatively little use of available public resources, tending not to seek the help of mental health specialists or other professionals to alleviate their problems.[55]

Family structure has changed as well. Many Canadian families include only a single parent with children. Others are blended, reconstituted, or two-career dual-earner couples. These variations mean that a family caregiver for disabled older parents may not always be available on a regular basis in the home. The incidence of caregiving by other relatives and friends in the community is, however, quite substantial. A national study in 1990 indicated a significant proportion of the elderly received help with transportation (48 percent of older women and 25 percent of older men) from individuals outside their household. Informal help with home maintenance and household work was also widely available. Able older individuals provide much of this assistance to their relatives, friends, and neighbors.[56, 60]

Female Responsibility. Women assume much of the responsibility for ongoing personal care to older relatives as in other countries. Yet, a high proportion also work outside the home, which allows limited time and energy for caregiving. Studies indicate that the need to care for elderly parents has caused a sizeable proportion of women to drop out of the workforce or work part-time. Women tend to strongly support public programs that help alleviate the stress in the home. It is worth noting that the costs for home care have been estimated to be equal to or greater than the costs for institutional care if the lost income of women is taken into account.[90]

Effects of Family Support. Formal training of family caregivers to increase competence and sense of control appears to make a distinct difference in quality of life for both the cared-for and the caregiver. It decreases the negative physical and psychological impact on the caregiver while delaying long-term institutionalization for the dependent older person. However, despite special training, caregivers tend to have higher than average levels of depression and anxiety.[65]

◆◆◆ PHYSICAL HEALTH CARE

The elderly appear to lead generally healthy lifestyles. Economic affluence and incidence of poverty in the older age groups are approximately comparable to the general population. The older age group accounted for more than half of all hospital days in 1990 and a high proportion of other health care costs. About 54 percent of those age 75–84, and 82 percent of those 85 and older, have some level of activity limitation.[8]

Public responsibility for special health care needs of the older population is largely decentralized to provinces and municipalities, within federal guidelines, as noted earlier. The Division of Aging and Seniors in Health Canada, the federal health department, serves as a center of information and national leadership on health care for older individuals. Provinces and territories provide the more immediate organizational structure and insurance for health care, home care, and long-term care, with services delivered through regional and community organizations.[9, 21]

Universal health care guarantees were implemented at the national level by the 1971 Canada Health Act (with more recent updates) with the proviso that programs must be comprehensive, accessible, portable between provinces, and publicly administered on a nonprofit basis. Although health care programs vary to some degree among provinces, all older individuals in need of health or long-term care have full access at very little out-of-pocket cost. Small user fees have been imposed in recent years but are usually affordable; individuals with minimal resources receive a subsidy to help cover costs. Older individuals have largely free choice in selection of physicians and other providers.[22, 41]

Prevention Emphasis

Preventive care is strongly emphasized throughout the health care system with several specific priorities:[5, 42]

- Primary prevention focuses on disease prevention, good nutrition, exercise, smoking cessation, appropriate use of medications, avoidance of injury, and minimizing the potential for osteoporosis—among other measures.
- Secondary prevention emphasizes early detection of disease and early treatment to avoid ill effects when possible.
- Tertiary prevention emphasizes treatment to delay disease progression and rehabilitation to promote optimal function when disease is already present.

Preventive care is provided for older individuals in the home as well as in health care facilities. Assessments to determine the type of preventive program needed, and the education required to improve preventive behavior, are undertaken by several types of health professionals: health education visitors in the home, physicians during office visits, and public health officers who coordinate major public interventions. Nursing homes also attempt to implement all three levels of preventive care as part of the rehabilitation process.[42, 59]

Internet access to the Canadian Health Network enables older citizens to secure information for healthier lifestyles, prevention of disease, self-care, and the performance of the health care system. It covers diseases such as Alzheimer's, medications, and available health care resources.[16]

Hospital and Outpatient Care

A substantial decline in overall use of hospitals has occurred since 1971 when universal health care insurance was established. Overall per capita patient days have gone down by 50 percent. Many hospitals in smaller cities have been closed. The consequence is a shortage of available hospital services in some rural and urban areas. The elderly are the most at risk since they use a high proportion of the acute care hospital services, at a rate 3 to 5 times greater than the younger population. Older patient use continues to increase as the population ages.[4]

Women fill a high proportion of formal health care occupations in Canada. In 1990 about 20 percent of physicians were women (a proportion that undoubtedly has increased since) as were 90 percent of nurses. Community home care helpers are predominantly female and part-time.[38, 90]

The dissatisfaction rate among rural physicians has been rising as shortages of resources have increased. The percentage of physicians "very satisfied" with their hospital facilities and services fell from 40 percent in 1991 to 17 percent in 1999. The proportion "very satisfied" with professional backup and specialty services dropped by more than 50 percent. They were unhappy with required on-call time, long distances to secondary referral centers, and too few general and family practitioners.[12]

Emergency Care.   Older citizens receive care in emergency departments of hospitals at about the same rate as younger people (as indicated in a southern Ontario study). However, older emergency patients are *admitted* at a much higher rate (45 percent compared to 12 percent for younger people). Emergency admittance of the elderly appears to be based largely on legitimate need for assistance.[39]

Specialized Geriatric Services.   Most regions of the country have developed specialized systems of hospital-based geriatric care. Community geriatric care is increasing. The primary goal of specialized geriatric services in Canada is to supplement the work of family physicians while improving the chances of continuing independence and effective functioning of the elderly. Many general practice physicians lack the knowledge and skills to deal with the medical management of complicated age-related problems. Consequently, they seek help from hospital-based geriatric specialists when possible.[77, 79, 94]

Geriatric assessment and treatment are usually based on two primary criteria:[62]

- Functional status: Has the individual suffered a recent decline, or is there an indication of high risk for future decline?
- Dependency: Is there evidence of serious dependency or instability with respect to activities of daily living?

If an individual shows evidence of poor response to these questions, specialized geriatric assessment and treatment are likely to be beneficial. A comprehensive evaluation is intended to identify problems that can be treated to prevent or delay admission to institutional nursing care.[47, 63]

Patients may go to a special day hospital in some locations for outpatient assessment, rehabilitation, and other treatment. Occupational, physical, and speech therapy are available to help improve overall function. Geriatric day hospitals are often associated with medical school departments of geriatric medicine.[3, 80]

Academic Programs In Geriatrics/Gerontology. Several universities have academic programs in gerontology and geriatrics. For example, the University of Toronto operates an Institute for Human Development, Life Course and Aging. The Institute is multidisciplinary with a social science focus. It is the home base for the Canadian Aging Research Network (CARNET), an affiliation of all of the leading aging specialists in Canada. Certificates are offered at the graduate level for masters and doctoral students, with most courses drawn from academic departments. The faculty members associated with the Institute have helped to make the University of Toronto the leading university in the country for research and education in aging.[94]

Pharmaceutical Care

The average older person in Canada filled 33 prescriptions for 5 medications in 1996. In part because of high prescription use, the incidence of adverse drug reactions among older people is roughly four times higher than among younger people. The elderly also use outdated drugs. Studies indicate that half of all physicians in Canada write at least one inappropriate prescription each year for an older person, resulting in unneeded or incorrect prescriptions for roughly 12 percent of the elderly. Twenty-five percent of drug-related hospital admissions in Canada are a result of prescribing errors. The problem can be minimized through careful medication reviews, computer record keeping, and close communication between physicians and pharmacists. A long-term experiment with such a system is underway in Montreal, Quebec.[30, 33, 89, 91]

The danger of inappropriate drug combinations increases with the number of physicians caring for a patient. About 21 percent of older patients in Quebec had four or more prescribing physicians, increasing the risk of inappropriate drug use by three times compared to individuals with only one physician. However, pharmacists maintain drug use profiles of patients and help alleviate this problem—when all prescriptions for a patient are received from the same pharmacy.[88]

◆◆◆ MENTAL HEALTH CARE

Most diagnosis and treatment of mental disorders of older people is through family physicians in the community, although specialized mental health teams also provide assessment and treatment in hospitals, outpatient clinics, and in the home. Psychiatry has greatly improved as a discipline and is providing helpful education and guidance to other professionals in the mental health field. During the late 1990s about 7 percent of medical students were specializing in psychiatry.[44]

Canada is characterized by an extreme maldistribution of mental health services, with urban areas much better served than the vast rural regions. Some provinces have done much better than others. For example, British Columbia has a provincewide network of mental health centers that provide outpatient assessment, counseling, treatment, and outreach services in more than 90 locations. Geriatric mental health teams respond to the special needs of older citizens. A Mental Health Information Line provides updates on mental health programs, specific mental illnesses, and general topics associated with mental health. The specialty fields of geriatric psychiatry and clinical psychology are available primarily in the larger medical centers.[19, 44, 86]

Approximately 80 percent of older nursing home residents have been diagnosed as having some form of mental disorder, notably dementia or depression. Yet, relatively few receive any form of psychiatric care other than psychotropic drugs prescribed by the medical director or other primary care physicians. Medical and nursing directors indicate that more mental health services are needed, especially for residents with dementia.[31]

Dementia patients cost more than twice as much to care for as other residents in nursing homes, when all costs for nursing home care and other care are considered. In the case of severe Alzheimer's disease the cost may be more than four times the average.[75]

Approximately 8 percent of all older Canadians were estimated to have some form of dementia in 1998—two-thirds of these with Alzheimer's disease. The proportion rises considerably for individuals 85 and older. About half live at home in their community, largely cared for by family and friends, many of whom suffer high levels of stress, depression, and anxiety as in other countries. Canada has well-developed support services for caregivers in much of the country. The needed support must generally be organized locally in consultation with family physicians.[30]

◆◆◆ LONG-TERM CARE

Canada has a long tradition of attention to long-term care, with special emphasis on keeping everyone at home who can function adequately without institutionalization. However, wide variations in organization, access, and quality are evident among and within the provinces. In most cases decisions are made about the type of care needed at "single point of entry" offices in each major community, as noted above for British Columbia.[2, 7, 73]

Major restructuring has been underway in the 1990s as a consequence in part of the effort to reduce government deficits resulting from the earlier economic downturn. The consequence has been curtailing of services to older people, especially those in outlying rural areas.[27]

Home Care Services

The primary goals of home care are to: (1) help frail elderly individuals avoid or delay admission to a nursing home or other chronic care facility, and (2) maintain quality of life at home despite disability. Services include homemaking, home visiting for assessment and surveillance, nursing care, support services such as oxygen, renal dialysis, intravenous chemotherapy, mechanical ventilation, and palliative care. A higher proportion of the elderly are "aging in place" than in earlier decades as a result of successfully meeting these goals.[8, 96]

Home care programs are operated largely by local public health departments, although some hospitals provide services to assist patients who have been discharged and need follow-up care. Private home health firms are also active. Community Care Access Centers coordinate local access to home care services and assist in placement of individuals designated by physicians as in need of service. In Ontario part of their role is to implement a system of "managed competition" as a businesslike approach to service provision—a change greeted with considerable skepticism by critics because of the potential negative effects on older clients. Greater burdens have been placed on families because of decreased access to formal home care. Many older individuals who might have managed at home may be forced to enter residential care or nursing homes.[27]

Physicians are actively involved in home care, making an average of four times more calls annually than in the United States. Professional care managers are available in some provinces to review the status of home care patients and make recommendations; they may also have the responsibility to serve as gatekeepers to institutional care in consultation with physicians.[7, 27, 82]

Emergency response systems are widely available and have helped to provide a sense of security in the home for many disabled older people. The Alberta government initiated a medical alert program in 1990 for low- and moderate-income renters, with grants for purchase of the equipment. Other provinces have taken comparable initiatives, usually implemented by local agencies. The Canadian Automated Building Association conducted a study to determine appropriate steps for enhancement of emergency response system, with the overall goal of increasing the potential for independent living.[84]

A recent initiative by Health Canada at the federal level is focusing on home care development as a vehicle to strengthen the home and community, in the interest of creating a fully integrated continuum of health care. Home care has been unevenly developed across the country and is not always accessible or fully integrated with the broader health care system.[20]

Nursing Home Care

Nursing homes are usually community institutions operated by local governments (about 50 percent) or nonprofit voluntary associations. Many are directly associated with assisted living units and independent living apartments with home care available on the premises. About 6.3 percent of the population over age 65 lived in some form of public or private institutional setting in 2000, down from 7.1 percent in 1991 but still higher than in most economically advanced countries. Average age of entry to nursing homes has steadily increased. The institutionalization rate varies slightly between provinces as a consequence of differences in demography and policies.[8, 53, 63, 83]

Services and level of support also vary somewhat by Province. Ontario has a Complex Continuing Care program that covers all older citizens in need of chronic care (as recommended by their attending physician). Services in hospitals and nursing homes are fully covered by insurance, although patients are assessed a co-payment to cover accommodation and meals when they have the resources.[23]

Public long-term care facilities are filled to capacity. High demand for space has meant that significant numbers of elderly patients reside in hospitals or at home for extended periods awaiting an opening in a nursing home. Those who can afford to pay for private institutional care may be able to move more quickly because space is more abundant. Residents in each case must pay for room and board from social security income or other available resources. They are allowed to retain $110 to $130 per month for personal expenses.[24, 57]

Quality. Generally speaking, the quality of care in nursing homes is very good, although few formal measures are available for full documentation. Overall staff quality and training appears to be good, providing a basis for high quality care and high resident satisfaction. Nurse aides are usually required to complete intensive community college training as a qualification for employment.[64]

Many Canadian provinces have adopted the use of the Minimum Data Set (similar to the instrument used in the United States) in all chronic care institutions. The goal is to systematically identify resident needs as a basis for improved care planning, using an instrument with 18 Resident Assessment Protocols to document patient characteristics, chronic and acute conditions, care patterns, and treatment progress. The data set has the potential to improve patient outcomes while also providing very helpful quality assessment and administrative information. A "continuum of care" concept focuses on provision of services in the community so that individuals need not fear having to move to another community for nursing care.[48, 73]

Palliative Care and the Hospice

Public and professional interest in hospices and palliative care has been increasing. The Canadian Society of Palliative Care Physicians was formed to provide education and support for hospice care in hospitals, nursing homes, and at home. One of the goals is training physicians with the skills necessary to provide pain and symptom relief as well as bereavement counseling for families of dying patients.[45]

◆◆◆ HOUSING AND COMMUNITY

Approximately 68 percent of older Canadians own their own homes, with seven out of ten of these homeowners free of mortgages. Most housing is financed by the private sector but with public mortgage insurance. The National Housing Act of 1944 encouraged the federal and provincial governments to improve housing and living conditions nationwide. Grants and subsidies of various kinds are provided by the Federal government to provinces and thence to localities, voluntary nonprofit groups, and for-profit organizations. Nearly half of all public housing expenditures go for renovation, upgrading, and adapting homes to elderly needs rather than for new construction.[8, 58]

Many housing projects are now organized with special consideration for older citizens. One variation is the two-family home, with one section or apartment designated for the elderly parent(s) or other relative, sometimes referred to as a *granny flat*. This allows for relative independence of the older person with help available from the younger family when needed. A variety of other schemes have been attempted to help keep elderly parents close to younger family members. Many older women still live alone in their own homes, while men tend more often to live in some type of family dwelling with other family members.[8]

Shelter is the single largest cost item for most older people, absorbing an average of 18 percent of income for couples, 24 percent for single older men, and 29 percent for single older women. (Mortgage or rent, maintenance and repairs, heat, light, property taxes, and other costs are included in the calculation.)[8]

Public Housing

The federally operated Canada Mortgage and Housing Association actively promotes better housing for older people through subsidies for home ownership, provision of low-rent housing, assistance to families who cannot otherwise locate affordable homes, management of large public-housing rental complexes, rent supplements, rehabilitation of older housing and emergency repair, and collaboration with the provinces on provision of housing. Almost half of all public housing was occupied by older people in 1994; they also received almost half of all rent supplement payments. Others lived in some form of public group housing other than nursing homes such as subsidized housing cooperatives, assisted living complexes, and retirement homes for the aged.[8, 63]

As social security and other income support systems have improved, public-housing policies have focused on alternatives other than direct provision or subsidization of housing. The older person or close relatives are expected to have sufficient income to purchase or rent what they need. But, housing assistance still remains available through "single point of entry" service offices enabling an older person or family members to secure needed support with minimal effort.[8, 71]

Institutional Residences

The relatively high rate of institutional residence noted earlier occurred in part because the public-funding system favored institutional care over home care. Even after considerable expansion of home care in the 1990s, nearly 10 percent of women over age 65 and almost 20 percent of women over 75 lived in some form of institutional care in 1997. About half as many men lived in institutional residences. The average age was 85.[96]

The most common types of institutional residences include chronic care hospitals, homes for the aged, and assisted living, as well as nursing homes. The lower average daily cost of hospital services in Canada is attributed in part to the extensive use of beds for long-term care. Individuals with the most severe health problems are likely to be in chronic care hospitals and the least severe in homes for the aged or assisted living.[8, 24, 34, 72]

Overall, the housing situation for the older population appears to be adequate except for the shortage of small assisted living units for single older women and nursing home spaces. The federal and provincial governments encourage the private market to fill gaps rather than rely on publicly sponsored housing. The continuing growth in numbers of older people and increasing life expectancy requires ongoing public attention to assure availability of adequate housing.[96]

◆◆◆ ECONOMIC AND FINANCIAL ISSUES

A guaranteed basic income, health care insurance, and support for long-term care provide a basic level of security for nearly all older individuals regardless of prior income status. The federal and provincial governments attempt to assure reasonably equitable treatment of everyone. These policies were put to the test in the 1996-98 period when the federal government cut health and social transfers to provinces by $7 billion. Since health care consumed one-third or more of provincial budgets, services were heavily affected and available resources declined.[27]

Income Support

Old Age Security is a universal income benefit for everyone age 65 and over who has resided in the country for at least ten years. Full benefits are available only for those who have lived and worked in the country for 40 years after age 18. Partial pensions are available for individuals who have lived only part of their lives in the country. A Guaranteed Income Supplement, Spouses Allowance, or Widowed Spouse's Allowance are available to low-income individuals who would not have sufficient income to meet the basic national standard without extra assistance. The Guaranteed Income Supplement is available only to recipients of the Old Age Security Pension without enough income to meet the federal standard. The Spouse's Allowance provides an income-tested benefit to low-income spouses age 60 to 64 married to Old Age Security pensioners with low pensions. The Widowed Spouse's Allowance is largely for older women who have no other source for a basic income.[15, 50, 51]

Six provinces and two territories further supplement income for those without sufficient Old Age Security and Guaranteed Income Supplement. On the other hand, repayment to the government of part of the pension is required for individuals who earn after-tax income of more than $53,215 (in 2000). Old Age Security and pension income are subject to income taxation at the same rates required of the younger population.[14, 50, 63]

The government proposed a major restructuring of Old Age Security and Guaranteed Income Supplement payments in 1996—merging the two programs into one Senior Benefits allocation with advantages for lower-income workers. Payroll tax costs would have been higher. However, improvement of the national economic situation led to dismissal of the change in 1999 before it was implemented, in part because the proposal was not popular with higher-income workers.[52]

Another program was initiated in 1998—with contribution rates from payroll taxes rising to 9.9 percent—to build a larger reserve fund than had existed previously. The additional contributions will be partly invested in a diversified investment portfolio managed by a Canada Pension Plan Investment Board. To be eligible for benefits retirees must have made contributions in four of the last six calendar years. A death benefit equal to six months of retirement payments up a maximum of $2500 (Canadian) was made available. Benefit payments to prior retirees were not directly affected by the changes.[52]

Health care deductibles and co-payments required of older people are adjusted for level of income and are therefore generally lower than for the younger population. Drug costs, for example, require much lower co-payments than for younger people, although with considerable variation by province.[63]

Private Pensions. In addition to the public programs about half of Canadians have private pension plans funded through their workplace. At retirement workers receive an average benefit of 25 percent of their monthly earnings (with a defined maximum per month). Private pensions are funded by a payroll tax that goes to a national private pension plan. Employers and employees contributed 1.8 percent of wages, up to an income cap of $25,800 annually in 1992. A surviving spouse receives a proportion of the pension income.[28, 63]

Financing Health Care Insurance

The older population particularly benefits from the provincial health insurance systems (referred to as *Medicare*). The plans cover the entire population but expenditures for the elderly are much higher than for younger people. Most physicians receive the bulk of their fees from the public system. Private health care provides a "safety valve" in some provinces for patients who can afford to pay and do not want to wait for services.[36]

The provincial health care insurance systems are less costly per capita or as a proportion of GDP than in the United States but are somewhat more expensive than in Europe or Japan. Overall, Canada spent about 11 percent of GDP for health care in 1997 compared to nearly 13.8 percent in the United States. Lower administrative expenses, a single-payer system, lower personnel costs, and less hospital technology than in the United States are all part of the explanation for lower costs. For example, administrative expenses were about 11 percent of health care spending in 1996 as compared to 24 percent in the United States. Physicians are paid considerably less as well, although nurses are paid somewhat more.[57, 69]

Financing Problems. As noted earlier, health care benefits were somewhat curtailed in the 1990s because of serious budget problems at provincial and federal levels. Lowered access to some forms of publicly insured health care has meant that private services must fill the gap if care is to be available to those who can pay. Consequently, private health care spending grew from 26 percent of health expenditures in 1993 to 31 percent in 1998. Private insurance companies that provide supplemental coverage, such as Liberty Health (formerly Ontario Blue Cross), have grown steadily even with increased premiums. Privatization is proceeding despite the stated preference (according to national surveys) by most people to keep their universal public system intact. The effort to balance provincial and federal budgets by cutting health care has been criticized because cutbacks have not always appeared to be undertaken with adequate consideration of equity and long-term consequences.[32, 85]

◆◆◆ VARIATIONS AMONG PROVINCES

Although information about each province is incomplete, the following illustrations highlight some of the additional similarities and differences among several provinces.

British Columbia

The British Columbia Continuing Care System is responsible for creating and managing a particularly impressive and comprehensive long-term care enterprise—as noted earlier. The system integrates residential and community based services for the elderly while taking full advantage of family contributions. Several levels of care are available:[49]

- Non-medical personal care.
- Three levels of intermediate care ranging from minimal to greater complexity.
- Extended care for very disabled and dependent individuals.

Each level can usually be provided either at home or in an institutional setting. Meals on wheels, homemaker services, adult day care, and respite care are available in homes. Costs are largely covered by provincial health insurance.[64]

Referrals to any of the continuing care programs can be made by a health professional, family member, a friend, or through self-referral. If the Continuing Care staff determine that an older individual is eligible for some level of assistance, an in-depth assessment is conducted. Specialized assessment and treatment centers in acute care hospitals are sometimes involved, usually in consultation with a personal physician. A plan is then developed for appropriate care. A case manager (usually a registered nurse) is assigned to manage each client. Services may be delivered through the agency or through for-profit or nonprofit local providers.[49]

Home Care. The Community Home Care Nursing Program provides comprehensive nursing care in group or private homes— seven days per week if needed. Home health and maintenance services are widely available throughout the province, growing substantially during the 1980s as limits on new nursing home beds were implemented. Although systematic quality measures were not in place for precise determination of how the programs operated, client satisfaction was high and political support was sufficient to secure the needed provincial budget support.[10, 40]

Services are delivered through 21 community offices, each headed by a community care manager. Each office manages an institutional care program, a community home care nursing program, and a community rehabilitation program. Home meal recipients are expected to pay for the cost of the food. A modest user fee is also required of those who can afford to pay for adult day care and homemaker services. Only 20 percent of home care clients have incomes high enough to require co-payment for services. The case managers determine individual service needs while acting as monitors and gatekeepers to specific facilities and services. The monitoring system plays a key role in cost control by helping to identify the least-cost satisfactory arrangements.[10, 64]

The Community Rehabilitation Program offers in-home consultation, equipment, and home modification focused on both prevention and treatment. Modifications facilitate easier functioning and can include hand-rails, ramps, widened doorways, and elevators, all of which are strongly encouraged as a means of lowering the risk of staying at home.[43, 49]

Outreach to remote rural areas is undertaken on a regular basis by case managers and clinical staff. When home care is not sufficient family care homes or small continuing care facilities are used. Home care and meal responsibility are sometimes contracted to a local provider.[49]

Nursing Home Care. Extended institutional care includes local nursing homes and extended care units in provincial hospitals. The single-entry-point office in each district takes inquiries, applications, and screens applicants for priority to enter a preferred facility. They must then wait in chronological order for an opening. A second choice facility may be used until an opening occurs in the preferred location. Rapid placement is possible in emergency situations. All costs except for a per diem rate or co-payment for room and board—usually drawn from a pension—are paid through provincial insurance.[49]

The British Columbia experience is of special interest as a successful example of public financing for nursing home and home health care. The system has been in place long enough for outcomes to be reasonably well understood.

Manitoba

Surveys indicate a high level of public support for a centrally administered comprehensive continuing care program. The system relies on an extensive information base about the elderly and their needs. Client-needs assessment and care coordination are the responsibility of a highly developed case management system which attempts to integrate income support, housing, home maintenance, and health care. Health services research is used to measure and monitor results while providing feedback to help improve the overall system. Social care is given equal status with medical care.[6]

Home Care. The provincial government concluded that development of home services was the best strategy for limiting the size and numbers of public nursing homes. Private facilities were allowed to increase in response to demand for space engendered by limitations on growth in public facilities.[64]

Home care services are provided free of charge—with funds allocated from provincial taxes and supplemented by a small federal subsidy. A wide array of services is available, including nursing visits, personal care, respite care, domestic help, meals, oxygen, several therapies, and day care, depending on the level of need.[6]

Local case coordinators have responsibility for assuring that clients receive appropriate service. Coordinators must have a bachelor's degree in nursing or social work and at least two years of community experience. In addition to administrative duties, their responsibilities include careful attention to family roles in the care process—attempting to avoid duplication with the work of formal home helpers. A regional care manager is responsible for planning, organizing, and managing services for groups of communities.[6, 67]

Nursing Home Care. The nursing home financing arrangement is based on five levels of disability (a so-called "case-mix" system) ranging from low-cost personal care to intensive nursing care. Occupancy rates approach 95–100 percent in both public and private nursing homes. Roughly 95 percent of those who enter nursing homes remain until death. Nursing home care requires co-payment for room and board for those who have a pension or other resources; other costs are covered by provincial insurance. About 75 percent of homes were nonprofit and publicly funded in 1995.[35, 64]

The per capita cost of nursing home care was considerably higher than in British Columbia or the United States—largely because of much higher staff compensation levels for better-trained nurses aides. Staff turnover is relatively low and relatively high levels of professionalism prevail. About 90 percent of all long-term care workers are unionized.[64]

Concern has been expressed in the public media that resources may not be adequate to sustain the comprehensiveness and quality of the mandated home care programs, given the growing numbers and longer lives of the older population. Eligibility requirements have been made more stringent as a result of budget limitations.[66]

New Brunswick

New Brunswick initiated a somewhat unique home health service in 1981 through the so-called Extra-Mural "hospital without walls" program. The mandate was to provide an alternative to hospitalization, facilitate early discharge from health care institutions, and provide care at home to terminally ill individuals.[79]

The home care emphasis appeared to be quite effective but it was unclear in the mid-1990s whether hospital admissions had actually been reduced or if palliative care had been enhanced. Use of physician services declined. Most referrals continued to be a result of some form of crisis rather than a consequence of planned admissions. The program reaches about 80 percent of the qualified elderly.[11, 79]

Ontario

The publicly funded long-term care system attempts to provide a continuum of health services and support for older people—under the policy direction of a Minister for Long-Term Care appointed for the first time in 1998. Community Care Access Centers are responsible for coordinating local home care and nursing home services while providing simplified access to long-term care. Roughly 66 percent of the nursing homes were private for-profit enterprises in 1998, 20 percent were municipal homes, and 14 percent were operated by charitable organizations.[27]

The rate of institutionalization was nearly 25 percent higher in Ontario than the average for other Canadian provinces in 1995 (absorbing 80 percent of long-term care resources) despite a policy emphasis on home care. The Ministry of Community and Social Services and the Ministry of Health both funded and supported institutional care and home health services—somewhat fragmenting the long-term care system. New legislation expanding community-based care and merging the services into a Service Coordination Agency was intended to alleviate the coordination problems.[61, 71, 79, 87]

The Sun Parlor Home for Senior Citizens, a county-operated continuing care home in the small community of Leamington, Ontario, is described in Illustration 10–1.

Illustration 10–1
SUN PARLOR HOME FOR SENIOR CITIZENS, LEAMINGTON, ONTARIO

The Sun Parlor Home is located in a 26 acre park-like setting in Leamington. Space is available for 208 residents, including individuals from outside the county who do not have ready access to such a facility. Healthier individuals and couples live independently in apartments with access to home care services provided by Sun Parlor staff. Others who need daily help with activities of daily living occupy assisted living units. The most seriously disabled live in a skilled nursing section, which includes an Alzheimer's locked wing with intensive nursing care and supervision. Any of the residents with potential for rehabilitation have direct access to physical therapy, occupational therapy, and other forms of rehabilitation.

The main building was completed in 1992 and was designed to maximize independence. Residents with the capacity to go out-of-doors have regular opportunities for walks or wheel chair trips in the parklike grounds. A library, several sitting and living rooms, a dining room, a craft and hobby room, a foot care clinic, and other medical support facilities are available.

The administrator and the other staff seemed thoroughly attuned to the needs of residents. We observed many kind words and ongoing helpfulness to residents. Nonetheless, because of health care resource cutbacks in Ontario, the home was required to reduce its budget by $1.5 million over 2½ years beginning in 1997. The province had "red-circled" the facility for targeted reductions. Other homes with fewer resources and greater demands were not required to cut expenditures to the same degree.

Restructuring has been underway for several years. The administrator identified several cost-cutting measures such as securing supplies through a bidding process to assure the best possible prices. Some services not deemed essential have been cut. However, residents tended to be somewhat more disabled than previously because of transfers from hospitals that had been closed. Proposals were under discussion to transfer some part of the savings from hospital closures to the nursing home, to offset increased costs.

The provincial government was in process of lowering government sponsorship of health and long-term care during the 1996–98 period. For example, the rule that all counties be required to maintain a public and nonprofit home for the disabled elderly was being reconsidered. This move toward privatization was directly affecting public facilities like Sun Parlor Home. The county was considering whether to sell the home to private investors. However, the public seemed very hesitant in 1997 to completely privatize both health care and housing for the vulnerable elderly.[27]

Mental health resources in 1997 were relatively limited in Ontario except in the major urban areas. The primary public focus was provision of services to individuals with major psychiatric disorders—which meant that the clientele of private psychiatrists tended to be the lower income segments of the population rather than the so-called "worried well." Most psychiatrists are compensated primarily from the single-payer provincial insurance system.[1]

Quebec

Quebec has a somewhat more liberal home care policy than other provinces. An older person does not necessarily need a medical referral to receive a home medical assessment—partially because it may be somewhat difficult to secure the services of a primary care physician for a home examination. Physicians are hesitant to see homebound patients even though the provincial rules call for their participation. Increased time per patient is obviously required for house calls. Primary care physicians are more willing to be involved when backed up by a clinical coordinator or case manager who maintains contact with the patient, coordinates home care services and health care institution visits, and arranges care.[25]

Hospice and Palliative Care. Quebec is noted for development of a national palliative care model at the Royal Victoria Hospital in Montreal. The program was modeled somewhat after St. Christopher's Hospice in London, England. Although the care is provided primarily in the hospital, patients are served at home whenever possible. Widespread use of volunteers helps to supplement a paid staff of physicians, nurses, social workers, psychologists, therapists, bereavement coordinators, and others. However, funding is a problem here as elsewhere, especially as health care budgets have tightened. Efforts to widen the range of responsibility to include local community organizations have been of some value, in part because churches and other local social groups have traditionally shared such responsibilities.[55, 68]

Saskatchewan

Saskatchewan has initiated a provincewide Palliative Care Services effort offered through district health boards under the home care program. It provides nursing services, homemaking, meal services, home maintenance and therapy, as well as symptom control, psychological support, bereavement counseling, and comfort to the dying individual and family. Specialized palliative care units are available in hospitals at Regina and Saskatoon.[17]

◆◆◆ LIFESTYLES: WORK, RETIREMENT, AND LEISURE

A high proportion of workers retire by age 62 and very few work after 65. Those who work tend to be part-time and intermittent—since they are generally able to receive adequate retirement benefits without earning additional income. Volunteerism by healthy older citizens is widespread. A New Horizons program emanating from the federal Health and Welfare ministry provides funding for senior groups to organize and support self-help community programs. Elderhostel, universities, senior centers, and many other educational programs encourage senior involvement in personal growth and learning.[63]

A National Advisory Council on Aging—with many older individuals as members—was created to advise the federal government on aging issues and quality of life for older people. The group reviews needs and problems, and recommends remedial action, encourages public discussion, and disseminates information deemed to be valuable to older citizens.[18]

Canadians are well-represented in the southern United States retirement communities described earlier. A number of RV parks and residential developments in Florida, Arizona, and Texas are inhabited primarily by temporary residents from Canada—who leave the colder climates up north to enjoy the warmth, sunshine, and abundant amenities of retirement communities. As long as they stay no longer than six months each year they can continue to draw full pension and health care benefits from their home province.

◆◆◆ NOTEWORTHY FEATURES AND MAJOR CHALLENGES

Quality of life has been a primary concern in several Provinces and is a major focus of researchers at the University of Toronto, whose work has helped identify the factors that contribute to success rates of public and private programs with close linkages to quality of life. Overall, the evidence indicates that public programs for the elderly are contributing to improved quality of life, although a number of issues continue to present problems.[81]

Noteworthy Features

The strong prevention orientation in the health care system helps older people to lead relatively healthy lifestyles. Single-payer public health and long-term care insurance is available to everyone without major out-of-pocket costs, if there is a willingness to wait for access to public facilities. Patients have relatively free choice of physicians and hospitals when space is available and can secure careful assessments to help minimize disease and illness. Geriatric specialists are available in most of the larger communities.

Long-term care has received major emphasis in most provinces, with special attention to avoidance of institutionalization whenever possible. Home care has a long tradition and helps facilitate aging in place. Physicians are much more involved in home care than in many other countries. Nursing homes tend to have high standards, and generally require greater training of nurse aides than elsewhere. Staff turnover is relatively low by international standards.

Housing is generally adequate for the older population, although shortage of space is sometimes a problem, particularly for single women needing access to assisted living and nursing homes. The public pension system means that older people face few financial risks, although their incomes may be modest depending on their access to private supplementary pensions and savings or investments. Overall, the Canadian support system for older citizens functions very well, generating relatively high levels of satisfaction and quality of life.

Major Challenges

Many hospitals were "mothballed" by provincial authorities in the early 1990s to cut health care expenditures. The closures included several specialized institutions for cancer treatment and heart treatment, decreasing access to care and putting many people out of work. Payments to remaining hospitals were also substantially cut. Rural communities were particularly impacted, in part because rural institutions tended to have fewer patients and a high per patient cost. The proportion of elderly also tends to be considerably higher than in urban communities.[24, 27, 54]

Services for the elderly have in the past been located inconveniently and were thus not optimally used. Creation of centralized Continuing Care Centers in most provinces was deemed an appropriate response, co-locating administration, home care, homemaker services, medical examination and treatment offices, adult day care, nursing care, respite care, retirement apartments, and associated services. British Columbia located new geriatric outreach centers in such facilities—with major advantages for the elderly and their families. The goal is to reduce the trauma of disability through improvements in continuity of services, thus limiting deterioration of disabled older clients.[27, 78]

An estimated 4 percent of Canadian elderly suffer from physical, emotional, or financial abuse or neglect. Although the proportion is relatively small, the number affected is quite substantial. Professionals who work with older people sometimes do not know how to deal with such problems—especially when they occur in a private home. Nurses are often in the best position to recognize signs of abuse and have taken an interest in learning more about identifying and intervening in such situations.[92]

Although the national economic situation improved somewhat in the latter part of the decade, financing programs for the rapidly expanding older population remains a major challenge. Privatization of some services—such as nursing homes and specialized medical services—has meant somewhat decreased equity and universalism of services for individuals at the lower end of the economic spectrum. Some of these services might not be accessible at all because of their lower public priority, if not for expansion of private enterprise.

◆◆◆ SUMMARY AND CONCLUSIONS

The ten provinces and territories assume most of the service responsibility for older citizens—with considerable variation in the details of implementation. Every province offers relatively generous income support, health care insurance, mental health care, nursing home care, home health care, and housing programs.

Federally sponsored Old Age Security and a Guaranteed Income Supplement, as well as work-related private pensions, mean that most older people have adequate retirement incomes. Since health care insurance is universal, care as needed is available without major out-of-pocket cost. Home health care is also nearly universal—although resource cutbacks have somewhat constrained services. Nursing home care is assured for those with chronic disabilities, although with some delay in access to public facilities. Personal or family responsibility for costs of room and board is required, except for those without resources. In non-emergency situations, access to some services requires waiting, regularly resulting in travel to nearby health centers in the United States with expenses paid from provincial health insurance.

Major stresses have been experienced by physicians, nurses, hospitals, and other providers as a consequence of service cutbacks. However, the impact on the elderly appears to have been modest and more a matter of inconvenience than serious damage to quality of life. Private enterprise is attempting to fill the gaps and has begun to provide many types of primary care, surgery, and nursing care services. Nonetheless, the public sector continues to be the primary provider of aging services.

British Columbia, Manitoba, and Ontario appear to have the most comprehensive and well-funded long-term care programs. These provinces have adopted case management as the primary mechanism for assuring that each older person at risk has guidance in securing full access to needed primary care, home health care, nursing home care, hospitalization, housing, and other community support services.

Canada has developed an impressive array of support programs for older citizens. While the economic downturn of the late 1980s and early 1990s led to major cutbacks in these programs, the basic structure and quality of services continue to place the nation in the front rank of countries with comprehensive aging policies and programs.

◆◆◆ REFERENCES

1. Anerson, Keith, Alistair Catterson, Michael Gaudet, Mamta Gautam, Peter J. Kerr, Marina Pecher, David Waiser, Junko Kaji, and Maurizio Fava (1997). A Cross-Sectional Study of Private Psychiatric Practices Under A Single Payer Health Care System, *Canadian Journal of Psychiatry*, 42 (4), 395–401.
2. Barer, Morris L., Clyde Hertzman, Robert Miller, and Marina V. Pascali (1992). On Being Old and Sick: The Burden of Care for the Elderly in Canada and the United States, *Journal of Health Politics, Policy and Law*, 17 (4), 762–82.
3. Baum, Carolyn M., and Mary Law (1997. Occupational Therapy Practice: Focusing on Occupational Performance, *Amercan Journal of Occupational Therapy*, 51 (4), 277–88.
4. Bay, K. S., M. J. Long, and J. C. Ross Kerr (1997). Utilization of Hospital Services by the Elderly: Geriatric Crisis in One Canadian Single Payer System, *Health Services Management Research*, 10 (1), 42–57.
5. Beckingham, A. C., and Susan Watt (1995). Daring to Grow Old: Lessons in Healthy Aging and Empowerment, *Educational Gerontology*, 21 (5), 479–495.
6. Berdes, Celia (1996). Driving the System: Long-Term-Care Coordination in Manitoba, Canada, *Journal of Case Management*, 5 (4) 168–72.
7. Boling, Peter A. (1997). *The Physician's Role in Home Health Care*, New York: Springer.
8. Brink, Satya (1995). Housing the Frail Elderly in Canada, in Jon Pynoos and Phoebe S. Liebig (eds), *Housing Frail Elders: International Policies, Perspectives, and Prospects*, Baltimore: Johns Hopkins University Press, 163–85.

9. Brotman, Shari L., and Mark J. Jaffe (1994). Are Physicians Meeting the Needs of Family Caregivers of the Frail Elderly? *Canadian Family Physician*, 40 (April), 679–85.

10. Brown, Arnold S. (1996). *The Social Processes of Aging and Old Age*, Upper Saddle River, NJ: Prentice Hall.

11. Brown, Murray (1995). Cost-Effectiveness: The Case of Home Health Care Physician Services in New Brunswick, Canada, *Journal of Ambulatory Care Management*, 18 (1), 13–28.

12. Buske, Lynda (2000). Growing Dissatisfaction Among Canada's Rural MDs, *Canadian Medical Affairs Journal*, 162 (4), 553.

13. Canadian Association on Gerontology (1997). The Association, *Newsletter*, 23 (1), 2.

14. Canadian Seniors Policies and Programs Data Base (2000a). *Policy or Program Name*, Online at www.sppd.gc.ca/scripts/sppd.

15. Canadian Seniors Policies and Programs Data Base (2000b). *Guaranteed Income Supplement (GIS)*, Online at www. sppd.gc.ca/scripts/sppdsrch.dll.

16. Canadian Seniors Policies and Programs Data Base (2000c). *Canadian Health Network*, Online at www.sppd.gc.ca/scripts/sppdsrch.dll.

17. Canadian Seniors Policies and Programs Data Base (2000d). *Palliative Care Services*, Online at www.sppd.gc.ca/scripts/sppdsrch.dll.

18. Canadian Seniors Policies and Programs Data Base (2000e). *National Advisory Council on Aging*, Online at www.HC-SC.GC.CA/seniors-aines/seniors/english/naca.

19. Canadian Seniors Policies and Programs Data Base (2000f). *Mental Health Services*, Online at www.sppd.gc.ca/scripts/sppdsrch.dll.

20. Canadian Seniors Policies and Programs Data Base (2000g). *Home Care Development*, Online at www .hc-sc.gc.ca.

21. Canadian Seniors Policies and Programs Data Base (2000h). *Division of Aging and Seniors*, Online at www.hc-sc.gc.ca/seniors-aines.

22. Canadian Seniors Policies and Programs Data Base (2000i). *Canada Health Act*, Online at www.hc-sc .gc.ca/medicare.

23. Canadian Seniors Policies and Programs Data Base (2000j). *Chronic Care (Complex Continuing Care)*, Online at www.sppd.gc.ca/scripts/sppdsrch.dll.

24. Carriere, Yves, and Lous Pelletier (1995). Factors Underlying the Institutionalization of Elderly Persons in Canada, *Journal of Gerontology*, 50B (3), S164–S172.

25. Clarfield, A. Mark, and Howard Bergman (1991). Medical Home Care Services for the Housebound Elderly, *Canadian Medical Association Journal*, 144 (1), 40–45.

26. Clark, Phillip G. (1993). Public Policy in the United States and Canada: Individualism, Familial Obligation, and Collective Responsibility in the Care of the Elderly, in Jon Hendricks and Carolyn J. Rosenthal, *The Remainder of Their Days: Domestic Policy and Older Families in the United States and Canada*, New York: Garland Publishing Company, 13–48.

27. Cloutier-Fisher, Denise, and Alun E. Joseph (2000). Long-Term Care Restructuring in Rural Ontario: Retrieving Community Service User and Provider Narratives, *Social Science and Medicine*, 50, 1037–45.

28. Cockerham, William C. (1991). *This Aging Society*, Upper Saddle River, NJ: Prentice Hall.

29. Cohen, Carole A. (2000). Caregivers for People with Dementia: What is the Family Physician's Role? *Canadian Family Physician*, 46 (February), 376–80.

30. Cohen, May, Christel A. Woodward, Barbara Ferrier, and A. Paul Williams (1996). Interest in Different Types of Patients, *Canadian Family Physician*, 42 (November), 2170–78.

31. Conn, David K., Victoria Lee, Allan Steingart, and Michel Silberfeld (1992). Psychiatric Services: A Survey of Nursing Homes and Homes for the Aged in Ontario, *Canadian Journal of Psychiatry*, 37 (8), 525–30.

32. Cournyer, Roger and Tina Cournyer (1997). Interviews by the authors, conducted in Hamilton, Ontario.

33. Courtman, Barbara J., and Sylvia B. Stallings (1995). Characterization of Drug-Related Problems in Elderly Patients on Admission to a Medical Ward, *Canadian Journal of Hospital Pharmacy*, 48 (3), 161–66.

34. Danzon, Patricia (1992). Hidden Overhead Costs: Is Canada's System Really Less Expensive? *Health Affairs*, 11 (1), 21–43.

35. DeCoster, Carolyn, Noralou P. Roos, and Bogdan Bogdanovic (1995). Utilization of Nursing Home Resources, *Medical Care,* 33 (12), DS73–83.

36. DeCoster, Carolyn A., and Marni D. Brownell (1997). Private Health Care in Canada, *Public Health Reports,* 112 (4), 298–307.

37. Department of Finance, Government of Canada (1996). *The Seniors Benefit: Securing the Future* (Brochure), Ottawa: Distribution Center, Department of Finance, Government of Canada.

38. Dowler, Judith M., Deborah A. Jordan-Simpson, and Owen Adams(1992). Gender Inequalities in Care-giving in Canada, *Health Reports,* 4 (2), 125–36.

39. Eagle, D. Joan, Elizabeth Rideout, Pamela Price, Cathy McCann, and Elizabeth Wonnacott (1993). Misuse of the Emergency Department by the Elderly Population: Myth or Reality? *Journal of Emergency Nursing,* 19 (3), 212–18.

40. Ellencweig, A. Y., A. J. Stark, N. Pagliccia, B. McCashin, and A. Tourigny (1990). The Effect of Admission to Long Term Care Program on Utilization of Health Services by the Elderly in British Columbia, *European Journal of Epidemiology,* 6 (2), 175–83.

41. Folland, Sherman, Allen C. Goodman, and Miron Stano (1997). *The Economics of Health Care,* Upper Saddle River, NJ: Prentice Hall.

42. Forbes, W. F., and M. J. MacLean (1992). Aspects of Preventive Health Care for Older Persons, *Canadian Journal of Public Health,* 83 (4), 303–5.

43. Fox, P. L. (1995). Environmental Modifications in the Homes of Elderly Canadians with Disabilities, *Disability and Rehabilitation,* 17 (1), 43–49.

44. Garfinkel, Paul E., and Barbara J. Dorian (2000). Psychiatry in the New Millennium, *Canadian Journal of Psychiatry,* 45 (1), 40–47.

45. Gibson, Brenda (1995). Volunteers, Doctors Take Palliative Care into the Community, *Canadian Medical Association Journal,* 153 (3), 331–33.

46. Havens, Betty, and Neena L. Chappell (1993). Canada, in Erdman B. Palmore (ed), *Development of Research on Aging: An International Handbook,* Westport, CT: Greenwood Press, 41–57.

47. Hébert, Rejean, Carol Brayne, and David Spieglehalter (1997). Incidence of Functional Decline and Improvement in a Community-Dwelling, Very Elderly Population, *American Journal of Epidemiology,* 145 (10), 935–44.

48. Hirdes, John P. (1997). Development of a Crosswalk from the Minimum Data Set 2.0 to the Alberta Resident Classification System, *Healthcare Management Forum,* 10 (1), 27–34.

49. Hollander, M. J., and P. Pallan (1995). The British Columbia Continuing Care System: Service Delivery and Resources Planning, *Aging Clinical Experience and Research,* 7 (2), 94–109.

50. Human Resources Development Canada (2000a). *Income Security Programs: Old Age Security Pension,* Online at www.hrdc-drhc.ge.ca/isp/oas/ispb185.shtml.

51. Human Resources Development Canada (2000b). *Income Security Programs: Spouse's Allowance (SPA).* Online at www.sppd.gc.ca/scripts/sppdsrch.dll.

52. International Social Security Association (1998). Proposed Seniors Benefit Dropped, *Trends in Social Security,* 1998 (2, 4), 6.

53. Jacobzone, S., E. Cambois, E. Chaplain, and J. M. Robine (1999). The Health of Older Persons in OECD Countries: Is It Improving Fast Enough to Compensate for Population Ageing, *Occasional Papers No. 37,* Paris: Organization for Economic Cooperation and Development.

54. Joseph, Alun, and Denise S. Cloutier (1990). A Framework for Modeling the Consumption of Health Services by the Rural Elderly, *Social Science and Medicine,* 30 (1), 45–52.

55. Jutras, Sylvia (1990). Caring for the Elderly: The Partnership Issue, *Social Science and Medicine,* 31 (7), 763–71.

56. Lapierre, Louise (1992). Measures of Outside Care Given and Received by Seniors, *Health Reports,* 4 (4), 355–66.

57. Lassey, Marie L., William R. Lassey, and Martin J. Jinks (1997). *Health Care Systems Around the World: Characteristics, Issues, Reforms,* Upper Saddle River, NJ: Prentice Hall.

58. Liebig, Phoebe S. (1995). Federalism and Suitable Housing for Frail Elders: Comparing the Policies of Four Nations, in Jon Pynoos and Phoebe S. Liebig (eds), *Housing Frail Elders,* Baltimore: Johns Hopkins University Press, 239–74.

59. Lilley, Susan A., and Claire Gaudet-LeBlanc (1992). Quality of Life in Long-Term Geriatric Care: The Dietitian's Role, *Journal of the Canadian Dietetic Association,* 53 (3), 194–98.

60. Lindsay, Joan (1994). Patterns of Caring for People with Dementia in Canada, *Canadian Journal of Aging,* 13 (4), 470–87.

61. Litwin, Howard, and Ernie Lightman (1996). The Development of Community Care Policy for the Elderly: A Comparative Perspective, *International Journal of Health Services,* 26 (4), 691–708.

62. Man-Son-Hing, Malcolm, Barbara Power, Anna Byszewski, and William B. Dalziel (1997). Referral to Specialized Geriatric Services: Which Elderly People Living in the Community Are Likely to Benefit?, *Canadian Family Physician,* 43 (May), 925–30.

63. Marshall, Victor W., and Blossom T. Wigdor (1994). Canada, in Jordan I. Kosberg (ed), *International Handbook on Services for the Elderly,* Westport, Connecticut: Greenwood Press, 66–79.

64. Miller, Robert H. (1993). Containing Use and Expenditures in Publicly Insured Long-Term Care Programs, *Health Care Financing Review,* 14 (4), 181–207.

65. Mohide, E. Ann, Dorothy M. Pringle, David L. Streiner, J. Raymond Gilbert, Gisele Muir, and Michelle Tew (1990). A Randomized Trial of Family Caregiver Support in the Home Management of Dementia, *Journal of the American Geriatric Society,* 38 (4), 446–54.

66. Monk, Abraham, and Carole Cox (1991). *Home Care for the Elderly: An International Perspective,* New York: Auburn House.

67. Monk, Abraham, and Carole Cox (1992). Lessons To Be Learned: Home Care in Other Countries, *CARING Magazine,* 11 (10), 35–39.

68. Mount, Balfour (1997). The Royal Victoria Hospital Palliative Care Service: A Canadian Experience, in Dame Cicely Saunders and Robert Kastenbaum (eds), *Hospice Care on the International Scene,* New York: Springer, 73–85.

69. National Center for Health Statistics (1998). *Health United States 1998,* Washington, DC: U.S. Bureau of the Census.

70. Neergaard, Lauran (2000). U.S. Health Care Delivers Little for the Money, *The Salt Lake Tribune,* June 21, A1, A4.

71. Neysmith, Sheila Marjorie (1994). Canadian Long-Term Care: Its Escalating Costs for Women, in Laura Katz Olson (ed), *The Graying of the World: Who Will Care for the Frail Elderly?* New York: Haworth Press, 163–88.

72. Olson, Laura Katz (1994). Introduction, in Laura Katz Olson (ed), *The Graying of the World: Who Will Care for the Frail Elderly?* New York: Haworth Press, 1–23.

73. Organization for Economic Cooperation and Development (OECD) (1996). *Caring for Frail Elderly People: Policies in Evolution,* Paris: OECD.

74. Organization for Economic Cooperation and Development (2000). Online at www.oecd.org.

75. Ostbye, Truls, and Evelyn Crosse (1994). Net Economic Costs of Dementia in Canada, *Canadian Medical Association Journal,* 151 (10), 1457–64.

76. Penning, Margaret J. (1995). Cognitive Impairment, Caregiver Burden, and the Utilization of Home Health Services, *Journal of Aging and Health,* 7 (2), 233–53.

77. Pereles, L., and M. L. Russell (1996). Needs for CME in Geriatrics, *Canadian Family Physician,* 42 (April), 632–40.

78. Phillips, John M. (1992). Geriatric Care Planning: Planning for Our Elderly, *The International Hospital Federation,* 28 (1), 15–24.

79. Pickles, B., A. U. Topping, and K. A. Woods (1994). Community Care for Canadian Seniors: An Exercise in Educational Planning, *Disability and Rehabilitation,* 16 (3), 181–89.

80. Powell, C., and M. Nixon (1996). Caring For Patients in Geriatric Day Hospitals, *Canadian Physician,* 42 (January), 110–17.

81. Raphael, Dennis, Ivan Brown, Rebecca Renwick, Maureen Cava, Nancy Weir, and Kit Heathcote (1997). Measuring the Quality of Life of Older Persons: A Model With Implications for Community and Public Health Nursing, *International Journal of Nursing Studies,* 34 (3), 231–39.

82. Richardson, Blair G. (1990). Overview of Provincial Home Care Programs in Canada, *Health Care Management Forum,* 3 (3), 3–19.

83. Rockwood, Kenneth, Paul Stolee, and Ian McDowell (1996). Factors Associated with Institutional-

ization of Older People in Canada: Testing a Multifactorial Definition of Frailty, *Journal of the American Geriatric Society*, 44 (5), 578–82.

84. Rodriguez, Luis (1992). Emergency Response Systems—The Canadian Perspective, *Home Health Care Service Quarterly*, 13 (3–4), 5–22.

85. Santis, Solange de (1998). Canada Government's Health Cuts Create Private-Sector Opportunities, *Wall Street Journal*, March 25, 1.

86. Stephenson-Cino, Patricia, Meir Steiner, Lester Krames, Ellen Bouchard Ryan, and Gail Huxley (1992). Depression in Elderly Persons and Its Correlates in Family Practice: A Canadian Study, *Psychological Reports*, 70 (2), 359–68.

87. Stewart, Ruth (1992). The Reform and Redirection of Long-Term Care in Ontario, *Caring Magazine*, 11 (10), 98–101.

88. Tamblyn, Robyn, Peter J. McLeod, Michal Abrahamowicz, and Rejean Laprise (1996). Do Too Many Cooks Spoil the Broth? Multiple Physician Involvement in Medical Management of Elderly Patients and Potentially Dangerous Drug Combinations, *Canadian Medical Association Journal*, 154 (8), 1177–84.

89. Tamblyn, Robyn, Andre Jacques, Rejean Laprise, Allen Huang, and Robert Perreault (1997). The Office of the Future Project: The Integration of New Technology Into Office Practice. Academic Detailing Through the Super Highway, *Clinical Performance and Quality Health Care*, 5 (2), 104–8.

90. Tarman, Vera Ingrid (1994). Age and Sex of Caregivers, *Canadian Family Physician*, 40 (May), 963–70.

91. Torrible, Susan J., and David B. Hogan (1997). Medication Use and Rural Seniors: Who Really Knows What They Are Taking? *Canadian Family Physician*, 43 (May), 893–98.

92. Trevitt, Corinne, and Elaine Gallagher (1996). Elder Abuse in Canada and Australia: Implications for Nurses, *International Journal of Nursing Studies*, 33 (6), 651–59.

93. United States Census Bureau (2000). *International Data Base*. Online at www.census.gov.

94. Wells, Donna L., Anita Saltmarche, Patricia Adolphus, and Kerry Marshall (1991). Getting Together: Administrative and Clinical Teamwork Creates a Geriatric Care Program for the Hospital, *Healthcare Management Forum*, 4 (1), 3–8.

95. Wister, Andrew V. (1992). Residential Attitudes and Knowledge, Use, and Future Use of Home Support Agencies, *Journal of Applied Gerontology*, 11 (1), 84–100.

96. Wister, Andrew, and Gloria Gutman (1997). Housing Older Canadians: Current Patterns, Preferences, and Policies, *Journal of Housing for the Elderly*, 12 (1, 2), 19–35.

Chapter 11

JAPAN
Challenges of Aging and Cultural Change

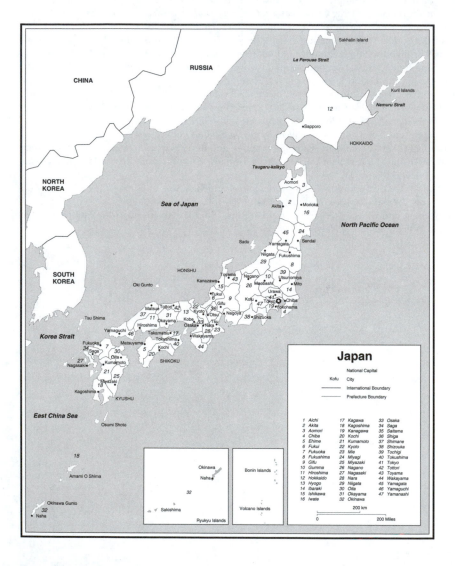

Japan

National Capital

Kofu   City

International Boundary

Prefecture Boundary

1	Aichi	17	Kagawa
2	Akita	18	Kagoshima
3	Aomori	19	Kanagawa
4	Chiba	20	Kochi
5	Ehime	21	Kumamoto
6	Fukui	22	Kyoto
7	Fukuoka	23	Mie
8	Fukushima	24	Miyagi
9	Gifu	25	Miyazaki
10	Gumma	26	Nagano
11	Hiroshima	27	Nagasaki
12	Hokkaido	28	Nara
13	Hyogo	29	Niigata
14	Ibaraki	30	Oita
15	Ishikawa	31	Okayama
16	Iwate	32	Okinawa

33	Osaka
34	Saga
35	Saitama
36	Shiga
37	Shimane
38	Shizuoka
39	Tochigi
40	Tokushima
41	Tokyo
42	Tottori
43	Toyama
44	Wakayama
45	Yamagata
46	Yamaguchi
47	Yamanashi

200 km

0   200 Miles

◆◆◆ INTRODUCTION

Japan is the third most densely populated nation in the world with more than 126.7 million people (in 1999); it has the second largest Gross Domestic Product and had the eighth largest GDP per capita in 1998. Only one-fifth of the land area permits agriculture; the remainder is mountainous. The Tokyo metropolitan region is particularly dense—containing 26 percent of the population. Income differences between workers are the smallest among advanced countries. In a recent survey, 80 percent of the Japanese considered themselves members of the middle class. Economic growth and prosperity have been the norm for several decades although during the 1990s there was a definite slowing of economic progress.[4, 72, 79]

The decline was accompanied by a crisis of confidence, exacerbated by rigidity in the financial system and political unwillingness to deal with many of the basic problems. A serious recession caused business failures, a huge loss in the stock market, and a general decline in real estate values. The financial problems made it difficult for government to deal with the rapid aging of the population.

Demographic Characteristics

Average life expectancy has been increasing rapidly since 1945, when it was 54 for women and 51 for men, to 80.1 in 1999—highest in the world. The increase in length of life is in significant part a consequence of improvements in health standards—and is reflected in the large numbers of older people, especially women—as indicated in the population pyramid in Figure 11–1. The relatively modest number of

FIGURE 11-1 Population Pyramids for Japan
Source: U.S. Census Bureau, *International Data Base,* 2000.

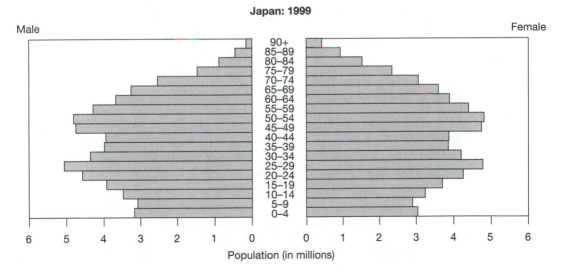

Japan: 1999

younger people is also reflected in the pyramid. The oldest old (85+) are increasing the most dramatically, as in other advanced countries, and will present great challenges to health care and long-term care in the years ahead.[23, 34, 43, 58]

Approximately 16.7 percent of the population was age 65 and older in 1999, and this age group is expected to grow to 26 percent or higher by 2025 when the post World War II babies reach retirement age. This is a faster growth rate than in any other economically advanced country, despite the fact that Japan did not experience a baby boom after the war. The large numbers in the upper-age categories of the population pyramid in Figure 11–1 illustrate the high proportion of older people. Women heavily outnumber men. Japan also has the lowest birthrate in the world—less than the replacement rate.[4, 7, 18, 24, 50]

Some estimates suggest that if current low birthrates continue total population numbers will drop from 125 million to fewer than 100 million by the year 2051 and less than 70 million by 2095. If major adjustments in policies and programs are not made, serious financial strain will be placed on the social security system, health care insurance, and long-term care programs.[9, 27, 31]

Rural regions tend to have higher proportions of older people than urban centers because younger people migrate to the cities in large numbers and older people tend to stay in their home communities. For example, only 4 percent of the population in suburbs are age 65 and over compared to 35 percent in some rural communities.[23, 51, 67, 72]

◆◆◆ HISTORICAL PERSPECTIVE

Japan has a very long and somewhat troubled history, especially because of the Japanese role in the twentieth century as a conqueror during World War II. The nation was relatively poor and isolated in earlier centuries. However, the energetic culture and value system have led to enormous social and economic progress in the postwar period.

Basic Values

Respect for the elderly has a long tradition in Japan and was explicitly written into an Act for the Welfare of the Aged in 1963: "Senior citizens shall be treated with dignity and respect as individuals who have contributed to the progress of society for many years, and who possess a wealth of knowledge and experience. With this in mind, they shall be guaranteed a high quality of life that is sound and secure." The responsibility of families to care for elderly members was inscribed in the Japanese Civil Code (item 877). Despite these formal declarations, there are clear signs that attitudes are changing among urbanized younger generations. For example, surveys in 1981 and 1992 show a decline from 73 percent to 56 percent in the belief that families should be responsible for care of older members. Younger citizens feel the government should take greater responsibility.[36, 67]

Japan has traditionally been a very status-conscious society. Great attention is paid to social rules that maintain and preserve status differences. Reputation or "saving face" is very important within and between social groups. Maintaining membership in social groups, in the family, at work, and in the community, while treating other members appropriately, has a very high social relevance. Any behavior that causes hurt to family or friends is considered a major transgression. Harmony, cohesion, cooperation, obligation, and obedience to norms and standards of behavior have long been central values. Social relationships are constantly monitored and regulated by the family and other social groups.[45, 71]

This may be among the reasons for the contrast between the "outer" self that is public and exposed to the community, and the "inner" or private self that is viewed as somewhat independent of outside influences. The outer self responds to the social pressures toward conformity while the inner self responds to personal values. The inner self is likely to be viewed positively by the older individual, as manifested by expressions that older age is good despite outer conditions that may be negative. Societal attitudes toward aging are sometimes negative and stereotypical whereas self-perceptions of aging may be positive. This illustrates the importance of balance among contrasting perspectives—thought to help create harmony in interpersonal relations and within the person.[38]

Families tend to be quite independent and even somewhat isolated from the larger community. Older people depend on "inside" social obligations of their family and tend to be isolated from "outside" services and influences. Family centeredness (or "filial piety") has traditionally been very strong. The family is linked together economically and psychologically to a greater degree than in most other economically advanced countries. Family interdependency has traditionally given the older person the right to be dependent on his or her family for care in times of disability.[69]

Social Security and Health Care

Universal social security and health care insurance were required by Article 25 of the post-World War II constitution. However, little government intervention on behalf of the older population was evident until an Employees' Pension Insurance act of 1954 and a National Pension Insurance act of 1959. The Law for the Welfare of the Aged in 1963 outlines basic principles for treatment of the elderly, followed by a Law for the Health of the Aged in 1982 providing new health care services. The pension system was reformed in 1989 and further improved in 1995.[14, 67]

The delay in developing adequate social security income guarantees has contributed to the tendency for men to remain in the workforce well past age 65. Furthermore, the increasing size of the service sector in recent decades is creating new opportunity for employment of older workers because younger workers are becoming less available.[33]

The Golden Plan

A major initiative was undertaken in 1989 as part of a ten-year strategy to promote health care and welfare services. The Golden Plan encouraged independence of older people through greater emphasis on home care, day care services, rehabilitation, short respite stays in elder care facilities, and reduction of long-term institutional care in geriatric hospitals. More attention was paid than previously to overall quality of life, individual autonomy, and involvement in decisions about the future. Services to the elderly were to be unified and coordinated to overcome fragmentation.[8, 31, 65, 70]

A new fundamental law on aging was approved by the National Diet in November 1995 to refine the goals of the Golden Plan and further advance public policies. The law provided the basis for expanded long-term care programs, increases in the number of home helpers and visiting nurses, increases in day service centers, expanded respite care, growth in nursing home spaces, more independent housing, and a series of other measures for overall enhancement of life quality for the older population.[41]

The Golden Plan emphasizes development of coping mechanisms to maintain independence during disability. Public assistance is provided to older individuals when important relationships change through death of a spouse or other events, helping to overcome loneliness and enhance interest in life. The community has traditionally taken responsibility for providing basic services such as health education, recreation, and other forms of social support.[17, 23, 41]

These changes were in part an outgrowth of developing research on aging, which began in earnest only after formation of the National Society for the Study of Geriatrics in 1953. A nationwide congress in 1959 led to the formation of the Japan Gerontological Society in 1960, which has since taken the lead in expanding research. Several major journals publish the results of this work—including the *Japanese Journal of Gerontology* and the *Japanese Journal of Geriatrics*.[40]

◆◆◆ SOCIAL SUPPORT SYSTEMS

Japanese society has traditionally placed great emphasis on individual responsibility and achievement within a family and group context. The extended life expectancy and generally good health of the older population are in part a function of a disciplined family and personal lifestyle. Sacrifice, suffering, and endurance are part of the core value makeup for older individuals.[69]

These traditions and values are directly associated with the long-held cultural expectation that care for older parents is a family responsibility. The eldest son has usually taken charge and received the bulk of the inheritance in exchange. However, only 15 percent of caregivers are men. Wives, especially the daughters-in-law, have cared for their husband's parents—a situation that is now changing rapidly as feminism has emerged. Mutual helping obligations are becoming less explicit, leaving older individuals somewhat more vulnerable. Decline in obligation to family and lowered inclination to be responsible for care of parents are altering the support system and possibly are a manifestation of negative attitudes toward aging among younger people.[3, 15, 16, 33, 38, 44, 66, 71]

A national survey conducted by the Ministry of Health and Welfare in 1988 indicated that 61 percent of older people wanted to live with their children and grandchildren, with the frail elderly or widowed having the strongest preferences. Another survey in 1992 indicated that children and grandchildren believed they should live near, *but not with*, their parents or grandparents. The very strong emphasis on achievement of high test scores by children if they are to continue their education has served to disrupt relationships with grandparents, who are no longer viewed as important sources of knowledge. Rather, children are required to spend many hours in school and at home study, thus having relatively little time for family activities.[64, 71]

The proportion of multigenerational households dropped from 80 percent in 1957 to 55 percent in 1994 and to about 35 percent in 1999. Families are thus getting progressively smaller—from an average of 5 members per household in 1945 to 2.84 in 1995. Improved job opportunities have increased mobility for younger members. Many families have only daughters and no eldest son to take responsibility for parents. The high cost of housing means that homes are relatively small. The multigeneration family thus increasingly requires more than one household to keep it durable; this often means that adult children provide part-time care for parents who live in separate households some distance from their children.[13, 16, 42, 51, 58, 72]

Although the family has traditionally provided protection for older members, in terms of housing, income, food, and personal services, the larger society is playing an increasingly significant role as the strength of family obligations declines. Modernization has led to a greater sense of individuality for both children and their parents—fostered in part by higher levels of education, higher living standards, and external influences from the mass media. New alternatives for housing have increased interest among the older population in living independently, as Western cultural patterns, for good or ill, gradually enter Japan.[16, 61, 72]

The feminist movement was much slower to develop in Japan than in other advanced countries. However, in recent years younger women are challenging traditional male domination in the family and at work. Age at first marriage for both men, 28.5, and women, 26.3 (in 1995), is among the highest in the world. The shortened reproductive period for couples contributes to the very low birthrate. The high cost of living is among the important reasons that couples delay establishing a family until they have attained an income level adequate enough to afford housing and support of children.[72]

Informal and Formal Caregiving

Despite the attitude changes, families continue to provide a high proportion of *informal care* for disabled older members; only 7 percent received some type of *formal care* in 1994. However, only about half of younger Japanese preferred family caregiving as an option; they would have chosen formal care if it were available. About 36 percent of women who provide informal care also work, which may affect their attitudes somewhat. Nevertheless, relying on friends or neighbors for assistance is regarded as somewhat shameful. If the family cannot provide needed support, the preference is for the help to come from local, regional, or national government.[15, 55, 61]

The quality of the relationship between the aged person and the family care providers is apparently an important predictor of preference for continuing to remain in the multigenerational home. A 1994 survey indicated that older individuals with strong family bonds generally preferred to avoid institutionalization. Older women indicated a fear of living alone and a greater preference than men for remaining in the family home. Males were more likely to prefer institutionalization, especially if they were in poor health and had weak family bonds.[64]

Overall, the survey revealed that the elderly are learning not to expect their children or grandchildren to care for them. This underlies the greatly increased recent support for public approaches to long-term care. Families are gradually accepting the importance of *formal home care services* as mechanisms to avoid higher rates of institutionalization.[42, 64]

Community and Government Roles

Education on resolution of aging problems is popular and widely available to older citizens. Communities frequently sponsor "Old People's Colleges," based on the theory that greater knowledge, supportive social networks of this type, and frequent social contacts will lower incidence of mortality and institutionalization. Ongoing social networks and social activities in the community have been demonstrated to result in greater longevity.[49, 83]

The government has begun to require study of aging in the elementary and secondary schools. A social studies course focusing on the need for income support, welfare, and other needs of an aging population, is prescribed by the Ministry of Education. The goal is to cultivate a benevolent attitude toward older people.[12]

Community Coordination of Services.   Teams of agency professionals were established in all municipalities in 1987 with responsibility for coordination of services to the elderly. Members included municipal directors of health and welfare, medical staff, public health nurses, and mental health counselors. The goal was to assure that services were available and accessible, while providing a liaison function among the local agencies. Evidence from a study in selected communities indicated that the goal was achieved: services became more accessible and were used by larger numbers of older individuals (especially those with dementia) in the coordinated communities.[19]

◆◆◆ PHYSICAL HEALTH CARE

All older individuals have full access to health care insurance at very little personal cost and regardless of income. They are not required to pay the same deductibles as younger people, although co-payments of 10 percent were instituted in 1992 for those able to pay. An annual free health checkup is universally available.[41]

Although physicians are relatively abundant, other health care and long-term care support personnel are not; Japan is lowest among economically advanced countries in the proportion of health care persons in the labor force. For example, the nation has only about one-third as many health and welfare workers per 1000 older population as Sweden. Expansion of health and long-term care programs for older people under the Golden Plan have been limited by a severe personnel shortage.[21]

Preventive Emphasis

Older Japanese are generally health conscious and lead relatively healthy lifestyles, eating low-fat diets, doing regular exercise, and undertaking stress-reduction activities. However, health threats are also present: relatively high alcohol consumption, high incidence of smoking, salty and pickled foods, limited protein intake, and relatively high stress. Health maintenance is clearly not universal.[2, 44, 54]

Prevention of illness has long been a major focus of the public health services and certainly one of the reasons for the enormous improvement in health status since 1946. Six new prevention measures were initiated as part of the Health Services for the Elderly Act in 1983. These are provided by municipalities or workplaces for all citizens age 40 and above, although there is wide diversity among municipalities in level of support for the preventive measures noted below:[49]

1. Physical examinations, including screenings for several kinds of cancer.
2. Health education including diet needs and cancer avoidance.
3. Health counseling for diabetes, obesity, dental health, and other problems.
4. Rehabilitation in the event of disabilities.
5. Home consultation and guidance.
6. Health notebook and medical record to be maintained to serve as an eligibility document for medical care.

More than 35 percent of the eligible older population took advantage of this service in 1993. Studies indicate a direct relationship between participation and longer survival. Hospital admission rates and in-patient health care costs are also lower for those who receive health checkups. The utilization of private physician services is higher. Long-term care patients in hospitals tend not to have used health checkups to the same degree as those who are not institutionalized.[48, 49]

The Golden Plan initiatives added a major new preventive care component with full implementation targeted for the year 2000. The campaign involves an alliance among medical providers, caregivers, and older people to promote the highest level of physical function. A specific goal was to decrease the mortality from cancer, heart disease, and stroke, while reducing the numbers who are bedridden. Several components of the campaign are:[34, 48]

- Education and enlightenment of the public and the elderly about ways to prevent the need for institutional care.
- A focus on injury prevention, rehabilitation, and a safe living environment.
- An emphasis on nutrition as a major health improvement element.

Illustration 11–1 summarizes some of the results in one rural community.

Illustration 11–1
KNOWLEDGE AND BEHAVIOR OF THE ELDERLY IN A RURAL COMMUNITY

Kuni village has a population of 2100 and is located in the mountains of rural Japan. A study of residents over age 65 revealed a high degree of self-reliance and substantial knowledge about health maintenance needs. Nearly 89 percent understood the health care system and 85 percent had regular health examinations. Sixty-four percent had sought information and counsel through health care education efforts. They knew about home health care (84 percent), but preferred to rely on family for assistance (83 percent). Nearly 69 percent preferred to stay at home even during a terminal illness. The study indicated that efforts to inform and prepare older citizens were relatively effective in this rural enclave.

Source: Data from Takei, Shimada, and Orimo, 1998: 569–570.

National nutrition surveys involving about 6,000 families throughout the country have been conducted for 50 years to measure adequacy of diets, although individuals over age 80 are not included. Results indicate that malnutrition among older individuals is a major issue contributing to morbidity and mortality.[9]

Special surveys of nutritional status have been carried out with centenarians and a volunteer sample of individuals age 65 or older in the Prefecture of Okinawa. The analysis indicated a correlation between nutrient intake and energy levels, suggesting a clear relationship between nutrition and overall physical function. However, there was no evidence in the study that nutrition necessarily had an impact on longevity.[9]

Clinic and Hospital Care

The distinction between clinics and hospitals is not as sharp in Japan as in most other countries. Clinics often have up to 20 patient beds and serve both out-patients and in-patients. Hospitals have 20 or more beds but also provide out-patient services. Two-thirds of physicians are employed by hospitals; one-third are either in clinic or office practice and do not treat hospitalized patients. More geriatric hospital beds are available on a per capita basis than in any other country, with lengths of stay averaging three or more months.[14, 41]

A 1994 census tabulation indicated 85 percent of clinics and 71 percent of hospitals were privately owned, most by physicians. The large specialty hospitals are largely public, however, and are usually associated with medical centers of medical schools. The average long-stay hospital room contains four to six beds; rooms with up to 12 beds are not uncommon. Amenities such as private rooms and high quality food service are exceedingly limited.[14, 20, 27]

Although Total Quality Management originated in Japan, the concepts have not been widely used in hospital or medical management. Formal academic programs in health care administration are very limited. Very few administrative staff have graduate training of any kind. Administrative staff, physicians, and nurses are not generally required to undertake continuing education to update their skills. Incentive systems to encourage quality and efficiency have also been very limited.[81]

The Physician Role

A Medical Service Law requires that physicians serve as chief executive officers of hospitals whether or not they have management training. Provision of health care services is thus dominated by physicians, who also directly sell most prescribed medications. They also serve as staff for most of the key positions in the Ministry of Health and Welfare. Senior staff are often resistant to change and have been slow to implement modernization. However, physicians are by no means united. Major differences of viewpoint and priorities between private and hospital practitioners are evident. Medical schools are very competitive, creating allegiances among their graduates that last throughout the professional lives of former students.[73, 76, 81]

Community-based clinic physicians are not usually specialized and do not have hospital privileges. They have tended, however, to secure higher earnings because of the large number of patients under their care whose expenses are paid through a fee-for-service reimbursement system. Hospital physicians are generally younger and earn an average of about one-third the income of their clinic-based peers.[70]

Regardless of practice location, physicians spend relatively little time with each patient, making only modest attempts to explain diagnoses and the proposed treatments to patients. Appointments are not usually scheduled in advance at clinics or outpatient units of hospitals and waiting times tend to be very long.[27]

Influence of the Status System.   Health care is heavily affected by the strict social status system described earlier. Lower-status individuals nearly always defer to, and are subservient to, those with higher status. Since physicians have very high status, the older patient with lower status always defers—and thus participates very little in medical decisions. Older consumers are assured low-cost access to services but have little influence on how the services are delivered. Although older citizens have tended not to complain about their health care, younger people have fewer inhibitions.[46]

An older individual is free to choose any out-patient department, clinic, or hospital. The large medical school hospitals are believed to provide the best care and are often crowded, whereas local clinics may be much less used—even though the primary aim of the most prestigious hospitals appears to be training of physicians rather than care and treatment of patients. This situation explains some of the major inefficiencies in the health care delivery system.[29, 73]

Geriatric Care Emphasis.   Attention to the needs of the elderly has not been a particularly high priority among any physician group. Geriatrics as a medical school specialty has been very slow to evolve because it has not been a traditional specialty, despite the evident need. However, the government began establishing geriatric health care facilities in the 1980s and 1990s. Several major goals were articulated:[29, 31]

- Increased efficiency and quality through better patient care—while containing health care costs.
- Expansion of nonhospital geriatric care facilities.
- Development of a multidisciplinary team approach which unifies services and achieves comprehensive coordination of health and social services.

The proposed team approach would actively involve families and older individuals in decisions through a contract between the patient and the service provider—including charges, universal access 24 hours a day, quality assurance, and easy to understand information. The plan of care would be monitored, evaluated, and flexible enough to accommodate changing needs. Each team would have representatives from appropriate professional groups such as home health care agencies, physicians, dentists, pharmacists, occupational and physical therapists, public health and other nurses, and social workers.[31, 34]

Pharmaceutical Care

The pharmacy distribution and pricing system is in process of reform. One of the goals is to increase pharmaceutical research and development. This could lead, along with other changes, to more cost-effective, higher-quality, and more competent family practice, as well as improved integration with the larger specialized health care system. The outcomes should have a positive impact on acute and long-term care for the elderly.[70]

Medical Records Technology

A field experiment using optical memory cards—about the size of credit cards—began in 1986 in Ishehara City, an urban area of 95,000 people located a short distance southwest of Tokyo. A card can hold a lifetime of data (four megabytes) including name, address, phone, blood type, and allergens, as well as clinical records such as health status, medical consultation reports, home visit reports, vaccination and prescription history, welfare reports, images such as x-rays, electrocardiograms, photographs, pathology images and endoscopy images. Access requires a password and personal photo identification. Data can be read by a microcomputer system in medical and hospital offices.[62]

The cards were to be used primarily as a means of avoiding repeated tests and paperwork, while providing medical practitioners with ready access to a wide range of information. The initial tests of the cards suggested both effectiveness and wide acceptance by local and national officials.[62]

◆◆◆ MENTAL HEALTH CARE

In part because it is widely considered a personality defect that reflects badly on the family, Japanese culture has tended to be prejudiced toward mental disorder. A mentally ill person and his or her family are under tremendous cultural pressure to avoid shame. Families therefore often keep seriously ill relatives out-of-sight. Avoidance of outpatient professional care is very common.[2]

An emphasis on community integration began in 1988 with the enactment of a new mental health law, updated in 1995. The U.S. Mental Health Centers Act of 1963 served as a guideline in the movement toward community mental health care. Hospital treatment remains the norm, although efforts have been undertaken to increase access to general and emergency care in the community. As of 1996 approximately 45 mental health centers and 852 public health centers offering some form of mental health care were available throughout the country but were generally not well equipped to handle serious emergency cases. Integration of long-term psychiatric patients into the community is a major challenge because of the aforementioned cultural constraints.[28]

The prejudice against mental disorder often results in the inappropriate commitment of mentally ill individuals to long-term care institutions; this requires only the concurrence of two psychiatrists, without a formal legal process. Psychotherapy by professional psychologists or psychiatrists is not widely available. Large psychiatric hospitals provide care for patients with severe problems. More than 300,000 psychiatric patients were hospitalized in 1996 with an average length of stay of 108 days. It is clear that prevalence rates of mental disorder are equal to or greater than in other countries.[2, 23]

Many individuals under psychiatric long-term care do not want to leave the hospital—because of the interpersonal and family issues noted above, lack of adequate psychosocial rehabilitation, insufficient support for managing activities of daily living, and few monitoring services for suicide prevention.[2]

Prevalence of Dementia

Rates of dementia have been growing as in other industrialized countries with prevalence estimates between 2.4 percent and 7.3 percent, depending on the source of data. Rates for individuals over age 85 are estimated to average 23 percent. A study in the small community of Hisayama, Kyushu, with a population having demographic characteristics very similar to the whole of Japan, indicated that 6.7 percent of the population age 65 and older, and one-third of individuals age 85 and older, suffered from dementia. A larger study among atomic-bomb survivors that included Hiroshima and Nagasaki found a rate of 7.2 percent. Hypertension, diabetes, head trauma, stroke, and history of cancer were identified as primary causal factors, especially for vascular dementia. Individuals with greater education had lower rates of Alzheimer's.[78, 82]

Another study was undertaken in the small city of Ohira indicating a 6.1 percent prevalence of dementia among residents over age 65, a minor depression rate of 2.4 percent and a major depression rate of 0.4 percent. Dementia co-existed with depression in 21 percent of the elderly with dementia. The rates of depression are generally lower than elsewhere in Japan and considerably lower than in other industrialized countries, attributed by investigators to close family bonds.[32]

Efforts are underway to improve understanding of dementia. For example, an index was developed to measure Dementia-Free Life Expectancy (Dem-FLE) as one measure of quality of life. A study in one urban community concluded that men at age 65 have an 11 percent probability of dementia in their remaining lifetime. They can expect to live another 18 years with 16 of those years free from dementia. Women at age 65 have a 22 percent probability of eventual dementia and can anticipate living an average of 23 additional years, 18 without dementia.[65]

Attitudes toward mental disorder remain a major obstacle to effective diagnosis and treatment. Although considerable progress has been made in urban areas of the country, a comprehensive community mental health program that serves the entire nation has yet to be developed. Most dementia sufferers and others with mental disorders continue to be cared for at home.[14, 23]

◆◆◆ LONG-TERM CARE

The Golden Plan has led to considerable progress toward more complete long-term care strategies—with ambitious goals for expansion of services. When fully implementated, there will be greatly improved options for disabled older individuals.[15]

Home Care

Increased emphasis on home care is a central component of the national strategy. Remaining at home is clearly the preference among the disabled older population. A Senile Welfare Law was approved in 1990 mandating that older individuals should receive home care if they have mental disorders or physical disabilities. Expanded formal home care is increasingly considered more cost-effective than institutionalization. Approximately 35 percent of the seriously disabled elderly remained at home as of 1994, partly because of a continuing shortage of spaces in institutional facilities rather than as a matter of personal or family preference.[15, 18]

Available Services.   Home services include:[22]

- Home care support centers that offer consultation, specialized assistance, and linkage to other local services.
- Home helpers whose job is to assist with activities of daily living.
- Home nursing care by trained nurses working for public or nonprofit agencies to assist with identification and resolution of medical problems.
- Rehabilitation therapists to help improve function for those with potential for progress.
- Nutrition consultants to enhance diets and meal programs.
- Durable medical equipment for loan to those who could benefit from such technology.
- Temporary respite accommodations to assist caregivers who need a break.
- Adult day care for disabled individuals whose caregivers work outside the home.

Prior to 1987, most home health visits were conducted by hospital nurses during their off hours. The primary focus was follow-up assistance to recently discharged patients—with little collaboration involving local social welfare offices. Since 1987 home visiting has become a responsibility of local social-welfare workers who work collaboratively with public health nurses. The rapid growth of home care has meant that social workers and nurses are in short supply and insufficient to meet the need.[1, 22, 34, 67, 75]

Home Support Centers.   The Golden Plan emphasizes formal care channeled through home support centers. By 1993 more than 4,330 centers were operating—with plans for 10,000 by the year 2000. Primary components of home support include:[17]

- Opportunity for participation in community activities.
- Enhancement of independence in activities of daily living.
- Prevention of social isolation.
- Improvement in self-esteem.
- Improvement in overall quality of life.

Home care support centers offer advice, provide information, and refer individuals to appropriate social agencies. Telephone access is available 24 hours a day. A case management team involves a staff of social workers, nurses, and other support personnel, in developing a care plan for each participating individual. Funding has been increased for training of new home aides and home care support network managers. The Golden Plan target for the year 2000 was 100,000 home helpers of various kinds. The centers are supplemented by technical service units that provide special beds, mattresses, toilet chairs, emergency alarm systems, wheelchairs, and other durable equipment. Policy makers view the community center effort as an important alternative to institutionalization for individuals who need support but do not require the level of care provided by nursing homes.[14, 17, 41, 51]

Home Nursing.   An expanded Home Nursing Care System was initiated in 1991 with a focus on involving family physicians in providing better service to the older population. Payment for services is made directly by health insurance agencies to the home nursing care units. Home nurse activities include health status screening, education about self-care, bathing, personal care, and supervision to assure appropriate care.[34]

Reimbursement rates for physician and nurse visits to homes have been increased as incentives to encourage greater participation; payment rates at 1994 levels were considered inadequate to attract a sufficient number of professionals. It remains to be seen whether resource increases of the late 1990s will alleviate the shortages.[22, 29]

Rehabilitation.   Rehabilitation services are intended to increase the capacity of disabled older individuals to live independently or with minimal support. Physiotherapists, occupational therapists, and other staff assist individuals to increase functional ability through activities such as walking, performing activities of daily living, exercise, and other efforts to increase quality of life. Rehabilitation is usually provided in community health centers or adult day care centers and may include transportation and meals.[75]

Day Care Centers

Comprehensive community adult day care services were considerably expanded as part of the Golden Plan. This has been crucial for caretakers who work but want to continue maintaining older relatives at home.[67]

Assisted Living

Assisted living homes are expanding rapidly to serve individuals who are moderately disabled and do not need skilled nursing. About 90 percent of the available units were privately operated in 1991. The most economical options are subsidized by national and local government as part of the public welfare system. Local government social-welfare offices determine who is eligible for subsidy, based on income, level of disability, and home environment. To secure subsidized accommodation the older person must have a low income, pay no income taxes, be in poor health, and have inadequate housing and/or be estranged from family. A monthly fee in proportion to income is charged for room, board, and other nonmedical services.[41, 47]

Privately operated lifelong care homes are increasingly available for those who can pay the rather high costs. Accommodation and food for either subsidized or for-profit private homes is not counted as a health care cost in national tabulations.[29, 34]

Geriatric Hospitals and Nursing Homes

Approximately 6.2 percent of the elderly were residents of some form of long-term care facility in 1993. Several types of facilities are available:[14]

- Geriatric hospitals.
- Health Care Facilities for Rehabilitation of the Elderly.
- Geriatric nursing homes.
- Special subsidized nursing homes.
- Nonsubsidized nursing homes.

A 1992 health care reform divided hospitals into two major categories: (1) those emphasizing acute care with special or advanced technology and (2) those providing primarily chronic care or long-term geriatric care. A significant proportion of both clinic and hospital beds were in the second category as of 1997, despite the steady growth in the other long-term care alternatives. Chronic care hospitals are reimbursed by health insurance agencies at lower rates than the standard rates for acute care. Roughly 42 percent of disabled older people, or 4.1 percent of all older individuals, resided in geriatric hospitals during 1993—with an anticipated decline to 12 percent of disabled individuals or 3 percent of the older population by the year 2000.[8, 47, 56]

Health Care Facilities for Rehabilitation of the Elderly were initiated in 1988 to provide for the residential and health care needs of frail, physically disabled, or mentally challenged older individuals. The facilities are intended to expand services for those not served by geriatric hospitals, geriatric nursing homes, and special nursing homes. Nursing care, personal care, and physical therapy are available. The ratio of qualified nurses to residents must be one to thirty-five. A part-time physician must be available for every 100 residents.[41] Illustration 11–2 describes a modern facility in Tokyo.

Illustration 11–2
THE FUKUEIKAI HOME FOR OLDER PEOPLE

A seven-story building houses 140 disabled residents, average age 81, mostly housed in four-bed rooms. The home, sponsored by the local government, required an average monthly fee of $3200 in 1996. Only individuals without family or estranged from family are qualified to reside here.

Residents are strongly encouraged to do as much for themselves as possible, such as bathing. Some in wheelchairs use a specially designed bath facility. Residents can garden, engage in various forms of recreation, and help keep the facility clean to the degree of their ability. Most residents consider themselves fortunate to be here. A waiting list of approximately 10,000 for this facility was on record because of a severe shortage of available spaces. In the meantime most of those on the list were residents of geriatric hospitals.

Source: Data from Beck, 1996: 164.

Geriatric nursing homes are a special category of health care facilities that offer less intensive care than geriatric hospitals but are more intensive than most nursing homes. They include consultation, treatment, physical therapy, dining, bathing, toileting, a lounge, and other support functions. Acute illnesses may require transfer to a nearby hospital.[29]

Special nursing homes are subsidized for lower-income older people and are essentially part of the local welfare system. The full range of nursing home services are provided, but emphasis is primarily on personal care. Nursing home spaces of this type have generally been in short supply.[29]

Private for-profit nursing homes are available for those able to pay from personal or family resources. Many high-quality facilities have specially trained nurses and physicians on staff; more modest private alternatives are also becoming more available.[30]

Quality of Care Issues

The increases in nursing homes and home care options are complicated by a severe shortage of professional workers as noted earlier. A major training program has been initiated to alleviate the shortages—but in the interim many staff lack adequate qualifications. Volunteers have helped to fill the gap but are not substitutes for trained care-takers. As a consequence, quality of care has suffered.[51]

A Society for Quality Assurance in Health Care was inaugurated in 1990 to implement quality management and continuous quality improvement in all types of facilities for the elderly. This initiative led to creation of a Council for Quality Health Care in 1995 as a collaborative enterprise between the Ministry of Health, the Japan Hospital Association, and the Japan Medical Association. The primary goal was to assess medical institutions, clarify health delivery problems, and provide consultation and training in quality improvement.[73]

The government helped sponsor a world home care and hospice organizational meeting in 1995. International experts were invited to help examine the quality of long-term care programs. A 1997 trade mission to Japan, sponsored by the embassies of various countries, included invited home care executives to provide consultation with business and health care leaders. An increase in networking and further personnel exchanges to upgrade quality of long-term care services resulted.[31]

The new quality orientation is in part a consequence of a change in the balance of influence among physician groups. Private clinic owners have in the past largely controlled the medical establishment. As senior physicians retire and are no longer in a position to obstruct improvements, younger and more progressive physicians in hospital-based or clinic practice are gaining influence. Many younger physicians are shifting their involvement from hospital in-patient and out-patient services to office practice in communities.[70]

Continuing Problems

Continuing problems include: provincialism and traditionalism in many older geriatric hospitals, shortages of basic amenities within institutional settings, lack of adequate training of long-term care professionals, lack of cooperation and communication between researchers and practitioners, slow development of quality of care criteria in the private long-term care sector, potential hazards from overprescribing by physicians and lack of data on the quality and cost-effectiveness of home care as opposed to institutional care. These problems are all partially addressed by the Golden Plan, but achievement of the needed changes remains to be completed.[18, 27, 29, 73]

Hospice and the End of Life

Medical tradition respects health care as a lifelong right and entitles older patients to treatment, whatever the outlook. Physicians are very reluctant to abandon life-sustaining measures and consign a patient to a hospice. A strong negative image of death prevails. Most physicians therefore aggressively treat patients irrespective of the probability of survival. About 80 percent of all deaths occurred in geriatric or general hospitals in 1999, although the strong preference of older people is to spend their final days at home. Patients and families are often not informed of the specific diagnosis. A 1994 survey indicated that 29 percent of dying patients were not told by their physician of their impending death. The lack of openness between physicians, patients, and families leads to suffering and pain at the end of life that might be somewhat alleviated by greater use of palliative care and the hospice concept.[25, 35, 63]

Medical ethics also limits end of life options for physicians. Japanese law recognizes death only when there is breath cessation, pupil dilation, and the cessation of the heart beat. Brain death is not considered sufficient. Consequently, organ/tissue donations are limited. University and hospital medical practice styles allow only limited commitment to organ/tissue transplants.[68]

The traditions do appear to be changing, however. Many physicians have begun to adopt a more progressive viewpoint and end of life issues have become a major subject of discussion in medical meetings.[11, 26]

Hospice Evolution.   The first hospice was organized in 1981. Palliative care units were officially recognized for insurance coverage in 1990, but only for cancer and AIDS patients. As of 1995, 20 palliative care units had been organized in hospitals around the country. Few physicians have yet been trained in palliative care.[63]

Living Wills.   Living wills have been a subject of considerable discussion in medical association meetings and in the popular press. A Japan Society for Dying with Dignity has been organized and is actively promoting the use of living wills. One study indicated that 94 percent of physicians respected the living will when they understood the concept.[1, 10]

Concepts such as euthanasia, death with dignity, and "do not resuscitate" conventions were not fully recognized as legitimate until the Japanese Medical Association officially came to terms with these concepts in 1992. Cultural taboos have severely limited formal discussions of these issues.[68]

Patient Rights.   Consumer group activity in support of patient rights has increased, as have the number of medical malpractice lawsuits. However, few claims have been successful. Younger and recently trained physicians are having a positive influence on the physician-patient relationship, including a commitment to informed consent and more responsible attention to patient wishes.[73]

◆◆◆ HOUSING AND COMMUNITY

Housing the older population has become a major public policy issue. The focus of public housing agencies in the past has been to subsidize the construction of multifamily homes without particularly emphasizing apartments or condominiums specifically for the elderly. The public sector has designed and encouraged certain adaptations to accommodate elderly needs—hand rails on stairs, ramps to entry ways, and elimination of stairs wherever possible. Initiatives were taken in 1964 and 1986 by the Housing and Urban Development Corporation (HUDC) to increase the supply of housing especially for the elderly, but it did not became a major priority until the early 1990s when the public began to realize that a housing crisis was emerging.[37]

Three primary independent living options were available in the 1980s and 1990s:[37]

1. Two-generation household units with a special room, kitchen, and toilet for the elderly member(s). Adjacent apartments or detached housing units enabling children to live next door to parents are relatively common.
2. Adjoining units in the home of an older person or couple for occupancy by an adult child or close relative.
3. Homes specifically designed for someone with disabilities, built in the same neighborhood where other family members are located.

Local governments have primary responsibility for implementation of housing programs and community services for older people. Federal and prefecture governments often provide partial funding. Private enterprise is encouraged to construct housing for those who can afford the cost. Large firms in the private housing market, including a few American companies, are gradually developing complexes of homes with dining and other services.[1]

Efforts have also been underway to design housing that is useful for both younger and older generations. Durable barrier-free units, adaptable and comfortable for use by multigeneration and older families, are being constructed. More flexible housing that promotes "aging in place" is receiving emphasis—an attractive option in Japan as it is elsewhere. Rehabilitation of older housing units is a part of this strategy.[37]

Housing units have generally been very small and crowded making multigeneration arrangements difficult. Many of these are now occupied by single older persons—9 percent of households in 1975 and 16 percent in 1994—proportions that are increasing as in other advanced countries.[64]

Supported Housing

Several major types of supported housing were available in 1997, with other variations emerging:[29, 35, 47]

- Private group homes with apartments for older persons who can afford the price and do not have serious health limitations.
- Public and private assisted living homes for individuals or couples with disabilities.
- Public "silver" housing which includes alarm and emergency call systems, enabling residents to continue living independently with surveillance by designated responders.
- Low-cost public room-and-board homes with daily services for somewhat disabled but otherwise healthy individuals over age 60 who are unable to live entirely independently.
- Subsidized facilities for lower-income older people with poor health status who do not need skilled nursing care but require ongoing assistance with activities of daily living.

Housing policies have thus evolved giving increased focus to the needs of older families. Housing units are built specifically for disabled older individuals with accompanying support services in the community. "Life care" or continuing care arrangements are gradually becoming available with both independent housing units and various levels of care in adjacent locations.[37]

The Ministry of Health and Welfare encourages families to adapt their homes to meet the needs of disabled members and provides loans for reconstruction costs. The federal government approved the National Sheltered Housing Program for the Elderly in 1988 to encourage construction of supported independent living homes for the frail and impaired elderly. The Golden Plan legislation contains provisions to increase further the number of publicly sponsored and supported residential alternatives.[67]

Residents of the public or subsidized facilities are required to pay monthly fees based on their income. Family members are also legally required to contribute on a sliding income scale when the older relative cannot pay directly.[67]

◆◆◆ ECONOMIC AND FINANCIAL ISSUES

The system of financial and related social support for the elderly has been gradually evolving since the end of World War II. Although local governments are given much of the responsibility, some estimates suggest that as many as 70 percent of local units are not financially capable of fulfilling the terms of the national Golden Plan.[58]

Income Support

The traditional age for receiving pensions was 60—based in part on the cultural belief that years after 60 were a "second childhood," permitting older individuals to be dependent. The eligible age for benefits from the largest public-pension program (Welfare Pension Insurance Program) was thus established as 60 for men and 55 for women. A high proportion of large and small business enterprises have similarly established a mandatory retirement age between 55 and 60, which means that those who want to continue working must find alternative employment.[40]

The Welfare Pension was established in 1961 to incorporate and expand earlier pension programs. Payments were relatively low for those who had not worked at high-paying jobs, although increases have occurred over time. The pension system remains less generous in Japan than in most other advanced industrialized countries. Many older individuals continue to be quite dependent on families for their economic well-being. Yet, the older population holds housing assets and other wealth that makes them as well off generally as younger people. A tax deduction for families caring for elderly parents over 70 was initiated at the national level in 1972 and at the local level in 1973. In both instances the goal was to further encourage traditional family support for older parents.[7, 29, 41, 53]

A 1985 reform created a new two-part system intended to help alleviate inequities. The first part is a national pension, which covered about 80 percent of the workforce in 1998, providing a basic benefit for all individuals who are either self-employed or employees. It guarantees a minimum retirement income of about 12 percent of the average worker's wage regardless of job status before retirement and includes benefits for spouses who have not worked. The second part is an employee pension depending on earnings and time worked. It pays about 30 percent of the average wage for those who have worked 40 years. These two programs cover about 90 percent of the population. Four smaller mutual aid associations cover the other 10 percent. Public assistance programs finance pensions for the relatively few older people who are not covered by other programs.[57]

The national treasury contributes about one-third of the pension funds. The remainder is generated through payroll deductions—approximately 19 percent in the year 2000. A pay-as-you-go arrangement means that payroll tax deductions will rise steadily as the number of retired people increases.[57, 67, 72]

Financing Health Care

As noted earlier, health insurance is essentially universal and comes from two primary sources:[34, 73, 77]

- Employment-related and mutual aid society coverage for most workers and their dependents (65 percent of the population).
- A National Health Insurance program for the self-employed, including farmers and their dependents (35 percent of the population).

Free medical care for the elderly was originally introduced in 1973, leading to a substantial increase in use of services. Consequently, a 10 percent co-payment was added in 1983 for those who could afford the cost. A special medical insurance plan for older citizens was introduced in 1991 to serve as the primary form of coverage for the older population.[22, 73, 77]

Under the National Health Insurance plan all participants under age 70 pay premiums based on their level of income and must make co-payments of 30 percent of in-patient and out-patient fees up to a limit of $480 per month (in 1999). Older individuals pay only $8 per month for in-patient care and $5 per day for out-patient care.[77]

Health care providers have traditionally operated under a fee-for-service reimbursement system. Clinic-based or private practice physicians are paid on the basis of "points" allowed for patient visits and procedures—with little account taken of specialized training, qualifications, type of facility, or geographic location. General practitioners earn substantially higher incomes (often two to three times more) than more specialized and salaried hospital-based physicians, who are often associated with medical schools. While the point system provides little incentive for specialized training, it has helped minimize the use of surgical services and contributed to lower medical care costs in comparison to other countries where more surgery is performed. The fee schedules are fixed at a uniform rate by the public health-insurance programs and provide an incentive for physicians to spend very little time with patients. Seeing as many as 100 patients each day is a direct consequence of the point-fee payment system.[31]

In 1997 health care consumed about 7.8 percent of Gross Domestic Product, representing a considerable increase from 5.3 percent in 1979. Rapid economic growth led to a major expansion in health services during the 1960s and 1970s but declining economic growth forced the government to curtail the increases in the 1980s. Changes in the health-insurance laws in 1986 shifted 10 to 30 percent (depending on the service) of the financial burden to beneficiaries.[29]

The overall cost of medications accounted for roughly 33 percent of health care expenditures for older people. Recent reforms have attempted to curtail the high drug costs by controlling the margin of profit for wholesalers and physician retailers.[29, 48, 50, 72]

Financing Long-Term Care

Estimates indicate that the number of older people needing some form of personal care and skilled nursing care will grow to 5 million by 2025, up from 2 million in 1993. By 2025 only about 2.4 workers will be available to support each retired older person. This could mean that payroll taxes may double to one-third of worker income. An increase in the pension and retirement age to 65 will make some difference, but will not solve the problem since a high proportion of workers already work well past age 65.[58, 77]

A Future Vision Committee was created under the Social Security Council in the mid-1990s with a mandate to design financing for a new long-term care insurance system. A public-opinion survey in 1995 indicated that 82 percent of the population favored some form of additional insurance. Consequently, the Care Insurance Law passed in 1997, providing for funding, benefits, and management, was scheduled for implementation in 2000.[20, 34, 74]

The law calls for access to institutional care for all who need it and emphasizes respite care, day care, home health assistance, and loans of durable medical devices. The funds would be generated through payroll deductions for every worker over age 40, with the balance to be raised through general taxation. The central government would cover half the cost, prefectures would finance one-fourth, and municipalities would be responsible for the remaining one fourth. Municipalities would operate and manage the home care services and institutional care system. Long-term care would become an entitlement. Responsibility of the family for care would be diminished, and care managers, in consultation with physicians, would assume much of the responsibility for assisting disabled older adults.[20, 52]

Home care services generally require a co-payment by the recipient or family based on a sliding income scale. The balance is paid by the prefecture or municipality. Because hospital expenses tend to be more fully covered by health-insurance funds than do other long-term care institutions, many families attempt to keep disabled relatives hospitalized. The high costs have made this preference increasingly difficult to support.[20, 29, 34]

Costs for geriatric hospitals, subsidized nursing homes, and Health Care Facilities for the Elderly are paid from public health-insurance plans and from government subsidies, based on a flat rate per resident. Nonmedical services are paid or co-paid by the patient from retirement income, savings, or from welfare funds in the case of low-income elderly. The least costly form of institutional care is provided in subsidized nursing homes for low-income elderly. Expenses are roughly one-third more in the Health Care Facilities for the Elderly, and are nearly twice as high in geriatric hospitals.[29, 34, 56]

A private long-term care insurance market has developed in conjunction with life-insurance plans and through special policies available from indemnity companies. The private market is estimated to be second only to the United States in policies sold, but still covers only a very small part of the older population.[56]

◆◆◆ LIFESTYLES: WORK, RETIREMENT, AND LEISURE

Enhanced lifestyle in older age has received major emphasis at the national and local levels and is among the primary bases for the emphasis on community support centers in the Golden Plan. Continued work after age 65 is encouraged in part because of the traditional work orientation of the Japanese, but also to help fill the needed jobs as the number of young people declines.

Continuing Work

Approximately 37 percent of men over age 65 were continuing to work full-time in late 1990s (compared to less than 17 percent in the United States)—the highest employment rate at this age of any country in the world. Employment of older women is increasing but is less than for men. The government has begun offering subsidies to firms that employ people over age 60, in conformance with the 1986 Law for Stabilized Employment of the Elderly. Several types of job location services, such as Silver Manpower Centers, help older individuals find full-time or part-time employment.[6, 40, 53, 59]

Nonetheless, companies continue to implement mandatory retirement ages for certain jobs. The lifetime employment pattern identified with Japan does not mean that an individual necessarily works at the same job with the same firm for his or her full working life. Workers may be re-employed in another job, or employment may shift to another position in a branch of the same company—usually at much lower pay. Older workers often move to another firm altogether, on a full- or part-time basis.[5, 6, 33, 44, 57, 67]

Retirement Planning

Preparing for retirement has not been particularly emphasized in the past because of the expectation that older people would be supported by families or would continue to work. The focus on long hours of work has been credited with giving workers little time to prepare for older age.[40]

The government and private enterprise are helping to inform older workers of the retirement issues and options available to them. Publicly sponsored continuing education courses focus on lifestyle patterns, mental and physical health maintenance, available public programs, hobbies and crafts, community activism, and strategies for enjoying the later years.[12]

A formal Pre-retirement Education and Life Planning (PREP) program was instituted in many corporations for employees age 50 and older, to help them plan for a productive and satisfying later lifestyle. The prototype program developed by Mitsubishi Corporation in 1977 is now widely adopted or adapted by other companies. As of 1992, 61 percent of the largest corporations operated some form of short-term PREP program of one to three days. Surveys indicated that employees were most interested in courses on retirement finances, health management, and creating satisfaction in later life. They had little interest in volunteer activities or community service.[43]

A national Respect for the Aged Day (September 15) is used as a time when education about aging and retirement is provided in the public schools. Older individuals are invited to present folktales, legends, history, and local culture to students. Formal expression of appreciation for grandparents is encouraged. The school children and older visitors eat together and discuss what it is like to be older and retired.[83]

Retirement preparation thus takes a number of forms. Given the very long life span of the Japanese, preparation for later life has become a high priority for the government, employers, and older citizens.

Leisure and Social Participation

The proportion of older people who participate in social clubs and other community activities has in the past been much smaller than in the United States and Western Europe. The Ministry of Education supports so-called Old Peoples Colleges catering to the interests of retirees, as noted earlier. Many older men and women travel widely in Japan and abroad. However, national organizations of older individuals—such as AARP in the United States—do not exist.[13, 67]

Senior Clubs.   The Ministry of Health and Welfare, under provisions of the Golden Plan, actively promotes the formation of senior centers and clubs. Senior-citizen clubs have been organized throughout the country, with more than one-third of the older population participating in local units. The club goals encourage an active and healthy lifestyle through education and organized health promotion. The focus is also on engaging in recreation and cultural activities. Volunteer work in the community is encouraged, particularly cleaning and beautifying public spaces. The clubs are often associated with the government-subsidized community centers, discussed earlier.[39, 41]

Mobility.   Migration to new communities in other parts of the country is unusual. Rather, older individuals, whether affluent or lower income, tend to remain where they are even when younger members of their family depart.[60]

Satisfaction with Life.   Older people tend to be more satisfied with their lives than are younger people according to a recent survey. They are also more satisfied with society in general than young people and tend to remain actively involved in family, continued learning, hobbies, watching TV, and continued work. Many engage in various arts—poetry, flower arranging, painting, growing miniature plants, calligraphy, and other activities such as the tea ceremony.[40, 69]

◆◆◆ NOTEWORTHY FEATURES AND MAJOR CHALLENGES

Quality of life for the older population of Japan is enhanced by a long and positive history of good treatment for older people, most recently emphasized by the Golden Plan. Yet, several major problems have not been fully resolved despite new initiatives.

Noteworthy Features

The Japanese have the greatest life expectancy of any nation, arising in part from a strong family and community support system, good nutrition, a focus on health maintenance activities such as exercise, and generally good health insurance and health care. Older people are respected more than in most countries and hold a revered role in their communities. The basic value system arising from a long and rich cultural history continues to encourage public policies supportive of older people. The Golden Plan is a recent example of this cultural commitment.

Most of the formal and informal support system is decentralized to the community and family level. Strong efforts are made in local communities to support and coordinate social involvement, physical activity, mental stimulation, good health care, and long-term care. A widespread system of home care services, channeled in part through home support centers, helps older people to remain in their homes until very advanced ages or until death. Senior clubs provide a supportive outlet outside the home. Overall, older people are very well treated.

Major Challenges

The continuing dominance of physicians in the health care system and in long-term care makes it difficult for consumers to have appropriate influence. Relatively low fees for office visits cause physicians to compensate by increasing the volume of patients—a practice that is particularly detrimental to older patients with chronic problems. The referral system is somewhat ineffective because local physicians are fearful of losing their patients to the high-status hospitals with specialist physicians. Since many older citizens feel dissatisfied with the services at community clinics, they choose prestigious hospitals for all their health care needs, even though these services are more expensive and often require long waiting times.[29]

The Japan Society for Quality Assurance in Health Care has helped develop criteria to measure quality of care and clarify problems in hospitals and other medical institutions—but implementation is in the early stages. Members of the Society provide advice and supervision on improvement techniques but must contend with the inflexibility of older managers.

Physicians may overprescribe because they benefit financially from the drugs they sell. Older patients are not always aware of the potential problem since many do not understand the medications. Most of their drug cost is covered by health insurance—so there has been little incentive for physicians to be cautious or for consumers to diminish consumption. Pharmaceutical costs consumed a very high proportion of health care costs in the late 1990s.[29]

Recent changes in rules may help obviate this situation. The Ministry of Health and Welfare has begun to enforce separation of prescribing and dispensing in the large national hospitals. However, local customs continue to allow many physicians in clinics and private offices to continue the dual practice.[70]

Pension costs will increase dramatically in the years ahead as the older population expands. The public costs and out-of-pocket costs for health care have increased significantly and are likely to continue rising. Estimates suggest that at current rates of increase—given the projected limited growth in the younger population—the required proportion of Gross Domestic Product for pensions and health care could grow 24 percent by 2020.[7, 27, 53, 73]

The new public long-term care insurance system for the elderly, instituted in 2000, is clearly a matter of some urgency but will also be very expensive and will require major increases in professional personnel. The shortage of long-term care services has been a major barrier to implementation of private insurance. The Golden Plan has provided a very rational basis for improving the options. However, implementation is limited by the constraints in financial and human resources.[20, 55, 80]

As noted earlier, coordination among clinic, hospital, and long-term care providers has been a major problem. Clinic-based physicians tend to focus on serving high volumes of patients—which appears to be of greater concern than patient well-being. Nurses and other health care workers are permitted to participate in health assessment or treatment on a very limited basis, simply taking orders from the physician in managing the flow of patients. Physicians can assign patients to institutional settings such as nursing homes or geriatric hospitals without a second opinion. Patients and families have relatively little influence on the process of care. The care of older patients is thus very often idiosyncratic and fragmented.[31]

Despite government and private efforts to build additional senior housing, a serious shortage of adequate space persists. Independent living and institutional housing options are not available to many who would prefer such accommodations. Both public and private enterprise have been active in building new complexes but have not been able to satisfy the demand. Given the rapid growth in the older population, housing is likely to continue as a major challenge for the indefinite future.

◆◆◆ SUMMARY AND CONCLUSIONS

Japan has the oldest population of any country and among the lowest birth rates—a profound challenge to both the younger population and the expanding number of older people living to very advanced ages. Although the social structure is changing toward fewer multigeneration households, the family retains greater responsibility for housing, income support, and long-term care than in other economically advanced countries. The strong family is highly valued as a primary means of social integration for older people.

The government initiated the Golden Plan as a tool for aggressively moving toward greater support for older individuals and families through strengthened community and national programs. An expanded network of community support centers offers home care, education, health promotion, opportunities for social well-being, and strengthened social and economic support close to the residential locations.

Physicians largely control the health care of the elderly through ownership and management of most clinics and hospitals. They also play a major policy role at the national level. The older population and their families have relatively little influence on the conduct of health care or long-term care. Universal health insurance covers most physician and hospital costs, minimizes co-payments, and covers most of the cost for pharmaceuticals. Quality of care has been a serious issue. However, quality improvement methods have been endorsed, especially by younger physicians, during the decade of the 1990s. The challenge is to improve quality without greatly increasing costs.

Financing of pensions, health care, long-term care, and housing will be a continuing challenge. Older citizens work to more advanced ages than in most other countries in part because of good health and in part because of inadequate pensions. The government encourages the practice as one means of helping to finance programs for the very old and disabled.

Despite the challenges, conditions for the older population have improved substantially in recent decades. Dependence on the family has decreased, allowing younger family members greater freedom from responsibility for daily care and support. Yet, the strength of the family does not appear to be greatly diminished.

◆◆◆ REFERENCES

1. Akimoto, Hazuki (1996). Long Term Care Problems in Japan (Term paper prepared for a graduate course in Health Policy and Administration), Washington State University at Spokane, WA.
2. Anders, Robert L., Masashi Kawano, Chizuru Mori, Hiroko Kohusho, Satoru Iguichi, and Satoru Yoshida (1997). Characteristics of Long-Term Psychiatric Patients Hospitalized in Tokyo, Japan, *Archives of Psychiatric Nursing*, (11) 3, 139–46.
3. Angel, Ronald J., and Jacqueline L. Angel (1997). *Who Will Care for Us? Aging and Long-Term Care in Multicultural America*, New York: New York University Press.
4. Associated Press (2000). Japan: Population Growth Slows, *The Arizona Daily Star*, March 24, A15.
5. Bass, Scott A., Robert Morris, and Masato Oka (eds) (1996). *Public Policy and the Old Age Revolution in Japan*, New York: Haworth.
6. Beck, Barbara (1996). A Gradual Goodbye, *The Economist*, 338 (7950), S5.
7. Bosworth, Barry, and Gary Burtless (1998). Population Aging and Economic Performance, in Barry Bosworth and Gary Burtless (eds), *Aging Societies: The Global Dimension*, Washington, DC: The Brookings Institution, 1–28.
8. Butler, Robert N., and Kenzo Kiikuni (eds) (1993). *Who is Responsible for My Old Age?* New York: Springer Publishing Company.

9. Chan, Ing-Ching, Makoto Suzuki, and Shigeru Yamamoto (1997). Dietary, Anthropometric, Hematological and Biochemical Assessment of the Nutritional Status of Centenarians and Elderly People in Okinawa, Japan, *Journal of American College of Nutrition* (16) 3, 229–35.

10. Chan, Y. (1992). Living Out Life's Final Stages by Terminal Patients, *Japan Times Weekly International Edition*, Oct. 26, 14.

11. Fair, Derek (1995). Comment on Attitudes of Japanese Physicians Towards Life Sustaining Treatment, *Lancet*, 346 (October 7), 971.

12. Falk, Ursula, and Gerhard Falk (1997). *Ageism, The Aged, and Aging in America*, Springfield: Charles C Thomas Publishers.

13. Freed, Anne O. (1992). *The Changing Worlds of Older Women in Japan*, Manchester, CT: Knowledge, Ideas, Trends, Inc.

14. Furuse, Tohru (1996). Changing the Balance of Care: Japan, in Organization for Economic Cooperation and Development, *Caring for Frail Elderly People: Policies in Evolution*, Paris: OECD, 239–46.

15. Harris, Phyllis Braudy, and Susan Orpett Long (1999). Husbands and Sons in the United States and Japan: Cultural Expectations and Caregiving Experiences, *Journal of Aging Studies*, 13 (3), 241–67.

16. Hashimoto, Akiko (1998). *The Gift of Generations: Japanese and American Perspectives on Aging and the Social Contract*, New York: Cambridge University Press.

17. Hashizume, Yumi, and Katsuko Kanagawa (1996). Correlates of Participation in Adult Day Care and Quality of Life in Ambulatory Frail Elderly in Japan, *Public Health Nursing* (13) 6, 404–15.

18. Horiguchi, Jun, Tsuruhei Sukegawa, and Yasushi Inami (1996). Survey of Living Conditions and Psychosomatic States of the Elderly in Japan Who Receive Home Help, *Psychiatry and Clinical Neurosciences*, 50 (5), 247–50.

19. Ida, Osamu, Kozo Tatara, Hitoshi Fujiwara, Yoshihiro Takashima, and Kenji Kuroda (1996). Percentage of Elderly and the Use of Welfare Services at City Welfare Offices in Japan, *Social Science and Medicine*, 43 (11), 1527–32.

20. Ikegami, Naoki (1997). Public Long-Term Care Insurance in Japan, *Journal of the American Medical Association*, 278 (16), 1310–14.

21. Imai, Kaori (1998). Bed-Ridden Elderly in Japan: Social Progress and Care for the Elderly, *International Journal of Aging and Human Development*, 46 (2), 157–70.

22. Imamura, Kyoko (1993). Japan's Experience in Long-Term Home Health Care of the Elderly, *Pride Institute Journal of Long Term Home Health Care*, 12 (1), 3–17.

23. Ineichen, Bernard (1996). Senile Dementia in Japan: Prevalence and Response, *Social Science and Medicine*, 42 (2), 169–72.

24. Jacobzone, S., E. Cambois, E. Chaplain, and J. M. Robine (1999). The Health of Older Persons in OECD Countries: Is It Improving Fast Enough to Compensate for Population Aging? *Occasional Papers No. 57*, Paris: Organization for Economic Cooperation and Development.

25. Kashiwagi, Tetsuo (1998). Palliative Care in Japan, in Derek Doyle, Geoffrey W. C. Hanks, and Neil MacDonald (eds.) *Oxford Textbook of Palliative Medicine* (2nd ed.), Oxford: Oxford University Press, 797–98.

26. Kashiwagi, Tetsuo (1995). Psychosocial and Spiritual Issues in Terminal Care, *Psychiatry And Clinical Neurosciences*, 49 (Supplement 1), S123–27.

27. Kawabuchi, Koichi (1996). Diversified Needs and Aging Population, *The Journal of the Japan Hospital Association*, 15 (July), 35–41.

28. Kishi, Yasuhiro, Hisashi Kurosawa, Yasutaka Iwasaki, Ritsuko Hirayama, and Shunkichi Endo (1997). Access to the Emergency Psychiatry System in Japan, *General Hospital Psychiatry*, 19 (2), 130–37.

29. Kobayashi, Yasuki (1994). Health Care Expenditures for the Elderly and Reforms in the Health Care System in Japan, *Health Policy*, 29 (3), 197–208.

30. Koff, Theodore (1999). Director, Gerontology Center Long Term Care Program, University of Arizona. Personal Communication.

31. Kolanowski, Ronald (1997). Japan's Gold Plan Emphasizes Home Care and the Consumer, *Caring Magazine*, 16 (4). 38–40.

32. Komahashi, Toru (and 16 colleagues) (1994). Epidemiological Survey of Dementia and Depression Among the Aged Living in the Community in Japan, *The Japanese Journal of Psychiatry*, 48 (3), 517–26.

33. Komine, Takao (1990). The Aging of the Labor Force in Japan, in Robert N. Butler, Mia R. Oberlink,

and Mal Schechter, *The Promise of Productive Aging: From Biology to Social Policy,* New York: Springer, 116–17.

34. Kosaka, Masato (1996). Developing a Health Service System for the Elderly in Japan, *Journal of Case Management,* 5 (4), 182–85.

35. Kosaka, Y., M. Yamaya, K. Nakajoh, T. Matsui, M. Yanai, and H. Sasaki (2000). Prognosis of Elderly Patients with Dysphagia in Japan, *Gerontology,* 46 (1), 111–12.

36. Kosberg, Jordan I. (1992). An International Perspective on Family Care of the Elderly, in Jordan I. Kosberg (ed), *Family Care of the Elderly: Social and Cultural Changes,* Newbury Park, CA: Sage Publications, 1–14.

37. Kose, Satoshi (1997). Housing Elderly People in Japan, *Ageing International,* 23 (3/4), 147–65.

38. Levy, Becca R. (1999). The Inner Self of the Japanese Elderly: A Defense Against Negative Stereotypes of Aging, *International Journal of Aging and Human Development,* 48 (2), 131–44.

39. Maeda, Daisaku (1990). Keeping Older People Productive, in Robert N. Butler, Mia R. Oberlink, and Mal Schechter (eds), *The Promise of Productive Aging: From Biology to Social Policy,* New York: Springer, 134–38.

40. Maeda, Daisaku (1993). Japan, in Erdman B. Palmore (ed), *Development and Research in Aging,* Westport, CT: Greenwood Press, 201–19.

41. Maeda, Daisaku (1996). Social Security, Health Care, and Social Services for the Elderly in Japan, in Fumio Takagi (ed), *Aging in Japan,* Tokyo: Japan Aging Research Center, 85–112.

42. Maeda, Daisaku, and Youmei Nakatani (1992). Family Care of the Elderly in Japan, in Jordan I. Kosberg (ed), *Family Care of the Elderly: Social and Cultural Changes,* Newbury Park, CA: Sage, 196–209.

43. Makino, Nobuo (1994). Preretirement Education and Life Planning Programs in Japan, *Educational Gerontology,* 20 (5), 503–10.

44. Manton, Kenneth G., Eric Stallard, and H. Dennis Tolley (1991). Limits to Human Life Expectancy: Evidence, Prospects, and Implications, *Population and Development Review,* 17 (4), 603–37.

45. Matsumoto, David (1996). *Unmasking Japan: Myths and Realities About the Emotions of the Japanese,* Stanford, CA: Stanford University Press.

46. Mosk, Carl (1996). *Making Health Work,* Berkeley: University of California Press.

47. Nagatomo, Itsugi, Kenji Kita, Morikuni Takigawa, Mitsuo Nomaguchi, and Kazuko Sameshima (1997). A Study of the Quality of Life in Elderly People Using Psychological Testing, *International Journal Of Geriatric Psychiatry,* 12 (6), 599–608.

48. Nakanishi, Noriyuki, Kozo Tatara, and Hitoshi Fujiwara (1996). Do Preventive Health Services Reduce Eventual Demand for Medical Care? *Social Science and Medicine,* 43 (6), 999–1005.

49. Nakanishi, Noriyuki, Kozo Tatara, Tosho Tatatorige, Shigeki Murakami, and Fumiaki Shinsho (1997). Effects of Preventive Health Services on Survival of the Elderly Living in a Community in Osaka, Japan, *Journal of Epidemiology and Community Health,* 51 (2), 199–204.

50. National Center for Health Statistics (1998). *Health United States 1998,* Washington, DC: United States Public Health Service.

51. Nishio, Harry Kaneharu (1994). Japan's Welfare Vision: Dealing with a Rapidly Increasing Elderly Population, in Laura Katz Olson (ed.), *The Graying of the World: Who Will Care for the Frail Elderly,* New York: Haworth Press, 233–60.

52. Nishiuchi, Masahiko (1999). Problems of the Elderly in Japan and Other Countries, *Pacific Friend,* 26 (11), 34–39.

53. Noguchi, Yukio, and David A. Wise (1994). Introduction, in Yukio Noguchi and David A. Wise (eds), *Aging in the United States and Japan: Economic Trends,* Chicago: University of Chicago Press, 1–5.

54. Noriyuki, Nakanishi, Kozo Tatara, and Hitoshi Fujiwara (1996). Do Preventive Health Services Reduce Eventual Demand for Medical Care? *Social Science and Medicine,* 43 (6), 999–1005.

55. Organization for Economic Cooperation and Development (OECD) (1994). *Caring for Frail Elderly People,* Paris: OECD.

56. Organization for Economic Cooperation and Development (OECD) (1996). *Caring for Frail Elderly People: Policies in Evolution,* Paris: OECD.

57. Organization for Economic Cooperation and Development (OECD) (1995). *The Labour Market and Older Workers,* Paris: OECD.

58. Oshima, Sumiko (1996). Japan: Feeling the Strains of an Aging Population, *Science*, 273 (5271), 44–45.

59. Quinn, Joseph F., and Richard V. Burkahuser (1994). Retirement and Labor Force Productivity, in Linda G. Martin and Samuel H. Preston (eds), *Demography of Aging*, Washington, DC: National Academy Press, 50–101.

60. Rees, Philip (1992). The Elderly Mobility Transition: Three Case Studies, in Andrei Rogers (ed), *Elderly Migration and Population Redistribution*, London: Belhaven Press, 183.

61. Rein, Martin, and Harold Salzman (1995). Social Integration, Participation, and Exchange in Five Industrial Countries, in Scott A. Bass (ed), *Older and Active: How Americans Over 55 Are Contributing to Society*, New Haven: Yale University Press, 237–62.

62. Sakashita, Y., Y. Ogushi, Y. Okada, M. Horie, Y. Ohta, Y. Hayashi, S. Suzuki, Y. Haruki, and T. Takahashi (1996). Health and Welfare Data on Optical Memory Cards in Isehara City, *Medical Informatics*, 21 (1), 69–79.

63. Sakonji, Mitsuaki, Chise Shimizu, Yae Shingo, and Eitaka Tauboi (1997). Hospice Care in Japan, in Dame Cicely Saunders and Robert Kastenbaum (eds), *Hospice Care on the International Scene*, New York: Springer, 219–31.

64. Sauvaget, Catherine, Ichiro Tsuji, Akira Fukao, and Shingeru Hisamichi (1997a). Factors Related to the Desire to Enter a Nursing Home among Elderly Japanese, *Journal Of Epidemiology*, 7 (2), 77–83.

65. Sauvaget, Catherine, Ichiro Tsuji, Y. Minami, Akira Fukao, Shingeru Hisamichi, H. Asano, and M. Sato (1997b). Dementia-Free Life Expectancy Among Elderly Japanese, *Gerontology*, 43 (3), 168–75.

66. Shibata, Hiroshi, and Atsuaki Gunji (1994). The Social Support System of the Japanese Elderly, *Journal of Cross-Cultural Gerontology*, 9 (2), 323–33.

67. Shimizu, Yutaka, and Junko Wake (1994). Japan, in Jordan I. Kosberg (ed), *International Handbook on Services for the Elderly*, Westport, CT: Greenwood Press, 227–43.

68. Shinagawa, Shinryo N. (1993). The "Seven Tunnels" of Japanese Medical Ethics, *HEC Forum (Kluner Academic Publishers)*, 39–43.

69. Silver, Catherine B. (1998). Cross-Cultural Perspective on Attitudes Toward Family Responsibility and Well-Being in Later Years, in Jacob Lomranz (ed), *Handbook of Aging and Mental Health: An Integrative Approach*, New York: Plenum Press, 383–415.

70. Smith, Blake W. H., Ray Demers, and Linda Garcia-Shelton (1997). Family Medicine In Japan, *Archives of Family Medicine*, 6 (1), 59–62.

71. Strom, Robert, Shirley Strom, Pat Collinsworth, Saburo Sato, Katsuko Makino, Yasuyuki Sasaki, Hiroko Sasaki, and Norihiro Nishio (1996). Intergenerational Relationships in Japanese Families, *International Journal of Sociology of the Family*, 26 (2), 1–15.

72. Takagi, Fumio (ed.) (1996). *Aging in Japan*, Tokyo: Japan Aging Research Center.

73. Takahashi, Toshiro (1997). The Paradox of Japan: What About CQI in Health Care? *The Joint Commission on Quality Improvement Journal*, 23 (1), 60–64.

74. Takei, Y., O. Shimada, and K. Orimo (1998). Awareness of and Attitude of Elderly Subjects Regarding Health Care and Welfare in Rapidly Ageing Population of Japan, *Family Practice* (Oxford University Press), 15 (6), 569–70.

75. Tamiya, Nanako, Shunichi Araki, Yasuki Kobayashi, Kohe Yamashita, Katsuyuki Murata, and Elji Yano (1996). Gender Difference in the Utilization and Users' Characteristics of Community Rehabilitation Programs for Cerebrovascular Disease Patients in Japan, *International Journal for Quality in Health Care*, 8 (4), 359–66.

76. Tanaka, K. (1996). The Kobe Earthquake: The System Responds. A Disaster Report from Japan, *European Journal of Emergency Medicine*, 3 (4), 263–69.

77. Tsuji, Ichiro, Aya Kuwahara, Yoshikazu Nishino, Takayoshi Ohkubo, Atshshi Sasaki, and Shigeru Hisamichi (1999). Medical Cost for Disability: A Longitudinal Observation of National Health Insurance Beneficiaries in Japan, *Journal of the American Geriatrics Society*, 47 (4) 470–76.

78. Ueda, Kazuo, Hideo Kawano, Yutaka Hasuo, and Masatoshi Fujishima (1992). Prevalence and Etiology of Dementia in a Japanese Community, *Stroke*, 23 (6), 798–803.

79. United States Census Bureau (2000). *International Data Bank*, Online at www.census.gov.

80. Weiner, Joshua M. (1994). Private Sector Initiatives in Financing Long-Term Care, in Organization for Economic Cooperation and Development (OECD), *Caring for Frail Elderly People*, Paris: OECD.
81. Wocher, John C. (1996). Hospital Management in Japan, *Japan Hospitals*, 15, 5–6.
82. Yamada, Michiko, Hideo Sasaki, Yasuyo Mimori, Fumiyoshi Kasagi, Shinji Sudoh, Junko Kieda, Yutaka Hosoda, Shigenobu Nakamura, and Kazunori Kodama (1999). Prevalence and Risks of Dementia in the Japanese Population: RERF's Adult Health Study of Hiroshima Subjects, *Journal of the American Geriatrics Society*, 47 (2), 189–95.
83. Yamazaki, Takaya (1994). Intergenerational Interaction Outside the Family, *Educational Gerontology*, 20 (5), 453–62.

Test Review for Final Exam

Questions from chp 18

*Demographics in the US.

    Changes in 2030

    Workers and retiree characteristics

    Poverty? Progress or regress?

    Sources of our retirement income and our social security benefits.

Pensions

    Gender and poverty relationships

Where do funds from health care?

What proportion of expenditures are for older people?

    Medicare.

What is our source for health insurance?

What are families like in Japan today?

What are the communities like in Japan?

Medicine for older people. Who owns medicine, hospitals, etc

Usage of clinics in America. How do they provide health.

When do we get our medicine in US? How are pharm dispensed of in Japan.   Life expectancy - Japan, US & UK.

    Geriatrics, housing in Japan. UK? US.

What are characteristics of the pop in the U.K. (65 and up)

Nat'l Health Services   What does the U.K. NHS policy provide?

What is palliative care?   How is geriatrics taught to physicians.

(Before one can be involved in geriatrics, a thorough assessment is made.)

Geriatric psychiatry in UK. Mental health in the U.K.

Home care supervisors? What are they?

What is the population in nursing homes in the UK?

Housing.   Income?   Cont'd on pg 258

Chapter 12

THE UNITED KINGDOM
Pioneering Geriatric and Hospice Care

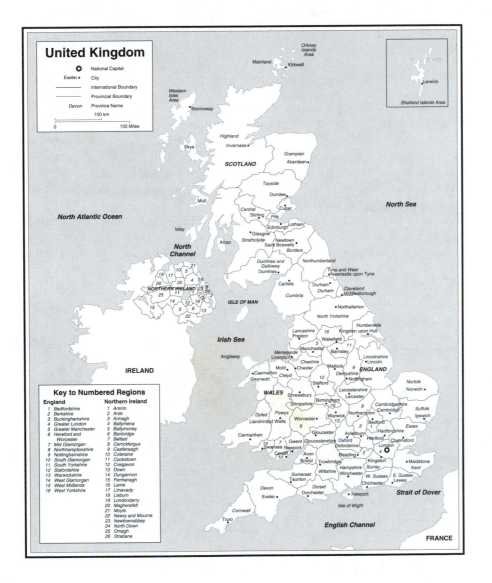

United Kingdom

- ✪ National Capital
- Exeter • City
- —— International Boundary
- —— Provincial Boundary
- *Devon* Province Name

100 km

0   100 Miles

Key to Numbered Regions

England	Northern Ireland
1 Bedfordshire	1 Antrim
2 Berkshire	2 Ards
3 Buckinghamshire	3 Armagh
4 Greater London	4 Ballymena
5 Greater Manchester	5 Ballymoney
6 Hereford and	6 Banbridge
Worcester	7 Belfast
7 Mid Glamorgan	8 Carrickfergus
8 Northhamptonshire	9 Castlereagh
9 Nottinghamshire	10 Coleraine
10 South Glamorgan	11 Cookstown
11 South Yorkshire	12 Craigavon
12 Stafordshire	13 Down
13 Warwickshire	14 Dungannon
14 West Glamorgan	15 Fermanagh
15 West Midlands	16 Larne
16 West Yorkshire	17 Limavady
	18 Lisburn
	19 Londonderry
	20 Magherafelt
	21 Moyle
	22 Newry and Mourne
	23 Newtownabbey
	24 North Down
	25 Omagh
	26 Strabane

◆◆◆ INTRODUCTION

The United Kingdom is an island nation with a population in year 2000 of more than 59 million—in England, Scotland and Wales. The country is densely populated, especially in the southeast where many of the larger cities are located. Roughly 92 percent of the population live in the cities. Per capita GDP is less than in many mainland European countries ($21,170 in 1998) but has been growing steadily during the recent decade of prosperity. Expenditures for pensions and health care are less generous than in most other economically advanced countries—but equity is emphasized to assure that everyone has good access to needed care. Geriatrics and the modern hospice were essentially invented here and are more developed than in any other nation.[47]

Demographic Characteristics

About 15.6 percent of the population was age 65 years or older in 2000, similar to most European countries and Japan but somewhat higher than in the United States, Canada, or the Netherlands. Life expectancy at birth was 77.4. The total number of older people is expected to increase roughly 30 percent by 2030, although the younger segment (ages 65 to 74) is not expected to increase substantially until after 2010. The 75–84 age range will rise by approximately 7 percent; those in the age 85 and over category will rise most dramatically—by 32 percent.[2, 6, 71, 73]

There are twice as many women as men over age 65, as the population pyramid in Figure 12–1 suggests—a circumstance arising in major part because of a high likelihood of early death among lower social-class men. Single older women are likely

FIGURE 12-1   Population Pyramids for the United Kingdom
Source: U.S. Census Bureau, *International Data Base,* 2000

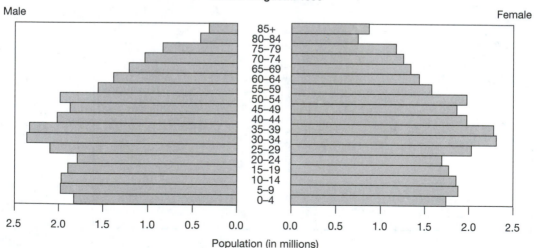

United Kingdom: 1999

to be from the lower social classes and have relatively low incomes. The figure also indicates the relatively comparable numbers of women and men in the lower- and middle-age categories—gradually changing to increasing numbers of women in the categories over age 65.[73]

Older people are nevertheless much better off than earlier generations. The younger age cohort (65 to 74) is more educated than older cohorts, has held better jobs, and has generally earned enough pension rights to retire in reasonable comfort. Mortality has declined here as elsewhere as has the birthrate—changes that are a consequence of healthier lifestyles, improved housing, better nutrition, and a relatively effective health care system. However, for a high proportion of those at advanced ages, infirmity, chronic disease, and poverty remain widely prevalent, especially among women.[82]

The demographic shift has important implications for the provision of health care and other services to the elderly. Public policy has changed quite dramatically, with an emphasis on averting unreasonably high public costs to support pensions, health care, and long-term care. Retirement age has increased and level of public resource allocation for pensions has declined.[41]

◆◆◆ HISTORICAL PERSPECTIVE

Prior to World War II, the United Kingdom had no national system of income support for the elderly, no public insurance for health care, and no provisions for public support of long-term care. Each family was responsible for securing services and insurance as best they could. Health care for most of the population was provided in modest and poorly supported institutions in local communities. Formal long-term care was provided through large and poorly maintained public institutions.[41]

The National Health Service

Toward the end of the Second World War resources were in very short supply and few people could afford health services. Political support was generated for an improved health care system, leading to legislation in 1946 establishing the National Health Service (NHS). The goal was to create comprehensive care for everyone regardless of income. The NHS quickly became the primary vehicle for universal provision of health care and long-term care, and it has served as an international model of universal care. Older people were major beneficiaries of the new system.[47, 53]

The organizational structure was controlled by the national government, from which grants were provided to communities for a significant proportion of costs. Physicians were paid fees based on the number of patients on their "list" rather than for services delivered. Hospitals became part of the national system and were the centers for development of an extensive system of geriatric care.[12]

All services to patients were initially free of charge, whether they were provided in the community by a general practitioner or in a hospital. By 1951 demand so exceeded expectations that legislation was enacted to charge patients for less critical services such as prescriptions and eye care, although emergency service remained free for the victims of accidents and urgent acute care. Long waiting lists became the norm for individuals with less urgent acute or chronic conditions—with serious implications for older people. Serious side effects and complaints became commonplace because of delays in care.[53]

Initiation of Reforms

The 1977 National Health Service Act was an attempt to control costs by limiting expenditures of local health authorities to the amounts authorized by the national government—with all NHS services to be provided free of charge for the elderly, disabled, children, and lower-income people. Charges were instituted for prescription medicines, dental treatment, and eye care for those able to pay, but about 80 percent of all prescriptions remained exempt from charges.[53]

Lengthy delays in provision of certain procedures for the elderly were considered by many critics to be highly objectionable. Other criticisms of NHS inadequacies again became widespread. The Thatcher government therefore launched a major reorganization of the NHS, based in part on recommendations in the Griffith report of 1983 suggesting the NHS become more businesslike. Privatization initiatives were implemented leading to the creation of private medical clinics, trust hospitals, and private for-profit nursing homes.[47]

Local government and National Health Service responsibility was diminished. Local authorities became service providers largely for lower-income elderly who had no other choices. The reforms culminated with the passage of the "Community Care Act" in 1990 and publication of a national health strategy report, "The Health of the Nation," in 1992, suggesting greater attention to the needs of the elderly. The reorganized health care system is clearly an effort to improve quality and service while containing public costs. New funds have been provided for research on older people. A "Better Government for Older People" project was launched to improve health care, social services, employment, housing, transport, and health education.[77, 81]

Long-Term Care

The evolving health care system did not draw a sharp distinction between medical treatment and long-term care. The National Health Service financed acute care in hospitals and chronic care in nursing homes with equal priority. However, a distinction was made between health care and social support. Nursing homes became part of the National Health Service whereas residential care facilities for the elderly were made part of the local social-service system. Thus, home care services were the responsibility of local governments, supplemented by partial support from federal grants.[1]

Major criticisms were leveled at the social-service systems during the 1970s and 1980s. Advocacy groups were formed to press for changes. For example, feminist groups complained that a high proportion of the service responsibility was left to female family members and poorly paid female workers, resulting in exploitation of women. Similarly, ethnic minority groups felt they were not adequately provided with services and were exploited in the service delivery system.[78]

◆◆◆ SOCIAL SUPPORT SYSTEMS

The changes noted above have led to greater focus on meeting individual needs of older people through family and community support, rather than reliance on local or national government. Education about management of health and self-care in the home are receiving greater emphasis.[77]

The Family Role

The family continues as the primary means of social and personal care, as well as the primary advocate for securing outside services. Studies have indicated that formal home care is less available to an older person who lives alone than when residence is with a spouse or other family member. Informal helpers in order of importance include: spouses, adult children (especially daughters), sisters, brothers, friends, neighbors, grandchildren, nieces and nephews and cousins.[9, 84, 85]

However, the real ability of the family to provide personal support has been weakening, as in other countries, for several reasons: an increasing proportion of women are at work and therefore less able to provide informal care. Geographical mobility for employment and residence means that younger families are less likely to be in close proximity to elderly parents. As a consequence, the demand for formal care-givers is increasing for those who have access to such services.

Community Responsibility

Recent policies have reenforced the responsibility of local jurisdictions for administering health and long-term care services, although the national government provides most of the financial support. Public housing programs for older people are similarly initiated at the community level with national funding.[82]

A provision in the Community Care Act of 1990 required the local health care systems to plan specifically for the social needs of older individuals. For example, older patients are not to be discharged from hospitals without a plan for their care when they return home or to group residential setting—usually managed by family members. The new emphasis is focused on assessing the needs of the individual and providing an appropriate package of services in the home whenever possible. The social consequences of chronic illness are thus to be more fully taken into account.[60, 82]

◆◆◆ PHYSICAL HEALTH CARE

The National Health Service policy toward patients is enumerated in a "Patients Charter"—indicating that every citizen has the right to receive health care based on physician-defined need, regardless of ability to pay, and within a specified time period after placement on a waiting list. Individuals over age 75 receive a free annual physical and mental examination designed to catch problems before they become chronic—certainly a noteworthy policy if well-conducted.[71]

However, older citizens have difficulty receiving their rightful attention because of resource limitations. The courts have been reluctant to get involved in determining priorities among competing claims for limited resources. For all practical purposes the level of resources invested by the government in health care is beyond the supervision of the courts. The Charter is thus more a statement of intent than a binding commitment. The NHS has become a large and somewhat inflexible bureaucracy with many inefficiencies; modernization has been a very slow process.[53]

The NHS has attempted to provide a continuum of care for the elderly, with home health care as the primary goal. Local governments are given responsibility for assuring that the continuum is fulfilled through adequate home care, group residential care, or nursing home care—through public or private means. Recent policy changes have increased the emphasis on private community-based services, usually accompanied by decreased publicly provided long-stay hospital and nursing home care. Admissions of elderly patients to public and private hospitals are increasing at about 4 percent annually; collectively the elderly account for about 65 percent of all admissions.[28, 71]

Many physicians practice in both the public and private systems. Individuals with private insurance, or adequate resources, need not wait for NHS service. As private providers, physicians serve as something of a safety valve when the NHS system is unable to provide timely service. About 11 percent of the population had private insurance in 1998. Roughly 20 percent of all surgeries are done privately, as are 30 percent of hip replacements. These options work well for the relatively *affluent* older population—but are of little use to those without private insurance or other resources.[54]

Consequences of the Community Care Act

As noted earlier, the 1990 Community Care Act represents a major shift toward greater community-based health care, with an emphasis on prevention of disease, privatization of services, greater accountability, quality assurance, and cost containment.

In the past a perverse incentive system had tended to favor hospital care over outpatient and home care. This was especially a problem when local general practitioners preferred not to deal with chronic problems or serious acute illness and instead assigned patients to hospitals. The more efficient practitioners and hospitals, which often emphasized home care, were financially penalized. They attracted more patients but did not secure more resources, forcing them to turn people away. The solution proposed in the Community Care Act was creation of an internal market that rewarded efficiency and penalized inefficiency, using NHS contracts as the motivating force.[12, 53]

The goal of greater efficiency, quality, and economy was accomplished in part by creating competition between hospitals and providers through a separation of purchaser and provider roles. The purchasers were the district health authorities and general practitioner groups. Money was allocated annually to the purchasers for the needed services. Hospitals and specialty groups were providers (especially the private Trust hospitals) and generated their income by offering services to purchasers at an acceptable negotiated quality and price as outlined in an NHS contract. The best quality and most efficient hospitals were to generate revenue by satisfying the purchasers who would send their patients. Providers generated resources based on the number of patients cared for and the quality of the care. The competition between providers was eventually expected to force improvements in the lower-quality facilities or cause them to close for lack of business.[53]

Care management receives major emphasis. The identification and monitoring of need is accomplished under the guidance of the care manager through a six step process: (1) screening, (2) assessment, (3) care planning, (4) monitoring, (5) review, and (6) case closure. The intent is to enable older individuals to achieve and maintain, or restore, an optimal level of social independence and quality of life. However, care managers are also expected to take into account cost effectiveness of services. Despite the logical nature of the care management process, it has been difficult to implement because of resistance by professional staff in local government units.[28]

Implementation of the Act. Application and enforcement of the Community Care Act varies considerably among regions, with a mixed effect on the older population. Targets were set for England and Wales requiring that 85 percent of community care funds be used for purchase of private services. The intent was to dismantle part of public system. Hospitals were encouraged to convert to private nonprofit "trusts." Supplemental private health insurance was also formally encouraged. Residential and nursing home care were to be increasingly means-tested so that individuals with resources would pay a greater part, or all, of the costs. However, the changes were resisted by local governments because a high proportion of consumers prefer the public NHS system to the private provision of services.[28]

While the 1990 reforms made the NHS more cost efficient in delivering medical care, more public bureaucracy evolved. From 1990 to 1993, the number of managers increased more than three-fold and administrative and clerical staff increased by 13 percent. The NHS services often required long waiting lists for procedures not considered urgent. In 1998, nearly 1.5 million people were awaiting admission to hospitals; 20 percent (most of them older citizens) had been required to wait a year or more. There was also some evidence that physically impaired older individuals were more likely to receive home health care and other services than those who were cognitively impaired. Specialist services for the cognitively impaired were simply less available in local communities.[21, 23, 28]

Evolution of Geriatric Medicine

Geriatrics as a medical specialty was founded in the United Kingdom and has been at the forefront of research, physician training, and training of other health care professionals who deal with the elderly. Geriatricians are trained to focus not only on accurate assessment and medical treatment, but also on rehabilitation and long-term care. Their goal is to optimize functional capacity and independence insofar as possible. However, approximately 75 percent of patients age 65 to 74 are cared for by general practitioners and not by geriatrics specialists. For those age 75 to 84 geriatricians care for about 56 percent, and beyond age 85 geriatricians care for about 75 percent.[51, 71]

The geriatrics specialty evolved through several major phases:[87]

1. Geriatric care was initiated in the 1930s at West Middlesex Hospital in London. Only about one-third of the patients in the long-term care wards were found by Dr. Marjory Warren to require continuing hospital care. One-third could be discharged immediately and, with appropriate therapy, one-third had the potential for discharge at a later date. Dr. Warren concluded that chronically ill older patients should no longer be admitted to acute medical wards but should instead be transferred to "geriatric" wards staffed by professionals trained in treatment of the elderly and with appropriate design and equipment. This early experience emphasized the need for thorough assessment prior to assignment of patients to either acute or chronic care facilities.

2. Specialized training of geriatric physicians was initiated and geriatric assessment units were organized during the 1940s and 1950s. Home health care with a geriatric component was also started, as was a system of geriatric day hospitals to serve those with serious acute or chronic health problems. Comprehensive geriatric assessment units were established in the new day hospitals.

3. An emphasis on prevention of chronic conditions was a primary focus during the 1960s. Advanced post-graduate education of geriatric specialists was developed as an important element in medical schools, nursing schools, and among other health care specialties. Community nurses were trained to identify high-risk individuals in the community. Attention was given to training and support for caregivers through respite care and day care. Psycho-geriatrics was created as a subdiscipline within the larger field of psychiatry. Greater emphasis was given to multidisciplinary research. Despite these developments, many senior physicians continued to doubt that geriatrics was a legitimate specialty and were unwilling to allocate the needed resources and hospital space.

4. The current phase is characterized as a maturing period for the discipline, with continuing emphasis on research and dissemination of geriatric care concepts to other countries. A recent study indicated that 25 percent of the elderly with five or more health problems, and 10 percent of those with severe disabilities, were still not receiving adequate geriatric care services. Despite the NHS requirement that each older person receive an annual physical and mental evaluation, many were being missed.[51, 82]

Training. Physician specialization in geriatrics requires a four-year graduate education program largely in residencies at approved hospital locations. Most geriatricians are also accredited in general internal medicine, which requires one additional year. Some receive a masters degree in gerontology during the training. Others receive training in research and pursue their career in an academic environment. Geriatric hospital wards have become the focus of training and research.[40]

A Diploma of Geriatric Medicine examination is available for general practitioners who want to gain some level of specialization. The diploma program was established by, and is supervised by, the Royal College of Physicians.[83]

Geriatric medicine has been informed in part by, and parallels, developments in social gerontology, which focuses on the social, psychological, and economic condition of the elderly. In both instances the emphasis is on the most disadvantaged and incapacitated elderly. Both fields attempt to differentiate the pathological effects of disease and its correlates from unproblematic "normal" aging. As self-care improves and the elderly remain healthy longer, less focus on pathology may result.[9, 82]

Multidisciplinary Collaboration. Geriatric physicians work extensively with other specialists as needed. For example, orthopedic surgeons must be involved when fractures occur. Geriatricians also conduct detailed consultation with family members and other caretakers, since fracture healing often requires immobility and rehabilitation for a lengthy time period.[62]

Practice Modes. Geriatric services are provided in three primary modes, referred to as: (1) traditional, (2) age-defined, and (3) integrated. Under the traditional mode, the diagnosis is by a general practitioner or by a specialist who refers patients to geriatric care if the initial diagnosis so indicates. In the age-defined mode, all patients age 65 and older are referred for geriatric care. Under the integrated model the decision about appropriate care is made by a medical team which includes a geriatrics specialist. When available, the integrated model is the most comprehensive and may best serve the patient. It also serves as a good training environment for medical students, who are very likely to see elderly patients whether or not they specialize in geriatrics.[71]

The advantage of having geriatricians made responsible for all of the older population presumably would be greater accuracy and comprehensiveness of diagnosis and treatment, while increasing experience and competence of these specialists in dealing with patients. The outcomes for the older patients should be better.[74] Outstanding examples of high quality specialist geriatric services are available in several locations, such as described in Illustration 12–1.

Illustration 12–1
THE VICTORIA GERIATRIC CENTER, GLASGOW, SCOTLAND

The Victoria Geriatric Center is a publicly sponsored facility with 469 beds and has been operational since 1971. Its mission is to give the highest priority to preserving and extending the independence of clients for as long as possible. Services include geriatric assessment/rehabilitation wards, long-stay nursing wards, out-patient clinical departments, and a day hospital. The out-patient and outreach units provide home help, home nursing, general practitioner services, and geriatric psychiatric care in private homes, residential homes, nursing homes and other hospitals. The building has no mobility restraints for patients, the majority of whom are over age 75.

The Center provides highly individualized care and services are integrated for each client so that the appropriate support is available at the right time. Intensive rehabilitation services attempt to optimize functional ability. More than half of clients return to their homes in the community.

Source: Data from Bruce, 1991: 29-31.

Community Role. Geriatricians have increasingly become involved in patient care and consultation at the community level as well as in hospitals. They are active in planning, establishing standards of care, conducting retirement education, screening for disease or disability, and managing services for the elderly. Preretirement education now includes a strong preventive component focusing on an active retirement that helps diminish disease or disability and promotes more positive attitudes toward later life.[33]

The system of geriatric care is not yet sufficiently developed to provide universal service to all older citizens. Trained geriatric physicians remain unavailable in many locations where the less-trained general practitioners must continue to assume primary responsibility. However, the United Kingdom continues to be the *only* country to develop a nationwide network of geriatric health care units staffed by trained and accredited physicians, nurses, and other geriatric specialists.[8, 26, 87]

Gender and Health

Elderly women in the United Kingdom, as in other countries, have higher levels of disability than men. Among women over age 75 twice as many are housebound (22 percent) as men (11 percent). Twice as many women have impaired mobility and severe disability (14 percent) as men (7 percent). A higher proportion of women have cognitive impairments after age 80. At ages 85 and over, 45 percent of women are severely disabled compared to 25 percent of men. Women have more nonlethal disabilities which cause impairment but are not necessarily life threatening, whereas men have a greater incidence of life-threatening health problems causing them to die earlier. Consequently, women are more likely to require informal care at home and longer-term health and welfare services.[2]

Disabled women are more likely than men to live with an adult child and are more likely to share their home with others. Half live alone—which means they are often somewhat dependent on relatives or need assistance from home helpers and visiting nurses. Women are more likely than men to have close friends as residential companions. A high proportion eventually must enter institutional care.[2]

Continuing Issues

The United Kingdom is attempting to identify measures for improving upon the current situation. An argument is underway over whether health status is actually improving into older age (compression of morbidity), or whether quality of life and health are deteriorating as people live longer. Is illness being postponed to a later age or is morbidity increasing with advanced age? The answers remain unclear in the United Kingdom as elsewhere.[5]

◆◆◆ MENTAL HEALTH CARE

The goals of the NHS contain provisions for an annual mental examination for individuals over age 75 to achieve early identification of problems and prompt treatment of mental disorders. Collaboration between physicians and mental health professionals in this process is encouraged. Public-sector out-patient screening is available at community mental health resource centers, general hospitals, or at home. Private-sector mental health care is rare because it tends not to be insured.[43, 65]

Psychiatry for the elderly has become a medical school and NHS specialty, with an emphasis on mental health care as a central part of primary health care at the community level. Many outdated mental hospitals have been replaced with specialty mental health services in general hospitals, day hospitals, nursing homes, and community mental health services.[42]

Smaller mental hospital units located in communities have expanded. For example, in Nottinghamshire a large hospital (Saxondale) was closed and a new multiunit complex was built to house those who could not function independently or in local facilities. Patients with less-severe problems returned to their homes.[42, 88]

Care management has become a primary integrating mechanism for mental health care as it is for physical health care. The addition of care management did not substantially increase costs. A controlled trial comparing case managed care with standard care for individuals with mental disorders found no significant differences in clinical outcomes.[31]

Depression is a particularly common diagnosis here as in other countries and is correlated with loss of mobility and chronic physical illness. Social isolation, loss of a loved one, and physical illness are the primary risk factors for severe depression. Suicide is most common among men over age 75 and among individuals who are divorced, single, or widowed. The highest incidence is poisoning by drug overdose, although hanging is a primary method among men.[17]

The rate of Alzheimer's disease is roughly the same in the United Kingdom as in other countries. Much of the long-term care burden is for older individuals with Alzheimer's and other dementias. Maldistribution of mental health professionals has been a major problem. Some areas have no specialists while other regions are abundantly served. Additional trained professionals are needed to help alleviate the shortages.[42, 88]

◆◆◆ LONG-TERM CARE

Allocation of long-term care resources changed dramatically over the decades of the 1980s and 1990s. Hospital care decreased substantially whereas formalized home care, residential care homes and private nursing homes greatly increased. For example, use of long-term care hospital beds declined by 20 percent between 1980 and 1990, while use of nursing homes (particularly in the private sector) increased by 41 percent. Use of residential care homes (also predominantly private) went up by 48 percent. These changes were in substantial part because of new rules and funding changes by the National Health Service and the Social Security system.[58]

Home Care

One policy goal of the Community Care Act as noted earlier was to maintain the elderly at home whenever possible. The Act requires local governments to direct more funds into community-based long-term care than into nursing homes. Social security funds go to local authorities for distribution, rather than directly to nursing homes as was earlier the case.[12]

Although the focus on community home care has been underway since 1971, the bulk of national funding continues to go to institutional care. Local governments were required by the 1971 rules to provide home care workers, visiting nurses, case management, and emergency support. Local social service departments were responsible for providing or arranging services. The services gradually increased during the next two decades but were particularly impacted by new resources as a consequence of the 1990 Community Care Act. Home help, district nurse visits, day care services, consultanting in geriatric practice, physical therapy, respite care, and other services have become much more available.[12, 78]

Local authorities have both management and budget responsibilities within national guidelines; because programs are implemented in a manner somewhat unique to each locality, services vary considerably from one locality to another. Some are centralized in local government units while others are relatively decentralized and privatized. Most of the funds continue to flow from the central government to the local units.[50]

Innovations. Considerable interest has been generated by a concept called "hospital-at-home," deemed to have four primary practical benefits: (1) better quality of care and improved health outcomes; (2) satisfying patient preferences to be cared for at home; (3) lower costs as compared to conventional in-patient care, and (4) earlier discharge of patients from hospitals. A cost comparison study indicated that costs per day for hospital-at-home care were lower than for in-patient care. However, living at home appeared to increase the total duration of acute episodes. The cost of standard hospital care was actually lower per episode than care at home with orthopedic cases in three experiments examined in London.[36]

Another example of special attention to home care has been underway in the county of Kent in southeast England. Several alternatives were examined: short-term residential and respite care, day care services, and support to informal caregivers. Individuals in the program were eligible for admission to a long-stay hospital or nursing home but preferred to remain at home. Each client received a personal budget for purchase of services, with the help of a community care organizer or case manager. Direct personal payment was required for services to the degree that income was available. Results indicated that very few individuals receiving these services entered hospitals or nursing homes except for short-term acute health problems. The goal of lower cost is also apparently being achieved.[75]

A concept referred to as Shared Care Recording has been implemented to help providers who visit the home know what other health care professionals are doing. The record has five sections: (1) basic information about the patient, (2) a care plan, (3) hospital discharge information, (4) a risk-assessment profile, and (5) record sheets for ongoing additions by providers of care. It is available to the patient as well as providers so that all parties have a basic understanding of what is needed and what has transpired.[89]

Training Requirements. Home care supervisors receive more training than in most other countries. Home health care nurses must meet strict standards. They undergo basic hospital training and supplementary training in home nursing offices. However, nonmedical home care personnel do not always have to meet training or qualification standards. Some local jurisdictions require 12 days to 2 weeks of in-service training at the beginning of employment. Standards are hard to enforce, however, because of a shortage of home care workers. Relatives can be paid for providing home care if the older person prefers that arrangement. A home care allowance goes to the disabled person who can dispense the funds to relatives while maintaining some independence and control.[50]

Volunteers. Volunteering has a long tradition in the United Kingdom, arising in part from cultural values and in part because of church traditions. Paid "volunteers" (often women in the community who help neighbors) perform many helping functions at very low wages with reimbursement by the local social services department. Day centers sponsored by a voluntary organization, "Help the Aged," provide home services in some locations, and "Age Concern England" lobbies the national government and European Community councils for improved aging programs. Public discussions on aging issues are also emphasized. More than 1000 local chapters provide direct assistance through day centers, transportation, and volunteer home helpers. A research unit produces policy documents for citizen and governmental consideration.[4, 82]

Nursing Homes

Roughly 3.5 percent of the population age 65 and older were residents of nursing homes in 1995. About 43 percent of the nursing homes were public, 47 percent were private, and 10 percent were sponsored by voluntary associations. However, about two-thirds of residents are funded from public sources, largely channeled through the social security system.[1, 12, 63, 80]

NHS and Community Care. NHS extended stay hospital units have been systematically closed, not only because of their high cost but also because they are viewed as compromising the well-being of residents—especially those who are diagnosed as terminally ill. Space shortages have meant that older individuals needing care were required to depend on home care services as the best alternative when geriatric nursing home care was not available.[75]

The Community Care Act of 1990 made nursing home and residential care much more of a private enterprise responsibility, as noted earlier, with greater means-testing required to secure access to NHS long-term care services. Most of the growth in residential long-term care services has been privately financed. Funding is lower than in most other advanced countries and is insufficient to expand long-term care spaces as rapidly as demanded by individuals who qualify. Since local governments have the principal responsibility, with varying requirements, availability of space is widely divergent from one jurisdiction to another.[45]

An important distinction exists between those who are considered NHS patients and those who are cared for in the community as nursing home residents. NHS care in hospitals is nationally sponsored and is generally provided free of charge to the individual, whereas community care is a patient responsibility to be paid from retirement income. Residents of nursing homes may, in some instances, have to sell their private homes to pay the costs. Consequently, there is a major incentive to stay in NHS hospitals. This issue has led to recommendations that chronic illness not be treated in NHS facilities.[53]

The NHS does not operate nursing homes as they are usually defined in the United States. Rather, nursing care functions are performed largely in long-term geriatric wards of hospitals. An effort has been underway to phase out this expensive form of long-term care. The social security system encourages and subsidizes private long-term nursing care, which has been subject to considerable criticism because evidence indicates that private entrepreneurs do not always provide quality care. The rights of residents are in some cases seriously compromised because of the profit motive and insufficient oversight. Physical abuse, drug abuse, lack of appropriate hygiene, fraud, and other problems have been identified.[44, 56]

A serious conflict of interest sometimes exists between the care-giving organizations and care receivers. Government efforts to contain costs means that regulation and adequate oversight are difficult because of staff shortages. Unfortunately, resources were not available in the late 1990s to fully implement the rules in the Community Care Act that would certainly help alleviate existing problems.[78]

Improvement Efforts. Researchers have devised a five point behavioral rating scale which classifies the elderly into categories related to need for various levels of care, as summarized in Table 12–1.

Physical and mental measurements are used to determine where each individual fits among the several categories of Table 12–1. The ratings can then be used to help older individuals, their families, and health professionals decide whether special long-term care is needed and what level of care is appropriate.[35]

Residential Care Homes

Nursing homes and residential care homes have in the past had separate systems of registration and regulation as well as different sources of funding. Residential homes receive lower reimbursement. A high proportion of residential homes are privately

TABLE 12–1   Ratings Scale of Individual Need for Long-Term Nursing Home Care

Impairment Level	Definition
1. *None*	Able to live at home without support.
2. *Mild*	Need for some support at home or in a residential facility.
3. *Moderate*	Need for residential care or substantial support at home.
4. *Substantial*	Need for high support in residential care or a nursing home.
5. *Severe*	High level of ongoing medical and social support needed in a skilled nursing facility.

Source: Data from Henwood, 1992: 33.

operated and owners may be unwilling to invest the resources necessary to achieve nursing home qualification. Many long-term care professionals have advocated bringing the two forms of care under the same regulatory and financing umbrella, as occurred in the United States when the "intermediate care" nursing facilities classification was eliminated. Supporters of integration believe that fewer premature deaths would result. The transfer from one supportive residence to another has been directly linked to deterioration of health status.[22]

Residential home managers have reported a dramatic increase in the number of frail, dependent, and chronically sick residents since the implementation of the 1990 Community Care Act, as the number of geriatric hospital beds was reduced. A recent survey found that almost half of people living in residential homes needed some degree of nursing care. Poorly trained care assistants were inappropriately responsible for pressure sore management, catheters, and insulin injections. The changes have caused increased responsibility for district nurses and GPs who are responsible for medical interventions in residential homes.[32, 70]

The problems could be prevented or alleviated, according to some critics, by increasing the possibility for homes to have dual registration as both nursing and residential homes. Many in residential homes do not have access to appropriate preventative, curative, and rehabilitative health services.[70]

Respite Care

Respite for caregivers is most often provided in private homes. The elderly person is temporarily moved and cared for by a woman who has a home care or nursing background. The respite caregiver receives compensation from the local social-service department that later bills the client or the social security system. Respite care decisions are made by care managers as part of their role in integrating services for each individual client. Experiments in Kent County (southeastern England) indicate that respite care integrated with home care diminishes entry to nursing homes and appears to somewhat extend length of life.[12]

Palliative Care and the Hospice

Palliative care is an important medical specialty in the United Kingdom and has contributed considerably to quality in the final months of life. As noted earlier, it is concerned primarily with the relief of pain and stress associated with incurable disease. Care of cancer patients was the original focus, but palliative care has broadened to include patients with many diseases who can benefit from support services. Approximately 220 palliative care units were available throughout the United Kingdom in 1996.[25]

The modern hospice concept was developed in the United Kingdom early in the twentieth century and has since been adopted in many countries, as noted earlier. The reincarnation began when religious organizations assumed responsibility for care of the incurably ill who were shunned by voluntary hospitals. Hospices now exist in many modes—primarily as home care services, as hospital in-patient units, and in nursing homes. Significantly more patients die at home rather than in hospitals or nursing homes as a consequence of hospice interventions.[20]

Shorter lengths of hospital residence and fewer deaths per admission may well be related to the steady growth in hospice home care and day care. The home hospice team interventions mean less need for hospitalization. Most patients clearly want to be cared for at home if possible.[25, 38]

Training Programs. Medical schools have begun to place greater emphasis on formal training about dying, death, and palliative care. Twenty-seven of the twenty-eight medical schools now offer courses on the subject. The content includes ethical issues in terminal and palliative care, use of physical therapy and drugs for pain relief, and the importance of teamwork. The local hospice is often used as a training mechanism. Periods of residency with a hospice are also common.[27]

Funding Issues. Funding continues to be a problem despite support from the NHS. About 60 percent of hospice costs are derived from donations of various kinds. A high proportion of the service is provided by home care teams including many volunteers, usually led by salaried nurses. A National Hospice Information Service helps secure funding and provides both training and information to professionals throughout the United Kingdom and the world.[38]

Withdrawal of Treatment. The traditional ethic among physicians has been to give priority to the diagnosis and treatment of patients in the interest of finding a cure. An ethical problem arises in cases when further treatment is not deemed to be beneficial, although the British House of Lords formally concluded *there is no absolute obligation* for physicians to keep patients alive when their condition and prospects of recovery are clearly without hope. Treatment can be withdrawn even with the full prior knowledge that such action will result in the patient's death. Considerable room for interpretation is left to physicians, who usually consult carefully with their colleagues and family members before withdrawing therapy.[53]

◆◆◆ HOUSING AND COMMUNITY

Approximately 90 percent of older people live in private homes which they or family members own. Roughly 71 percent of those over age 85 continued to live in private homes as of 1997, while 29 percent were in group residential or nursing homes. However, private homes may be small and poorly equipped; one-fourth of them had no central heating in 1990. As age increases, repairs, maintenance, and improvements become a problem for those who live on modest resources. The situation is alleviated somewhat by voluntary associations which offer assistance through special efforts such as "Staying Put" and "Care and Repair" projects. Resources may be donated or secured through grants provided (beginning in 1986) to the sponsoring organizations by the federal Department of Environment. Costs of rental housing are rising, which can become a serious problem for older individuals or couples whose income is fixed or falling as they age.[49, 61, 72]

Housing for older people was in particularly short supply and of poor quality until 1948 when formal housing policies were implemented through the National Housing Assistance Act. The legislation required that local government authorities arrange homes for the elderly as needed. In the beginning, newly constructed units were large group homes and were intended for the poorest and most infirm older individuals. Since then housing policies have not targeted the older population particularly, even though a succession of studies indicate that such households are more likely than homes of younger families to lack basic features such as indoor plumbing and bathing facilities.[10, 41]

More recently public policies have encouraged nonprofit associations and public housing authorities to sponsor, build, and manage various types of special housing, such as sheltered units with a warden to help in times of need. Some units are designed for active older people who can comfortably function in a private apartment—with nearby common areas for socializing, dining, and other services. Individuals with disabilities are provided with small apartments linked to interior hallways and intensive services, including three meals per day, laundry, and personal care support for activities of daily living (similar to assisted living facilities in the United States).[10, 29]

More intensively supported housing provides meals, extra monitors or wardens, home assistants, and communal living facilities—at greater cost than a private home but much less costly than nursing home or hospital care. Evaluations indicate that here, as in other countries, supported housing arrangements are quite satisfactory to residents, although they may have less contact with former friends and some family members. Loneliness is often a problem.[10, 72]

Moves from one kind of unit to another are resisted. Older residents prefer to stay in one place. Newer housing projects have therefore been designed for independent living and all levels of disability, with home help available as needed.[12, 13, 52]

Home health and personal care are now central elements in the design of both public and private housing. A home help charge must be paid by about 30 percent of the user population with higher incomes. Home health care has become especially crucial for the one-third of the elderly population (50 percent for those over age 80) who lived alone in 1994.[12, 41]

A Special Challenge: Housing for Older Women

Half of elderly women lived alone in 1994 as compared to only 20 percent of men (both proportions are higher than in the United States and most other countries). This is not the result necessarily of abandonment by family members. Rather, a high proportion of older women indicate they prefer to live alone if they have sufficient resources. Nearly 80 percent occupy an owned home. The value of these homes can often be translated into income through "equity release" arrangements or home equity loans, thus increasing available income flow. However, the increase in disposable income does not apparently have a major impact on long-term well-being nor does it pay for much of the cost of residential care.[2, 34]

Use of Technology

Emergency Response Systems have become commonplace in housing built specifically for the elderly. A response "warden" is available to answer emergency calls 24-hours a day. More recently, the systems have become widely available for private homes and group facilities as well, with professional monitoring by private companies. Increased use may have the effect of lowering the cost per housing unit. The systems have the capacity to monitor activity or passivity in a housing unit to detect when a resident is incapable of sounding the alarm. Equipment has been standardized to fit national criteria for use in a variety of housing units, further increasing potential for lower cost and decreasing the need for monitors in every housing unit.[29]

An automated telephone assessment system has been developed to monitor the status of individuals recovering at home or in a hospital or nursing home. A series of sensors that detect and transmit evidence of movement are placed in the home, enabling ongoing measurements by an occupational therapist (or other specialist) of ability to perform activities of daily living. The system is sufficiently new that evaluations have not been completed. About 20 percent of the population age 80 and older do not have home telephones and cannot take advantage of alarms.[19, 72]

Status of Housing

The quantity and quality of housing for the elderly have clearly improved, as has the technology that supports independent living. However, direct government support has actually declined as incentives have increased for private construction and management. The experiences described above have very useful potential for application in other countries.[10]

◆◆◆ ECONOMIC AND FINANCIAL ISSUES

The public system of providing for the elderly uses the lowest proportion of GDP among the countries reviewed. Greater retirement income inequality is also evident. Affluence has grown for the middle- and upper-income groups but lower-class incomes have not kept pace.[34, 77]

Income Support

Social security programs developed slowly after World War II. Poverty among the older population was the rule. Changes since then have considerably modernized the social security system, making it more equitable and efficient with fewer older people in poverty. Public pension systems provided more than half of retirement income in the mid-1990s, a higher proportion than in the United States but lower than among the other economically advanced countries of Europe.[2, 6, 37, 41]

Nonetheless, older people generally have lower average overall incomes than in the other countries. Household income of older people in the other countries averaged 93 percent of all households, but averaged only 76 percent in the United Kingdom. As a consequence of increasing prosperity during the 1990s, the size of the middle-income group has grown while the lower-income group has diminished.[30, 45]

The public cost of social security and pensions has increased steadily with growth in retired workers. To counteract the rising public costs the government has cut back on social security and is relying more on occupationally based pensions—although a very modest income floor has been established for those with lower incomes. The basic social security pension was actually cut from 20 percent of average per capita income in 1990 to 15 percent in 1998—increasing the inequality not only between men and women but between upper- and lower-income older citizens as well. Older males have improved incomes from higher occupation and personal pensions, whereas older females have had to rely largely on public pensions.[2, 6, 15]

Changes in Pension Policy. The pension change as implemented during the 1980s had four major parts:[15]

1. The basic state pension is financed through payroll taxes and available to everyone whether or not they have worked. Retired workers receive greater benefits than those who have not worked. The pension can be paid as a lump-sum benefit at retirement or can be taken as a monthly benefit.
2. An earnings-related social security benefit is available to workers on a monthly basis upon retirement, also financed by payroll taxes which include employer contributions.
3. Employer pension plans which can substitute for public social security with the payroll contributions going into the company plan rather than to government social security.
4. Private pensions investments are available as a substitute for the social security benefit—much like the 401 (k) plans in the United States, with special tax incentives to encourage participation.

The latter option was new in 1988 and quickly became very popular, with 25 percent of the higher-income workforce participating by 1994. It was costly to the national Treasury, however. The incentives were of great advantage to participants whereas the cost to nonparticipating taxpayers was substantial, in part because of investment manager costs that were largely unregulated. Many investors were badly advised and lost the value of their contributions. Men tended to benefit much more than women, and higher-income workers benefited much more than lower-wage earners.[15]

Since traditional social security benefits were scaled back, noninvestors in the private pension scheme are worse off than they might have been. The proportion of government funds spent on social security is expected to drop from 4.2 percent of GDP to 3.3 percent early in the twenty-first century. The new government policy has had the effect of transferring public resources to the private sector—to the disadvantage of public pensions. Consequently, about 40 percent of younger workers have opted out of the government social security system in favor of the private investment accounts.[15, 30]

The differential between men and women is in substantial part a consequence of pension disparity for women at work. Most men receive both social security payments and an employee pension. Women who do receive pensions generally get less because of lower occupational pay scales.[2]

Financing Health Care

Health care expenditures have been more effectively controlled than in most countries. Only about 6.6 percent of gross domestic product went for health care in 1997, the smallest proportion of GDP among economically advanced nations. The relatively low cost is a consequence of several factors: (1) community-based health and long-term care, (2) a single NHS payer, (3) relatively low compensation for service providers, and (4) systematic rationing of nonemergency services. However, the United Kingdom is determined to improve services so as to achieve a standard equal to the European average. Plans are to increase funding by $30 billion during the six years after 2000 to bring the proportion of GDP for health care to about 8 percent. Among the immediate plans is to greatly boost the salaries of mid-level nurses.[11, 41, 67]

Private health insurance is available and widely used by middle- and upper-income citizens. Private health care will certainly become more widespread if government funding remains limited. A two-tier system is evolving, with private services of higher quality available for those who can afford to pay for private insurance or out-of-pocket, and public services of lower quality for those who cannot. Such an arrangement is clearly disadvantageous to lower social classes.[12, 46, 76]

Financing Long-Term Care

Long-term care has been heavily dependent on public support, with government sources covering over two-thirds of costs in 1995. Long-term care consumed an estimated 1.3 percent of GDP, excluding care provided by family and other unpaid caregivers.[39, 45]

Home Care. Roughly 79 percent of home care was paid for with public funding in 1992—most provided directly by local government social-service departments or health departments. Local social-service departments may charge user fees, which vary widely around the country, whereas health departments (largely staffed by district nurses paid by the NHS) do not charge. The Social Security system provides an Attendance Allowance or a Disability Living Allowance for purchase of services by individuals who are severely disabled but able to live at home with an attendant. The amount varies with the degree of disability and need.[45]

Nursing Homes. The fees for private nursing home care must be paid from personal or family income if available. Those unable to pay privately can receive additional public support based on means-testing. As noted earlier, public geriatric hospitals are largely free of personal cost but tend to be very crowded and in great demand, despite their inadequacies.[77]

Private Long-Term Care Insurance. Private long-term care insurance became widely available only in the early 1990s. Eight insurance companies offered varying long-term care products but policies were not affordable by most older people. Consequently, relatively few families are prepared to use long-term care insurance.[57]

Prescription Drugs

Expenditures for pharmaceuticals are among the lowest per capita in Europe. Generic prescription drugs are supplied by the National Health Service and are closely controlled. Strict limitations are established for payment of costs of nongeneric brand-name drugs.[18]

◆◆◆ LIFESTYLE: WORK, RETIREMENT, AND LEISURE

Lifestyles for older people are highly varied here as elsewhere. Lower-income individuals have relatively limited choices and usually choose to follow the lifestyle developed over many years in their community. Middle- and upper-income groups tend to be more mobile, often traveling extensively around the United Kingdom, Europe, and elsewhere.

Continuing Work

Continuing work with reasonable incomes is difficult for individuals over age 65. Education beyond elementary school was not widespread among older individuals. Three-quarters of males over age 60 in 1997 left school and went to work by age 15. Women had even less schooling. Consequently, much of the current retired population is ill-prepared to continue in the workforce even if jobs were available.[41]

The official retirement age for both men and women is 65—with the shift from work to retirement involuntary for most workers. Average incomes are such that amenities are often limited. For example, less than half of the elderly owned an automobile in 1991—a much lower proportion than in most other economically advanced nations. Of course cars are somewhat less needed in urban areas with good public transportation where most older people live.[9, 10, 12, 59, 80]

Full-time work after age 65 has declined steadily since the implementation of social security programs after 1946. Nonetheless, low incomes mean a relatively high incidence of full- or part-time work continuing at low wages. The change is in part a result of early retirement efforts instituted in many industries to deliberately reduce the work force during the 1970s and 1980s—policies that have changed considerably in the 1990s as unemployment has diminished.[41]

Elements of Successful Aging

British researchers have initiated a focus on successful aging. Several indicators similar to those found in the United States have been identified:[7]

- Good physical and mental health.
- Adequate income.
- Social support.
- Autonomy.

- Sense of control over one's destiny.
- Satisfying social relationships.
- An active lifestyle.
- Quality of home and environmental setting.

"Success" is of course relative, since it is in part a function of culture and personal values rather than objective measures of individual well-being.

A certain segment of the older population finds continuing education an important contributor to successful aging. The Open University has a substantial number of older students (75,000 in 1993) studying a great variety of subjects. Most pursue learning in an effort to remain active and stimulated while enhancing their capacity to enjoy life. Older people tend to be among the most successful academically in the overall population of Open University students.[68]

◆◆◆ NOTEWORTHY FEATURES AND MAJOR CHALLENGES

Several significant achievements related to quality of life for older people are noteworthy in the United Kingdom—although major challenges remain.

Noteworthy Features

The universal health care system established after World War II has been highly beneficial to the older population, despite its inadequacies. Individuals over age 75 are entitled to free annual physical examinations and have most needed medications paid for. Geriatric medicine and social gerontology are more developed here than in most countries and certainly contribute to better health care and greater social provision for older people.

Similarly, mental health care for older people has received major attention—much more on a par with physical health care than in most countries. Home care is well developed, providing support to large numbers of older people. Home care workers receive more extensive training than in most countries. The "hospital at home" concept has been a useful experiment with apparent positive results.

Palliative care and the hospice were largely British inventions—now widely disseminated to other countries. The quality of end-of-life care has been vastly improved by the involvement of trained palliative care physicians and other professionals.

Housing for older people has improved, although with much remaining to be done. Income support has also been improved and is universal, although at a level that continues to leave many older individuals, particularly women, at the poverty level. Overall, great progress has been made in improving the welfare of older people during the last 50 years of the twentieth century.

Major Challenges

Ageism continues to be a significant problem. Devaluation and disenfranchisement of the elderly goes on despite the efforts of Age Concern and other organizations to fight prejudices. Ageism denies many older people access to opportunities and manifests itself in the refusal of some public hospitals to admit coronary care patients aged 75 and over. Geriatric units are sometimes located in older hospital buildings with large wards occupied by six to twenty patients—conditions that would be unacceptable for many younger people.[14, 55]

Age discrimination in the NHS has continued despite explicit directives from the government that withholding treatment based on age is not appropriate. Blatant age discrimination with regard to older female breast screening has been detected; women between the ages of 50 and 64 were automatically invited for mammograms, but once they reach 65 they were not, despite the fact that an older woman is more likely to develop breast cancer. Government spending limits, as well as financial incentives for physicians and hospitals to limit costs, are undoubtedly part of the cause for both age discrimination and rationing.[74, 86]

Although the partial privatization of pension funds has been helpful to many current and potential retirees during the prosperous period of the 1990s, others have not fared so well. All taxpayers were forced to pay for part of the additional benefits realized by participants. Furthermore, as noted, many of those who entered the new system were badly advised and did not benefit. Low-income workers were the primary losers because public pensions on which they have to rely actually declined. One-third of pension recipients were on welfare in 1998. However, because of the cutbacks in public pensions, the country does not face the same kind of major fiscal problem of financing the pension system that exists in some other countries.[6, 15]

Older women would do much better, according to some investigators, if they had improved and more equitable access to several types of basic resources: greater material amenities, especially adequate income and satisfactory housing; greater access to health care for chronic conditions; and more consistent personal caretakers in the home to provide ongoing social support. Because of earlier cultural patterns, a high proportion of older women do not have adequate access to these options. Greater attention to the needs of older women would help solve the dependency problem and improve the quality of lifestyles.[2]

A growing care gap is emerging. Some critics argue that many older people with disabilities do not receive sufficient services to meet their basic needs. Families, especially women, are left with the burden of caring for relatives with very limited outside resources.[78]

Among the other problems of the current system is the competition for resources between health care and other social services. Despite the lofty goals of the Community Care Act, it has been very difficult to provide the level of resources needed to make the mandated changes in all communities.[28]

The problem is particularly pronounced when older patients have been hospitalized and treated for an acute problem. They no longer need acute care but cannot secure follow-up residential care. Many remain in the hospital simply because there are no available alternatives for rehabilitation or convalescence. Indeed, some commentators argue that the recent emphasis on community care may be in substantial part because of the slow pace of residential care evolution. An essential ingredient of the home care system is more genuine collaboration between health care provided through NHS, and social services provided by local authorities.[4, 44, 69]

Waiting lists for entry to hospitals for surgery or other forms of acute care are

continuing despite the many changes during the 1990s. Waiting for hospital procedures seems to have increased rather than declined because of insufficient resources
to accommodate all needs.[69]

Part of the rationale for rationing is the belief that *the values of the larger society
should predominate, rather than the interests of the elderly*. If a shortage of health care
resources means that everyone cannot be served equally, there may be a higher value
in providing care to younger individuals with greater life expectancy. The counter-argu-
ment suggests that discrimination on the basis of age is unethical and assumes that
the value of life is determined by its length. Since the quality of life may very well be
best at the later stages, this argument may be difficult to justify.[24, 86]

Some health and social-services programs have not been well targeted to meet
the needs of those most at risk. The frail elderly who are unable to fend for themselves
adequately depend upon the fairness, integration, and coordination of health care
and long-term social care. Although this is generally understood among professionals in the public services, it has not always been achieved either in community-based
services delivered to the home or in residential or nursing homes.[35]

Inequity is especially a problem for ethnic minorities who make up about 3
percent of the older population and are generally ill-informed about aging policies
and services. Most are first-generation migrants. They are clearly underrepresented
in nursing homes and other residences for the elderly. Their primary contact with the
health care system is through general practitioners who would be in the best position to provide them with information and direct them to services.[65]

The goals of the Community Care Act discussed earlier have thus not been
fully realized. Much remains to be done to adequately integrate services that respond
to individual needs.[48, 79]

Debate of the Age

Partially in response to these problems, the government launched a Royal Commission on Long-Term Care and initiated a formal national "Debate of the Age" in 1998,
focusing on implications of the graying of the country. The final report was presented January 1, 1999, arguing that equality and adequacy of services can only come
with better national policies for the integration of health care, social services, and
housing. The report suggested that chronological age should be eliminated as a criterion for certain forms of physical and mental health care, to overcome the rationing
of health treatments.[16, 64]

Public policy in the late 1990s was clearly more supportive of improved aging
policies, research, and some services at the same time that public pensions were
declining. The groundwork has been established for progress in the years ahead.[81]

◆◆◆ SUMMARY AND CONCLUSIONS

The system of public support and care for older people has a long and progressive history in the United Kingdom and has become increasingly responsive to those with the

greatest needs. Social support systems, community services, and housing have been much improved despite the remaining inadequacies.

The government has attempted to control costs by decreasing use of hospitalization, localizing services, and emphasizing private provision of nursing and residential care. The results of these changes remain to be fully measured and interpreted.

Geriatrics as a medical specialty has been pioneered and developed here, as has the hospice concept for end-of-life care of the dying. These innovations have had a major positive impact in the United Kingdom and in many other countries around the world. Both concepts have greatly improved treatment and quality of life for the most frail and needy elderly.

Services to the older population are relatively cost-effective compared to other economically advanced countries. However, government restraint on costs has made ageism, rationing, and long waiting lists evident. Local social and health services are under great pressure. Physicians, nurses, and other health care personnel are often overtaxed. Considerable inequity continues, despite efforts by government and voluntary organizations to correct the problems.

The interests of the elderly are clearly represented in the political system. With coaching from special interest groups such as "Age Concern," the national government has responded by redesigning financial support, increasing community services, encouraging the construction of housing, upgrading health care, and expanding private long-term care. The goals of the Community Care Act of 1990 were highly supportive of the older population and are in the process of realization. Although there is much to criticize, the system of services is among the most complete and equitable among modern nations.

◆◆◆ REFERENCES

1. Alber, Jens (1992). Residential Care for the Elderly, *Journal of Health Politics, Policy and Law,* 17 (4), 929–57.
2. Arber, Sara, and Jay Ginn (1994). Women and Aging, *Reviews in Clinical Gerontology,* 4 (4), 349–58.
3. Baldock, John (1991a). The National Context of Social Innovation: England and Wales, in Robert J. Kraan, John Baldock, Bleddyn Davis, Adalbert Evers, Lennarth Johansson, Martin Kragren, Mats Thorslund, and Catherine Tunissen, *Care for the Elderly: Significant Innovations in Three European Countries,* Boulder, CO: Westview Press, 45–69.
4. Baldock, John (1991b). Strengthening Home-Based Care, in Robert J. Kraan, John Baldock, Bleddyn Davis, Adalbert Evers, Lennarth Johansson, Martin Kragren, Mats Thorslund, and Catherine Tunissen, *Care for the Elderly: Significant Innovations in Three European Countries,* Boulder, CO: Westview Press, 141–85.
5. Bone, Margaret R., and Andrew C. Bebbington (1998). Policy Applications of Health Expectancy, *Journal of Aging and Health,* 10 (2), 136–53.
6. Bosworth, Barry, and Gary Burtless (1998). Population Aging and Economic Performance, in Barry Bosworth and Gary Burtless (eds), *Aging Societies: The Global Dimension,* Washington, DC: The Brookings Institution, 1–28.
7. Bowling, Ann (1993). The Concepts of Successful and Positive Aging, *Family Practice* (Oxford University Press), 10 (4), 449–53.
8. Bruce, Sandra (1991). Health Care for the Elderly: What Can We Learn From Britain? *Michigan Hospitals,* 27 (11), 29–33.

9. Caldock, Kerry, and G. Clare Wenger (1993). Sociological Aspects of Health, Dependency, and Disability, *Reviews in Clinical Gerontology*, 3 (1), 85–96.
10. Clapham, David (1995). Housing Frail Elders in Great Britain, in Jon Pynoos and Phoebe S. Liebig (eds), *Housing Frail Elders: International Policies, Perspectives, and Prospects*, Baltimore: The Johns Hopkins University Press, 68–88.
11. Cochrane, Sue (1997). Link Up, Check Up, Speak Up, *Nursing Times*, 93 (29), 38–39.
12. Coleman, Barbara J. (1995). European Models of Long-Term Care in the Home and Community, *International Journal of Health Services*, 25 (3), 455–74.
13. Coolen, Jan (ed) (1993). *Changing Care for the Elderly in the Netherlands*, Assen/Maastricht, The Netherlands: Van Gorcum.
14. Coupland, Nikolas, and Justine Coupland (1993). Discourses of Ageism and Anti-Ageism, *Journal of Aging Studies*, 7 (3), 279–301.
15. Daniel, Caroline (1998). Great Britain's Experience: Privatization Has Its Downside, *Washington Post National Weekly Edition*, August 17, 1998, 10–11.
16. Dean, Malcolm (1998). Britain to Debate How to Plan for an Ageing Population, *The Lancet*, 351 (9105), 811.
17. Dennis, Michael S., and James Lindesay (1995). Suicide in the Elderly: The United Kingdom Perspective, *International Psychogeriatrics*, 7 (2), 263–74.
18. Dickson, Michael (1994). Paying for Prescriptions in Europe, in Organization for Economic Cooperation and Development, *Health: Quality and Choice*, Paris: OECD, 83–110.
19. Doughty, Kevin, and Jan Costa (1997). Continuous Automated Telecare Assessment of the Elderly, *Journal of Telemedicine and Telecare*, 3 (Supplement 1), 23–24.
20. Duke S. (1997). An analytical study of the changing health of a hospice population 1978–89, *Palliative Medicine*, 11 : 145–51.
21. Economist (1998). The Health Service at 50: Bevan's Baby Hits Middle Age, *The Economist*, 348 (8075), 55–57.
22. Editor (1997). Elderly care counts. Single care home plan loses ground, *Nursing Times*, 93 (30) : 14–15.
23. Ely, Margaret, Carol Brayne, Felicia A. Huppert, and Daniel W. O'Conner (1997). Cognitive Impairment: A Challenge for Community Care. A Comparison of the Domiciliary Service Receipt of Cognitively Impaired and Equally Dependent Physically Impaired Elderly Women, *Age and Ageing*, 26 (4), 301–8.
24. Evans, J. Grimley (1997). The Case Against, *British Medical Journal*, 314 (March 15), 822–25.
25. Eve, Ann, Anthony Smith, Peter Tebbit (1997). Hospice and palliative care in the UK 1994–95, including a summary of trends 1990–95, *Palliative Medicine*, 11 : 31–43.
26. Farquhar, M. (1993). Elderly People's Use of Services: A Survey, *Nursing Standards*, 7 (47) : 31–36.
27. Field, David (1995). Education for Palliative Care: Formal Education About Death, Dying and Bereavement in UK Medical Schools in 1983 and 1994, *Medical Education*, 29 (6), 414–19.
28. Filinson, Rachel (1997). Legislating Community Care: The British Experience, with U.S. Comparisons, *The Gerontologist*, 37 (3), 333–40.
29. Fisk, Malcolm J. (1992). Local Authority and Housing Association Perspectives on ERS in the United Kingdom, *Home Health Services Quarterly*, 13 (3/4), 159–75.
30. Ginn, Jay, and Sara Arber (1999). Changing Patterns of Pension Inequality: The Shift from State to Private Sources, *Ageing and Society*, 19, 319–42.
31. Gray, A. M., M. Marshall, A. Lockwood, and J. Morris (1997). Problems in Conducting Economic Evaluations Alongside Clinical Trials, *British Journal of Psychiatry*, 170 (1), 47–52.
32. Greengross, Sally (1997). Age of No Concern, *Nursing Times*, 93 (8) : 22.
33. Greveson, Gabrielle (1994). In the Community, *Age and Ageing*, 23 (3), 515–17.
34. Hancock, Ruth (1998). Housing Wealth, Income and Financial Wealth of Older People in Britain, *Ageing and Society*, 18 (1), 5–33.
35. Henwood, Melanie (1992). *Through a Glass Darkly: Community Care and Elderly People*, Research Report No. 14, London: King's Fund Institute.
36. Hensher, Martin, Naomi Fulop, Sonja Hood, and Sarah Ujah (1996). Does Hospital-at-Home Make Economic Sense? Early Discharge vs. Standard Care for Orthopaedic Patients, *Journal of the Royal Society of Medicine*, 89 (10), 548–51.

37. International Social Security Association (1998). United Kingdom, *Trends in Social Security*, 1998 (1), 20.

38. Jackson, Avril, and Ann Eve (1997). Hospice in Great Britain, in Dame Cicely Saunders and Robert Kastenbaum (eds), *Hospice Care on the International Scene*, New York: Springer, 143–50.

39. Jacobzone, Stephen (1999). Ageing and Care for Frail Elderly Persons: An Overview of International Perspectives, *Occasional Papers #38*, Paris: Organization for Economic Cooperation and Development.

40. James, O. F. W. (1994). In Training, *Age and Ageing*, 23 (3), S43–S45.

41. Johnson, Malcolm L. (1994). Great Britain, in Jordan I. Kosberg (ed), *International Handbook on Services for the Elderly*, Westport, CT: Greenwood Press, 154–74.

42. Jolley, David (1997). Services for Older People With Mental Health Problems: Inequalities and Strategies to Help the 'Have-Nots,' *Dementia and Geriatric Cognitive Disorders*, 8 (2), 132–35.

43. Kafetz, K.M. (1994). In Collaboration with Old Age Psychiatrists, *Age and Ageing*, 23 (3), S34–35.

44. Kraan, Robert J., John Baldock, Bleddyn Davis, Adalbert Evers, Lennarth Johansson, Martin Kragren, Mats Thorslund, and Catherine Tunissen, (1991). *Care for the Elderly: Significant Innovations in Three European Countries*, Boulder, CO: Westview Press.

45. Laing, William (1993). *Financing Long-Term Care: The Crucial Debate*, London: ACE Books (Age Concern).

46. Lancet, The (1997). Health Inequality: the UK's Biggest Issue, *The Lancet*, 349 (9060), 1185.

47. Lassey, Marie L, William R. Lassey, Martin J. Jinks (1997). *Health Care Systems Around The World: Characteristics, Issues, Reforms*, Upper Saddle River, NJ: Prentice Hall, 220–39.

48. McCormack, Brendan (1998). Community Care for Elderly People: Will Improve Only When There are National Standards and Explicit Funding, *British Medical Journal* (International Edition), 317 (7158), 552–53.

49. Messado, Jaqueline (1990). Development of Agency Services in the U.K., in *Supporting Older People in General Housing*, Oxford: The Oxford Conference at Wadham College, 11–14.

50. Monk, Abraham, and Carole Cox (1991). *Home Care for the Elderly: An International Perspective*, New York: Auburn House.

51. Mulley, Graham P. (1999). Journals of Geriatric Medicine and Gerontology, *Age and Ageing*, 28, 1–2.

52. Nazarko, Linda (1997). The Road to Hell, *Elderly Care*, 9 (2), 35.

53. Newdick, Christopher (1997). Resource Allocation in the National Health Service, *American Journal of Law and Medicine*, 23 (2/3), 291–318.

54. Nicholson, Bryan (1998). Private Care Eases Public Burden, *Management Today*, August, 5.

55. Olde Rikkert, Marcel (1997). A Travel Account of an 11 City Tour of British Geriatric Units, *Age and Ageing*, 26 (3) : 233–35.

56. Olson, Laura Katz (1994). Introduction, in Laura Katz Olson (ed), *The Graying of the World: Who Will Care for the Frail Elderly?* New York: Haworth Press, 1–23.

57. Organization for Economic Cooperation and Development (OECD) (1994). *Caring for Frail Elderly People*, Paris: OECD.

58. Organization for Economic Cooperation and Development (OECD) (1996). *Caring for Frail Elderly People: Policies in Evolution*, Paris: OECD.

59. Organization for Economic Cooperation and Development (OECD) (1995). *The Labour Market and Older Workers*, Paris: OECD.

60. Proctor, Susan (1995). The Move to Community Care and the Impact of Long-Term Disability on Health Service Provision: Some Implications for Library Services, *Health Libraries Review*, 12 (4), 235–41.

61. Pynoos, Jon, and Phoebe S. Liebig (1995). Housing Policy for Frail Elders: Trends and Implications for Long-Term Care, in Jon Pynoos and Phoebe S. Liebig, *Housing Frail Elders: International Policies, Perspectives, and Prospects*, Baltimore: The Johns Hopkins Press, 3–15.

62. Reid, J. (1994). In Collaboration with Orthopaedic Surgeons, *Age and Ageing*, 23 (3), S31–33.

63. Ribbe, Miel W., Gunnar Ljunggren, Knight Steel, Eva Topinkova, Catherine Hawes, Naoki Ikegami, Jean-Claude Henrard, and Palmi V. Jonnson (1997). Nursing Homes in 10 Nations: A Comparison Between Countries and Settings, *Age and Ageing*, 26 (S2), 3–12.

64. Richards, Tessa (1998). Ageing Costs: Evidence to Royal Commission Emphasizes Need for Explicit Standards, *British Medical Journal*, International Edition, 317 (7163), 896.

65. Shah, Ajit (1997). Down Under and Over the Top: Geriatric Psychiatry in Melbourne and London, *International Journal of Geriatric Psychiatry*, 12 : 263–66.

66. Shah, Ajit (1998). The Psychiatric needs of Ethnic Minority Elders in the UK, *Age and Ageing*, 27 (3), 267–69.

67. Sibbald, Barbara (2000). UK Pumps $30 Billion into Health Spending, *Canadian Medical Affairs Journal*, 162 (4), 553.

68. Slater, Robert (1995). *The Psychology of Growing Old*, Philadelphia: Open University Press.

69. Spicker, P., and J. Hanslip (1997). Matching Services to Needs in the Health Care of Elderly People, *Health Services Management Research*, 10 (2), 113–20.

70. Summer, Pauline (1997). Primary concerns, *Nursing Times*, 93 (8) : 54–55.

71. Thomas, Anita (1994). In Acute Medicine: The Integrated Model, *Age and Ageing*, 23 (3), S22–S24.

72. Tinker, Anthea (1997). Housing and Household Movement in Later Life: Developing the Range of Housing Options in the United Kingdom, *Journal of Housing for the Elderly*, 12 (1 & 2), 9–17.

73. United States Census Bureau (2000). *International Data Base*, Online at www.census.gov/cgi-bin/ipc/idbpyry.pl.

74. Vallon, A.G. (1994). In Acute Medicine: The Age-defined Model, *Age and Ageing* 23 (3), S25–26.

75. Waddington, Paul (1996). Toward Care in the Community: A Carer's Tale, *British Journal of Nursing*, 5 (1), 48–50.

76. Walker, Alan (1993). A Cultural Revolution? Shifting the UK's Welfare Mix in the Care of Older People, Chapter 4, in Adalbert Evers and Ivan Svetlik (eds), *Balancing Pluralism: New Welfare Mixes in Care for the Elderly*, Vienna: Avebury, 67–88.

77. Walker, Alan, Jens Alber, and Anne-Marie Guillemard (1993). *Older People in Europe: Social and Economic Policies*, European Observatory, Commission of the European Communities.

78. Walker, Alan, and Lorna Warren (1994). The Care of Frail Older People in Britain: Current Policies and Future Prospects, in Laura Katz Olson (ed), *The Graying of the World: Who Will Care for the Frail Elderly?* New York: Haworth Press, 129–62.

79. Warden, John (1998). Community Care is Failing Elderly People, *British Medical Journal*, International Edition, 316 (7128), 332.

80. Warnes, Anthony M. (1994). Cities and Elderly People: Recent Population and Distributional Trends, *Urban Studies*, 31 (4/5), 799–816.

81. Warnes, Anthony M. (1999). A Decade of Gerontology's Development in Britain, *Contemporary Gerontology*, 5 (2), 120–24.

82. Warnes, Anthony M. (1993). United Kingdom, in Erdman B. Palmore (ed), *Developments and Research on Aging: An International Handbook*, Westport, CT: Greenwood Press, 335–53.

83. Webster, S. G. P. (1994). In Continuing Care, *Age and Ageing*, 23 (3), S36–S38.

84. Wenger, G. Clare (1997). Review of Findings on Support Networks of Older Europeans, *Journal of Cross-Cultural Gerontology*, 12, 1–21.

85. Wenger, G. Clare, and Dorothy Jerrome (1999). Change and Stability in Confidant Relationships: Findings from the Bangor Longitutinal Study of Ageing, *Journal of Aging Studies*, 13 (2), 269–94.

86. Williams, Alan (1997). The Rationing Debate. Rationing Health Care By Age: The Case For, *British Medical Journal*, 314 (March 15), (7083), 820–25.

87. Williamson, J. (1994). In the Past, *Age and Ageing*, 23 (3), S9–11.

88. Wistow, Gerald, and Marian Barnes (1995). Central Nottinghamshire, England: A Case Study of Managed Innovation in Mental Health, in Rockwell Schulz and James R. Greenley (eds), *Innovating in Community Mental Health*, Westport, Connecticut: Praeger, 109–31.

89. Wolf, Rogan (1997). Shared Care Recording in Community Care, *Nursing Times*, 93 (28), 52–53.

Chapter 13

THE NETHERLANDS
Integrated and Comprehensive Services

◆◆◆ INTRODUCTION

The Netherlands is the smallest and most densely populated among the countries considered in this volume. Most of the population lives in urban centers. However, the Dutch have been highly industrious and creative in expanding opportunities within the small landmass—most notably draining and reclaiming large areas from the sea to form the "polders." Much of the country is below sea level. They have also developed one of the most integrated, comprehensive, and well-financed support systems for the older population among modern nations. The consequence is a strong record in preventing poverty while providing a relatively seamless security net of income support, health care, long-term care, and housing. Government policy has guided deliberate public and private efforts to optimize quality of life.[12, 33]

Surveys indicate that roughly 70 percent of the population believes that the federal, provincial, and local governments have direct responsibility to assure adequate income and ongoing care for older people. Deliberate decentralization of responsibility has shifted most of the operational details to the community and family, although taxes are collected centrally and redistributed via provinces and municipalities. The public generally supports the necessary taxation to finance benefits, although questions are regularly raised about the generosity of some benefits because of the high tax burden imposed on households, individuals, and families.[32]

Demographic Characteristics

The Netherlands had a population of 15.9 million in 2000. Approximately 13.5 percent are over age 65; 3.1 percent are over age 80—many more women than men as indicated by the population pyramids in Figure 13–1. More than 17.8 percent are expected to be in the older age categories by 2010 and 23 percent by 2025—as suggested by the larger numbers in the age 40 to 64 categories of the pyramids. Those over age 80 will increase rapidly to nearly 5 percent in 2010, and 7 percent by 2025, then expand at about the same rate as the general population.[15, 39]

Life expectancy was 80.6 for females and 75.2 for males in 2000, among the highest in the world. As elsewhere the proportion of older women was much higher than older men. Older men are almost twice as likely to be married as women. About 48 percent of older women are widows, compared to only 16 percent of men.[4, 15, 32, 43]

Eighty-two percent of older people live independently in their own homes. Another 10 percent live in adapted service homes, 5.5 percent in residential care (assisted living) homes, and 2.7 percent are in nursing homes. The Netherlands has a well-developed system of geriatric care with specialists in nursing home care, social geriatrics, and geriatric psychiatry.[15]

◆◆◆ HISTORICAL PERSPECTIVE

The government has historically taken major responsibility for the welfare of older people. Basic income support, health care, long-term care, and housing have been features of social policy for decades. The health care insurance system evolved from

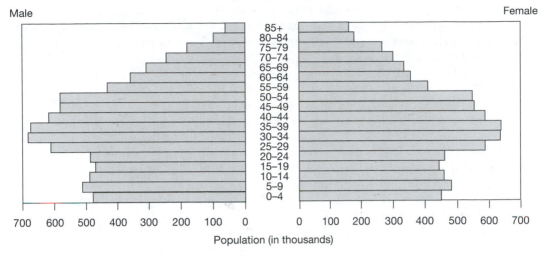

FIGURE 13–1   Population Pyramids for The Netherlands
Source: U.S. Census Bureau, *International Data Base,* 2000

mutual-aid societies associated with medieval guilds of the nineteenth century. During World War II, health insurance organized by sickness funds was introduced. After the war a series of modifications were added with a focus on private insurance options. The General Old Age Pensions Act was passed by the national parliament in 1957. A series of other laws have supplemented the guaranteed income and initiated comprehensive health care, long-term care, housing, and lifestyle enhancements.[16, 18]

Public sickness insurance funds and private insurance were financed through payroll tax deductions and together paid about 90 percent of health care costs. The Exceptional Medical Expenses Compensation Act (referred to as ABWZ) of 1968 established a national fund supported by income taxes to finance community mental health care, residential care, nursing homes, and home care. The Act contributed substantially to the improvement of long-term care services and other support for disabled elderly.[15, 16, 32]

The Dekker Commission on "Structure and Financing of the Health Care System," appointed in 1987, recommended increased emphasis on ambulatory care, more cost-efficient hospital services, improved coordination of all services, and greater privatization of insurance. The general policy has been referred to as "substitution": home care was substituted for institutional care when possible; hospitals shifted patients to nursing homes; nursing homes transferred those who could manage to residential homes; and the least disabled were moved from professional care to informal care if it were available. Each shift was toward a lower cost option and greater quality of life.[15, 35]

A change from conservative to more liberal political leadership led to further adjustments in policy during the early 1990s. The Plan Simons replaced some of the alternatives in the Dekker Commission report, with more focused attention to insurance equity and improved quality of care. Private and public insurance inequities were brought into balance. The insurance emphasis thus changed from expanding public insurance coverage and services toward a major focus on private insurance and market-based cost containment as a means of both improving services and lowering costs.[21, 37]

The entire population was to receive a comparable benefits package funded by payroll deductions. Supplemental private insurance was available at competitive rates with sickness fund insurance. Payroll taxes supported 82 percent of the costs for public insurance while 18 percent was covered by premiums for private insurance.[21]

During the 1990s the policy emphasis shifted toward greater focus on prevention of chronic illness, with a goal of lowering the proportion of disabled older people living in institutional settings. Nonetheless, as of 2000 the demand for residential home and nursing home spaces remained very high. The new policies have restricted the construction of additional residential care and nursing homes units and high demand has meant shortages of nurses and other support personnel. Only geriatric nursing homes specializing in mental health problems have been allowed to significantly increase their capacity. However, critics have argued that it may not be possible to sufficiently increase ambulatory care and home care to make them viable substitutes for institutional care.[2, 15]

◆◆◆ SOCIAL-SUPPORT SYSTEMS

The Netherlands has a long tradition of family solidarity and community responsibility to older people—as the previous section emphasizes. The great majority of support, including home care for disabled older people, is from the family, although community and national resources interact more with family resources than in most other countries. Women work outside the home in large numbers as in other countries (63 percent as compared to 68 percent in the United States, 65 percent in the United Kingdom and 61 percent in Germany), making family home care a major challenge. When adult children are not available to provide support, siblings and siblings-in-law often provide the needed support. Neighbors or friends are generally not involved in direct ongoing caregiving but often become active in times of crisis or when a spouse dies. However, changing demographic realities mean that capacity for family support is likely to diminish because of declining family size and greater mobility of younger family members.[7, 11, 12, 15, 36, 37]

One indication of diminished support is the high proportion of single older households: more than 40 percent of older women live alone compared to 14 percent of older men. Roughly 18 percent of men and 13 percent of women live with their children. Extended family households are diminishing while single older households are increasing. This may explain in part why the use of formal home care support services is much higher in the Netherlands than in most other countries. Despite the obstacles, family support remains strong; older individuals living alone do not appear to exhibit strong feelings of loneliness, although they are less satisfied than when living with a marital partner.[7, 10]

Communities tend to be highly integrated and supportive. An extensive network of local community centers provides information and assistance with health care, mental health care, housing, long-term care and social/recreational opportunities. The primary goal is to bridge the gap between the elderly and the local organizations providing various forms of care or service. Municipal social security departments are responsible for awarding benefits and special allowances such as transportation and needed equipment. Able older people reciprocate by helping to maintain the community infrastructure, part of the explanation for the neat and well-kept appearance of most community environments.[37]

◆◆◆ PHYSICAL HEALTH CARE

The elderly are covered by the same basic public or private insurance as younger citizens, without evident discrimination. Public sickness funds and private insurance companies offer coverage for acute and chronic care. Supplemental private insurance is purchased by young and old to cover deductibles and services not provided by the public insurance package.[12]

Public health services supported by national and local governments are provided in decentralized local units with a focus on health promotion and disease prevention. The elderly are a specific target of public health efforts. Although the health care system is guided and regulated by the national government, private practitioners, nonprofit hospitals and nursing homes provide most of the care.[15]

Primary and Hospital Care

Primary health care is provided primarily by general practitioners who act as gatekeepers to specialty and hospital care. The older person has little choice of physicians because they are on a practitioner "list" of all patients in the immediate geographic area of the primary care physician's office. Referral to specialists occurs only when the GP concludes that he or she is unable to adequately diagnose and/or treat the patient. Private and generally nonprofit hospitals (often affiliated with a church) provide some out-patient services as well as in-patient secondary and tertiary care. Although the elderly comprise only 13.5 percent of the population, they use 44 percent of hospital days. Home health care services are often provided from hospitals and nursing homes, including physician visits, skilled nursing care and personal care.[15]

Geriatric Specialization

Geriatrics was officially encouraged as a medical specialty beginning in 1982 and has since expanded rapidly. Four subspecialties have been created: clinical geriatrics, nursing home medicine, social geriatrics, and geriatric psychiatry. Clinical geriatricians are the most highly trained and tend to be hospital based. Nursing home geriatricians provide daily care in nursing homes. Social geriatricians care for patients primarily at home or in residential care settings. Geriatric psychiatrists work primarily with older patients through the community mental health care system. A high proportion of the new geriatric specialists are women who constitute 60 percent of medical school students and generally prefer to work part-time—in nursing homes and home health care—rather than in hospitals.[14, 15]

Seventeen hospital geriatric departments had been initiated by 2000. For example, the University Hospital-Utrecht includes a 24-bed geriatric in-patient unit plus an out-patient clinic, as described in Illustration 13–1.

Illustration 13–1
GERIATRIC SERVICES AT UNIVERSITY HOSPITAL-UTRECHT

Patients using the geriatrics unit are usually 75 years of age or older and include only those with complex problems. Patients with modest problems are treated in general medical departments. The emphasis is on quality of life rather than simply prolonging life. Several special adaptations facilitate comfort of patients. The unit has special bathrooms and an accessible living room adjacent to the nurse's station. Directional signs are in large print to compensate in part for impaired vision. Confused patients are able to walk freely around the unit, secured by a coded entry and exit system.

The staff includes geriatricians, nurses trained in geriatrics, physical therapists, occupational therapists, psychologists, and dieticians. A geriatric nurse serves as the care coordinator. Consultations with other medical specialties such as ophthalmology and speech pathology are available as required. Every effort is made to help recovery of functions, maintenance of autonomy, and ongoing association with family.

Source: Data from Schuurmans, 1996: 539–540.

The Geriatric Nurse Specialist. Greater emphasis on geriatric nurse specialist training was initiated in 1989. A master's degree in nursing science, special education in geriatrics, extensive experience with the elderly, and primary care internships were required. Advanced training is largely in the hospital setting rather than in academic departments of universities. Geriatric nurses support patient care while coordinating consultations with physicians, undertaking education in geriatric care, and conducting research. Nurses take the lead in development of a care plan for each patient. They also provide basic information on nutrition, mobility, and home care needs.[34]

A law passed in 1992 clarifies education requirements, physician and nurse responsibilities, and provides for greater interdependence of physicians and nurses. Nurses were given greater rights to function as independent practitioners.[34]

Pharmaceutical Care

During the period since World War II the pharmacy profession has begun to embrace pharmaceutical care with a greater focus on direct patient assistance in the appropriate use of drugs. "Social pharmacy" has emphasized the responsibility and involvement of pharmacists with drugs in society, collaboration with physicians, and direct work with patients.[9]

Pharmaceutical care has evolved through several major stages to become increasingly effective in managing use of drugs with the elderly:[9]

- An improved collaborative relationship between pharmacists and physicians.
- Greater focus by the pharmacist on the individual and social needs of the patient, rather than only the effects of drugs.
- Improvements in pharmacy education and information provided to the patient.
- Careful observation of patient drug use through use of computers and registration of all drugs.

Medication evaluation instruments were developed to assist pharmacists and physicians with surveillance of drug use, thus adding specific understanding of the effects of drugs, misuse, failure to take prescriptions, and a variety of other attributes of medications. The instruments provide the data for medication counseling by pharmacists in hospitals and community pharmacies.[9]

Computerized registration is used in 90 percent of pharmacies to manage and control use of medications. Prescription services are covered by insurance under a carefully regulated system to control costs. Ninety-three percent of the population typically uses the same pharmacy over a prolonged time period, which facilitates integrated and full information shared between physicians, hospitals, and pharmacists. Pharmacists have achieved a status almost equal to physicians and have become members of the health care team to a greater degree than in most other countries—a situation which is directly beneficial to older patients who take multiple prescriptions.[22]

Compliance with instructions about use of drugs is a significant problem, as is polypharmacy (taking several prescriptions at once). Computerized registration enables pharmacists and physicians to more closely monitor patients. Compliance is greater, and misuse of drugs is less, when the pharmacist or physician helps the older patient understand the purpose of a drug.[22]

◆◆◆ MENTAL HEALTH CARE

Treatment of mental disorders is relatively well developed in the Netherlands, based on international standards. Diagnosis and treatment of relatively minor disorders is usually managed by general practitioners in the primary care system. Psychiatrists, psychologists, and social workers are trained in geriatrics and are available to supplement the work of primary care physicians.[6, 32]

The number of mental health hospital beds is declining as the government develops regional community mental health services. Treatment for serious cases is increasingly provided in supportive housing, half-way houses, day hospitals, nursing homes, out-patient clinics and crisis intervention centers. Most nursing homes have day clinics for mentally ill residents. Departments of geriatric medicine in hospitals provide diagnosis and treatment. Regional Institutes for Mental Welfare provide out-patient care and help support day care centers. Private insurance or the Exceptional Medical Expenses Act cover the majority of costs.[6, 15, 43]

Incidence of Depression

Depression is among the most prevalent medical conditions (as in other countries) among older people, especially for men. Physicians have diagnosed minor or major depression in 8 to 14 percent of elderly patients, depending on the criteria used. The incidence of major depression is estimated at about 4 percent. A strong correlation is evident between physical illness and depression.[23, 25]

Controlled studies suggest, however, that about one-third of general practitioners are not adequately able to diagnose or treat patients with depression. The research indicates that only about one-quarter of patients later diagnosed as having major depression were identified by general practitioners, resulting in inadequate and inconsistent diagnoses and care. Diagnosis is improved considerably when practitioners use a short version of a Geriatric Depression Scale designed for detection of disorders.[1, 19, 24, 26]

Suicide. About one-third of suicides are among the elderly, usually following a period of serious depression. Suicide represented about 1 percent of all deaths in 1990 and was higher among men than women. Widowed or divorced individuals are at greater risk than married people. The majority of cases are associated with major and irreversible life events, such as severe physical suffering, the death of a spouse, the threat of dependency, institutionalization, loss of an active position in society, severe psychological distress, alcohol or drug addiction, or severely disturbed social relations. Most cases are preventable, given adequate understanding of the state of mind of the older person.[19]

Dementia

Rapid growth of the population over age 85 means more cases of dementia. The overall incidence in this older group was 6.9 percent in a study conducted by Leiden University; women are two-thirds of the older population and three times as many women as men suffer dementia.[13]

Studies indicate that men at age 65 will on average have dementia for 6 months of their remaining 14.5 year life expectancy; i.e., over 95 percent of their life will be dementia free. Women suffer somewhat higher levels largely because they live longer. At 65, women's life expectancy is 19 years, and they can expect to live 93 percent of their post-age 65 years dementia free. Following the onset of dementia, men and women can expect to spend 20-25 percent of their remaining life in a nursing home, although those with mild cases, the great majority, typically remain at home.[29]

Caregiver Stress. The stress of caregiving for a demented relative is high, as noted in earlier chapters. Support groups help families cope, but care providers often experience chronic fatigue, depression, isolation, and declining health. Only about 7 percent of caregivers participate in support groups located throughout the country. Professionals—usually nurses, social workers, or psychologists—work with support groups to teach caregivers how to provide good care and yet experience occasional respite from the responsibility. Periodic group meetings provide information updates, allow for exchange of experiences, affirm the value of caregiving, and offer advice on how to cope with problems. The professionals help prevent the development of physical or psychological problems, while improving the quality of care for the patients and lowering likelihood of nursing home placement.[6]

◆◆◆ LONG-TERM CARE

A relatively higher proportion of the elderly received long-term care in residential care (5.5 percent) or a nursing home (2.7 percent) setting in 2000. However, there is a clear distinction between "residential care" (service houses or homes for the aged, similar to assisted living) and intensive care nursing homes. Both residential homes and nursing homes also provide support to nonresident individuals living at home—assistance such as hot meals, help with bathing and other limitation problems, respite care, recreation, emergency assistance, day care, support for home care of terminal patients, and temporary admission in times of illness. Most nursing homes and home health organizations are available 24 hours per day.[2, 4, 15, 16]

Home Care

Dutch citizens have indicated a strong preference for home care—through powerful advocacy organizations. Publicly supported home health care evolved from earlier charitable assistance by private organizations, although home health services are now provided largely by public district nursing units. Pro-competition legislation has promoted a variety of private for-profit home care agencies as well, thus providing greater choice to consumers while forcing the public agencies to offer better services. About 30 percent of the disabled population age 75 or older was receiving some form of formal home help or home health care in 1998.[12, 42]

Overall, about 10 percent of all older people received home help, health care, or both. The proportion rises to one-fifth for individuals over age 80 living in supported housing and one-third for those who live in private homes. Home assistance is used an average of 5 hours per week for 3 to 4 years. Formal assistance from agencies replaces some of the support formerly provided by a spouse but does not usually replace assistance provided by children. Most of the users are in the lower-income categories.[12]

A Long-Term Care Social Insurance Act provides the most comprehensive coverage of any country except possibly Germany, with a strong emphasis on home care and supportive housing. The focus of the Act was increased quality of care, efficient service delivery, and cost containment. The burden of care was shifted toward local communities, with supervision by care managers. The government provides supplemental funding, regulates, and coordinates services but does not get involved directly in delivery of care.[4, 8]

The care manager coordinates care in the home, with GP primary care, with specialized and hospital care, and nursing home care if needed. Specialized education in case management has been implemented and job opportunities are increasing. The demand for case managers is likely to rise as the concept of "a continuum of care" is more widely adopted.[43]

Home services must be prescribed by a general practitioner. Physician visits are paid for by sickness funds, whereas nursing services and other forms of home help are funded under the Exceptional Medical Expenses Act. The older person pays an average of less than 10 percent of costs out-of-pocket.[4, 16, 43]

The home care industry is represented by the National Association for Home Care, and is closely tied with home health care organizations that serve every community. More than half of the older population belong to health care organizations and pay an annual membership fee of roughly $25, giving them special access to home care and preventive care, as well as primary and hospital care.[40]

Home nursing care and personal care are provided by nonprofit nursing care organizations. Household services are provided by separate home help organizations. The Central Home Help Association and the National Cross Association (community nursing) are the largest provider organizations. Some fragmentation of care occurs because these two groups do not always cooperate. Proposals for merger have been under discussion. Approximately 80 smaller private home nursing organizations were also offering services in 1995.[4, 27]

Skilled nurses and other qualified personnel are difficult to recruit because their prestige is relatively low, the work load is high, compensation is more limited than in some other fields, and there is a shortage of young people in the population. A special category of home helpers is available for older individuals who do not need personal care but require assistance with household activities. The individual must contract with them directly; payment comes from a special government subsidy.[4, 15, 16, 36]

Training of Home Care Workers. Training of district home health nurse supervisors is comparable to hospital nurses: four years of nurses training and two years of experience in the public health services. Practical nurses, who do most of the home visiting, have three years of hospital training and six months in the public health services. Both categories of nurses are relatively well compensated by international standards, even though other occupations in the Netherlands may offer higher remuneration. Home helpers have much less training and are less well paid. They are required to take on-the-job training at the beginning of their employment, and incentives are in place to encourage continuity in the job. Nevertheless, turnover rates averaged 25 percent per year in 1990.[27]

Homes for the Aged (Assisted Living) and Nursing Homes

Homes for the aged or service houses have traditionally provided housing and basic personal care services but very little medical or nursing care. However, this is changing somewhat as such homes add nursing care units for residents who prefer not to move. Most residents have their own small apartments with a kitchen and bathroom. Nursing homes, on the other hand, serve chronically ill patients who need extensive complex nursing care but very little specialist physician care. Separate wards are available for rehabilitation and special care of Alzheimer's patients. Since hospice care was not yet widely available in the late 1990s, nursing homes generally served terminal patients who did not need hospitalization.[15, 32]

Residential homes and nursing homes continue to have high occupancy rates despite the increasing emphasis on home care. Waiting lists require as much as 40 weeks for admission to a residential home and up to 17 weeks for a nursing home. Overnight and weekend respite admissions alternatives provide some flexibility and rest for caregivers at home. Except in extreme situations, the age for entry to nursing care at home or within institutions has been raised from age 65 to 75.[4, 15]

Experiments with Long-Term Care Alternatives

The Dutch have a long tradition of formal experimental tests of health and long-term care options leading to innovations that are later incorporated as formal policies. Four types of long-term care demonstration experiments were conducted in the 1980s and 1990s:[5, 38]

1. A publicly funded personal budget was provided for care in the home to be allocated by the patient under the guidance of a case manager. The goal was to optimize flexibility in meeting individual needs while enabling continuing independence (undertaken in Rotterdam).
2. Coordination was increased between informal home care and formal community service providers within a region through a flexible service package (in Groningen and Bevelanden).
3. Integration of planning and execution of home care, day care, meals, and other services involving various home service groups, health professionals, and volunteers was increased through self-governing care networks (in Nieuwegein and Venlo).
4. A care manager helped create greater coherence in care of disabled elderly, whether in sheltered housing, homes for the elderly, or nursing homes, enabling older individuals to remain in one home rather than moving to more intensive care as disability increased (in the Hague and Enschede).

The demonstrations indicated which alternatives worked most effectively, with findings used to improve current programs.

The Groningen Activity Restriction Scale. Dutch researchers have developed and tested a scale for measuring disability affecting usual activities of daily living and instrumental activities of daily living. The scale has proven highly useful as a method of precisely describing and measuring the degree of disability caused by chronic health conditions. It also helps assess the need for home care or other forms of support.[18, 35]

Multipurpose Centers. Several communities have experimented with multipurpose care centers offering a variety of services such as temporary respite care, adult day care, out-patient physical therapy, meals, and other options. Funding is provided from a mixture of local, provincial, and national sources. The results of these tests revealed rather clearly that multipurpose centers are beneficial to older people and are more efficient for providers of care.[36]

Case Management. Case management research has indicated that nursing home placement can often be avoided if disabled elderly are provided with adequate resources and a case manager who serves as an advisor and "care consultant." The consultant is responsible for evaluating the living situation and available options, while also helping calculate a budget for health care. The older person works with the case manager in the use of insurance funds to secure quality health care at the lowest cost.[43]

Results indicated that only 38 percent of the people in the case management participant group moved to a home for the aged, compared to 73 percent of the control group. Moreover, the cost of services for the participant group was lower and participants scored higher than the control group in ability to undertake activities of daily living. This kind of evidence supports both the concept of case management and the use of a personal health care budget allowance.[43]

Evaluations also indicate that as individuals adjust to using their allocation, they prefer greater assistance from professionals and less help from family and friends—in part because of increasing disability and in part because they do not want to burden their informal caregivers although they have funds to pay them. Using professional help appears to increase feelings of independence and autonomy. However, professional help also reflects a decrease in the size of the informal support network with advancing age and greater disability.[41, 42]

Overall results from the various experiments indicated that home care was not consistently more effective than institutional care. However, older individuals with fewer disabilities were able to continue living at home with increased and more integrated home care. Somewhat fewer individuals entered nursing homes, and the quality of home health services improved. However, costs for home care increased. Professional and voluntary help were better used in part because of the case manager role. Quality of life for older people clearly increased.[4, 5]

Use of Supportive Technology

Use of technical aids such as alarm systems, canes, wheelchairs, grab-bars, and shower chairs is widespread—helping to increase the potential for independent living and substituting for more expensive home health or nursing home care. Women tend to use technology aids like wheel chairs and other mobility assistance more than men. Technology is used more in nursing homes, or in other forms of sheltered housing, than in homes for the aged or in private homes. Sheltered housing often provides technical devices as part of the service. Individuals with some form of informal care in the home tend to use technology more than those with no assistance.[20]

Essential technical equipment was provided by the health insurance funds without personal cost until 1994. A cost-saving cutback was implemented requiring older citizens with resources to be responsible for the purchase of equipment. Those with higher incomes obviously had greater access to needed equipment than lower-income individuals regardless of insurance compensation.[20]

Occupational therapists are principally responsible for advising older individuals about using supportive devices, usually in association with hospitals, nursing homes, or rehabilitation centers. They are unlikely to work in home care agencies, which means that home help aids and visiting nurses typically have the responsibly for informing disabled elderly of the options available to them. Several barriers continue to impede optimum use of technology—negative attitudes, lack of knowledge about services, poor functional status, and poor housing conditions.[20]

Hospice

Use of hospices was not widespread until the 1990s and remains well behind many other countries. Local hospice centers have been opened in some communities to serve as relief and support facilities for terminal patients and their families, usually with volunteer staffing. Advocates are urging eventual expansion of services throughout the country.[38]

◆◆◆ HOUSING AND COMMUNITY

The Dutch have worked vigorously to integrate the elderly with the remainder of the community. Good housing in an appropriate community setting is considered a core priority. Several basic principles underlie public policies.[3]

- Older people should be both encouraged and enabled to live independently as long as possible.
- Housing should be adapted to fit the unique needs of older people as they age and become less mobile and functional.
- Additional support such as alarm systems, access to home caretakers, and provision of home health care should be provided as necessary to maintain independence.
- Residential and nursing home care should be deemphasized in favor of maintenance of the elderly in private dwellings insofar as possible.

The country has long had something of a housing shortage, with essentially all forms of accommodation filled to capacity, although the situation improved somewhat in the 1990s. Since housing and associated community services are relatively expensive about 20 percent of the elderly with lower incomes received rent subsidies in 1993. Support sometimes was in the form of funds to adapt their housing to accommodate disabilities, to avoid forcing them to move to alternative housing. Home repair resources have been available as well.[30, 32, 40]

Several major housing types are summarized in Table 13–1. Most older individuals have been lifelong residents of the same community and live in private homes in close proximity to children, other relatives, and friends. Two-thirds of the population age 75 or older lived in rental houses or apartments owned by local housing associ-

TABLE 13–1   Range of Housing Types and Level of Disability

Types	Degree of Disability
Standard private homes	Low
Adapted private homes	∧
Sheltered housing	∧
Service or assisted living apartments	∧
Cluster apartments with assistance	∨
Homes for the aged	∨
Apartments associated with nursing homes	∨
Nursing homes	High

Source: Data from Vliet, 1995: 107.

ations. When disability occurs they are supported and cared for in this context. A relatively small proportion (primarily the oldest old) requires high-support accommodations.[15, 32]

Adapted Homes

About 5 percent of older people live in private homes "adjusted" to the needs of slightly or seriously disabled individuals—with ramps to accommodate wheel chairs, easy entry, and technology for ready use by disabled individuals. A high proportion of such homes are managed by local public housing corporations, and residents must pay a designated proportion of their retirement income for rent. More affluent disabled individuals reside in privately operated and well-appointed commercial adjusted apartments or condominiums where they can receive ongoing home assistance.[16]

Sheltered Housing

Another 5 percent live in sheltered housing, also adjusted, but with daily home help services, meals, and 24-hour alarm systems. The homes are often part of a complex that may also include independent living and/or a nursing home. Each residence is likely to have an emergency communication system directly linked to a caretaker. Meals and social activities can be secured through home care agencies or from a nearby home for the aged or nursing home.[16]

The Anton Pieckhofje housing project in the city of Haarlem, a shelter with minimal restrictions, is described in Illustration 13–2.

Illustration 13–2
THE ANTON PIECKHOFJE RESIDENTIAL COMPLEX

The two-story project was built by a nonprofit housing corporation as an experiment with advanced concepts in elderly housing for individuals with mental or physical disabilities. Six separate buildings house six demented individuals in separate rooms but with a common living/dining room, a kitchen, a large bathroom, and a guest room. Entrance to each dwelling is through a secured interior passageway accessible to all residents and connected to an interior courtyard.

One caregiver is available for each dwelling during the day and two caregivers are available at night for the entire complex. Home care is available for each dwelling as needed for housekeeping. Residents have their own furniture, can keep pets, and can be visited anytime by friends and family. The use of medication is minimal, and no strict daily regimen governs residents. Individuals do their own laundry, cleaning, and meal preparation to the degree of their ability and interest. They can go shopping with an escort. Furthermore, three-room dwellings for spouses and other caregivers are available on the second floor of the complex to maintain social contact and support as much as possible.

Source: Data from Vliet, 1995: 102-103.

Service and Cluster Apartments and Homes for the Aged

Homes for the aged have a long tradition beginning with church sponsorship in the Middle Ages. In the 1950s and 1960s the national government began to support the construction of new accommodations to meet the growing demand. Roughly 7 percent of the older population were residents of some form of home for the aged in the 1970s and 1980s, with complexes ranging in size from a few small apartments to more than 100 units. Most units consisted of a living room and bedroom combination, kitchenette, and bathroom.[32, 37, 40]

Service or assisted living apartments are somewhat more recent but have many characteristics similar to homes for the aged. Provincial governments have responsibility for financing and supervision of the new units, although with some federal government support. Residents must pay rent from retirement funds that collectively cover about 40 percent of costs.[16]

The homes have more recently become strictly "need-tested" with carefully defined levels of disability required for entry. Intensity of care has increased so that less disabled individuals are accommodated in less costly adjusted and sheltered housing described above. Homes for the aged and service houses have provided enough support to accommodate aging in place, with special care units in some complexes for individuals with dementia. Admission policies and procedures for homes for the aged, service houses, and nursing homes have been integrated to help assure the accommodation fits the level of need.[16]

Nursing Homes

The national government strictly limits the allocation of nursing home spaces, defines qualifications for entry, and has encouraged expansion of services into the community, as noted earlier. Roughly one-fourth of day care patients eventually become permanent residents of nursing homes. Some nursing homes also provide medical and occasional nursing care for residents of homes for the aged and provide home health care to other community residents.[16]

Many of the relatively new units have received international recognition for their creative and functional design. Hallways have been converted to streetlike settings with plants and decoration. Atriums are used to create an outdoorlike atmosphere. Deliberate efforts are made to have the buildings fit the social needs of residents. Services are close at hand, and members of the outside community are encouraged to use facilities such as dining rooms, which also serve as public restaurants. Some have a bar or lounge for social drinking before and after meals, following the tradition in most towns.[31]

Long-Term Care in Hospitals

Hospitals serve as the temporary home for substantial numbers of disabled older people, especially those at the most advanced ages or with the most severe physical or mental problems. Seventeen hospitals, especially university-related hospitals, have special geriatric units.[15, 16]

Elderly Service Centers

Local service centers for the elderly were initiated in 1963 with an emphasis on (1) sociocultural activities, (2) services such as meals on wheels, laundry services, and foot care, and (3) information and advice. Most municipalities now have such centers, although their specific functions vary widely. Sociocultural activities are initiated by local residents, with services often provided by volunteers. Full-time staff (usually social workers) are responsible for providing information and advice. The centers have focused strongly in recent years on coordination of services to increase convenience of access.[16]

◆◆◆ ECONOMIC AND FINANCIAL ISSUES

The government has progressively developed a series of national policies to provide comprehensive financial support for the older population, to supplement the social benefits discussed above.

Income Support

A comprehensive pension system was initiated in 1957 with a minimum income established guaranteeing that no older person would live in poverty. Federally collected payroll taxes and supplementary taxes are allocated to municipal governments for distribution. Everyone who has worked all of their adult years is assured a pension of 80 percent of average salary at the time of retirement, a higher benefit than in most countries.[32]

Individual retirement resources still vary widely depending on work history and accumulated assets. Supplemental pensions through the workplace contribute an average of more than 25 percent of retirement income; personal savings account for about 18 percent; Social Security provides about 55 percent; and the rest comes from other sources.[32]

The Social Security system and other services have been characterized as "passionate ageism." The strong Dutch labor union movement has been instrumental in developing public policies. However, because of the high cost to current workers, proposals are under consideration to minimize early retirement and encourage extension of work life to a more advanced age.[32]

Health Care Finance

Overall costs of health care were 9.3 percent percent of GDP in 1997, despite global budgeting for hospitals and fee regulation of physicians. Eighty percent of the resources were generated through payroll taxes and general taxation; private health care insurance accounted for the other 20 percent. Long-term care (home care and nursing home care) and mental health care are funded through the Exceptional Medical Expenses Act financed by employer taxes. Services such as hearing aids, eye glasses, physical therapy, and certain other medical needs require a co-payment.[34]

The sickness funds insured approximately 61 percent of the population who had relatively lower incomes in 1997; the other 39 percent with higher incomes had the choice of purchasing private health insurance. Private insurance typically provided more complete coverage than was available through sickness funds. In addition to paying for health care, the insurance programs provide families with an ongoing replacement income when the wage earner(s) is/are ill or incapacitated.[18]

Cost-Control Initiatives

Legislation in 1993–1994 encouraged greater competition between sickness insurance funds. The government has shifted greater responsibility to the individual and the private sector, in part because organized consumer groups demanded that the health care system respond more to individual needs.[43]

The cost-containment efforts reduced hospital bed capacity and increased ambulatory and out-patient care. Information systems were further developed to monitor utilization and generate more detailed cost data as the basis for improved efficiency. The global budgeting system for hospitals and fee regulation for physicians were strengthened. Fewer referrals to specialists by general practice physicians were encouraged.[21]

Substituting lower-cost community long-term care for higher-cost institutional care is among the cost-control strategies. The revised policies attempt to enhance services while tightening the management structure. Coordination between professionals working with an individual at home is intended to create more efficient care while diminishing errors. These options are collectively designed to maintain or improve health and prolong the time disabled individuals can remain at home, while at the same time lowering costs.[5]

A deliberate attempt was made in the 1990s to focus on "aging in place." Long-term care insurance is guaranteed for every older person and is financed from taxes adjusted by income level. Supplemental insurance is available to cover dental care, physical therapy, and other services not covered by the guaranteed insurance. Older individuals can choose their insurer and their care providers, thus promoting competition based on cost and quality. Risk is transferred from the government to insurers and providers, as managed competition attempts to do in the United States.[16]

◆◆◆ LIFESTYLE: WORK, RETIREMENT, AND LEISURE

The older Dutch population tends to be very active in maintaining their health. Although few continue to work in formal jobs after retirement, they contribute in many ways to maintenance and enhancement of towns and the countryside.

Very few people worked beyond age 65 and only 20 percent worked beyond age 60 in the mid-1990s—the lowest among advanced industrial countries. Many of the men and women who continue are employed only on a part-time basis or as volunteers.[28]

Volunteerism is actively supported through public and private initiatives. Younger retirees are heavily engaged in helping support their older neighbors, in private homes, homes for the aged, nursing homes, and in hospitals. Support groups are organized to help needy groups in the community. Organizations of older persons arrange group trips within the country and elsewhere and develop other activities on the basis of common interests. Older citizens with special professional or technical skills provide organized consultation and advice in their field within the country and in other countries—at no salary except for expenses. Senior citizens can take advantage of a Senior Citizen's Pass that provides for discounts at a wide range of recreational and transportation facilities.[32]

The government encourages educational initiatives for older citizens through universities and communities, although most continuing education activity is initiated by organizations of older individuals based on their collective interests. Courses are available on retirement, political involvement, and other topics of common interest. Some special courses are offered through so-called "universities of the third age."[32]

◆◆◆ NOTEWORTHY FEATURES AND MAJOR CHALLENGES

The Netherlands is clearly well advanced in providing for older people, despite some continuing challenges.

Noteworthy Features

The Dutch system of services for the older population is among the most integrated, comprehensive, and well-financed combination of programs anywhere—collectively leading to a long life expectancy and high quality of life. The formal programs are supported by strong family solidarity and integrated, responsible, community programs. Essentially every community supports a network of community centers providing information, assistance, and recreational opportunities. Older people reciprocate by vigorously providing service to their communities.

Geriatrics specializations are highly developed in all major categories of health care for the elderly. Social pharmacy emphasizes the appropriate use of drugs and involves pharmacists as very active participants in elderly health care—as full partners with physicians, nurses, and other health professionals. Computerized registration is used to help avoid inappropriate prescriptions and harmful use of drugs.

Mental health care for older people is more advanced than in most countries, under the direction of highly trained geriatric psychiatrists, psychologists, and social workers. Home care and institutional long-term care are closely coordinated and highly developed. Long-term care insurance is part of the larger package of benefits and pays most of the costs except for room and board charges in supported housing.

Good housing for the elderly has been central to public policy. Consequently, high quality and appropriate housing is available to most older people, although shortages mean that some individuals must wait for months to secure access to supported homes. Many of the facilities are highly advanced and have received international recognition.

Major Challenges

Several major challenges are clear: financing the comprehensive support system for the increasing older population; adjusting to the movement of government toward greater privatization and individual responsibility; and increasing voluntary support from families and communities to offset the lowered federal support. The transition to greater individual, family, and community responsibility is generated in part by the realization that as the number and proportion of older individuals increases it will be difficult for the federal government to finance resources and support.[17]

The change represents a considerable transition from the previous focus on national government responsibility. Communities and families have a long history of assuming a major part of the support role and thus support the idea of lowered federal involvement in day-to-day activities. It remains to be seen whether local governments, families, and individuals can maintain the quality of life for older people that has already been achieved.

◆◆◆ SUMMARY AND CONCLUSIONS

The Dutch people have been diligent in designing a comprehensive system of services. Geriatric health services for older people are intended to improve primary and chronic care. Physicians are securing training in geriatrics enabling them to understand and manage chronic health care. Computerized pharmacies help to minimize problems with misuse of medications, while increasing quality of drug treatment.

Long-term care programs increasingly emphasize home care and are improving the alternatives to institutional care. Case management is enhancing coordination of services, improving outcomes and decreasing costs. Mental health care for the elderly is improving. A generally high satisfaction rate suggests the system of care is quite effective from the older person's perspective.

Income support essentially guarantees that no older individuals will live in poverty. Subsidized repair and upgrading of housing provides assurance that the quality of living space and community environment will not fall below a certain standard. Several types of housing are available to fit the needs of individuals with various types and degrees of disability.

The Dutch have systematically used scientific methods to study and evaluate a wide range of programs in an effort to test their usefulness and value to the older population. Outcome studies serve as very useful illustrations of public policies and programs that appear to work. These have led directly to major policy and program changes of benefit to quality of life for the older population.

◆◆◆ REFERENCES

1. Beekman, A.T.F., D.M.W. Kriegsman, D.J.H. Deeg, and W. van Tilburg (1995). The Association of Physical Health and Depressive Symptoms in the Older Population: Age and Sex Differences, *Sociology, Psychiatry, and Psychiatric Epidemiology*, 30, 1, 32–38.

2. Berg Jeths, Anneke van den, and Mats Thorslund (1994). Will Resources for the Elder Care Be Scarce? *Hastings Center Report*, 24 (5), 6–10.

3. Blom, Rik (1990). Staying Put in the Netherlands, in *Supporting Older People in General Housing*, Oxford: The Oxford Conference at Wadham College, 26–32.

4. Coleman, Barbara J. (1995). European Models of Long-Term Care in the Home and Community, *International Journal of Health Services*, 25, 3, 455–74.

5. Coolen, Jan (ed) (1993). *Changing Care for the Elderly in the Netherlands*, Assen/Maastricht, The Netherlands: Van Gorcum.

6. Cuijpers, Pim, Clemens M. H. Hosman, and Joep M. A. Munnichs (1996). Change Mechanisms of Support Groups for Caregivers of Dementia Patients, *International Psychogeriatrics*, 8, 4, 575–87.

7. Dautzenberg, Maaike G. H., Jos P. M. Diederiks, Hans Philipsen, Fred C. J. Stevens (1998). Women of a Middle Generation and Parent Care, *International Journal of Aging and Human Development*, 47 (4), 241–362.

8. Edvartsen, Trond O. (1996). Possibilities and Problems in Cross-Country Comparative Analysis of Long-Term Care Systems, in Roland Eisen and Frank A. Sloan (eds), *Long-Term Care: Economic Issues and Policy Solutions*, Boston: Kluwer Academic Publishers, 25–44.

9. Foppe van Mil, J. W., Dick F. J. Tromp, James C. McElnay, Lolkje T. W. de Jong-van den Berg, and Rein Vos (1999). Development of Pharmaceutical Care in the Netherlands: Pharmacy's Contemporary Focus on the Patient, *Journal of the American Pharmaceutical Association*, 39 (3), 395–401.

10. Gierveld, Jenny De Jong, and Theo Van Tilburg (1999). Living Arrangements of Older Adults in the Netherlands and Italy: Co-residence Values and Behavior and Their Consequences for Loneliness, *Journal of Cross-Cultural Gerontology*, 14 (1), 1–24.

11. Groenou, Marjolein Broese van, and Theo van Tilburg (1997). Changes in the Support Networks of Older Adults in the Netherlands, *Journal of Cross-Cultural Gerontology*, 12 (1), 23–44.

12. Groenou, Marjolein Broese van, and Theo van Tilburg (1996). The Personal Network of Dutch Older Adults: A Source of Social Contact and Instrumental Support, in Howard Litwin (ed), *The Social Networks of Older People: A Cross-National Analysis*, Westport, CT: Praeger, 163–82.

13. Gussekloo, J., T. J. Heeren, G. J. Izaks, G. J. Ligthart, and H. G. M. Rooijmans (1995). A Community Based Study of the Incidence of Dementia in Subjects Aged 85 Years and Over, *Journal of Neurol Neurosurg Psychiatry*, 59 (5), 507–10.

14. Heiligers, Phil J. M., and L. Hingstman (2000). Career Preferences and the Work—Family Balance in Medicine: Gender Differences Among Medical Specialists, *Social Science and Medicine*, 50, 1235–46.

15. Hoek, J. Frank, Brenda W. J. H. Penninx, Gerard J. Ligthart, and Miel W. Ribbe (2000). Health Care for Older Persons, A Country Profile: The Netherlands, *Journal of the American Geriatric Society*, 48 (1), 214–17.

16. Huijsman, Robbert (1993). Care Provisions for the Elderly: A Review, in Jan Coolen (ed), *Changing Care for the Elderly in the Netherlands*, Assen/Maastricht, The Netherlands: Van Gorcum, 23–45.

17. Kees, C. P., and M. Knipscheer (1992). The Netherlands in European Perspective, in Hal L. Kendig, Akiko Hashimoto, and Larry C. Coppard (1992). *Family Support for the Elderly*, New York: Oxford University Press, 147–59.

18. Kempen, Gertrudis I. J. M., Johan Ormel, Els I. Brilman, and John Relyveld (1997). Adaptive Responses Among Dutch Elderly: The Impact of Eight Chronic Medical Conditions on Health-Related Quality of Life, *American Journal of Public Health*, 87, 1, 38–44.

19. Kerkhof, A. J. F. M., A. Ph. Visser, R. F. W. Diekstra, and P. M. Hirschhorn (1991). The Prevention of Suicide Among Older People in the Netherlands: Interventions in Community Mental Health, *Crisis*, 12 (2), 59–72.

20. Klerk, Mirjam M.Y., de, Robbert Huijsman, and Joseph McDonnell (1997). The Use of Technical Aids by Elderly Persons in the Netherlands: An Application of the Anderson and Newman Model, *The Gerontological Society of America*, 37, 3, 365–73.

21. Lassey, Marie L., William R. Lassey, and Martin J. Jinks (1997). *Health Care Systems Around the World: Characteristics, Issues, Reforms*, Upper Saddle River, NJ: Prentice Hall.

22. Lau, Hong S., Karin S. Beuning, Ennie Postma-Lim, Liesbeth Klein-Beernink, Anthonius de Boer, and Arjan J. Porsius (1996). Non-compliance in Elderly People: Evaluation of Risk Factors by Longitudinal Data Analysis, *Pharmacy World and Science*, 18, 2, 63–68.

23. Marwijk, H.W.J. van, G.H. de Bock, J.M.A. de Jong, and A.A. Mulder (1994a). Management of Depression in Elderly General Practice Patients, *Scandinavian Journal of Primary Health Care*, 12, 162–68.

24. Marwijk, H.W.J. van, Geertruida H. de Bock, Jo Hermans, Jan D. Mulder and Machiel P. Springer (1996). Prevalence of Depression and Clues to Focus Diagnosis, *Scandanavian Journal of Primary Health Care*, 14, 142–47.

25. Marwijk, H.W.J. van, Henriette L. Hoeksema, Jo Hermans, Adrian A. Kaptein and Jan D. Mulder (1994b). Prevalence of Depressive Symptoms and Depressive Disorder in Primary Care Patients Over 65 Years of Age, *Family Practice*, 11 (1), 80–84.

26. Marwijk, Harm W. J., Paul Wallace, Geertruida H. de Bock, Jo Hermans, Adrian A. Kaptein, and Jan D. Mulder (1995). Evaluation of the Feasibility, Reliability and Diagnostic Value of Shortened Versions of the Geriatric Depression Scale, *British Journal of General Practice*, 393 (45), 195–99.

27. Monk, Abraham, and Carole Cox (1991). *Home Care for the Elderly: An International Perspective*, New York: Auburn House.

28. Organization for Economic Cooperation and Development (OECD) (1995). *The Labour Market and Older Workers*, Paris: OECD.

29. Perenboom, Rom J.M., Hendriek C. Boshuizen, Monique M.B. Breteler, Alewijn Ott, and Harry P.A. Van de Water (1996). Dementia-Free Life Expectancy (DemFLE) in the Netherlands, *Social Science and Medicine*, 43, 12, 1703–7.

30. Pynoos, Jon, and Phoebe S. Liebig (1995). Housing Policy for Frail Elders: Trends and Implications for Long-Term Care, in Jon Pynoos and Phoebe S. Liebig (eds), *Housing Frail Elders: International Policies, Perspectives, and Prospects*, Baltimore: The Johns Hopkins University Press, 3–44.

31. Regnier, Victor (1994). *Assisted Living Housing for the Elderly: Design Innovations from the United States and Europe*, New York: Van Nostrand Reinhold.

32. Schuyt, Theo N. M., and Gerard h. van der Zander (1994). The Netherlands, in Jordan I. Kosberg (ed), *International Handbook on Services for the Elderly*, Wesport, CT: Greenwood Press, 288–304.

33. Siegenthaler, Jurg K. (1996). Poverty Among Single Elderly Women Under Different Systems of Old-Age Security: A Comparative Review, *Social Security Bulletin*, 59 (3), 31–44.

34. Schuurmans, Marieke J. (1996). The Clinical Nurse Specialist in Geriatrics in Utrecht, The Netherlands, *Nursing Clinics of North America*, 31, 3, 535–47.

35. Suurmeijer, Theo P. B. M., Dirk M. Doeglas, Torbjorm Moum, Serge Briancon, Boudien Krol, Robbert Sanderman, Francis Guillemin, Anders Bjelle, and Wim J. A. van den Heuvel (1994). The Groningen Activity Restriction Scale for Measuring Disability: Its Utility in International Comparisons, *American Journal of Public Health*, 84 (8), 1270–73.

36. Talsma, Akkeneel, and Ivo L. Abraham (1997). Nursing and Health Care for an Aging Society: The Case of the Netherlands, *Journal of Gerontological Nursing*, 23 (9), 37–44.

37. Tunissen, Catherine, and Mat Knapen (1991a). The National Context of Social Innovation: The Netherlands, in Robbert J. Krann, John Baldock, Bleddyn Davies, Adalbert Evers, Lennarth Johansson, Martin Knapen, Mats Thorslund, and Catherine Tunissen (1991), *Care for the Elderly: Significant Innovations in Three European Countries*, Frankfurt am Main/Boulder, Colorado: Campus/Westview, 7–27.

38. Tunissen, Catherine, and Mat Knapen (1991b). Strengthening Home-Based Care: The Netherlands, in Robbert J. Krann, John Baldock, Bleddyn Davies, Adalbert Evers, Lennarth Johansson, Martin Knapen, Mats Thorslund, and Catherine Tunissen (1991), *Care for the Elderly: Significant Innovations in Three European Countries*, Frankfurt am Main/Boulder, Colorado: Campus/Westview, 93–120.

39. United States Census Bureau (2000), *International Data Base*, Online at www.census.gov/cgi-bin/ipc/idbpyry.pl.

40. Vliet, Willem Van (1995). Housing for an Aging Population in the Netherlands, in Jon Pynoos and Phoebe S. Liebig, *Housing Frail Elders: International Policies, Perspectives, and Prospects*, Baltimore: The Johns Hopkins University Press, 89–111.

41. Wenger, G. Clare (1997). Review of Findings on Support Networks of Older Europeans, *Journal of Cross-Cultural Gerontology*, 12 (1), 1–21.

42. Wielink, Gina, and Robbert Huijsman (1999). Elderly Community Residents' Evaluative Criteria and Preferences for Formal and Informal In-Home Services, *International Journal of Aging and Human Development*, 48 (1), 17–33.

43. Willems, Dries (1996). The Case Manager in Holland Behind the Dikes: A Hole Filler or Bridge Builder? *Journal of Case Management*, 5 (4), 146–52.

Chapter 14

GERMANY
Confronting Aging and Social Integration

◆◆◆ INTRODUCTION

Germany is the most spacious country in Western Europe with the largest population (82 million) and the greatest economy (third in the world after the United States and Japan). The rejoining of Eastern and Western Germany in the early 1990s has created considerable stress because of the depressed condition of the economy in the eastern states and the much lower incomes. Serious cultural differences had emerged during the 50 plus years of communist domination. Per capita Gross Domestic Product grew to $22,835 in 1998—twelfth in the world. The nation has played a central role, if not always positive, in the history of Europe and the world, and has long been a leader in science and technology. Researchers have been entrepreneurs in scientific medicine, and the government has been an innovator in social services for older citizens.[9, 31]

Each level of government is part of the social welfare system for older people with implementation largely the responsibility of local government under guidelines established by state and national legislation. Both providers of services and consumers have a major voice in public policy, via professional organizations, advisory groups, and health care organizations (especially sickness funds and physician associations). The consequence is a wide array of services, with the source of the funding strictly separated from the service providing agency.[9, 36]

Demographic Characteristics

As of 2000, 16.1 percent of the population was age 65 or older with relatively rapid increases anticipated over the immediate future—as Figure 14–1 suggests when numbers in the age 50 through 64 segments of the population pyramid are considered.

FIGURE 14–1 Population Pyramids for Germany
Source: U.S. Census Bureau, *International Data Base,* 2000

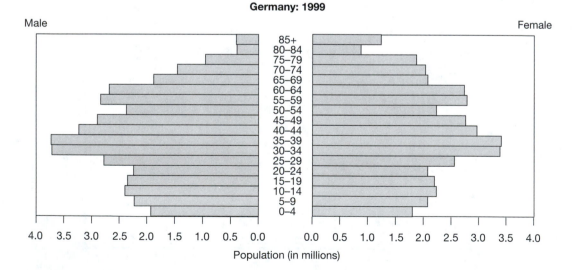

The pyramid also indicates the much higher numbers of women than men in the age 75 and over categories—more pronounced for Germany than many other countries because of the large numbers of men killed in World War II.[40]

The United Nations estimates that the older population will grow to approximately 22 percent by 2020 and 28 percent by the year 2040 when the baby boom generation is largely retired—among the highest in the world along with Japan. The old age dependency ratio is expected to grow from .25 to .48 (the highest in the world) during the same period. Under these circumstances, national income devoted to social security pensions will nearly double from 16.4 percent in 1992 to 31 percent by 2040 unless changes are made in the retirement pension system.[5, 45]

Germany had among the lowest birthrates in Europe as of 1996 (1.3 births per woman age 15–49). The working age population is steadily declining as a proportion of the whole, and the overall population will decline at the current birthrate without heavy inmigration. Life expectancy at birth was about 73 for men and 80 for women (an average of 77.2 in 2000)—somewhat lower than other European countries and Japan but higher than the United States.[5, 22]

◆◆◆ HISTORICAL PERSPECTIVE

The nation has a long history of public social protection for all citizens. Social solidarity is a very important value and has led to a wide range of programs to provide retirement income support, health care, long-term care, disability arising from accidents or illness, unemployment compensation, and housing benefits. The system of social protection has three primary dimensions:[36]

1. Social insurance for pensions, health care, long-term care, accidents, and unemployment.
2. Social equalization benefits for housing and other basic needs.
3. Public welfare in the form of social assistance to those with inadequate pensions or low incomes.

Until the Social Welfare Act of 1961, institutional long-term care was available largely through social-welfare organizations in generally poor quality facilities. However, welfare or social-assistance benefits do not generate public respect to the same degree as payroll tax-financed health insurance or pension benefits. After the 1961 Act, greater focus was given to housing for older people, including construction of higher quality nursing homes. In the 1970s funding was further increased to upgrade quality in both residential apartments for the elderly and nursing homes, with funding and management largely at the local level. The long-term care provisions approved in 1994 substantially increased resources for care of the older disabled population.[24, 36]

The Social Safety Net

The combination of the three forms of protection noted above established a relatively secure safety net—viewed by citizens as a constitutional obligation of the various levels of government. Citizens accept the compulsory obligation to contribute to funding of health care as well as residential and long-term care, through payroll and other taxes. Older people have a choice of physicians, hospitals, long-term care facilities, and other forms of care—within available space and funding. Health insurance funds pay the costs for medical care and hospitalization but pension income must be used to help pay for lodging and food when an older individual lives in institutional facilities. Public-welfare subsidy was needed for about two-thirds of nursing home residents until passage of the new long-term care legislation.[24, 36]

Public policies have supported various forms of involuntary early "retirement" in the form of disability payments (for individuals unable to work at their primary job), unemployment benefits (for those who cannot secure another job), and full retirement benefits (for those with 35 or more years of work). Many of these provisions were instituted partially as a result of the decline in job opportunities during the 1970s and 1980s. The retirement system became a safety valve to open job opportunities for younger workers.[30]

Labor costs have become very high compared to other countries in part because of the payroll taxes to support social security, health care, and long-term care. High unemployment (almost 10 percent in 1997) impinged heavily on employee contributions to sickness funds thus diminishing ability to cover expenses. The integration of eastern Germany has also placed a heavy burden on the sickness funds that serve that region.[20, 35, 42]

A Scientific Perspective

Germany has long taken a scientific approach to social issues. An example of this with respect to aging is the Berlin Aging Study, a multidisciplinary and longitudinal study of aging initiated in 1988 before unification. A sample of 1908 elderly individuals was drawn randomly from the state registry records and was perfectly stratified by age and gender. The periodic measurements are multidisciplinary and include data on internal medicine and geriatrics, psychiatry, psychology, and socioeconomics. Some of the following data is drawn from various dimensions of the study.[4, 26]

Production of pharmaceuticals has long been an important outcome of the scientific orientation. Germany ranks first among nations as an exporter of medications of many types. Older and younger citizens are heavy users of these products as well; nearly 20 percent of sickness fund expenses are for pharmaceuticals, with eleven types of medication prescribed per year on average for each older individual.[24]

◆◆◆ SOCIAL-SUPPORT SYSTEMS

Public policy emphasizes the importance of self-reliance, independence, and personal choice. Older citizens are expected to manage on their own and with family assistance as long as they are physically and mentally able. The family remains the primary unit for provision of social support and is strongly preferred by older individuals in comparison to community or government forms of support. Friendship bonds and support are also very strong. Membership in and support from voluntary associations is less important than in many other countries.[9, 15]

The decline in household size to 2.4 is a consequence of smaller families, divorce, and greater female employment. The extended family has diminished in importance. These changes lower the potential for family caregiving at a time when the need is increasing. Relative affluence and desire for mobility among early retirees may have diminished their interest in serving the caregiving function for older parents.[16, 36]

As in other countries, older women are more likely to be single and more dependent than men; approximately 75 percent of older men are married whereas 70 percent of older women are single. Availability and proximity of children are diminished. Although over 80 percent of older people had living children in 1992, only about 30 percent live in the same state because of high workforce mobility. Despite distances, surveys indicate that 84 percent of older people have daily or weekly contact with children and grandchildren.[9]

Churches and other voluntary organizations play a relatively strong role in helping to maintain family structures and other forms of social support. For example, six nationwide nonprofit welfare organizations support over half of institutions for the elderly, offering 65 percent of all the spaces, and with responsibility for nearly all of the home nursing services.[9]

◆◆◆ PHYSICAL HEALTH CARE

Health care is financed and supported by more than 1000 autonomous sickness (insurance) funds—which collectively cover 90 percent of the population. Some serve specific geographic regions while others serve employees of major organizations or groupings of organizations. The balance, roughly 8 percent of the more affluent population, have private insurance and 2 percent have government employee coverage.[42]

Ambulatory physicians, hospitals, sickness funds, and other elements of the health care system are represented on a national advisory group referred to as Health Concern. This group recommends policies and legislation to improve the overall health care system and has played an influential role in evolution of high quality health care for older people.[42]

Physician and Nurse Roles

Older patients can freely select ambulatory care physicians, but are usually referred by their primary care physicians for specialist treatment in hospitals. Physician associations receive allocations from the sickness funds and serve as the centralized reimbursement mechanism for fee-for-service ambulatory care physicians in each of the 16 regions. Hospital physicians are usually salaried and paid directly by the hospitals. Regional associations of physicians play a major role in management of health care and also monitor the volume and value of services, writing of prescriptions, and referral patterns.[42]

Physicians not only provide primary and specialty medical care but also undertake many of the duties of trained nurses in other countries, in part because of a substantial surplus of physicians. Nurses have relatively less status and training in Germany than in many other countries. As one consequence, a severe shortage of trained nurses exists. The poor status of nurses is problematic for an aging society, which needs the professional nursing skills associated with long-term care. Further professional evolution and greater incentives may be needed to attract and retain an adequate pool of nurses.[7, 28]

Geriatrics. Geriatric medicine has been slow to develop, having been regarded as of less importance than other medical specialties. Relatively few physicians or nurses are trained or experienced in specialized care for the elderly. Comprehensive geriatric assessment as practiced in some other countries is therefore not widely available. Consequently, most care for the elderly is provided by general practitioners who have been the primary caregivers. This is especially a challenge for the adequate diagnosis of such problems as dementia, which ordinarily requires special training and knowledge.[16, 18]

In those instances where geriatric assessment teams have been formed, the physician plays the primary role with relatively little input or involvement from nurses, social workers, or psychologists. Psychologists may be responsible for undertaking psychological tests, but under physician direction. Social workers are involved primarily with the caretakers of the elderly, and less involved with care or counseling of older people themselves. Nurses are likely to provide care functions, but have little real involvement in assessment or rehabilitation.[16]

A longitudinal study at the University of Heidelberg hospital evaluated comprehensive geriatric assessment and home care for frail elderly patients. A home intervention team consisted of a geriatrician, a physiotherapist, an occupational therapist, a social worker, and three nurses. Results indicated the assessment procedures are leading to better results for patients.[29]

Hospitals

Out-patient surgery has been available on a very limited basis in ambulatory settings, although it was estimated to be appropriate for about 9 percent of all surgeries. The greater openness of specialist services and hospitals, provided for as part of 1995 legislative changes, may lead to more care through out-patient clinics. Hospitals were allowed to undertake pre-admission diagnosis and post-discharge care beginning in 1993 (heretofore reserved to office-based physicians). Acute care cases in hospitals will be further reduced, whereas intensity of care per case will increase as the hospitalized population rises in age and acuity.[7, 28, 44]

A 1991 law increased benefits for the most severely handicapped and noninstitutionalized older population—to help avoid the need for extended hospitalization. The average length of stay was 19.2 days for the older handicapped population of Augsburg, Germany, for example, compared to a national average of 15.8 days for all older people.[23]

Advancing Technology

Every older person received a "smart card" beginning in 1995 containing patient information and providing access to treatment from any physician (ambulatory or specialist) or hospital. The card had a microchip memory with personal medical records to help avoid duplication of tests and other services. Security of patient information is a major concern and is being incorporated in the card.[42]

Experiments have been conducted with "tele-health" care systems to provide emergency access for disabled older people living at home. The television and phone linkages include:[13]

- An alarm service linked to a tele-care center by a video-telephone, enabling professional staff to observe as well as hear clients.
- Information, assistance, and counseling to provide ongoing personalized television and phone contact outside the home.
- Home health care on-demand including respite care.
- Training, education, rehabilitation, and exercise routines for clients at home.
- Caregiver support and training.

Evaluations indicate a high level of satisfaction among clients of the system. However, the videophone service functions better when it is integrated with the larger network of available services. The technology is helpful to the degree that it improved access to local services but remains to be widely implemented.[13]

The German health care system has been considered of high quality with equitable standards of care for older people. Patients and physicians generally evaluate the system quite positively. However, nurses tend to be somewhat critical because they have not so far been treated as professionally as they would prefer.[28, 42]

◆◆◆ MENTAL HEALTH CARE

Mental health care has been undergoing a slow process of reform. Conditions for older individuals with mental disorders were widely considered inhumane until the 1960s when the government appointed an expert commission to investigate and make recommendations for improvements in the system of care. The recommendations were published in 1975, slowly leading to major changes. Mental health care continues to be considered of secondary importance to physical care.[33]

Important outcomes of the changes included a decrease in use of large mental hospitals in favor of more community-based services. Seriously ill patients were moved to community general hospitals, with treatment responsibility left largely to a growing number of community-based private psychiatrists and psychologists. Dependent patients may live in sheltered homes or apartments, although some have become homeless. The number of psychiatric beds available in general hospitals has gradually increased—albeit at a much slower rate than called for by public policy decisions.[34]

The mental health care system did not yet have in place a comprehensive and multidisciplinary approach to diagnosis and treatment in the late 1990s, although methods were improving for early detection of the various forms of dementia and other disorders. Formal tools for integrating services between communities and states were generally minimal. The current system of care allocates responsibility to a wide range of agencies. Most of the preventive efforts are undertaken with guidance from local public health boards and community practitioners. When private for-profit or voluntary organizations are available, much of the responsibility is allocated to them by the public health boards. General practice physicians assume responsibility for many patients without necessarily referring to specialists, even when patients may benefit from specialized care.[8, 33, 44]

In the city of Bonn—capital city of the country from 1949 until the late 1990s—schizophrenia was largely ignored as a serious and treatable problem until the deinstitutionalization process began in 1975. Changes were initiated by individuals and small organizations rather than public authorities in the city or federal government. After a prolonged period of review, a plan was developed to meet the needs of schizophrenic patients through "community-oriented psychiatry." Residential facilities were created, day care centers were established, training workshops were organized, and a comprehensive approach to diagnosis, treatment, and care was developed.[34]

Reluctance to Secure Treatment

The elderly in Germany are generally more reluctant than are younger people to admit mental health problems and seek treatment. Few are receptive to psychotherapy. They tend to prefer natural remedies, often rejecting the use of psychotropic drugs. Such attitudes may be responsible in part for higher institutionalization rates among individuals with a mental disorder (especially dementia) compared to those having physical disabilities alone.[3, 25]

The system of care is complicated for the older patient. Treatment of diagnosed problems is covered by health insurance, but rehabilitation is covered only by pension funds. Social care is the responsibility of local welfare programs. It is thus much easier to secure diagnosis and short-term treatment than to secure rehabilitation and social care while recovering from serious disorder. As a consequence the chronically mentally ill tend to be poorly served. This was especially the case in eastern Germany before unification.[33]

Treatment of Dementia

The incidence of dementia, especially Alzheimer's disease, is increasing here as elsewhere. About 5 percent between ages 65 and 70 had some form of dementia in 1993. The incidence increased to 20 percent for those aged 80 to 85. About 60 percent of patients with moderate or severe dementia depended permanently on caregivers, and 80 percent of the caregivers were family members.[27]

Availability of family caregivers is diminishing, as noted earlier. Caregiver burnout is an ongoing problem as well. Moreover, physicians may be reluctant to provide the drug treatment and support that would make home care effective. Consequently, the need for nursing homes to house and care for severely disabled dementia patients is increasing.[27]

Specialist Training

A new curriculum was established in the 1980s for training of psychiatrists, with greater emphasis on psychology and psychotherapy. The number of trained specialists in office practice increased nearly three times between 1980 and 1993. Case managers—usually social workers or psychiatric nurses—have also been trained to work with mentally ill older people, and play a major social support role under the general supervision of a psychiatrist or psychologist. However, little evidence is available that case management makes a major difference in treatment outcomes for patients.[33]

Special Legal Initiatives

A guardianship law was approved in 1990 to provide protection of rights, income, and property for the severely disabled. Older people with mental disorders have access to legal assistance if they or their families feel rights have been violated by the mental health care system. For example, compulsory confinement in a mental institution can only be ordered by a court after very clear indications that the ill individual is a danger to him- or herself or to others. The "gray panthers," a senior citizen advocacy organization, actively promotes the rights of older people in general, but especially of institutional residents.[22, 33]

Evidence of Progress

Services in the community are much improved. The number of trained nurses, occupational therapists, psychologists, and psychiatrists has increased to a level that satisfies the requirements of most regions. Institutional and community supported housing for the mentally ill is generally adequate, although a shortage of psychiatric beds continues in general hospitals. Lack of cooperation between general practitioners and mental health specialists is an ongoing problem—to the disadvantage of older mental patients. However, public attitudes towards individuals with mental disorders appear to have improved considerably.[33]

The Berlin Aging Study. The Berlin Aging Study provides strong evidence that the intellectual abilities of the elderly continue into advanced old age. In the absence of serious disease, capacity to function intelligently remains possible until quite advanced age. Individuals with higher levels of intellectual capacity tend to decline at a slower rate than those with less capacity.[26]

At the most advanced ages in the Berlin aging study (85–103 years old), decline tends to be more visible and causes considerable intellectual dysfunction despite higher intelligence—especially among women. However, large differences between individuals continue to be evident. Among younger and older cohorts overall functional ability was directly related to educational level, sensory capacity (vision, hearing), ability to undertake instrumental activities of daily living, and incidence of chronic conditions. That is, the healthiest individuals with the most education were able to function better.[39]

◆◆◆ LONG-TERM CARE

An increased emphasis on home care has become national policy here as elsewhere. About 75 percent of older disabled individuals are cared for at home by families. Roughly 10 percent were receiving formal home care assistance and 7 percent were institutionalized in 1998, in nursing homes, residential care, hospitals, or other institutions. About 16 percent of those over age 85 were in nursing homes.[1, 20, 21]

Adult children have in the past been expected to help pay for any institutional care costs of parents who do not have the resources. The precise implications of the changes in family capacity to provide care are difficult to determine because of insufficient national data. Most information has been generated by states without a national standard. For example, the number of facilities offering residential care for the elderly has not been clear. However, studies sponsored by the Organization for Economic Cooperation and Development indicate that while numbers institutionalized have increased over the years rates of institutionalization have stabilized.[1, 16, 20]

Public Long-Term Care Insurance

The 1994 Long-Term Care Insurance Act has begun to generate additional data and is already changing the traditional pattern of family responsibility by providing resources for both nursing home care and home care. Preventive care and rehabilitation are especially emphasized. The program provides coverage under the same general model as current health insurance, with financing through payroll taxes. Individuals with higher incomes, who purchase private insurance, are exempted from payroll tax contributions.[36]

The Law specifically allows for the three usual types of nursing home sponsorship: (1) public facilities supported by the state or local government, (2) profit-making private enterprise facilities, and (3) nonprofit charitable private facilities. Private for-profit and nonprofit homes predominate.[36]

To qualify for benefits the older individual must need daily care at one of three major levels:[1]

1. Individuals with considerable incapacity who need daily care at home can receive 25 visits per month from a professional caregiver or can opt for a cash benefit allowing them to pay for care provided by family members.

2. Those with heavy care needs at least three times per day can secure 50 visits per month from a professional caregiver or can opt for a cash benefit for family care.

3. Those with constant care needs who require nursing home residence will have all health care costs paid but must cover basic food and lodging from pension or family funds.

The long-term care insurance plan contributes to a greater sense of security and a higher quality of life for disabled older people and their families. Although it remains to be fully evaluated, the program appears to be one of the most advanced among the countries considered here.

Home Care

Home care in Germany has a long history, although it was not especially well organized until the 1970s. Social-welfare organizations deliver home services of various kinds to ill individuals, including the elderly. Meals-on-wheels and social activities are offered in some localities. Home care staff includes nurses, social workers, home helpers, lay volunteers and young men who serve in the community as an alternative to military service. However, until the 1994 Act national policies did not encourage uniformity and comprehensiveness of services. Most funding came from community and state sources rather than the federal government.[24, 36]

Recent surveys indicate several types of continuing need:[1, 12]

- Home care was needed by 3 percent of individuals between ages 70–74; 6 percent at ages 75–79; 11 percent at ages 80–85; and 26 percent after age 85.
- 20 percent lived alone and needed some form of outside care.
- 34 percent lived in two person households and thus had some support at home.
- 46 percent lived in households with two or more other individuals. The primary caregivers in each case were the spouse (37 percent), a daughter (26 percent), daughter-in-law (9 percent), and other relatives and friends (27 percent).

Home health care and social support in the broader sense have been slow to evolve because no mechanism was available to pay the costs except social assistance programs—until the 1994 legislation described above. Although case management is reasonably well developed for mental health treatment it has rarely been used as a mechanism to assist older individuals with home health care. Increasing numbers of private enterprise home health agencies have been formed to provide 24-hour service to disabled older individuals for a fee.[10, 44]

Cooperation between hospitals and home care programs has been limited. Rehabilitation is largely confined to home care programs and nursing homes, although a few major hospitals with geriatric staff (in Berlin, Heidelberg, and Frankfurt especially) have well developed rehabilitation departments and generally appear to be of very high quality.[7]

Nursing Homes

As in other countries the average age and disability of nursing home residents has been steadily increasing. Hospitals discharge older patients after shorter visits because of health care funding constraints. The average cost for nursing home care doubled between 1977 and 1992, and is far more than the income available from an average pension. This forced a high proportion of institutional residents to seek social-welfare assistance until implementation of the 1994 legislation. About 70 percent of those in nursing homes in 1997 were receiving social assistance in some form because their income was insufficient to cover required fees.[20, 36, 44]

Hospice Care

Modern hospice services have had a relatively slow beginning. The first recorded use was at the Paul-Lechler Hospital in Tubingen during the 1960s. A documentary on the British approach to the hospice was televised in 1971 and triggered a debate about the desirability of expanding use.[14]

The first in-patient unit was established in 1983 at the University Hospital in Cologne and the first multidisciplinary care group was initiated in Munich in 1985— both modeled on the British experience. Since then palliative care units and in-patient hospices have been started in several parts of the country, many associated with nursing homes. The pattern so far has been to care for patients within institutional settings rather than at home.[41]

A German Association of Palliative Care Medicine was founded in 1995. The Medical School of Hanover recently began training general practice physicians in palliative care—especially in pain control and training of family members to care for terminally ill relatives at home and as attendants in hospitals. Volunteer hospice associations provide psychosocial support, cooperating with visiting nurses, physicians, and home health aides. More than 1000 local associations had been formed by 1996. Multidisciplinary teams had yet to become commonplace in the 1990s, although there was certainly close cooperation between physicians, nurses, ministers, and other support professionals. The sickness funds had not yet agreed to fully pay for team members other than physicians, skilled nurses, and home health aides. Reimbursement for institutional care was not uniform among sickness funds. The 1994 long-term care insurance program provides additional reimbursement.[14]

Patient self-determination is not widely practiced, nor is informed consent. Living wills and "do not resuscitate" orders are not in vogue as yet, in part because physicians appear to prefer retaining control of such decisions. It seems clear, however, that concern for the dying is increasing among physicians and the general public— with accompanying steady growth in palliative care and hospices.[14]

◆◆◆ HOUSING AND COMMUNITY

Publicly sponsored construction of housing was a major government policy immediately after World War II. In the late 1940s and 1950s approximately 70 percent of all new housing was public. During the 1960s and 1970s tax incentives and subsidies were initiated to encourage owner occupation of single family units, enabling many older people at all income levels to own their homes. Rent controls and rent subsidies for low-income older people were also the norm to keep housing costs for renters reasonable during a period of serious housing shortages.[10, 32]

Inadequate housing for the elderly has been a major policy issue for some time. Many older families and individuals lived in substandard homes during the 1990s. Eastern Germany had many older and poor housing areas. A high proportion of housing had been rental units under the communist system. The federal government began a new public housing program in the 1990s with a special focus on low-cost homes for the elderly and other lower-income segments of the population. An estimated 3 million new units were needed to meet demand and to replace poor units, especially for single older women.[10]

The older population generally tends to live in older housing throughout the country, whether owned or rented, because of relatively low mobility. Housing renewal policies in western Germany, coupled with general urban renewal, means that very few slums exist. Home ownership was in the range of about 38 to 48 percent among the older population in 1994, considerably lower than in most other economically advanced countries.[10, 17]

The government has emphasized the importance of intermixing homes for older people with younger families rather than construction of retirement enclaves. However, the high mobility of younger people means they depart in large numbers from smaller communities to the large cities in search of good jobs and more diverse lifestyles—leaving a high proportion of older people in many such communities.[9, 22]

Institutional Housing

Three primary types of institutional housing are available for older people with disabilities: sheltered housing or service houses, group homes, and nursing homes. Voluntary nonprofit associations sponsor 17 percent of the resident spaces and publicly supported homes account for 19 percent—largely in small units averaging about 40 spaces. Rental costs are usually subsidized for lower-income residents in sheltered housing and group homes. Service houses tend to have a higher concentration of support services than sheltered homes but otherwise little difference is evident. The most disabled individuals tend to be in nursing homes, but there is otherwise no consistent distinction between characteristics of residents in the three types.[2, 10]

Until implementation of the new long-term care insurance, an extended hospital stay was sometimes the only alternative for seriously disabled individuals because of shortages of supported housing and the lack of adequate home care. The recent changes considerably alter housing options. Lower-income disabled older people can now receive benefits in cash enabling them to purchase the care they choose at home or in an institutional setting.[2, 36, 44]

The presumption is that the 1994 law will largely solve the long-term care housing problem, although it is too soon to make that judgment. Allocation of adequate funding is likely to be difficult if demand grows as predicted.

◆◆◆ ECONOMIC AND FINANCIAL ISSUES

The social security system has taken a different approach than in the United States—in part because of high unemployment and the need to create openings for younger workers. The average retirement age in 2000 was 60 although the official age was 65 for men and 60 for women. No penalty existed for early retirement and no incentives were provided for continued work.[11, 30]

Income Support

Pensions require more public resources than in any other country as a proportion of national income (16.4 percent in 2000)—placing a major burden on the working population who must pay most of the payroll deductions. Public pensions contribute 70 percent of retirement income, also considerably higher than in most other countries. The average payroll deduction for social security was 19.4 percent in 1997 and is expected to rise to 22 percent in 2030. The 1994 changes in long-term care funding increased social security contributions of workers while somewhat decreasing the annual cost of living adjustments.[5, 11, 22, 38, 45]

An additional pension reform act was passed in 1997 for implementation in 1999. If a pension is claimed before age 63, the recipient will have a reduced future pension of .3 percent per month up to a maximum reduction of 10.8 percent. The reform also raised the official retirement age to 65. Early retirement with full benefits can occur only after 35 years of full-time work except for severely disabled individuals who can retire at age 60 with reduced benefits. Disability benefits will no longer be allowed as a form of unemployment payment for older workers; real disability must be demonstrated. Part of the revenue for pensions will be raised through the Value Added (sales) Tax to supplement payroll taxes.[5, 19]

The revised pension system is designed to assure a retirement income of between 64 percent (the minimum) and 90 percent of wages at the time of retirement. Individuals with fewer than 35 years of work will receive the lower pensions. Women can draw upon the social security income of a husband upon his death and receive 60 percent of the husbands benefit. They can also receive pension benefits credit for the years spent raising children and can make voluntary contributions to the pension system. Distinctions between retirement benefits for male and female workers are to be eliminated by the year 2012. In the short term this particularly affects women who have tended not to stay in the work force for the full required period. In 1990, women earned only 42 percent of the male average and were 72 percent of the welfare-assistance clientele. Many older German women are relatively poor because benefits were not available during their younger years. Among those age 75 and over receiving welfare assistance, 83 percent were women.[5, 19, 22, 43]

Considerable inequity in retirement incomes thus remains since pensions are the primary source for 80 percent of retirees. However, despite the inequities, the pension system is generally much more successful at protecting older individuals (especially women) from poverty than is the case in the United States or the United Kingdom. The 1997 reforms are intended to eventually correct most of the inequities.[6, 19]

Health Care Finance

Health insurance coverage is essentially universal. Nongovernment employees earning less than $43,746 (in February 1997) were mandated to belong to a sickness fund. The funds are supported by payroll deductions (12.8 percent of wages in 1995) with half paid by the employer and half by the employee. Retired individuals on pensions have 50 percent of the premiums withdrawn from their pension checks; the other 50 percent is paid as a subsidy by current workers. The health care system used 10.8 percent of GDP in 1997.[42]

In 1997 sickness fund allocations were approximately as indicated in Table 14–1.

Hospital Reimbursement. Hospitals have traditionally been reimbursed by the sickness funds or private insurance on the basis of patient days. However, new policies have (1) limited increases in hospital budgets to the average growth rate of incomes for sickness fund members and (2) partial use of a cost-per-case arrangement much like the Diagnosis Related Group system in the United States. Two types of sickness groups are differentiated: (1) 200 types of surgery and 10 diagnostic techniques are covered by fee-for-service, including diagnosis, food, housing and overhead, and (2) 80 types of more complex surgeries are covered on a cost-per-case basis. Nonsurgery cases are to be paid from the global hospital budget. Hospitals have the choice of staying with the global or maximum budget approach or switching to the new cost-per-case system. Capital needs for buildings and equipment continue to be provided by state and local governments, with very little federal contribution.[42, 44]

The change in incentives encourages hospitals to discharge patients as early as possible and encourages home care. Although the changes present advantages for patients, concern arises about the welfare of older individuals who may not have adequate family or other home care support.[44]

TABLE 14–1   Allocation of Insurance Funds to Services

Service	Proportion of Funds
Hospital Care	34%
Ambulatory Care	18
Prescriptions	13
Dental	9
Medical appliances	7
Nursing Homes	3
Maternity Care	2
Visits to Spas	2
Miscellaneous (travel, funerals, other services)	5
Income supplements during sickness	7

Source: Data from Wahner-Roedler, Knuth, and Juchems, 1997: 1063.

Physician Payment. Office-practice physicians submit their bills to regional physician associations for reimbursement based on a fee schedule. Each type of physician service has an assigned value, with the more complex procedures such as radiological examinations having a higher value. Hospital physicians receive salaries based on specialization, work role, and time in rank. Individuals who have high levels of training, administrative responsibilities, and greater time in service receive higher salaries.[42]

Payment for Pharmaceuticals. Pharmaceutical prices are governed by a "Reference Price System," managed by a committee of physicians and sickness fund managers. Generic drugs are used as base price, effectively lowering the cost of brand name drugs. If prescription costs exceed a target expenditure as specified in a 1992 law, the deficit is to be paid by physicians and the pharmaceutical industry—to discourage overprescribing. The rules have encouraged physicians to hospitalize older patients who need large doses of drugs—with costs paid from the hospital budget.[42, 44]

Choice of Sickness Funds. A 1992 provision allows older individuals (and others) to choose the sickness fund from which they secure their insurance—an opportunity that was not widely possible before. By 1996 roughly 95 percent of consumers could choose among 16 funds during an annual three-month open enrollment period. This is a considerable advantage to older individuals because the payroll tax varies among the funds, and the level of benefits is better in some than in others. Competition is intended to lower costs and increase benefits.[44]

Financing Long-Term Care

The 1994 long-term care act provides insurance financed with additional compulsory payroll contributions of about 1.7 percent of salary (in 1996) from the employer and employee. Sickness funds are responsible for managing the allocations and administering the program. However, a national pooling of resources makes the costs and benefits uniform throughout the country.[1]

Payroll taxes are expected to grow as the number of elderly needing long-term care increases. However, housing and maintenance, whether at home or in nursing homes, is largely financed by participant payments except for social-welfare recipients—helping somewhat to contain long-term care costs.[42, 44]

The actual net growth in expenditures for long-term care are expected to decline somewhat because some of the earlier payment burden is lifted from the sickness funds and social assistance. The 1994 law is expected to increase efficiency, equity, and coordination. Members of the middle class who did not qualify for social assistance and had to finance long-term care privately will particularly benefit.[1]

A 1991 change in the health insurance laws provided for an increase in home health care benefits to 25 visits by home care professionals per month. Although responsibilities of families are relieved somewhat, most recipients of benefits opt for cash payments which means that families continue to have the primary role, albeit with some compensation. Costs for long-term nursing home care and home care have become the fastest growing components of health care in Germany as in the United States.[1, 36]

◆◆◆ LIFESTYLES: WORK, RETIREMENT, AND LEISURE

Nearly everyone retires by age 65. Only 5 percent of older men are engaged in any kind of paid economic activity, considerably fewer than in most other economically advanced countries. The proportion of men working between the ages of 60 and 64 is also lower than in most countries.[30]

The great majority of older individuals in the western German states are able to live satisfying lifestyles. Opportunities are available for a wide range of leisure activities—education, travel, sports, and cultural opportunities. Universities offer "third age" courses, often taught by retirees. Roughly 15 percent of older Germans participate in educational programs sponsored by people's "high schools" or "senior universities." For those with special skills, volunteer opportunities are also widely available in both unpaid and paid capacities as consultants. Councils of the elderly have been formed at the municipal level to sponsor activities for peers and to represent older people in the local legislatures.[9]

Studies suggest that most retirees continue the leisure activities already a part of their lifestyle rather than undertaking new initiatives. Most remain in their home communities participating in family life, local clubs, and preferred forms of recreation. Those who enjoyed travel before retirement are likely to do more of it. Considerable migration of older individuals from the east to the western part of the country has been documented—many to secure better housing and to be closer to family members or friends. Others move for environmental and cultural reasons. Some migration from urban to rural or suburban locations has been documented in western Germany.[27, 37]

A federal Senior's Bureau was established in 1992 to encourage self-help and volunteer programs in each state. German's have a long tradition of community involvement and work hard to maintain the beauty and quality of their neighborhoods. The Bureau also encourages communication and linkages among existing programs.[22]

◆◆◆ NOTEWORTHY FEATURES AND MAJOR CHALLENGES

Germany has in many respects been a world leader in economic and social support for older people. However, the reunification with eastern Germany created significant challenges in the 1990s.

Noteworthy Features

Germany has been a pioneer in creation of funding mechanisms for universal physical health care, mental health care, and long-term care—together providing the basis for a relatively secure safety net. Everyone has free choice of primary care physicians and hospitals, with a choice among sickness funds or private insurance to pay the costs. The 1994 Act discussed earlier may be the most comprehensive effort among modern nations to provide long-term care for disabled older people, who are generally quite satisfied with the health care and social support system.

The income support arrangements are also among the most generous in the world, with a minimum guarantee of 64 percent of final salary as retirement income. Most retirees have much more than the minimum. Strong efforts are underway to improve incomes for older women, who have generally received considerably less than men. Adequate retirement incomes and health care mean that the great majority of older people (less so in eastern Germany) have the resources to lead satisfying lifestyles. A Senior Bureau and the Gray Panthers at the national level lead the way in helping to assure that good opportunities are available.

Major Challenges

As noted earlier, Germany suffered serious economic decline in the late 1980s and 1990s, partially as a consequence of the general recession in Europe, and partially because of the high costs incurred for integration and development of eastern Germany. The cost of labor associated with a high wage scale and high payroll taxes has become a barrier to economic growth. High cost German goods and services do not compete well with lower-cost goods or services from other countries. Many companies have moved part of their production outside the country as a consequence.[1]

Financing of services for the elderly is thus more difficult. The group of older people who became unemployed or took forced early retirement during the late 1980s and 1990s, from eastern Germany particularly, do not have the same level of income support that was available to earlier cohorts in western Germany.[22]

Families share a substantial proportion of the burden of health and long-term home care. Public insurance does not cover all of the costs, which is not a major problem for middle- and upper-income members of the population but a significant issue for those with lower incomes.[1]

Accessibility of services is a challenge for older people most in need. Services tend to be used most heavily by individuals who are well informed and know how to access what they want. Some of the states have integrated various support services into centrally located social-service centers for populations of 15,000 to 50,000 residents but the practice is not universal throughout the country. The primary focus has been accessibility to ambulatory medical treatment rather than other social services, because health care financing is available through the sickness funds.[22]

Integration of geriatrics into health care is incomplete, although more emphasis has been given to geriatric research than in the past and more training of geriatricians is underway. A serious shortage of well-trained nurses continues. Better facilities are needed for geriatric care with greater integration of the various specialties. Coordination among specialties has not always been well managed. The 1994 long-term care insurance program has facilitated important advances.[36]

◆◆◆ SUMMARY AND CONCLUSIONS

In keeping with Germany's leadership among nations in the provision of social benefits and services to citizens, legislation in 1994 provides for universal long-term care insurance. Public commitment to paying for services is a direct outcome of the widely supported communal solidarity principle between the government and the people, which helped generate previous programs offering universal retirement income, health care insurance, and unemployment benefits.

The great increase in the older population is presenting major challenges to maintenance of the social safety net—retirement income, health care, mental health care, long-term care, and housing. The anticipated decline in the size of the labor force because of low birthrates will lead to declining population in the years ahead. Equitable treatment for the lower-income eastern German and large minority populations is likely to remain a continuing challenge.

The health care system is among the best in the world, despite serious problems of integration and collaboration among primary care physicians and specialists, and continuing shortcomings in the provision of mental health care and geriatric care. German health care specialists are viewed internationally as excellent. Improvement may be needed in delivering care to the older patient. More adequate long-term care insurance will contribute to the development of geriatrics and to further integration and completeness of the service system.

The economic and social integration of Europe is likely to have a major impact on the overall support system for older citizens and will encourage dissemination of innovative elements from the German system. Experiences of other countries will also be valuable to Germans. Older people in other nations have benefited from the successful experience of sickness-insurance mechanisms, pharmaceutical research, and other medical research

Quality of life is clearly improving for the older population. The government and the population appear committed to continuing the progress despite the obstacles.

◆◆◆ REFERENCES

1. Alber, Jens (1996). The Debate About Long-Term Care Reform in Germany, in Organization for Economic Cooperation and Development (OECD), *Caring for Frail Elderly People: Policies in Evolution,* Paris: OECD, 261–78.
2. Alber, Jens (1992). Residential Care for the Elderly, *Journal of Health Politics, Policy and Law,* 17 (4), 929–57.
3. Angermeyer, M. C., and H. Matschinger (1996). Public Attitude Towards Psychiatric Treatment, *Acta Psychiatrica Scandinavica,* 94 (5), 326–36.
4. Baltes, Paul B., and Jacqui Smith (1997). A Systematic-Wholistic View of Psychological Functioning in Very Old Age: Introduction to a Collection of Articles From the Berlin Aging Study, *Psychology and Aging,* 12 (3), 395–409.
5. Bosworth, Barry, and Gary Burtless (1998). Population Aging and Economic Performance, in Barry Bosworth and Gary Burtless (eds), *Aging Societies: The Global Dimension,* Washington, DC: Brookings Institution Press, 1–28.
6. Burkhauser, Richard V., Greg J. Duncan, and Richard Hauser (1994). Sharing Prosperity Across the

Age Distribution: A Comparison of the United States and Germany in the 1980s, *The Gerontologist*, 34, 2, 150–60.

7. Castleden, C. M. (1994). A Visit to Germany, *Journal of the Royal College of Physicians*, 28, 5, 434–38.

8. Cooper, B., H. Bickel, and M. Schaufele (1996). Early Development and Progression of Dementing Illness in the Elderly: A General-Practice Based Study, *Psychological Medicine*, 26 (2), 411–19.

9. Dieck, Margaret, and Hans Thomae (1993). Germany, in Erdman B. Palmore (ed), *Developments and Research on Aging*, Westport, CT: Greenwood Press, 113–31.

10. Dieck, Margaret (1995). Housing Elders in Germany, in Jon Pynoos and Phoebe Liebig (eds), *Housing Frail Elders: International Policies, Perspectives, and Prospects*, Baltimore, MD: Johns Hopkins Press, 112–33.

11. Economist (2000). Germany's Age-old Problem, *The Economist*, June 10, 54.

12. Eisen, Roland, and Hans-Christian Mager (1996). Long-Term Care—An Inter- and Intra-generational Decision Model, in Roland Eisen and Frank A. Sloan (eds), *Long-Term Care: Economic Issues and Policy Solutions*, Boston: Kluwer Academic Publishers, 251–84.

13. Erkert, Thomas (1997). High-Quality Television Links for Home-Based Support for the Elderly, *Journal of Telemedicine and Telecare*, 3 (Supplement 1), 26–28.

14. Farnon, Christa (1996). A Personal Exploration of the German Hospice System, *The American Journal of Hospice and Palliative Care*, 13 (4), 32–37.

15. Field, Dorothy (1999). A Cross-Cultural Perspective on Continuity and Change in Social Relations in Old Age: Introduction to a Special Issue, *International Journal of Aging and Human Development*, 48 (4), 257–61.

16. Goldmeier, John (1994). Geriatric Rehabilitation in the United States and the Federal Republic of Germany: A Comparison, *International Psychogeriatrics*, 6 (2), 185–97.

17. Holt-Eakin, Douglas, and Timothy M. Smeeding (1994). Income, Wealth, and Intergenerational Economic Relations of the Aged, in Linda G. Martin and Samuel H. Preston (eds), *Demography of Aging*, Washington, DC: National Academic Press, 102–45.

18. Hornung, W. Peter, and Gerhard A. E. Rudolf (1995). What Provision is Made by Practicing Physicians for Psychogeriatric Patients in Western Germany, *International Psychogeriatrics*, 7 (1), 105–14.

19. International Social Security Association (1998). Germany, *Trends in Social Security: An International Update*, 1998 (1), 16.

20. Jacobzone, Stephane (1999). Ageing and Care for Frail Elderly Persons: An Overview of International Perspectives, *Occasional Papers*, Paris: Organization for Economic Cooperation and Development.

21. Jacobzone, Stephane, E. Camois, E. Chaplain, and J. M. Robine (1998). The Health of Older Persons in OECD Countries: Is It Improving Fast Enough to Compensate for Population Ageing? *Occasional Papers*, Paris: Organization for Economic Cooperation and Development.

22. Karl, Fred (1994). Germany, in Vernon I. Kosberg (ed), *International Handbook on Services for the Elderly*, Westport, CT: Greenwood Press, 123–38.

23. Kliebsch, Ulrike, Harald Siebert, and Hermann Brenner (2000). Extent and Determinants of Hospitalization in a Cohort of Older Disabled People, *Journal of the American Geriatric Society*, 48 (1), 289–94.

24. Lassey, Marie L., William R. Lassey, and Martin J. Jinks (1997). *Health Care Systems Around the World: Characteristics, Issues, Reforms*, Upper Saddle River, NJ: Prentice Hall.

25. Linden, Michael, Ann L. Horgas, Reiner Gilbert, and Elisabeth Steinhagen-Thiessen (1997). Predicting Health Care Utilization in the Very Old, *Journal of Aging and Health*, 9 (1), 3–27.

26. Lindenberger, Ulman, and Paul B. Baltes (1997). Intellectual Functioning in Old and Very Old Age: Cross-Sectional Results From the Berlin Aging Study, *Psychology and Aging*, 12 (3), 410–32.

27. Moller, Hans-Jurgen (1995). Dementia Treatment: A German Perspective on Psychosocial Aspects and Therapeutic Approaches, *International Psychogeriatrics*, 7 (3), 459–70.

28. Muller-Mundt, Gabriele (1997). Trends in Hospital Restructuring and Impact on the Workforce in Germany, *Medical Care*, 35 (10), OS132–OS142 (Supplement).

29. Nikolaus, T., N. Specht-Leible, M. Bach, C. Wittmann-Jennewein, P. Oster, and G. Schlierf (1995). Effectiveness of Hospital-Based Geriatric Evaluation and Management and Home Intervention Team (GEM-HIT), *Z. Gerontol Geriat*, 28 (1), 47–53.

30. Organization for Economic Cooperation and Development (1995). *The Labour Market and Older Workers*, Paris: Organization for Economic Cooperation and Development.

31. Organization for Economic Cooperation and Development (2000). Online at www.oecd.org.

32. Pynoos, Jon, and Phoebe S. Liebig (1995). Housing Policy for Frail Elders: Trends and Implications for Long-Term Care, in Jon Pynoos and Phoebe S. Liebig (eds), *Housing Frail Elders: International Policies, Perspectives, and Prospects*, Baltimore: The Johns Hopkins University Press, 3–44.

33. Rossler, Wulf, Hans-Joachim Salize, and Anita Riecher-Rossler (1996). Changing Patterns of Mental Health Care in Germany, *International Journal of Law and Psychiatry*, 19 (3/4), 391–411.

34. Schmid, Rudolf (1995). Bonn, Germany: A Public Initiative for Private Community Care, in Rockwell Schulz and James R. Greenley (eds), *Innovating in Community Mental Health*, Westport, Connecticut: Praeger, 98–108.

35. Schneider, Markus (1994). Evaluation of Cost-Containment in Germany, in Organization for Economic Cooperation and Development, *Health: Quality and Choice*, Paris: OECD, 63–82.

36. Schulte, Bernd (1996). Social Protection for Dependence in Old Age: The Case of Germany, in Roland Eisen and Frank A. Sloan (eds), *Long-Term Care: Economic Issues and Policy Solutions*, Boston: Kluwer Academic Publishers, 149–70.

37. Serow, William J., Klaus Friedrich, and William H. Haas (1996). Residential Relocation and Regional Redistribution of the Elderly in the U.S.A. and Germany, *Journal of Cross-Cultural Gerontology*, 11, 293–306.

38. Siddiqui, Sikandar (1997). The Impact of Health On Retirement Behavior: Empirical Evidence from West Germany, *Health Economics*, 6 (4), 425–38.

39. Smith, Jacqui, and Paul B. Baltes (1997). Profiles of Psychological Functioning in Old and Oldest Old, *Psychology and Aging*, 12 (3), 458–72.

40. United States Census Bureau (2000). *International Data Base*, Online at www.census.gov/cgi-bin/ipc/idbpyry.pl.

41. Voltz, Raymond, Akira Akabayashi, Carol Reese, Gen Ohi, and Hans-Martin Sass (1997). Organization and Patient's Perception of Palliative Care: A Crosscultural Comparison, *Palliative Medicine*, 11 (5), 351–57.

42. Wahner-Roedler, Dietlind, Peter Knuth, and Rudolf-H. Juchems (1997). The German Health-Care System, *Mayo Clinic Proceedings*, 72, 11, 1061–68.

43. Walker, Alan, and Tony Maltby (1997). *Ageing Europe*, Philadelphia: Open University Press.

44. Wasem, Jurgen (1997). A Study on Decentralizing from Acute Care to Home Care Settings in Germany, *Health Policy*, 41 (Supplement), S109–S129.

45. Williamson, John B., and Fred C. Pampel (1993). Paying for the Baby Boom Generation's Social Security Pensions: United States, United Kingdom, Germany and Sweden, *Journal of Aging Studies*, 7 (1), 41–54.

Chapter 15

SWEDEN
Adaptation in a Welfare State

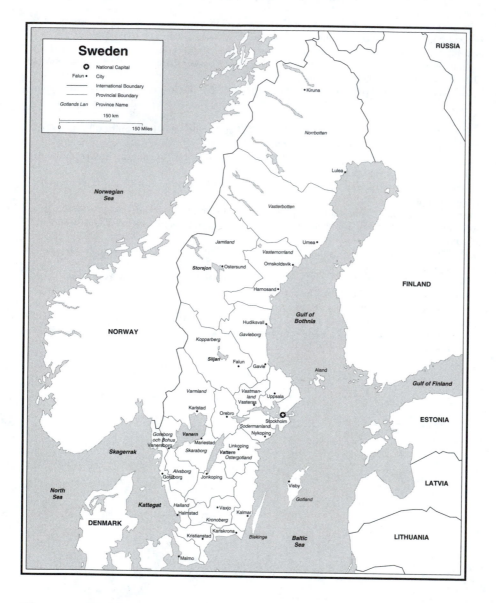

◆◆◆ INTRODUCTION

Sweden is the northernmost country we discuss in this volume. Most of the population lives in the southern counties, while the colder northern areas are sparsely populated. The more urbanized counties have a rich array of services while the northerners are less well served. In this modern nation, advanced industrialization and high productivity have been the norm for many decades—with high living standards for nearly everyone. Social inequality is lower than in most countries and poverty has largely been eliminated. The country has been an international leader in the effort to treat women equally; more than 80 percent of women between age 18 and 65 are employed.[24]

Sweden has been characterized as the quintessential "welfare state." The range and level of publicly provided social services are the most generous in the world. The social sector is heavily financed by government (67 percent of GDP was expended in the public sector in the mid-1990s), which means Sweden has the highest tax rate among modern nations. Unemployment benefits, family allowances, public assistance, and health care benefits are all part of the social benefit package. Ninety-three percent of hospital visits and 87 percent of physician office visits were funded by government-sponsored insurance in the early 1990s.[21, 24]

Programs for the elderly are widely supported by a younger population that generally has a positive image of aging. Attitudes may actually have improved over the years as older citizens have become more vigorous and healthy. An active older life is very much the norm. Sweden might be viewed as one clear prototype for the future with respect to population aging and the complex of programs for adding *length* and *quality* to the lives of older people.[35]

Demographic Characteristics

Sweden had the highest proportion of older population of any country—about 17.3 percent in 1999—and is expected to reach 23 percent by 2020—as suggested by the bulge in the 45 and over categories in the population pyramids of Figure 15–1. More than 4.3 percent of the population was over age 80—the highest proportion in the world. The pyramid also highlights the much higher proportion of older women than men.[38, 39]

Average life expectancy was 79.3 in 1999—third in the world after Japan and Canada. Newborn children in the 1990s can expect to live 90 years on average. If conditions of life and health continue to improve, the typical newborn baby could conceivably have an average life expectancy of 100 years.[1, 13, 34, 38]

Sweden is relatively well off with a GDP per capita of $21,213 in 1998—eighteenth in the world. The population of 8.9 million people is concentrated in urban areas of the south. The dependency ratio (proportion of retired to working age population) was approximately .25 in 2000 and is expected to reach .37 in 2040. Medical costs for care of older people, especially those with dementia, are consequently expected to rise significantly.[39, 41]

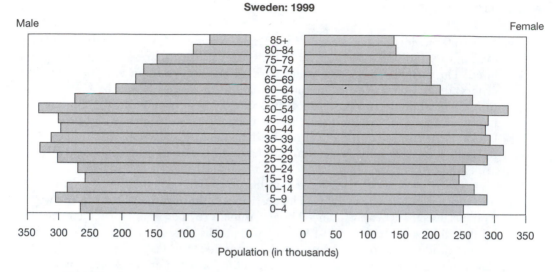

FIGURE 15–1   Population Pyramids for Sweden
Source: U.S. Census Bureau, *International Data Base,* 2000.

However, the growth in older population should level off and even decline early in the twenty-first century because of the relatively low birthrates. Rapid increases in the aged population appear to be over. Services are in place and the needs are more satisfied than in most countries. Because of slow economic growth in the 1990s, resources to support social services have been limited, resulting in major cutbacks.[1, 7, 24]

◆◆◆ HISTORICAL PERSPECTIVE

The welfare approach has a long and progressive history. The first pension systems were introduced in 1914, well before most other countries. Social welfare provisions have gradually become more comprehensive, including a wide range of public services emanating from federal, county, or municipal governments—with relatively little contribution from private sources or voluntary agencies except the immediate family.[23]

However, as resources became limited in the 1980s and 1990s the government began to shift greater responsibility for some functions to local jurisdictions, families, and individuals. Property values have fallen, bankruptcies have increased, and banks have suffered major losses. Employers have laid off workers, contributing to relatively high rates of unemployment (8 percent in 1997). Since employers pay all of the 33 percent of payroll tax for social security and other benefits, they cannot afford to keep employees when production declines. Less emphasis on institutionalization, greater emphasis on home care, and more support for family caregivers, have become the norms.[26, 42]

The 1982 Social Services Act and the 1983 Health and Medical Services Act provided the framework for reform and decentralization of services. Both Acts also reemphasized the universality of access and set standards for service quality. However, public services are now more specifically targeted to the frail and dependent elderly. As growth began to slow in the 1980s, a more conservative government reconsidered public policies. Among other changes, the proportion of elderly receiving public home help services dropped from 38 percent of those 80 and older in 1975, to 21 percent in 1994.[2, 5, 23, 25]

◆◆◆ SOCIAL-SUPPORT SYSTEMS

Personal independence is among the priorities supported by most people—directly contributing to the relatively low rate of marriage. Men and women who do marry tend to wait until older ages than in most countries, averaging age 30 for men and 27 for women in 1990. However, a high proportion of nonmarried individuals co-habitate, functioning much like married couples. Approximately half of marriages end in divorce, among the highest in the world. One outcome of fewer marriages and high divorce rates is diminished capacity of families to provide support for older disabled members.[1, 24]

The relatively low marriage rate has also been characteristic of earlier generations. Women in their 20s during the depression era of the 1930s are now in their 80s or older, and 20 percent of these women were never married. Older males marry and remarry at a higher rate. This means that many older single women have no children, considerably fewer resources than men or married couples, and greater difficulty securing home help or other assistance. Older women have more close contacts in their families than men, take more preventive health measures, have more minor health problems, and more often suffer mental illnesses.[10, 11]

Changing Family Patterns. The proportion of older people with children increased steadily during the twentieth century, rising from 67 percent in 1935, to 73 percent in 1954, and to 81 percent in 1994; the proportion is expected to increase even further in the early twenty-first century. The rate of marriages is increasing, and marriages are lasting longer on average, often to 40 or 50 years. Greater age equality between spouses as well as greater longevity are among the underlying reasons. Four and five generation families are relatively common. Kinship networks are strong and extended. About 63 percent of the elderly had at least one child living within 15 kilometers in 1994. Roughly one-third see family members every day and more than two-thirds at least once per week.[2]

Informal Care vs. Formal Support. Children, other family members, friends and neighbors other than a spouse prefer not to provide everyday care. Instead, families tend to strongly support and seek assistance from the formal support system in the community. Many older individuals prefer to rely on the formal system rather than informal support from relatives. When relatives do provide daily care, they can be compensated, and can be paid by the social-insurance system for periodic respite from caregiving responsibilities.[8, 37]

Only a small number of older people lived with their children in the 1990s.

Most continue to live with a spouse into very old age or they live alone; 59 percent of noninstitutionalized individuals aged 80 and above (mostly women) lived alone in 1994. They seem to prefer depending on their own income and maintaining their own households. The elderly tend to have relatively strong friendship circles: 69 percent see friends every week, and 17 percent every day. The rates are even higher for those living alone, especially among women. Being a burden to family is generally considered undesirable. Independence is an important value in older age as it is at younger ages.[1, 2, 12]

Community Responsibility

The so-called Adel Reform of 1992 made municipalities responsible for providing or subsidizing needed housing, social services, and health care for impaired elderly. The county (roughly equivalent to a state or province in other countries) had previously had direct responsibility. However, public perceptions indicated that management and services should be located closer to the neighborhoods in which older people reside—especially near sheltered housing, old-age homes, and nursing homes. Home health care was thus made an entitlement provided by municipalities, although counties continue to have some responsibility. Dissatisfaction with municipal services can serve as the basis for a grievance lodged with county administrative courts.[5, 13, 23]

An extensive and subsidized municipal transportation network for the disabled is available in most communities and is widely used. Costs are relatively low. In rural communities mail carriers provide banking and other services to individuals who do not have transportation. Eligibility for some of the services requires formal assessment of need.[34]

Overall, it is clear that the social-support system is highly developed with public agencies available to provide assistance. Families tend to be supportive, but older individuals prefer the *independence* of formal home care rather than depending on family whenever possible. The cutbacks in services during the 1990s have, however, made this more difficult.[24]

◆◆◆ PHYSICAL HEALTH CARE

Health care has been a tax-financed entitlement since about 1900 and is universally available to everyone. Public health programs have been in place since at least 1867. The National Institute for Public Health was created in 1938 and has been a very active force in health promotion and disease prevention—part of the explanation for high life expectancy and low infant mortality. The first insurance scheme financed through payroll taxes was initiated in 1947. The older population thus has access to a comprehensive and relatively integrated array of health services with very little out-of-pocket cost.[21]

It is worth noting that Sweden has a formal policy requiring that older individuals have equal access with younger people to all health services. Age is not to be taken into account when resources are allocated. However, when given a choice in national surveys, the public places greater value on allocating limited resources to younger as compared to older people.[18]

Geriatric Services

Geriatric medicine and programs in multidisciplinary gerontology have been available in Sweden since the early 1970s. Several hospitals and university academic departments were established as centers of training and research. Specialty clinics and geriatric assessment units are widely accessible. Most patients are frail and quite elderly. Geriatric assessment is particularly targeted toward patients who are candidates for entry to nursing homes. Specialists indicate a high commitment to patient autonomy, improvement of function, prevention or postponement of functional decline, improved long-term institutional care, and cure of disease when possible.[33]

Multidisciplinary assessment teams usually include a physician, a nurse, an occupational therapist, a physiotherapist, and a social worker. In some instances speech therapists, nutritionists, or psychologists may be consulted as well. Each focuses on the patient's condition and needs from the vantage point of their specialty, while consulting closely and sharing information with other team members. For example, the therapy specialists concentrate on investigation of functional skills, general abilities, limitations, and disabilities. The results are shared with other team members as part of the comprehensive assessment and are used to teach the patient how to overcome disabilities or adjust the environment to accommodate limitations. Special areas of concern for each specialist are summarized in Table 15–1.[33]

The excellent reputation of Swedish scholars in the field of geriatrics is well known in the international academic community. As one example, the Department of Geriatric Medicine at the University of Gothenburg has been conducting a longitudinal study of aging among a sample of older people in that city (the second largest urban area in the country) since 1971. Among the findings were an indication that potential for dementia could be identified well in advance of onset, allowing for earlier treatment, and that 60 percent of individuals over age 70 have some form of cardiovascular illness.[31]

Pharmaceutical Services

All pharmacies are part of the National Corporation of Swedish Pharmacies and have the exclusive right to sell drugs. Pharmacists serve as advisors to physicians on all medication-related issues. A drug information system has been created to help assure that drugs are well documented and tracked for each older patient. The system is particularly useful in avoiding some of the drug-overuse problems that are common in the United States and other countries.[21]

Training of Health Care Professionals

Training of health professionals is among the best in the world. For example, nurses are better trained and more highly rewarded here than in most countries. Consequently, their numbers in relationship to the population are relatively higher. Nurses have major responsibilities in local public health and in other services for the elderly. Still, a nursing shortage exists in the care-taking institutions because of greater opportunities elsewhere.[21]

TABLE 15–1   Specialist Roles in Geriatric Assessment

Specialist	Subjects for Evaluation and Treatment
Physician	Physical examination and functional ability Tests for disease and health conditions Evidence of incontinence, polypharmacy, pain, etc. Treatment of disease and conditions
Nurses	Activity, sleep, rest Excretion function Food and fluid intake Locomotion Motivation Personal hygiene Respiration and circulation
Social Worker	Access to community services Economic well-being Housing status Social networks and support Legal status Social status and security Quality of life Assistance with social and economic problems
Physiotherapist	Ability to move and navigate Balance and coordination Need for aides and appliances Improvement of physical function
Occupational therapist	Cognitive function Communication skills Ability to wash, dress, eat, toilet Ability to manage financial affairs Household abilities Training to improve function
Psychologist or psychiatrist	Cognitive function Emotional state Evidence of mental illness Treatment of mental disorders

Source: Data from Sletvold et al., 1996: 354.

◆◆◆ MENTAL HEALTH CARE

Mental health care changed significantly in the 1980s and 1990s. Large mental hospitals have been replaced in substantial part by mental health wards in general hospitals and community-based care. An expanded network of out-patient facilities has been developed. However, the changes have been difficult for severely ill patients such as schizophrenics who need daily assistance and care; community mental health centers have difficulty meeting their needs.[4]

Treatment Facilities

Counties have had primary responsibility for mental health treatment but have delegated much of the work to mental health clinics in municipalities. Each clinic is headed by a senior psychiatrist who supervises a staff of 8 to 16 professionals. Physicians or psychiatrists see about 15 percent of patients; others are treated by psychologists (15 percent), psychiatric social workers (30 percent), and psychiatric nurses (40 percent). All facilities serve older individuals, with costs largely covered by health insurance.[4]

Dementia

Dementia is a significant problem for families in Sweden as it is elsewhere. It causes major stress to caregivers, especially spouses and adult children, even when home help is available from home health services. Many of the occupants of homes for the aged, service houses, and nursing homes have some form of dementia.[9, 19]

Ethical and Legal Issues

Lack of respect for the unique needs of patients has been among the complaints about the mental health care system. Many physicians and other health care providers behave impersonally toward older patients, under the assumption that they "know best"—with little allowance for patient input. The national parliament passed a Health and Medical Care Act in 1983, in response to public complaints, affirming that medical care should be based on respect for the patient's self-determination and integrity. The Act further mandated that whenever possible mental health care should be planned and implemented in consultation with the patient. Autonomy and informed consent were to be the watchwords.[3]

◆◆◆ LONG-TERM CARE

Long-term care has long been a major public issue. Public policy has been focused on creating services to help older people age-in-place while minimizing the need for institutional care.

Home Health Services

Home care has become very popular; nearly 20 percent of older people received such assistance in the early 1990s. The services include shopping, cleaning, cooking, laundry, health care and personal care, depending on the need. Use of home care increased with age according to a 1991 survey: 13 percent received home services at ages 75–79; 25 percent at 80–84; 39 percent at 85–90; and 44 percent at 90 and older. Among the older population with special care needs, about half indicated they had received some form of public home care; over half had received help from family members. Cash allowances were provided to disabled elderly to pay a family care-giver or for outside providers. A close relative can receive paid leave from employment for up to 30 days for emergency care when a disabled family member is in crisis or ter-minally ill.[2, 35]

Several experiments have been conducted to determine the value of home care services. In Sundsvall, for example, individuals requiring support were able to delay entry to nursing homes by nearly three years (from an average age of 80 to age 83). Waiting lists for entry to homes for the elderly ended, and waiting lists for nursing homes dropped considerably, although there continued to be a shortage of spaces. Studies indicated that as many as half of the elderly requesting nursing home admis-sion could be adequately supported at home if they wished.[1, 5, 6]

Cutbacks in resources have forced reductions. Only 9 percent of older people were receiving home services in 1998, with a focus on personal care for older and more frail individuals who live alone. Night patrols continued to assist clients who may need after-hours attention. The recipient pays only a fraction of the cost, although personal costs have been rising as public support has declined.[34, 36]

Training. Home helpers receive three years of training in home care and prac-tical nursing. They can perform simple medical tasks as well as housekeeping and personal care. Community nurses may have formal training in geriatrics and are pre-pared to perform complex medical tasks in the private home and or in residential care facilities, in consultation with physicians. The policy is to provide a flexible service to clients that can meet their needs and enhance the quality of their lives.[20]

Home helpers have much more attractive income potential than in most coun-tries, with wages comparable to the national average for similar kinds of work. Up to 60 days of paid leave is available per year. They can work in teams or more inde-pendently—which may mean relative isolation from co-workers and supervisors. Child care is often a problem for younger women. The work is sometimes physically and emotionally demanding. As a consequence, absenteeism rates are high, as is turnover, especially among younger workers.[5, 23, 34]

Care Managers. Home care is coordinated by a care manager who is a key ele-ment in improving quality and efficiency. Care managers are responsible for the first assessments of individual needs in the home and manage the follow-up care. Most are trained in university programs designed for the specific needs of elder care man-agement. The training program has some similarities to social work but has greater content in health care and is considered a separate profession. Care managers work in tandem with physicians, nurses, therapists, and social workers.[5, 13]

Day Care and Other Community Services

A comprehensive system of day-care centers is available for disabled individuals. The goal is to provide an alternative to nursing home admittance while prolonging con-tinuing residence in the community. The services are available to anyone who needs assistance regardless of other characteristics. Older participants have a strong role in management and planning. The centers offer a variety of programs, including medical appointments, transportation, grooming, bathing, hair care, podiatry, art, music, cooking, exercise, mental stimulation, and meals, as well as social opportunities with friends and neighbors. Many centers are directly affiliated with sheltered housing or nursing homes but serve other members of the community as well. Individuals are not excluded because of incontinence or disruptive behavior, although a high proportion of clients go from the day-care setting to a nursing home.[13, 17, 35]

Long-Stay Residential Care

The proportion of older people living in institutional settings of any kind declined by about 34 percent during the 1980s. Whereas the population over age 80 increased by 30 percent in the 10 years from 1982 to 1992, the proportion of residents in homes for the aged and nursing homes decreased by 15 percent. The overall institutionalization rate was about 9 percent in 2000 (but 25 percent for people aged 80 and older) for all forms of residential care.[2, 5, 12, 16, 34]

Several types of residential alternatives are available:[20, 25]

1. Extended stay in general hospitals.
2. Geriatric clinics, used for assessment, rehabilitation, recovery, and respite.
3. Central nursing homes, usually large facilities for very dependent individuals (100 to 200 beds) adjacent to county hospitals.
4. Smaller local nursing homes located in municipalities with larger individual spaces and a "homelike" atmosphere.

Long-Stay Hospitals. A sharp decline in long-stay hospitalization began after the reforms of 1992, as municipalities assumed greater responsibility. The decrease ranged from 9 percent to 37 percent depending on location, greatly diminishing the proportion of older individuals in long-stay hospitals.[34]

Central Nursing Homes. Central nursing homes are diminishing in importance as well, with the local nursing home as a replacement. Frail individuals have sometimes been required to move from one type of facility to another, creating a difficult disruption.[2]

Smaller Nursing Homes. The emphasis on creating homelike settings has expanded. New homes tend to be small with few residents per room or single rooms and additional private space. Most are publicly owned and operated by municipalities.[25, 34]

The population of the smaller nursing homes has gradually changed to older and more disabled residents who are nearing the end of life. The period of residency has shortened. Most have illnesses from which they cannot recover, although rehabilitation continues to be provided by the homes and through geriatric departments of hospitals.[34]

Hospice Care

The formal introduction of hospice services did not begin until 1991, but growth has been steady since then. The emphasis is on provision of services in the home rather than in formal institutions.[35]

◆◆◆ HOUSING AND COMMUNITY

The official housing policy since 1967 has emphasized access to healthy, spacious, suitably equipped and affordable housing in well-planned communities. Three types of subsidies are offered: (1) low interest loans, (2) tax benefits, and (3) housing allowances for families with children and retirees with lower incomes. Roughly 40 percent of retirees received allowances in 1994. The combination of these measures made the system one of the most generous and costly in Europe, absorbing approximately 3.5 percent of GDP. The reforms in the 1990s have substantially decreased benefits, somewhat increasing the personal costs of housing for older individuals.[22]

The federal government offers incentive grants to municipalities to build homes designed for maximal independence as disability increases. Government funds are also provided for improvements to existing homes. Home ownership is relatively low in Sweden compared to other countries: only 25 percent of older couples or individuals own their dwellings.[5, 6, 14]

Municipal social-service agencies have been made responsible for all public housing and associated social services in addition to long-term care—including all forms of group housing except cooperative apartments. A conscious policy attempts to avoid concentrations of older people. Rather, the focus is on integrating populations of all ages. However, this policy has not been universally enforced in many of the latest housing developments targeted to the older population.[22]

Supported Housing

The several residential alternatives with some level of built-in personal assistance include:[5, 19, 23, 25, 34]

1. Congregate apartments with full food and support services. Twenty-four hour a day support is available for a monthly fee paid from retirement or social-welfare income.
2. Service (assisted living) apartments constructed largely since 1970. Residents receive housing allowances from the local government to help cover the cost of rent. They have access to home helpers and health care to supplement assistance provided by families. Many of the service-house complexes also contain a restaurant, day centers and recreation areas that provide activities and services for in-house residents as well as others in the community. The activities are often organized and run by the elderly for themselves and their peers.
3. Cooperative housing units organized by the National Association of Pensioners and national cooperative housing organizations. The blocks of apartments are

limited to individuals or families over age 55. Residents join owners associations that help manage common dining areas, communal rooms, hobby areas, and other common sections. Most residents buy the apartments and pay their own way.

4. Group housing for individuals with dementia or other serious disability are usually of modest size for 6 to 8 individuals, each with a private room and shared common areas. Residential staff is available to provide assistance around the clock.

Service apartments have become the key element of publicly provided homes for those unable to afford or manage in a privately owned home. Most residents are of advanced age and in need of personal assistance and occasional medical care. Nearly all take advantage of the home help services. About one-third of the elderly were receiving a housing allowance in 1994 for one of the options noted above.[5, 23, 35]

Availability of homes especially adapted for disabled elderly was quite limited in the 1980s, but special incentives to cooperatives and other private organizations led to construction of significant numbers of new units in the 1990s—most of them for purchase at favorable rates. However, the increase in numbers of frail elderly has meant some shortage of spaces for the less frail who would like supported housing.[13, 35]

Emergency Response Systems

Local governments pay for emergency alarm phone systems as one method for helping to maintain safety and independence. The emergency phones can automatically call for help by pulling or pressing a portable alarm trigger or by pressing an automatic dialing button adjusted to notify a family member. Speaker phones enable conversation without handling the receiver. There appears to be much greater potential for use of modern alarm and communication systems.[32]

◆◆◆ ECONOMIC AND FINANCIAL ISSUES

Sweden has the highest rate of taxation among economically advanced nations, except for Denmark, at about 50 percent of incomes. Much of the tax is levied at the county and municipal levels for health care and other social services. The decentralization process has made tax collection and expenditures on public services much closer to the people.[24]

As noted earlier, the ability of the economy to support social services was severely hampered by the major recession of the early 1990s, which caused the unemployment rate to grow from 1.9 percent in 1987 to 8 percent ten years later in 1997—considerably higher than ever before in history. Young people have been most directly affected but pensions were also impacted.[24, 26]

Means-testing for social-welfare benefits has traditionally been minimal. Everyone received more or less the same benefits regardless of income. The guiding philosophy of government has been to promote equality of incomes supported at a middle-class standard. However, the policy began to change in the 1990s, with greater attention given to the older population having the greatest need.[25, 34]

Income Benefits

The social security system provides a national minimum pension benefit to all older individuals who have resided in the country for 40 years. An earnings-related supplementary pension is available as well. Most employees are also covered by a work-related pension negotiated between employers and unions. Together the three pension types provide an average of 75 percent of gross preretirement income. The system is based on pay-as-you-go financing.[24]

Calculation of earnings begins at age 16, with 42 working years required for a full pension at age 56. The pension system perpetuates a certain degree of income inequality that existed prior to retirement, especially for women. Most pension expenditures are financed through employer taxes rather than from employees—although recent changes have required equal contributions from employees.[24, 30, 35]

The basic pension is financed in part from general taxation and in part from payroll contributions. Under the revised 1999 scheme the basic pension will be allocated only to retired individuals whose supplementary benefits are very low. The revised supplementary pension provides for a minimum pension averaging 60 percent of the monthly income earned in the final 15 years of employment. Both types of pension were indexed to the consumer price index until 1994 when the rate of increase in wages became the index. In addition to the supplementary income, each individual has a personal account consisting of 2.5 percent of their total income going into retirement accounts; the funds can be invested in private pension funds or other investments. The collective changes are expected to increase inequality since they are more advantageous to higher-income employees.[13, 24, 25, 29]

Upon retirement an individual can choose to withdraw the entire amount of the retirement reserve, or it can be allocated on a monthly basis based on earnings of the larger fund. A minimum pension is guaranteed for those who may have worked at low wages or for less than the required number of years for a full pension. The new system allocates greater responsibility and rights to the individual worker.[15]

About 95 percent of retired men received the earnings-related benefit in 1995, although it was available to only 60 percent of women. Roughly 27 percent of lower income retirees also qualified for a housing benefit. A widow's benefit is available if other sources of income are insufficient to provide the basic minimum. As a consequence of these programs, very few older people require other forms of social assistance. Poverty has essentially been eliminated, and the variation in income among social groups is relatively low as compared to most other countries. However, the cost-of-living is high and has recently risen somewhat faster than pension increases.[30, 35]

The major pension reform also helped support needed long-term care. Allowances for parents and caretakers of disabled relatives are counted fully as income. Care of small children and military service are counted the same as working for wages.[15, 29]

The national social security fund is considered by outside observers to be well managed. A substantial reserve has been created that is about 5.5 times larger than the annual payments to retirees. Investments are made in corporate stocks as well as government bonds, housing bonds, and long-term capital projects. The national budget is balanced without relying on the social security fund.[40]

Health and Long-Term Care Insurance

The cost of most health and long-term care services is insured by municipal social-service agencies as a universal benefit and is financed through payroll deductions, with contributions from both employers and employees. The proportion of GDP for health care was 9.6 percent in 1997, with more than half devoted to some form of care for the elderly.[21, 26]

Allocations to home care have substantially increased in the recent period, while expenditures for nursing home care have diminished. However, roughly 70 percent of the long-term care funds continued to go for various forms of institutional care in 1996, while the balance went to home and community care.[13, 23]

About 80 percent of the cost of health and long-term care services for older people were from county and municipal taxes, with federal contributions only 2 percent. Users fees and other revenues covered the remaining 18 percent, including portions from private health insurance and and 4 percent from patient fees. However, the federal government contributes substantial additional resources for research, education, and mental health care.[13, 35]

◆◆◆ LIFESTYLE: WORK, RETIREMENT, AND LEISURE

Retirement and a leisurely later life are considered a right in the Swedish social system. The national value system assumes that full retirement should be the norm.

Work

Only about 8 percent of individuals over age 65 continued to work full-time during the mid-1990s: 11 percent among the age 65–69 group and 5 percent among those 70 to 79. However, substantial numbers work part-time—to a degree in response to a shortage of workers in some fields. No penalty is levied on pensions for part-time work.[27, 35]

However, social security legislation now encourages later retirement. The longer pensions are delayed, the higher the income. Retirement before age 61 is discouraged and a legal right to work until 67 is official policy. Healthy individuals thus have an incentive to work as long as they prefer. Although the proportion of people retiring at earlier ages has increased since 1980, most workers currently continue to the official retirement age of 65, a pattern at variance with other European countries, where early retirement is more commonplace.[29]

Retirement and Leisure

A high proportion of the older people remains active and fully involved in the life of their family and community. There are opportunities for abundant recreation, travel, sports, and other forms of productive activities in the highly developed and prosperous Swedish environment. The Red Cross actively promotes voluntary activities in communities. Senior clubs are widely available as the focus of organized activities. Churches are also active in supporting volunteer and social opportunities.[35]

An estimated one-third of older people are active in political affairs, channeled in part through two national senior citizen organizations which are regularly consulted by government officials on legislation related to aging. Good government is a very important public value.[35]

Interest in living life to its fullest continues well into old, old age as Illustration 15–1 indicates.

Illustration 15–1
CENTENARIAN LIFESTYLE AND QUALITY OF LIFE

Sweden has the highest proportion of centenarians of any country. In the interest of learning more about these older citizens, researchers at Lund University in southern Sweden undertook an interview study in one county with 143 individuals who had passed their 100th birthday. They described the group from physical, social, and psychological viewpoints.

Eighty-two percent were women and 25 percent still lived in private homes or service apartments. Thirty-seven percent lived in old age homes and 38 percent were in nursing homes. More than half could manage the usual activities of daily living with only modest help, although all received some assistance at least once per week, 80 percent from formal caretakers and 20 percent from family and friends. Roughly one-third had been manual laborers, another third white-collar workers, and another third had been self-employed.

As younger individuals these centenarians had been generally more responsible, capable, easygoing, and less prone to anxiety than the general population. More than half drank wine, liquor, or beer (75 percent of the men and 48 percent of the women) but smoking rates were very low. They were not generally encumbered by disease in their lives before age 80. The prevalence of stroke and diabetes was low, but 39 percent had one or more disorders of the circulatory system. Hip fractures were also common—for 39 percent of women and 11 percent of men. Only 20 percent had good vision and hearing and 27 percent were demented. However, more than half considered their current life to be of good quality. They clearly had genetic structures and stable personalities that enabled them to survive better than the general population.

Source: Data from Samuelsson et al., 1997: 223.

Quality of Life

Quality of life appears to have been good for the centenarians described in the illustration—an attitude that appears to be widespread. Surveys indicate that 78 percent of the older population generally feel they are treated with respect in older age. A survey by Eurobarometer (the research arm of the European Union) comparing countries, suggests that older Swedes rate themselves as being treated better than the older population in any other country in Europe except in Denmark. Even those who live alone appear to feel quite satisfied with their lives. A few indicate serious dissatisfaction with income or services available to them.[2, 35]

The overall quality of services has improved substantially in recent years, despite cutbacks in national resources allocated to programs for the elderly, undoubtedly contributing to the high level of overall satisfaction. The reforms appear to have improved the rationality as well as quality of the remaining services. The shift of many key benefits to municipal responsibility appears to have contributed to improved quality and satisfaction—with greater local control and management responsive to perceived needs. A move toward privatization of selected services is underway in many municipalities. The federal government has deliberately changed the rules to allow for greater individual initiative. Block grants have been provided to municipalities encouraging the local governments to experiment with new forms of service provision.[35]

◆◆◆ NOTEWORTHY FEATURES AND MAJOR CHALLENGES

Sweden is clearly among the most generous and supportive nations in the treatment of the older population—generating high levels of satisfaction. However, several challenges are also evident.

Noteworthy Features

Social equality is higher than in most other countries and poverty among older people has been largely eliminated. Kinship support networks remain strong and are supplemented by home care and other services. Younger relatives can receive compensation for care-taking when a parent or other older relative needs assistance.

The health care system provides for tax-financed universal insurance and an integrated array of services available to everyone, with relatively little out-of-pocket cost. Older individuals are guaranteed equal access with younger people. Geriatric medicine and multidisciplinary social gerontology are highly developed, with a strong commitment to individual autonomy and avoidance of institutionalization whenever possible. Pharmaceutical services are managed through a national system—with a highly developed information system to minimize misuse of medications. Nurses receive more advanced training and better compensation than in most other countries.

The long-term care system is focused on a continuum of care, with emphasis on keeping disabled older individuals in their homes for informal and formal support. Home helpers receive more training and better compensation than in most countries. Nonetheless, the very large numbers of older people means that families and home care agencies cannot always provide the range of needed intensive care, thus requiring an array of high quality day care and institutional care options. A generous and universal pension system enables most older individuals to pay for their housing, food, and basic needs whether in private homes or institutions. Other personal care and health care costs for long-term care are covered by public insurance.

Preventive health care, abundant social support, good housing, and satisfying lifestyles mean that many people live well past age 100; Sweden has the highest proportion of centenarians of any country. An active and relatively healthy long life is the norm—making Sweden a prototype for productive and successful aging.

Major Challenges

The major reforms of the late 1990s suggest a public preference for limitations on taxes. Municipalities, counties, and the federal government are searching for avenues to economize on expenditures while still providing the basic services. Service levels were lowered and largely financed from the existing tax revenues. Private enterprise initiatives were encouraged to replace some public services, possibly leading to a two-tiered system as in many other countries. Increases in pension levels are to be linked to increases in GDP rather than based on the consumer price index. Services are being targeted somewhat more toward those who meet means-testing criteria. These changes suggest a major redirection of public policy that may detract from the tradition of social equity.[19, 24]

Recruitment and training of staff for the various programs in support of the elderly is among the greatest challenges although higher unemployment levels of the late 1990s may help alleviate the problem somewhat. The low social status, modest rates of pay, and the difficult nature of the work has made these occupations less attractive than other more rewarding alternatives.[19]

Despite the universality of the care system, wide variation between communities in completeness and quality of services is evident. The larger municipalities of the south appear to be doing much better than the smaller and more rural communities—especially in the north. Municipalities have varying levels of resources despite federal and county government efforts to promote equity.[19, 24]

◆◆◆ SUMMARY AND CONCLUSIONS

Sweden has a relatively small population but has taken full advantage of its resources to create one of the most advanced support systems for the elderly in the world. Life expectancy is third highest in the world and per capita income is near the top. Length of life is continuing to increase, with a consequent rise in the numbers of older and frail elderly who need some form of ongoing support. A survey of centenarians indicates an amazing degree of independence and optimism.

The level of taxation is high but the quality of services appears to be considered worth the price—if high satisfaction of older citizens is any measure. Public policy decisions have begun to support a fairly radical change in service provision—from highly centralized financing and organization at the national and county levels, to decentralized and private services at the municipal level. A state of transition is underway toward more local responsibility, control, and private enterprise. One consequence may be greater social inequity between social classes and between communities.

Expenditures for social services are the highest in the world as a proportion of gross domestic product. The Swedish population has continued to support these high costs, especially for programs focused on the older population, over many decades. It seems quite likely that the support will continue, possibly at a more modest level, with equality, universality, comprehensiveness, and public funding as guiding principles.

◆◆◆ REFERENCES

1. Andersson, Lars (1992). Family Care of the Elderly in Sweden, in Jordan I. Kosberg (ed), *Family Care of the Elderly: Social and Cultural Changes*, Newbury Park, CA: Sage, 271–85.
2. Andersson, Lars, and Gerdt Sundstrom (1996). The Social Networks of Elderly People in Sweden, in Howard Litwin (ed), *The Social Networks of Older People: A Cross-National Analysis*, Westport, CT: Praeger, 15–29.
3. Andersson, Margareta (1996). Respect for the Patient's Integrity and Self-Determination—An Ethical Imperative Called Upon in the Swedish Health and Medical Care Act, *Medical Law*, 15 (2), 189–93.
4. Brinck, Ulf (1994). Psychiatric Care and Social Support for People with Long-Term Mental Illness in Sweden, *International Journal of Social Psychiatry*, 40 (4), 258–68.
5. Coleman, Barbara J. (1995). European Models of Long-Term Care in the Home and Community, *International Journal of Health Services*, 25 (3), 455–74.
6. Coolen, Jan (ed) (1993). *Changing Care for the Elderly in the Netherlands*, Assen/Maastricht, The Netherlands: Van Gorcum.
7. Daatland, Svein Olav (1996). Adapting the "Scandinavian Model" of Care for Elderly People, in Organization for Economic Cooperation and Development (OECD), *Caring for Frail Elderly People: Policies in Evolution*, Paris: OECD, 247–59.
8. Davey, Adam, Elia E. Femia, Dennis G. Sea, Steven H. Zarit, Gerdt Sundstrom, Stig Berg, and Michael A. Smyer (1999). How Many Elders Receive Assistance: A Cross-National Comparison, *Journal of Aging and Health*, 11 (2), 199–220.
9. Grafstrom, Margaret, and Bengt Winblad (1995). Family Burden in the Care of the Demented and nondemented Elderly—A Longitudinal Study, *Alzheimer Disease and Associated Dementias*, 9 (2), 78–86.
10. Gustafsson, Tove M., Dag G. L. Isacson, and Mats Thorslund (1998). Mortality in Elderly Men and Women in a Swedish Municipality, *Age and Ageing*, 27 (5), 585–93.
11. Helset, Anne (1993). Elderly Women in the Nordic Countries; Level of Living and Situation in Life, *Scandanavian Journal of Social Medicine*, 21 (4), 223–26.
12. Hilleras, Pernilla K., Anthony F. Jorm, Agneta Herlitz, and Bengt Winblad (1998). Activity Patterns in Very Old People: A Survey of Cognitively Intact Subjects Aged 90 Years or Older, *Age and Ageing*, 28 (2), 147–52.

13. Hokenstad, Merl C., and Lennarth Johansson (1996). Eldercare in Sweden: Issues in Service Provision and Case Management, *Journal of Case Management*, 5 (4), 137–41.

14. Holtz-Eakin Douglas, and Timothy M. Smeeding (1994). Income, Wealth, and Intergenerational Economic Relations of the Aged, in Linda G. Martin and Samuel H. Preston (eds), *Demography of Aging*, Washington, DC: National Academy Press, 102–45.

15. International Social Security Association (1998). Sweden, *Trends in Social Security*, 1998 (3), 24–25.

16. Jacobzone, S., E. Cambois, E. Chaplain, and J. M. Robine (1999). The Health of Older Persons in OECD Countries: Is It Improving Fast Enough to Compensate for Population Aging? *Occasional Papers*, Paris: Organization for Economic Cooperation and Development.

17. Jarrott, Shannon E., Steven H. Zarit, Stig Berg, and Lennarth Johansson (1998). Adult Day Care for Dementia: A Comparison of Programs in Sweden and the United States, *Journal of Cross-Cultural Gerontology*, 13 (2), 99–108.

18. Johannesson, Magnus, and Per-Olov Johansson (1996). The Economics of Ageing: On the Attitude of Swedish People to the Distribution of Health Care Resources Between the Young and the Old, *Health Policy*, 37 (3), 153–61.

19. Johansson, Lennarth, and Mats Thorslund (1991). The National Context for Social Innovation: Sweden, in Robert J. Kraan, John Baldock, Bleddyn Davis, Adalbert Evers, Lennarth Johansson, Martin Kragren, Mats Thorslund, and Catherine Tunnissen (eds), *Care for the Elderly: Significant Innovations in Three European Countries*, Boulder, CO: Westview Press, 28–44, 122–27.

20. Kraan, Robert J., John Baldock, Bleddyn Davis, Adalbert Evers, Lennarth Johansson, Martin Kragren, Mats Thorslund, and Catherine Tunnissen, (1991). *Care for the Elderly: Significant Innovations in Three European Countries*, Boulder, CO: Westview Press.

21. Lassey, Marie L., William R. Lassey, and Martin J. Jinks (1997). *Health Care Systems Around the World: Characteristics, Issues, Reforms*, Upper Saddle River, NJ: Prentice Hall.

22. Lundin, Lars, and Bengt Turner (1995). Housing Frail Elders in Sweden, in Jon Pynoos and Phoebe S. Liebig (eds), *Housing Frail Elders: International Policies, Perspectives, and Prospects*, Baltimore: The Johns Hopkins University Press, 45–49.

23. Monk, Abraham, and Carole Cox (1991). *Home Care for the Elderly: An International Perspective*, New York: Auburn House.

24. Olsen, Gregg M. (1999). Half Empty or Half Full? The Swedish Welfare State in Transition, *Canadian Review of Sociology and Anthropology*, 36 (2), 242–63.

25. Organization for Economic Cooperation and Development (OECD) (1996). *Caring for Frail Elderly People: Policies in Evolution*. Paris: OECD.

26. Organization for Economic Cooperation and Development (2000). *Labor Force Statistics*, Online at www.oecd.org.

27. Organization for Economic Cooperation and Development (OECD) (1995). *The Transition from Work to Retirement*, Paris: Organization for Economic Cooperation and Development.

28. Samuelsson, S.-M., B. Bauer Alfredson, B. Hagberg, G. Samuelsson, B. Nordbeck, A. Brun, L. Gustafson, and J. Risberg (1997). The Swedish Centenarian Study: A Multidisciplinary Study of Five Consecutive Cohorts at the Age of 100, *International Journal of Aging and Human Development*, 45 (3), 223–53.

29. Scherman, Karl Gustaf (1995). Major Changes in Sweden's Pension System, *Ageing International*, 7 (2), 27–31.

30. Siegenthaler, Jurg K. (1996). Poverty Among Single Elderly Women Under Different Systems of Old-Age Security: A Comparative Review, *Social Security Bulletin*, 59 (3), 31–44.

31. Steen, B., and H. Djurfeldt (1993). The Gerontological and Geriatric Population Studies in Gothenburg, *Zeitschrift Fur Gerontologie*, 26 (3), 163–169.

32. Stenberg, Bo (1992). The Swedish Model of Social Alarm Systems for the Care of the Elderly, *Home Health Care Quarterly*, 13 (3–4), 135–48.

33. Sletvold, Olav, Reijo Tilvis, Arsoell Jonsson, Marianne Schroll, Jon Snaedal, Knut Engedal, Kirsten Schultz-Larsen, and Yngve Gustafson (1996). Geriatric Workup in the Nordic Countries, *Danish Medical Bulletin*, 43 (4), 350–359.

34. Sundstrom, Gerdt, and Mats Thorslund (1994a). Caring for the Elderly in Sweden, in Laura Katz Olson (ed), *Graying of the World: Who Will Care for the Frail Elderly?* New York: Haworth Press, 59–86.

35. Sundstrom, Gerdt, and Mats Thorslund (1994b). Sweden, in Jordan I. Kosberg (ed), *International Handbook on Services for the Elderly*, Westport, CT: Greenwood Press, 401–14.

36. Sundstrom, Gerdt, and Maria Angeles Tortosa (1999). The Effects of Rationing Home-Help Services in Spain and Sweden: A Comparative Analysis, *Ageing and Society*, 19 (2), 343–61.

37. Tornstami, Lars (1992). Formal and Informal Support to the Elderly in Sweden, in Hal Kendig, Akiko Hashimoto, and Larry C. Coppard (eds.), *Family Support for the Elderly: The International Experience*, New York: Oxford University Press, 138–46.

38. United States Census Bureau (2000). *International Data Base*, Online at www.census.gov/cgi-bin/ipc/idbpyry.pl.

39. Vaupel, James W., and Hans Lundstrom (1994). Longer Life Expectancy? Evidence from Sweden of Reduction in Mortality Rates at Advanced Ages, in David A. Wise (ed), *Studies in the Economics of Aging*, Chicago: The University of Chicago Press, 79–94.

40. Williamson, John B., and Fred C. Pampel (1993). Paying for the Baby Boom Generation's Social Security Pensions: United States, United Kingdom, Germany, and Sweden, *Journal of Aging Studies*, 7 (1), 41–54.

41. Winblad, B., G. Ljunggren, G. Karlsson, and A. Wimo (1996). What Are the Costs to Society and to Individuals Regarding Diagnostic Procedures and Care of Patients with Dementia? *Acta Neurologica Scandinavia*, 168 (Supplement), 101–04.

42. Zeitzer, Ilene R. (1994). Recent European Trends in Disability and Related Programs, *Social Security Bulletin*, 57 (2), 21–26.

Chapter 16

FRANCE
Personalized Care and Fragmented Services

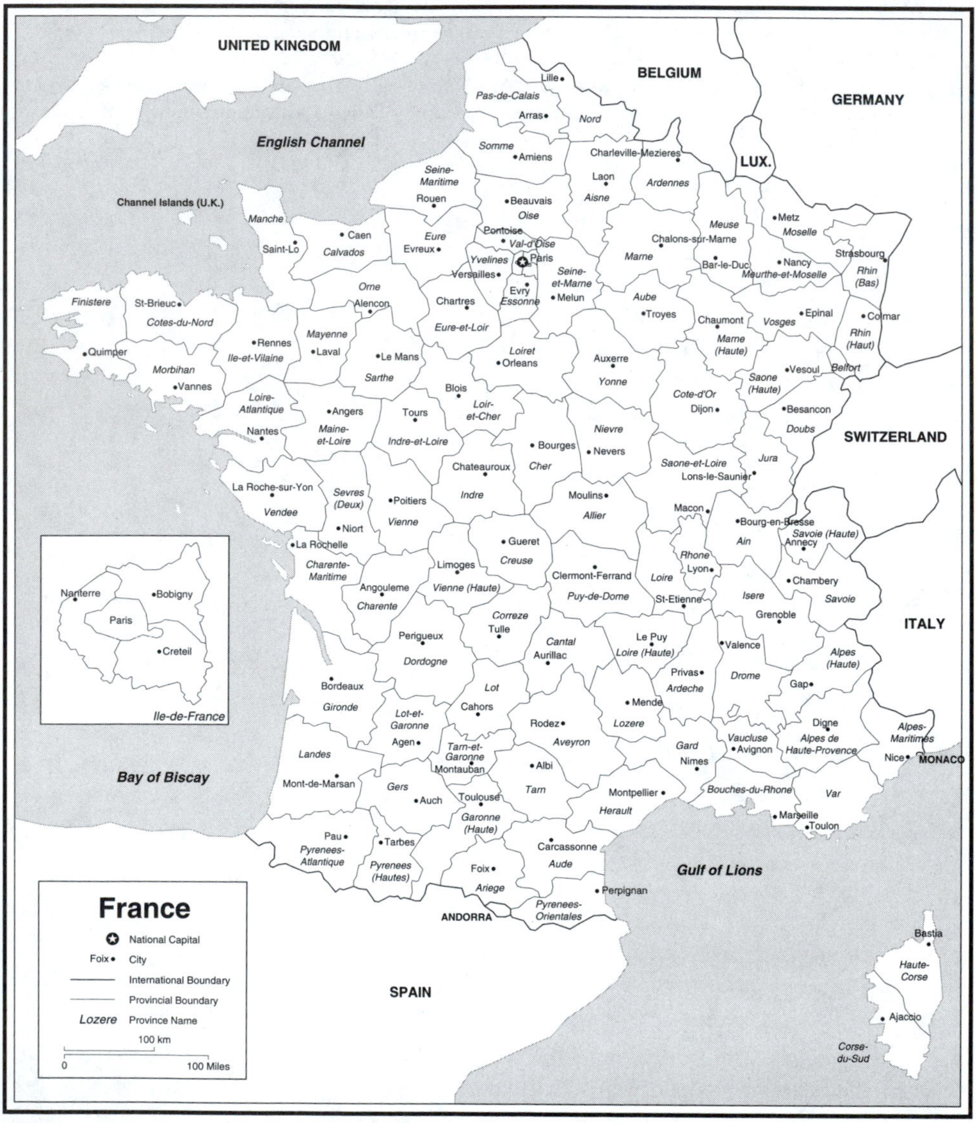

UNITED KINGDOM
BELGIUM
GERMANY
LUX.
SWITZERLAND
ITALY
MONACO
ANDORRA
SPAIN
English Channel
Channel Islands (U.K.)
Bay of Biscay
Gulf of Lions
Lille
Nord
Pas-de-Calais
Arras
Somme
Amiens
Seine-Maritime
Rouen
Beauvais
Oise
Charleville-Mezieres
Ardennes
Laon
Aisne
Manche
Saint-Lo
Caen
Calvados
Eure
Evreux
Pontoise
Val-d'Oise
Paris
Yvelines
Versailles
Evry
Essonne
Seine-et-Marne
Melun
Marne
Chalons-sur-Marne
Meuse
Bar-le-Duc
Metz
Moselle
Nancy
Meurthe-et-Moselle
Strasbourg
Rhin (Bas)
Finistere
Quimper
St-Brieuc
Cotes-du-Nord
Morbihan
Vannes
Rennes
Ile-et-Vilaine
Orne
Alencon
Chartres
Eure-et-Loir
Mayenne
Laval
Le Mans
Sarthe
Loiret
Orleans
Aube
Troyes
Chaumont
Marne (Haute)
Vosges
Epinal
Colmar
Rhin (Haut)
Auxerre
Yonne
Loire-Atlantique
Nantes
Angers
Maine-et-Loire
Tours
Indre-et-Loire
Blois
Loir-et-Cher
Cote-d'Or
Dijon
Saone (Haute)
Vesoul
Belfort
Besancon
Doubs
Bourges
Cher
Nievre
Nevers
Chateauroux
Indre
La Roche-sur-Yon
Vendee
Sevres (Deux)
Niort
Poitiers
Vienne
La Rochelle
Saone-et-Loire
Lons-le-Saunier
Jura
Moulins
Allier
Macon
Bourg-en-Bresse
Ain
Savoie (Haute)
Annecy
Gueret
Creuse
Limoges
Vienne (Haute)
Charente-Maritime
Angouleme
Charente
Clermont-Ferrand
Puy-de-Dome
Loire
Rhone
Lyon
St-Etienne
Chambery
Savoie
Isere
Grenoble
Correze
Tulle
Perigueux
Dordogne
Cantal
Aurillac
Le Puy
Loire (Haute)
Valence
Drome
Alpes (Haute)
Gap
Privas
Ardeche
Bordeaux
Gironde
Lot
Cahors
Lot-et-Garonne
Agen
Mende
Lozere
Rodez
Aveyron
Digne
Alpes de Haute-Provence
Alpes-Maritimes
Nice
Landes
Mont-de-Marsan
Tarn-et-Garonne
Montauban
Albi
Tarn
Gard
Nimes
Vaucluse
Avignon
Gers
Auch
Toulouse
Garonne (Haute)
Montpellier
Herault
Bouches-du-Rhone
Marseille
Var
Toulon
Pau
Pyrenees-Atlantique
Tarbes
Pyrenees (Hautes)
Foix
Ariege
Carcassonne
Aude
Perpignan
Pyrenees-Orientales
Bastia
Haute-Corse
Ajaccio
Corse-du-Sud
Nanterre
Bobigny
Paris
Creteil
Ile-de-France
France
National Capital
Foix
City
International Boundary
Provincial Boundary
Lozere
Province Name
100 km
0
100 Miles

◆◆◆ INTRODUCTION

France is the second largest nation in Europe and is also second in population with nearly 59 million people in 2000. It has long been a cultural and political leader among Europeans. Per capita GDP was $22,091 in 1998—near the middle among economically advanced countries. Government is decentralized; the central authorities set policies and collect taxes, then allocate resources and responsibility to departments (comparable to states) and prefects (like counties). Direct management and payment for publicly provided services are at the local level.[22, 36]

The French generally subscribe to the "third age" value that retirement is the prime of life with opportunity for independence and pursuit of a long and leisurely later life. However, this is in many respects an individualistic society. The value orientation is to maintain the ability of each older person to manage independently, based on the belief that problems of older age should be postponed as long as possible. Social status and valued roles in the family and community are sustained until serious disability takes over.[10, 15, 35]

This positive attitude toward aging is part of the basis for government policies supportive of the older population. Health care programs are universally available. Public health, hygienic measures, and other health improvements were implemented earlier here than in many countries. A World Health Organization report recently ranked France first in the world for overall health care. Long-term care is generally available for those who need it, at home or within institutions. And social institutions have been created to support activities of older people in the community.[22, 27]

Demographic Characteristics

The population has been aging somewhat more rapidly than neighboring European countries and has the greatest prevalence of centenarians except for Sweden and Denmark. The oldest age groups are predominantly women, as the population pyramid in Figure 16–1 indicates.

The larger numbers of both men and women in the age categories between 55 and 64 suggests that the numbers of very old people will continue to increase over the next 25 years, as longevity rises. Even larger numbers in 25 to 54 age categories means that the proportion of older population will continue to be very large well into the twenty-first century. Life expectancy was 78.6 (about 83 years for women and 74 for men) in 1999 and has been steadily increasing as in other countries. Approximately 16 percent of the population was age 65 or older in 2000—a proportion that is expected to reach 20 percent by 2015.[10, 11, 29, 43]

◆◆◆ HISTORICAL PERSPECTIVE

The Laroque Report of 1962 marked the beginning of modern policies affecting older people. It emphasized maintenance of the elderly in their homes, outlined a more positive and independence-oriented approach to members of the "third age,"

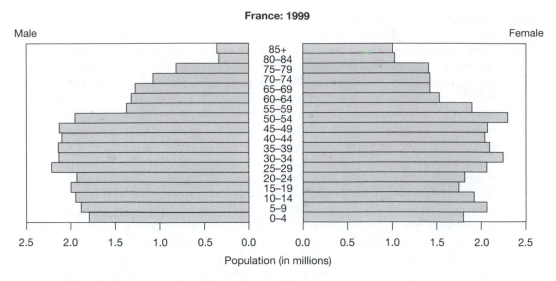

FIGURE 16–1 Population Pyramids for France
Source: U.S. Census Bureau, *International Data Base,* 2000.

and suggested the need for increased resources as well as better coordination of services. The report recommended that old people's homes be replaced with more flexible support in the community. Near universal health care insurance was initiated in 1967 and was extended to 99 percent of the population by 1978. Retired individuals were not required to pay deductibles. Patients were required to pay physicians directly for their care and personally submit bills to the local Social Security department for reimbursement, which often takes a considerable time period and therefore becomes a financial burden to individuals with minimal incomes.[33]

Despite a formal emphasis on elderly independence and home care, the number of people living in institutions continues to increase because home care services have not evolved rapidly enough to fulfill demand. The system of health and long-term care services is very complicated and constantly in process of adjustment, presenting a continuing challenge to older people.[22]

Competition between federal ministries and among local government departments—the powerful public bureaucracies—contributes to the complexity. A National Committee of Pensioners and Elderly Persons was created in 1981 to advise the Ministries of Health and Social Affairs on needed policy and program changes. The resulting Braun report of 1988 identified many of the continuing problems and offered recommendations for simplification and adjustment. The government has implemented many of the suggestions, improving policies and programs in the process.[16]

The first phase focused on support of families and implementation of expanded home care, with emphasis on avoiding institutionalization whenever possible. Community care was strengthened. Services were to be delivered at the local level of government; improved housing was given high priority; home help and meals were to be provided; senior clubs were to be organized; and health centers were to be opened in local neighborhoods throughout the country.[16]

A second phase focused more on changes in the larger system. The Boulard and the Schopflin reports recommended means testing of benefits to replace the universal income allowances—as a way of providing more adequately for low-income elderly. Both reports also recommended greater public support for informal care, increased housing resources, and greater coordination of service provision.[33]

◆◆◆ SOCIAL-SUPPORT SYSTEMS

The family remains a very strong force in society despite the high value placed on individualism and independence. A high proportion of younger families continue to live in close proximity to older parents, although this is less true in rural regions where many younger people have departed for jobs in the cities. Surveys suggest that roughly 71 percent of the elderly feel that the family is the primary social network. About 83 percent of those in good health receive occasional assistance from family in meeting their daily needs; this rises to 94 percent when disability occurs. Daughters and daughters-in-law are most often the primary caregivers. About one-fourth of sons provide some primary care, and both sons and sons-in-law are often secondary caregivers.[2, 6, 10]

The 1990 national census indicated that about 3 percent of those aged 75 or older live with family members other than a spouse. This proportion rises to 17 percent among single older women. Adult children and grandchildren are the usual helpers with domestic tasks such as laundry, cooking, and caring for the household. Reciprocity is an important element of family involvement. Older individuals tend to help their children financially to the extent of their ability, with gifts, loans, help with housing and furnishing, or in times of crisis. They provide occasional childcare, help around the house, give professional advice, and help with household chores to the extent of their ability.[2]

Older adults indicate they are generally very satisfied (82 percent) with their social relationships. Regular family gatherings and family vacations are highly valued, especially those involving grandchildren. Children often spend extended periods with grandparents and get to know them and be known by them. Furthermore, older individuals who engage extensively with family and appreciate the close relationships tend to have a lower likelihood of depression and other mental health problems than those with weaker family ties.[1, 11]

Friends and neighbors are viewed as more important than family for some leisure activities and in combating loneliness, especially among older people without children. Roughly half of the elderly over age 75 report having received regular assistance from friends and neighbors for such activities as shopping and transportation.[2]

◆◆◆ PHYSICAL HEALTH CARE

National health policy has in the past emphasized scientific and acute or curative medicine rather than disease prevention. For example, the government did not initially subscribe to the World Health Organization's basic principles on health promotion, except for preventive care for mothers and children, school health, and occupational health programs. Primary care professionals emphasized immunizations and rehabilitation but without much attention to public health measures. More recently the Social Security system has begun to emphasize flu vaccinations and cancer screening for the elderly. The health care system has improved significantly in the last decade.[24, 27]

Primary Care

The primary health care system is grounded in four basic principles:[24]

1. Freedom of patients to select their general practitioner and specialist physicians.
2. Physicians should have the freedom to practice as they please, wherever they choose.
3. Each physician has the right to prescribe medications according to his or her best judgment.
4. Confidentiality between patient and physician is paramount.

These principles have helped to establish a strong commitment of physicians to sensitive patient care—to the great advantage of the older population. Physicians tend to take the needed time to fully examine patients and respond to their needs. The openness between physician and patient is quite exceptional compared to most other countries. Furthermore, physicians generally lead a much less harried professional life than in other countries. Office-based local physicians do not usually see their patients in the hospital, which is the domain of salaried hospital specialists. Primary health care is generally of good quality, whether it is provided by private medical practitioners or hospital out-patient departments.[24]

A patient health care booklet or medical record is kept by individuals age 75 and over and serves as the continuing record of health status, medications, and care. This booklet is taken by the patient to any point of care, for continuous updates.[24]

Hospitals

Older individuals have the freedom to select either public or private hospitals. Both are reimbursed through the health insurance mechanism. Public hospitals operate on a global budget and private hospitals are paid on a fee-for-service basis. Public hospitals were dominant with about 80 percent of the beds until the 1990s. Private hospitals expanded steadily during the 1990s because a cap was placed on growth of new public hospitals. By the late 1990s public hospitals were down to about 65 percent of all bed spaces, whereas private not-for-profit hospitals and private for-profit hospitals provided the rest of the beds. Public hospitals are staffed by salaried physicians. Private hospitals rely primarily on private fee-for-service physicians. University hospitals tend to be the most prestigious and have the most developed geriatric services.[15, 24, 29]

Geriatric Assessment and Care

Some public hospitals, or wards within hospitals, specialize in long-stay elderly patients who are disabled. Multidimensional geriatric assessment has been implemented in selected university hospitals but is not widespread in general or private hospitals, which ordinarily offer only subacute and long-term care. Bichat University Hospital in Paris, for example, has used comprehensive geriatric assessment to improve diagnosis, treatment, and earlier discharge. The medical, social, financial, and dependency status of patients are compiled upon admission, allowing for better understanding and more appropriate care in the hospital and at home. Patients using the service are discharged an average of four days earlier than those who were not comprehensively evaluated near the beginning of their hospitalization.[23, 29]

Illustration 16–1 describes a unique effort by Vaugirard Hospital in the most populated district of Paris to implement an advanced approach to geriatric care.

Illustration 16–1
GERIATRIC CARE IN THE VAUGIRARD HOSPITAL DISTRICT

Vaugirard Geriatric Hospital was opened in 1991 with 340 beds—55 devoted to geriatric rehabilitation. A survey had earlier been used to determine the health care needs of the older population in the district. The hospital was then designed as much as possible to meet patient preferences. A gerontology network was established to link together all professionals in the district as a coordination and communication mechanism with the hospital.

Admission is preceded (whenever possible) by careful analysis of individual needs and preferences. The hospital then attempts to fulfill the defined needs. Upon discharge the return home is coordinated with local professionals to assure delivery of meals, housekeeping, and other home care services.

Patients are treated as "guests at a luxury hotel." Families are warmly welcomed at any time. Social workers and psychologists are employed to give specific attention to patient and family needs. Staff is selected for their interest in geriatric care, and they receive specific training to enhance their attitudes and skills. They receive several types of fringe benefits to improve the working environment and encourage retention of good employees. Volunteers are available to assist the patient and staff and to support appropriate care at home.

The patient medical record booklet (as noted earlier) is used as a continuing record of out-patient and in-patient care, including any social issues that may be relevant. Every attempt is made to minimize the time in the hospital while optimizing home care. The linkage of the hospital to local professionals helps to establish ongoing preventive care and health promotion. A "guide to professionals" enables hospital staff to identify the appropriate local contacts and link them to patient needs. The experiment appears to work well although no definitive evaluation had been reported when this was written.

Source: Data from Le Faou and Jolly, 1995: 19-20.

Geriatrics Training. Optional course work in geriatrics has been available in selected medical schools since the 1970s and formal medical courses in geriatric care have been obligatory in most medical schools since 1997. General practitioners who want to increase their knowledge and skills may take special competency training. Specialists can receive certification in geriatrics by taking an examination after two years of fellowship training.[29]

Emergency Care

The older population is generally well served by a highly developed national emergency-response system. Each response unit is under the direct supervision of trained emergency physicians who work with fire department ambulance crews. The system is referred to as the Mobile Hospital Emergency and Intensive Care Services (SMUR) and has one national emergency phone number. SMUR is closely interconnected with fire and police services as well as hospital emergency departments. Direct early involvement of trained physicians should be a considerable advantage for older individuals who have multiple problems possibly interacting with a stroke or heart attack.[28]

Pharmaceuticals

The freedom of physicians to prescribe medications, described earlier, was constrained somewhat in 1995 by prescription standards to help lower costs and avoid overprescribing. Guidelines have been developed limiting the use of medications judged to be unnecessary or inappropriate. The procedures are supervised by a panel of Social Security physicians charged with enforcement. Drug prices are set by government regulations.[24]

Eating, Drinking, and Health: A French Paradox?

The incidence of heart disease is lower in France than in other economically advanced countries, despite a high consumption of fatty foods, low incidence of exercise, and a relatively high rate of smoking. The lower rates of disease clearly contribute to greater life expectancy and better health. High consumption of vegetables and red wine appear to have some influence. The virtues of a heavily vegetable diet are well documented, but the value of wine consumption is less understood. Flavonoids in red wine appear to boost good cholesterol, while absorbing harmful cholesterol.[14]

    A study of the Epidemiology of Vascular Aging among a volunteer sample of

1389 older residents in the Nantes region indicated that no negative or positive effects in cognitive functioning were associated with moderate drinking among men. However, for women the findings suggested moderate drinking had a beneficial effect on cognitive function. A lower incidence of vascular disease was found among moderate drinkers as compared to nondrinkers.[8]

A larger study of dementia and wine consumption in the Bordeaux region showed similar results. Moderate wine drinkers generally had a lower rate of dementia than nondrinkers, suggesting that wine may protect against dementia to some degree.[37]

◆◆◆ MENTAL HEALTH CARE

Mental health care has evolved steadily since World War II, with a decrease in focus on mental hospitals as the primary source of treatment and an increase in community-based approaches emphasizing community care. A psychiatric team was assigned in 1960 to provide care to all of the mentally ill in defined subdivisions of each department (state). The team diagnosed problems, provided consultation, recommended hospitalization as needed, and undertook programs of rehabilitation for all age groups. Government-sponsored health insurance covered most of the costs.[4]

The transformations were accompanied by a major increase in the number of psychiatrists and psychologists entering public or private practice in private office or clinic settings. Older individuals with mental disorders have full access to the services in most parts of the country. Specialists in geriatric psychiatry are not widely accessible, however. Relatively little special emphasis has been given to the mental health problems of the older population, except for ready access to general psychiatric consultation.[4, 15]

Depression

Depression is a major problem among the elderly here as elsewhere. A longitudinal epidemiological study of community residents in the Bordeaux region (the so-called PAQUID study) indicated that depression is among the primary factors leading to dependence and inability to undertake independent activities of daily living. The findings indicated that both depression and cognitive impairment tended to decrease mobility and increase the probability of early death. Self-perceptions of poor health are predictors of depression and thus contribute to early mortality as well. Men appeared to be more affected by depression than women; they are in somewhat greater danger of early death if they lack sufficient social contacts. Lack of social support appears to lead to depression.[3, 12]

Dementia

Individuals with some form of dementia occupy about half of all space in nursing homes and other institutions. Researchers have developed a version of the so-called Canberra Interview for the Elderly that produces a diagnosis or assessment of dementia and depression according to the Diagnostic and Statistical Manual (III-R) of the American Psychiatric Association. The measurement provides reliable and valid assessments of populations and serves as the basis for research comparability between countries.[26]

A study of patients in the largest geriatric hospital in France (Charles Foix Hospital in Paris) revealed that one-third of patients had some form of dementia. About 15 percent of them had Alzheimer's. The other primary diseases regularly overlapping with dementia were stroke (30 percent), hypertension (26 percent), respiratory tract infections (24 percent), and iatrogenic (treatment-caused) disease (23 percent). These findings are similar to results from studies in the United States and other countries.[17]

Studies using the PAQUID instruments have measured "dementia-free life expectancy." At age 65 the study indicated an average dementia-free life expectancy of 16.9 years, with a total life expectancy of 17.7 years—or an average expectation of .8 years *with* dementia. Women generally have a lower expectation of dementia than men, a finding at variance with studies in some other countries.[39]

The Value of Intellect and Independence

Social scientists have sought to determine the possible linkage between social circumstances, educational level, and mental decline in older age. A French study concluded that individuals age 75 and over tended to decline less if they had higher levels of education. Those with greater education are more able to continue developing verbal skills after with the physical deterioration associated with advancing age.[25]

Use of Pharmaceuticals

Use of pharmaceuticals for treatment of mental health problems is very popular. France has one of the highest per capita drug consumption rates in the world. For example, a study comparing use of drugs for insomnia problems in France and Quebec indicated a French consumption rate that was twice the Canadian rate for psychotropic drugs. In both instances, however, women and the elderly were the primary users, usually with prescriptions written by general practitioners rather than specialists.[30]

Ethical and Legal Issues

Abuse of the elderly is a problem here as elsewhere as revealed in a 1990 study in the Department of Lille in Northern France. Although relatively small numbers of older people are affected, examples were detected of physical mistreatment, psychological abuse, inadequate living conditions, infringement of personal rights, and a variety of other abuses. However, none of the abused individuals were willing to file formal complaints against the perpetrators, mostly their own children. They were in many cases fearful of losing their living arrangement and had no reasonable alternatives. Specific legal rights for dependent elderly are very limited, although civil and penalty codes do exist to protect all citizens from abuse.[13, 21]

Physician responsibility towards elderly mental patients is defined in law. The consent of the patient must be obtained for any procedure, and the physician is required to provide straightforward, honest, and intelligible information. When the patient is mentally impaired, a protection system is available but must be specifically requested.[13]

Protection can include guardianship under supervision of a judge when serious incompetence exists. The appointed person is ordinarily a family member but can also be unrelated. The primary focus is protection of a person's property rather than the integrity of the individual.[13]

◆◆◆ LONG-TERM CARE

Long-term care received increased emphasis in 1970 when reforms were implemented. General hospital wards, old age homes, and mental hospitals had been the primary locations for institutional long-term care. Since 1975, nursing homes, retirement homes, home health care, and chore services have received greater emphasis and development.[22]

Home Care

Relatively generous home health care benefits were implemented by a 1981 law allowing four home visits per day for individuals with serious disabilities. Legislation in 1988 limited such benefits largely to individuals age 75 and over, with financing through social security insurance. Local social-welfare offices provided support and coordination. Medical and nursing services in the home were also expanded and paid for through insurance. Additional legislation in 1995 expanded and integrated public payments for both home care and institutional care.[10, 32]

Home nursing care is available on a public or private basis. Home meal services and respite care are also widely available. Emergency alarm systems are used in some areas of the country. Although access to services has increased steadily since the 1970s, evaluations in 1994 indicate many gaps in programs for older individuals in greatest need. Day care has been very slow to develop, although centers are available in some communities and in a few geriatric hospitals.[10, 15, 29, 31]

Nearly one-third of individuals age 75 or older who live at home receive some form of nonmedical home help. Home services are usually initiated after a recommendation by the responsible physician or social worker. Public payment is provided by municipal welfare departments for lower-income individuals. Private services are available for those covered by insurance or those who can pay from personal or family resources.[2, 15]

Old Age Homes and Nursing Homes

Publicly operated homes predominate for lower-income disabled older individuals. A fixed amount of the required cost is from health-insurance funds but must be supplemented by private payments from residents and families for room and board when possible or from welfare funds otherwise. Some public homes have been criticized for poor design, inadequate "homelike" environments, and poor quality of care.[31, 32]

Private nonprofit or for-profit old age homes (similar to assisted living) are available for those who have pensions, public housing allowances, or other private income. Most residents do not need daily nursing care. However, some facilities have a nursing care section which can receive reimbursement from health-insurance funds.[15]

Both old age homes and nursing homes operate under a formal policy (approved in 1986) of involving residents in governance and management through resident councils. Many facilities have a very strong commitment to comfort, security, and support for the frail individuals under their care. Good food and wine are sometimes available in accordance with the cultural traditions of residents.[22]

About 6.5 percent of the older population lived in nursing homes in 1999. Family availability appears to make a substantial difference in nursing home admission, according to an earlier study. Older people with two adult children were less likely than average to enter nursing homes. With one child accessible the proportion entering a home rose to 9 percent; and with no children it was 23 percent. Many older individuals apparently live in nursing homes simply because they have no other source of care.[2]

Hospice

Hospice and palliative care started at Paris University Hospital in 1987, using the British experience as a model. Since then, hospices have evolved very quickly to a system of 37 units around the country (in 1995). However, hospices serving individuals at home remained insufficient and underfunded. The great majority of older individuals continue to die in hospitals.[29, 40]

◆◆◆ HOUSING AND COMMUNITY

Most of the older population continue to live in private homes. The government has provided funds to renovate homes in the interest of keeping disabled older people from entering institutional housing. However, publicly sponsored specialized housing has not been given a high priority. Nonprofit organizations have attempted to fulfill some of the needs. Homes of older people tend to be of generally lower quality than housing inhabited by the younger population.[15, 41, 42]

Sheltered and Assisted Living Homes

Sheltered housing and assisted living homes are available in many locations. The accommodations are usually studio apartments with private bath and kitchen, and with access to group dining, social activities, emergency alarms, home help, and home health care services. Housing allowances were available to about 10 percent in of the elderly in 1994 to assist with payment of rent.[15]

◆◆◆ ECONOMIC AND FINANCIAL ISSUES

The various levels of government have constructed a rather complete network of services for the older population, although without the degree of equity or integration achieved by some other European countries. Guarantees exist for income, health care, and long-term care, but the quality and completeness of services varies substantially depending on income level and location in the country.[10]

Income Benefits

The system of pensions is much more fragmented than in most economically advanced countries—with two primary levels and a third welfare-based level. The first level is financed from payroll taxes paid jointly by employers and workers. It provides 50 percent of the average income of the 25 best earning years. The basic pension is related to the level of earnings and the length of the work life—with 40 years required for a full pension at age 60. Annual increases are based on the rise in a cost-of-living index.[5]

The second level is a complementary occupational pension, also financed from payroll taxes and is available to groups of workers who have agreements with employing organizations. About one-third of the workforce is covered by smaller plans for specific socioeconomic groups. A third benefit is for individuals who have not worked at all, or have worked less than the required years, and is subject to a means-test.[15]

Social-assistance programs at the local level provide support for older individuals at the bottom of the income ladder, paying for basic maintenance, home help services, and residence in retirement or long-term care homes. Only those with no other source of support receive assistance. Social workers are responsible for assessing the need and determining whether families can pay part of the cost. Because of system complexity, an older individual often receives part of the needed support from several local, regional, and national funding sources.[33]

The government developed a formal policy in the early 1990s to raise the incomes of older people at the lower end of the income ladder. The legislation indexes retirement income to wage or price increases, whichever is higher. The effect was to increase overall living standards of the older population. As a consequence, the proportion of the elderly in poverty declined substantially to less than 10 percent in 1998.[29, 44]

A special preretirement allowance was created in 1998 by the national parliament to apply in case of unemployment prior to the official retirement age and applicable after 40 working years. The fund guarantees a minimum income to anyone who qualifies. The policy was designed to help older workers during the recent period of high unemployment, while at the same time relieving the stress on unemployment funds.[18]

The pension system preserves social class and gender differences. Varying plans exist for salaried workers, independent workers, farmers, civil servants, and other groupings. Gender inequalities are *profound*, in substantial part because three of every four men work the number of years required for a full pension, whereas only one of every three women do.[15]

Health Care Insurance

The health care system was among the most expensive in Europe in 1998, using 10.3 percent of GNP. In 1994, the government placed a 3.4 percent annual cap on increases in health care spending to counteract annual increases of 7 percent.

All older individuals are covered by mandatory health insurance funded largely by a flat tax. Co-payments are required for physician services but private insurance policies available to everyone for a monthly fee generally cover such costs. Lower-income older citizens are exempt from most co-payments and have coverage for prescriptions as well as primary, hospital, and long-term health care insurance. When the family has insufficient resources to pay room and board costs, the local welfare system pays the bill. Retired individuals were required to pay 1.4 percent of their Social Security income and 2.4 percent of their other pension income for health insurance in 1993.[7, 9, 15, 29, 45]

The larger health care system is managed primarily through the national social security system (as are retirement benefits, family allowances, disability allowances, workmen's compensation, and occupational health). Roughly 75 percent of all payments to providers come through the largest national insurance fund. Benefits are actually paid to recipients by local Prefect Social Security committees that also have responsibility for local management and monitoring of health care providers.[24]

Public and nonprofit hospitals are paid directly from Social Security funds, based on an annual global budget. For-profit institutions are paid based on fees for services. This complex arrangement has given the profit-making hospitals a distinct growth advantage, especially after public hospital growth was deliberately constrained. Recent legislation has placed them partially under a global budgeting system as well.[24]

Patients pay their physician (or pharmacist) directly and are reimbursed by the insurance plan for about 75 percent of the cost. Supplementary private insurance covers most of the balance, including deductibles and co-payments. Lower-income elderly, cancer patients, AIDS patients, and individuals with other costly chronic diseases are exempt from charges.[15]

Long-Term Care Insurance

Long-term care insurance was initiated in 1988 although the first effort was not entirely successful because costs were much higher than anticipated. A more adequately financed plan was initiated in 1994 with payment variations depending on the level of disability. A new "autonomy" benefit was approved in 1995 for implementation in 1997, with financing shared by national and department governments, and intended to help those at lower income levels who are dependent. Potential recipients must pass a means-test in advance, conducted by a socio-medical team at the local level.[33, 34]

Medically necessary care provided at home by physicians, nurses, and therapists is fully reimbursed on a fee-for-service basis by National Health Insurance. However, nurse aides, meals, daycare, and equipment are not reimbursed and must be paid privately. A Certificate of Need is necessary prior to construction of a new nursing home. A careful licensure and inspection process helps assure an adequate level of quality.[29]

Payment for Pharmaceuticals

Pharmaceuticals are subsidized for everyone—with payment from National Health Insurance and supplements (for some medications) from private insurance. Prescription drug costs were considerably higher than in any other country in Europe in the early 1990s. Drugs on an approved list are fully or partially covered, depending on the type of therapy. Essential drugs for cancer treatment, for example, required no co-payment. For the majority of drugs, such as antibiotics, a 30 percent co-payment was required, although not for lower-income older people. A 60 percent co-payment was need for so-called "comfort" drugs such as tranquilizers.[29]

◆◆◆ LIFESTYLE: WORK, RETIREMENT, AND LEISURE

A good lifestyle and leisure in retirement are very important French values, as noted earlier. Public policy has attempted to enhance satisfying alternatives.

Work

The majority of salaried workers begin to draw retirement benefits at age 60, receiving 80 percent of their preretirement income. Gradual retirement is also encouraged through part-time work until a later age. One effect of the early retirement policy was to limit options for older workers who wanted to continue, resulting in loss of work incentives, neglect of retraining for new job skills, and increased costs for social security support of relatively young retirees. Many employers appear to hold somewhat negative attitudes towards continuing employment of older workers.[15, 19, 35, 38]

Retirement

A study of retirees in the Paris region indicated that satisfaction is closely associated with the degree of physical impairment, mental health status (especially among women), engagement in an active lifestyle, and maintenance of good relationships with family and friends. Good physical health, participation in physical activities such as sports, involvement in social life, and productive use of leisure time were predictors of high retirement satisfaction.[20]

More than 20,000 "Third Age" clubs have been organized throughout the country. Regional and national committees representing the clubs provide advisory functions to public officials on issues related to retirement and older age. Some clubs are focused on recreation, while others have broader functions. Exercise and sports activities have become very popular. Volunteerism in community activities is also commonplace. Educational opportunities specifically for the elderly—available on a wide variety of topics through Universities of the Third Age—were initiated in Toulouse in 1973.[10, 15]

◆◆◆ NOTEWORTHY FEATURES AND MAJOR CHALLENGES

Older people are held in high regard by the French and are treated with respect by their families, communities, and larger support systems. Coordination problems between the agencies responsible for health and social care nonetheless create obstacles to older individuals who have trouble navigating through the bureaucracy.

Noteworthy Features

Attitudes toward aging are more positive than in many other countries. A supportive social system, coupled with relatively healthy diets and lifestyles, enables older people to be satisfied during their later lives. The family remains a very strong force in providing most of the informal long-term care for older members.

Physicians tend to take time for older patients—who have freedom to select whomever they please as a primary care giver, with their expenses paid through universal insurance. Openness and confidentiality between physician and patient are greater here than in most countries. A highly developed emergency medical system, with full-time physicians as part of the team, means that older people in trouble can usually secure help quickly. The mental health care system serves older patients well, although it challenges them with complexity and bureaucratic barriers. Progress has also been achieved in providing formal long-term care, at home and in high-quality nursing homes.

The French place great value on a good retirement and quality of life in older age, as reflected in the widespread formation of "Third Age Clubs" throughout the country. Public policies provide a reasonably comprehensive array of programs to make the good life possible.

Major Challenges

Although a high proportion of residents of long-term care institutions have dementia, they are not provided for to the extent recommended by the various public reports. Formal long-term institutional care has received much greater continuing financial support than maintenance of independence in the home. Families of dependent elderly have not received the attention they would prefer.[11]

A shortage of nursing homes is evident in some parts of the country. Costs remain high for lodging and board when borne by the individual or family. Day care, day hospitals, respite care and hospice services remain underdeveloped in many communities.[29]

Geriatric health care continues to be relatively underdeveloped, although the requirement that new physicians take geriatric courses (beginning in 1997) should eventually improve services. Continuing medical education in geriatrics is now required as well, which should increase knowledge and skills over time. A shortage of university faculty in geriatrics is an impediment to rapid progress in most parts of the country. A full specialization in geriatrics was not yet available in 1998.[29]

Very rapid increases in the older population mean that financing pensions is likely to become difficult in the years ahead, assuming the pay-as-you-go system continues. The share of national income required could double by 2040. Medical care costs will similarly rise dramatically. Despite the efforts to improve income, nearly 10 percent of the older population remained below the official poverty level in 1998—especially widows and divorced women age 75 and over.[29]

◆◆◆ SUMMARY AND CONCLUSIONS

French public policies toward the elderly are generally progressive. The family structure is strong and supportive of older members. However, public social support at the individual level is often complex because of fragmented program organization and the need to deal with a variety of agencies to secure needed benefits.

The primary health care system is attentive to the needs of older people and largely covers costs with very little out-of-pocket expenditure except for short-term physician costs, which are later reimbursed. Specialization of professionals in geriatric health care has expanded considerably but remains less developed than in many other advanced countries. Mental health care improved substantially in the 1990s, but is not especially prepared to deal with the unique problems of the older population. A vigorous emphasis on home care and an effort to reform and improve nursing homes are gradually improving long-term care. Training of support staff in public and private agencies has been enhanced.

Housing programs received substantial support during the 1980s and 1990s—including mechanisms for improvements to private homes and construction of new sheltered and assisted living residences. However, the means-testing procedure and the variety of agencies that must be involved make it difficult to secure benefits.

Incomes have increased for all segments of the older population, but particularly for those at the lower end of the scale. Retirement satisfaction appears to be quite high. Most older people remain in good health until relatively advanced age and have satisfying lifestyle options, providing the basis for a long, leisurely, and high-quality later life.

◆◆◆ REFERENCES

1. Antonucci, Toni C., Rebecca Fuhrer, and Jean-Francois Dartigues (1997). Social Relations and Depressive Symptomatology in a Sample of Community-Dwelling French Older Adults, *Psychology and Aging*, 12, 1, 189–95.
2. Attias-Donfut, Claudine, and Alain Rozenkier (1996). The Lineage-Structured Social Networks of Older People in France, in Howard Litwin (ed), *The Social Networks of Older People: A Cross-National Analysis*, Westport, CT: Praeger, 31–53.

3. Barberger-Gateau, Pascale, Anicet Chaslerie, Jean-Francois Dartigues, Daniel Commenges, Michele Gagnon, and Roger Salamon (1992). Health Measures Correlates in a French Elderly Community Population: The PAQUID Study, *Journal of Gerontology, SOCIAL SCIENCES*, 47 (2), S88–95.

4. Bleandonu, Gerard (1995). Psychodynamic Psychiatry and the Treatment of Psychosis in the French Community, *Bulletin of the Menninger Clinic*, 59 (3), 372–84.

5. Bosworth, Barry, and Gary Burtless (1998). Population Aging and Economic Performance, in Barry Bosworth and Gary Burtless, *Aging Societies: The Global Dimension*, Washington, DC: The Brookings Institution, 1–27.

6. Clement, Serge (1993). Sibling Configuration and Support to Old Parents in the Rural South-Western Area of France, *Social Science and Medicine*, 37 (2), 139–51.

7. Dickson, Michael (1994). Paying for Prescriptions in Europe, in Organization for Economic Cooperation and Development, *Health: Quality and Choice,* Paris: OECD, 83–110.

8. Dufouil, Carole, Pierre Ducimetiere, and Annick Alperovitch (1997). Sex Differences in the Association Between Alcohol Consumption and Cognitive Performance, *American Journal of Epidemiology*, 146 (5), 405–12.

9. Fielding, Jonathan E., and Pierre-Jean Lancry (1993). Lessons from France—"Vive la Difference," *Journal of the American Medical Association*, 270 (6), 748–56.

10. Fontaine, Anne (1993). France, in Erdman B. Palmore (ed), *Development of Research on Aging: An International Handbook*, Westport, CT: Greenwood Press, 103–11.

11. Frossard, Michel, and Anne-Marie Guillemard (1994). French Old Age Polices and the Frail Elderly, in Laura Katz Olson (ed), *The Graying of the World: Who Will Care for the Frail Elderly?* New York: Haworth Press, 180–209.

12. Fuhrer, R., C. Dufouil, T. C. Antonucci, M. J. Shipley, C. Helmer, and J. F. Dartigues (1999). Psychological Disorder and Mortality in French Older Adults: Do Social Relations Modify the Association? *American Journal of Epidemiology*, 149 (2), 116–26.

13. Gromb, Sophie, Gerard Manciet, and Anaud Descamps (1997). Ethics and Law in the Field of Medical Care for the Elderly in France, *Journal of Medical Ethics,* 23 (4), 233–38.

14. Hackman, Robert M. (1998). Flavonoids and the French Paradox, *USA Today*, 127 (2640), 58–59.

15. Henrard, Jean-Claude (1994). France, in Jordan I. Kosberg (ed), *International Handbook on Services for the Elderly*, Westport, CT: Greenwood Press, 104–23.

16. Henrard, Jean-Claude, Bernard Cassou, and Dominique Le Disert (1990). The Effects of System Characteristics on Policy Implementation and Functioning of Care for the Elderly in France, *International Journal of Health Services*, 20 (1), 125–39.

17. Holstein, Josiane, Giles Chatellier, Francois Piette, and Robert Moulias (1994). Prevalence of Associated Diseases in Different Types of Dementia Among Elderly Institutionalized Patients: Analysis of 3447 Records, *Journal of the American Geriatric Society*, 42 (9), 972–77.

18. International Social Security Association (1998a). France, *Trends in Social Security*, 1998 (3), 18.

19. International Social Security Association (1998b). France, *Trends in Social Security*, 1998 (4), 17.

20. Iwatsubo, Yuriko, Francis Derriennic, Bernard Cassou, and Jean Poitrenaud (1996). Predictors of Life Satisfaction Amongst Retired People in Paris, *International Journal of Epidemiology*, 25 (1), 160–70.

21. Jarde, O., B. Marc, J. Dwyer, P. Fournier, H. Carlier-Pasquier, and L. Lenoir (1992). Mistreatment of the Aging in the Home Environment in Northern France: A Year Survey, *Medical Law*, 11 (7–8), 641–48.

22. Lassey, Marie L., William R. Lassey, and Martin J. Jinks (1997). *Health Care Systems Around the World: Characteristics, Issues, Reforms*, Upper Saddle River, NJ: Prentice Hall.

23. Ledesert, B., P. Lombrail, P. Yeni, C. Carbon, and M. Brodin (1994). The Impact of a Comprehensive Multi-Dimensional Geriatric Assessment Programme on Duration of Stay in a French Acute Medical Ward, *Age and Ageing*, 23 (3), 223–27.

24. Le Faou, Anne-Laurence, and Dominique Jolly (1995). Health Promotion in France: Toward a New Way of Giving Medical Care, *Hospital Topics*, 73 (2), 17–21.

25. Leibovici, Didier, Karen Ritchie, Bernard Ledesert, and Jacques Touchon (1996). Does Education Level Determine the Course of Cognitive Decline? *Age and Ageing*, 25 (5), 392–97.

26. Mulligan, R., A. Mackinnon, P. Berney, and P. Giannakopoulos (1994). The Reliability and Validity of the French Version of the Canberra Interview for the Elderly, *Acta Psychiatrica Scandanavica*, 89 (4), 268–73.

27. Neergaard, Lauran (2000). U.S. Health Care Delivers Little for Money, *The Salt Lake Tribune,* June 21, A1, A4.

28. Nemitz, B. (1995). Advantages and Limitations of Medical Dispatching: the French View, *European Journal of Emergency Medicine,* 2 (3), 153–59.

29. Nourhashemi, F., B. Vellas, L. K. Gray, D. Mischlich, F. Forette, B. Forette, J-M Vetel, F. Kuntzmann, R. Moulias, and J. L. Albarede (1998). Health Care for Older Persons, A Country Profile: France, *Journal of the American Geriatrics Society,* 46 (11), 1431–33.

30. Ohayon, Maurice M., and Malijai Caulet (1996). Psychotropic Medication and Insomnia Complaints in Two Epidemiological Studies, *Canadian Journal of Psychiatry,* 41 (7), 457–64.

31. Olson, Laura Katz (1994). Introduction, in Laura Katz Olson (ed), *The Graying of the World: Who Will Care for the Frail Elderly?,* New York: Haworth Press, 1–23.

32. Organization for Economic Cooperation and Development (1996a). *Ageing in OECD Countries: A Critical Policy Challenge,* Paris: Organization for Economic Cooperation and Development.

33. Organization for Economic Cooperation and Development (1996b). *Caring for Frail Elderly People: Policies in Evolution,* Social Policy Studies No. 19, Paris: Organization for Economic Cooperation and Development.

34. Organization for Economic Cooperation and Development (1994). *Caring for Frail Elderly People,* Paris: Organization for Economic Cooperation and Development.

35. Organization for Economic Cooperation and Development (1995). *The Labour Market and Older Workers,* Paris: Organization for Economic Cooperation and Development.

36. Organization for Economic Cooperation and Development (2000). Online at www.oecd.org.

37. Orgogozo, J.-M., J.-F. Dartigues, S. Lafont, L. Letenneur, D. Commenges, R. Salamon, S. Renaud, and M. B. Breteler (1997). Wine Consumption and Dementia in the Elderly: A Prospective Community Study in the Bordeaux Area, *Review of Neurology,* 153 (3), 185–92.

38. Phillipson, Chris (1998). *Reconstructing Old Age: New Agendas in Social Theory and Practice,* Thousand Oaks, CA: Sage Publications.

39. Ritchie, Karen, Jean-Marie Robine, Luc Letenneur, and Jean-Francois Dartigues (1994). Dementia-Free Life Expectancy in France, *American Journal of Public Health,* 84 (2), 232–36.

40. Salamagne, Michele (1997). Hospice in France, in Dame Cicely Saunders and Robert Kastenbaum (eds), *Hospice Care on the International Scene,* New York: Springer, 130–42.

41. Sykes, Roger (1990). The Client Group—Characteristics and Trends, in *Supporting Older People in General Housing,* Oxford: the Oxford Conference, Wadham College, 33–51.

42. Tinker, Anthea (1994). The Role of Housing Policies in the Care of Elderly People, in Organization for Economic Cooperation and Development, *Caring for Frail Elderly People,* Paris: Organization for Economic Cooperation and Development, 57–82.

43. United States Census Bureau (2000). *International Data Base.* Online at www.census.gov/cgi-bin/ipc/idbpyry.pl.

44. Walker, Alan, Jens Alber and Anne-Marie Guillemard (1993). *Older People in Europe: Social and Economic Policies,* Brussels: European Observatory, Commission of the European Community.

45. Zeitzer, Ilene R. (1994). Recent European Trends in Disability and Related Programs, *Social Security Bulletin,* 57 (2), 21–26.

Part IV

ALTERNATIVES FOR OPTIMAL AGING AND QUALITY OF LIFE

In Part IV we compare the characteristics and experience of eight countries as they have attempted to develop appropriate policies and programs contributing to optimal aging and quality of life in older age. Chapter 17 contains detailed comparisons among the eight countries that help clarify the status and progress of conditions, policies, and programs. The available information is not always entirely complete or up-to-date for every country but it provides a basis for reasonably accurate comparisons.

Chapter 18 draws from the successful experience of all countries to construct an outline of policies and programs that have the potential to optimize quality of life for older people. Any summary suggesting an "ideal model" must be somewhat cautious and preliminary because successful programs in one country might not work effectively in another—for cultural, economic, or political reasons. Furthermore, policies and programs have not always been adequately tested and evaluated. What appears to be good policy may not always have been fully realized in practice.

No country appears to have a perfect system. However, some have clearly been doing considerably better than others in selected policy and program categories. All are challenged by a rapidly growing older population and limited resources. Each country can presumably learn from the successful and unsuccessful experiences in other countries.

Chapter 17

COUNTRY COMPARISONS
Indicators of Effectiveness

◆◆◆ INTRODUCTION

Similarities and major diversity are evident among the economically advanced countries discussed in the previous chapters. All have one thing clearly in common: the proportion of older population is increasing, as illustrated in Table 17–1.

TABLE 17–1   Changing Proportions of Older Citizens

Country	1950	1985	2000	2020 (Projected)
United States	8.1%	11.9	12.7	17.3
Canada	*	*	12.5	*
Japan	4.9	10.3	16.7	23.8
United Kingdom	10.7	15.1	15.6	18.7
The Netherlands	*	*	13.5	*
Germany	9.4	14.7	16.1	22.3
Sweden	10.3	17.9	17.3	22.8
France	11.4	13.0	16.0	19.1

*Data was not available for Canada and the Netherlands in years 1950, 1985, and projected to 2020.
Source: Data from United States Census Bureau, 2000; Social Security Administration, 1997: xlvi; Nishio, 1994: 236.

Although the direction of the trend in the first two decades of the twenty-first century is clearly upward (column 4), the projections are based on certain assumptions about life expectancy that may not be entirely dependable. If mortality continues to decline because of healthier lifestyles and improved medical care, the future size of the older population could be considerably larger, as is already evident in Sweden and Japan.[34]

In the year 2000 the countries with the highest proportion of older people were Japan, Sweden, Germany, the United Kingdom, and France (proportions above 15 percent); the United States, Canada, and the Netherlands have somewhat lower proportions. The "older" countries are already experiencing greater pressure on their pension, health care, and long-term care systems than the "younger" countries—and are in the process of considering financing and benefit reforms to avoid unreasonable future tax burdens.[4]

◆◆◆ ECONOMIC AND SOCIAL COMPARISONS

Ability of countries to support programs for the older population is indicated in part by Gross Domestic Product per capita, summarized in Table 17–2.

The differences between countries in GDP per capita are not substantial since all of these countries are economically advanced—although the United States is clearly well ahead of the others, and the United Kingdom and Sweden are the least wealthy per capita.

Common Attributes

Several attributes common to all countries are listed in Table 17–3.

The common patterns and variations outlined in the table suggest the usefulness of examining the policies and programs in each country to identify what seems to work well and the potential application of that experience in other countries.

TABLE 17–2   GDP Per Capita, 1998

Country	GDP Per Capita (Converted to U.S. Dollars)
United States	30,514
Canada	24,468
Japan	24,109
United Kingdom	21,170
The Netherlands	23,082
Germany	22,835
Sweden	21,213
France	22,091

Source: Data from Organization for Economic Cooperation and Development, 2000. These comparisons are based on purchasing power parities that eliminate the price differentials between countries.

TABLE 17–3 Common Country Characteristics Related to Aging

- Steadily increasing life expectancy.
- Improved levels of physical health compared with earlier decades—generally associated with higher levels of education and affluence.
- Decline of multigeneration families in the same household accompanied by higher proportions of older people (especially women) living independently.
- Health insurance that generally assures older individuals access to health care, with major variations in completeness and quality of coverage, especially for long-term care.
- Increases in supported housing programs of various kinds to compensate for losses in ability to undertake activities of daily living.
- Expansion and refinement of social security and pension systems to provide widespread basic income support and minimize poverty among the segment of the population that has not worked at good jobs.

Source: Data in part from Tokarski, 1993: 63–64.

Life Expectancy

Life expectancies at birth and at age 65 are summarized in Table 17–4.

As data in the table indicate, Japan, Canada, and Sweden are at the top in life expectancy, although women can expect a longer life in France than in Sweden. The United States, Germany, and the United Kingdom rank at the lower end for both men and women. France and the Netherlands are in the middle. Life expectancy at age 65 varies considerably from life expectancy at birth. Japan, France, and Sweden are at the top, with the United States and Canada in the middle. The United Kingdom, Germany, and the Netherlands are lower.

TABLE 17–4 Life Expectancy in Eight Countries, at Birth and at Age 65, for Males and Females, 1999

Country	Life Expectancy at Birth	Life Expectancy at Age 65	
	Average (1999)	Men (1994)	Women (1994)
United States	76.2	15.5	19.0
Canada	79.4	15.8	19.9
Japan	80.1	16.8	21.3
United Kingdom	77.4	14.4	18.6
The Netherlands	78.2	14.8	18.8
Germany	77.2	14.7	18.4
Sweden	79.3	16.0	19.8
France	78.6	16.2	21.0

Source: Data from National Center for Health Statistics, 1998; United States Census Bureau, 2000.

The differences between countries are relatively slight. The bottom rank of the United States in life expectancy at birth for both men and women is a reflection in part of the high rate of infant mortality and early death among low-income and minority populations. For example, the American southern states with higher poverty and higher minority populations than the national average tend to have both high infant mortality and lower life expectancy than other states.

The relatively low rank for Germany is heavily a consequence of the much lower life expectancy in eastern Germany following the communist era (also the case for most eastern European countries). It will take several decades to entirely overcome this deficit. In Japan and Sweden, on the other hand, poverty and infant mortality tend to be very low, and minority populations are very small. Diets have been relatively good in both countries, with lots of vegetables and fish. Both countries also have a strong record of preventive health care for children and adults. The explanation for particularly high female life expectancy in France is not clear, although a diet high in vegetables may be an influence.[17]

The differences between Canada and the United States in life expectancy at birth (Canada does better) may be traced in part to differences in poverty (Canada has less) and minority populations (Canada has fewer). The health care insurance and long-term care systems in Canada are also more universal than in the United States—which may contribute to less morbidity and greater longevity.

Higher life expectancies at age 65 in Sweden, Japan, and France may reflect positive factors—good diet, good health care, and good social-support systems. However, the basis for the outcome is not entirely clear. Lower age 65 life expectancies in Germany probably reflect the east German situation as noted above, whereas in the United Kingdom the older population may not always be well served by a modestly funded health and long-term care system that has discriminated against older people by imposing rationing on selected services. The reasons for a somewhat lower than average life expectancy at age 65 in the Netherlands are unclear since all of the ingredients for high life expectancy appear to be present.

The birthrate is a major factor in the future ability of countries to afford programs for the elderly. At present several of these countries have a birthrate below replacement. That is, fewer children will be born to counterbalance the number of deaths. Sweden, Germany and Japan have the lowest birthrates, well below replacement and indicating a decline in future populations. This could create major problems in financing pensions and other social protection for the older population. France, the Netherlands and the United Kingdom are expected to continue moderate population growth, whereas Canada, and the United States will grow more rapidly, in part because of immigration from other countries.[4]

◆◆◆ MAJOR QUALITY-OF-LIFE CATEGORIES

Individual Freedom and Independence

All of the countries place considerable emphasis on individual freedom and initiative. However, government policies or cultural practices in some countries limit choices more restrictively than in others. For example, choice of physicians (particularly specialists) and hospitals is generally available in the United States, Canada, Sweden, and France, but choice is more constrained (especially for specialists) in Japan, the United Kingdom, Germany, and the Netherlands. The advent of widespread managed care in the United States has somewhat diminished freedom to choose physicians causing widespread dissatisfaction among physicians and patients.

Physicians have substantial control over medical care and patients in Japan—with little patient initiative allowed. The expectation in the Netherlands is for an older individual to see the physician close at hand in the community. Each GP physician in the United Kingdom has a "list" of patients and is responsible for any referrals to specialists. In Germany, general practitioners cannot treat their patients in hospitals but exercise control over access to specialists.

These are only illustrations of limitations on individual freedom and independence. In general, these countries have few constraints.

Family and Community

The culture of every country places great emphasis on the importance of family support. The degree of actual dependence varies widely however. Policies in some countries, especially in Sweden, Canada, Germany, and the United States, promote a high level of independence for older people, whereas Japan, the United Kingdom, France, and the Netherlands show evidence of somewhat greater integration with and dependence on families. Japan is at one extreme and Sweden is at the other among these countries. Despite their differences, the two countries have in common the greatest average life expectancies among the nations of the world.[12]

Families in every country continue to assume primary responsibility for support and ongoing care, although with a declining tendency to share three generation households. Older couples and individuals prefer to live separately whenever they have the income and capacity, with the exception of Japan; but even in Japan this tendency is increasing. Some are minimally supported because they have no children or because they outlive them. Between 20 and 30 percent of older people are childless in most countries.[21]

Cultural differences in the interpretation of family responsibility also play a role. Sweden, the United States, and Canada appear to encourage nuclear family independence through housing and pension policies, whereas this seems to have been less true in Japan, the Netherlands, Germany, France and the United Kingdom. In Sweden, for example, a strong commitment to independence for women has meant that most women work and are not available for full-time care-taking. On the other hand, family responsibility for long-term care has been encoded in a series of laws in Japan and Germany, although recent policy changes have altered the rules; government responsibility comes increasingly into play when families are simply not available to assume the primary caretaker role.[21]

Health Care

The United Kingdom, Sweden, the Netherlands, Canada, and the United States have well-developed geriatric health care programs, whereas Japan, France, and Germany have not given as much attention to specialized health care for the older population. In most instances health care providers treat older people much like anyone else, despite evidence that aging bodies benefit from specialist knowledge about the unique physical and mental changes that occur with aging.

Sweden, the Netherlands, Canada, and the United Kingdom have attempted to decentralize the management of health care, and have moved toward greater privatization although heretofore they were noted for centralized control. The governments of these countries have apparently concluded that government control and management are more costly and less effective than local and private control. However, in Japan the trend is in the opposite direction, in part because local control by private physician managers of clinics and hospitals has not apparently been of sufficient benefit to the elderly. Consequently, consumers are choosing to seek health care whenever possible from salaried physicians in public hospital out-patient units rather than from local private clinics.

Several countries are experimenting with the "managed care" approach to cost cutting as practiced in the United States. Elements of managed care in the hospital setting are at work in the Netherlands and Sweden, accompanied by considerable public regulation. It remains very unclear whether managed care is improving or harming health care for older people and whether it is effectively cutting costs over the long term.

Mental Health Care

No country has achieved comprehensive care for the older population with mental disorders. The relevance of mental health to physical well-being and quality of life is neither well understood nor appreciated in most countries. The "best" methods of treatment for the older population are not widely pursued. However, Sweden, the Netherlands, France, Canada, the United Kingdom, Germany, and United States have made major strides in upgrading services. Japan has not made as much progress, in part because mental disorder continues to be poorly understood and viewed as a negative reflection on the family.

Depression and dementia rates are relatively comparable in every country, especially among older individuals living in institutional settings. The suicide rate among the older population is higher in the United States and Japan than in other countries, without a clear rationale. No common contributing factors have been identified. However, suicide is directly related to depression which appears to be somewhat higher than average in these two countries.[2]

Long-Term Care

It has been difficult in every country to keep pace with the growing number of very old individuals who need assistance with activities of daily living, personal care, and chronic health care. Home health care has been a growth industry in every country. The addition of nursing home spaces has not kept pace with demand. Nursing homes are often understaffed, and tend to be very costly in all countries.

Home Care. Community home care has been justified on the basis of at least two primary assumptions: (1) it has the potential to be more cost efficient than institutional care thus saving investment in more expensive nursing homes, and (2) it may be more effective at optimizing the quality of life for the individual served, especially in contrast to institutional care. All countries have adopted these assumptions and have been systematically substituting home care for nursing home care whenever possible. However, experiments in several countries over a period of years seem to indicate that home care is less expensive than nursing home care *only* when the older person is capable of *self-care* for much of the time or is cared for in part by an unpaid family member or other helper. When more than eight hours per week of paid skilled nursing or other care is required, institutional care may be less expensive.[15, 16]

Costs have risen dramatically causing some countries to begin limiting access to home care for less needy individuals. Alternative approaches are under examination such as means-testing of benefits for home nursing and home help in the United States, Japan, Sweden, and Germany. Until the late 1990s, Sweden provided widely accessible home health care free of personal cost. However, fees were instituted because of resource shortages. Access to home help services now requires some level of private payment depending on income. In the Netherlands all older people have access to health and homemaker services 24 hours per day but the more affluent must pay an annual fee and additional fees. The United Kingdom has attempted to provide universal home health service 24 hours per day, but resource shortages mean that access and funding vary widely depending on the location in the country. In each country public programs have difficulty recruiting and retaining home health workers because of the relatively low rates of pay and status. Home care is thus faced with serious challenges.

New methods of providing home care have been tested in experiments intended to examine cost efficiency and effectiveness. For example, direct cash payments to disabled older individuals who meet certain criteria enable them to personally purchase needed home care services from either home help or health care agencies or family members in the United Kingdom, Germany, and Sweden. Evidence indicates that those receiving the benefits tend to economize on services while appreciating the opportunity for choice. Providers of services are presumed to be available on call, which is not always the case given the high demand. A care (or case) manager has been widely used to help provide the link between services and consumers.

Institutional Care. The rate of residence in assisted living homes and nursing homes varies considerably from one country to another as indicated in Table 17–5.

The differences between assisted living, skilled nursing, or long-term hospital residence and care have become somewhat fuzzy because of varying definitions among countries. The breakdown in the table is based on a definition of nursing home that includes 24-hour-per-day nursing care as well as assistance with activities of daily living, personal care, one or more therapies, and room and board. Residential or assisted living homes usually do not have 24-hour skilled nursing available but sometimes have ready access to nurse aids or licensed practical nurses. Long-term hospital residence is usually less intense than acute care and somewhat like skilled nursing home care.[26]

Some of the countries have emphasized assisted living while limiting use of

TABLE 17–5   Estimated Rates of Institutional Care in Selected Countries, 2000

Country	Proportion in Assisted Living, Nursing Homes, or Long-Term Stay Hospitals
United States	5.7
Canada	6.2
Japan	6.0
United Kingdom	5.1
The Netherlands	8.8
Germany	6.8
Sweden	8.7
France	6.5

Note: the definition of assisted living or residential care and nursing home care varies somewhat between countries. For example, Japan uses hospitals as locations for skilled nursing care much more than other countries, which is not counted in many calculations. Consequently, investigators reach somewhat varying results).
Source: Data from Jacobzone et al, 1999a: 49; Jacobzone, 1999b: 56.

nursing homes, as in the United Kingdom, Sweden, the Netherlands, and France. The United States and Japan have until recently made greater use of proprietary nursing homes (or hospitals in Japan) and less use of residential care. However, the situation began to change rapidly in the 1990s in all countries as costs, shortages of space, and concerns about quality of life in nursing homes have risen. All countries are now giving greater emphasis to assisted living for anyone who can function with a reasonable quality of life outside the nursing home setting.

Quality of Care. Two primary dimensions are considered paramount in judging quality whether in a private home or institutional setting: (1) the quality of professional and personal care based on needs assessments, adequacy of the care plan, and implementation of the plan, and (2) the quality of life in the home or institutional setting, in terms of the social, psychological, and physical living environment. Each country focuses on optimizing these two dimensions.[10]

Maintaining and enhancing quality of care has been a major issue because of the pressure to provide care for growing numbers of individuals in the context of limited resources. Cost containment limits facility investments and wages for staff, with clear quality-of-life implications. Moreover, standards providing the basis for ongoing evaluation of quality have only been partially developed and implemented in most countries. The new German long-term care insurance scheme contains a required quality measurement mechanism to be undertaken by managers of any nursing home receiving insurance benefits.[10]

A recent study in ten countries, based on a Resident Assessment Instrument, indicated little consistency between assessments of functional capacity and nursing home placement. Rather, institutionalization rates were interpreted to be a result of such factors as: (1) differences in organization and financing of long-term care services (2) the amount of responsibility assumed by families, and (3) the availability of nursing home beds. Countries with good financing tended to have more people in nursing homes. If more nursing home beds were available, they tend to be filled. When families assume greater responsibility, fewer people go to nursing homes.[26]

Service Sharing. Sweden and the Netherlands have developed a combination of publicly supported assisted living (so-called service houses), nursing homes, and community services which focus on maximizing independence. At the same time, they economize on costs by sharing services between assisted living residences, nursing homes, and the community. Residents in each case are encouraged to do as much as possible for themselves, with minimal dependence on staff. Each type of senior housing unit is designed to be integrated with the community setting to avoid isolation from social activities.[5]

Hospice Care. The hospice as a form of care for terminally ill individuals has become nearly universal in economically advanced nations, although there are wide variations in extensiveness and structure. The British have the most advanced system in Europe. However, lack of understanding of the concept, and consequent resistance to hospice development, represents a barrier for many medical practitioners, insurance executives, and government officials in every country. Use of drugs for pain control continues to be resisted by many physicians despite the evidence of effectiveness.[11]

Attention to the process of dying is widely viewed as having a lower priority than medical support for those who have the potential for recovery. The result is a continuing challenge in financing hospice services in every country. Further education on death and dying, the hospice philosophy, and the financial benefits which flow from use of the procedures, is likely to be required if medical practitioners and public officials are to be convinced that palliative care has sufficient merit to become a permanent part of the effort to enhance quality of later life.[11]

◆◆◆ HOUSING AND COMMUNITY

Home ownership by older families or individuals varies widely among countries. The ownership rate is more than 78 percent in the United States and Canada, 50 percent in France and the United Kingdom, about 33 percent in Germany and The Netherlands, and approximately 25 percent in Sweden (no data were available for Japan). Public policy favors ownership in Canada, Germany, and the United States, with tax deductions for interest payments and other available subsidies. Although similar policies exist in other parts of Europe and in Japan, public rental housing has been given much greater priority.[2, 32]

Although the United States and Japan provide housing subsidies for many lower-income older individuals, support for public housing has not been considered an essential part of the package of services to the same degree as in the European countries and Canada. Subsidies are available for design, construction, and management of public housing specifically for the older population, notably in the United Kingdom, Sweden, and The Netherlands. Home care services are often designed to complement the public accommodation. Private enterprise does the great majority of housing construction and rental in the United States.[3, 24]

◆◆◆ ECONOMIC AND FINANCIAL ISSUES

Income support, health insurance, and long-term care financing have been evolving rapidly in all of the countries. The European Union incorporated income and support guarantees into two major cooperative agreements—the Maastricht Treaty and the Social Charter on the Fundamental Rights of Workers, both written in 1992. The agreements include the following language:

- "Every worker of the European Community must, at the time of retirement, be able to enjoy resources affording him or her a decent standard of living."
- "Every person who has reached retirement age but who is not entitled to a pension or who does not have other means of subsistence must be entitled to sufficient resources and to medical and social assistance specifically suited to his or her needs."[33]

These proclamations indicate wide acceptance of progressive policies toward older people in the European countries. Generally greater public funds have been devoted to the various forms of social protection such as social security, health care insurance, and long-term care, as illustrated in Table 17–6 for 1993. Changes during the 1990s have altered the allocations somewhat but the pattern is likely to persist well into the twenty-first century.[20]

TABLE 17–6   Social Expenditure as a Proportion of Gross Domestic Product (1993)

Country	Proportion of Total Public Funds for Social Protection
United States	15.6
Canada	19.7
Japan	12.4
United Kingdom	23.4
The Netherlands	30.2
Germany	28.3
Sweden	38.0
France	28.7

Source: Data from Olsen, 1999: 245, based on data from the Organization for Economic Cooperation and Development.

TABLE 17–7 Contribution Rates in Eight Countries for Social-Support Programs in 1997

Country	Total Payroll Tax (%)		Individual Payroll (%)		Employer Payroll (%)
United States	18.15	=	7.65	+	10.5
Canada	14.03	=	5.9	+	8.13
Japan	27.8	=	13.37	+	14.43
United Kingdom	22.0	=	12.0	+	10.0
The Netherlands	55.25	=	44.65	+	10.60
Germany	41.86	=	20.20	+	21.66
Sweden	35.85	=	5.95	+	29.90
France	50.65	=	15.26	+	35.39

Source: Social Security Administration, 1997: xlvii.

The table shows that the United States and Japan spent less than half of the proportions of GDP expended in Sweden and much less than in other European countries; however, as noted earlier, the proportions of older people are also significantly lower in Canada and the United States. Expenditures in Japan are rising rapidly as the older population increases—but continuing reliance on families for social protection has helped to make costs lower.

Table 17–7 summarizes the payroll-tax contribution rates of each of the countries examined here, for old age and disability benefits (pensions), health care, death benefits, maternity allowances, family allowances, occupational injury, and unemployment.

The table indicates wide difference in contributions from employers and employees. Part of the difference is the much greater European use of payroll deductions for family allowances, universal health care, and unemployment benefits. Some countries pay for health care from general taxation budgets (Canada, the United Kingdom, and partially in Sweden) rather than through payroll taxes.

A correlation is evident between the proportion of older people and the overall costs for income benefits and health care—with income-benefit requirements generally higher in the countries with older populations (except Japan). However, higher costs for health care are noteworthy in the United States and Canada despite a lower proportion of older people than in most European countries or Japan.[19, 31]

Income Support

The average proportion of GDP going to public pensions in Europe was about 9 percent in 1996, as compared to 6.5 percent in the United States. These differences exist in part because of the varying goals of each system. For example, in the United States and Japan social security payments are intended primarily to keep older individuals from living in poverty. Public benefits are minimal, especially for individuals who worked in lower-paid occupations. Sources of income above this minimal level are considered the responsibility of the individual, the family, or the employer and are implemented through personal savings or employer pension plans. In much of Europe, on the other hand, public pensions are intended to continue a standard of living roughly at the level when working. Hence, costs and benefits are considerably higher and poverty is considerably lower. One consequence of the differences is a higher proportion of older individuals who must work to survive in the United States and Japan as compared to Europe. Retirement incentives clearly discourage older workers from continuing in the labor force in much of Europe—through mandatory retirement policies, relatively high-pension income, and tax penalties for continued work.[3]

Projections indicate the proportion of GDP required for pensions will rise to an average of 14–15 percent in most economically advanced countries early in the twenty-first century, although some countries with older populations such as Germany, France, and Sweden have already reached that level. Public pension needs in the United States, Canada, and the United Kingdom will increase more slowly because of the alternative sources of income noted above.[1]

Primary features of income security systems are summarized in Table 17–8.

As the table indicates, the proportion of personal income going toward income security is roughly correlated with the proportion of the population beyond retirement age, that is, France, Germany, Sweden, the Netherlands and the United Kingdom have higher assessments than the United States and Canada. Japan does not fit the pattern because of higher dependence on families, higher incidence of older workers, and a lower average public pension. Reforms of pensions schemes have recently been instituted or proposed in most countries because of their impending inadequacy as the proportions of older people increase.

As column two of the table indicates, expected retirement age is 65 in most countries except for Germany (age 63), the Netherlands (age 60) and France (age 60). The retirement age expectations are in process of change in most countries; age requirements are gradually moving upward as part of the reform process—again, to lower the cost of income-support schemes while increasing payroll contributions.

TABLE 17–8   Characteristics of Public Income Security Systems, 1996

Country	Total Payroll Tax for Income Security (% of income)	Expected Retirement Age
United States	12.4	65
Canada	6.0	65
Japan	17.3	65
United Kingdom	22.0	65
The Netherlands	32.25	60
Germany	17.8	63
Sweden	20.06	65
France	16.45	60

Source: Data from Beck, 1996: 9; Social Security Administration, 1997: xlvii.

Income Support Variations. Most pension systems have two parts: (1) a basic minimal social security pension available to everyone, and (2) an earnings-related supplementary payment based on years of employment and pay scale. The latter provision discriminates against lower-paid occupations and women who do not work outside the home during many of their most productive years.[33]

The ability of public social security to finance pensions is heavily impacted by the incidence of unemployment, which was a major issue in most of the European countries during the 1980s and 1990s. Unemployment generates a major problem when retirement income is almost entirely dependent on financing through pay-as-you-go payroll taxes. Consequently, countries such as the United Kingdom, the Netherlands, and Sweden have reformed their systems to cut back on public benefits—shifting more of the responsibility to private pension approaches.[20, 36]

Alternatives for the Future. Partly in response to the noted financing problem, social security systems in most advanced nations are projected to provide a lower proportion of income in the future. Retiring workers will receive fewer benefits from social security, requiring other pension sources or investments to increase—if living standards are to be sustained. Private pensions are becoming more widely supported and are now partially financed through government contributions, as in the United Kingdom. If such changes are not made, the World Bank has projected that many social security systems could become insolvent by 2030 or earlier, as the bulk of the baby-boom generations reach retirement age.[20, 35]

Levels of publicly provided income support, health care insurance, and long-term care insurance are highly controversial and serve as grist for major political differences within most economically advanced countries. A Europe-wide survey found that 75 percent of retired individuals feel that the governments *do not do enough* for older people, in terms of pensions, health care and long-term care. Others feel that *too much* is being done for the elderly, at the expense of other age groups in the population. In the Netherlands feelings were so strong that retirees formed new political parties to press their case, winning seven parliamentary seats in the 1994 elections.[1]

Pension levels actually regressed in the United Kingdom during the 1990s, becoming less equitable and less advantageous for lower-income workers and women. The reformed pension program was linked more directly to level of earnings with a relatively low basic pension guarantee for those who have not worked or were earners of low wages. Consequently, increased numbers of women and former lower-status older individuals received less than poverty-level income. This group remains well below the average income for comparable individuals in other countries.[1, 33]

The challenges are particularly acute in the countries with the oldest populations, such as Japan, Germany, France, the Netherlands, and Sweden but are somewhat less severe in the United States, Canada, and the United Kingdom. Moreover, the disparity between higher- and lower-income retired workers has been increasing in most countries, in substantial part because of greater improvements in retirement benefits of higher-income workers. However, governments have generally been slow to resolve the inequities because of the public financial commitment required.[21, 33]

TABLE 17–9   Proportion of GDP for Health Care and Per Capita Costs (1997)

Country	Proportion of GDP for Health Care	Per Capita Cost (in U.S. dollars)
United States	13.8	3633
Canada	11.0	2069
Japan	7.8	1581
United Kingdom	6.6	1246
The Netherlands	9.3	1728
Germany	10.8	2134
Sweden	9.6	1360
France	10.3	1972

Source: Data from National Center for Health Statistics, 1998: Table 116.

Financing Health Care

The proportion of GDP for health care and the per capita costs in each country are summarized in Table 17–9.

The United States spent far more for health care than any other country in 1997 with a per capita cost more than twice most countries. Per capita costs for the *older* population and the proportion of *all* health care costs devoted to the elderly were much higher in each country than for younger people, as indicated in Table 17–10.[28]

There is no direct relationship between the proportion of population age 65 or older and the proportion of health expenditures for the older population, in part

TABLE 17–10   Proportion of Health Care Expenditures for Care of the Older Population (1997)

Country	Proportion of Expenditures for Older People
United States	37%
Canada	*
Japan	43
United Kingdom	42
The Netherlands	40
Germany	32
Sweden	39
France	41

*No data were available for Canada.

Sources: Data from Organization for Economic Cooperation and Development, 1996: 54; U.S. Bureau of the Census, 1998, 1999.

because resources spent for health care are based on political decisions; health expenditures correlate with the affluence of the country.

Expenditures have been rising steadily in all countries except in the United Kingdom; they are expected to continue climbing over the next few years unless policies are changed. For example, estimates indicate that unless something drastic is done to change growth patterns, 17 percent of GDP will go to health care by 2007 in the United States, rising from $1,147 billion in 1998 to $2,113 billion in 2007—nearly doubling. Health insurance premiums are expected to rise at a rate of more than 8 percent annually. The largest single category of increase is for prescription drugs; hospital costs, home health care, and nursing home costs will rise more slowly because of Medicare and Medicaid cost controls.[6]

European countries and Canada have more complete reimbursement systems for health care at lower cost than in the United States. Canada, France, Germany, the United Kingdom, and Sweden cover both acute and long-term health care under national health insurance plans. The Netherlands and Japan have separate long-term care insurance programs. Room and board costs in nursing homes must be paid from social security, private pensions, or other income to the extent possible in all countries.[32]

Financing Long-Term Care

The Netherlands, United Kingdom, Canada, France, Germany, and Sweden support more extensive provisions for financing institutional care than do the United States and Japan. Japan expanded coverage in the late 1990s for implementation in 2000. The German system implemented in 1994 allocates funding from a special segment of health insurance resources for both home care and nursing home care.[1, 27]

Each country is challenged by efforts to integrate various sources of funding to complete a package of needed services. Lack of adequate coordination between financing systems sometimes means gaps in coverage. Care managers have alleviated some of the problem by assuming responsibility for integrating budgets and services.[27]

Costs for nursing home care vary widely although accurate comparable data are not easily obtained. For example, average cost of care for an older person is estimated to be 1.5 times higher in the Netherlands than in the United States, assuming all services are equal. However, since the Netherlands places greater emphasis on residential care, and only the most seriously disabled enter nursing homes, residents are likely to be more seriously ill on average than in the United States. Rehabilitation also appears to receive more emphasis in the Netherlands. Variations like these make precise comparisons in costs very difficult.

The French, German, United Kingdom, Swedish, and Canadian systems have not required stringent means-testing for entry to subsidized nursing home care, as compared to the systems in the Netherlands, the United States, and Japan, where means-testing is used as the basis for providing coverage of anyone who doesn't have the resources. Every country is struggling to design a cost-effective system that does not rely purely on high-cost public social insurance.[13]

◆◆◆ LIFESTYLE: WORK, RETIREMENT, AND LEISURE

Nearly all countries have experienced a gradual decrease in the proportion of older people who continue working. Japan has the highest proportion of working older men and women, followed by the United States, Sweden, and Canada. Fewer older individuals work in European countries. However, as the decline in the number of working-age adults proceeds, most countries are reevaluating retirement age and are increasing incentives for continued work beyond age 65.[2, 22, 25]

However, there is considerable resistance to a reversal of the early retirement pattern by some segments of the older population in many European countries, particularly among blue-collar workers in physically demanding jobs. Part-time employment prior to full retirement has become very common in a few countries, most notably in the United States, even though part-time jobs pay less and have lower status than many older workers are accustomed to.[1]

The changes of recent years have made retirement at 65 for men the official policy of most countries. Women can officially retire earlier in Japan, the United Kingdom and France, although several other countries have also encouraged women to retire earlier than men. Current policies in most countries focus on equal treatment for men and women.[21]

The Active Aging Movement

Active aging is getting support in every country, not only through continued employment but in other realms as well. A recent survey in the United States indicated that 40 percent of the new retiree population would like to continue some form of work and have a strong interest in being active and involved in community endeavors—rather than simply taking it easy.[14]

Public policy changes are increasing opportunities for training, education, and preventive health care as well. For example, Third Age Clubs have become widespread in France as mechanisms for participation in community activities, national life, and for leisure activities. Similar movements are evident in each of the other countries—with cultural variations. However, changes in attitudes among younger people and alterations in public policies are also required. Appropriate involvement of the older population could do much to lower the social costs of retirement while increasing tax revenues needed to pay the costs for pensions, health care, and long-term care.[21, 33]

◆◆◆ NOTEWORTHY ACHIEVEMENTS AND QUALITY OF LIFE

All of the countries are moving diligently to improve the conditions that contribute to quality of life for older people. However, some countries appear to have moved further, and provided better conditions, within some quality-of-life categories. Individual choice is high in all of these countries but may occasionally be restricted. For example, the United States, Canada, Sweden, and France appear to provide the greatest individual choice in selection of personal physicians, whereas the other four countries offer somewhat less choice. Japan, the United Kingdom, Germany, and the Netherlands place some formal or informal restrictions on the ability of older individuals to select primary care and specialist physicians—less the case in the other countries.

Family support remains strong in all of the countries but appears to be greatest in Japan, the Netherlands, Germany, and France. The important role of the family in caring for older members is part of cultural tradition. In each case public policy also directly supports the family responsibility. However, the family role is changing, and diminishing somewhat, in all these countries as adult children become more mobile and more women enter the work force. Consequently, community and national programs are increasing to fill the gap.

Canada, Germany, the Netherlands, Sweden, and France appear to have the most comprehensive and supportive health care programs for older people. In each case, high quality care is available for everyone with minimal out-of-pocket cost. In the United States, Japan, and the United Kingdom either quality or access is a problem to some degree—especially for lower-income segments of the older population.

Only the Netherlands and Sweden appear to have high-quality mental health care especially tailored to older people as an integral part of the larger health care system. In the other countries access is limited or serious taboos constrain use of services, particularly in Japan. Mental health care for older people has not achieved an equal footing with physical health care in most countries.

Home care appears to be most accessible in Canada, the United Kingdom, the Netherlands, and Sweden, although all of the other countries have increased the emphasis and resources devoted to in-home services. The evidence seems clear that most older individuals much prefer remaining at home with formal and informal services, rather than entering either assisted living care or a nursing home. The four countries noted have responded to this priority with greater comprehensiveness and effectiveness than have the United States, Japan, Germany, or France.

Nursing home services and insurance appear to be of somewhat higher quality in Canada, Germany, the Netherlands, and Sweden, than in the other countries. However, even in these countries a shortage of long-term care workers creates problems. As noted earlier, Germany has recently established a new funding mechanism to improve a system that was judged to be inadequate. Canada, the Netherlands, and Sweden have a longer tradition of emphasizing public support for good nursing home care. Until recently Japan has provided little public support and has a severe shortage of nursing homes, with large numbers of disabled older individuals lodged in multiple-bed wards of geriatric hospitals.

The Netherlands and Sweden appear to have the most comprehensive housing policies, especially for older individuals with lower incomes. Very few older citizens live in substandard housing. In both cases major efforts are made to integrate senior housing with community services—to provide ready access for daily needs and encourage continued participation of older people in social affairs. Service houses providing support for activities of daily living and personal care are widely available with public subsidy. Consequently, relatively few disabled older individuals must move to nursing homes. Japan has a serious shortage of affordable housing for older citizens but has recently begun to vigorously develop assisted living facilities for those with moderate and low incomes.

Income-support programs are available in all countries, with considerable variation. Canada, Germany, the Netherlands, Sweden, and France appear to have the most adequate public support and very little poverty among older people. The United States, Japan, and the United Kingdom have rather substantial numbers of older people with very low incomes because public pensions are modest for those from lower-paid occupationals, especially women.

Overall, Canada, the Netherlands, and Sweden appear to have the most comprehensive public policies—and thus older populations with the greatest potential for high quality of life. Germany and France occupy the middle ground, while the United States, Japan, and the United Kingdom have less comprehensive and adequate policies in several categories of support for quality of life.

◆◆◆ CONTINUING CHALLENGES

None of the countries have met *all* of the challenges of rapidly aging populations, as discussed in earlier chapters. Several common policy issues are widely evident.

Age Discrimination

Despite the relative affluence and social progressiveness of the countries reviewed and compared, age discrimination remains a major obstacle to full integration of older citizens into social and economic life. Workplace, pension, and retirement policies continue to make equal treatment difficult. Formal policies against discrimination remain unfulfilled in every country.

Long-Term Income Security

At least four options are available to help finance pensions for the increasing older population: (1) benefit reductions, (2) increases in payroll-tax revenues, (3) increases in the retirement age, and (4) greater advance funding through private and public investment for future retirees, rather than relying on paying-as-you-go policies. Variations of each possibility have been tried, with no clear pattern of success evident across all countries. Decisions in favor of one or more of these procedures will be required in each country during the early years of the twenty-first century.

Quality of Health Care

Barriers exist to use of some health services because of gaps in coverage and negative attitudes of providers. For example, essential prescription drugs are not fully covered by insurance in several countries and increasing co-payments make access somewhat difficult for older people with lower incomes. Physician providers offer limited service to the elderly in several countries as they attempt to see more patients than is reasonable for adequate diagnosis and treatment of chronic disease. Shortages of space and rationing of surgical services are a major problem in several countries. Patients with certain serious problems such as cancer are regularly sent from Canada to the United States, for example, for needed services because the services are over-taxed at home.

Nearly all countries have a need for greater attention to geriatric care, including the training of more physicians with a geriatrics specialization, more hospitals with geriatric wards, and greater provision for financing geriatric care. Furthermore, integration of specialized age-related health and social services at the community level has not generally been fully achieved. Public health and social care administration are usually separated at national, regional, and local levels. Health services tend more often to be financed at the national level and social services more often financed and managed at the local level.[27]

Long-Term Care

Few countries are satisfied with policies and support systems for long-term care, despite the progress of recent years. Most countries have not achieved a level of services that meet the need because of the high costs of long-term care. Consequently, families with disabled relatives are often under great stress as they attempt to care for older members, especially in the case of dementia or other very serious illnesses.

Experiments and surveys in the Netherlands, the United Kingdom, the United States, and Sweden indicate integrated home care is viewed as generally satisfactory by older consumers. However, the declining size of families, with fewer younger members to provide informal care for disabled older persons, and the shortage of home help and health care professionals, make the home care emphasis somewhat difficult to fully implement in all countries.

Geographical Inequities

The more vigorous and capable communities tend to provide good services whereas those with poor leadership and fewer resources may not serve their constituencies well. Wide variations between regions and communities in service adequacy and quality have been observed in the United Kingdom, France, Sweden, Germany, Japan, Canada, and the United States. Relative uniformity seems to prevail in the Netherlands. State responsibility for Medicaid in the United States has meant wide variations in completeness and quality of services among states and communities. Some states have minimal programs whereas others with greater wealth and farsightedness serve the older population quite well.

◆◆◆ SUMMARY AND CONCLUSIONS

Both common patterns and major variations are evident among the eight countries under discussion. Older individuals are healthier and living longer in every country. Extended families are declining in importance, as nuclear families become more prominent and a higher proportion of women are at work. Income and social support for older families are improving in every country. Physical health care, mental health care, and long-term care programs have been upgraded. Special housing for older people is expanding and helping to improve living conditions.

Some countries are doing better than others in several quality-of-life categories. The achievements correlate somewhat with the proportion of public resources spent for social protection, with some notable exceptions. The Netherlands, France, Germany, and Sweden spend the most per capita, followed by the United Kingdom, Canada, the United States, and Japan. Although Canada spends less than the European countries, quality of life for older people appears to be high. Germany has high expenditures but does not do uniformly well, in part because of the continuing lower social and economic level in the East German states.

All countries face the continuing challenges of age discrimination, uncertain long-term income security, gaps in health care, inadequate mental health care, shortages of long-term care, and geographical inequities. None has fully solved the problems of aging populations or achieved the quality of life that the older population might prefer.

◆◆◆ REFERENCES

1. Beck, Barbara (1996). The Luxury of Longer Life, *The Economist,* January 27, 3–16.
2. Blair, Cornelia, Mark A. Siegel, and Jacquelyn Quiram (1998). *Growing Old in America,* Wylie, TX: Information Plus.
3. Borsch-Supan, Axel (1994). Aging in Germany and the United States: International Comparisons, in David A. Wise (ed), *Studies in the Economics of Aging,* Chicago: University of Chicago Press, 291–325.
4. Bosworth, Barry, and Gary Burtless (1998). Population Aging and Economic Performance, in Barry Bosworth and Gary Burtless (eds), *Aging Societies: The Global Dimension,* Washington, DC: Brookings Institution, 1–27.
5. Carella, Joseph (1996). Scandanavians Champion Resident Independence, *Contemporary Long Term Care,* 19 (9), 140–41.
6. Goldstein, Amy (1998). A Transfusion from Patient's Wallets May Be in Order, *The Washington Post National Weekly Edition,* September 21, 31.
7. Hoek, J. Frank, Brenda W. J. H. Penninx, Gerard J. Ligthart, and Miel W. Ribbe (2000). Health Care for Older Persons, A Country Profile: The Netherlands, *Journal of the American Geriatric Society,* 48 (1), 214–17.
8. Jacobzone, Stephane (1999a). Ageing and Care for Frail Elderly Persons: An Overview of International Perspectives, *Occasional Papers No. 38,* Paris: Organization for Economic Cooperation and Development.
9. Jacobzone, S., E. Cambois, E. Chaplain, and J. M. Robine (1999b). The Health of Older Persons in OECD Countries: Is It Improving Fast Enough to Compensate for Population Ageing? *Occasional Papers No. 37,* Paris: Organization for Economic Cooperation and Development.
10. Johne, Gabriele (1996). The Assessment and Regulation of Quality in Long-Term Care, in Roland Eisen and Frank A. Sloan (eds), *Long-Term Care: Economic Issues and Policy Solutions,* Boston: Kluwer Academic Publishers, 285–305.
11. Kastenbaum, Robert, and Marilyn Wilson (1997). Hospice Care on the International Scene: Today and Tomorrow, in Dame Cicely Saunders and Robert Kastenbaum (eds), *Hospice Care on the International Scene,* New York: Springer, 267–72.
12. Kees, C. P., and M. Knipscheer (1992). The Netherlands in European Perspective, in Hal L. Kendig, Akiko Hashimotot, and Larry C. Coppard (1992), *Family Support for the Elderly: The International Experience,* New York: Oxford University Press, 147–59.

13. Laing, William (1993). *Financing Long-Term Care: The Crucial Debate*, London: ACE Books (Age Concern).

14. Lewis, Robert (1999). Older Workers Vow to Stay on the Job, *AARP Bulletin*, October, 4.

15. Monk, Abraham, and Carole Cox (1992). Lessons to Be Learned: Home Care in Other Countries, *CARING Magazine*, 11 (10), 35–39.

16. Monk, Abrahm, and Carole Cox (1995). Trends and Developments in Home Care Services: An International Perspective, in Leonard W. Kaye (ed), *New Developments in Home Care Services for the Elderly*, New York: The Haworth Press, 251–70.

17. National Center for Health Statistics (1998). *Health United States 1998*, Washington, DC: U.S. Bureau of the Census.

18. Nishio, Harry Kaneharu (1994). Japan's Welfare Vision: Dealing with a Rapidly Increasing Elderly Population, in Laura Katz Olson (ed), *The Graying of the World: Who Will Care for the Frail Elderly?* New York: Haworth Press, 233–60.

19. O'Connell, Joan M. (1994). The Relationship Between Health Expenditures and the Age Structure of the Population in OECD Countries, *Health Economics*, 5 (6), 573–78.

20. Olsen, Gregg M. (1999). Half Empty or Half Full? The Swedish Welfare State in Transition, *Canadian Review of Sociology and Anthropology*, 36 (2), 241–63.

21. Organization for Economic Cooperation and Development (1996). *Ageing in OECD Countries: A Critical Policy Challenge*, Paris: Organization for Economic Cooperation and Development.

22. Organization for Economic Cooperation and Development (1995). *The Transition from Work to Retirement*, Paris: Organization for Economic Cooperation and Development.

23. Organization for Economic Cooperation and Development (2000). Online at www.oecd.org.

24. Regnier, Victor (1994). *Assisted Living Housing for the Elderly: Design Innovations from the United States and Europe*, New York: Van Nostrand Reinhold.

25. Rein, Martin, and Harold Salzman (1995). Social Integration, Participation, and Exchange in Five Industrial Countries, in Scott A. Bass (ed), *Older and Active: How Americans Over 55 Are Contributing to Society*, New Haven: Yale University Press, 237–62.

26. Ribbe, Miel W., Gunnar Ljunggren, Knight Steel, Eva Topinkova, Catherine Hawes, Naoki Ikegami, Jean-Claude Henrard, and Palmi V. Jonnson (1997). Nursing Homes in 10 Nations: A Comparison Between Countries and Settings, *Age and Ageing*, 26 (S2), 3–12.

27. Schulte, Bernard (1996). Social Protection for Dependence in Old Age: The Case of Germany, in Roland Eisen and Frank A. Sloan (eds), *Long-Term Care: Economic Issues and Policy Solutions*, Boston: Kluwer Academic Publishers, 149–70.

28. Social Security Administration (1997). *Social Security Programs Throughout the World*, Washington, DC: U.S. Government Printing Office.

29. Tokarski, Walter (1993). Later Life Activity from European Perspectives, in John R. Kelly (ed), *Activity and Aging: Staying Involved in Later Life*, Newbury Park: Sage, 60–68.

30. United States Census Bureau (1998). *National Data Book*, Washington, DC: U.S. Government Printing Office.

31. United States Census Bureau (2000). *International Data Base*. Online at www.census.gov.

32. Walker, Alan, Jens Alber, and Anne-Marie Guillemard (1993). *Older People in Europe: Social and Economic Policies*, Brussels: European Observatory, Commission of the European Community.

33. Walker, Alan, and Tony Maltby (1997). *Ageing Europe*, Philadelphia: Open University Press.

34. Wise, David A. (1994). *Studies in the Economics of Aging*, Chicago: University of Chicago Press.

35. World Bank (1994). *Averting the Old Age Crisis: Policies to Protect the Old and Promote Growth*, Washington, DC: The World Bank.

36. Zeitzer, Ilene R. (1994). Recent European Trends in Disability and Related Programs, *Social Security Bulletin*, 57 (2), 21–26.

Chapter 18

QUALITY OF LIFE
Focusing on the Priorities

◆◆◆ INTRODUCTION

Wide agreement exists among citizens and leaders in economically advanced countries on several basic priorities for achieving quality of life among older people:

- Freedom and choice should be optimized—older individuals ought to have substantial control over their lifestyle in later life.
- Older individuals should receive ongoing informal support in the context of family and community whenever possible.
- Every older person should have ready access to health care, mental health care, and long-term health care at modest personal cost.
- Older individuals and couples should have good housing that fits their needs— in a pleasant community setting with required services close at hand.
- Disabled older individuals unable to manage in a private home should have access to residence in supportive homelike environments as close to family and friends as possible.
- Basic income support should be universally available and adequate to meet primary needs and insure a good quality of life.
- Lifestyle choices should allow older individuals to continue working if they wish, remain active in community and society, enjoy retirement and leisure, and achieve their potential for a high-quality later life.

Within each country disagreement exists about which of the priorities are most important when resources are scarce and when all preferred choices cannot be achieved. Political consensus that leads to clear policies and programs is difficult. Major gaps and program inadequacies are evident in nearly all countries.[18]

Divergence in Policies

The degree to which the priorities are implemented not only varies considerably among countries, but also diverges from one jurisdiction to another *within* countries. Rural and urban regions tend to be at different stages of development in most countries, with generally more developed services in the affluent urban regions— with some notable exceptions. Rural retirement enclaves in recreational areas may have excellent services.

In Germany older residents of the western states have generally greater access to resources and services than older people in the eastern states; many years will be required to overcome the deficits created by the earlier years of communist control. Nearly all countries have internal variations although not usually as extreme as in Germany. The costs of creating reasonable uniformity throughout a country can be enormous, although some countries such as the Netherlands have been reasonably successful. Estimates indicate that implementation of the current priorities at 1999 levels of spending for all of the additional older people in the United States could absorb as much as 60 percent of the United States federal budget by 2020—if changes are not made.[2, 23]

Basic Questions

Several basic questions can be raised about the appropriateness of providing government-sponsored pensions, health care, long-term care, and other support to all older people in every country:

- How much should society tax itself to publicly subsidize programs for older people?
- Is there a danger that the growing commitment of federal resources to programs for the aged will crowd out *other* fundamental needs, such as education for young people, managing natural resources, research, and other public priorities?
- Should means-testing be used to give greater benefits to older people with lower incomes and greater need, while requiring those with resources to pay more of their own way?
- Should the age of eligibility for income support and other benefits be raised as the health and functioning of the older population improves?

These questions are under examination in every country, especially during periods of economic downturn when tax revenue goes down and unemployment goes up, as in most of Europe, Canada, and Japan during the 1990s. Choices were made in some countries to cut back on programs that citizens had learned to expect, notably in Sweden and the United Kingdom. Cutbacks raise serious equity questions because the most vulnerable often suffer most—especially the large population of very old women without sufficient resources to pay their own way.

◆◆◆ COMPONENTS AND RESPONSIBILITIES

The discussion in the following pages identifies the components and responsibilities apparently required for an equitable and optimum quality of life for older people—based on the collective experience of the countries under consideration. A summary is presented in Table 18–1.

Individual Initiative and Choice

The individual usually has major responsibility to take the initiative and make choices in democratic societies. However, learning how to be independent, disciplined, and informed is part of the socialization and education responsibility of the family, community, and larger educational system. Parents learn what they know about values, attitudes, beliefs, and socialization of their children as part of their own experiences and training. The adequacy of the socialization process is a direct predictor of ability to be independent, or interdependent, while making good choices as we age.

The larger culture and social system has major influence on the values, attitudes, beliefs, and behaviors of families, and the relative independence of individuals, even though democratic societies usually do not try to forcefully impose cultural values, attitudes, beliefs, or behavior. However, the tendency of governments to pre-

TABLE 18–1   Quality of Life Components and Responsibilities

Components	Primary Responsibility
Individual Initiative and Choice	The Individual, Family, Community
Social Support	Family, Community, Government
Health and Health Care	The Individual, Family, Private Enterprise, Community, Government
Mental Health and Care	The Individual, Family, Community, Private Enterprise, Government
Long-Term Care —Home Care —Assisted Living or Residential Care —Nursing Home Care	The Individual, Family, Community, Private Enterprise, Government
Housing and Community	The Individual, Private Enterprise, Community, Government
Income Support	The Individual, Government, Private Enterprise
Satisfying Lifestyle	The Individual, Family, Community

fer uniformity and universality appears to be greater in some countries than others—one of the reasons that policies and programs for older people are more nationally comprehensive in countries such as Canada, the Netherlands, Germany, and Sweden.

Social Support

Social support is surely among the most crucial requirements for quality of life in older age. It is usually provided in some form by family and community without any need for intervention by regional or national governments. However, if the family structure is weak or does not remain available, as is clearly the case for some older individuals in all countries, the community and/or government must intervene to fill the gap if dependent older individuals are to survive and thrive. Some communities fail because they are dysfunctional, poor, or not capable of responding with resources and assistance—regularly the case in certain locations within most countries. Regional or national authorities then become the primary recourse for needed assistance, illustrated by response efforts of Area Agencies on Aging in the United States and outreach service centers in other countries, to help provide formal social support in the private home, retirement home, or nursing home.

Many European countries try to assure social support by integrating housing for older citizens into the core of the community infrastructure through special housing and long-term care centers. Assisted living homes are built near the community center, have public restaurants, and share services with independent living apartments and nursing homes nearby. Social support is encouraged by proximity to other people and by the use of case managers who keep track of each older person while assuring them needed social and other support.

Health and Health Care

Good health is much more a result of effective personal health practices than a consequence of contacts with the health care system. An older individual can usually maintain health and prolong life through good nutrition, appropriate exercise, avoiding toxins, and otherwise practicing self-discipline, except on occasions when the body is unavoidably attacked by diseases such as cancer.

Private enterprise has a role to play in preventing disease, maintaining good health, and caring for individuals who become ill. Nutritional food is heavily promoted by major food companies, nutritional food stores, and in a variety of advertising forms. Health clubs have proliferated to encourage and support proper exercise patterns. Major campaigns have been undertaken by public and private groups to discourage smoking, drinking, drug use, and avoidance of other toxins. Public health organizations of local, regional, and national governments are engaged in health promotion and disease prevention within every country.

Most countries now assume that health care should be available to all older people, but the mode of delivery may be private, public, or a combination. Some countries rely much more than others on private practitioners and private hospitals as the delivery mechanisms for preventive and acute care, whereas a public system predominates in others. Every country is attempting to make these services more comprehensive and cost effective, in the interest of avoiding unsupportable cost increases.

The prevailing pattern is for governments to play a major role in either: (1) directly providing disease prevention and acute care services, or (2) establishing rules, regulations, and procedures to assure the availability of insurance and care under private auspices. The United States is the only country among those examined here that does not attempt to guarantee universal health insurance for every younger person; Medicare and Medicaid are supposed to achieve the goal for the older population. However, because of major gaps in coverage and services the two public programs do not entirely solve the problem. Other countries also have shortages of services or insufficient insurance coverage but generally attempt to assure that lower-income individuals have access to emergency care and acute care even though they may have to wait for services.

Private enterprise has no incentive to insure or care for lower-income individuals who cannot afford insurance or direct payment. Government involvement has therefore seemed essential to *every* country in designing the rules and guaranteeing care. Countries with the most successful health care programs are consistently dependent on government rules or programs to assure equitable, universal, and reasonably uniform health care delivery.

Mental Health and Care

Maintenance of mental health may be primarily an individual responsibility, but is heavily a consequence of positive experiences in the family and community. However, the mental realm is less generally understood, and mental health care continues to be less available in most countries than physical health care. Yet it is very clear that mental disorder contributes directly to poor physical health and greatly diminishes quality of life in older age.

The most common serious disorders for older people—depression and dementia—appear to be only partially related to heredity or family background. It is not likely that either can be entirely avoided through good mental health practices. Individuals with these and other serious disorders are often unable to look after their own welfare. Family members may not have sufficient understanding of the problem to be very good at resolving the difficulties either.

Well-trained mental health professionals can be of great assistance in diagnosing and alleviating problems through application of their knowledge and use of modern prescription drugs. The costs can be substantial, which means that most private-insurance providers do not have sufficient incentive to offer full coverage. Private mental health care professionals are therefore not available to diagnose and alleviate many of the most serious problems. Government in some form must provide care or finance the needed services if they are to be available.

The trend, as indicated in earlier chapters, has been to develop mental health services at the community level, rather than at the regional (state) level or in large public hospitals. The Dutch have attempted to integrate physical and mental health services—with considerable success. France has initiated a regional system with publicly sponsored mental health care providers located in communities throughout the country. The United States has a system of community mental health centers that partially respond to many older individuals needing assistance. Nursing homes in the United States are officially required under Medicare and Medicaid rules to provide mental health services but usually do not have the professional personnel to respond.

None of the countries provides sufficient services to meet the demand. Yet, it seems clear that an adequately developed community-level system of services would greatly improve quality of life for older people. Since many expensive physical health problems have a mental health origin or are aggravated by mental disorder, greater investment in diagnosis and treatment of mental disorders is likely to lower the cost of physical health care somewhat.

Long-Term Care

Individuals and families in all countries usually do their best to manage disabilities at home. They call upon external resources only when they feel unable to fulfill the needs, and they much prefer help in the home if available. Institutionalization is avoided except when there is no other reasonable alternative. Public or private home health agencies and nursing homes are available in all countries, with wide variation in access and quality. Only the relatively affluent are able to pay the costs of either home care or institutional care on a sustained basis. Hence, the clear need for community and/or government reimbursement to assist those with lower incomes.

All countries provide some form of public support for home care, assisted living, and nursing home care—although with great variation in organization and resource allocation. Achieving the "right" amount and balance of various forms of long-term care and/or insurance is a major policy issue in every country. The appropriate balance between the various levels of care is not always clear—although every country is attempting to de-emphasize nursing home care in favor of home care or assisted living. Home care generally provides the best quality of life and may be the least expensive, depending on how it is managed.

Some form of assisted living is usually the second preference after home care for disabled individuals who do not need skilled nursing care—with the potential to maintain choice and relative independence at lower cost than nursing home care. Nursing homes and hospitals are choices of last resort when no other reasonable options are available.

The need for long-term care will continue to grow as populations of very old people increase. Private for-profit or nonprofit enterprise plays a major role in most countries, with governments helping finance the costs via sponsorship of insurance or direct payment. Decentralized management of programs and facilities has been gaining support even in countries that have traditionally been centralized, such as Sweden and the United Kingdom. A regulatory system is required to assure high quality care whether through public or private providers. Ample evidence in the United States and elsewhere indicates that without government regulation and inspection some unscrupulous private home care and nursing home operators will shortcut care so as to gain larger profits. Professional staff in public or nonprofit home care agencies and nursing homes are also in need of regular oversight as an incentive to maintain high standards.

The public burden for nursing home care is expected to increase substantially. A high proportion of older and seriously disabled individuals will not have adequate resources, insurance, or other outside assistance to share costs. The decrease in average family size in every country, and increasing employment of women, somewhat lowers the potential for family home care. Furthermore, Social Security payments, pensions, and savings are not expected to increase sufficiently to cover the rising costs of assisted living or nursing home care for all who need it. In the United States, Social Security, and Medicare are most critical to maintenance of independence, and yet they also appear to have limited potential to cover rising nursing home costs.[8]

Consequently, a public insurance program of the kind available in Germany, Sweden, and the Netherlands appears to be the best option. Payroll taxes are used to raise the needed revenue. All individuals with insufficient resources who need home care or nursing home care are eligible to receive a subsidy. Room and food costs are paid from pension income insofar as possible.

Housing and Community

The best housing and environment for older people in any country contains several basic attributes:[20]

1. Privacy, with a locked door, private bathroom, and kitchen for food storage and preparation.
2. Choice of furnishings, pictures, and other adjustable attributes.
3. Independent living insofar as possible, through self-care but with ability to call for help when needed.
4. Attention to individuality and uniqueness in terms of personal preferences for food, recreation, and social life.
5. Opportunity for stimulation, new experiences, and creativity in terms of art, music, and other sensory pleasures.
6. Homelike environment of the larger facility—in the case of grouped assisted living or other apartments—with a living room area, comfortable dining, access to various forms of recreation, and a pleasant exterior environment.
7. Maintenance of personal dignity and respect from staff and other residents.
8. Safety and security so as to minimize fear and avoid accidents.

Some governments have appeared sensitive to the mix between therapeutic goals, the social context, organizational needs, and the physical setting. The design and operation of public housing and care facilities have taken these factors into account. If any part is left out, a facility will have difficulty providing a high quality of life for residents.[20]

The great majority of older individuals assume full responsibility for achieving these attributes in their personal housing, remaining in a private home throughout their lives except for possible short periods of hospitalization or rehabilitation. They stay in a preferred community setting regardless of its merits and inadequacies, although many live in older housing and often in distressed communities. Several countries such as Sweden and the Netherlands have diligently tried to upgrade accommodations with various forms of publicly financed repairs, upgrading, and/or construction of new spaces, whereas other countries have left the responsibility largely to the private market, as is the case in the United States and Japan.

Only with major disability does housing become a special challenge in most countries, especially true for older women who are disproportionately short of good incomes and housing options. Those who do not have access to family support, or prefer to be independent, must deliberately choose to move to some form of assisted living or nursing home accommodation. Several countries include housing allowances as part of the basic support package for older people.

Public or private income-support programs in most countries provide for basic housing needs but may not be adequate in the event of a chronic condition. At this point governments have a clear role in helping with housing finance, construction, or rental supplements to meet the additional requirements. Private enterprise has no incentive to build housing for low income older people without a subsidy.

Income Security

Every country considered here has a publicly sponsored and mandated pension system that guarantees a retirement income for anyone who has worked. Most countries require a basic pension with work-related supplemental pensions that depend on years worked and level of wages. In some cases the public pension system provides sufficient income for comfortable living, as in Canada, Germany, the Netherlands, France, and Sweden. In other cases, the United Kingdom, United States, and Japan, the public social security income is modest and must be supplemented with personal savings or a supplementary pension to achieve a reasonable quality of lifestyle.

A few countries guarantee an adequate basic income to everyone, regardless of their employment status and whether or not they have worked. This has a special advantage for the substantial numbers of older women who have not worked at good wages and must otherwise live in poverty during their later years. This remains a major problem in the United States, Japan, and the United Kingdom. A government role in establishing an adequate minimum income is obviously crucial.

In most cases the income-support system is funded on a pay-as-you-go basis—a satisfactory arrangement as long as the number of workers greatly outnumbers the number of retirees. As retirees become more numerous, the required payroll contributions must increase for the smaller proportion of continuing workers—a major problem already for Germany, Japan, and Sweden, all with older populations and declining workforces.

The World Bank recommended in 199r5 that the pay-as-you go social security systems be replaced in part by mandatory and privately managed savings arrangements. At retirement the money accumulated would go to each retiree based on their contribution. This approach is quite similar to many private pension schemes already in existence, such as the Teachers Retirement and Annuity Association and

College Retirement Equities Fund for educators, the largest single private retirement fund in the world. The United Kingdom, The Netherlands, and Sweden have adopted variations of this approach, and similar options are under consideration in the United States as this is written.[1]

As noted previously, some danger exists that the additional required pension costs will crowd out public spending for other needs such as education, environmental protection, and transportation. There is major uncertainty about adequacy of government policy and management for income security in countries with generous benefits. Programs for the younger population could suffer in the interest of adequately supporting the older generations. Governments clearly have a major role in encouraging, regulating, creating stability, and providing for continuity of any income plans.[27, 28, 30]

Every country is attempting to increase cost effectiveness of public programs to avoid undue increases in public funding. The tendency is to add co-payments and deductibles for health care and long-term care. As a consequence, the burden of payment is increased for the individual. If incomes are adequate this may not be a major issue, but it is a serious problem for moderate- and lower-income retirees.

Out-of-pocket costs for health care in the United States were estimated to be twice as high in the 1990s as they were before the advent of Medicare in 1965. Two major options appear to be viable for solving this problem: (1) increasing basic pension incomes sufficiently to cover the co-payments, deductibles, and direct costs of health care, or (2) subsidizing these costs as part of the health and long-term care insurance package. The first option has been used in many countries and appears to help maintain financial security, individual independence, and autonomy. In the United States the second option is used via Medicaid to pay Medicare deductibles for some lower-income older individuals.

Satisfying Lifestyle

A satisfying lifestyle is in some sense the summary category or product of the components and responsibilities noted above. When all the elements are positive, older age is likely to be of high quality. A satisfying lifestyle is ultimately unique and individualistic—depending on the values, attitudes, beliefs, interests, and achievements of the person. The factors that produce the desired result vary in each country, depending on cultural traditions and priorities. In Japan close family relationships continue to appear critical to many older people with other friendships of less importance, whereas in the somewhat less family-oriented cultures of Europe and North America occasional interactions with family may be sufficient and outside friendships more extensive.

However, older individuals almost invariably value family and friendships regardless of country or culture. They want regular interaction with and support from their spouses, children, grandchildren, siblings, and close friends. Without these close relationships, quality of life and a satisfying lifestyle may be elusive.

A satisfying community setting is also obviously important. Ready access to services is crucial for daily needs and in times of crisis. Recreation and entertainment are of major importance to good health and personal pleasure. A high-quality community environment will contribute to aesthetic satisfaction and ease in securing other community requirements. Community government and local leadership can contribute greatly to elderly well-being by taking needs of older people and their preferences into account in designing and supporting the community infrastructure. Governments can contribute to good lifestyles by assuring that the components for quality of life are available when private sources of funding and institutional services are for some reason not forthcoming.

◆◆◆ CRUCIAL CHANGES AND QUALITY OF LIFE

Resolution of several major issues would greatly improve the quality of later life for large numbers of older individuals in every country.

Increasing the Efficiency and Quality of Care Systems

Systems of care for older individuals are sometimes based on tradition and outmoded rules. Several countries have successfully experimented with alternatives that seem to work better and be less expensive than previous models. For example, the Netherlands has created integrated community programs that attempt to achieve the best combination of home care, assisted living, and nursing home care in one community location, using many of the same facilities and personnel for each activity. The arrangement is similar in many respects to continuing care retirement communities in the United States. The use of this concept in Oregon with rigorous case management and improved medical management has considerably lowered costs and yet appears to improve quality of life for the older individuals involved. The number of required nursing home spaces has decreased in each case.[3, 26]

Geriatric Assessment and Care Management

The geriatric care management process has been developed as a specific approach for improving quality of care, preventing some illness and disease, and increasing efficiency. The procedure requires a highly trained geriatric care manager, usually a registered nurse or physician, to build and maintain good team relationships in the health care setting. The goals are to:[11]

- Improve preventive actions, health promotion, diagnosis, and care using a specific care plan.
- Reduce lengths of stay in hospitals and nursing homes.
- Help assure that institutional resources are efficiently used, including analysis of alternatives that might lower costs.
- Help patients make the transition to alternative lower-cost care settings.
- Improve the overall quality of patient care.

High-risk patients are identified early through careful screening so that appropriate resources can be applied to improve their care while minimizing length of stay. Improved physician practice patterns, discharge planning, end-of-life planning for patients who are diagnosed as terminally ill, and other patient care issues, can be implemented to improve efficiency. Systematic outcome evaluation can be used to measure effectiveness of the ongoing patient management system. Evaluation studies indicate that improved patient care and significant cost savings can be achieved using these tools.[19, 22]

Overcoming the Disadvantages of Older Women

As emphasized previously, a high proportion of older women in most countries do not have adequate retirement income, access to good housing, or support for long-term care. In the United States many do not have sufficient supplementary health care insurance to cover co-payments and deductibles, except when covered under the policy of a spouse or by Medicaid. Others have not worked outside the home or had medical insurance benefits in their workplace (where they are likely to have worked for considerably lower incomes than men), and thus have less access to retirement income. Upon the husband's death, if they were married, they may lose a substantial part of his retirement income. Consequently, paying basic expenses and affording good housing are often very difficult without direct family assistance.

Improving Care and Treatment of Dementia

A high proportion of older people, including nursing home residents in every country, have Alzheimer's disease or other forms of cognitive disorder. The incidence of these diseases is increasing steadily as the population lives longer. Many individuals and families cannot afford the costs of home care because neither private insurance or public programs are prepared to pay for enough of the relatively high personal and financial burden. Sweden, Germany, and the United Kingdom have provisions for social security credit for caretakers, to minimize making them dependent on welfare in later life. Many older individuals with serious dementia must enter nursing homes supported with public funds because they have no other choice of housing. The cost is likely to be considerably higher than would be the case for adequate home or assisted living support. Better understanding of the disease and an improved care system would enhance the well-being of dementia victims and their families.[15, 18]

Case or Care Management

Case management has been adopted in many countries as an important method of improving services and lowering costs. The role has been used extensively in several countries for better management of home health and nursing home care, especially when no family members are available with the requisite understanding. Training programs have been designed to prepare social workers, nurses, and others with the needed knowledge and skills for helping older individuals who may have difficulty understanding and using the care system. A key function is coordination of various resources and services to create sensible, more efficient, and more helpful packages of care.

Use of Means-Testing

Means-testing has been widely used to identify individuals or families with limited ability to pay required costs for services. Individuals with legitimate needs can then be given the support and resources to assure their well-being. This procedure is in contrast to financing systems that pay costs for the relatively affluent population—who can afford to pay their own way and are better at identifying resources—while neglecting many very old and less-aggressive lower-income individuals. The problem has been partly managed in most countries by increasing basic pension levels or providing a cash allowance to raise standards of living and thereby increase access to services. A means-testing system can require contributions from those who can afford to pay some part of the cost while assuring assistance for those with little income, even though it is often perceived as intrusive.

Optimizing Independence

Rigorous means-testing can unfortunately sometimes deprive the older individual of independence and decision power. The United Kingdom and a few other countries have initiated a publicly provided "personal budget" for individuals in need of long-term care. The budget is controlled by the individual—sometimes with the help of a care manager—who allocates the funds to purchase the preferred form of care. Results of controlled experiments indicate that the elderly decision makers tend to select lower-cost options that result in a decline of institutional care in favor of home care. Optimizing independence in other ways is likely to increase individual well-being and quality of life.[6]

Limiting "Unnecessary Care"

Minimizing overzealous medical care may improve efficiency and improve quality of life for mentally alert older people who place personal limits on the application of medical interventions or technology. Most acute or chronically ill older individuals are at the mercy of health care providers because they do not understand how much health care is needed under varying circumstances. They do not know when to say "no" to physicians, hospitals, and other health care professionals, even when they have their full cognitive abilities.[5]

Improved education on health care alternatives for consumers, and education for health professionals to make them more open to patient participation in decisions, are likely to increase as sophistication of the older population increases. Advance health care directives, statements of patient preferences, and medical directives are steps in this direction and can help patients limit decisions and actions they would prefer to avoid. Many of the very high costs near the end of life could thus be lowered.[5]

Limiting Transfers to Hospitals

Hospital death with associated intense life-extending efforts can be very demeaning and expensive. It is generally more satisfactory to dying individuals and families if death occurs at home or in a nursing home. Yet, a high proportion of older individuals who live at home until a final crisis are transferred to hospitals where they die—often after heroic efforts to extend their life for even a few days. Fewer nursing home residents are transferred to hospitals near death. A high proportion of lifetime health care costs are associated with the last year of life, largely because of terminal hospital care. However, failure to move to a hospital during a health crisis has major ethical implications for families and physicians when there is any uncertainty about the possibility of survival. Hence, transfers from home to hospital continue to predominate in every country.[17]

Wider Use of Hospice

Hospice care clearly improves end-of-life quality and is widely viewed as a cost-saving procedure, as demonstrated in studies comparing hospice and nonhospice care. However, hospice costs depend heavily on the level of care provided and are strongly affected by location of the patient, whether at home (usually less expensive) or in an institution (usually more expensive), and availability of family and other caretakers to shoulder some of the care burden. Financing of hospices is not yet sufficient in most countries to assure widespread availability because of doubts or misunderstanding within the medical establishment. Reimbursement by Medicare, Medicaid, and some private insurance in the United States has contributed to greater use.[21, 24, 29]

Insurance Reforms

Access to dependable, trustworthy, and efficient insurance has become a controlling factor for health and long-term care, and thus has major influence over quality of life. Some countries have made their insurance systems relatively user-friendly, whereas others allow the older person to be constantly challenged by complexity and uncertainty. For example, in the United States older individuals need supplementary insurance to cover costs not paid by Medicare. Lower-income individuals must deal with the complexities of both Medicaid and Medicare. In France complexity also reigns because of multiple insurance and payment requirements. On the other hand, the single-payer insurance plans in Canada and most European countries appear to be less complex and more easily used.[12, 13, 16]

Assurance of Intergenerational Equity

The high costs of income security, health care, and long-term care have consequences for intergenerational equity in every country. Inequity and conflict can arise when there is an appearance of overly generous public benefits supporting the older generations, while younger generations must pay high taxes and yet are unable, from their viewpoint, to secure adequate public services for themselves and their children. Public benefits to support retirees are likely to become much more burdensome for future generations of workers as the older population increases. In 1995 there were about 3.5 active workers per retiree in the United States, but in 2020 this ratio will have dropped to about 2 workers per retiree as in most other countries, if no changes are made in the official retirement age.[4, 7]

These issues are even more profound in Europe and Japan where the population is aging faster than in the United States and Canada. Younger workers and younger families have a larger tax burden for support of services to the older population. The system of reciprocity between generations is in danger of becoming unbalanced unless some of the measures noted above are implemented to diminish the cost burden. Income security and service systems must be supported by the younger working population, the older working population, and the retired population with good incomes, if the perception of intergenerational inequity is to be avoided. Healthier older people have the potential to be more productive and more valued as contributors to family, community, and the larger society than in the past.[9, 25]

Studies in the economics of aging suggest that most of the public costs associated with an older population can be managed quite adequately in times of reasonable economic growth. Increases in health care and long-term care costs are not attributable only to the aging of the population. Rather, inflation of medical costs, increased use of health care per person, and greater intensity per use are primary causes. Health care and long-term care costs have the potential to be much better managed.[10, 14]

◆◆◆ SUMMARY AND CONCLUSIONS

A high quality of life in older age is a primary goal in every country. However, some countries have done more than others to minimize inequities—making it possible for most older people to have adequate choice, social support, health care, mental health care, long-term care, good housing, income security, and satisfying lifestyles. On the other hand, no country has achieved a perfect arrangement. The United States does well in some categories that contribute to quality of life but does poorly in others, allowing substantial numbers of older people to subsist with a low-quality lifestyle.

The following basic policies and programs would help greatly to improve the situation in every country:

- Optimizing independence and personal choice.
- Increasing the efficiency and quality of care systems.
- Focusing on geriatric care management that looks after the whole person.
- Greater attention to the special needs of older women.
- Better means of caring for and treating individuals with dementia.
- More assistance to dependent older people through case or care management.

- Greater use of means-testing to assure that those most in need secure help.
- Limiting unnecessary medical care that creates stress and is unduly costly.
- Limiting unnecessary transfers to hospitals especially in the period before death.
- Expanding use of the hospice concept to improve the quality of end-of-life experience and death.
- Undertaking reforms that make insurance more user friendly.
- Financing and managing programs for the older population to assure inter-generational equity and fair treatment for all generations.

All of the potential policy and program changes outlined above and in Chapter 17 have some application in *all* countries but are particularly relevant to the United States. Quality of life can clearly be achieved for the great majority of the older population.

◆◆◆ REFERENCES

1. Beck, Barbara (1996). The Luxury of Longer Life. *The Economist,* January 27, 3–16.
2. Besharov, Douglas J., and Keith W. Smith (1999). Neglecting the "Oldest Old," *The Washington Post National Weekly Edition,* 16 (34), 23.
3. Bodenheimer, Thomas (1999). The American Health Care System: The Movement for Improved Quality in Health Care, *New England Journal of Medicine,* 340 (6), 488–92.
4. Cole, Thomas R. (1994). Intergenerational Equity in America: A Cultural Historian's Perspective, in Chris Hackler (ed), *Health Care for An Aging Population,* Albany: State University of New York Press, 19–32.
5. Conrad, Alfred F. (1994). Elder Choice and Health Care Costs, *Health Systems Review,* 27 (4), 39–40.
6. Coolen, Jan (ed) (1993). *Changing Care for the Elderly in the Netherlands,* Assen/Maastricht, The Netherlands: Van Gorcum.
7. Cooper, Glenn, and Peter Scherer (1998). Can We Afford to Grow Old? *OECD Observer,* 212 (June/July), Online at www.oecd.org/publications/observer/212/Article5_eng.htm
8. Friedland, Robert B. (1996). Demographic, Economic, and Health Factors Likely to Affect Public Policy, *Journal of Long Term Home Health Care,* 15 (4), 24–37.
9. Guillemard, Anne-Marie (1996). Equity Between Generations in Aging Societies: The Problem of Assessing Public Policies, in Tamara K. Hareven (ed), *Aging and Generational Relations Over the Life Course,* New York: Walter de Gruyter, 208–24.
10. Hargrave, Terry D., and Suzanne Midori Hanna (1997). Aging: A Primer for Family Therapists, in Terry D. Hargrave and Suzanne Midori Hanna (eds), *The Aging Family: New Visions in Theory, Practice, and Reality,* New York: Brunner/Mazel Publishers, 39–60.
11. Hottinger, Margaret, Cynthia L. Polich, and Marcie Parker (1991). At Risk: A Look at Managing Medicare Losses, *Health Care Financial Management,* 45 (5), 22–32.
12. Iglehart, John K. (1999a). The American Health Care System: Medicaid, *New England Journal of Medicine,* 340 (5), 403–8.
13. Iglehart, John K. (1999b). The American Health Care System: Medicare, *New England Journal of Medicine,* 340 (4), 327–32.
14. Kosterlitz, Julie (1997). When We're 64, *National Journal,* 29 (39), 1882–85.
15. Kovach, Christine R. (1996). Alzheimer's Disease: Long-Term Care Issues, *Issues in Law and Medicine,* 12 (1), 47–56.
16. Kuttner, Robert (1999). The American Health Care System: Health Insurance Coverage, *New England Journal of Medicine,* 340 (2), 163–68.
17. Merrill, Deborah M., and Vincent Mor (1993). Pathways to Hospital Death Among the Oldest Old, *Journal of Aging and Health,* 5 (4), 516–35.

18. Organization for Economic Cooperation and Development (1996). *Ageing in OECD Countries: A Critical Policy Challenge,* Paris: Organization for Economic Cooperation and Development.

19. Parker, Marcie, David W. Heiss, and Michael J. Harris (1993). Geriatric Care Management Reduces Medicare Losses, *Health Care Financial Management,* 47 (10), 22–26.

20. Regnier, Victor (1994). *Assisted Living Housing for the Elderly: Design Innovations from the United States and Europe,* New York: Van Nostrand Reinhold.

21. Rhymes, Jill A. (1991). Home Hospice Care, *Clinics in Geriatric Medicine,* 7 (4), 803–16.

22. Rowe, John W. (1999). Geriatrics, Prevention, and the Remodeling of Medicare, *New England Journal of Medicine,* 340 (9), 720–21.

23. Samuelson, Robert J. (1999). The Seduction of Surpluses, *Newsweek,* CXXXIV 134 (2), 74.

24. Scitovsky, Anne A. (1994). "The High Cost of Dying" Revisited, *Milbank Quarterly,* 72 (4), 561–91.

25. Shoven, John B., Michael D. Topper, and David A. Wise (1994). The Impact of the Demographic Transition on Government Spending, in David A. Wise (ed), *Studies in the Economics of Aging,* Chicago: University of Chicago Press, 13–40.

26. Snow, Kimberly Irvin (1996). Downsizing and Diversion: Strategies to Reduce Medicaid Long-Term Care Expenditures, *Journal of Case Management,* 5 (1), 19–24.

27. Swardson, Anne (2000). A Pension Crisis Looms in Europe, *The Washington Post National Weekly Edition,* 17 (27), 17–18.

28. Vanston, Nicholas (1998). The Economics of Ageing, *OECD Observer,* June/July (Issue 212), 10–14.

29. Watt, Kevin (1996). Hospice and the Elderly: A Changing Perspective, *American Journal of Hospice and Palliative Care,* November/December, 47–48.

30. World Bank (1994). *Averting the Old Age Crisis: Policies to Protect the Old and Promote Growth,* Washington, DC: The World Bank.

Appendix A

GERONTOLOGY JOURNALS AND OTHER PUBLICATIONS

AARP Bulletin
Abstracts in Social Gerontology (Sage)
Advances in Gerontological Research
Age and Ageing (British)
Aging and Society
Aging and Work
Aging International
Aging Magazine
American Journal of Geriatric Psychiatry
American Journal of Public Health
Archives of Gerontology and Geriatrics
Canadian Journal on Aging
Care of the Elderly
Clinical Gerontologist
Current Literature on Aging
Current Problems in Geriatrics
Death Education
Developmental Psychology
Educational Gerontology
Experimental Aging Research
Experimental Gerontology
Generations
Geriatric Nursing
Geriatrics
The Gerontologist

Gerontology (British)
Gerontology and Geriatrics Education
Gerontology, Drugs, and Aging
Gerontology News
Health Care for Women International
Human Development
International Journal of Aging and Human
    Development
International Psychogeriatrics
International Social Science Journal
Journal of Aging and Health (Sage)
Journal of Aging and Identity
Journal of Aging and Social Policy (Haworth)
Journal of Applied Gerontology (Sage)
Journal of Cross-Cultural Gerontology
Journal of Elder Abuse and Neglect (Haworth)
Journal of Geriatric Nursing
Journal of Geriatric Psychiatry
Journal of Geriatric Psychiatry and Neurology
Journal of Gerontological Nursing
Journal of Gerontological Social Work
    (Haworth)
Journal of Gerontology
Journal of Gerontology: Biological Sciences
Journal of Gerontology: Medical Sciences

Journal of Gerontology: Psychological Sciences
Journal of Gerontology: Social Sciences
Journal of Health and Social Behavior
Journal of Housing for the Elderly
Journal of Long-Term Care Administration
Journal of Long-Term Health Care
Journal of Marriage and the Family
Journal of Minority Aging
Journal of Nutrition for the Elderly
Journal of Palliative Care
Journal of Religious Gerontology
Journal of Social Issues
Journal of Social Psychiatry
Journal of the American Geriatrics Society
Journal of the American Medical Association
Journal of Women and Aging (Haworth)

Long-Term Care Facilities
Modern Maturity
New England Journal of Medicine
OMEGA, The International Journal of Death and Dying
Physical and Occupational Therapy in Geriatrics
Psychology and Aging
Research on Aging (Sage)
Retirement Life
Reviews in Clinical Gerontology (British)
Social Forces
Social Science and Medicine
Topics in Geriatric Rehabilitation
Women and Aging

Appendix B

USEFUL INTERNET WEB SITES

WWW:

aarp.org — Ageline prepared by the American Association of Retired Persons: wide range of information on programs and benefits for older Americans.

aarp.org/answers.html — A guide to publications and other resources from the American Association of Retired Persons.

aapr.org/cyber/guide1.htm — An AARP guide to Internet resources related to aging which also provides links to other helpful sites.

ageinfo.org — National Aging Information Center: wide range of information on aging issues.

aoa.dhhs.gov — United States Administration on Aging: information on aging issues, studies and programs, including list of local agencies.

aoa.dhhs.gov/aoa/pages/jpostist.html — Internet and e-mail resources on aging.

census.gov — Source of a wide range of information about the older population published by the United States Census Bureau.

elderhostel.org — Information on Elderhostel educational programs for older people.

geodesicmeditech.com — Contains a self-administered drug test that allows older individuals to know of potential drug interactions or problems.

healthfinder.org or health.gov — Healthfinder: the federal government's gateway to health and medical information, with links to many other sites.

heartinfo.org — Provides information and answers questions on cardiovascular problems.

hcfa.gov — Health Care Financing Administration: detailed information on Medicare and Medicaid.

mcs.net/grossman/macareso.htm — Internet resources on aging.

medicare.gov — Medicare web site: detailed Medicare information.

Ncoa.org — Information from the National Council on Aging.

nig.nl — GeronLine containing a wide range of information about gerontology.

nih.gov/health — National Institutes of Health: information on diseases and recommendations for other Web sites.

nlm.nih.gov — National Library of Medicine: link to Medline with full access to publications on health and aging.

nlm.nih.gov/databases/freemedl/.html — National Library of Medicine Medline: direct access to free information via Medline.

nsclc.org — National Senior Citizens Law Center: information on legal issues and legal assistance for older people.

oecd.org — Extensive information from the Organization for Economic Cooperation and Development on older populations and policies in the economically advanced countries.

oncolink.upenn.edu — Information, treatment and discussion about cancer for patients.

pbgc.gov — Pension Benefit Guaranty Corporation: information on pension benefit issues.

realage.com — Contains a 110 item questionnaire producing a health quotient score.

senior.com — SeniorCom: directory for Internet information for older citizens.

senior.com/npo/nssc.html — National Senior Service Corps: volunteer opportunities for older citizens.

seniorlaw.com — Senior Law Home Page: information on Medicare, Medicaid, estate planning, trusts, and the rights of the elderly.

seniornet.org — Seniornet: Internet locations of interest to older citizens.

ssa.gov — Social Security: detailed information on Social Security.

va.gov — Veterans Affairs Department: information on veterans benefits of all kinds.

youfirst.com — Contains a 33-item test which assigns a health age, contrasting with chronological age.

INDEX